THE ROUGH GUIDE TO
DEVON & CORNWALL

written and researched by

Robert Andrews

ROUGH
GUIDES

Contents

Introduction to

Devon & Cornwall

Stretching sinuously into the Atlantic, Britain's westernmost counties of Devon and Cornwall have always captured the imaginations of artists, writers, surfers and hikers – anyone, in fact, who's drawn to wild landscapes, dramatic coastline and a benign climate. The two counties have a markedly different look and feel to the rest of the UK: Devon's rolling swards of pasture, narrow lanes and cosy thatched cottages are a counterpoint to Cornwall's craggy charm and deep Celtic roots. The essential elements, however, are shared, first and foremost being the sea – a constant theme, whether experienced as a restless force raging against rocks and reefs, or as a more serene presence, bathed in rich colours more readily associated with sun-baked Mediterranean shores.

You're never very far from the coast in Devon and Cornwall, where the panoramic sequence of miniature ports, placid estuaries, embattled cliffs and sequestered bays is linked by one of the region's greatest assets, the **South West Coast Path**, stretching from the seaboard of Exmoor to Poole Harbour in Dorset. Most visitors are primarily enticed by the magnificent **beaches** strewn along the deeply indented coast, ranging from grand sweeps of sand confronting ranks of surfer-friendly rollers to intimate creeks and coves away from the crowds. The **resorts** also come in all shapes and sizes, from bijou fishing ports to full-blown tourist towns offering every facility, and from genteel Victorian health resorts to spartan outposts squeezed between cliffs.

Inland, the peninsula has a trio of wildernesses – **Exmoor**, **Dartmoor** and **Bodmin Moor** – which appeal equally to activity enthusiasts and wildlife watchers. Elsewhere, Devon and Cornwall also boast some supreme specimens of English rural life – unsung hamlets far from the beaten track, where clustered cottages, steepled churches and brilliant flower displays perfectly complement the lush meadows and tidy dells surrounding them.

ABOVE ST MICHAEL'S MOUNT (P.247)

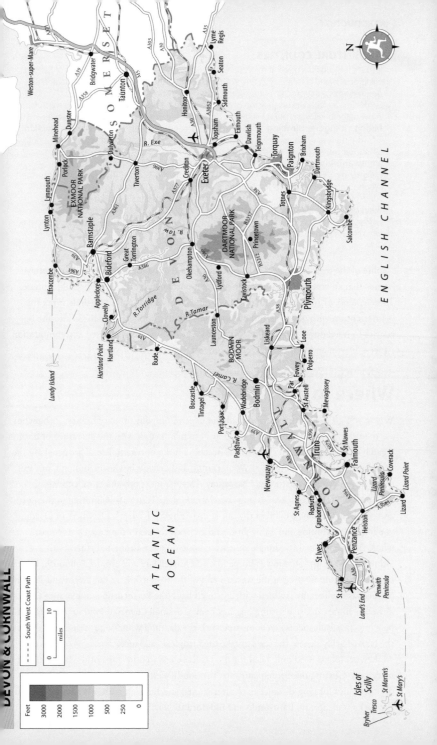

DEVON & CORNWALL

Feet
3000
2000
1500
1000
500
250
0

- - - - - South West Coast Path

0   10
miles

N

ATLANTIC OCEAN

ENGLISH CHANNEL

SOMERSET

DEVON

CORNWALL

EXMOOR NATIONAL PARK

DARTMOOR NATIONAL PARK

BODMIN MOOR

Weston-super-Mare
Bridgwater
Taunton
Minehead
Dunster
Porlock
Lynmouth
Lynton
Ilfracombe
Barnstaple
Bideford
Appledore
Clovelly
Hartland Point
Hartland
Bude
Boscastle
Tintagel
Port Isaac
Padstow
Wadebridge
Bodmin
Newquay
St Agnes
Redruth
Camborne
St Ives
St Just
Land's End
Penwith Peninsula
Penzance
Helston
Lizard
Lizard Peninsula
Lizard Point
Coverack
St Mawes
Falmouth
Truro
Mevagissey
St Austell
Par
Fowey
Polperro
Looe
Liskeard
Launceston
Lydford
Tavistock
Okehampton
Great Torrington
Dulverton
Tiverton
Crediton
Exeter
Honiton
Sidmouth
Topsham
Exmouth
Dawlish
Teignmouth
Torquay
Paignton
Brixham
Dartmouth
Kingsbridge
Salcombe
Totnes
Princetown
Plymouth
Seaton
Lyme Regis

R. Exe
R. Taw
R. Torridge
R. Tamar
R. Camel

Lundy Island

Isles of Scilly
Bryher
Tresco
St Martin's
St Mary's

ADVENTURE COUNTIES

If you're looking for a piece of the action, Devon and Cornwall have it all. The tracts of rugged wilderness inland combine with miles of cliffy coastline and beaches to make the region the destination of choice for adventure enthusiasts of every hue. Devon's Tarka Trail and Cornwall's Camel Trail are only the best-known of a web of **cycle tracks** weaving across the peninsula, some of them following old mining trails. Dartmoor and Exmoor provide ideal terrain for **hiking**, **riding** and **climbing**, while the rivers Dart and Fowey are popular with the **kayaking** crowd. Other water-based activities include **sailing** from the south-coast ports of Dartmouth, Salcombe and Falmouth, **coasteering** along the sea cliffs of northern and western Cornwall, and **swimming** from just about anywhere. The waters around the Lizard and Penwith peninsulas and the Isles of Scilly offer some of the country's premier **dive sites**, while Croyde, Woolacombe, Polzeath and Newquay on the north coasts of Devon and Cornwall can boast some of the finest **surfing** – not to mention more select sports such as **kitesurfing** and **waveskiing**. Newbies will find facilities for renting and instruction throughout the region, while action addicts can sate their appetites with a choice of **adventure centres** offering day, weekend and week-long sessions.

Some of the region's greatest cultural treasures are to be found in the various **stately homes** that are open to the public, many with **gardens** that thrive in the mild climate. There's plenty of interest in the towns and cities too: **castles** and **cathedrals** vying for your attention with **galleries** and **ancient markets**. It's not necessary to stick to the bigger centres to track down top-quality **restaurants** or the most sophisticated **accommodation**, either – Devon and Cornwall excel at both, often in the remotest spots.

Where to go

Where you go in Devon and Cornwall will depend on your primary interest. If **beaches** are the priority, you can pick just about any stretch of coast with the guarantee of finding a patch of sand or rocks to swim from. Beaches on the northern littoral are generally the first choice for surfers, notably at **Woolacombe** and **Croyde** in Devon and, in Cornwall, those around **Bude**, **Padstow** and **Newquay**. Devon's most popular seaside towns are on the more **sheltered** southeast-facing coast, where there is superb swimming to the north and south of **Torquay**, capital of the self-styled "English Riviera". Elsewhere in Devon, you'll find less coming and going around the classic resorts of the East Devon coast, where the predominantly shingle shores are backed by sandstone-red cliffs, as at **Sidmouth**. In Cornwall, crowds home in on **St Austell Bay** and around **Falmouth**, but the beaches are more inviting at the western end of the region, where the Lizard and Penwith peninsulas are liberally studded with sheltered bays like **Porthcurno** and **Kynance Cove**, as well as more extensive surfing beaches such as **Sennen Cove** and **Poldhu**. All, however, pale into insignificance when compared with the dazzling white-sand strands found on the **Isles of Scilly**, where the sea can take on a tropical brilliance.

Likewise, hikers need only head for the nearest coast to find some of the best **walking** in Britain. Circling the entire peninsula, the South West Coast Path allows endless opportunities for long-distance or shorter jaunts, and links up with other routes such as the **Tarka Trail**, around **Barnstaple** and **Bideford** in North Devon, and the **Camel Trail**, which weaves inland from the coast at **Padstow** to **Bodmin Moor**. Unsurprisingly, it is the moors that hold the greatest range of paths and bridleways, and of these **Dartmoor** has the densest concentration, though more cultivated **Exmoor** should not be discounted.

The pleasures of Devon and Cornwall are not confined to the great outdoors, however. History and culture can be soaked up at the region's main centres, not least in **Exeter**, which features stunning medieval architecture and a first-rate museum. Devon's leading part in England's maritime history is in evidence here and at **Plymouth**, which has preserved its medieval core around the old harbour despite severe bomb damage during World War II. On a smaller scale, the nautical tradition is perpetuated in such estuary ports as **Dartmouth**, **Salcombe** and **Fowey** on the south coast, all favourite anchorages of the yachting set.

The West Country's past is evident in the numerous **ruins** scattered throughout the peninsula. These range from the primitive hut circles and Iron Age remains on the moors and remote Isles of Scilly, to **castles** from diverse eras – fragmentary but dramatic, as at **Tintagel**, fabled home of King Arthur on the north Cornish coast, or immaculately preserved, such as at **St Mawes** and **Pendennis Castle** in South Cornwall. The region's former wealth, derived above all from mining and wool, is reflected in a rich assortment of stately homes, usually tucked out of sight in splendid countryside, as at **Hartland Abbey**, in North Devon, and **Lanhydrock**, on the edge of Bodmin Moor. The endowments of landowners and merchants helped to fund some of Devon's most striking examples of ecclesiastical architecture too; for example at **Crediton** in mid-Devon, while Cornwall's

myriad **Methodist chapels** are testament to the markedly different style of popular religion proselytized by John Wesley in the eighteenth century. **Truro**'s twentieth-century cathedral – a bold neo-Gothic statement – has, literally, raised the profile of Cornwall's county town.

The region's modernity is well evident a few miles west at **St Ives**, whose branch of the **Tate** celebrates the various schools of art that colonized the area in the twentieth century. Other flagship attractions in the region highlight the diversity of the natural environment with an accent on conservation – most famously the ambitious **Eden Project** near St Austell, a clay pit converted into a complex of immense greenhouses and cultivated terraces marrying technology with ecology on an eye-popping scale.

For many people, however, the magic of Devon and Cornwall lies in the multitude of **remote villages** dotted along the coast, often sandwiched between rocky headlands, where a few fishing vessels still operate and timeless tranquillity sets the tone. There are any number of well-known examples – **Boscastle** and **Port Isaac**, on Cornwall's northern coast, **Polperro** in South Cornwall, or **Beer** in South Devon – but the best ones are usually serendipitous discoveries. Drop in on these places when the crowds have gone, and you'll find their authentic charm shining through.

When to go

With the highest average year-round temperatures in Britain, Devon and Cornwall make a viable destination in all seasons. This makes an even more compelling case for avoiding the peak **summer months**, if at all possible. Admittedly, the sea is at its warmest and the possibility of rain at its lowest in July and August, but this is also the season of congested roads and paths, packed beaches and reduced availability for accommodation. The **school holiday period** – from mid-July to early September – is the busiest time. Other busy periods include the **Easter** holiday and, to a lesser extent, around Christmas and New Year. At other times, **weekends** see most movement, and Saturday in particular – "changeover day" for the weekly renters – is traditionally the worst day for traffic.

On the other hand, don't expect to enjoy all that the peninsula has to offer in the middle of **winter**. Wet weather can ruin any outdoor pursuit, and in the case of walking can be downright risky. This is particularly true on the coast and on the moors, where mists and blinding rain can descend amazingly quickly. Attractions, including stately homes, often close during the winter months, and many accommodation options are also shut between October and Easter. Public transport services, too, are severely curtailed. All the same, you can still find good weather in winter, when you'll have many places pretty much to yourself, and when experienced surfers will appreciate the bigger swells. In the Isles of Scilly, you'll also be timing your visit perfectly for the **flower harvest**.

Spring sees the famous plants and shrubs of the peninsula's south coast at their most spectacular, while the turning of the colours in **autumn** is also a visual feast, especially on the moors. However, you'll have to guard against the strong winds, which can still blow fairly cold, and only the hardiest will dare to try a dip in the sea.

Author picks

Years spent combing the South West peninsula have thrown up some gems that don't always appear in the tourist brochures. Every visit reveals a new crop. Here's a recent selection of our author's favourites:

Ports of call The south coasts of Devon and Cornwall specialize in yachting ports and fishing villages that are well-nigh irresistible: these include Salcombe (see p.102), Polperro (see p.204) and Fowey (see p.205).

Pubs and pints West Country beers and ciders are some of the finest in the country: try some at Exeter's *Rusty Bike* (see p.54), the *Peter Tavy Inn* on Dartmoor (see p.131) or the *Blue Anchor* in Helston (see p.234).

Alimentary pastimes The time is long past when the region's most famous dining experiences were cream teas and pasties. Try *Herbie's* (see p.53) in Exeter for vegetarian, *Rockfish* (see p.100) in Dartmouth for fish and chips, and *Gidleigh Park* (see p.125) for a pull-out-all-the-stops splurge.

Coastal pursuits The coastal path can be tough going, but there are some delightful spots where it's enough just to sit and gape at the scenery. Among these are Berry Head (see p.91), Cape Cornwall (see p.255) and Hartland Point (see p.194) – once seen, never forgotten.

Church interludes Some of the most amazing architecture and craftsmanship is to be found in the lesser-sung churches of the region. St Neot on Bodmin Moor (see p.329), St Mary's in Totnes (see p.94) and St Petroc's in Padstow (see p.299) are just three examples.

Cool campsites There's nothing like sleeping under the stars and waking to a beautiful view. Some of the region's most appealing campsites include *Little Meadow* (see p.188), *North Morte Farm* (see p.185), *Henry's* (see p.237), *Lower Pennycrocker* (see p.310), *Upper Lynstone* (see p.313) and *South Penquite* (see p.325).

> Our author recommendations don't end here. We've flagged up our favourite places – a perfectly sited hotel, an atmospheric café, a special restaurant – throughout the Guide, highlighted with the ★ symbol.

FROM TOP FOWEY (P.205); CAPE CORNWALL (P.255); *RUSTY BIKE PUB* (P.54)

15

things not to miss

It's not possible to see everything that Devon and Cornwall have to offer in one trip – and we don't suggest you try. What follows is a selective and subjective taste of the region's highlights: outstanding natural features, outdoor activities, festivals, museums, historical attractions and beautiful architecture. All highlights are colour-coded by chapter and have a page reference to take you straight into the Guide, where you can find out more.

1 BEACHES OF NORTH CORNWALL

Pages 291, 294, 302, 304 & 312

The numerous and varied patches of sand on the North Cornwall coast are wilder and less sheltered than others on the peninsula, but generally more scenic.

2 EDEN PROJECT

Page 209

The hype, for once, is justified – Eden is everything it's cracked up to be, and well worth a visit. Come early to avoid the crowds.

3 EXETER CATHEDRAL

Page 45

With its imposing, carved west front and immense vaulted ceiling, the cathedral is the region's greatest medieval monument.

5

6

10

11

Johannes ora pro nobis

Martyn et
fenestram fieri

12

10 NATIONAL MARITIME MUSEUM, FALMOUTH
Page 224
There's no getting away from boats in Cornwall, and this museum is crammed to the rafters with craft of every description.

11 ST NEOT CHURCH
Page 329
Fifteenth-century church on the southern edge of Bodmin Moor, rich in historical detail and boasting fine stained glass.

12 HIKING ON DARTMOOR
Page 112
Solitude and untrammelled nature are the biggest lures for walkers on southern England's greatest expanse of wilderness.

13 ISLES OF SCILLY
Page 268
These islands offer the ultimate getaway and above-average hours of sunshine.

14 WALKING ON THE COAST PATH
Page 162
Britain's longest waymarked footpath, the South West Coast Path, is the best way to explore the region's ever-changing seaboard.

15 LANHYDROCK
Page 323
This stately home on the edge of Bodmin Moor ranks among the region's grandest.

Itineraries

The following itineraries suggest a framework for enjoying the best that Devon and Cornwall have to offer. They dip into Devon's historical treasures and Cornwall's rich mythology, as well as allowing you to leg-stretch, swim and kayak amid some of England's finest coastal scenery.

ON THE WATER

Whether you're on the river or the coast, water sets the tone for much of the region, and is one of its greatest attractions. Even the rain has a different texture… Allow a week or so to cover all the following suggestions.

❶ **The Exe estuary** Walk or cycle along the Exe from Exeter to Topsham, and, if you've got the energy, continue along the estuary to Exmouth from where a ferry crosses to South Devon. See p.49 & p.64

❷ **The River Dart** Spend the morning on a steam train following the Dart from the edge of Dartmoor as far as Totnes, and the afternoon on a cruise down to Dartmouth. See p.94 & p.123

❸ **Kingsbridge to Salcombe** Board a ferry from the South Hams capital to the sailing resort of Salcombe, which has stupendous coastal walking to either side. See p.102

❹ **The Fal estuary** A variety of boat trips exploring the estuary are offered in Falmouth, also home to the National Maritime Museum Cornwall. See p.226

❺ **Newquay** The UK's surfing capital has dozens of other aquatic activities on hand, not to mention some of Cornwall's best beaches. See p.292

❻ **Bude** This watersports hotspot also has a canal with walking and cycling trails. See p.311

ON THE ARTS AND LITERARY TRAIL

The peninsula's combination of light, landscape and sea has been a powerful inspiration to generations of artists and writers. Reawaken your creative side in some of the same environments. You could fit all the stops below into five or six days, but it's worth spending longer if you can.

❶ **Verity, Ilfracombe** Artist and entrepreneur Damien Hirst has left his mark on this harbour resort with his giant statue of a semi-flayed pregnant warrior striding out to sea. See p.185

❷ **Tarka Country** Follow in an otter's footsteps, as described in Henry Williamson's classic *Tarka the Otter*. The 180-mile Tarka Trail provides access for bikers and hikers. See p.179

❸ **St Ives and Newlyn** Cornwall's Far West has attracted legions of pioneering open-air painters and abstract artists, much of whose work can be viewed in Tate St Ives. See p.261

❹ **Zennor** D.H. Lawrence revelled in this wild spot, where he settled during World War II. It's little changed – you can sink a pint in his memory at the bar where he drank. See p.258

❺ **Falmouth** Sample some of Cornwall's up-and-coming artistic talents in Falmouth, home to a distinguished art college. See p.222

❻ **Fowey** This estuary town where Daphne du Maurier once lived trades on its literary links and hosts an annual arts extravaganza. See p.205

ABOVE WATERGATE BAY (P.294)

⑦ Greenway Agatha Christie fans won't want to miss the Queen of Crime's former holiday mansion on the banks of the Dart, perfectly preserved in its 1950s appearance. **See p.101**

HISTORY AND MYTHOLOGY

There's no clear line between historical fact and mythological tale on this far-flung peninsula, where heroes, sorcerers and armies have tussled for centuries; this tour takes in some of the most interesting of the related sights, over a four- or five-day period.

❶ Boscastle Explore the world of sorcery and superstition in this harbour town's entertaining Museum of Witchcraft and Magic. **See p.309**

❷ Tintagel Castle The cradle of Arthurian legends, this ruined fortress – actually Norman in origin – is redolent of epic deeds, and has great views to boot. **See p.306**

❸ Chysauster One of Britain's finest and most evocative surviving Iron Age villages lies on a panoramic hillside above Penzance. **See p.258**

❹ Pendennis Castle Guarding the entrance to Falmouth and the Carrick Roads estuary, this grand fortification endured one of the Civil War's harshest sieges. **See p.225**

❺ Hound Tor This Dartmoor site has literary, historical and legendary associations, involving Sherlock Holmes, phantom hounds and the remains of a medieval village. **See p.116**

THE GREAT OUTDOORS

Most of the pleasures of Devon and Cornwall are out in the open air, whether it's walking, surfing or swimming. Allow a week to ten days for this itinerary.

❶ Dartmoor Southern England's greatest wilderness has everything that the outdoor enthusiast could wish for – not just walking but riding, caving, kayaking and climbing. **See p.108**

❷ Exmoor Less wild than Dartmoor, this National Park also has England's highest sea-cliffs. **See p.152**

❸ The Camel Trail This walking and biking route extends along the River Camel from Padstow into Bodmin Moor – mostly flat, it is always inspiring. **See p.301**

❹ Watergate Bay The northern coast has some superb surfing spots in both counties. This beautiful bay has a range of adventure activities to keep you on your toes too. **See p.294**

❺ The coast path around the Lizard The route around Cornwall's southern claw brings you along wild-flower-speckled paths to beaches with wind- and sea-sculpted rock formations and through delightful villages. **See p.238**

❻ The Isles of Scilly You could have a self-contained holiday on this remote archipelago, offering first-class beaches and some very classy restaurants. **See p.268**

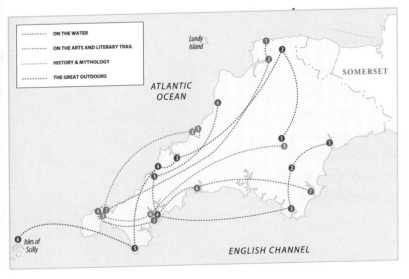

RIVER DART, DARTMOUTH

Basics

Getting there

**Getting to Devon and Cornwall is easily
accomplished whether you're travelling
by road, train or plane. Bus and train
travellers from northern England,
Scotland or Wales might need to change at
Birmingham or Bristol. For all rail and bus
timetable information, consult Traveline
(☎0871 200 2233, ⌨traveline.info).**

By plane

Exeter and Newquay have the region's main airports
for anyone intending to **fly** to the South West. There
are scheduled flights **to Exeter International
Airport** (☎01392 367433, ⌨exeter-airport.co.uk)
from London City, Manchester and Newcastle in
England; Edinburgh and Glasgow in Scotland;
Belfast City and Dublin in Ireland, and some
European airports in France, the Netherlands and
Spain; nearly all are run by Flybe (⌨flybe.com).

Flybe also operates flights **to Newquay Airport**
(☎01637 860600, ⌨newquaycornwallairport.com)
from Belfast City, Birmingham, Edinburgh, Glasgow,
London Gatwick, Liverpool, Manchester and
Newcastle, though only those from London and
Manchester are year-round.

Skybus (☎01736 334220, ⌨islesofscilly-travel
.co.uk) operates flights to St Mary's, in the **Isles of
Scilly** – year-round from Land's End airport and
Newquay, March to November only from Exeter.

Fares vary according to specific dates and how
far in advance you book; for example, a return ticket
from London to Newquay can cost £90–150 for a
midweek flight; flight-time is around 1hr 10min.

By train

All rail lines into the region – from London, Salisbury,
Birmingham and Bristol – pass through Exeter. The
main line then goes through Totnes and Plymouth
to Bodmin, St Austell, Truro and Penzance. The cost
of **tickets** varies according to how far ahead you
book and the restrictions imposed. There are three
main types of ticket on UK trains: Advance (the
cheapest, for a specified date and time of travel and
with limited availability), Off-peak (usually for trains
departing at weekends or outside the busiest times
on weekdays) and Anytime (the most expensive and
flexible option, for use on any train); all prices given
below are for off-peak travel. It may be cheaper to
buy two singles online instead of a return, especially
for advance tickets.

From London Paddington

From **London Paddington**, Great Western
Railway (GWR) runs all trains to Exeter, Plymouth
and Penzance, with one or two departures every
hour. Journey time to Exeter St David's is 2–3
hours, and standard-class one-way fares are
£40–60 for an Advance or Off-peak ticket and up
to £125 for an Anytime ticket. Services from
London to Plymouth, taking 3–4 hours, cost
£45–75 for an Advance or Off-peak one-way
ticket, around £130 for Anytime. You can reach
Penzance from London Paddington in 5–6 hours,
with Advance or Off-peak one-way tickets costing
£55–85, Anytime up to £140.

From London Waterloo

From **London Waterloo**, South West Trains take
longer – around three and a half hours – to reach
Exeter, running via Salisbury and Honiton in East
Devon, and depart roughly hourly. Tickets cost £16
for an Advance or Off-peak one-way journey, and
around £72 for an Anytime. **Megatrain** uses South
West Trains for its discounted service to Exeter,
running four times daily (Mon–Sat); tickets, best
booked online, cost £15–21 one-way according to
availability.

From Birmingham New Street

CrossCountry operates train services from
Birmingham New Street station, running once or
twice hourly to Exeter in around two and a half
hours, and charging £45–85 for an Advance or
Off-peak ticket, around £90 for an Anytime (both
one-way). Services to Plymouth take around three
and a half hours, with Advance or Off-peak tickets
costing £55–120 and Anytime roughly £125
(one-way fares). To Penzance, trains take about five
hours thirty minutes; Advance or Off-peak tickets
cost around £72 and Anytime are about £155. Most
journeys to Penzance require a change at Exeter or
Plymouth.

With a bike

Trains carry **bikes** for free, but restrictions apply on
some lines during peak times and it's always worth
checking in advance for the train you want. As a
rule, high-speed trains – that is, those with a
limited number of stops (including all GWR trains
from London to Exeter and beyond) – require bike
reservations, while others don't. In any case, as
space is limited to two to six per train, reservations
are advised at least 24 hours in advance, and
particularly for 7–10am and 3–7pm journeys.
Non-reserved bikes are carried on a first-come,

first-served basis as long as there is space. South West Trains from London Waterloo to Exeter require advance reservation for bikes at least 24hr before travel, while most CrossCountry trains can only carry three bikes, making reservations highly recommended. Bikes cannot be carried with a Megatrain ticket, but folding bikes can be carried without reservation on any train. There are also some restrictions for taking bikes on trains within Devon and Cornwall (see p.22).

By bus

National Express **buses** connect Devon and Cornwall with London, Bristol, Birmingham, Manchester, Newcastle, Sheffield, Southampton and other major UK centres. Megabus operates a budget service from London and Birmingham to Exeter, and from London to Plymouth and Penzance. Both companies also serve places en route such as Newquay and St Ives. Online fares booked ahead are always cheaper than those bought on the day of departure – usually, the earlier you book, the cheaper it is.

From London

From **London's Victoria Coach Station**, there are National Express departures every two hours or so to Exeter (4–5hr; £9–14 one-way); some services carry on to Torquay, Paignton and Totnes. There are seven to eight departures daily from London to Plymouth (5–6hr; £12–28 one-way), with some coaches continuing to St Austell (3 daily; 7hr–8hr 15min; £41–47), Truro (4 daily; 7hr 30min–8hr 45min; £48) and Penzance (5 daily; 8hr 45min–9hr 45min; £13–42). Ilfracombe, Barnstaple, Bodmin, Newquay, Falmouth and St Ives are connected by less frequent daily services from London.

Megabus also operates a bus service from Victoria Coach Station leaving five times daily for Exeter (4hr 25min–5hr) and Plymouth (5hr 40min–7hr 15min), and once daily for Torquay (6hr), Newquay (7hr 15min), Redruth (7hr 30min) and Penzance (8hr 25min), with fares as low as £6–10 for all destinations.

From Birmingham

From Birmingham, there are four National Express buses daily to Exeter (3hr 50min–5hr; around £7–30 one-way), five daily to Plymouth (5–6hr; £10–38 one-way), and one daily to Penzance (9hr 15min; £63 one-way). Two daily Megabus services connect Birmingham with Exeter and Plymouth, with tickets as low as £12.

From Bristol

From Bristol, there are five daily buses to Exeter (around 2hr; £6–15 one-way) and Plymouth (2hr 30min–3hr 15min; £16–23 one-way), and one daily to Penzance (7hr; £48 one-way). Services are operated by National Express and Megabus.

By ferry

Travellers from France and Spain can cross over to Plymouth by **ferry** with Brittany Ferries (☎0330 159 7000, ⓦbrittany-ferries.co.uk) from Roscoff in Brittany (1–2 daily; 4hr 15min–8hr) and Santander in Spain (1 weekly; 19hr).

By car

By road, most use the **M5** motorway, which swoops south from Birmingham and links with the M4 from London outside Bristol. The M5 terminates at Exeter, from where roads radiate out to different parts of Devon and further west. You can expect around ninety minutes' driving between Bristol and Exeter, depending on the volume of traffic. The A30 or the faster A303 (which branches off the London–Southampton M3) offers a more dawdling but arguably more picturesque route from London and Salisbury to Exeter, from where the A30 extends all the way to Land's End.

Bank holiday weekends and high summer see intense traffic, particularly on the M4 and M5 around Bristol. Saturday is "changeover day", when holidaymakers on weekly rentals clog up the roads in and around the region, and should be avoided if possible. You can get up-to-date **information** on bottlenecks and other possible delays from the **AA** Roadwatch service (☎0906 888 4322, ⓦtheaa.com) and the **RAC** (ⓦrac.co.uk); calls to AA Roadwatch cost 65p per minute from a landline (mobile charges vary). Both organizations also provide a free online route-planning service with traffic reports. Local radio stations (see p.38) provide useful traffic news, too – frequencies are sometimes posted up at the side of major roads.

If you want to lower driving costs, you might consider sharing a ride: Liftshare (ⓦliftshare.com) puts members in touch with others travelling the same way.

TRANSPORT OPERATORS AND INFORMATION

Cornwall Public Transport Information ☎0300 123 4222, ⓦcornwallpublictransport.info. Cornwall County Council's public transport information service.

CrossCountry ☎ 0844 811 0124, Ⓦ crosscountrytrains.co.uk.
Fares, schedules and bookings on CrossCountry trains.

First ☎ 0345 602 0121, Ⓦ firstgroup.com. For First bus and train
schedules throughout the region.

First Kernow ☎ 0345 602 0121, Ⓦ firstgroup.com/cornwall. For
First Kernow bus routes, schedules and service updates in Cornwall.

Great Western Railway ☎ 0345 700 0125, Ⓦ gwr.com. For GWR
train schedules and ticket purchase.

Journey Devon Ⓦ journeydevon.info. Devon County Council's public
transport information service.

Megabus/Megatrain ☎ 0900 160 0900, Ⓦ megabus.com.
Budget buses and trains to Exeter and Cornwall from London and
Birmingham. Calls cost 65p/min plus access charges.

National Express ☎ 0871 781 8181, Ⓦ nationalexpress.com. For
information on long-distance coach services.

National Rail Enquiries ☎ 0345 748 4950, Ⓦ nationalrail.co.uk.
For all train timetables, information on passes and links for ticket
purchases.

South West Trains Ⓦ southwesttrains.co.uk. For trains to Honiton
and Exeter via Salisbury.

Stagecoach ☎ 01392 427711, Ⓦ stagecoachbus.com/southwest.
For Stagecoach bus services in the region.

Traveline Southwest ☎ 0871 200 2233, Ⓦ travelinesw.com.
Invaluable resource for all public transport schedules.

Getting around

**While having your own car does provide
the freedom to explore more remote
parts of the region, it can also be a
cumbersome burden in Devon and
Cornwall's towns and villages, which
are prone to traffic restrictions,
snarl-ups and limited parking. There
are viable alternatives to cars both for
longer and shorter journeys, however,
not least an extensive public transport
network – though services can be
woefully sporadic in some of the most
attractive parts of the region. The
peninsula is also well supplied with
walking and cycling routes. Additionally, you may need to make use of ferry
services and air routes to the Isles of
Scilly or Lundy.**

Although general points are covered below, you'll
find detailed listings of transport schedules and
frequencies in the Guide. Comprehensive
transport timetables for the region are listed in
free booklets available from tourist offices and
travel shops. For local and national rail and bus
timetable information, consult Traveline (☎0871
200 2233, Ⓦ travelinesw.com).

By train

The **train network** in Devon and Cornwall is a mere
shadow of the system that covered the region in
Victorian times. The main spine survives today,
running from Exeter through Plymouth, Bodmin
and Truro to Penzance, and this provides a quick
and efficient way to travel through the peninsula.
With rare exceptions (such as Bodmin Parkway),
stations are centrally located. A few **branch lines**
remain, too, providing unique opportunities to see
some of the region's most scenic countryside; all are
operated by Great Western Railway.

Branch lines

From Exeter, the **Avocet Line** runs the brief distance
south alongside the Exe estuary to Exmouth, while
Tarka Line trains run northwest to Barnstaple,
making a handy link to mid- and North Devon. From
Plymouth, the **Tamar Valley Line** runs north to
Gunnislake, close to a cluster of sights as well as to
Dartmoor. In Cornwall, the **Looe Valley Line** links
Liskeard, on the main line, with Looe, on the south
coast; the **Atlantic Coast Line** goes northwest from
Par in St Austell Bay to Newquay; and the **Maritime
Line** runs between Truro and Falmouth. The **St Ives
Bay Line** constitutes perhaps the most beautiful West
Country track, running from St Erth (the last stop on
the main line before Penzance) along the Hayle
estuary to St Ives. The website Ⓦ greatscenicrailways
.com contains details for eight of these branch lines.

Private lines

There are a few restored **private lines** (or tourist
railways) running in summer and school holidays,
too: chiefly the **Dartmouth Steam Railway** (see
p.90), tracing the Dart estuary from Torbay to
Kingswear, which is connected by ferry to
Dartmouth, and the **South Devon Railway** (see
p.94) between Totnes and Buckfastleigh on the
edge of Dartmoor. They're touristy but fun, and
provide useful links in the transport network.

Rail passes

Although they're not valid on private lines, **rail
passes** are a worthwhile investment if you're going to
make regular use of the trains. Covering all
non-heritage lines in Devon and Cornwall, a
Freedom of Devon and Cornwall Rover allows
three days' travel in seven at a cost of £47, or eight
days' travel in fifteen at £72. A **Devon Day Ranger** is
valid for one day's travel throughout Devon and costs
£10, and a **Devon Evening Ranger** for use after 6pm
costs £5. A **Ride Cornwall Ranger** allows one day's

travel on trains as well as most buses in Cornwall, and costs £10 for adults, £20 for a family (up to two adults and three children). A further discount on all these passes is given for holders of a 16–25, Two Together, Senior or Disabled railcard. The passes, which are generally not valid for weekday travel before 9am, can be obtained from any staffed train station.

With a bike

Bikes can be carried for free on all trains, though as availability is usually limited to just two spaces, reservations at least 24 hours beforehand are recommended.

By bus

While National Express provides a long-distance service linking the main centres of Devon and Cornwall, the chief companies running **bus services** in Devon are Stagecoach and First, and in Cornwall, First Kernow. Most villages in the region are covered at least once daily, though others, for example on the moors or on remote sections of coast, may be visited just once or twice weekly, or on school days only.

Tickets and passes

Day-return **tickets** are cheaper than two singles, and family/group tickets for up to five people valid for one day are also discounted. If you're going to be using buses extensively, you might want to consider buying a **pass**: a **South West Explorer** ticket covering travel on the complete Stagecoach South West network for one day (£7.70); a **Devon Day** ticket covering all bus operators in Devon apart from First for one day (£8.50); or a **Megarider Gold** covering Stagecoach South West services for a week (£27). There are also cheaper versions covering local areas such as North Devon, Torbay, Dartmouth, Exmouth and Plymouth. **First Kernow** offer tickets covering travel on all First buses throughout Cornwall for one day (£12), two days (£18), three days (£24), a week (£26) and a month (£100). The **Ride Cornwall Ranger** (see pp.21–22) covers bus as well as train travel.

You can buy all of the passes listed here at some **travel agents** and **tourist offices**, and on board the buses themselves.

By ferry

With its long coastline and profusion of rivers, the South West peninsula has a number of **ferry** services, which can save long detours by road or on foot, and often link up with train routes. Some are equipped just for foot passengers and bicycles – for example, the Exe estuary crossing between **Exmouth** and **Starcross** (see p.65) and the tourist service between **Fowey** and **Mevagissey** (see p.206). Others transport cars, such as the **Dartmouth–Kingswear** crossing (see p.100), and the **King Harry Ferry** on the Roseland Peninsula (see p.220). A network of passenger ferries links **Truro**, **Falmouth** and **St Mawes** in and around the Carrick Roads estuary (Ⓦ falriverlinks.co.uk).

Between around Easter and October, there's a regular boat service **to the Isles of Scilly** from Penzance, operated by Isles of Scilly Travel (Ⓣ 01736 334220, Ⓦ islesofscilly-travel.co.uk), and **to Lundy Island** (see p.195) from Ilfracombe and Bideford by Lundy Island Ferries (Ⓣ 01271 863636, Ⓦ lundy island.co.uk).

By car

Though a **car** is often the fastest way to get around Devon and Cornwall, the nature of the region's roads and the level of summer traffic mean that you may often get entangled in frustrating hold-ups. The peninsula's three **main roads** – the A39, running along the north coast; the A30, which cuts through the middle as far as Land's End; and the A38, which takes the southern route through Plymouth, joining the A30 near Bodmin – can get seriously clogged in holiday season, with caravans and camper vans adding to the congestion.

On leaving the main roads, you'll often find yourself in narrow, winding **country lanes**, flanked by high hedges and with minimal visibility, often used by farm vehicles and where a low speed is unavoidable. Other rural hazards include horses and riders, straying sheep and ponies, and hunt followers on the moors.

Car parks

Drivers will often find that the best policy is to deposit your vehicle at the first available **car park** whenever you reach a destination – negotiating convoluted one-way systems can be a nightmare and parking spaces on streets are few and far between. Car parks, though, are relatively expensive (at least in the tourist hotspots); most are pay-and-display, so a small cache of change is useful to have to hand.

Car rental

Car rental companies are distributed throughout the region; a selection is detailed in the Guide. The companies listed here have branches in Exeter,

Plymouth, Newquay, Falmouth and Penzance. Prices start at around £80 per week. Alternatively, consider renting a **camper van** – it's a more expensive option, but you'll save money on accommodation. Local operators include O'Connors Campers (☎01837 659599, ⓦoconnorscampers .co.uk), South West Camper Hire (☎01392 811931, ⓦswcamperhire.com) and Cornish Campers (☎01726 842800, ⓦcornishcampers.co.uk); prices range from £400 to £1000 per week according to season and model.

Telephone numbers for **taxis** are provided for the major centres throughout the Guide.

CAR RENTAL COMPANIES

Avis ☎ 0808 284 0014, ⓦ avis.co.uk.
Enterprise ☎ 0800 800227, ⓦ enterprise.co.uk.
Hertz ☎ 020 7026 0077, ⓦ hertz.co.uk.
Holiday Autos ☎ 020 3740 9859, ⓦ holidayautos.co.uk.
Thrifty ☎ 01392 207207, ⓦ thrifty.co.uk.

By bike

A significant stretch of the **National Cycle Network** – NCN – links Bristol and Bath with Land's End in Cornwall (NCN3), making biking through the region a particularly attractive possibility. Known as the **West Country Way**, the Bristol–Padstow route connects and overlaps with the **Cornish Way**, which runs between Bude and Land's End. Parts of the West Country Way run along the **Tarka Trail** in North Devon (see p.179) and the **Camel Trail**, which runs between Bodmin Moor and the Camel estuary at Padstow (see p.301), two first-class walking and cycling routes. The West Country Way also connects with the **Devon Coast to Coast** route (NCN27), running across the peninsula between Ilfracombe and Plymouth (much of it on disused railway lines and along the western flank of Dartmoor), and the **Cornwall Coast to Coast** route between Portreath and Devoran. Other **cycleways** have been developed on the **Mining Trails** around Redruth (see p.289) and the **Clay Trails** around St Austell and the Eden Project (see p.213).

Resources and bike rental

For more information on the West Country and Cornish Ways, and on the entire National Cycle Network, contact **Sustrans** (☎0117 926 8893, ⓦsustrans.org.uk). See ⓦdevon.gov.uk/travel, for cycle trails and town routes in Devon, and ⓦvisitcornwall.com for information on bike rental, routes and cycling events. Bike **rental outlets** are found throughout the region, especially around the main trails. A selection is included in the Guide; expect to pay £10–15 per day including helmet; a deposit and proof of identity are generally required.

It's usually possible to carry bikes on trains in Devon and Cornwall (see opposite), and to arrange for luggage transfers (see p.34).

On foot

England's longest national trail, the **South West Coast Path** tracks the peninsula's coast all the way round from Minehead in Somerset to Poole in Dorset, and offers an unrivalled way to experience the coast and sea. The path was conceived in the 1940s, but it is only in the last forty years or so that – barring a few significant gaps – the full 630-mile route has been open, much of it on land owned by the National Trust, and all of it well signposted with the acorn symbol shared by all national trails. Local shops stock **maps** of the route (the Ordnance Survey 1:25,000 *Explorer* series is the most useful) and there are several guides giving detailed directions. There is a series of four describing different stretches of the path, and including Ordnance Survey maps, simply called *South West Coast Path*; they're published by Aurum Press (ⓦquartoknows .com) and obtainable from local bookshops. Walkers should get a reliable local **weather** check from a nearby tourist office before setting out each day, and carry waterproofs and rations; good footwear is important, since even the gentlest coastal sections cross uneven ground.

Consult the website of the **South West Coast Path Association** (☎01752 896237, ⓦsouthwest coastpath.org.uk) for general information and updates on the route, or one of the independent

DEVON AND CORNWALL MILEAGE CHART

	Exeter	Penzance	Plymouth	Torquay	Truro
Exeter	—	120	42	23	94
Penzance	120	—	78	102	26
Plymouth	42	78	—	24	52
Torquay	23	102	24	—	76
Truro	94	26	52	76	—

websites providing route descriptions and news updates, for example Ⓦexplorethesouthwestcoast path.co.uk. The **South West Coast Path Association** publishes an annual guide to the route (£14), including practical information such as accommodation, refreshment stops and **tide tables** (these can also be bought from local tourist offices, newsagents, souvenir shops and bookshops for around £1.50). The South Devon stretch in particular requires careful timing, as there are six ferries to negotiate and one ford to cross between Exmouth and Plymouth. **Accommodation**, which is relatively plentiful along the way, should also be booked ahead – including campsites, though campers have the flexibility of asking farmers for permission to pitch in the corner of a field.

The South West Coast Path also touches on other long-distance paths in the region, including the **Saints' Way**, linking Cornwall's coasts between Padstow and Fowey, and the **Two Moors Way**, which connects Exmoor and Dartmoor between Lynmouth and Ivybridge – local tourist offices have route maps of both. Walkers may want to take advantage of luggage transfer outfits (see p.34), while useful tips on accommodation, eating and drinking, transport links and other services on long-distance trails can be found at Ⓦramblefest.com.

Tours

Taking a **tour** allows you to see and learn a lot quickly, and with minimum effort. Most are conducted in minibuses by guides who possess an expert knowledge of the area and mix personal experience with history and context. Some of the best focus on individual **themes**, such as the archeology of Penwith, Arthurian links in Cornwall and wildlife on the moors, giving you a deeper insight into one particular area, and a new angle on the region as a whole. Specialist tours tend to change frequently, but local tourist offices can update you on what's currently on offer. For general tours, try Cornwall Welcome Tours (Ⓦcornishwelcometours .co.uk), Unique Devon Tours (Ⓦuniquedevontours .com) or Tours of Excellence (Ⓦtoursofexcellence .com). For history tours there's Cornish Heritage Safaris (Ⓦcornishheritagesafaris.co.uk).

Accommodation

You'll find a fantastic range of accommodation to suit every pocket and taste throughout the region, from chic five-star retreats to backpacker hostels, and from boutique B&Bs to campsites. Examples of the typical, old-fashioned seaside lodging still exist in abundance, but many of these have been converted into sleek, modern places with bike storage and serving free-range eggs for breakfast.

At peak periods – Christmas, New Year, Easter, public holidays and all school holidays (particularly the six-week summer break from late July to early Sept) – you should always **book ahead**. Many establishments will insist on a minimum three-day or week-long stay in summer. Single rooms can be hard to come by at any time of year – single travellers will most often be given a double room at about two-thirds of the cost that two people would pay. If you're economizing, hostels, university rooms, campsites and camping barns are all options.

Local **tourist offices** will sometimes make bookings in hotels and B&Bs over the phone, a service that may be free or incur a charge. Tourist offices are usually abreast of vacancies, and when offices are closed, a list of nearby options may be pinned up on the door. There are also several dedicated websites listing all kinds of accommodation with the option of booking online (see p.39). Note that **smoking** is banned in almost all hotels and B&Bs, though it may be allowed in the garden.

Hotels

Hotels in Devon and Cornwall come in all shapes and sizes. Many are little more than B&Bs with fire doors, some are dismally furnished and desperately old-fashioned, while others are the acme of comfort, character and quality. On the whole, though, you can expect at least a bar, restaurant and parking space. Some places offer a pool, sauna, gym or games room at correspondingly higher prices.

Designer-led **boutique hotels** can be found in seaside or rural locations, often marketed at urbanites on weekend breaks (and therefore often booked up at weekends). Some may offer **spa breaks** and various therapy and **beauty treatments** for some serious pampering, while others are known for their cuisine. Foodies and weekend-breakers will also be interested in the growing number of "**restaurants with rooms**" in the region – essentially quality restaurants which have two or three guest rooms available. These are usually of a high standard with prices to match, but staying over lets you off a late-night drive at the end of a meal, and you're virtually guaranteed a top-notch breakfast.

B&Bs

Most ubiquitous of the accommodation options in the West Country are **B&Bs**, often quite modest private homes with a couple of rooms available. On the whole these offer more personal service than more expensive places; owners are generally friendly and informative, and will often give you a fairer picture of a place than the tourist office can. As a rule, B&Bs (also known as guesthouses) are cheapest where they're remotely located; some of the best deals are on **rural farms**, where prices can be as low as £25 per person; more commonly, prices start at around £35 per person in double or twin rooms, with singles paying a supplement. Rooms at this price usually have tea- and coffee-making facilities and a TV, though for an en-suite bathroom you may pay a few pounds more – and even then these may amount to little more than a cupboard with a toilet and shower. Rooms with shared facilities (sometimes described as "standard" rooms) will often have a sink.

There's a great uniformity of style in B&Bs; most are decked out in either functional or chintzy furnishings and offer identical breakfasts of juice, toast, cereals, a fry-up ("Full English Breakfast") and tea or coffee. Amenities are generally minimal, though some have guest lounges and gardens, and some provide evening meals. As elsewhere in the country, the region has seen an increase in upmarket "**boutique**" **B&Bs**, where guests can expect all the comforts and style of a chic hotel but in a more intimate, informal setting. In most places, you're expected to vacate your room by 10 or 11am for cleaning, whether or not you're staying a second night.

Hostels and bunkhouses

YHA hostels

There are 17 **YHA youth hostels** in the area covered by this Guide, all of them listed at the relevant places in the text. Outside the cities, some close during the winter months but may open for groups with advance booking. It's always advisable to call ahead to check opening hours and availability – they are often booked up weeks in advance, particularly in summer and at weekends, with groups sometimes booking an entire hostel. You'll find the majority of the hostels clean, and many are well equipped with laundries, internet access and bike rental; most have canteens and/or **self-catering facilities** too. On the minus side, most places still operate a curfew and are closed during the day.

Sleeping arrangements are pretty similar in all hostels: **dormitories** rarely have more than eight bunk beds, many are en suite and there are usually twin and family rooms available. Increasingly, hostels have a few camping pitches, some with bell-tents to rent. Expect to pay around £22 for a dorm bed in high season, less in winter, or a little more per person for a double or twin room; bed linen is free, but towels are not provided.

Membership of the **Youth Hostel Association** is not required to stay in their hostels, but members

---

ACCOMMODATION PRICES

Throughout this book, accommodation has been priced according to the nightly cost of the least expensive **double room** in high season. Prices for dorm beds and (if available) double or twin rooms are given for **hostels**. For **campsites**, we quote the price of a spot for a two-person tent, pitched yourself; if a campsite uses a different pricing system (eg per person), we make this clear.

Tariffs in hotels and B&Bs reflect the level of comfort, their location and the season. Within the same establishment, rooms with panoramic views or four-poster beds generally cost more, while most hotels and some B&Bs reduce their rates in low season. Hotels, in particular, often dispense with fixed tariffs altogether, and quote rates according to availability and demand – it's always useful to check **online** to see if you're getting the best deal. Low-season, midweek and last-minute bookings can be especially good value. Most hotels and B&Bs additionally offer **discounts** for stays of two or more nights, or "special breaks" – usually referring to packages including meals – and in B&Bs and smaller hotels these can often be negotiated. In any case, the combined dinner, bed and breakfast rates offered by numerous hotels and some B&Bs can work out to be an excellent deal. In some places, particularly in rural areas or on the Isles of Scilly, half- or full-board is obligatory, especially in summer.

Pretty much all hotels and pubs, and an increasing number of B&Bs, accept **credit and debit cards**, but smaller campsites usually don't – we've noted in the Guide all establishments that don't take cards.

receive a rate discounted by up to £3 per person. Membership costs £20 per year for individuals (£10 for under-26s) or £30 for family membership, with good discounts if paying by direct debit; contact the YHA (📞0800 019 1700, 🌐yha.org.uk) or join online or at one of the hostels. Most members of hostelling associations in other countries have automatic membership of the YHA.

Independent hostels

While YHA hostels may often be located in highly scenic spots, **accessibility** can be a problem when they are hidden away in remote rural settings that are difficult, if not impossible, to reach by public transport. Most of the **independent hostels**, on the other hand, are conveniently located in the centres of towns and villages, and they usually stay open all year. They have a less institutional atmosphere, and may offer as good a range of facilities – kitchen, laundry, internet access and bike rental – as you'll find in the YHA hostels. On the downside, they can sometimes be scruffy, and you may not be comfortable with the fact that dorms are occasionally mixed-sex. **Prices** are usually lower than those at YHA hostels, with discounts negotiable for longer stays, and linen is usually supplied (sometimes for an extra charge).

Bunkhouses

Often located on remote moorland, **bunkhouses** make useful bases for outdoor pursuits. Some are run by or affiliated to the YHA, others are annexed to pubs or campsites, and they can range from basic dorms with cooking and bathroom facilities to swish, fully equipped and well-heated rooms. The cost is usually £15–20. Most will provide bed linen, but check. Always call ahead, as they're often used by groups.

Self-catering

Self-catering holiday properties can be a cheaper alternative to hotels and B&Bs, though some are chic and luxurious, with prices at the top of the scale. There are thousands of properties on offer, ranging from flats by the sea to rustic barn conversions, and the best are often booked a year in advance. **Prices** can range from £200 to £2000 a week, according to size and season, and always include bed linen and towels. In high season, most are rented by the week only – usually Saturday to Saturday – though some operate more flexible rental periods, and three-night breaks are often available. The companies listed below have photos

FIVE FORMIDABLE FORTRESSES

Dunster Castle Part stately home, part castellated stronghold on the edge of Exmoor. See p.164

Pendennis Castle Falmouth. Superbly positioned on the Fal estuary, this extensive site is the venue for jousts and other entertainments. See p.225

St Michaels Mount Penzance. This doughty edifice perched on a granite promontory in Mount's Bay is besieged by the sea at high tide. See p.247

Tintagel Castle Tintagel. Saturated in Arthurian myth, there's little remaining of this rocky redoubt, but the site retains its power. See p.306

Totnes Castle Classic Norman motte-and-bailey construction at the heart of this Devon town. See p.94

and full details of individual properties online and in brochures. Local tourist offices, newspapers and notice boards are also worth consulting.

For something a little different you might consider renting a **yurt** for a week; a number of places offer these fully insulated and equipped Mongolian-style tents accommodating two to six people; for example Yurtworks (📞01208 850670, 🌐yurtworks.co.uk) on Bodmin Moor. Other alternatives exist, such as the cob-, wood- and straw-built **roundhouses** available from the Living Well Centre (🌐thelivingwellcentre.co.uk), near Penzance.

HOLIDAY PROPERTY AGENCIES

Airbnb 🌐 airbnb.com. All kinds of accommodation are available through this online booking service, usually self-catering.

Beach Retreats 📞 01637 861005, 🌐 beachretreats.co.uk. Upmarket and contemporary holiday homes close to North Cornwall beaches.

Breakwater Holidays 📞 01288 352338, 🌐 breakwater -holidays.co.uk. Specializes in quality accommodation in and around Bude, North Cornwall.

Cartwheel Holidays 📞 01392 877842, 🌐 cartwheelholidays .co.uk. Directory of farmhouses and other rural breaks throughout the region.

Classic Cottages 📞 01326 555555, 🌐 classic.co.uk. Country properties throughout the West Country.

Coast and Country Cottages 📞 01548 843773, 🌐 coastand country.co.uk. Holiday lodgings in Devon's South Hams district, from barn conversions to waterside apartments.

Cornish Cottage Holidays/Devonshire Cottage Holidays 📞 01326 573808, 🌐 cornishcottageholidays.co.uk and

W devonshirecottageholidays.co.uk. Thatched cottages and seaside nooks galore.

Cornish Cottages ☎ 01326 240333, **W** cornishcottagesonline .com. More than 200 properties, mainly on the coast.

Cornish Farm Holidays W cornishfarmholidays.co.uk. Properties to rent and B&Bs on farms across Cornwall.

Cornish Traditional Cottages ☎ 01208 895354, **W** corncott .com. Self-catering cottages throughout the county.

Devon Farms ☎ 01626 833266, **W** devonfarms.co.uk. Self-catering accommodation and B&Bs on farms throughout Devon.

Forest Holidays ☎ 01503 220370, **W** forestholidays.co.uk. Modern woodland cabins near Liskeard.

Helpful Holidays ☎ 01647 433593, **W** helpfulholidays.com. Dartmoor-based company, offering everything from apartments to manor houses throughout the West Country.

Hoseasons ☎ 0345 498 6060, **W** hoseasons.co.uk. Long-established, country-wide company offering a range of self-catering properties including country lodges and caravans on holiday parks.

Landmark Trust ☎ 01628 825925, **W** landmarktrust.org.uk. Memorable accommodation in 60 historic properties in the region, from cottages to castles, including 24 on Lundy Island.

National Trust Holidays ☎ 0344 800 2070, **W** nationaltrust holidays.org.uk. National Trust lodgings, often in historic and idiosyncratic properties.

Unique Home Stays ☎ 01637 881183, **W** uniquehomestays .com. High-end accommodation in luxury holiday homes from love nests to ecolodges, including options for house parties and groups.

Camping

Camping has been popular in Devon and Cornwall since tents were invented, and you'll find sites on every part of the coast and inland. Many are mega-parks dominated by caravans and motorhomes, but the ones we've recommended in the Guide are for the most part smaller-scale and tent-friendly. Most are closed in the winter months (usually Oct–May), though some stay open with reduced facilities – always call first. Busier sites sometimes require a minimum two- or three-night or even week-long stay at peak times. The website **W** ukcampsite.co.uk is useful for locating sites, allowing you to narrow your search to specific requirements, and also has recent reviews. **Prices** vary from £5–10 per person in farmers' fields to £35 per pitch for the best-equipped places in high season, where there might be a pool, sports facilities and nightly enter-tainment. Some **YHA hostels** also offer camping facilities, charging around £10–15 per person. Campers can use all the hostel's other facilities, including the kitchen (if one is available). Always book ahead, as camping places are restricted – and the same goes for all other campsites in high

season. Lastly, **W** campinmygarden.com, which connects you with mainly small-scale operators offering pitches on an informal basis, is ideal for a night or two with the locals, averaging around £7 per person per night.

Camping barns

Other options on or around Dartmoor and Exmoor are **camping barns**, usually rudimentary but weather-tight structures fitted with showers, toilets and often basic self-catering facilities, with sleeping platforms on which to roll out your sleeping bag. Costing £6–10 per night, many are run by, or associated with, the YHA (see p.25) – though you don't need to be a YHA member to stay in these. Bed linen and blankets are usually available, but most people just roll out their sleeping bag and bed mat. Camping barns are often rented out to groups, so always call first. Places in YHA-affiliated barns can be booked by phoning **☎** 0800 019 1700.

Wild camping

By and large, **camping rough**, or "**wild camping**", is not so easy. The majority of land is privately owned and on most of the rest – for instance on parkland or National Trust property – it's illegal, though it's always worth asking around, as some easy-going farmers will provide a pitch. Expect a hostile reception if you camp without asking. The website **W** nearlywildcamping.org has a directory of locations where camping is both legal and wild.

On Dartmoor, you are allowed to camp out for a maximum of two nights as long as you're out of sight of houses and at least 100m distant from roads, away from reservoirs and archeological sites, and not on farmland or on certain commons, as specified on the website **W** dartmoor-npa.gov.uk, where you can download a useful map showing all camping options (also available as a leaflet). Open fires are forbidden, but you can use **stoves**, taking due care especially after a spell of dry weather. Free camping is not allowed on the other moors unless permission by landowners is granted first, and overnight camping in any of the region's car parks is also prohibited.

Food and drink

The foodie revolution that has swept the nation in the last few years has found particularly fertile ground in Britain's West Country. Eating out in Devon and Cornwall has improved

immeasurably as a result, and it's now possible to find a wide range of quality restaurants – several of them Michelin-starred – serving adventurous Modern British cuisine. Alongside these are more modest places offering traditional local meals and pub food aplenty, often including pasties – a permanent feature of the culinary landscape in the region. Despite the peninsula's reputation for quality seafood, however, don't always expect perfect fish and chips to munch along the quayside – there is as much junk food about as you would expect to find in any English holiday region.

Even the smallest villages in Devon and Cornwall may have surprisingly sophisticated **restaurants**, while the larger towns will have the gamut of Indian, Thai, Chinese and Italian places. What really marks out the menus of Devon and Cornwall, however, is the **fish**, ranging from the salmon caught in the rivers of Exmoor and Dartmoor to the freshest seafood from the local ports. Despite drastic reductions in the catches and restrictive quotas, the region's fishing industry is still relatively strong, and good seafood restaurants abound, not least in the Cornish port of Padstow, where TV chef Rick Stein has established an empire that draws food fans from far and wide. Restaurants aren't the only places to sample the freshest seafood, though – crab sandwiches are sold at stalls and in many pubs, making an excellent light lunch. For restaurants, reviews, recipes and food facts, see Ⓦeatoutdevon.com, Ⓦeatoutcornwall.com, Ⓦfoodfromcornwall.co.uk and Ⓦsugarvine.com/devonandcornwall.

The speciality **meat** found in most of Devon and Cornwall's restaurants is lamb, cooked all ways, while Exmoor and Dartmoor are renowned for grouse and other game. Though it may not rise above a nut roast, almost everywhere now offers a **vegetarian** option, while an increasing number of cafés and accommodation establishments now cater to **special diets**, too – vegan, gluten-free, dairy-free, etc.

Delicatessens and **wholefood shops** can be found in remote villages as well as in the towns. **Farmers' markets** are always a good source of the best local produce, setting up in many towns and villages once or twice monthly (contact local tourist offices for dates and places).

Regional specialities

Sometimes claimed to be Cornwall's greatest export, **pasties** were originally made as a full meal-

---

FIVE RESTAURANTS WORTH A DETOUR

Fifteen Cornwall Watergate Bay. See p.297
Gidleigh Park Dartmoor. See p.125
Paul Ainsworth at No. 6 Padstow. See p.301
The Fish House Newquay. See p.297
Number 7 Fish Bistro Torquay. See p.87

---

in-one for miners to take underground, with vegetables at one end and jam at the other. The crimped edge was a practical addition – the miners could hold it without washing their hands, then throw it away. At home, each member of the family would have their own tastes catered for, marking the corner of their pasty with their initials.

If you're in search of a good pasty, forget about the stodgy lumps stuffed with gristle and mince that you'll see in chiller cabinets, and head for the local baker's. Ideally, the pasty should have a rich, short pastry, neatly crimped on the rounded edge and filled with gravy-soaked steak, turnip and potato. You can also find a wide range of **non-traditional fillings** in some delis.

Other local specialities include **Stargazy pie** (also known as Starry Gazy pie), a fish pie with the heads and tails of the fish – traditionally pilchards or mackerel – sticking out of the pastry. Tradition has it that this originated after a local fisherman returned from a fierce storm with seven types of fish, which were then cooked in a pie with their heads sticking out for easy identification. In Devon, you may come across **cobbler**, a baked meat dish with a scone topping, and you'll also find casseroles of pork or rabbit cooked in cider.

Sweet dishes include fruity **Cornish heavy cake** and **saffron cake**, a loaf baked with currants and saffron – though, these days, genuine saffron is rarely used (and when it is, it's probably been imported). Everywhere in the West Country, from quaint tearooms to farmhouses and cafés, you'll be tempted by **cream teas**: fluffy scones thickly spread with clotted cream and strawberry jam. The best advice is to surrender to the temptation at least once. The two counties have long disputed which of them is responsible for originating the tradition, and each has its particular method: in Devon the cream is spread on each half of the scone, then the jam is spread on top; in Cornwall it's vice versa.

The region's **ice cream** is equally prized – we've mentioned the best places to sample it in the

Guide. Lastly, it's also worth looking out for local cheeses, most famously **Cornish Yarg** – mild, creamy and wrapped in nettles or wild garlic leaves.

Drinking

Devon and Cornwall boast some of the snuggest **pubs** in the land, often of the thatched and inglenook variety, and equipped with old slate floors, beamed ceilings and maritime paraphernalia. Most pubs are open all day from 11am until 11pm (usually noon–10.30pm on Sun), but often close between around 3pm and 6pm in winter. We have provided kitchen hours in the Guide where pubs are recommended for their food; service hours in rural and coastal pubs, in particular, can vary from season to season though, so it's always worth checking online or by phone.

As for liquid refreshment, the region is dominated by the St Austell brewery, responsible for superlative **beers** such as HSD, Tribute and Admiral's Ale. In recent years the brewery has branched out into new areas that have proved popular, for example Mena Dhu, a stout using a blend of six malts, and Korev lager. Truro-based Skinner's, Sharp's (producer of the UK's top-selling bottled beer, Doom Bar) from Rock, near Padstow, and Devon's Otter breweries are among the leading local independents. There are shining examples of smaller operations, too, notably the *Blue Anchor* pub at Helston (see p.234), where renowned Spingo bitter is brewed on the premises.

Among local **ciders**, Cornish Rattler from Healey's Cyder Farm outside Newquay has achieved nationwide fame, and you're all but guaranteed to see other local ciders and perries (pear ciders) advertised in farm shops. You might also look out for home-made **scrumpy** – a cloudy and potent version of cider weighing in at around 8 percent ABV.

Look out, too, for local **wines** such as Sharpham (see p.97), from around Totnes, or Camel Valley (see p.324), from near Bodmin. If you're interested in wines and wine-making, you can tour either of these vineyards. Note that some restaurants allow you to **bring your own bottle** of whatever alcohol you fancy ("BYOB").

You'll occasionally come across **meaderies** in the South West – usually bawdy, faux-medieval halls that serve meals alongside the various types of mead (an alcoholic drink made from fermented honey) on offer, which can be surprisingly strong. They're pretty tacky places, but are relatively cheap and can be a good laugh.

Festivals and events

The demands of the tourist industry combine with authentic local traditions to ensure a full programme of annual festivals and events, especially over the summer. As nearly every village stages an annual event of some sort, and carnivals surface year-round, it would be impossible to detail them all. The main events listed below are arranged according to the week in which they occur, as most are fixed to weekends or specific days; contact the local tourist office or see festival websites for precise dates. You can also find information on all the main events on the websites ⓦ visitdevon .co.uk and ⓦ visitcornwall.com.

Unsurprisingly, given the region's long seaboard, a large proportion of events in Devon and Cornwall focus on the sea. The smartest of these are the various **regattas** that take place throughout the summer; larger ones, such as at Dartmouth and Fowey, get jam-packed. A peculiarity of Cornwall is **gig races** – rowing-boat races held in the summer between teams from different West Cornwall villages or from different islands in the Isles of Scilly. Foodies might take more interest in the **Newlyn Fish Festival** in late August (see box, p.248) and Falmouth's **Oyster Festival** in October (see box, p.226); in both cases the quaysides have all sorts of seafood on display, cookery demonstrations and Celtic entertainment.

Other festivals are firmly tied to the land,

> ### FIVE FEISTY FESTIVALS
> **Sidmouth FolkWeek** Folk and roots music take over this stately East Devon resort every summer. See p.72
> **Tar Barrelling** Ottery St Mary. Reckless but compulsive viewing, burning barrels are carried through town on Bonfire Night. See p.75
> **Golowan** Penzance. An effervescent celebration of Cornish culture and local creativity. See p.247
> **Boardmasters** Newquay. Surfing thrills and spills combine with great music on the beach. See p.296
> **Obby Oss** Padstow. This rowdy May Day romp sees masked and costumed capers with a dark medieval flavour. See p.300

especially those with an element of fertility ritual such as Padstow's May Day **Obby Oss** celebration (see box, p.300), when a weird and wonderful hobbyhorse in a circular hooped skirt prances its way through the town, and Helston's **Flora Day** (see box, p.234) on May 8, which has smartly turned out couples dancing to the tune of the *Furry Dance*. Dance features strongly in both events, as it does in many other Cornish festivities such as the midsummer **Golowan Festival** in Penzance (see box, p.247), a week-long community celebration with pagan elements, featuring fireworks and cultural events. Devotees of Cornwall's Celtic heritage flock to Newquay's **Lowender Peran** festival (see box, p.296), over five days in October.

For a winter festival, you'd be hard-pressed to beat the **tar barrels** at Ottery St Mary in early November (see box, p.75), when people rush through the narrow streets with flaming barrels on their shoulders.

Arts festivals

Probably the most famous of the West Country's **arts festivals** is the **Dartington Summer Festival** (see p.97), throughout August, where you might take in three concerts a night ranging from classical to contemporary jazz and world music in the antique setting of Dartington Hall. The **Fowey Festival of Arts and Literature** (see p.206) in May includes plenty of walks, concerts, workshops and exhibitions as well as talks by literati and others, while the **St Ives September Festival** (see p.262) has an eclectic brief, with the emphasis on music.

The biggest and best known of the region's **folk music festivals** is **Sidmouth FolkWeek** (see box, p.72), which attracts a diverse audience in early August. Near Wadebridge, in Cornwall, **St Endellion** hosts two **classical music festivals**, for a week at Easter and around ten days in July/August (see p.306). At the other end of the spectrum, Newquay's Electric Beach Festival in July and Board-masters Festival in August feature indie bands and DJs (see box, p.296).

Lastly, many towns and villages pull out all the stops when it comes to **Christmas illuminations** – those at Mousehole (see p.249), near Penzance, are especially awesome.

A festival calendar

MARCH/EASTER

Easter Festival St Endellion, Easter. A week of classical music concerts.

Vibraphonic Exeter, March. A feast of live music, mainly urban, jazz and reggae.

APRIL

Exeter Festival of Food and Drink Second/third week. The South West's premier food and drink jamboree, held over a weekend.

MAY

English National Surfing Championships Watergate Bay, late April/early May. One of the longest-running surfing competitions in the UK.
World Pilot Gig Championships Isles of Scilly, late April/early May. Thrilling boat races.
Obby Oss Padstow, early May. May Day shenanigans.
Fowey Festival of Arts and Literature First/second week. Eight days of books, talks and walks.
Flora Day Helston, May 8 or previous Sat. Ancient fertility dance through town.

JUNE

Gala Week Budleigh Salterton, late May/early June. Mainly family-oriented events, including dog shows and a barbecue.
Tavistock Steam Fair Sunday in first/second week. Vintage and classic cars alongside steam rollers and traction engines.
Royal Cornwall Show Wadebridge, second week. Agricultural show with folk dancing, military bands, flower displays and much more.
GoldCoast Oceanfest Croyde, second/third week. A weekend of water and beach sports, with live bands.
Golowan Festival Penzance, third week. Cultural binge lasting nine days.
Exmouth Festival Fourth week. Ten days of concerts, dance, poetry, sand sculptures and workshops in late May/early June.

JULY

Ways With Words Dartington, first/second week. One of the UK's top literary gatherings, lasting ten days.
Stithians Show Second/third week. Cornwall's biggest one-day agricultural show, including food, crafts, traditional music and lots of animals.
Honiton Fair and Hot Penny Day 1st Tues after July 19. The town's annual fair traditionally kicks off with catching heated pennies.

PUBLIC AND BANK HOLIDAYS

January 1
Good Friday (late March or early April)
Easter Monday (late March or early April)
First Monday in May
Last Monday in May
Last Monday in August
December 25
December 26
(Note that if Jan 1, Dec 25 or 26 falls on a Saturday or Sunday, the next weekday becomes a public holiday.)

Ale Tasting and Bread Weighing Ashburton, third week, Saturday. Medieval fair with procession.

Launceston Agricultural Show Third/fourth week. Livestock, local produce and crafts.

Plymouth Regatta Third/fourth week. Sailing, music and barbecues over a week in and around Plymouth Sound.

Port Eliot Festival St Germans, late July. Literature, music and cabaret over four days on the Rame peninsula.

Budleigh Music Festival Budleigh Salterton, late July/early Aug. Classical concerts over eight days.

Padstow Carnival Late July/early Aug. A week of events, stalls and family entertainment.

St Endellion Summer Festival Late July/early Aug. Classical concerts in a church over ten days.

Dartington Summer Festival Late July to late Aug. A month of concerts, mainly classical, but also world, folk and jazz.

AUGUST

Beer Regatta First/second week. Competitions and street entertainment.

Sidmouth FolkWeek Late July/early Aug. One of the country's top folk festivals.

Henri Lloyd Falmouth Week First/second week. Including a regatta to rival Cowes, this sailing and carnival week features displays of maritime prowess and fireworks.

Paignton Regatta First/second week. Talent shows, tribute bands and fireworks, as well as boating events and swimming races.

Boardmasters Festival Newquay, second/third week. Five days of surfing, skating and live music on Fistral Beach and Watergate Bay.

Fowey Royal Regatta Second/third week. Races, air displays, carnival floats and fireworks.

Bude Carnival Third Sat. Competitions by day, followed by an evening procession.

Torbay Royal Regatta Third/fourth week. Six days of sailing and shore-based events, and fireworks.

Newlyn Fish Festival Fourth week. Seafood galore, to eat and to see prepared in culinary demonstrations.

Cornwall Folk Festival Wadebridge, last weekend. Live folk and roots music, attracting major musicians.

Dartmouth Royal Regatta Late Aug. Races and displays in the Dart estuary over three days.

Bude Jazz Festival Late Aug/early Sept. Mainly trad bands appear over four days.

SEPTEMBER

Widecombe Fair Widecombe-in-the-Moor, second Tuesday. Famed Dartmoor fair, which has now grown to include agricultural displays, competitions and morris dancing.

Ladies' County Gig Championships Newquay, second week. Boat-racing thrills and spills.

Agatha Christie Festival Torbay, second/third week, alternate years. A week of Christie-related events, with readings, tea parties and murder mysteries.

St Ives September Festival Second–fourth week. Top-ranking arts festival, with music, theatre, literature and exhibitions over a fortnight.

Men's County Gig Championships Newquay, fourth week. Boat-racing on traditional Cornish gigs.

Looe Music Festival Last weekend. Big-name rock and folk acts on five stages, the main one facing out to sea.

OCTOBER

Exmouth Carnival Second week. Floats and family fun, with an illuminated costumed procession.

Goose Fair Tavistock, second Wed. Traditional gathering with stalls and family amusements.

Beer R&B Festival Second/third week. Three days of blues and jazz.

Two Moors Festival Exmoor and Dartmoor, fourth week. Classical music in village halls and churches.

NOVEMBER

Lowender Peran Newquay, first week. A five-day celebration of Celtic culture, with music and dance at the fore.

Tar Barrel Rolling Ottery St Mary, Nov 5. Flaming barrels carried through the streets in a local Bonfire Night tradition.

Teignmouth Jazz Festival Second/third week. A weekend of jazz and blues by the sea.

DECEMBER

Tom Bawcock's Eve Mousehole, Dec 23. Featuring choirs and the consumption of Stargazy pie.

Outdoor activities

There's plenty of scope for experiencing the outdoor life in Devon and Cornwall, from hiking to mountain biking, and caving to kayaking. The biggest draw for most visitors is the coastline, chiefly for its beaches, which number among Britain's finest – if the water is too cold for total immersion, you can still experience the waves on board a boat. The range of outdoor pursuits extends far beyond the obvious pastimes though; see the websites Ⓦ exploredevon.info and Ⓦ www .adventure-cornwall.co.uk for inspiration for activities and extreme sports.

Beach life

The West Country's biggest asset for visitors is its hundreds of miles of **coastline**, most of it more or less unspoilt and studded with many of Britain's cleanest **beaches** and bathing waters. The region won sixteen prestigious **Blue Flag** awards in 2016 (see box, p.33), awarded annually on the basis of various criteria including facilities and environmental standards, as well as water quality. This was a decrease from previous years. Focusing on water quality alone, the **Marine Conservation Society** recommends many more than these – over half of the total number of beaches listed in the region – which have achieved "Excellent" or "Good" classification according to EU standards introduced in 2015. You can check all beaches granted Blue Flag status and Seaside Awards at ⓦtheseasideawards.org, or search for beaches at ⓦgoodbeachguide.co.uk.

The shores are certainly not free of problems, however, with various forms of **pollution** affecting a number of beaches; untreated sewage is still discharged close to the shore in some places and is washed back onto the sands. Both the local water companies have put considerable investment programmes in place to deal with the continuing scandalous condition of some coastal stretches, but they're still regularly criticized by groups such as Surfers Against Sewage (ⓦsas.org.uk). See ⓦbeach live.co.uk for up-to-the-minute reports on bathing water quality.

Most beaches are closed to **dogs** from Easter to September; however, there's a map showing beaches open throughout the year in the leaflet *Beach Guide for Dog Owners*, available from tourist information centres or on ⓦgoodbeachguide.co.uk.

Beach safety

Remember that the **currents** around the peninsula are powerful and can quickly pull you out to sea; it's best not to swim alone or too far out. Between June and September, the most popular beaches are under lifeguard surveillance and a system of **flags** is in operation: a red flag indicates danger and means that the beach is closed for swimming and surfing; the zone between two red-and-yellow flags designates an area safe for swimming, body- and paddle-boarding; while the area between black-and-white chequered flags is reserved for surfing, wave skis, canoes and windsurfing. An orange windsock signifies high winds, when it is inadvisable to go out on inflatables.

Note that all beaches around the Devon and Cornwall coasts – including the Isles of Scilly – are subject to **tides**, which dramatically transform the appearance of the seashore. Low tide can leave you feeling like you're sitting in a bath after the water has run out, while sudden high tides can pose a significant risk by cutting off your return from a rock or strip of sand. Take local advice, see the website ⓦeasytide .ukho.gov.uk or buy tide-time booklets (usually £1.50 or less) from tourist offices or newsagents.

Coasteering

North Devon and North and West Cornwall offer some of the UK's best areas for **coasteering**, the adrenaline-fuelled sport of negotiating sea cliffs and rocky stretches of coast by all means possible. Half-days and longer sessions can be booked from specialist agencies – contact the local tourist office for which ones. Xtreme Coasteering leads sessions on the north coasts of Devon and Cornwall (☎07412 603116, ⓦxtremecoasteering.co.uk). Coasteering South West also operates in North Devon (☎01271 871337, ⓦcoasteeringsouthwest.co.uk).

Diving

With some of the clearest waters around the UK, Devon and Cornwall offer a wealth of **scuba diving** and **snorkelling** possibilities. Dive sites are scattered around the coasts, with those around West Cornwall and the Isles of Scilly especially rich in opportunities for poking around shipwrecks and reefs.

Numerous places offer **tuition** and equipment rental (usually around £15 for a couple of hours' taster) – make sure that instructors have the appropriate PADI qualifications. The British Sub-Aqua Club (☎0151 350 6200, ⓦbsac.com) lists approved schools and instructors, as well as information on local dive sites and services.

Sailing

The sight of sailors messing around in boats in every port in Devon and Cornwall is an inspiration for anyone yearning to try their hand at **sailing**. Richly endowed with inlets, estuaries and creeks, the peninsula is ideal for first-timers and old salts alike. The more sheltered south coast offers the best conditions: particularly around Teignmouth, Dartmouth, Salcombe and Plymouth in Devon, and Fowey and Falmouth in Cornwall.

A residential course is the best option for **tuition**, with a range of specialist schools listed by the Royal Yachting Association (☎023 8060 4100, ⓦrya.org .uk). For the slightly less daunting experience of sailing on **lakes**, contact the South West Lakes Trust (☎01566 771930, ⓦswlakestrust.org.uk), which offers a range of watersports including sailing at four sites in Devon and Cornwall.

FIVE AMAZING SURF BREAKS

Croyde North Devon. See p.181
Fistral Newquay. See p.295
Polzeath North Cornwall. See p.304
Sennen Cove Penwith. See p.254
Woolacombe North Devon. See p.184

Surfing

The north coast of Devon and Cornwall has some of the country's most outstanding **surfing beaches**, which, thanks to wetsuits, are used year-round by surf enthusiasts. The most popular areas are Woolacombe Bay and Croyde Bay in Devon, and the areas around Bude and Newquay, and the beaches at Polzeath, Constantine Bay, Porthtowan, Perranporth, Portreath and Sennen Cove in Cornwall. In summer, you'll find plenty of kiosks on the beaches renting out **surf equipment** – boards and wetsuits each cost about £10 per full day (plus a deposit); details of dedicated watersports equipment rental outlets are given in the Guide. **Surfing courses** are also readily available, with two- to three-hour lessons costing about £30, and private tuition £40–60 for two hours or so, including all equipment. Surfing GB (🖲 surfinggb.com) has a selection of approved surfing schools in the South West and lists events. Updated reports on **surf conditions** and forecasts are available at 🖲 get aforecast.com and 🖲 magicseaweed.com, the latter with live webcams relaying images of the major surfing beaches.

Windsurfing, kitesurfing and paddleboarding

While **windsurfing** has ebbed in popularity in recent years, it's still practised all over the South West, especially in sheltered spots such as the Exe estuary, Plymouth Sound and the Carrick Roads estuary. Basic tuition in a group starts from £15 per hour, and you'll pay around the same to rent equipment for one hour (usually around £20 for two hours). The Royal Yachting Association (📞 023 8060 4100, 🖲 rya.org.uk) lists schools in the area, while the South West Lakes Trust (📞 01566 771930, 🖲 swlakestrust.org.uk) offers windsurfing, among other watersports, at four inland sites in Devon and Cornwall.

Kitesurfing, on the other hand, attracts increasing interest among extreme sports fans on the peninsula's beaches. Equipment can be rented and tuition given at various activity centres, such as Cornwall's Extreme Academy on Watergate Bay (📞 01637 860543, 🖲 watergatebay.co.uk). The British Kitesurfing Association (📞 01305 813555, 🖲 britishkitesports.org) has lists of recognized schools and suitable beaches.

Paddleboarding has also become more common at beach resorts and on lakes and rivers in the South West, with options to rent equipment or join a course at all the most popular spots, often at the same places offering windsurfing. The British Stand Up Paddle Association (📞 0330 113 6266, 🖲 bsupa.org.uk) lists providers of equipment and courses.

Biking

Touring Devon and Cornwall **by bike** makes an efficient, ecofriendly and relaxing way to discover the hidden corners of the peninsula. As well as the various **cycleways** (see p.23), there are numerous opportunities for off-road biking (particularly on the moors), for which you should be fully equipped with waterproofs, maps and liquids – as with hiking, preparation is paramount, not least with regard to bad weather. Bike **rental outlets** are listed in the Guide for all the major centres and the main trails. Note that bikes can be carried on trains when there is availability (see p.22).

Caving and climbing

The granite landscape of the West Country's moors is ideal for **caving** and **rock climbing**, neither of which should be undertaken without expert guidance or adequate equipment. On Dartmoor especially, **Sheeps Tor**, **Haytor** and the **Dewerstone** offer some of the country's best climbing and bouldering opportunities. The British Mountaineering Council website 🖲 thebmc.co.uk lists climbable cliffs and crags, and activity centres in the region offer day, weekend and week-long courses

---

BLUE FLAG BEACHES IN 2016

North Devon
Westward Ho!
South Devon
Blackpool Sands
Breakwater (Torbay)
Challaborough Bay (Bigbury)
Dawlish Warren
Meadfoot (Torbay)
Oddicombe (Torbay)
Sandy Bay (Exmouth)

North Cornwall
Carbis Bay
Polzeath
Porthmeor (St Ives)
Porthminster (St Ives)
Porthtowan
Trevone Bay (Padstow)
Widemouth Bay (Bude)
South Cornwall
Gyllyngvase (Falmouth)

for caving and climbing enthusiasts – for example Essential Adventure (☎01752 418038, ☒essential -adventure.co.uk) and Isca Outdoor (☎01392 340484, ☒iscaoutdoor.co.uk). Contact local tourist offices and National Park visitor centres for a full list.

Fishing

The **rivers** of Dartmoor and Exmoor are much prized for their fishing opportunities, and are well stocked with wild brown trout, sea trout and the occasional salmon. Always enquire about **licences**: many local **clubs** offer temporary membership, allowing you to use their streams and rivers (around £15 for a day). The website ☒fishingnet.com has details of fishing venues, fisheries and angling clubs in the region. For fishing in **lakes**, you can also go to one of the four sites in Devon and Cornwall managed by the South West Lakes Trust (☎01566 771930, ☒swlakestrust.org.uk).

Sea-angling is another popular activity, and in summer you'll find numerous outfits advertising two- or three-hour excursions to fish for bass, mackerel or even shark. Fishing Cornwall (☎07853 391090, ☒cornwall-fishing.co.uk) conducts coastal fishing excursions around Looe, Cornwall, the region's **shark-fishing** centre (see p.200) – always returning the sharks to the ocean.

Hiking

In addition to the **long-distance footpaths** crossing the region (see pp.23–24), the South West also boasts a multiplicity of shorter **hiking routes**, most notably the network of tracks over Exmoor, Dartmoor and Bodmin Moor, and around the region's river estuaries. The excursions outlined in the Guide present a cross-section of the kinds of walks you can find, with terrains ranging from bare moorland to wooded valley. These are more general descriptions than specific route guides, however, and the walks should not be undertaken without a proper 1:25,000 or 1:50,000 **map** (see p.38) and a **compass**. Ask at local tourist offices for leaflets – either free or costing around £1 each – detailing circular routes, which take in places of interest.

If you're not on a circular route, you'll probably have to rely on public transport to get you home at the end; on the moors, **bus routes** often link up with walking routes – local bus timetables sometimes even suggest walks, with good directions. Coastal transport routes lend themselves to spurts of hiking on the South West Coast Path, too, with frequent intersections of path and bus route.

The website ☒greatscenicrailways.co.uk details walks that can be accessed from the peninsula's branch rail lines, also indicating pubs en route.

All walks should be approached with forward planning and suitable **equipment**. Supportive, waterproof hiking boots are ideal – moorland is particularly uneven terrain – and you should carry a waterproof jacket with hood, a warm, dry change of clothing on wet days and around two litres of water per person on a hot day. For longer hikes, something to eat is also essential. You might also consider using a **luggage-transfer** service; for example Luggage Transfers (from £15 for 2 bags; ☎0800 043 7927, ☒luggagetransfers .co.uk), covering Dartmoor, Exmoor and the whole of the South West Coast Path. Some B&Bs also offer this service.

Take advice on the **weather** (local tourist offices, local press, radio and TV, and ☒metoffice.gov.uk are useful sources of information). Bad conditions can set in fast, and fogs are a particular hazard on the coast and moors. **GPS receivers** can be a useful back-up to a map; some display location details superimposed on Ordnance Survey maps.

If you're inexperienced, consider joining one of the regular **organized walks** on Exmoor and Dartmoor and along the coast. These are of varying length and difficulty: contact local tourist offices and moorland visitor centres for details.

Kayaking and canoeing

The rivers and seas around the South West peninsula offer ample scope for **kayaking and canoeing**, whether you fancy drifting lazily along a meandering stream or battling against rapids or surf in whiteknuckle escapades. **Inland**, the rivers Exe and Barle on Exmoor, Dart on Dartmoor and Fowey in South Cornwall are all favourite venues for taking up the paddle, and you'll find operators – mainly active in the winter months – in and around Dulverton, Princetown and Fowey. The waters here can get very fierce and expertise is required; the local tourist offices can inform you of qualified instructors. For a calmer experience, the four sites in Devon and Cornwall managed by the South West Lakes Trust (☎01566 771930, ☒swlakestrust.org.uk) offer canoeing and

---

MOST EXHILARATING WALKS

Hound Tor Dartmoor. See p.116
Ilfracombe to Combe Martin on the coast path North Devon. See p.187
Rough Tor and Brown Willy Bodmin Moor. See p.328

HEALTH HAZARDS FOR HIKERS

Apart from hiking injuries, the main hazards facing walkers in the West Country (as elsewhere in the UK) are overexposure to the sun, snakes and ticks. Take the usual precautions to avoid **sunburn**: wear a hat, and use sunscreen.

Among the resident snakes, **adders** (also known as vipers) are the only dangerous species: distinguished by a zigzag stripe along its back, the adder is rare to encounter, and bites are uncommon. If you should be unlucky enough to be bitten, it is extremely unlikely to be fatal, though you should seek medical attention as soon as possible.

Ticks are an irritation in many areas of Britain and may cause Lyme disease if left untreated. They occur in wooded areas and where there is thick vegetation, for instance bracken; the creatures are brushed (or fall) onto your exposed skin, where they burrow in to suck your blood. They are small, the bites are painless, and victims are often unaware they have been bitten. The best prevention is to avoid exposing skin while walking, but note that pets are more prone to catch ticks than humans, and can easily pass them on to humans.

If you find one, the best advice is to go to a **doctor** to have the tick removed. If you do decide to remove a tick yourself, don't apply any oil or lotion or squeeze it; the correct method is to twist it gently anticlockwise using tweezers, cleansing the area thoroughly with antiseptic afterwards. Always keep the extracted tick to show to a medical authority.

A further possible hazard is **toxocara**, a small parasite carried in the faeces of some animals (especially dogs). It can cause blindness and is therefore something to be aware of in areas frequented by dogs – for example, picnic areas where children might play.

---

kayaking **on lakes**. For a single kayak, expect to pay around £18 for two hours' rental, £35 for a day.

On the coast, **sea-** and **surf-kayaking** are increasingly popular; you can opt for more sheltered spots around, for example, Exmouth, St Austell Bay and Falmouth, or brave the waves from typical surfing beaches on the northern coast, such as Polzeath and Bude. Some outfits offer sea-kayaking trips to Lundy Island; for example Sea Kayaking South West (W seakayakingsouthwest.co.uk). Surf-kayakers should observe the same safety procedures as surfers, and always allow others plenty of space.

British Canoeing has details of approved centres in the region (T 0300 011 9500, W britishcanoeing .org.uk); see also W gocanoeing.org.uk for courses, events and activities.

Horseriding

Dartmoor and Exmoor are particularly ideal for **horseriding**. Stables can be found in some of the most scenic parts of the moor, as well as in coastal areas, and are detailed in the Guide. Expect to pay about £25 per hour for riding or tuition. Check the directory of approved riding schools and trekking centres on the website W bhs.org.uk.

SPECIALIST OPERATORS AND ACTIVITY HOLIDAYS

Adventure Okehampton T 01837 53916, W adventure okehampton.com. The YHA's adventure centre on the edge of Dartmoor offers a range of activity holidays for individuals and families, including biking, climbing and pony trekking.

Adventureline Walking Holidays W adventureline.co.uk. Guided walking packages including accommodation, on Dartmoor, the Cornish coast and the Isles of Scilly.

Classic Sailing T 01872 580022, W classic-sailing.co.uk. Sailing holidays around Devon, Cornwall and the Isles of Scilly, from luxury to more hands-on trips.

Contours Walking Holidays T 01629 821900, W contours.co.uk. Self-guided hikes on the Tarka Trail, Dartmoor Way, Saints' Way, Two Moors Way and Coast Path, with accommodation and transport arranged.

Dartmoor Llama Walks T 01364 631481, W dartmoorllamawalks .co.uk. Moorland walks accompanied by luggage-carrying llamas and alpacas.

Devon Cycling Holidays T 01392 271426, W devoncycling holidays.co.uk. Escorted and bespoke cycling tours, including the Devon Coast to Coast and around the Exe estuary; also offers cycle hire, bike transport and luggage transfer.

Elemental UK T 01326 318771, W elementaluk.com. A range of activities on land and sea are available at Falmouth and Newquay, from bouldering to coasteering.

Encounter Cornwall T 07976 466123, W encountercornwall .com. Two- or three-hour accompanied canoe excursions on the River Fowey, or tailor-made options.

Encounter Walking T 01208 871066, W encounterwalking holidays.com. Self-guided walking holidays in Devon and Cornwall.

Footpath Holidays T 01985 840049, W footpath-holidays.com. Guided and self-guided walks in North Cornwall, South Devon and the far west, with accommodation arranged, including New Year breaks.

Global Boarders T 01736 369995, W globalboarders.com. Surfing holidays in West Cornwall and Newquay, with beach transfers and stylish accommodation – good for families.

Let's Go Walking/Biking ☎ 01837 880075, 🌐 letsgowalking
.com and 🌐 letsgobiking.com. Self-guided walking and biking
holidays in the West Country, including cycling Devon's Coast to Coast
route. Luggage transport and accommodation arranged.

Lundy Diving ☎ 07971 462024, 🌐 lundydiving.co.uk. Diving and
fishing trips from Ilfracombe, North Devon, with access to dive sites
around Lundy Island.

Riding Holidays Cornwall ☎ 01288 331204, 🌐 riding-holidays
-cornwall.co.uk. Self-catering accommodation attached to stables at
Morwenstow – near Bude, Cornwall – for week-long riding holidays and
short breaks.

Shoreline Extreme Sports ☎ 01288 354039, 🌐 shoreline
activities.co.uk. Year-round outdoor activities including archery,
sea-kayaking and rock climbing, based in Bude, North Cornwall.

Spirit of Adventure ☎ 01822 880277, 🌐 spirit-of-adventure
.com. Try hiking, kayaking and climbing, or a combination of different
activities, on an adventure weekend, with high-quality bunkhouse
accommodation in the heart of Dartmoor.

Way2Go4 Walking Holidays ☎ 01288 331416, 🌐 way2go4.com.
Week-long or short-break guided and self-guided walking holidays on
the North Devon/Cornwall border, in standard or superior farmhouse
accommodation.

Travel essentials

Climate

As the most southerly and westerly part of the UK,
and one surrounded by ocean on all sides, Devon and
Cornwall have a unique climate. The peninsula enjoys
some of the country's greatest levels of sunshine, but
also the strongest winds. Rainfall along the coasts is
comparatively low, but once you get to the higher
reaches of the moors, it increases dramatically.

Costs

If you're watching your budget – hostelling or
camping and buying some of your own food in
shops and markets – you can get by on as little as
£30–60 a day, but a more realistic average daily
budget is £60–120, including B&B accommodation
and some travel costs, while on £120–150 a day
you'll be living pretty comfortably: staying in a
decent hotel and dining out every night.

National Trust and English Heritage sites

Many of the most treasured sites in Devon and
Cornwall – from castles, abbeys and great houses to
tracts of protected landscape – come under the
control of the private **National Trust** (🌐 national
trust.org.uk) or the state-run **English Heritage**
(🌐 www.english-heritage.org.uk), whose properties
are denoted in the Guide with "NT" or "EH". Both these
organizations charge an entry fee for nonmembers
at the majority of their historic properties, and these
can be quite high, especially for the more grandiose
National Trust estates. Note that there are **reduced
entry rates** for anyone arriving at NT properties by
bike or on public transport.

If you think you'll be visiting more than half a dozen
places owned by the National Trust or more than a
dozen owned by English Heritage, it's worth taking
out annual **membership** for free entry to the organizations' respective sites. For the National Trust, it costs
around £65 for individuals, £105 for joint membership, £32 for anyone aged 13–25, or £70–112 for
families. For English Heritage, membership costs £52
for individuals, £93 for a couple, £44 for students.
Many **stately homes** remain in private hands, and
charge entry prices comparable to National Trust's.

Entry fees

Attractions owned by the local authorities generally
have lower admission charges; municipal art
galleries and museums, for example, are usually
free. Almost all the region's **churches** are free –
Exeter Cathedral being a notable exception – but
they may suggest a voluntary donation and charge
a small fee for a photographic permit.

AVERAGE MONTHLY TEMPERATURES AND RAINFALL

	Jan	Feb	Mar	Apr	May	Jun	Jul	Aug	Sept	Oct	Nov	Dec
PLYMOUTH												
Max/min (°F)	48/39	48/38	51/41	55/43	61/48	64/52	68/56	68/56	65/53	59/49	53/44	49/40
Max/min (°C)	9/4	9/4	11/5	13/6	16/9	18/11	20/13	20/13	18/12	15/9	12/6	10/5
Rainfall (mm)	108	84	78	67	64	57	62	67	74	113	113	119
NEWQUAY												
Max/min (°F)	48/39	47/39	50/41	54/43	59/47	63/52	66/56	66/56	63/53	58/49	53/44	49/40
Max/min (°C)	9/4	9/4	10/5	12/6	15/9	17/11	19/13	19/14	17/12	14/10	11/7	9/5
Rainfall (mm)	109	79	75	65	65	62	70	67	77	112	125	112

ROUGH GUIDES TRAVEL INSURANCE

Rough Guides has teamed up with WorldNomads.com to offer great travel insurance deals. Policies are available to residents of over 150 countries, with cover for a wide range of adventure sports, 24hr emergency assistance, high levels of medical and evacuation cover and a stream of travel safety information. Roughguides.com users can take advantage of their policies online 24/7, from anywhere in the world – even if you're already travelling. And since plans often change when you're on the road, you can extend your policy and even claim online. Roughguides.com users who buy travel insurance with WorldNomads.com can also leave a positive footprint and donate to a community development project. For more information, go to Ⓦ roughguides.com/travel-insurance.

The majority of fee-charging attractions have **reductions** for senior citizens, full-time students and children under 16, with under-5s being admitted free almost everywhere.

Emergencies

Dial ☎ 999 for all **emergencies**, including the police, fire service, ambulance and coastguard. For non-emergency cases, call ☎ 101 (24hr) for **police** in Devon and Cornwall, or see Ⓦ www.devon -cornwall.police.uk.

Health

Although the South West does not present particular **health hazards** that are exclusive to this part of the country, there are some tips that are worth remembering whether or not you are covered by health insurance (see box above). Remember that the sun can be deceptively strong in the South West, especially (but not only) in the summer months, so you should use a suitable **sunscreen** (SPF 30+ is recommended). On beaches, "jelly shoes" – available at many seaside shops – are a good safeguard against the **weaver fish**, which lurks under the sand at low tide and can cause painful stings from the venomous spines along its dorsal fin. If stung, you should wash the wound in hot water, allowing it to bleed freely, and seek medical attention. Ticks, snakes and toxocara can also be hazards (see box, p.35).

More generally, it's worth packing any prescription medication that you normally take, as well as carrying contact details of your own doctor. Should health issues arise, you can consult the **NHS website** Ⓦ nhs.uk, packed with information on most problems and providing details of local GPs, pharmacies and walk-in centres. Dial ☎ 111 if you need urgent medical help or advice when it's not life-threatening, or ☎ 999 in an **emergency**.

Hospital Accident and Emergency departments are mentioned in the Guide in the relevant chapters.

Insurance

A typical **travel insurance policy** provides cover for the loss of baggage, tickets and – up to a certain limit – cash or cheques, as well as cancellation or curtailment of your journey. Most of them exclude so-called dangerous sports unless an extra premium is paid: in England this can mean most watersports, rock climbing and mountaineering, though probably not activities such as hiking and kayaking.

Internet

Wi-fi is commonly available in bars, cafés and accommodation. If you need to access a terminal and printing facilities your best bet is to ask wherever you are staying; alternatively, head for a public library, where nonmembers are charged around £4 for two hours online. Note there may be a queue to use the computers in libraries, which you can often avoid by booking. Libraries also have free wi-fi.

LGBT travellers

Most of the region's LGBT action is in the two main cities – Plymouth and Exeter – leaving the rest of the area with a somewhat limited, low-key scene. LGBT listings and news can be found at PinkNews (Ⓦ pinknews.co.uk) and Gay Times (Ⓦ gaytimes .co.uk). For information and links, go to Ⓦ gaybritain .co.uk and Ⓦ gaytravel.co.uk.

Maps

The handiest general **map** of the South West is the *A–Z Devon Cornwall Visitors' Atlas and Guide*, showing the region at a scale of 2.5 miles to the inch (around one mile to the centimetre). Produced by Geographers' A–Z Map Company, and available from most newsagents in the region, it has visitor information and large-scale town plans at the back. *Philip's Street Atlas: Cornwall* reproduces the county at a scale of 1.75 inches to the mile (about a quarter-mile to the centimetre), with towns at 3.5 inches to the mile (about an eighth of a mile to the centimetre). Walkers, however, should get hold of one of the two series published by Ordnance Survey (Ⓦ ordnancesurvey.co.uk): the 1:50,000 maps of the *Landranger* series, and the more detailed 1:25,000 maps of the *Explorer* series.

All the above are on sale at outdoors shops and bookshops in the region, or from dedicated **map outlets** such as Stanfords, whose nearest branch is in Bristol (29 Corn St, Bristol BS1 1HT; Ⓣ 0117 929 9966, Ⓦ stanfords.co.uk). Online map services include Ⓦ maps.google.co.uk, Ⓦ bing.com/maps and Ⓦ streetmap.co.uk, all of which have satellite images and road maps of the whole area.

The media

Local publications are often an excellent source of up-to-date information and entertainment listings. **National TV channels** have some local news and current affairs programmes, while **radio stations** based in Devon and Cornwall are useful for weather and traffic bulletins.

One of the South West's most widely read local **newspapers** is the daily *Western Morning News* (Ⓦ plymouthherald.co.uk), based in Plymouth and covering most of Devon and Cornwall – a sort of Middle-England paper with national as well as local news. The same company publishes the weekly *North Devon Journal, Mid-Devon Gazette, The Cornishman, Cornish Guardian* and *West Briton*, the last three covering respectively Penwith, mid-Cornwall and the Lizard, and East Cornwall; all are strong on local news, events and general tittle-tattle. **Magazines** geared toward the region include the monthly glossies *Inside Cornwall, Cornwall Today, Devon Life* and *Devon Today* – all of them with articles on food, culture, local events and other aspects of living in the West Country. You'll pick up more practical information from **free newspapers and magazines** relating to specific regions; for example *Exmoor* and *Enjoy Dartmoor*, which contain information on walks, wildlife, accommodation and services, and can be found in tourist offices and local pubs and hotels.

Providing the usual mix of chat and chart music, **local radio stations** can be useful sources of information on traffic and sea conditions, weather and local events. The BBC's **Radio Cornwall** (95.2, 96 or 103.9FM) and **Radio Devon** (95.7 or 103.4FM) are staid but authoritative, with the accent on local issues; phone-ins tend to feature complaints about the state of the roads and problems with gulls. The main independent stations are **Heart FM** (96.2–107FM) in Devon and Cornwall, **The Breeze** (105.5FM) in South Devon, and **Pirate FM** (102.2 or 102.8FM) in Cornwall; all have national and local news, traffic, weather and surf reports, and a fairly mainstream musical output.

Money

Britain uses the **pound sterling** (£), divided into 100 pence (p). Coins come in denominations of 1p, 2p, 5p, 10p, 20p, 50p, £1 and £2. Notes are in denominations of £5, £10, £20 and £50. You can rely on **credit and debit cards** for most daily expenditure, though many B&Bs and smaller campsites will not accept them (in which case they will generally accept **cheques** or **transfers**).

Opening hours

Many **paying attractions** stop admitting visitors 45 minutes to an hour before closing. Larger and more important **churches** are almost always open during daylight hours, but you'll often find country churches locked up unless they're particular tourist attractions – most in any case close at 4 or 5pm. **Shops** generally open from 9am to 5.30pm Monday to Saturday, with many bigger stores and supermarkets open on Sunday as well (often with reduced hours). When all else is closed, you can normally find a garage selling basic items. In summer, food shops in tourist areas often stay open until 10 or 11pm.

Phones

Public telephone kiosks are still fairly common in towns and villages throughout the South West peninsula, though many do not accept coins. **Mobile phones** are not always to be relied upon – parts of the region are out of range or have only a weak signal – for example, stretches of the north coast of Devon and Cornwall, West Cornwall, the Isles of Scilly and the moors.

Shopping

Devon and Cornwall have always attracted artisans and craftspeople keen to merchandise their wares, ranging from candles in Totnes to sword-and-sorcery trinkets in Tintagel. Fishermen's **smocks** are well in evidence throughout Cornwall, and you'll also find a bewildering range of objects fashioned from **serpentine** from the Lizard peninsula. It's worth checking out Devon's **pannier markets** – covered bazaars where a motley range of items is sold alongside local foodstuffs – and you'll find other markets in most towns, including **farmers' markets** for local produce, which usually take place once or twice monthly.

Tourist information

While **regional tourist boards** (see below) can supply maps and general information via their websites, local **tourist offices** are best for practical, up-to-date information. Funding restrictions have meant that these local visitor centres are not as ubiquitous as they once were, and many of those that survive are now privately run, but they continue to be well supplied with material on public transport, local attractions and accommodation. It's worth noting, however, that much of the material available relates only to places that have paid for their entries and listings in the official brochures. All the same, as a rule, the (often overworked) staff are knowledgeable and helpful, and it's worth grabbing whatever accommodation and dining info they have. **Opening hours** for most tourist offices are Monday to Saturday from 9am to 5pm; in high summer, many are open daily, while in winter some are open at weekends only or even close altogether. Larger offices will have internet access, some will book accommodation, and many also sell tickets for tours, ferries and National Express coaches.

REGIONAL TOURIST BOARDS

Visit Cornwall Ⓦ visitcornwall.com.
Visit Devon Ⓦ visitdevon.co.uk.

USEFUL WEBSITES

Ⓦ **bbc.co.uk/devon and** Ⓦ **bbc.co.uk/cornwall** Invaluable websites for local news, weather and travel, as well as events, attractions and other information relating to the two counties.
Ⓦ **chycor.co.uk** Mainly useful for all kinds of accommodation in Cornwall.
Ⓦ **cornwall.gov.uk** Official county website, worth exploring for its tourism and transport pages and more.

Ⓦ **cornwall-online.co.uk and** Ⓦ **devon-online.com** With a wealth of information on places, activities and attractions, these websites present a range of accommodation in the region, including farm holidays, weekend breaks, camping and self-catering.
Ⓦ **devon.gov.uk** Good all-round site covering everything from museums to the economy, environment and transport.
Ⓦ **devonmuseums.net and** Ⓦ **museumsincornwall.org.uk** Up-to-date info on museums and exhibitions.
Ⓦ **www.english-heritage.org.uk** General information for visiting historic attractions run by English Heritage.
Ⓦ **gps-routes.co.uk** Useful directory of walking and cycling routes with downloadable maps.
Ⓦ **lemonrock.com** For events, gigs and festivals, with links and interactive features.
Ⓦ **lotstodo.co.uk** Useful descriptions and details of some of Devon's top attractions, including kids' favourites, with links.
Ⓦ **metoffice.gov.uk** Detailed five-day forecasts for the region.
Ⓦ **nationaltrust.org.uk** Background and visiting details for National Trust properties.

Travellers with disabilities

Concessionary rates for **travellers with disabilities** are patchy, but one of the better deals is the **Disabled Persons Railcard**, which knocks a third off the price of most railway tickets. The card costs £20 and is valid for one year. Call ☎0345 605 0525 or apply at Ⓦ disabledpersons-railcard.co.uk. Good sources of information for leisure activities and holiday accommodation in the UK are Ⓦ accessatlast .com, Ⓦ goodaccessguide.co.uk and Ⓦ tourismforall .org.uk. See also the *Rough Guide to Accessible Britain* (Ⓦ accessibleguide.co.uk), free to view online and download as a PDF.

Travelling with children

Devon and Cornwall are ideally suited to **family holidays**, with dozens of family-targeted attractions in every area. The great outdoors, of course, is the biggest draw, though options may be limited in bad weather – the websites Ⓦ dayoutwiththekids.co.uk and Ⓦ 101-things-to-do-on-a-rainy-day-in-cornwall .co.uk are useful resources. Paying attractions can be highly expensive: always ask about **family tickets** (usually for two adults and up to three children), which are especially good value in National Trust and English Heritage sites. You can also save money using family rail passes. Many **accommodation** options, including hostels, offer family rooms.

Exeter and mid-Devon

KNIGHTSHAYES COURT

1

Exeter and mid-Devon

One of the West Country's oldest settlements, Exeter is also the most vibrant of Devon and Cornwall's cities, and one where you may be tempted to spend more than a day or two. The county capital's former importance in Devon's flourishing wool industry is perpetuated today in its role as a major commercial centre, while its plethora of bars and restaurants, its numerous cultural events and festivals, and a strong student presence make it a compelling stop. Easily accessible from Exeter, mid-Devon holds a few scattered points of historical and architectural interest that merit a detour, all in or around the small towns of Tiverton and Crediton.

Exeter's premier sight is also its most visible: rising above the concrete of the modern centre, the city's **cathedral** represents the apotheosis of one of the most brilliant periods of English architecture. The other unmissable attraction is the dense collection of art and artefacts in the **Royal Albert Memorial Museum** – an excellent overview of the city and county, which has a respected ethnographic section. As well as its traditional sights, Exeter's range of accommodation, pubs, clubs and restaurants makes it a fun place to soak up the more contemporary cultural scene, and an ideal base for visiting other places in this part of Devon.

North of Exeter, sandwiched between the wild moorland to the north and south, mid-Devon has preserved its profoundly rural nature, its valleys and meadows still largely farmed and dotted with sheep. Accessible by train or via the A396, **Tiverton** is inland Devon's biggest town, and lies within easy reach of two grand country houses: **Knightshayes Court**, a showcase for the work of Victorian architect and designer William Burges; and, to the south, **Killerton**, famous for its extensive collection of costumes. Elsewhere in the region, there's little to tempt you to stay in one place, but there are some destinations worth visiting in passing, notably **Crediton** – on the A377 northwest of Exeter, and on a train line – home to one of Devon's grandest churches.

GETTING AROUND   EXETER AND MID-DEVON

By train Exeter is the hub of the region's rail network, served by frequent trains on the main line to Plymouth and Penzance, and the departure point for branch lines to Barnstaple, Exmouth and, on summer Sundays, Okehampton.

By bus Good bus services link the city to most places in mid-Devon, though having your own vehicle is useful for reaching the area around Tiverton. Bus travellers can save money by purchasing a Devon Day or Explorer ticket (see p.22).

Exeter

A major transport hub and the terminus of the M5 motorway, Devon's county town, **EXETER**, is the first stop on many a tour of the West Country. Despite having much of its ancient centre gutted by World War II bombs, the city retains plenty of its medieval heritage, not least its sturdy **cathedral**, whose flanking Norman towers are Exeter's most recognizable landmark. Other remnants of the old city include a clutch of **medieval churches**, fashioned – like the sparse remains of the castle and city walls – in the local

| Exploring the River Exe and the Exeter Canal p.49 | Walking tours of Exeter p.50 Exeter's festivals p.53 |

EXETER CATHEDRAL

Highlights

❶ Exeter Cathedral One of the country's greatest cathedrals, rich in architectural interest and boasting the longest continuous Gothic ceiling anywhere. **See p.45**

❷ Royal Albert Memorial Museum A delightfully miscellaneous treasure-trove, this Exeter museum boasts informative sections covering everything from Devon pottery to Tahitian mourning dress. **See p.47**

❸ A trip along the Exeter Canal and the Exe estuary Explore the Exeter Canal and River Exe by bike or boat or on foot, with pub stops along the way. **See p.49**

❹ Knightshayes Court This Victorian Gothic house holds striking works by the medievalist designer William Burges, and also has fine gardens. **See p.55**

❺ Coldharbour Mill Museum Devon's wool industry played a crucial role in the county's history, and this ex-mill entertainingly reveals its finer points and provides context. **See p.56**

❻ Church of the Holy Cross Devon's former cathedral is an imposing fifteenth-century structure in Crediton made of red sandstone. **See p.57**

HIGHLIGHTS ARE MARKED ON THE MAP ON P.44

1

pinkish-red sandstone, and a fascinating network of **subterranean passages**. The history and geography of the whole region is covered in the town's fine **Royal Albert Memorial Museum**, while away from the centre, the **Quay** is the starting point for canalside walks and bike rides during the day and a lively focus for diners and pub-goers in the evening.

Brief history

Previously a settlement of the Celtic Dumnonii tribe, Exeter was fortified by the **Romans** in around 50–55 AD – the most westerly outpost of Rome in the British Isles – and renamed Isca Dumnoniorum. Little of note has been excavated from this period, though, suggesting that it was primarily a military occupation. The city was refounded by **Alfred the Great** at the end of the ninth century, and grew to become one of the largest towns in Anglo-Saxon England, profiting from its position on the banks of the River Exe as the major outlet for the inland wool industry. The **Normans** strengthened the old Roman walls, rebuilt the cathedral and expanded the wool trade, which sustained the city until the eighteenth century. Woven in rural Devon, the serge cloth was dyed and finished in Exeter and then exported from the quays on the Exe to France, Spain and the Netherlands. By the first quarter of the **sixteenth century**, Exeter was one of the largest and richest towns in England – only York, Norwich, Bristol and Newcastle were more important outside London. Although the Countess of Devon

EXETER & MID-DEVON

Barnstaple

EXMOOR NATIONAL PARK

0   5
miles

N

South Molton

Bampton

B3226

B3137

A361

A396

Knightshayes
Court
🏛 **4**

Chulmleigh

A377

Witheridge

B3137

A361

River Taw

B3042

Tiverton

Coldharbour
Mill

Eggesford

EGGESFORD
FOREST

Grand Western Canal

5

A384

Winkleigh

Tarka Line

Bickleigh

Cullompton

A3072

A396

M5

Sampford
Courtenay

A3072

Coleford

A377

Crediton

River Exe

B3181

Killerton
🏛

Yeoford

6

A30

Broadclyst

Exeter

DARTMOOR
NATIONAL
PARK

A30

1
2

Crealy Great
Adventure Park

Clyst St
Mary

3

HIGHLIGHTS

1 Exeter Cathedral
2 Royal Albert Memorial Museum
3 A trip along the Exeter Canal
    and the Exe estuary
4 Knightshayes Court
5 Coldharbour Mill Museum
6 Church of the Holy Cross

diverted most of the shipping trade to Topsham by building a weir across the Exe in around 1285, Exeter's role as a major port was restored by the construction of the Quay and the **Exeter Ship Canal** between 1564 and 1566 – the first canal to be built in England since Roman times.

The Civil War to modern times

During the **Civil War**, Exeter – unusually for the West Country – held predominantly Parliamentarian sympathies, but was besieged and taken by the Royalists in 1643, becoming their headquarters in the west and sheltering Charles I's queen. The city fell to a Roundhead army in 1646, which stayed in occupation until the Restoration. Exeter subsequently entered its most prosperous age; the scale of its cloth trade moved the traveller and diarist Celia Fiennes, who visited in 1698, to marvel at the "incredible quantity of [serges] made and sold in the town… The whole town and country is employed for at least twenty miles around in spinning, weaving, dressing and scouring, fulling and drying of the serges. It turns the most money in a week of anything in England". Trade ceased during the **Napoleonic Wars**, and by the time peace was restored, the focus of textile manufacturing had shifted to England's northern industrial towns; Devon's wool industry never regained its former importance.

The severe bombing sustained during **World War II** miraculously spared the city's cathedral, but much of the historic centre was lost, to be replaced by bland reconstruction. In recent years, however, an infusion of energy provided by the university and the tourist trade has prevented Exeter from sliding into provincial decline, and a raft of fashionable new hotels and restaurants testify to its economic wellbeing today.

Exeter Cathedral (St Peter's)

Cathedral Close, EX1 1HS • Mon–Sat 9am–5pm (last entry), Sun 11.30am–5pm (last entry) • £7.50 • **Tours** Mon–Fri 11am, noon, 1pm & 2.30pm, Sat 11am, noon & 1pm, Sun 12.30pm; 1hr • Free • ☎ 01392 285983, ⓦ exeter-cathedral.org.uk

In the centre of town, but aloof from the commercial bustle, **Exeter Cathedral** is a striking place to kick off an exploration of the city. Begun around 1114, the structure was thoroughly remodelled between about 1275 and 1369, resulting in one of the country's finest examples of the Decorated Gothic building style. Seen from afar, the two massive Norman towers, built (unusually) on the transepts, are the stately building's most distinctive feature; close up, it is the facade's ornate Gothic screen that commands attention, its three tiers of sculpted figures – including the kings Alfred, Athelstan, Cnut, William the Conqueror and Richard II – begun around 1360, and now badly eroded.

The interior

On entering the cathedral, you're confronted by the longest unbroken **Gothic ceiling** in the world, an arresting vista of rib-vaulting that has been compared to an avenue of stately trees (the effect heightened by the multiplicity of shafts on each of the stout piers and of mouldings on the arches). The bulbous bosses running along the length of the ceiling are vividly painted – one shows the murder of Thomas à Becket.

High up on the left side, a **minstrels' gallery** is sculpted with angels playing musical instruments, below which are figures of Edward III and Queen Philippa. The walls of the aisles are densely packed with tombs and memorials that show a range of styles – most eye-catchingly in the right transept, where the fourteenth-century sepulchre of Hugh Courtenay, Earl of Devon, and his wife, is carved with graceful swans and a lion. A door from here leads to the **Chapter House**, with a fine wooden ceiling and several discordant 1970s sculptures. In the left transept, the fifteenth-century **astronomical clock** shows the earth with the moon revolving around it, turning on its own axis to show its phases, and the sun represented by a fleur-de-lys. The minute dial above was added around 1760.

▲ A377   ▲ **1**, **2**, University, Bill Douglas Cinema Museum, Lemon Grove, Exeter Northcott Theatre & A377 Barnstaple   St James Park Train Station ▲

EXETER

Exeter
St David's
Train Station

3

NEW NORTH ROAD

Bury
Meadow

HOWELL ROAD

ELMGROVE ROAD

1 **4**

YORK ROAD

BLACKALL ROAD

HOWELL ROAD

QUEEN'S CR.

LONGBROOK STREET

HELE ROAD

6

NEW NORTH ROAD

LONGBROOK T.

CHURCH L.

ST DAVID'S HILL

5

BONHAY ROAD

River Exe

7

BYSTOCK RD

RICHMOND ROAD

MALDON ROAD

QUEEN STREET

Exeter Central
Train Station

Northernhay
Gardens

Rougemont
Castle

Rougemont
Gardens

Market

CASTLE ST

DRINKING
Double Locks	6
George's Meeting House	4
Rusty Bike	1

Royal Albert
Memorial Museum

NORTHERNHAY ST.

IRON BRIDGE

Exeter
Phoenix

3

Library

2

Underground
Passages

PARIS ST

i

Bus
Station

NIGHTLIFE
The Cavern	3
Move	5
Timepiece	2

PAUL STREET

EXE STREET

BARTHOLOMEW ST E.

NORTH STREET

HIGH STREET

GANDY ST.

HIGH STREET

Princesshay
Shopping Centre

REDCOAT STREET

The
Guildhall

Mol's
Coffee
House

3

2

Playing Fields

BONHAY ROAD

BARTHOLOMEW ST.

St Petrock's

CATHEDRAL YARD

Bike Shed Theatre

MARY ARCHES ST.

Farmers'
Market

CATHEDRAL CLOSE

SOUTHERNHAY WEST

SOUTHERNHAY EAST

BARNFIELD ROAD

Barnfield
Theatre

5

8

St Nicholas
Priory

FORE STREET

Corn
Exchange

GEORGE'S ST

SOUTH STREET

Exeter
Cathedral
(St Peter's)

PALACE ST

SOUTHERNHAY
GARDENS

WESTERN WAY

6

St Mary
Steps

7

KING ST

SMYTHEN ST

STEPCOTE HILL

MARKET STREET

PRESTON STREET

4

9

MAGDALEN STREET

10

WESTERN WAY

TUDOR ST

WEST STREET

NEW BRIDGE ST

FROG STREET

QUAY HILL

i

P

HOLLOWAY STREET

BULL MEADOW ROAD

11

FAIRPARK RD

ROBERTS RD

OKEHAMPTON

STREET

ACCOMMODATION
Braeside	6
Crealy Meadows	12
Globe Backpackers	11
Hotel du Vin	10
Langford Bridge	2
Park View	3
Raffles	4
Southernhay House	8
Telstar	5
Townhouse	7
University of Exeter	1
White Hart	9

Medieval
Bridge

EDMUND STREET

COMMERCIAL ROAD

THE QUAY

COWICK ST

ALPHINGTON ST

Custom
House

THE QUAY

3

Quay House

Exeter
St Thomas
Train Station

River Exe

HAVEN

ROAD

N

8

EATING
Ask	3
The Conservatory	2
The Cosy Club	6
The Glorious Art House	7
Harry's	1
Herbie's	4
On The Waterfront	8
Rendezvous	5

0   200
yards

▼ M5, A30 Okehampton, A38 Plymouth & **6**   Exeter Canal ▼

The Choir is dominated by a spectacularly ugly 60ft bishop's throne, built in oak around 1316, whose intricate canopy is said to be the largest of its kind in Britain. Decorated with foliage and grotesque beasts, the **misericords** here are thought to be the oldest in the country, dating from around 1260, and include a carved elephant – allegedly inspired by the elephant given to Henry III by the French king and kept at the Tower of London. On the way out of the cathedral, note the simple plaque to R.D. Blackmore, author of *Lorna Doone*.

To make the most of your visit you can pick up a free **audioguide**, join a **guided tour** or soak up the ethereal atmosphere at **evensong** (Mon–Fri 5.30pm, Sat & Sun 4pm; 45min).

Cathedral Close

Outside the cathedral, a studious-looking statue of the locally born theologian Richard Hooker surveys **Cathedral Close**, an area of green surrounded by a motley mixture of architectural styles from Tudor to Regency, though most display Exeter's trademark red

1

brickwork. One of the finest buildings is the Elizabethan **Mol's Coffee House**, impressively timbered and gabled. Said to have been named after a local Italian woman in the sixteenth century, it's now a leather shop.

The Guildhall

High St, EX4 3LN · Mon–Fri 10.30am–4pm, Sat 10.30am–1pm; may be closed for official functions, so call to check · Tours on arrangement, call to prebook; 1hr · Free · ☎ 01392 665500

Exeter's pedestrianized High Street has a scattering of older buildings among the usual roster of shops and cafés, most notably the fourteenth-century **Guildhall**. Marked out by its elegant Renaissance portico (built in the 1590s from Beer stone), this is claimed to be England's oldest municipal building still in regular use, and easily ranks as Exeter's finest civic building. The key attraction is the panelled main chamber, where the city's councillors meet, entered through an impressive oak door and adorned with giant portraits of such worthies as George II and General Monck, the Devon-born Civil War veteran. The chamber is topped by a fine example of a collar-and-brace timber roof built 1460–1470, its trusses supported by brackets in the form of bears holding a ragged staff, symbol of the earls of Warwick.

Just down from the Guildhall, almost opposite the impossibly narrow Parliament Street (just 25 inches wide at the High Street end), **St Petrock's** church is one of the six surviving medieval churches in Exeter's central area, though its interior (rarely open) was extensively remodelled by the Victorians.

Royal Albert Memorial Museum

Queen St, EX4 3RX · Tues–Sun 10am–5pm · Free · ☎ 01392 265858, ⓦ rammuseum.org.uk

After the cathedral, Exeter's most compelling attraction is the excellent **Royal Albert Memorial Museum**, just north of the High Street near Central station. The neo-Gothic building exudes a Victorian spirit of wide-ranging curiosity, though a modern, user-friendly approach has been adopted, with eye-catching presentations and a discreet sprinkling of twenty-first-century technology.

The ground floor

History, geology and archeology predominate on the museum's **ground floor**. Earliest times are thrillingly illustrated in the archeology and geology rooms where a wide-screen film simulates the formation of the local landscape in the Permian, Triassic and Jurassic periods, and numerous examples from the prehistoric fossil record are on show in display cases, including giant ammonites and fossilized horse and mammoth teeth. The earliest human imprint is represented by finds from the numerous Bronze Age barrows excavated in Devon, notably a substantial haul from Hembury, near Honiton, including arrowheads, flint axe-heads and rudimentary tools like "chippers" and "bashers".

The extensive **Making History** gallery evocatively gathers together art and artefacts, from the Roman coins, glassware, jewellery and pottery of Exeter's legionary fortress through medieval flutes to eighteenth-century costumes and World War II memorabilia. It's quite a lot to take in, with wildly contrasting eras and spheres of interest cheek by jowl. Among them are some of the objects for which Exeter and the West Country were famous; for example pocket watches, clocks and silverware. There's also some slightly weird Martin-ware pottery made by the Martin brothers – among the most successful of the "art potters" of the late nineteenth and early twentieth centuries.

The first floor

On the **first floor**, an echo of the original Victorian character of the museum is present in **Sladen's Study**, decked out in period fashion to display the collection of starfish, sea urchins, sea cucumbers and other echinoderms assembled by the nineteenth-century

1

zoologist William Percy Sladen. Elsewhere, **In Fine Feather** has 140 stuffed birds from around the world in a single display case, and a veritable menagerie of other specimens from tiny, iridescent beetles to large ferocious-looking mammals can be inspected in other rooms.

The **art gallery** has temporary exhibitions as well as a permanent collection of West Country art – mainly landscapes by local painters alongside work by other artists associated with Devon such as Turner, Reynolds and Opie (some paintings are also displayed on the ground floor). The **World Cultures** gallery is particularly strong on items from the Pacific, West Africa and the Congo River area.

Rougemont Castle

Rougemont Gardens, EX4 3PU • Daily 7.30am–dusk • Free

At the top of Castle Street stands the red-stone gatehouse of **Rougemont Castle**, the original fortress erected by William the Conqueror soon after his invasion of England. The castle was later rebuilt and augmented but little else remains today beyond banks and ditches. A plaque commemorates the last people to be executed for witchcraft in England; the women were tried here in the 1680s and hanged in nearby Heavitree.

Beyond the gatehouse, **Rougemont Gardens** and the adjoining **Northernhay Gardens** (also accessible from Queen Street) contain an impressive stretch of **city walls**, incorporating elements of Roman, Saxon, Norman and medieval construction; pick up a free leaflet from the tourist office for a self-guided walk around the walls.

Underground Passages

2 Paris St, EX1 1GA • Tours June–Sept & school hols Mon–Sat 9.30am–5.30pm, Sun 10.30am–4pm; Oct–May Tues–Fri 10.30am–4.30pm, Sat 9.30am–5.30pm, Sun 11.30am–4pm; 35min; call ahead to check availability • £6, children £4; no under-5s • ☎ 01392 665887

Round the corner from the north end of the High Street is the unprepossessing entrance to a network of **underground passages** that were first excavated in the fourteenth century. Masons at work on the cathedral in the 1340s were enlisted to improve the water supply intended for the cathedral precincts, laying down new lead pipes and creating conduits for which the vaulted "Cathedral Passage" visible today formed a kind of maintenance tunnel. The townspeople were entitled to a third of this precious piped water supply, but the city went to the trouble of building its own network, which was upgraded in the 1490s to form what is now called the "City Passage". You can explore the interlinking passages on a diverting 25-minute **guided tour** preceded by a ten-minute film presentation (last tour starts one hour before closing). The narrow stone corridors require much stooping and are not recommended for claustrophobes.

St Nicholas Priory

The Mint, EX4 3BL • Currently closed for renovation • ☎ 01392 665858

Off Fore Street, a tiny lane leads to **St Nicholas Priory**, originally part of a small Benedictine foundation that became a merchant's home after the Dissolution. The interior has been restored to show how it might have looked in Tudor times, including a parlour with a splendidly plastered ceiling, the kitchen, the Norman cellar and the Great Chamber with its arch-braced timber roof. The Priory was closed for renovation at the time of writing, so check before visiting.

Stepcote Hill

To the east of Fore Street, King Street leads to cobbled **Stepcote Hill**, sloping down towards the river. It's difficult to imagine today that this steep and narrow lane was once the main road into Exeter from the west. At the bottom, surrounded by some wobbly timber-framed houses, **St Mary Steps** is one of Exeter's most ancient churches, with a fine seventeenth-century clock showing a knight and two red-coated retainers on its tower, and a late Gothic nave. The rather incongruous-looking timber-framed house across the street is known as the **House That Moved**, a (probably) fifteenth-century merchant's house that was transferred here in its entirety in 1961 when the city-centre bypass was built through its original location.

The Quay

At the bottom of Fore Street, off New Bridge Street, the red ruins of the city's **medieval bridge** lie in a small park tucked away from the traffic swirling over the more modern bridges across the River Exe. Walk along the riverbank (or follow Commercial Road) to reach the old port area, **the Quay**; now mostly devoted to leisure activities, the area gets busy in the evening, but it's worth a wander at any time for its shops and cafés.

The most opulent building here is the **Custom House**, built in 1681, which still preserves its ornamental plaster ceilings upstairs, along with panels explaining the development of the local wool trade. The ground floor is occupied by a tourist information desk (see p.52) and a room where a short video on Exeter's history is screened (free).

Further along the Quay, a handsomely restored pair of five-storey warehouses, dating from 1835, are prize examples of the industrial architecture of the period, with hatches and winches hanging from their windows. You can cross the River Exe via a pedestrian suspension bridge or by the hand-pulled **Butts Ferry** (Easter–Oct daily 11am–5pm; Nov–Easter Sat & Sun 10am–dusk; 40p). On the west bank you'll find the start of the **Exeter Canal**, which dates from the sixteenth century and was the first in Britain to use pound locks (vertical guillotine sluice gates).

Bill Douglas Cinema Museum

The Old Library, Prince of Wales Rd, EX4 4SB • Daily 10am–5pm • Free • ☎ 01392 724321, ⓦ bdcmuseum.org.uk • Roughly a 20min walk from the centre, or take bus #D from the High St

Exeter's most offbeat attraction is the **Bill Douglas Cinema Museum**, on the university's Streatham Campus to the northwest of the town centre, off New North Road. Both a

---

EXPLORING THE RIVER EXE AND THE EXETER CANAL

From the Quay, the **River Exe** and the **Exeter Canal** run parallel towards Topsham (see p.63) and beyond, a highly attractive tract that you can explore by land or on the water. Check ⓦ exe-estuary.org for an overview of the routes available and the wildlife to see.

The main **walking and cycling route** follows a part of the Exe Valley Way, passing the *Double Locks* pub (see p.54). From Exeter Quay it's a five-mile stretch to *Lock Keepers Cottage*, where there's a café open in July and August (Wed–Sun; ⓦ topshamlockcottage.co.uk). About 50m from here, the on-demand Topsham Ferry crosses over to Topsham (9.30am–5.30pm: April–Sept Mon & Wed–Sun; Oct–March Sat & Sun; £1.20 each way, bikes 60p; ☎ 07801 203338), from where an off-road cycle path traces the east side of the estuary to Lympstone, A La Ronde (see p.64) and Exmouth (see p.64). Alternatively, staying on the west bank will bring you a further mile along the towpath to the *Turf Locks Inn* for food and refreshment, and a mile beyond that to Powderham Castle (see p.81). There's a ferry between the *Turf Locks Inn* and Topsham (see p.63).

Exeter Cruises ☎ 07984 368442, ⓦ exetercruises .com. Runs hourly canal trips from Exeter Quay (April, May & Sept Sat & Sun; June–Aug daily; £6 return) as far as the *Double Locks* pub (see p.54) – a 45-minute round trip.
Saddles & Paddles 4 King's Wharf, The Quay ☎ 01392 424241, ⓦ sadpad.com. Bike and canoe rental is available from Saddles & Paddles, which charges £15 per day for bikes, £15–20 for two hours on single and double kayaks, and £25 for two hours on Canadian (open) canoes. Booking advisable.
Stuart Line Cruises ☎ 01395 222144, ⓦ stuartlinecruises.co.uk. Runs an Exeter Canal cruise from Exmouth 1–3 times monthly May–September, taking around 2hr 30min (£10).

1

WALKING TOURS OF EXETER

Exeter's tourist offices have free leaflets for self-guided walks around the city; alternatively you can join a free 1hr 30min **guided walk** conducted by Red Coat guides (☎01392 265203, ⓦexeter.gov.uk/guidedtours). Taking place daily throughout the year, they focus on themes including "Exeter Old and New" and "Ghosts and Legends" and don't require booking. Most start from Cathedral Close (outside the Mol's Coffee House) at 11am and 2pm, with additional tours in summer at 10.30am, 2.30pm and 7pm; quayside tours kick off from outside the Custom House on the Quay. Call, consult the website or pick up a leaflet from the tourist office for details.

---

public museum and a research facility, the Centre explores the development of visual media from Chinese shadow puppetry to Harry Potter. Much of the collection was assembled by Peter Jewell and the great Scottish film-maker **Bill Douglas** – best known for his epic account of the Tolpuddle Martyrs, *Comrades* (1987) – and includes examples of early moving image forms like magic lanterns, peep shows and optical toys. One of the two rooms holds memorabilia, from Hollywood cigarette cards and British film posters to Chaplin comics and kitsch Disney toys. Pick up a guide or audioguide for brief commentaries on the various items.

Crealy Great Adventure Park

Sidmouth Rd, Clyst St Mary, EX5 1DR • Daily: late May to early Sept 10am–5.30pm; early Sept to late May 10am–5pm • £6–20 according to season; online discounts available • ☎01395 233200, ⓦcrealy.co.uk • Exit Junction 30 from M5 or take bus #52A

A big hit with families, **Crealy Great Adventure Park**, on the eastern outskirts of town, has more than sixty indoor and outdoor rides and attractions, and a menagerie of animals from emus to monkeys and meerkats. White-knuckle rides such as the Twister rollercoaster provide the thrills, while interactive shows and the nature trail offer gentler amusements. It's a great rainy-day attraction, though most kids aged 5–12 will appreciate it rain or shine. Tickets can be validated for repeat entries over six days.

ARRIVAL AND DEPARTURE

EXETER

By plane Exeter International Airport (☎01392 367433, ⓦexeter-airport.co.uk) lies 6 miles east of Exeter at Clyst Honiton, off the A30 (connected hourly by bus #56). UK destinations served by the airport include Belfast, Edinburgh, Glasgow, Manchester, Newcastle, the Channel Islands and the Isles of Scilly, and there are also links to European cities such as Amsterdam, Dublin, Malaga and Paris.

By train The most useful of Exeter's four train stations are Exeter Central – smack in the middle of town on Queen Street – and Exeter St David's – further northwest on Bonhay Road, closer to some of the city's cheaper B&Bs. Trains on the London Waterloo–Salisbury line stop at both, as do Tarka Line services to Barnstaple and trains to Exmouth. Travellers from London Paddington, Bristol or Birmingham will have to get off at Exeter St David's, connected to the centre by city bus #H every 15–30 minutes, or a 20min walk. Trains for Exmouth leave from Exeter St David's and stop at Exeter Central and St James Park (northeast of the centre), while trains for Okehampton leave from St James Park, making a stop at Exeter Central.

Destinations Barnstaple (Mon–Sat hourly, Sun 7–8 daily; 1hr 15min); Crediton (Mon–Sat hourly, Sun 7–11 daily; 20min); Exmouth (1–2 hourly; 30–50mins); London (2–3 hourly; 2hr–3hr 30min); Okehampton (mid-May to mid-Sept Sun 4 daily; 50min); Penzance (1–2 hourly; 3hr–3hr 30min); Plymouth (2–3 hourly; 1hr); Tiverton (2–3 hourly; 15min).

By bus Long-distance buses use the bus station on Paris Street, near the tourist office and Princesshay shopping centre.

Destinations Barnstaple (Mon–Sat hourly; 2hr–2hr 30min); Bude (Mon–Sat hourly, Sun 3 daily; 2hr 20min); Crediton (Mon–Sat 3–4 hourly, Sun every 30min; 30min); Exeter Airport (hourly; 20–30min); Exmouth (Mon–Sat every 15min, Sun every 30min; 40min); Honiton (Mon–Sat 1–3 hourly, Sun 1–4 daily; 1hr–1hr 25min); London (10–11 daily; 4hr 30min–5hr); Okehampton (Mon–Sat hourly, Sun 5 daily; 55min–1hr 10min); Plymouth (12–14 daily; 1hr 15min–1hr 50min); Sidmouth (Mon–Sat every 30min, Sun 1–2 hourly; 55min); Tiverton (Mon–Sat 3–4 hourly, Sun every 2hr; 40min–1hr 15min); Torquay (hourly; 1hr 15min); Uffculme (Mon–Sat hourly, Sun 5 daily; 55min–1hr 10min).

1

GETTING AROUND

Exeter's sights are easily visited **on foot**; the furthest from the centre is the Bill Douglas Cinema Museum, on the university campus a mile or so north. Almost everything else you'll want to see lies between the cathedral and the quayside.

By bus If you envisage using the city buses during an intensive one-day visit, pick up leaflets with timetables and routes from the bus station and buy a £3.60 "Day Rider" all-day ticket here or on board. Useful routes include bus #G (Mon–Sat), which goes down to the Quay from the High Street and Fore Street hourly until 3.15pm, and services #D and #H, which run frequently north to the university campus and the Northcott Theatre from the High Street.
By taxi Apple Taxis, Exeter St David's station (☎ 01392 666666); Z Cars, South St (☎ 01392 595959); both operate 24hr.

By car Most car rental agencies have offices at the airport, such as Avis (☎ 0844 544 6015, ⬤ avis.co.uk), or in the Marsh Barton Trading Estate off Alphington Rd (bus #B from the bus station or the High St), including Enterprise (29 Marsh Green Rd East; ☎ 01392 421400, ⬤ enterprise .co.uk), and Thrifty (12 Marsh Barton Rd; ☎ 01392 207207, ⬤ thrifty.co.uk).

INFORMATION

Tourist information Dix's Field, across from the bus station and behind Princesshay car park (April–Oct Mon–Sat 9am–5pm; Nov–March Mon–Wed & Fri 9.30am–4.30pm, Thurs & Sat 9.30am–4pm; ☎ 01392 665700, ⬤ heartofdevon.com/exeter). There's a smaller office in The Custom House on Exeter Quay (April–Oct daily 10am–5pm; Nov–March Sat & Sun 11am–4pm; ☎ 01392 271611).

ACCOMMODATION

HOTELS

★**Hotel du Vin** Magdalen Street, EX2 4HY ☎ 01392 790120, ⬤ hotelduvin.com. A red-brick former eye hospital has been reincarnated as a contemporary hotel with quirky details and eye-catching murals. Rooms are full of funky charm – those higher up are bigger and better (and rooms at the back are quieter). There's a French-inspired bistro, a spa and a great indoor/outdoor pool. Parking is very limited. £119
White Hart 66 South St, EX1 1EE ☎ 01392 279897, ⬤ marstonsinns.co.uk. Centrally located old coaching inn with period trappings and friendly service. The courtyard and bar are especially atmospheric, but most of the bedrooms are in a modern annexe. Parking available. £84

B&BS

Braeside 21 New North Rd, EX4 4HF ☎ 01392 256875, ⬤ guesthouseinexeter.co.uk. Close to the sights and Exeter Central station (and about 10min from St David's), this B&B is perfectly positioned for a night or two in the city. Some rooms and bathrooms are small but all are modern and functional. The friendly couple who own it have lots of local tips. £70
Park View 8 Howell Rd, EX4 4LG ☎ 01392 271772, ⬤ parkviewexeter.co.uk. Equidistant between the two train stations, this Georgian guesthouse in a quiet spot has airy, spotless rooms of various sizes – the top-floor rooms are biggest – overlooking either a park or the back garden, and mostly en suite. It's a bit dated, but offers a good choice at breakfast. £65
★**Raffles** 11 Blackall Rd, EX4 4HD ☎ 01392 270200, ⬤ raffles-exeter.co.uk. Victorian B&B full of character and crammed with military chests, risqué paintings and other

items from the owner's antiques business. There's a handsome guests' lounge, a garden and parking space (£5 per car). £78
Southernhay House 36 Southernhay East, EX1 1NX, ☎ 01392 435324, ⬤ southernhayhouse.com. Though extravagant, a stay in this centrally located hotel in a tastefully renovated Georgian townhouse is worth the expense for its breezy feel and chic, eclectic style that blends period and modern decor. It has just ten rooms, all with modern facilities, though some are small. Extras are pricey, but breakfasts are beautifully cooked and there's a great bar and restaurant offering delicious food. £154
Telstar 77 St David's Hill, EX4 4DW ☎ 01392 272466, ⬤ telstar-hotel.co.uk. Convenient for St David's station and the centre of town, this place has calming and tasteful decor and very helpful staff. Some of the rooms are smaller and have shared bathrooms, but there's a comfortable lounge with an open fire. Breakfasts are excellent, and there's (limited) parking. £65
Townhouse 54 St David's Hill, EX4 4DT ☎ 01392 494994, ⬤ townhouseexeter.co.uk. Appealing Edwardian guesthouse, midway between the train stations and adjacent to a churchyard. The bright, mainly spacious rooms are named after literary characters, and breakfast includes home-made and free-range products. £85

HOSTEL AND UNIVERSITY ACCOMMODATION

Globe Backpackers 41 Holloway St, EX2 4JD ☎ 01392 215521, ⬤ exeterbackpackers.co.uk. Exeter's only hostel is centrally located, clean and relaxed, with bunk beds in dorms for eight or ten people and private rooms sleeping four (with shared bathroom). There are good kitchen facilities with free tea and coffee. Dorms £17.50; doubles £45

University of Exeter Streatham Campus, off New North Rd, EX4 4QR ☎ 0300 555 0214, ⓦ eventexeter .co.uk. Clean, basic B&B accommodation in single or double rooms convenient for St David's station. You can stay at Reed Hall, a conference centre where eight rooms are available throughout the year, or in a hall of residence during the Easter and summer breaks. Both places enjoy amazing views. Book well ahead. **£52**

CAMPING

Crealy Meadows Sidmouth Rd, Clyst St Mary, EX5 1DR ☎ 01395 234888, ⓦ crealymeadows.co.uk. A couple of miles east of Exeter, this campsite lies right next to Crealy Great Adventure Park (see p.50), so is particularly favoured

by families. Everything is clean and orderly, and there are glamping options (from £295 for two nights) in Safari or Medieval tents, complete with solid wood furniture, wood-burning stoves, fridges and sinks. Entertainments are laid on every evening during peak season, and campers get discounted entry to Crealy Park (free for glampers). Bus #52A from Exeter. Closed early Nov to March. **£15**

Langford Bridge Newton St Cyres, EX5 5AQ ☎ 01392 851459, ⓦ langfordbridge.co.uk. Between Exeter and Crediton off the A377 (3.5 miles northwest of Exeter), this small site beside a stream is clean and quiet, and a 20min walk from the excellent *Beer Engine* pub and Newton St Cyres railway station (on the Tarka Line). No credit cards. **£15.50**

EATING

Ask 5 Cathedral Close, EX1 1EZ ☎ 01392 427127, ⓦ askitalian.co.uk. Pastas and pizzas (£8–13) are the main event at this capacious, child-friendly Italian restaurant – part of a chain, but housed in an atmospheric old building overlooking the cathedral. If there's no space by the large windows, eat in the low-beamed back rooms or on the red-brick veranda. Mon–Sat 11.30am–11pm, Sun 11.30am–10.30pm.

The Conservatory 18 North St, EX4 3QS ☎ 01392 273858, ⓦ theconservatoryrestaurant.co.uk. This calm, pastel-hued haven offers generous portions of Mediterranean food, such as roast hake fillet (£17) and baked courgette stuffed with sun-dried tomatoes and couscous (£16). There's a great-value lunchtime menu of two courses for £10. One wall is dominated by a Tudor panel dating from around 1600. Tues–Thurs noon–2pm & 5.30–8.30pm (last orders), Fri & Sat noon–2pm & 6–9pm (last orders).

The Cosy Club 1 Southernhay Gardens, EX1 1SG ☎ 01392 848744, ⓦ cosyclub.co.uk. The institutional setting of this place in a former hospital wing is offset by the zany decor – a retro confection of flouncy lampshades, mismatched furniture, anatomical prints and animal skulls. It's a great spot for brunches, coffees, tapas (£12 for 3) and burgers (around £9), though it gets packed at weekends. Mon–Wed & Sun 9am–11pm, Thurs–Sat 9am–11.30pm; food served 9am–10pm.

The Glorious Art House 120 Fore St, EX4 3JQ ☎ 01392 490060, ⓦ theglorious.co.uk. As the name suggests, this café-gallery on three floors of a narrow sixteenth-century

building has an arty, homespun, retro style, and an exuberantly old-school ambience, making it a fun spot for a snack lunch or a pot of tea with a slice of cake on charming old crockery. The menu includes baguettes, bagels and organic soups for £5–6, and salads, curry, tagine and homity pie for £7–8. The top floor is a gallery with exhibitions of local art. Mon–Sat 8am–5.30pm, Sun 10am–4pm.

Harry's 86 Longbrook St, EX4 6AP ☎ 01392 202234, ⓦ harrysrestaurants.co.uk. Good-value Mexican and Italian staples (£10–14) are on the menu in this converted Victorian stonemason's studio that preserves a lively, upbeat feel without sacrificing its period atmosphere. It gets very busy at weekends, and is worth booking at any time. Food served daily 9–11.30am, noon–2pm & 6–9.30pm.

★ **Herbie's** 15 North St, EX4 3QS ☎ 01392 258473. The city's favourite veggie and wholefood restaurant has fast and friendly service, an eclectic and creative menu that draws in plenty of non-vegetarians, and organic ales and wines to boot. Mains range from stoneground pizza and Greek Pie (both £10) to the Larder Plate (veggie meze, £14.75). Mon 11am–2.30pm, Tues–Fri 11am–2.30pm & 6–9.30pm, Sat 10.30am–3.30pm & 6–9.30pm.

On The Waterfront The Quay, EX2 4AP ☎ 01392 210590, ⓦ waterfrontexeter.co.uk. In a great setting with a lively atmosphere, this popular spot has a cosy vaulted interior, but most opt for the tables out on the quayside. Pizzas (small or large, £10–20) are the biggest draw on the menu, alongside a selection of tapas (£4), burgers (£10–14) and steaks (£14–18). There's live

---

EXETER'S FESTIVALS

Exeter's **Festival of Food and Drink** (ⓦ exeterfoodanddrinkfestival.co.uk; £8 for one day, £20 for whole event) takes place over a long weekend in mid- or late April, and features stalls of local produce for sale, cookery demonstrations and (separately ticketed) evening concerts. **Vibraphonic** (ⓦ vibraphonic.co.uk), spread over three weeks in March, highlights urban music, taking in jazz, hip-hop, soul and reggae. For details of all city festivals, contact the tourist office, call the festivals and events office (☎ 01392 265200) or see ⓦ heartofdevon.com/exeter.

1

acoustic music on Tues and Thurs from 7pm (April–Oct). Daily 10am–11.30pm; food served 10am–10pm.
★**Rendezvous** 38–40 Southernhay East, EX1 1PE ☎01392 270222, ⊛rendezvous-winebar.co.uk. This basement wine bar and restaurant provides a peaceful bolt hole for a satisfying meal in a smart, friendly environment. The varied menu might include plaice goujons to start,

mains like guinea fowl and pork tenderloin, and passion fruit cheesecake for dessert, and there's a superb wine list. Prices are high-ish, but the lunch and early evening menu (two courses for £16) is a good deal. You can eat or drink in the garden in fine weather, and there's live music on the first Friday of the month. Food served noon–2.15pm & 6.30–9.15pm.

DRINKING

Double Locks Canal Banks, Alphington, EX2 6LT ☎01392 256947, ⊛doublelocks.com. A pleasant 2.5-mile walk, boat ride or cycle along the canal banks from the Quay brings you to this brick-built inn, which has a large food menu, a beer garden and, in summer, weekend barbecues and occasional live music. Young's ales are served, alongside rotating local brews and ciders. Daily 11am–10.30pm, closes earlier in winter.
George's Meeting House 38 South St, EX1 1ED ☎01392 454250, ⊛jdwetherspoon.co.uk. In an atmospheric converted chapel from 1760, this

Wetherspoons pub has a range of good-value bar food available until 11pm. There's an outdoor garden, and usually a crowd at night. Mon–Thurs & Sun 8am–midnight, Fri & Sat 8am–1am.
★**Rusty Bike** 67 Howell Rd, EX4 4LZ ☎01392 214440, ⊛rustybike-exeter.co.uk. There's an excellent vibe at this wood-decor pub/restaurant with vintage table-football and a range of gins, malt whiskies and tequilas alongside local beers and ciders. An impressive range of locally-sourced dishes is available, and there's a patio. Mon–Sat 5–11pm, Sun noon–10.30pm.

NIGHTLIFE

★**The Cavern** 83 Queen St/Gandy St, EX4 3RP ☎01392 495370, ⊛exetercavern.com. A local institution, this underground venue has been at the centre of Exeter's live music scene for decades (mainly punk, electro and indie) and also has DJ nights (indie, drum'n'bass, dubstep, etc.). It opens for daytime snacks too (not Sun). Mon–Sat 11am–5pm, club nights 8pm–late.
Move 4 The Quay, EX2 4AP ☎07447 494764, ⊛move-exeter.co.uk. Drop into this waterside venue for a

soundtrack of house, dubstep, drum'n'bass and rap, as well as live bands. There's usually discounted entry for early birds. Mostly weekends 8pm–3am.
Timepiece Little Castle St, EX4 3PX ☎01392 493096, ⊛timepiecenightclub.co.uk. Formerly a prison, this venue on two floors now hosts club nights and student nights throughout the week, with turntables whirling to techno, Latin, urban and indie music. There's outdoor seating in the courtyard. Usually 7.30pm–2am.

ENTERTAINMENT

THEATRES
Barnfield Theatre Barnfield Rd, Southernhay, EX1 1SN ☎01392 271808, ⊛barnfieldtheatre.org.uk. The home of Exeter's Little Theatre Company is also used by a range of local amateur and professional companies for theatrical and musical productions.
Bike Shed Theatre 162 Fore St, EX4 3AT ☎01392 434169, ⊛bikeshedtheatre.co.uk. Small basement venue staging diverse events from comedy and quizzes to experimental productions by guest companies.
Exeter Northcott Theatre Stocker Rd, Streatham campus, University of Exeter, EX4 4QB ☎01392 726363, ⊛exeternorthcott.co.uk. Exeter's main performance venue for mainstream and traditional drama as well as cabaret, concerts, dance and opera.
Exeter Phoenix Bradninch Place, Gandy St, EX4 3LS

☎01392 667080, ⊛exeterphoenix.org.uk. This arts and media centre hosts plays, concerts and various workshops as well as art films and installations. Exhibitions are usually free, and there's an excellent café-bar (Mon–Sat 10am–11pm) with an outdoor terrace and snacks.

MUSIC VENUES
Corn Exchange Fore St/Market St, EX1 1BW ☎01392 665938, ⊛sites.exeter.gov.uk/cornexchange. Mainstream venue for regular folk and rock concerts, tribute acts and comedy evenings.
Lemon Grove Cornwall House, Streatham campus, University of Exeter, EX4 6TG ☎01392 723511, ⊛exeterguild.org/lemongrove. The university's club – aka the *Lemmy* – is open term-time only and hosts a variety of live acts from metal to rap.

DIRECTORY

Hospital Royal Devon and Exeter Hospital's main site is on Barrack Rd, Wonford, EX2 5DW (☎01392 411611), where there's an Accident and Emergency Department. Bus #H

from High St.
Left luggage Apple Taxis, on the forecourt of Exeter St David's station, will stash your gear (£4/item for 24hr).

1

Markets In addition to the few stalls on Sidwell St, at the top of the High St (Mon–Sat 8.30am–4.30pm), Exeter has some appetizing foodie markets. There's a Farmers' Market on Thursdays (9am–2pm) at the junction of South and Fore streets, plus evening street-food markets on the Quay on the first Thursday of the month, and across the river in Piazza Terracina on the third Thursday (both April–Oct 5.30–9.30pm and usually with live music; ⓦ streetfoodexeter.co.uk). Exeter Quay also hosts a crafts market, usually on the first Sunday of the month (Easter–Sept 10am–5pm).

Police Exeter Police Station, Heavitree Rd, EX1 2LR (☎ 101, ⓦ devon-cornwall.police.uk).

Post office 28 Bedford St, Princesshay shopping centre (Mon–Sat 9am–5.30pm).

Tiverton and around

At the heart of a rich agricultural region of red soil and lush meadows, **TIVERTON** lies thirteen miles due north of Exeter. The town owes its fortune to textiles, its mills powered by the Exe and Lowman rivers that meet here. Pedestrianized Fore Street leads westwards down Angel Hill to the Exe Bridge, from where you can see the last remaining textile factory, a prominent landmark that was opened as a cotton mill in 1792 by a lace and textile entrepreneur, John Heathcoat.

The locality's one-time wealth is reflected in the number of churches in town: no fewer than eleven. They include **St George** on St Andrew Street, constructed partly of Purbeck stone in 1733 and reckoned to be Devon's finest Georgian church, and **St Peter** on St Peter's Street, whose south porch has Gothic tracery depicting the Assumption of the Virgin Mary flanked by images of the benefactor and his wife.

Tiverton Museum of Mid-Devon Life

Beck's Square, EX16 6PJ · Feb to late Dec Mon–Fri 10.30am–4.30pm, Sat 10am–4pm · £4.50 · ☎ 01884 256295, ⓦ tivertonmuseum.org.uk

Across from the bus station, **Tiverton Museum of Mid-Devon Life** outlines the background of the town's cloth industry and includes lace-making machinery from Heathcoat's factory. The collection takes in the domestic and social history of the whole region, illustrated through a variety of items from agricultural implements – mantraps and farm wagons – to cooking utensils, brewing equipment and a reconstructed room belonging to a wool merchant of 1600.

Grand Western Canal

Just off Canal Hill on the Cullompton road, a mile southeast of the town centre, lies the western end of the **Grand Western Canal**, originally conceived as a means of linking the English and Bristol channels, though only the Tiverton–Taunton stretch was completed (in the early 1800s). The waterway fell into decline following the growth of the railway in the 1840s, but has been restored and now forms the focus of a country park and nature reserve. The canal can also be accessed from Tiverton Parkway station, half a mile distant. Pick up a leaflet describing walks along the canal banks from Tiverton's tourist office (for boat trips, see p.56).

Knightshayes Court

Bolham, EX16 7RQ · **House & garden** Daily: March–Oct 10am–5pm; Nov–Feb 11am–4pm · £9.30; NT · **Park** Daily dawn–dusk · Free, but parking £1/hr or £4/day · ☎ 01884 254665, ⓦ nationaltrust.org.uk/knightshayes · From Tiverton, taxis are around £5. Alternatively, take bus #398 to Bolham, or #348 or #349 to Lea Rd; from either stop it's nearly a mile walk, though from Bolham it's a steeper uphill climb

A couple of miles north of Tiverton off the A396, the Victorian Gothic pile of **Knightshayes Court** was partly designed by the flamboyant and idiosyncratic architect William Burges for John Heathcoat Amory (1829–1914), MP for Tiverton and grandson of John Heathcoat (see above). Burges' offbeat ideas, however, led to him being replaced in 1874 by J.D. Crace, whose contributions were considerably blander

1

than his predecessor's. Characteristic of Burges' work are the corbel figures in the hall stairwell, and the hall itself, an imitation of a medieval vaulted room, holding a bookcase designed by Burges and painted by the Pre-Raphaelites Burne-Jones and Rossetti. More of Burges' work can be seen in the sumptuous library, in the magnificent arched red drawing room with its Burges-designed marble chimneypiece, and in the bedroom, splendidly decorated with wall paintings of more than eighty birds.

Coldharbour Mill Museum

Uffculme, EX15 3EE · Tours Tues–Sun 10am–4pm in school hols; term-time Fri–Sun 10am–4pm; 30min · £6.75 · ☎ 01884 840960, ⓦ coldharbourmill.org.uk · From Tiverton, Tiverton Parkway station or Exeter, take bus #1

Seven miles east of Tiverton on the B3440 (and signposted from junction 27 of the M5), **Coldharbour Mill Museum**, outside the village of Uffculme, was a fully-fledged working mill for nearly two hundred years until its closure in 1981. Now reduced to supplying its shop with wool, the mill still provides a fascinating insight into the techniques and machinery of the wool industry in the nineteenth century, when it was the area's major employer. You can only visit on one of the informative **tours**, which take in working examples of steam engines of the era.

ARRIVAL AND DEPARTURE
TIVERTON AND AROUND

By train Tiverton Parkway train station lies six miles west of the town centre, connected by bus #1 (Mon–Sat hourly, Sun 4 daily; 20min).
Destinations Bristol (1–2 hourly; 1hr); Exeter (1–2 hourly; 15min); Plymouth (1–2 hourly; 1hr 20min).

By bus Tiverton's bus station is centrally located near the museum at Phoenix Lane, with services to Exeter (Mon–Sat 3–4 hourly, Sun 11 daily; 40min–1hr 30min) and Uffculme (Mon–Sat 1–2 hourly; Sun 4 daily; 35min).

INFORMATION AND ACTIVITIES

Tourist information Tiverton Museum, Beck's Square (Mon–Sat: April–Sept 9.30am–4.30pm; Oct–March 10am–4pm; ☎ 01884 230878, ⓦ exploretiverton.co.uk).
Bike rental Abbotshood Cycle Hire, *Globe Inn*, Sampford Peverell, on the canal (5 miles east of Tiverton, one mile east of Tiverton Parkway train station); ☎ 01884 821214, ⓦ abbotshoodcyclehire.co.uk. £9.50 per day.

Canal trips and boat rental Tiverton Canal Co, The Wharf, Canal Hill (☎ 01884 253345, ⓦ tivertoncanal .co.uk). Excursions on horse-drawn barges are offered (2hr 30min; £12.40), as well as boat rental (rowing boats £15/2hr; Canadian canoes £20/2hr; motor boats for up to 6 people £90/4hr). There's also a visitor centre here, a shop and the *Ducks Ditty* café.

ACCOMMODATION AND EATING

Bridge Guest House 23 Angel Hill, EX16 6PE ☎ 01884 252804, ⓦ bit.ly/BridgeGuestHouse. All the rooms in this modernized red-brick Victorian house overlook the River Exe, with a narrow garden running along the banks. En-suite bathrooms are cramped, but excellent breakfasts are served and there's (limited) parking. No credit cards. **£68**

Flying Pickle 40 Gold St, EX16 6PY ☎ 01884 242661. This smart delicatessen has everything you need for brunches and lunches – West Country hams, cheeses and pickles to take away, plus sandwiches, salads, coffees and cakes in the café or the comfy upstairs area. Breakfasts are good too, and there are some tables outside. Mon–Sat 8am–4pm.

DIRECTORY

Markets Tiverton's Pannier Market between Fore Street and Newport Street is open Mon for a flea market and Tues, Fri & Sat for general wares and food – including cheap snacks.

Electric Nights Streetfood market (ⓦ electricstreetfood .wordpress.com) takes place here on the first Saturday of the month from 5.30pm (May–Oct), and includes live music.

Killerton

Broadclyst, EX5 3LE · **House** Daily: mid-Feb to mid-March & mid-Nov to Dec 11am–4pm; mid-March to Oct 11am–5pm · **Chapel & garden** Daily: Jan to mid-Feb 11am–4pm; mid-Feb to Dec 10am–5.30pm · £10.50; NT · **Park** Daily 8am–7pm or dusk · Free · ☎ 01392 881345, ⓦ nationaltrust.org.uk/killerton · Take any Exeter–Tiverton bus to Killerton Turn, then walk for 15min

1

Twelve miles south of Tiverton off the B3181, **Killerton** is attractively set on a hillside amid a landscaped garden of lawns, champion trees and herbaceous borders. The elegant eighteenth-century house is famous for its **fashion collection**, one of the largest in the South West. Exhibitions on the first floor, drawn from more than 20,000 items in storage, are changed each year (recent themes include natural fibres and the development of dyes).

The extensive grounds include the **bear's hut**, a summerhouse named after a pet bear once housed within, and the **ice house**, constructed in 1808 and capable of storing up to three years' worth of ice. Open-air **drama productions** are staged in the gardens in summer.

Crediton

At the precise geographical centre of Devon, **CREDITON** was established as an important settlement and market town in Saxon times, serving as the meeting point of trade routes from Okehampton, Exeter, Tiverton and Barnstaple. Today the only item of note in what is now a mere village is its splendid, red, collegiate **parish church**. Once you've taken in the church, there's little reason to hang around unless you're looking for refreshments or stuck for a bed for the night.

Church of the Holy Cross

Church Lane, EX17 2AH • Daily 9am–dusk • Tours : Usually Sat 10am (check first); 30min–1hr • Free • ☎ 01363 773226,
ⓦ creditonparishchurch.org.uk

The cathedral dimensions and pinnacled central tower of the **Church of the Holy Cross** appear in a different scale to the rest of Crediton. The present building was started at or near the site of the town's monastery church in the mid-twelfth century, though only the base of the present tower remains from that period. Most of what you see today dates from a reconstruction in the early Perpendicular style between 1410 and 1478; as a result of this, what might have been a gloomy interior is now flooded with light coming in through two rows of generous windows (including those of the clerestory). The plain glass here replaced the original stained glass blown out by a landmine in 1942.

The south choir aisle gives access to the **Chapter House**, dating from around 1300; the lovely old room now displays a collection of local knick-knacks – pieces of seventeenth-century armour, a few musket barrels and the like.

ARRIVAL AND DEPARTURE
CREDITON

By train Crediton's train station is off the A377 Exeter road just south of town, a stop on the Tarka Line between Exeter and Barnstaple.
Destinations Barnstaple (Mon–Sat hourly, Sun 7 daily; 1hr); Exeter (Mon–Sat hourly, Sun 7–11 daily; 15min);

Okehampton (mid-May to mid-Sept Sun 4 daily; 30min).
By bus Buses stop on the High Street, and go to Barnstaple (Mon–Sat 9 daily; 2hr) and Exeter (Mon–Sat 4–5 hourly, Sun every 30min; 25–40min).

ACCOMMODATION AND EATING

★**Taw Vale** 2 Taw Vale Terrace, Station Rd, EX17 3BU ☎01363 777879, ⓦtawvale.co.uk. This detached Georgian house at the southern end of town (very near the train station) offers spotless and spacious rooms, one with its own patio shaded by a grapevine. The generous breakfasts include home-made jams and marmalades. £78
Three Little Pigs Parliament Square, EX17 2BP ☎01363 774587, ⓦthethreelittlepigscrediton.com.

Idiosyncratic pub and restaurant, with everything from stuffed animals to musical instruments and model trains hanging from its walls and ceiling. Doom, Tribute and guest ales are served, and the food (served noon–3pm & 6–9pm) ranges from salads and pizzas to lamb shank, with most dishes under £10. You can sit at tables in the square when weather permits. Mon–Thurs 11.30am–10.30pm, Fri & Sat 11am–midnight, Sun 11.30am–9pm.

East Devon

VIEW FROM BEER HEAD

2

East Devon

The country between the Exe estuary and the Dorset border holds some often overlooked gems that are worth digging out, including some stunning coastline – part of the fossil-rich Jurassic Coast – and a sprinkling of old-fashioned, Regency-style seaside resorts. Inland, the lush, agricultural countryside sheltering drowsy villages and ancient churches seems equally detached from twenty-first-century stresses. While the majestic red cliffs and shingle beaches of East Devon are popular with young families in August, the region is relatively free of the congestion that afflicts other parts of Devon. The area also hosts some of the West Country's most rambunctious festivals, involving stonking rhythm and blues, folk music mayhem and flaming tar barrels.

Immediately south of Exeter, at the head of the broad and marshy Exe estuary, the small port of **Topsham** is closely linked to the county capital, but with a very separate identity tied to its seafaring past. Further south, the Gothic fantasy of A La Ronde sits above the estuary, one of the most delightful architectural curiosities in the West Country.

At the mouth of the estuary, **Exmouth** is as busy as things get in this region, a family resort embellished by some elegant Georgian terraces, and a good starting point for walks and cycle rides. East along the coast, **Budleigh Salterton** has a wide stony seafront, while forays inland can be made to East Budleigh and Otterton. Back on the coast, a mile east of Otterton, the beautifully sited beach at Ladram Bay is the biggest crowd-puller in the area.

Sidmouth is the most appealing of East Devon's seaside resorts, an elegantly aged Regency town with considerable architectural charm. There are cliff-backed beaches to either side, and the coast path provides an ideal way to reach more isolated stony strands, such as Branscombe, a secluded hamlet with a monumental church. Further east, **Beer** is an immediately likeable village with an intriguing network of subterranean caverns to explore.

East Devon's only substantial inland centre is **Honiton**, home to an absorbing lace museum and not far from one of Devon's most impressive churches at **Ottery St Mary**, an expression of the largesse of the local merchants.

GETTING AROUND   EAST DEVON

By train It's easy to explore the area via public transport, though train routes are limited to the branch line from Exeter St David's to Exmouth – the Avocet Line, a lovely ride along the Exe estuary – and the less frequent service from Exeter to Honiton.

By bus The most useful bus routes from Exeter are #9 and #9A to Sidmouth, #X52 to Beer, and #57 to Topsham and Exmouth, while the #56B provides a useful Sunday service linking Exeter, Ottery St Mary, Honiton and Sidmouth between late May and mid-September.

By bike Useful publications for cyclists include the *Cycling in East Devon* leaflets (free from tourist offices), which describe road routes and shortcuts.

SIDMOUTH FOLKWEEK

Highlights

❶ A La Ronde A unique neo-Gothic folly created by two eighteenth-century women travellers and crammed with offbeat souvenirs collected on their Grand Tour. **See pp.64–65**

❷ The coast path from Sidmouth to Beer This hilly stretch of coastline takes in the thickly grown Hooken Undercliff, pebble beaches and a stupendous view from chalky Beer Head. **See pp.70–72**

❸ Sidmouth FolkWeek One of the country's most exuberant folk music festivals, not least for its seaside setting. **See p.72**

❹ Beer Quarry Caves Delve deep underground to view the achievements of the men tasked with quarrying the Beer stone that was used in some of Britain's greatest monuments. **See p.72**

❺ Branscombe Make a stop in this secluded hamlet, home to a fine church, a delightful beach and a brace of fine pubs. **See p.73**

❻ St Mary's Church A contender for Devon's most glorious church, beautifully sited on a hill in Ottery St Mary; the interior is a visual feast. **See p.75**

HIGHLIGHTS ARE MARKED ON THE MAP ON P.62

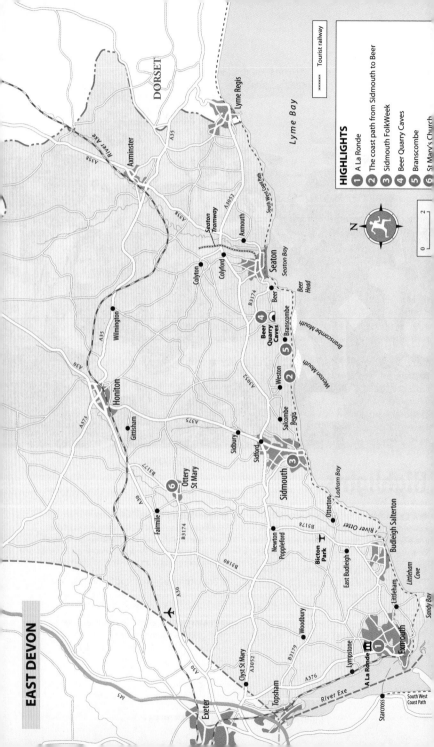

EAST DEVON

DORSET

Lyme Bay

HIGHLIGHTS

1. A La Ronde
2. The coast path from Sidmouth to Beer
3. Sidmouth FolkWeek
4. Beer Quarry Caves
5. Branscombe
6. St Mary's Church

--- Tourist railway

N

0   2

Lyme Regis

River Axe

Axminster

Seaton Tramway

Axmouth

South West Coast Path

Colyton

Colyford

Seaton

Seaton Bay

Beer Head

Beer

Branscombe

Branscombe Mouth

Wilmington

Weston

Weston Mouth

Honiton

Salcombe Regis

Gittisham

Sidbury

Sidford

Sidmouth

Ottery St Mary

Fairmile

Ladram Bay

Otterton

Newton Poppleford

Bicton Park

River Otter

Budleigh Salterton

East Budleigh

Littleham Cove

Woodbury

Littleham

Sandy Bay

Clyst St Mary

Lympstone

A La Ronde

Exmouth

Topsham

Exeter

River Exe

Starcross

South West Coast Path

Topsham

Five miles south of Exeter, **TOPSHAM** was the county capital's main port from the first century on, prospering from the European (and later the transatlantic) wool trade. When this faltered at the end of the eighteenth century, the port was sustained by shipbuilding and its subsidiary activities, such as chain- and rope-making. Today Topsham has a pleasant, well-to-do air, with former warehouses and seventeenth-century merchants' houses along the central Fore Street and the Strand, including good examples of the Dutch-influenced gabled architecture introduced by merchants trading with Holland.

Further down the Strand, the sea wall offers **birdwatching** opportunities at low tide when there are views across the reedy mud flats – look out for curlews, godwits and avocets. Closer to the centre, at the bottom of the steps behind the church of St Margaret's on Fore Street, boatyards and ships' chandlers line the riverfront.

Topsham Museum

25 The Strand, EX3 0AX • 2–5pm: April–July, Sept & Oct Mon, Wed, Thurs, Sat & Sun; Aug Mon–Thurs, Sat & Sun • Free • ☎ 01392 873244, Ⓦ devonmuseums.net/topsham-museum/devon-museums

You'll pick up plenty of background information on the town's shipbuilding and trading traditions at **Topsham Museum**, housed in a seventeenth-century house and former sail loft. Exhibits include a model of Topsham as it was in 1900, four restored river boats, a selection of local craftwork and records of families prominent in the serge-cloth trade. Twentieth-century interest is provided in the form of memorabilia relating to the film star Vivien Leigh, sister-in-law of the museum's founder.

ARRIVAL AND DEPARTURE   TOPSHAM

By train Topsham's train station lies a 10min walk northeast of Fore Street and the High Street.
Destinations Exeter (Mon–Sat every 30min, Sun hourly; 15–25min); Exmouth (Mon–Sat every 30min, Sun hourly; 15min).
By bus Buses stop on the High St and at the train station, and run to Exeter (3–4 hourly; 25min) and Exmouth (2–4

hourly; 25min).
On foot/by bike You can reach Topsham from Exeter Quay on foot or by bike along the Exe Valley Way, which follows the Exeter Canal, crossing to Topsham on the Topsham Ferry (see p.49). Topsham is on the south-coast NCN2, which intersects with the Exe Valley Way at Bridge Road. You can rent bikes from Route 2 (see p.64) for £16 per day.

TOURS

Sea Dream II ☎ 07778 370582, Ⓦ topshamtoturfferry .co.uk. From Trout's Boatyard, between the *Lighter Inn* on the Quay and St Margaret church steps, *Sea Dream II* ferries passengers to the *Turf*, a waterside pub and hotel less than a mile downstream (4–6 times daily: Easter–June & Sept Sat & Sun; June–Aug daily; £5 return). In winter, they also run 1hr–1hr 30min birdwatching cruises in conjunction with the Royal Society for the Protection of Birds (see Ⓦ rspb.org.uk or call ☎ 01392 432691 for details; £15), a

chance to see avocets as well as brent geese and black-tailed godwits.
Stuart Line ☎ 01395 222144, Ⓦ stuartlinecruises.co.uk. From behind the Antiques Warehouse on Lager Quay, Stuart Line runs hour-long river cruises down to Exmouth (late March to mid-Oct; £6), departing 1–3 times a week at different times, depending on the tide; a Round Robin ticket (£10) allows you to take any of the frequent trains back.

ACCOMMODATION

★ **Reka Dom** 43 The Strand, EX3 0AY ☎ 01392 873385, Ⓦ rekadom.net. This waterside seventeenth-century merchant's house has real character, with three suites including one in an old water tower with a separate sitting

room and serene estuary views. Stewed fruits, home-made yoghurt and fish are offered at breakfast, which costs an extra £10 each and can be taken in your room. No credit cards. **£105**

EATING

Bridge Inn Bridge Hill, EX3 0QQ ☎ 01392 873862, Ⓦ cheffers.co.uk. On the eastern edge of town,

overlooking the muddy River Clyst and right on the NCN2 cycle route, this sixteenth-century pub is said to be

Topsham's oldest building, and claims to be the only one ever visited by the Queen in an official capacity – in 1998, when she bought some ale to take back to Philip. A good selection of guest beers and bar snacks is served in the small rooms inside, and there's a garden. Mon–Thurs noon–2pm & 6–10.30pm, Fri & Sat noon–2pm & 6–11pm, Sun noon–2pm & 7–10.30pm.

The Café 76 Fore St, EX3 0HQ ☎ 01392 877827. All-day breakfasts, bacon baguettes and delicious cakes are served in a large room with wooden tables and a relaxed atmosphere. Daily specials might include bubble and squeak, aubergine and spinach frittata, and homity pie (£8.25). No credit cards. Mon–Sat 9.30am–4.45pm, Sun 10am–4.45pm.

The Galley 41 Fore St, EX3 0HU ☎ 01392 876078, ⓦ galleyrestaurant.co.uk. This inviting restaurant boasts dark wood beams and exposed brick walls, and specializes in seafood, from tandoori monkfish with curried prawns to champagne-battered sea bass. Most mains are around £19, and there are fixed-price lunches for £13–22. Tues–Sat noon–2.30pm & 6.30–9pm.

Route 2 1 Monmouth Hill, EX3 0JQ ☎ 01392 875085, ⓦ route2topsham.co.uk. Named after the bike route that passes through town, it's a cyclists' heaven, but non-bikers will also find this a great spot to linger over coffees, snacks and home-made ice cream. Breakfasts, burgers and soups are popular menu items (mains around £8), as are the local beers. Bikes are repaired and available to rent next door. Daily 8am–5pm.

Exmouth and around

At the southeastern corner of the Exe estuary, **EXMOUTH** claims to be the oldest seaside resort in Devon and signs of its early gentility are evident in some graceful examples of Georgian architecture. However, there are few surprises in the repertoire of resort attractions, and the town is primarily a holiday base – no more, no less. Its terraces rise above lawns, rock pools and two miles of **sandy beach** – a rare thing in East Devon.

The town's finer architecture is set back from the beach, notably on **the Beacon**, ascending from Alexandra Terrace, where such folk as Lady Nelson and Lady Byron once stayed (installed at 6 and 19 The Beacon, respectively). At the western end of town, the old **port** is now a luxury marina, though there are still some working fishing boats in evidence, and it's the departure point for a range of **boat trips** (see opposite).

Brief history

Exmouth was unmentioned in history books before a Viking raiding party landed on a marauding invasion in 1001, fanning out to burn and pillage as far as Exeter. By 1200 Exmouth was an important port, and it later became a noted smugglers' haunt. From the time of the Napoleonic Wars, the town evolved as a resort and the central core preserves much of the feel of that era.

The beach

Exmouth's white-sand **beach** is undoubtedly the town's biggest attraction. Orcombe Point at its eastern end marks the start of the **Jurassic Coast** (see box opposite), where you can join the South West Coast Path or, at low tide, walk around the red cliffs to Sandy Bay. It's also a good beach for swimming, though you should pay attention to the red warning flags, as the offshore tides can stir up strong currents. As a reward for your exertions, head for the **ice-cream stand** – a family-run local institution – halfway along the beach, near a line of brightly coloured beach huts.

A La Ronde

Summer Lane, EX8 5BD • Mid-Feb to Oct 11am–5pm • £8.40; NT • ☎ 01395 265514, ⓦ nationaltrust.org.uk/a-la-ronde • Buses #57 & #58 to Summer Lane from Exeter or Exmouth

On a hillside overlooking the Exe estuary, resembling something out of a fairy tale, the lantern-roofed Gothic folly of **A La Ronde** lies a couple of miles north of Exmouth and four miles south of Topsham, along a signposted turn-off from the A376 (a five-minute walk from the bus stop). An extravagant flight of fancy dating from the 1790s, A La

Ronde was the achievement of two cousins, Jane and Mary Parminter, who were inspired by a European Grand Tour to construct this sixteen-sided house – possibly based on the Byzantine basilica of San Vitale in Ravenna – filled with mementos of their travels. To these, the Parminters added a number of their own eccentric creations, such as the shells with which they covered the gallery and staircase at the top of the house; they're very delicate, so only viewable via a touchscreen.

A little further up the lane, the tiny Congregational chapel of **Point-in-View** and its adjoining almshouses were built in 1811 on the instructions of the Misses Parminter, for "four spinsters over fifty years of age and approved character".

2

ARRIVAL AND DEPARTURE

EXMOUTH AND AROUND

By train With a good rail link with Exeter on the Avocet Line, Exmouth's train station is a short walk north of the centre, off Marine Way. There are regular services to Exeter (Mon–Sat every 30min, Sun hourly; 35min) via Topsham (10min).

By bus The bus station sits next to the train station a few minutes north of the centre of town off Marine Way; bus #57 links the town frequently with Exeter.

Destinations Budleigh Salterton (Mon–Sat 2 hourly, Sun hourly; 25min); Exeter (Mon–Sat 4 hourly, Sun 2 hourly; 50min); Sidmouth (Mon–Sat hourly; 1hr); Topsham (Mon–

Sat 4 hourly, Sun 2 hourly; 25min).

By boat Providing a useful way to get to or from South Devon without passing through Exeter, a water-taxi service (☏07970 918418, ⦿exeplorerwatertaxis.co.uk) runs between Dawlish Warren (see p.81) and Exmouth (April to early Sept; £4 return; no bikes), while the Exe to Sea Cruises ferry service (☏01626 774770 or ☏07974 772681, ⦿exe2sea.co.uk) crosses the estuary to Starcross (March to mid-May and mid-Sept to Oct 10.40am–4.40pm; mid-May to mid-Sept 10.40am–5.40pm; £4.50 one-way, £5.50 day return, bikes £1). Both run hourly.

INFORMATION AND TOURS

Tourist information AJ's Taxis, 42 The Strand (Mon–Sat: May–Aug 10am–4pm; Sept–April 10am–2.30pm; ☏01395 830550, ⦿exmouth-guide.co.uk).

Stuart Line Exmouth Marina ☏01395 222144, ⦿stuart linecruises.co.uk. Offers cruises to Topsham (late March to mid-Oct; £6), Torbay (late May to Sept; £12.50) and along the Jurassic Coast (April–Oct; £10), as well as three-hour

birdwatching trips in the Exe estuary (Nov–Feb; £12.50) and 1–2hr river cruises (all year; £7.50). A Round Robin ticket (£10) allows you to cruise up to Topsham and return by train.

Tiger Charters ☏07836 792626, ⦿tigercharters.co.uk. Runs wreck-fishing trips from late March to Oct, costing £45/£55 for a six- or eight-hour excursion; booking essential.

ACTIVITIES

Bike Hire Exmouth Cycle Hire, 1a Victoria Rd, off the Strand (☏01395 225656, ⦿exmouthcycles.com; £12/day).

Watersports Edge, The Pier Head, Exmouth Marina (☏01395 222551, ⦿edgewatersports.com), and Liquid

Motion, based at *Exmouth Country Lodge & Campsite* (see p.66; ☏01395 276599, ⦿exmouthwatersports.co.uk) provide equipment rental and tuition for kayaking, paddle-boarding and wind- and kitesurfing. Wetsuits and surfing gear can also be rented from beach kiosks.

THE JURASSIC COAST

The 95-mile stretch of the East Devon and Dorset coasts between Exmouth and Studland Bay has been named the **Jurassic Coast** in honour of the long geological record vividly revealed here, and designated a UNESCO Natural Heritage Site. Despite the name, some 185 million years are represented, covering the Triassic, Jurassic and Cretaceous periods (together forming the Mesozoic Era). The Dorset section of the coast is the most rewarding area for fossil-hunters, but the East Devon stretch is the oldest, and includes the richest mid-Triassic reptile sites in Britain. The coast is distinguished for its diversity, ranging from the red sandstone of the sea stacks at **Ladram Bay** – the reddish colouring hereabouts is due to the presence of iron – to the white chalk of **Beer Head**, and the areas where landslides have created "**undercliffs**", thickly grown with trees and other vegetation. The best way to explore the coast is either by sea – **boat trips** are available in summer from all the major resorts – or on foot along the **coast path**. For more information, pick up a free leaflet or the official guide (£4.95) from local tourist offices, or see ⦿jurassiccoast.com.

ACCOMMODATION

★ **Exmouth Country Lodge & Campsite** Maer Lane, Littleham, EX8 5DB ☎ 01395 276626, ⓦ prattshayes.co.uk. A couple of miles east of the centre and just half a mile from the beach, this is the town's nearest campsite, set on National Trust land. It's small but clean and well equipped, and there's a bunkhouse and private rooms available too (from £49). It's half a mile along Maer Lane from the *Clinton Arms*

pub (bus #95). Camping __£14__, bunks __£25__

Royal Beacon Hotel The Beacon, EX8 2AF ☎ 01395 264886, ⓦ royalbeacon.co.uk. Though it's slightly dated and in need of a lick of paint, this hotel has more than a touch of Regency elegance. Some rooms are in a newer block, but it's worth spending £15 extra for the more spacious rooms with a sea view. There's a bar and a fine-dining restaurant, and limited parking. __£105__

EATING

Redwing Bar & Dining Church Rd, Lympstone, EX8 5JT ☎ 01395 222156, ⓦ redwingbar-dining.co.uk. Hidden away in an estuary village close to A La Ronde, this pub and restaurant with contemporary decor serves good local ales and tasty butternut squash risotto (£10), burgers (about £12), and more expensive steaks, and there's a set lunch and early-evening menu (£13.50). The various eating areas include a conservatory and patio, and it's child-friendly. Kitchen Mon–Sat noon–2pm & 6–9pm, Sun noon–2.30pm & 6–9pm.

River Exe Café ☎ 07761 116103, ⓦ riverexecafe.com. Here's a novel way to view the local avocet and seal populations – from a barge in the middle of the estuary between Exmouth and Starcross. It also offers great food (local crab, mackerel and scallops, or simple fish and chips) and local wines, beers and ciders; prices range from £7 for bouillabaisse to £15 for Exmouth mussels. Call first to arrange a pick-up by water-taxi. April–Sept daily 11.30am–11pm (weather dependent).

Budleigh Salterton and around

Bound by red sandstone cliffs to the west and the pebblestone ridge of the Otter estuary in the east, **BUDLEIGH SALTERTON**, four miles east of Exmouth along the B3178, is the apotheosis of Devon respectability. The motto on its coat of arms, *Beau Sejour* ("Have a good stay"), has been taken to heart by the legions of elderly folk who have settled here, giving the place a slow, somnolent feel. The town takes its name from the salterns, or saltpans, in which monks evaporated sea water during the thirteenth century – long since disappeared. In the twentieth century, Budleigh's whitewashed cottages and houses attracted such figures as Noël Coward and P.G. Wodehouse, and it is the old-fashioned flavour associated with these names that constitutes the principal charm of the place today.

Fairlynch Museum

27 Fore St, EX9 6NP • Easter–Oct Tues–Sun 2–4.30pm • Free • ☎ 01395 442666, ⓦ devonmuseums.net/fairlynch-museum/devon-museums

East Devon has several examples of nineteenth-century *cottages orné* – ornamental rustic cottages in a roughly Gothic style – including this one, which now houses the excellent **Fairlynch Museum**. Built around 1811, the thatched building features a fine collection of Victorian and Edwardian costumes and locally made Edwardian dolls. Geological exhibits include examples of radioactive nodules found in local cliffs, and there's a diverse array of historical relics in a damp, low-ceilinged "smuggler's cellar". Upstairs you can see beautiful examples of lace, a regional speciality, and there are occasional lace-making demonstrations.

The beach

At the bottom of Fore Street, Marine Parade faces a wide arc of beach where you can still see the wall shown in the iconic *Boyhood of Raleigh*, painted here by John Everett Millais in 1870. The original work, which depicts a salty sea dog spinning a

2

BUDLEIGH SALTERTON'S FESTIVALS

The **Budleigh Music Festival** extends over eight days in late July, featuring mainly classical concerts in local churches and village halls. Tickets cost £17 (lunchtime concerts are free) – see ⓦ budleighmusicfestival.co.uk or contact the tourist office for details. A **Literary Festival** also takes place here over a long weekend in September – for more information, see ⓦ budlitfest .org.uk. The Festival's current President is Hilary Mantel, and past guests have included Margaret Drabble and Ben Okri; tickets are £9 or £12 per event.

yarn to the young Walter Raleigh and his half-brother, Humphrey Gilbert, another sailor-to-be, is now in London's Tate Britain. The Octagon, the house where Millais stayed, stands next to the Fairlynch Museum. The western end of the beach is traditionally used by naturists, marked by "clothing optional" signs.

ARRIVAL AND DEPARTURE   BUDLEIGH SALTERTON AND AROUND

By bus Exmouth and Budleigh Salterton are linked by buses #157 and #357; #157 also runs to East Budleigh, Otterton, Bicton Park and Sidmouth.
Destinations East Budleigh (Mon–Sat hourly, Sun 4 daily; 5min); Exmouth (Mon–Sat 2 hourly, Sun hourly; 20min); Otterton (Mon–Sat hourly, Sun 4 daily; 15min); Sidmouth (Mon–Sat hourly, Sun 4 daily; 40min).

INFORMATION AND ACTIVITIES

Tourist information Fore St (Mon–Sat: Easter–Sept 10am–4pm; Oct–Easter 10am–1pm; ☏ 01395 445275, ⓦ visitbudleigh.com). Has information on local activities, including walking and birdwatching.
Budleigh Salterton Riding School Dalditch Lane, Knowle ☏ 01395 442035, ⓦ devonriding.co.uk. A mile or so northwest of Budleigh, this place (closed Mon), provides horseriding tuition and rides on nearby Woodbury Common (£26/hr, £37/2hr), and also offers holiday cottages (from £440/week).

ACCOMMODATION

Pooh Cottage Bear Lane, EX9 7AQ ☏ 01395 442354, ⓦ poohcottage.co.uk. Close to the cycle track to Exmouth and a mile inland of Budleigh Salterton, this is a quiet, sheltered campsite with a good pub nearby. Closed Nov to mid-March. Per person <u>£10</u>
Rosehill Rooms and Cookery 30 West Hill, EX9 6BU ☏ 01395 444031, ⓦ rosehillroomsandcookery.co.uk. Plushly refurbished Victorian country house a 5–10min walk up Budleigh Salterton's High Street, where the bright, spacious rooms have sofas and modern bathrooms. Healthy breakfasts are eaten around a large refectory table. Ask about cookery courses held here. <u>£115</u>

EATING

Bowmers 7 High St, EX9 6LD ☏ 01395 442676, ⓦ bowmers.com. The modern, clean lines of this café/restaurant make a refreshing contrast to Budleigh's prevailing 1950s feel. Drop in for coffee and cake, or a set-price lunch (£15 for two courses, £18 for three). In the evening you'll pay around £16 for mains of Creedy Carver duck, chargrilled lamb or local seafood. There's live music most Thurs evenings. Wed 10am–3pm, Thurs–Sat 10am–3pm & 6–11pm, Sun noon–3pm.
Otterton Mill Fore St, Otterton, EX9 7HG ☏ 01395 567041, ⓦ ottertonmill.com. Out of town, on the Sidmouth road, this is the place for local organic produce to eat in or take away. The bakery provides tasty bread for the excellent café/restaurant, where a range of wholesome snacks and hot dishes is available at lunchtime (most dishes £6–8.50). Live jazz, blues and folk concerts take place most Thurs evenings, when dinners are served (booking essential). March–Nov Mon–Wed & Fri–Sun 10am–5pm, Thurs 10am–5pm & 6pm–late; Dec–Feb Tues–Sun 10am–4pm.

East Budleigh

A mile and a half north of Budleigh Salterton, the small village of **EAST BUDLEIGH** is famed for its connection with Walter Raleigh, who was born just outside in the manor of Hayes Barton. Once a bustling port, it's now a tidy, sleepy spot, with a stream running alongside the main street.

All Saints

High St, EX9 7ED • Daily 9am–dusk • Free • ☎ 01395 444276 • Bus #157 from Budleigh Salterton

Walter Raleigh's father was warden at the church of **All Saints**, at the top of the village. Inside you can see the family's pews (the front two on the left), as well as a collection of superbly carved sixteenth-century bench ends, among the oldest in the country.

Bicton Park

East Budleigh, EX9 7BG (1.5 miles north of East Budleigh, off the B3178) • Daily: mid-March to mid-Sept 10am–5pm; mid-Sept to mid-March 10am–4.30pm • £9.95 • ☎ 01395 568465, ⓦ bictongardens.co.uk • Bus #157 from East Budleigh and Budleigh Salterton

East Devon's showiest garden, **Bicton Park** is famed for its formal arrangement and specialist greenhouses. Spread over some sixty acres, the sweeping lawns, arboretum and exhibition hall displaying bygone items of rural and agricultural life provide plenty of diversion. However, horticulturalists and amateur gardeners alike are most drawn to the immaculate, set-piece gardens – mainly nineteenth-century in origin, though the Italian Garden dates back to the 1730s.

Otterton Mill Centre

Otterton, EX9 7HG (around 2 miles north of Budleigh Salterton) • March–Nov daily 10am–5pm; Dec–Feb Tues–Sun 10am–4pm • Free • ⓦ ottertonmill.com • Take bus #157 from Budleigh Salterton, or walk along the river

Located in the handsomely thatched and timbered village of **OTTERTON**, the **Otterton Mill Centre** is the last working mill on the river. You can view the flour-milling process (check the website for milling days), and the end-products are sold in the shop and café/restaurant (see p.67). There's also a craft centre and gallery of local art, plus weekly live-music evenings.

Sidmouth and around

Nestled in the Sid valley six miles northeast of Budleigh Salterton, **SIDMOUTH** is the region's architectural aristocrat. Characterized by its Regency terraces, with castellated parapets and Gothic windows, the seaside resort boasts nearly five hundred listed buildings, most of them from the first forty years of the nineteenth century. The town's "silvery, pink and creamy" facades inspired poet and architecture buff John Betjeman to extol "Devon Georgian" as "the simplest, gayest, lightest, creamiest Georgian of all".

Brief history

Sidmouth's fashionability among the upper classes grew after the Duke of Kent retired here in 1819; his family, including his daughter, the future Queen Victoria, moved into Woolbrook Cottage, now the *Royal Glen Hotel*. What had previously been a low-key fishing village subsequently enjoyed the patronage of such figures as Grand Duchess Hélène of Russia, sister-in-law of the tsar, and Empress Eugénie, wife of Napoleon III. The twentieth century saw the resort transmogrify from Edwardian opulence to something much cosier – a location for P.G. Wodehouse films and home of preservation societies – but it was also injected with a shot of energy in the form of the folk festival, which has grown since it started in 1955 into quite a rambunctious affair (see box, p.72).

The Esplanade

The strongest echoes of Sidmouth's regal connections survive today along **the Esplanade**, at the end of the shop-lined High Street and its continuation, Fore Street. Most people come here to promenade among the deckchairs and benches which, in summer, are almost permanently occupied by people contemplating the pebbly beach

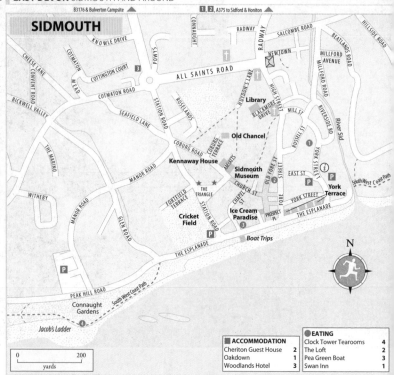

■ ACCOMMODATION	
Cheriton Guest House	2
Oakdown	1
Woodlands Hotel	3

● EATING	
Clock Tower Tearooms	4
The Loft	2
Pea Green Boat	3
Swan Inn	1

below. Here and elsewhere in the town, wrought-iron balconies with curved canopies rise above the numerous hanging baskets and lavish flower displays that have helped make Sidmouth a multiple winner of floral awards.

Though the town **beach** makes absorbing viewing, the best area for bathing is west of the centre at **Jacob's Ladder**, a stretch of gently shelving shingle (sandy at low tide) that's backed by crumbly red cliffs and overlooked by lush gardens and a tearoom housed in a clocktower.

Sidmouth Museum

Church St, EX10 8LY • April–Oct: Mon 1–4pm, Tues–Sat 10am–4pm • Free • ☎ 01395 516139, ⓦ sidvaleassociation.org.uk

Housed in the Sid Vale Heritage Centre, the **Sidmouth Museum** holds absorbing displays of Regency prints, a miscellany of Victoriana, illustrations of the complicated geology of East Devon and a comprehensive collection of local lacework (lace-making demonstrations are usually held here on Thursdays). Next to the museum, restored **Kennaway House**, dating from 1805, also hosts occasional exhibitions.

East along the coast path

East of Sidmouth, the **coast path** climbs steeply up Salcombe Hill. You'll find plenty of places to pause for a swim but the best **beaches** are at **Weston Mouth**, about two and a half miles east of Sidmouth's Esplanade, and **Branscombe Mouth**, a couple of miles further on by Branscombe village (see p.73), where the grassy cliffs and wide, stony shores are managed by the National Trust.

ARRIVAL AND DEPATURE

By bus Service #157 runs between Sidmouth, Budleigh Salterton and Exmouth, while buses #9 and #9A connect Sidmouth with Exeter via the inland A3052. Eastward, the #899 service (Mon–Sat) links Sidmouth with Branscombe, Beer and Seaton. Most bus stops are on the Triangle, just up from the seafront on Station Rd.

Destinations Beer (Mon–Sat 3–6 daily; 35min); Branscombe (Mon–Sat 3–5 daily; 20min); Budleigh

SIDMOUTH AND AROUND

Salterton (Mon–Sat hourly, also late May to mid-Sept Sun 4 daily; 40min); Exeter (Mon–Sat every 30min, Sun 1–2 hourly; 55min); Exmouth (Mon–Sat hourly, also late May to mid-Sept Sun 4 daily; 55min); Honiton (Mon–Sat hourly, also Sun late May to mid-Sept 3 daily; 35min); Ottery St Mary (Mon–Sat 5 daily, also late May to mid-Sept Sun 3 daily; 30min); Seaton (Mon–Sat 1–2 hourly, Sun 7 daily; 40min).

GETTING AROUND

By bus The free Sidmouth Hopper bus service (late May to Sept) provides a useful means of getting around, leaving hourly from the Triangle.

By bike Between Easter and Sept, bikes can be rented from W.V. Fish, at 71 Temple St (☎ 01395 512185), for £12 per day.

INFORMATION AND TOURS

Tourist information Ham Lane car park (May–Sept Mon–Sat 10am–5pm, Sun 10am–4pm; Oct–April Mon–Sat 10am–1.30pm; ☎ 01395 516441, ⊛ visitsidmouth .co.uk). Sells pamphlets about the many walks in the area, and the *Blue Plaque Guide* (£4), which documents the town's historic houses.

Boat trips Between May and Aug Stuart Line (☎ 01395 222144, ⊛ stuartlinecruises.co.uk) operates boat trips in Sidmouth Bay (£6). Departures are from the beach in front

of the *Bedford Hotel*; call or consult the website for times and dates.

Walking tours Between Easter and Oct, you can soak up the town's historical and architectural heritage on free two-hour walking tours from outside Sidmouth Museum (see opposite): on Tues for the western side of town, Thurs for the eastern side (both starting at 10.30am) and Wed for the seafront, with a focus on the local geology (2pm).

ACCOMMODATION

Sidmouth has **accommodation** to suit all pockets; more expensive places lie nearer the sea, while most of the cheaper guesthouses are about a mile back from the Esplanade, on or around Vicarage Road at the north end of the High Street. Many places are booked up months ahead for **Sidmouth FolkWeek**. The best **campsites** are east of Sidmouth, along or off the A3052; take any bus for Beer or Seaton.

Cheriton Guest House 9 Vicarage Rd, EX10 8UQ ☎ 01395 513810, ⊛ cheriton-guesthouse.co.uk. This B&B has spotless, mostly spacious rooms (one with a balcony), with those at the back overlooking a leafy garden leading down to the River Sid. There's a lounge and car park, and the seafront is less than a 10min walk, reached from the High Street or through the Byes riverside park. **£80**

Oakdown Gatedown Lane, Weston, EX10 0PT ☎ 01297 680387, ⊛ oakdown.co.uk. Spacious, well-maintained campsite some three miles east of Sidmouth off the A3052 (there's some road noise). "Glamping" pods are also

available, and pubs are nearby. There's a three-night minimum stay on bank holidays and seven nights during FolkWeek. The free Sidmouth Hopper bus service stops here in summer. Closed early Nov to mid-March. **£20.40**

Woodlands Hotel Station Rd, EX10 8HG ☎ 01395 513120, ⊛ woodlands-hotel.com. One of Sidmouth's most charming hotels, a few minutes' walk up Station Road from the Esplanade, this large *cottage orné* was built in its present form around 1809, but parts date back over seven hundred years. There are antiques in the bedrooms, a huge conservatory and gardens. **£130**

A WALK AROUND SIDMOUTH'S OLD TOWN

Away from the seafront, you can take in Sidmouth's best architectural features on a leisurely amble. Some of the best terraces can be seen at **York Terrace**, on the seafront east of Fore Street, and on and around **Fortfield Terrace**, off Station Road, where dignified white facades with covered balconies are fronted by lawns and flowerbeds. One curiosity on Coburg Terrace is the **Old Chancel**, a private house standing tall and turreted beside the bowling green, made up of parts rescued from a church after it was remodelled in 1860; living quarters were added to the original chancel, which retains its Perpendicular window, resulting in a bizarre Victorian–medieval pastiche.

2

SIDMOUTH FOLKWEEK

With its diverse range of musicians, harmonious setting and eclectic atmosphere, **Sidmouth FolkWeek** (late July/early Aug) is one of the country's premier folk festivals. Folk and roots acts, workshops and ceilidhs take place in venues ranging from 1000-seater marquees to pubs and hotels around town, as well as spontaneous sessions and plenty of pavement busking.

Tickets for the whole festival cost £308 or £214 (including or excluding the headline acts at the Ham Marquee, respectively); weekend tickets are £134 or £88, and day-tickets are £42 (excluding the Ham concerts). Anyone with a ticket that doesn't cover Ham Marquee events gets discounted prices for these (it's worth booking early). There are also substantial **discounts** when buying advance tickets before the end of April – they usually go on sale the previous December. In addition to the concerts, there are **workshops** and **talks**, and a plethora of **craft stalls**.

Accommodation is at a premium and also needs to be booked well in advance. For more details and to book, visit the website ⓦ sidmouthfolkweek.co.uk, or call Sidmouth's tourist office (☎ 01395 516441).

EATING

★ **Clock Tower Tearooms** Connaught Gardens, EX10 8RZ ☎ 01395 515319, ⓦ clocktowercafesidmouth .co.uk. Overlooking Jacob's Ladder beach, this is a great spot for stews, pies and local crabcakes, as well as teas and humongous cakes, all of which can be enjoyed in a lovely walled garden or upstairs for sea views. Daily: Aug 9.30am–6pm; Sept–July 10am–5pm.

The Loft 3–5 Old Fore St, EX10 8LS ☎ 01395 489681, ⓦ theloftsidmouth.co.uk. Located above shops in Sidmouth's shopping precinct, this place is the perfect stop for breakfast or a light lunch. You'll find pizzas, pastas and gourmet burgers on the menu (around £10), or you can order an antipasti board or seafood selection (both around £13 for one person, £22 for two). There's a friendly, laid-back atmosphere, and a roof garden. Tues–Fri 10am–3pm, Sat 10am–3pm & 6pm–late.

Pea Green Boat The Esplanade, EX10 8BB ☎ 01395 514152, ⓦ thepeagreenboat.com. Tiny café/restaurant on the seafront, offering brunches, sandwiches and generous salads, and more substantial dishes such as thin-crust pizzas, gourmet burgers, and smoked haddock and leek carbonara (all £12–15). With some tables outside, it makes an ideal mid- or post-stroll stop, and a lively venue for dinner. Mon–Sat 10am–10pm, Sun 10am–4pm; food served Mon–Sat 10am–3pm & 5–8.30pm, Sun 10am–3pm.

★ **Swan Inn** 37 York St, EX10 8BY ☎ 01395 512849, ⓦ rampubcompany.co.uk. Popular with locals, this convivial, wood-beamed pub offers real ales, bar meals and a garden – it's a fun place during FolkWeek. Mon–Sat 11am–11pm, Sun noon–11pm; kitchen daily noon–1.45pm & 6–8.45pm.

Beer and around

Seven miles east of Sidmouth, the tiny fishing port of **BEER** is one of the gems of the Devon coast. The allure of the village – whose name is a corruption of the old English word *bearu* meaning small wood – derives largely from its location, huddled in a narrow cove between gleaming white headlands, with a gurgling stream running through its centre. The village was once a smugglers' eyrie; local inlets were used by such characters as Jack Rattenbury, whose famous exploits were chronicled in his 1837 book *Memoirs of a Smuggler*.

Beer Quarry Caves

Quarry Lane, EX12 3AT · Tours daily: late March to Sept hourly 10am–4.30pm (until 5.30pm during school hols); Oct every 2hr 10am–3.30pm; last tour 1hr before closing · £7.70 · ☎ 01297 680282, ⓦ beerquarrycaves.co.uk

A mile or so west of the village, **Beer Quarry Caves** were worked continuously from Roman times until 1900, with the extracted Beer stone used in countless Devon churches and houses, not to mention Winchester Cathedral, Westminster Abbey, St Paul's Cathedral and the Tower of London. You can only enter on an hour-long **walking tour**, which takes in a chapel 200ft underground and the etched signatures of quarrymen going back to the year of Queen Victoria's accession.

Beer Head

Soaring above stony beaches southeast of Beer, the cliff path climbs for a mile up to **Beer Head**, a majestic 426ft vantage point at the most westerly end of the south coast's chalk-white cliffs. From here, you have the choice of sticking to the clifftop or descending to an area known as **Hooken Undercliff**, the result of a landslip in 1790 and now a thickly grown wilderness that provides sanctuary for birds and other wildlife as well as a means of accessing the pebbly beach.

ARRIVAL AND INFORMATION

By bus Beer is linked with Sidmouth and (less frequently) Branscombe by bus #899 and with Exeter by #X52.
Destinations Branscombe (Mon–Sat 3–4 daily; 20min);

BEER AND AROUND

Exeter (Mon–Sat 3 daily; 1hr 10min); Sidmouth (Mon–Sat 3–6 daily; 40min).
Tourist information See ⓦ beer-devon.co.uk.

ACCOMMODATION

Beer Head Caravan Park Common Hill, EX12 3AH ⓣ 01297 21107, ⓦ beer-head.com. Beautifully located site with limited tent pitches but panoramic views and plenty of room for caravans (from £510/week). Snacks and meals are available. The site is easily reached along Common Lane, half a mile beyond the *Anchor Inn* at the bottom of Fore Street. Closed Nov to mid-March. **£20**
Durham House Fore St, EX12 3JL ⓣ 01297 20449, ⓦ durhamhouse.co.uk. Handsome Victorian B&B that retains its neo-Gothic entrance, stained glass and tiling.

Rooms are airy with modern facilities, and breakfast choices include croissants and eggs Benedict. Two-night minimum stay June–Sept. Free parking. No credit cards. **£80**
YHA Beer Bovey Combe, EX12 3LL ⓣ 0845 371 9502, ⓦ yha.org.uk. East Devon's only youth hostel is in a secluded site half a mile northwest of Beer. There are 4–6 beds per dorm, and there are family rooms (£99) with shared or private bathrooms. Meals are available, or you can use the kitchen. To reach the hostel, follow signs for Beer Quarry Caves, turning right about 300m from the end of Fore St. Dorms **£26**

EATING

Dolphin Hotel Fore St, EX12 3EQ ⓣ 01297 24506, ⓦ dolphinhotelbeer.co.uk. Meals are consistently good at this hotel, pub and restaurant, with an emphasis on local seafood. Apart from the crab, skate and scallops usually available, you can opt for smoked chicken linguine or chargrilled steak (mains £10–15), and there's a renowned carvery (March–Nov Sun noon–6pm; £9.50). The lounge bar

has a livelier atmosphere than the restaurant, and also offers a lunchtime bar menu. Daily noon–2pm & 6–9pm.
Steamers New Cut, off Fore St, EX12 3DU ⓣ 01297 22922, ⓦ steamersrestaurant.co.uk. The top restaurant in Beer has rather dated decor, but a great menu that includes local scallops and grilled venison steaks, with most dishes £15–20. Tues–Sat 10am–2pm & 6.45–9pm, Sun hours variable.

Branscombe

The inland hamlet of **BRANSCOMBE**, four miles east of Sidmouth, is worth a wander, with thatched cottages strung along a meandering valley and, in a sheltered spot below the road, the surprisingly large twelfth-century church of **St Winifred**, with a prominent Norman tower. Inside are an unusual triple-decker pulpit from the eighteenth century and fragments of medieval wall painting.

EATING

BRANSCOMBE

★**Fountain Head** Branscombe Mouth, EX12 3DP ⓣ 01297 680359, ⓦ fountainheadinn.com. At the higher, less visited end of the village, this unspoilt fourteenth-century tavern serves superb local beers and

ciders and generous portions of food, including fresh crab sandwiches (£7). There are barbecues every evening in July and Aug. Mon–Sat noon–2pm & 6.30–9pm, Sun noon–2.30pm & 7–9pm.

FESTIVITIES IN BEER

Beer attracts huge crowds during **Regatta Week** (ⓦ beer-regatta.co.uk) in August, where the highlight is the Beer Luggers race, and during the rocking **R&B Festival** (ⓦ beerblues.co.uk) held over three days in mid-October. Local accommodation in both these periods may be hard to come by.

Honiton

The market town of **HONITON**, East Devon's biggest inland centre, was once an important coaching stop on the London-to-Exeter road, with as many as 35 coaching inns. It was also famed as the most rotten of the parliamentary "rotten boroughs", when the purchasing of votes was commonplace among the small electorate – a practice stopped by the 1832 Reform Act. A couple of disastrous fires in the eighteenth century destroyed most of the town's medieval fabric, which was replaced with the fine red-brick Regency houses visible today.

Allhallows Museum

High St, EX14 1PG · Late March to Sept Mon–Fri 9.30am–4.30pm, Sat 9.30am–1pm; Oct Mon–Fri 9.30am–3.30pm, Sat 9.30am–12.30pm · Free · ☎ 01404 44966, ⓦ honitonmuseum.co.uk

Honiton's chief attraction is **Allhallows Museum**, housed in the oldest building in town, a fourteenth-century chapel later used as a schoolroom and dining hall and now holding three galleries stuffed with examples of the fine **lace** with which Honiton is synonymous. Other exhibits include the bones and tusks of the Honiton Hippos, which date back some 100,000 years. Lace-making demonstrations take place on weekdays between June and August.

ARRIVAL AND DEPARTURE
HONITON

By train Honiton is on the main London–Salisbury–Exeter line. The station lies a few minutes from the centre off Church Hill, a continuation of New Street, which leads south from Fore Street.
Destinations Exeter (hourly; 30min); London (hourly; 2hr 55min); Salisbury (1–2 hourly; 1hr 20min).
By bus Honiton is most easily reached on buses #4, #4A, #9 and #56B from Exeter, #4 and #4A from Ottery St Mary, #9

and #56B from Sidmouth, and #20 from Taunton. Bus stops are on the High Street.
Destinations Exeter (Mon–Sat 1–3 hourly, Sun 1–4 daily; 50min–1hr 40min); Ottery St Mary (Mon–Sat 2 hourly, also late May to late Sept Sun 3 daily; 25min); Sidmouth (Mon–Sat hourly, also late May to late Sept Sun 3 daily; 40min); Taunton (Mon–Sat 5 daily; 1hr 25min).

INFORMATION

Tourist information The website ⓦ visithoniton.com has information on what to see and where to sleep and eat in the area.

ACCOMMODATION AND EATING

★ **Forest Glade** 6 miles northeast of Honiton, near Kentisbeare, Cullompton, EX15 2DT ☎ 01404 841381, ⓦ forest-glade.co.uk. Campers should head for this peaceful, well-sheltered site in the Blackdown Hills, accessible from the A373 (call for directions). It has an indoor pool and access to woodland walks. Camping pods (£33) also available. Closed Nov to mid-March. **£19.50**

★ **The Holt** 178 High St, EX14 1LA ☎ 01404 47707, ⓦ theholt-honiton.com. Tasty lunchtime snacks, tapas and a range of evening meals are on the menu, including slow-roast pork belly, venison steak and grilled cod fillets, all at £15–19. The downstairs flagstoned bar serves a range of local Otter ales (the Otter brewery is owned by the same family). Tues–Sat 11am–3pm & 5.30–11pm; kitchen noon–2pm & 6.30–9pm (Fri & Sat until 9.30pm).

HONITON LACE

For over four hundred years, **lace** has been made in Honiton and the surrounding area. The industry originated in the sixteenth century when Flemish refugees introduced the craft, and escalated in importance when Parliament forbade the import of foreign-made lace at the end of the seventeenth century. The locally produced lace was primarily used for collars, cuffs, edgings and wedding veils. Although there's been no commercial production for the last century or so, some locals still make lace as a hobby. Samples are available to buy at Honiton's **Allhallows Museum** (see above).

Splatthayes 3 miles west of Honiton; Buckerell, EX14 3ER ☎01404 850464, ⓦwww.splatthayes.co.uk. This B&B in a quiet village has four large rooms with views of the garden. There's a log-burner in the lounge, dietary preferences are catered for at breakfast, and the owners are friendly and welcoming. No credit cards. **£75**

Ottery St Mary

Five miles southwest of Honiton, **OTTERY ST MARY** sits on the banks of the River Otter in a lovely valley that runs to the sea at Budleigh Salterton (see p.66). The river was eulogized by Samuel Taylor Coleridge ("Dear native brook! Wild streamlet of the West!"), who was born in the locality and whose father was the local vicar from 1760 until 1781. Ottery was also the occasional home of William Makepeace Thackeray, who set his novel *Pendennis* here. The town fans out from a medieval central hub, but most of the elegant buildings date from Georgian times.

St Mary's Church

The College, EX11 1DQ • Daily 8.30am–6pm except during services • Free • ☎01404 812062, ⓦotterystmary.co.uk

Ottery's strong ecclesiastical heritage is embodied in **St Mary's Church**, extravagantly sized for such a small town. It was the work of Bishop Grandisson of Exeter, who in 1335 bought the existing church, then owned by Rouen Cathedral, and rebuilt it using Exeter Cathedral as his model, copying such features as the idiosyncratic positioning of two towers over the main transept (the weathercock atop one tower is said to be the oldest in situ in Europe). In the richly decorated interior, look out for the astronomical clock in the south transept, one of the oldest still in working order, possibly dating from Grandisson's reconstruction.

ARRIVAL AND INFORMATION
OTTERY ST MARY

By bus Ottery St Mary is linked to Exeter and Honiton by buses #4, #4A and #4B, and to Sidmouth by #382 (in summer the #56B links all four places on Sun). Bus stops are on Broad Street and The Square.

Destinations Exeter (Mon–Sat 2 hourly, also late May to late Sept Sun 3 daily; 30–50min); Honiton (Mon–Sat 2 hourly, also Sun late May to late Sept 3 daily; 25min); Sidmouth (Mon–Sat 5 daily, also Sun late May to late Sept 3 daily; 30min–1hr).

Tourist information 10B Broad St, EX11 1BX, downhill from the church off Silver Street (May–Nov Mon–Fri 9.30am–4pm, Sat 10am–1pm; Dec–April Mon–Sat 9.30am–1pm; ☎01404 813964, ⓦotterystmarytourism .co.uk).

EATING

★**The Rusty Pig** Yonder St, EX11 1HD ☎01404 815580, ⓦrustypig.co.uk. Part breakfast café, part restaurant, part butcher's, this informal place uses the best local ingredients for top-rated breakfasts, lunches and, in the evening, pizzas (all under £10) with toppings like smoked ham hock, pork and anchovy, and spicy goat's cheese. Pizzas are also available to take away. Alternatively, go for one of the fixed-price dinners (£25 for two courses, £33 for three). Thurs & Fri 9.30am–3pm & 4–9pm, Sat 9.30am–3pm.

TAR BARRELLING IN OTTERY ST MARY

If possible, try and time your visit to Ottery St Mary to coincide with Bonfire Night (Nov 5), when instead of fireworks the ancient ritual of **tar barrelling** is enacted (ⓦotterytarbarrels .co.uk). The practice is thought to have originated in the seventeenth century, with the aim of ridding the streets of the devil. Each pub sponsors a wooden barrel, which is soaked in tar for about three days before the event. The barrels are then set alight and carried on people's backs through the town until the flames die down. A huge bonfire is lit at the lower end of town, a funfair adds to the merriment and the drink flows freely. The event takes place on the preceding Saturday when November 5 falls on a Sunday.

South Devon

DARTMOUTH HARBOUR

South Devon

The wedge of land between Dartmoor and the Channel is one of Devon's most alluring areas, a mix of traditional seaside resorts, striking coastline and – stretching between the Dart and Plym estuaries – the rich agricultural hinterland of the South Hams. Apart from the Torbay resorts, the chief towns of the region are all on rivers, between which some of Devon's comeliest villages are nestled at the end of long, straggling lanes. Among the coastal resorts, Dawlish and Teignmouth have retained their Regency and Victorian character, but most visitors are attracted to Torbay – the collective name for the towns of Torquay, Paignton and Brixham, spread along the ten-mile arc between the two promontories of Hope's Nose and Berry Head. This coast's sheltered climate and sparkling bay views have earned it the rather optimistic tag of "the English Riviera".

3

Of the Torbay towns, it's **Torquay**, with its marina, tiered seafront and strings of fairy lights, that most closely measures up to the Riviera moniker; **Paignton** happily fills the role of a traditional English bucket-and-spade resort; while **Brixham** is still essentially a fishing port, albeit one overwhelmed by the tourist deluge every summer. Inland from the Torbay conurbation, things get much quieter around **Totnes**, a historic riverside town that makes an agreeable base for exploring the whole region. From here you can take a bus or a boat eight miles downstream to the classic estuary town of **Dartmouth**, more touristy but still with a strong maritime tradition – and a great place to eat fish. Dartmouth and Totnes have preserved numerous relics of their medieval past, such as the slate-hung facades for which this part of South Devon is known. South of the Dart rivermouth lie some enticing beaches, notably in Start Bay, where a wildlife reserve and the rocky headland of Start Point deserve lengthy explorations on foot.

Outside the towns, the South Hams is a hilly patchwork of fields that extends southwest of the River Dart as far as Plymouth, cut through by a splay of rivers flowing off Dartmoor. The area enjoys a sheltered, mild climate (a "hamme" is a sheltered place in Old English), which encourages subtropical plants as well as the vines that produce the celebrated Sharpham wine. From **Kingsbridge**, "capital" of the South Hams, you can board a boat to the mouth of the Kingsbridge estuary, where the sailing resort of **Salcombe** makes the best base for trips around the dramatic coast to either side. To the west, the coast path gives access to some choice beaches dotted around **Bigbury-on-Sea**.

GETTING AROUND   **SOUTH DEVON**

By train On one of the West Country's loveliest stretches of rail, with views over the Exe estuary (and frequently subject to spray in blowy weather), trains from Exeter run down the coast as far as Teignmouth before striking inland for Totnes. To get to Torbay, you may need to change at Newton Abbot (see ⓦ therivieraline.com for the Exeter– Torbay stretch).

By bus Paignton and Newton Abbot are the main hubs for bus services in South Devon. Frequent #2 buses connect Exeter with Dawlish, Dawlish Warren and Teignmouth, while #11 links Dawlish and Teignmouth with Torquay. #X46 runs a faster service between Exeter and Torquay, and

---

VIEW FROM TOTNES BRIDGE, TOTNES

Highlights

❶ Berry Head, Tor Bay At the southern end of the "English Riviera", this limestone promontory boasts fortifications from the Napoleonic Wars, a conservation area beloved of birdwatchers and sublime views across the bay. **See p.90**

❷ Totnes Historic atmosphere with a New Age veneer makes this riverside town a compelling stop. **See p.92**

❸ River trip on the Dart A mellow way to explore the river, with departures from Totnes and Dartmouth. **See p.94**

❹ Seafood in Dartmouth A culinary hotspot, Dartmouth has a superb selection of waterside restaurants and cafés. **See p.100**

❺ Start Bay Stretch out on the beaches at Blackpool Sands and Slapton Sands, or explore the wildlife at Slapton Ley nature reserve. **See p.100**

❻ Overbeck's Museum and Garden Delightfully idiosyncratic museum in Sharpitor displaying all kinds of curios and with sections on maritime history and local wildlife, surrounded by lush gardens. **See p.104**

HIGHLIGHTS ARE MARKED ON THE MAP ON P.80

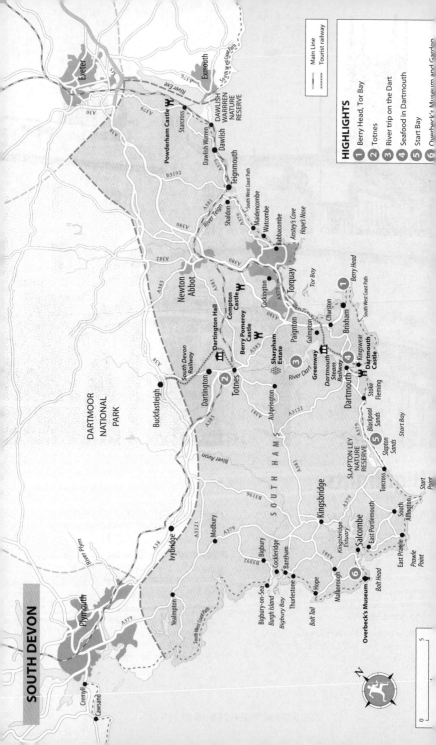

SOUTH DEVON

Main Line
Tourist railway

Exeter
Exmouth
River Exe
South West Coast Path
DAWLISH WARREN NATURE RESERVE
Powderham Castle
Starcross
Dawlish Warren
Dawlish
B3192
A379
Teignmouth
A381
River Teign
Shaldon
A379
Maidencombe
Watcombe
A380
Anstey's Cove
Hope's Nose
Babbacombe
A382
A383
Newton Abbot
A381
Tor Bay
A380
Compton Castle
Dartington Hall
Berry Pomeroy Castle
Cockington
Torquay
A3022
Paignton
Galmpton
Berry Head
South West Coast Path
Churston
Brixham
South Devon Railway
Dartington
2 Totnes
Sharpham Estate
3 River Dart
Greenway
Dartmouth Steam Railway
4 Kingswear
Dartmouth Castle
Dartmouth
Ashprington
A381
A3122
Stoke Fleming
Blackpool Sands
5 Slapton Sands
Start Bay
Buckfastleigh
DARTMOOR NATIONAL PARK
River Avon
A38
A3121
A384
A381
A361
A3196
SLAPTON LEY NATURE RESERVE
Torcross
Start Point
Kingsbridge
Kingsbridge Estuary
A379
Salcombe
East Portlemouth
South Allington
East Prawle
Prawle Point
Modbury
A379
Ivybridge
River Plym
Plymouth
A38
A379
Bigbury-on-Sea
Burgh Island
Bigbury Bay
Bantham
Thurlestone
Cockeridge
Bigbury
B3392
Hope
Bolt Tail
Malborough
6 Overbeck's Museum
Bolt Head
South West Coast Path
Cremyll
Cawsand

N

0   5

SOUTH HAMS

#12 is the main link between Newton Abbot, Torquay, Paignton and Brixham. Most buses for Salcombe, the South Hams and points west leave from Kingsbridge, though services can be extremely sporadic.

By ferry Between March and Oct, travellers between East Devon and South Devon can make use of the Starcross Ferry (see p.65), which links Starcross, on the western side of the Exe estuary, with Exmouth (foot passengers only). Regular ferries link Torquay and Brixham, and seasonal river ferries also link Totnes and Dartmouth, and Kingsbridge and Salcombe.

By car Road users following the A379 from Exeter touch the shore only at the small village of Starcross (also a rail stop). Car traffic into Torbay can be intense, while roads threading through the South Hams are mostly tiny – negotiating them can be a lengthy business.

INFORMATION

Tourist information There's reams of regional information on ⓦ visitsouthdevon.co.uk.

Tide times Local tide times – useful for coast-walkers – are available at tourist offices or on ⓦ easytide.ukho.gov.uk.

Dawlish and around

Small and sedate **DAWLISH**, a couple of miles south of the Exe estuary, is a traditional Devon seaside resort much favoured by nineteenth-century holidaymakers, but today makes a quieter, scaled-down contrast to the flashier resorts further south. It's a charmingly understated place, probably now best known for the black swans that congregate on the lawns around Dawlish Water in the centre. The sand and shingle town beach runs alongside a granite railway viaduct built by Brunel, with the passing trains providing occasional excitement – you'll find more seclusion at the broader, cliff-backed beach at **Coryton Cove**, a few minutes' walk south.

Dawlish Warren National Nature Reserve

Beach Rd, Dawlish Warren, EX7 0NF • **Reserve** Daily dawn–dusk • Free • **Visitor centre** April–Aug Wed–Fri 2–4pm, Sat & Sun 2–5pm; Sept–March Sat & Sun 1–4pm • **Guided walks** See website or call ahead for times; 1hr 30min–2hr • £3–4 • ☎ 01626 863980, ⓦ teignbridge.gov.uk, ⓦ devonwildlifetrust.org • Dawlish Warren station is on the Exeter–Dawlish train line, and bus #2 stops here

North of Dawlish, a sandy spit jutting into the estuary holds the **Dawlish Warren National Nature Reserve**, harbouring a range of wildfowl and wading birds – best seen in autumn and winter – as well as a huge variety of flowering plants, mosses, liverworts and lichens (see p.342). You can get some background at the **visitor centre**, but the best way to take it all in is by joining one of the sporadic **guided walks** conducted by the reserve's rangers. In winter, the Royal Society for the Protection of Birds runs **Avocet Cruises** on the Exe estuary starting from Topsham (see p.63). There's a long sandy Blue Flag **beach** here too, backed by dunes and popular with families.

Powderham Castle

Kenton, EX6 8JQ, three miles north of Dawlish Warren off the A379 • Mon–Fri & Sun: late March to mid-July, Sept & Oct 11am–4.30pm; mid-July to Aug 11am–5.30pm • £11.50, under-17s £9.50; gardens only £8.50, under-17s £6.50 • Tours mid-July to late Aug regularly from 11am, last tour 3pm; late March to mid-July, Sept & Oct regularly from 11.15am, last tour Mon–Thurs & Sun 3.30pm, Fri 2.30pm; 1hr • **Deer Park Safari** Wed & Thurs (daily in school hols) 1.45pm; 35min • £2.50 • ☎ 01626 890243, ⓦ powderham.co.uk • Bus #2 from Exeter or Dawlish

Home to the eighteenth earl of Devon, **Powderham Castle** is a pleasing melange of Gothic, Georgian and Victorian styles. Enhanced by colourful anecdotes, the **guided tours** point out Baroque bookcases, portraits by Joshua Reynolds, an eighteenth-century music room designed by James Wyatt and a restored Victorian kitchen. Note that you can usually only see inside the castle on a tour. The grounds are good for walks and there is a park holding some 400 fallow deer, viewable on a tractor-drawn **Deer Park Safari**.

The castle makes an easy destination for cyclists from Exeter or Dawlish (both 30–45min), on the **Exe Estuary Trail** (NCN2).

> **TEIGNMOUTH JAZZ FESTIVAL**
>
> Teignmouth Jazz Festival (ⓦteignmouthjazz.org) takes place over a long weekend in mid-November, with trad jazz, swing and contemporary bands playing in theatres, pubs and clubs. Tickets (around £80 for the weekend, or individually priced at £12–15 per gig) are available from the festival website.

Teignmouth

At the mouth of the River Teign, **TEIGNMOUTH** (pronounced "Tinmuth") is a traditional and atmospheric seaside town, with narrow lanes leading down to the river. On the seafront, to either side of the pier that once segregated male and female bathers, the narrow, unexceptional bathing beach is backed by **the Den**, a tidy swathe of lawns and flowerbeds and miniature golf courses. Overlooking the gardens are some of the town's most graceful Georgian and Victorian villas, several dating from Teignmouth's evolution as one of Devon's first seaside resorts at the end of the eighteenth century.

There's still a thriving harbour here, and this estuary side of town has a clutter of boats moored in the river and fishing vessels hauled up onto the pebbly **Back Beach**. The water here is too oily to invite a dip, and fast currents make swimming around the estuary mouth risky, but Teignmouth's main **beach** is safe enough. From Back Beach, a passenger ferry crosses the Teign to Teignmouth's sister resort, **Shaldon**, throughout the year (£1.50; ☏07896 711822, ⓦteignmouthshaldonferry.co.uk).

ARRIVAL AND DEPARTURE
TEIGNMOUTH

By train Teignmouth's station lies a few minutes north of the harbour on Exeter Rd (A379).
Destinations Dawlish (1–3 hourly; 5min); Exeter (1–3 hourly; 15–40min); Newton Abbot (1–3 hourly; 8min); Torquay (1–2 hourly; 20min).

By bus Stops are on the Esplanade and Wellington St, with services to Dawlish (#2 & #22; 2–4 hourly; 15min), Exeter (#2; 1–4 hourly; 50min–1hr 10min) and Torquay (#22; hourly; 50min).

INFORMATION

Tourist information The Pavilions theatre on the Den, TQ14 8BG, has an information point (Mon–Sat 10am–3pm, also for 1hr prior to performances; ☏01626 249049, ⓦvisitsouthdevon.co.uk).

ACCOMMODATION AND EATING

★**The Crab Shack** 3 Queen St, TQ14 8BY ☏01626 777956, ⓦcrabshackonthebeach.co.uk. Overlooking Back Beach (and with some outdoor tables), this is the place to come for the freshest local seafood in a fun atmosphere. There's excellent cod and chips (£11.50) on the menu, though the accent is on shellfish – from whelks and winkles to a bucket of crab claws (£16) or a lobster platter (£34). Chunky sandwiches are also available to take away from its offshoot around the corner. Mon–Fri & Sun 6–9pm, Sat noon–2pm & 5.30–9.30pm.

Minadab Cottage 60 Teignmouth Rd, TQ14 8UT ☏01626 772044, ⓦminadab.co.uk. A thatched *cottage orné* dating from 1820, this B&B lies outside the centre on the northern outskirts of town (on the Dawlish road). The three rooms are elegant and clean, with modern bathrooms. Breakfasts include fresh fruit and home-made bread and preserves, and there are lots of complimentary extras. Two-night minimum stay June–Aug. No under-12s. **£75**

Torquay and around

Five miles south of the Teign estuary, **TORQUAY** owes much of its appeal to its combination of hills and extensive palm-planted seafront, with views across the whole of Tor Bay. The town is associated with crime writer **Agatha Christie** (see box, p.86) and fictional TV hotelier Basil Fawlty, whose anachronistic attitudes reflect Torquay's forced adaptation to mass tourism (and the *Gleneagles Hotel* on Anstey's Cove, an inspiration for *Fawlty Towers*, is still going strong).

Torquay is liveliest around the **Old Harbour**, where the quayside bars and cafés attract idling crowds during the day and on summer evenings. The marina here is packed with pleasure craft, and with stalls advertising **boat trips** (see p.87), weather permitting – in summer, most nearby beaches can be accessed this way.

Activity enthusiasts should make use of the impressive range of **waterskiing, surfing** and **sailing** facilities at the harbour and nearby coves and beaches, many of which are accessible via pleasant coastal walks. Away from the seafront are hilly residential areas full of creamy villas on quietly elegant streets, with subtropical greenery and sea views all around.

Brief history

The sheltered location and clement weather were both factors in Torquay's elevation from a group of fishermen's cottages to an important naval base during the Napoleonic Wars, and Napoleon himself was a visitor (though without setting foot on land) when he was held for seven weeks aboard HMS *Bellerophon* in Tor Bay following his defeat at Waterloo. Torquay then became a fashionable haven for invalids – among them the consumptive Elizabeth Barrett Browning, who lived here 1838 to 41 – and the flow of holidaymakers increased with the extension of the railway from Newton Abbot in 1848.

3

Living Coasts

Beacon Quay, TQ1 2BG • Daily: April–June & early Sept to Oct 10am–5pm; July to early Sept 10am–6pm; Nov–March 10am–4pm; last entry 1hr before closing • £11.05, under-16s £8.30; combined ticket with Paignton Zoo (see p.90) £22, under-16s £15• ☎ 01803 202470, ⓦ livingcoasts.org.uk

On the southern edge of the Old Harbour, **Living Coasts** is a zoo and aquarium focusing on coastal habitats, with reconstructed beaches, cliff faces and an estuary, as well as underwater viewing areas and a huge meshed aviary. It's educational and fun: you'll see such aquatic birds as avocets, redshanks, puffins, penguins, guillemots and terns, as well as octopus, puffer fish, otters and seals. There are talks throughout the day, and the penguins' breakfast and lunch are worth catching at 10.30am and 2.30pm. About half the displays are outdoors.

Torre Abbey

King's Drive, TQ2 5JE • March–May & Oct–Dec Wed–Sun 10am–5pm; June–Sept daily 10am–5pm; last entry 4pm • £7.85 • ☎ 01803 293593, ⓦ torre-abbey.org.uk

Tucked out of sight above Abbey Sands, **Torre Abbey** was founded in 1196 and became the chief power in these parts until it was razed by Henry VIII in 1539. Only the gatehouse, tithe barn, chapterhouse and tower have survived, which now form part of the superimposed seventeenth- and eighteenth-century construction that holds one of Devon's finest galleries.

The collection includes silver, glass and sculpture, and minutely detailed marine paintings by, among others, the Teignmouth artist Thomas Luny. Other highlights include a series of Pre-Raphaelite window designs by Edward Burne-Jones, proof copies of William Blake's haunting illustrations for the Book of Job and a small but eclectic choice of twentieth-century art – a refreshing modern interlude among all the antiques.

Outside the main building, you can admire the square, crenellated gatehouse and the handsome brick **Spanish Barn** just beyond, named after the 397 Spanish prisoners captured from one of the Armada warships and imprisoned here in July 1588, now used for exhibitions.

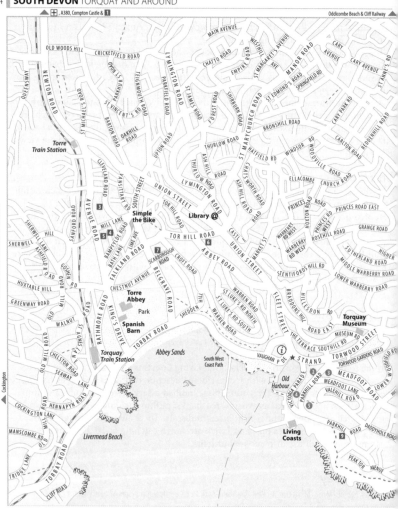

Torquay Museum

529 Babbacombe Rd, TQ1 1HG • Mon–Sat 10am–4pm, also Sun late June to early Sept 10am–4pm • £6.45 • ☎ 01803 293975, ⓦ torquaymuseum.org

In contrast to the finery of Torre Abbey, **Torquay Museum**, a few minutes uphill from the harbour, contains a more down-to-earth but no less absorbing miscellany of objects relating to the area. The collection includes exhibits from natural history and prehistory, including, on the second floor, an important collection of objects found in Kents Cavern (see opposite), of which the highlight is part of a human jawbone said to be Europe's oldest securely dated modern human fragment, around 41,000 years old.

Also on the second floor, the **Agatha Christie Gallery** explores the crime writer's life and achievements (see box, p.86), from early photos of the young Agatha Miller with sister Madge, dog and "Nursie", to her writing career, represented by manuscripts, book covers and items connected to TV and film adaptations.

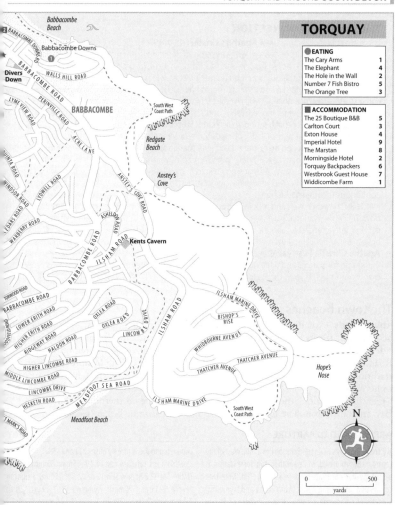

● **EATING**

The Cary Arms	1
The Elephant	4
The Hole in the Wall	2
Number 7 Fish Bistro	5
The Orange Tree	3

■ **ACCOMMODATION**

The 25 Boutique B&B	5
Carlton Court	3
Exton House	4
Imperial Hotel	9
The Marstan	8
Morningside Hotel	2
Torquay Backpackers	6
Westbrook Guest House	7
Widdicombe Farm	1

3

Kents Cavern

89–91 Ilsham Rd, TQ1 2JF • Tours daily: April–June, Sept & Oct regularly 9.30am–5pm; July & Aug regularly 9.30am–5.30pm; Nov–March 11am, 12.30pm, 2pm and 3.30pm; 45min–1hr • £10, under-16s £9 • ☏ 01803 215136, ⓦ kents-cavern.co.uk • Take bus #11, #22 or #32 to St Matthias church, then walk 400m

About a mile from the harbour off Babbacombe Road, you can explore **Kents Cavern**, a cave system excavated in the nineteenth century that shows signs of human habitation stretching back some 500,000 years. The tours are informative and entertaining, though most of the finds discovered here are on show in Torquay Museum (see opposite). Composed of white limestone dyed reddish brown by leaking iron oxides, the caves are adorned with stalagmites, stalactites and delicate "frozen waterfall" formations. They make a great wet-weather, child-friendly attraction with showy audiovisual effects and an underground exhibition filling in some of the history.

3

THE CHRISTIE CONNECTION

There are constant reminders of **Agatha Christie** (1890–1976) in South Devon, as the provincial life of the upper classes here was so often depicted in her murder mysteries. Born and raised in Torquay, she married Colonel Archie Christie in 1914, divorced him in 1928 and subsequently married the distinguished archeologist Max Mallowan, with whom she pursued an interest in Mesopotamia and its finds, making frequent visits there. She was inspired to write crime stories after making a bet with her sister Madge as to who could write the best mystery tale, discovering a talent for ingeniously – and eventually formulaically – plotted murder yarns that usually featured one of her principal sleuths, **Hercule Poirot** or **Miss Marple**.

Christie's formidable output – she once described herself as "a sausage machine, a perfect sausage machine" – relied on rather predictable scenarios and cardboard-thin characters, but this hasn't dented her success. To date, her 78 crime novels have sold more than a billion copies in English alone, with as many again sold in translation, and many filmed. Her play **The Mousetrap** opened in 1952 and is still going strong, making it the world's longest-running continuous theatre production.

In 1938 she purchased and rebuilt **Greenway**, a solid country residence overlooking the Dart, now run by the National Trust (see p.101). Fans should also seek out the **Torquay Museum** (see p.84), where a separate gallery is devoted to the author's life and work. Torbay's tourist offices have a leaflet detailing a themed walking trail and all the local Christie connections, and the **Agatha Christie Festival** (ⓦagathachristiefestival.co.uk) features talks, walks, film screenings, theatre performances and a tea dance over a week in mid-September on odd-numbered years; on even-numbered years there are events on Dame Agatha's birthday, September 15.

The town beaches

Abbey Sands, extending below the main promenade, is the handiest of the local beaches, but it gets busy in summer and it disappears to almost nothing at high tide. Walking northeast from the Old Harbour, a footpath signposted off Parkhill Road winds round the coast to the pebble-and-sand, Blue Flag **Meadfoot Beach**, traditionally the more "select" of Torquay's beaches, where Agatha Christie bathed in her youth.

Continue east along the coast path for **Hope's Nose**, the northernmost point of Tor Bay, and north from here to Anstey's Cove and Babbacombe Beach (see p.88).

ARRIVAL AND DEPARTURE   TORQUAY

By train Torquay's main train station lies a mile west of the centre on Rathmore Rd, while another stop, Torre station, is a mile further north at the top of Avenue Rd. Note that connections at Newton Abbot (from Exeter and Plymouth) sometimes necessitate a wait of 30min or more, so it may be quicker to take the #12 bus or a taxi from there.
Destinations Dawlish (1–3 hourly; 25min); Exeter (1–3 hourly; 35–55min); Newton Abbot (1–3 hourly; 12min); Paignton (1–3 hourly; 10min); Teignmouth (1–3 hourly; 20min).
By bus Most buses stop at the Old Harbour, including the #X46 between Exeter and Torquay and the frequent #12 service linking with Newton Abbot, Paignton and Brixham. National Express and Megabus coaches stop at the bus station about a mile from the harbour on Lymington Road,

connected to the centre by buses #31 and #34.
Destinations Brixham (every 10–15min; 55min); Exeter (Mon–Sat 1–2 hourly, Sun 12 daily; 1hr 15min); Paignton (every 5–15min; 25min); Plymouth (1–2 hourly; 2hr); Teignmouth (hourly; 50min); Totnes (1–3 hourly; 55min).
By taxi Riviera Taxis ⓞ01803 212600; Torbay Taxis ⓞ01803 211611.
By ferry Ferries operated by Brixham Express (ⓞ07553 359596, ⓦbrixhamexpress.com) and the cheaper Western Lady (ⓞ01803 293797, ⓦwesternladyferry.com) shuttle between Torquay's Old Harbour and Brixham all year about 6.30pm weekdays, 5.30pm on Sat and 5pm on Sun (Mon–Sat 1–2 hourly, Sun 7–16 daily; 25–35min; £2–5 one way, £3–6 return, bikes free). Sailings may be cancelled in bad weather.

GETTING AROUND

By bus Torquay has a decent bus network covering all areas you'll want to visit. The most useful services are #12 for Paignton and Brixham; #22 and #32 for Babbacombe,

and #62 for Cockington, all running frequently from the Strand, Torquay Harbour.

INFORMATION AND ACTIVITIES

Tourist information Vaughan Parade, Old Harbour (Mon–Wed, Fri & Sat 9.30am–2pm; ☎01803 211211, ⍵english riviera.co.uk). You can pick up discount vouchers for some local attractions as well as maps, transport timetables and information on events and entertainments here.

Bike rental Simply the Bike, 100 Belgrave Rd (☎01803 200024, ⍵simplythebike.co.uk), charges £11 per half-day or £17 per day.

Boat trips Apart from the daily excursions to Brixham (see p.91), boat trips from Torquay harbour include cruises to Dartmouth (£8.75; ☎01803 555872, ⍵dartmouthrailriver .co.uk) and mackerel- and wreck-fishing expeditions (£15–20; ☎07966 507882, ⍵mackerelfishingtorquay.co.uk). Various wildlife and evening cruises are also advertised, most operating April–Oct.

ACCOMMODATION

The 25 Boutique B&B 25 Avenue Rd, TQ2 5LB ☎01803 297517, ⍵the25.uk. As the name suggests, this place puts design at the forefront – rooms feature zebra-striped or purple-hued walls – but doesn't jettison essential comforts and practicalities. The pricier suites have mood lighting, iPads, Apple TV, rainhead showers and posh toiletries, while breakfasts include home-made yoghurt and smoothies. It's about a 10min walk from the seafront. No under-18s. Two-night minimum stay. **£115**

★**Carlton Court** 18 Clevedon Rd, TQ2 5BE ☎01803 297318, ⍵carlton-court.co.uk. In a quiet neighbour-hood, this Victorian villa has bright, spacious rooms equipped with fridges and modern bathrooms. The suites (£109) are like small apartments, with underfloor heating. There's an extensive subtropical garden and ample parking. No under-16s. **£90**

Exton House 12 Bridge Rd, TQ2 5BA ☎01803 293561, ⍵extonhotel.co.uk. Small, clean and calm B&B, a 10min walk from the train station and 20min from the Old Harbour. Rooms are spotlessly clean and the lounge has a balcony. Free pick-up from bus and train stations. **£65**

Imperial Hotel Parkhill Rd, TQ1 2DG ☎01803 294301, ⍵thehotelcollection.co.uk. It's let down by its shabby 1960s exterior, but this is still one of Devon's swankiest hotels, with aristocratic trimmings and period atmosphere (it was the model for the Majestic in Agatha Christie's *Peril at End House*). *The Regatta* restaurant makes a grand setting for a formal and fairly expensive meal, while there's

a more relaxed bar area for snacks or a cream tea; both offer panoramic bay views. Go for a sea-facing guest room if you can (they usually cost considerably more). There's also a health club included in the price with tennis and squash courts, pools, sauna and solarium. **£134**

The Marstan Meadfoot Sea Rd, TQ1 2LQ ☎01803 292837, ⍵marstanhotel.co.uk. Classic Victorian villa with a grand piano and antiques in the lounge and elegantly furnished guestrooms with modern, en-suite bathrooms. Uphill from the Old Harbour, it's ideally placed for Meadfoot Beach and the coast path, and the garden has a hot tub and a small pool – perfect de-stressers after long perambulations. No under-4s. **£89**

★**Torquay Backpackers** 119 Abbey Rd, TQ2 5NP ☎01803 299924, ⍵torquaybackpackers.co.uk. One of Devon's best independent hostels, providing cheap, clean and friendly accommodation in a central location a 10min walk from Torquay's train stations. Dorms are four- or six-bed and there's a double with shared bathroom; more rooms are available at a second property nearby, run by the same owners. Washing, cooking and free internet facilities are on hand. Booking essential. Dorms **£18**, doubles **£38**

Westbrook Guest House 15 Scarborough Rd, TQ2 5UJ ☎01803 292559, ⍵westbrookguesthouse.uk. Nice and central, off Belgrave Rd, this is a straightforward, unpretentious B&B, ideal for a night or two. The modern, en-suite rooms are spotless and well appointed, and there's parking. **£70**

EATING

★**The Elephant** 3–4 Beacon Terrace, TQ1 2BH ☎01803 200044, ⍵elephantrestaurant.co.uk. One of the region's best dining experiences, this classy but relaxed ground-floor brasserie offers lunchtime menus at £14.50 for two courses or £17 for three, while in the evenings mains average £19. Book ahead. Tues–Sat noon–2pm & 6.30–9pm.

★**Number 7 Fish Bistro** 7 Beacon Terrace, TQ1 2BH ☎01803 295055, ⍵no7-fish.com. The place to come for the freshest seafood and a lively atmosphere, overlooking the harbour. Choose from whatever the boats have brought in, from scallops simmered with mushrooms, vermouth and lemon to crab and lobster grilled with garlic and

brandy (mains mostly £15–20). Booking essential. Tues 6.30–9.45pm, Wed–Sat 12.45–1.45pm & 6–9.45pm: June–Oct also Mon 6.30–9.45pm; July–Sept also Sun 6.30–9.45pm.

The Orange Tree 14 Parkhill Rd, TQ1 2AL ☎01803 213936, ⍵orangetreerestaurant.co.uk. A procession of brilliantly executed and smartly presented works of culinary art issues from the kitchen of this sober and civilized place. The emphasis is on game, poultry and other meat dishes (around £18), though there are a couple of seafood and vegetarian options too. The delicious desserts include chocolate fondant and crème brûlée. Mon–Sat 7pm–late.

3

DRINKING

The Hole in the Wall 6 Park Lane, TQ1 2AU ⌖01803 200755, ⓦholeinthewalltorquay.co.uk. Reputedly the town's oldest pub, this was Irish playwright Sean O'Casey's local when he lived in Torquay. There's a bar menu and a separate restaurant (worth booking) where you can dine on seafood, steaks and pies. Live music plays on Tues, Thurs & Sun. Daily 11.30am–midnight.

Babbacombe and around

The one-time village of **BABBACOMBE** is a peaceful spot with lofty sea views. The main attraction is its 240ft **cliff railway** (mid-Feb to Oct; £2 single, £2.20 return; last departure 5pm, or 6pm June–Sept; ⌖01803 328750, ⓦbabbacombecliffrailway.co.uk) to the arc of **Oddicombe Beach**, awarded Blue Flag status in 2016.

Just a few minutes' walk south of Oddicombe Beach, the long sand-and-shingle expanse of **Babbacombe Beach** has deckchairs and changing cabins as well as facilities for **diving**. Above it, the car park near the *Cary Arms* was once the site of a beach house where a local resident was murdered in 1884, for which John "Babbacombe" Lee was convicted. After three unsuccessful attempts to hang him, his death sentence was commuted to life imprisonment; he was released in 1907. The "man they could not hang" was immortalized in various books and by Fairport Convention's ballad *Babbacombe Lee*.

Half a mile southeast, **Anstey's Cove** is a tiny, sheltered pocket of shingle and rock good for swimming, and you can reach more secluded cliff-backed coves with sand-and-shingle beaches three or four miles north up the coast from Babbacombe at **Watcombe** and **Maidencombe**.

GETTING AROUND   BABBACOMBE AND AROUND

By bus Babbacombe can be reached on buses #22 and #32 from Torquay as well as via the Cliff Railway from Oddicombe Beach. Bus #22 carries on to Watcombe and Maidencombe, and Watcombe is also connected by #31 and #34 from Babbacombe.

ACTIVITIES

Diving Divers Down, 139 Babbacombe Rd, Babbacombe (⌖01803 327111, ⓦdiversdown.co.uk), offer accompanied and unaccompanied dives and tuition.

ACCOMMODATION AND EATING

The Cary Arms Babbacombe Beach, TQ1 3LX ⌖01803 327110, ⓦcaryarms.co.uk; map pp.84–85. Away from the hullaballoo of Torquay's centre, this seaside pub and hotel has beamed ceilings, bare stone walls, books and board games. Soak up great views across the bay while enjoying a range of local ales as well as snacks and meals (most mains £13–18). Kitchen daily noon–3pm & 6.30–9pm.

Morningside Hotel Babbacombe Downs, TQ1 3LF ⌖01803 327025, ⓦthemorningsidehotel.co.uk; map map pp.84–85. This out-of-the-centre option (easily accessed on bus #32) is ideally placed for Babbacombe and Oddicombe beaches. It has a garden, bar, conservatory restaurant (for lunches only) and bright, spacious rooms – some, costing slightly more, with views over the bay. **£79**

Cockington

A mile or so west of Torquay's main train station, Torbay suddenly turns deeply rural at the showcase village of **COCKINGTON**. Though frequently overrun by crowds, it's worth a wander if you can stomach the chocolate-box imagery, the result of an overzealous preservation programme dating from the 1930s. The core of the original Saxon village can still be discerned, however, and the only completely "modern" building you'll see is the *Drum Inn*, concocted by Edwin Lutyens in 1934 in traditional thatched style as part of a much larger development project that never materialized.

Cockington Court

TQ2 6XA • Daily: April–Sept 10am–5pm; Oct–March 10am–4pm • Free • ☎ 01803 607230, ⓦ cockingtoncourt.org

Cockington's main crowd-puller is **Cockington Court**, whose picturesquely landscaped grounds lie uphill to the left from the crossroads at the centre of the village. This much-remodelled house now holds a complex of craft studios and souvenir shops, and there's a glass-blowing workshop and an organic garden in the grounds; you're free to wander round.

More interestingly, atop a grassy mound next to the house is the parish church of **St George and St Mary**, a good-looking thirteenth- to fourteenth-century red-sandstone construction whose interior has a triple barrel-vaulted ceiling and a Renaissance pulpit, though the intricate wooden screen is recent. The surrounding **parkland** filled with woodland walks and lakes makes ideal picnicking country.

GETTING AROUND   COCKINGTON

By bus Bus #62 (or marked "Cockington") heads to the village every 40min (Mon–Fri) from Torquay Harbour and Belgrave Rd; otherwise take bus #12 for Paignton and get off just south of Torquay train station on Torbay Rd, from where it's a pleasant mile-long stroll up Cockington Lane.

ACCOMMODATION

Lanscombe House TQ2 6XA ☎ 01803 606938, ⓦ lanscombehouse.co.uk. This country house has four elegant rooms overlooking a walled garden, and period furnishings. It's linked to Torquay's centre by bus #62 (Mon–Fri), otherwise it's under a mile's walk from both the seafront and Torquay train station. Two-night minimum stay. No under-16s. Closed mid-Oct to Easter. **£105**

Compton Castle

Compton, TQ3 1TA • April–Oct Tues–Thurs 10.30am–5pm • £6.30 (cash only); NT • ☎ 01803 661906, ⓦ nationaltrust.org.uk/compton-castle • Take a bus to Marldon, then walk 1.5 miles north

Three miles west of Torquay, signposted off the A380 near Marldon, **Compton Castle** has been home to the seafaring Gilbert family – related to Sir Walter Raleigh – for most of the last six centuries. Buttressed and battlemented, its dramatic exterior has proved a favourite with film-makers (1995's *Sense and Sensibility* was shot here), while the more modest interior includes Elizabethan portraits in the reconstructed Great Hall and a vast fireplace in the old kitchen.

ACCOMMODATION   COMPTON

Widdicombe Farm A380 near Compton, TQ3 1ST ☎ 01803 558325, ⓦ widdicombefarm.co.uk. Accessed from the Torbay ring road, this sheltered, well-equipped campsite is for adults only, with a three-night minimum stay in peak season. Facilities are clean and there's a bar/restaurant and laundrette. Mid-March to late Oct only. **£20**

Paignton

Three miles south of Torquay, not so much a sister-resort as a poor relation, **PAIGNTON** lacks the gloss – and the pretensions – of its neighbour. Its beach, pier, arcades and other seaside amusements identify it as a traditional family resort, though it is somewhat spoiled by the torrents of traffic flowing through. From **the Esplanade**, lawns back on to the level pink sands of the main town beach. At its southern end, a small harbour nestles in the lee of the aptly named **Redcliffe headland**, quite a lively spot in summer with restaurants and boat tours, while to the south, the wide, shell-specked **Goodrington Sands** is the best spot for a paddle or a dip, backed by a low sea wall and a long strip of park.

Paignton Zoo

Totnes Rd, TQ4 7EU • Daily: March, April & early Sept to Oct 10am–5pm; May to early Sept 10am–6pm; Nov–March 10am–4.30pm; last entry 1hr before closing • £15.40, under-16s £11.55; combined ticket with Torquay's Living Coasts (see p.83) £22, under-16s £15 • ☎ 01803 697500, ⓦ paigntonzoo.org.uk

A mile inland from the seafront, **Paignton Zoo** is the town's most famous attraction, its 80 acres divided into savanna, forest, wetland, tropical forest and desert zones, all with hands-on displays. There's plenty to take in and the various habitats are imaginatively presented, with an emphasis on ecology and conservation. The hot and humid **Crocodile Swamp** holds crocs from Cuba and the Nile, as well as boa constrictors and pythons, while the **Wetland** zone has a series of lakes and a large walk-through aviary, and the **Forest** zone features endangered Asiatic lions and Sumatran tigers.

Dartmouth Steam Railway

Train station, Torbay Rd, TQ4 6AF • April–Oct, plus some dates in Feb, March, Nov & Dec 4–9 daily • £16 return to Dartmouth, Round Robin £25.50, bikes free • ☎ 01803 555872, ⓦ dartmouthrailriver.co.uk • Bus #100 runs from the Strand in Torquay (daily 10am; free) to Paignton station

Paignton is the northern terminus of the **Dartmouth Steam Railway**, which runs from next to the main-line train station, near the harbour, to the village of Kingswear, across the Dart from Dartmouth. The accent is on Victorian nostalgia, with railway personnel in period uniforms, but even without the trappings it's a nice way to view the countryside, the line connecting with Goodrington Sands before veering inland and trundling alongside the Dart estuary. There's also a stop at **Greenway Halt**, linked to Greenway by a thirty-minute woodland walk or a free shuttle bus (see box, p.101). The full Paignton–Kingswear stretch takes thirty minutes, and from Kingswear there are frequent ferry crossings to Dartmouth. You can also buy a Round Robin ticket, which additionally covers the river trip up the Dart to Totnes and the bus from Totnes back to Paignton.

ARRIVAL AND DEPARTURE   PAIGNTON

By train Paignton's train station is close to the beach, pier and harbour on Victoria Street.
Destinations Exeter (1–3 hourly; 40min–1hr 10min); Newton Abbot (1–3 hourly; 15min); Torquay (1–3 hourly; 5min).

By bus The bus station is opposite the train station, across Victoria Street. Bus #12 is the most useful service for Torquay and Brixham, #100 and #GOLD for Totnes.
Destinations Brixham (every 5–15min; 25min); Torquay (every 5–15min; 25min); Totnes (2–4 hourly; 25min).

INFORMATION

Tourist information There are information points at the *Flagship Inn*, Esplanade Road, and Torbay Bookshop, 7

Torquay Rd (for both ☎ 01803 211211, ⓦ englishriviera .co.uk).

ACCOMMODATION

P&M Paignton Residence 2 Kernou Rd, TQ4 6BA ☎ 01803 523118, ⓦ paignton-residence.com. Crisply contemporary B&B near the centre with neutrally coloured, en-suite rooms – one with its own sauna, another with a Japanese soaking tub – and all equipped with flatscreen TVs, digital radios and iPod docking stations. **£85**

Whitehill Country Park Stoke Rd, TQ4 7PF ☎ 01803

661961, ⓦ beverley-holidays.co.uk. The heights above Paignton hold most of Torbay's campsites, including this, quieter and more secluded than most but still equipped with a heated outdoor pool, play areas for children and modern washing facilities. Wooden pods (£52) are available for two or four people. It's 2.5 miles from Paignton's seafront (bus #25). Late March to Sept only. **£26**

EATING

Restaurant 59 59 Torquay Rd, TQ3 3DT ☎ 01803 527347, ⓦ restaurant59.co.uk. Large portions of "English-style tapas" are served at this relaxed and friendly place, such as battered cod bites, baked camembert, paella, and pulled pork and apple (mostly £4–6). The menu also has pizzas (£7–11), sharing platters (£14) and some

luscious desserts, and there are vegan and gluten-free options. Tues–Thurs 4pm–late, Fri & Sat noon–late.
TJ's Café-Bistro 44 Cliff Rd, TQ4 6DL ☎ 01803 527389, ⓦ tjsrestaurant.co.uk. This harbourside spot with a heated terrace overlooking the boats suggests there might be something in the "Riviera" tag after all. The menu ranges

from braised belly pork to fish of the day (around £11), alongside a superb range of tapas (£4–7). 6pm–late: April & May Thurs–Sat; June–Sept Wed–Sat, but daily in school hols; Oct–March Fri & Sat.

Brixham

From Paignton, it's about five miles round the bay to **BRIXHAM**, the smallest and quaintest of the Torbay trio, with a lively harbour sheltered in the lee of Berry Head. Fishing has always been Brixham's lifeblood; once the major fish market in the West Country, it still supplies restaurants in London and beyond. You'll find all manner of cockles, whelks and crab sticks at the harbourside stalls, and no shortage of fresh seafood at local pubs and restaurants.

The Golden Hind

The Quay, TQ5 8AW • Feb–Oct daily 10am–4.30pm, longer hours in summer • £7 • ☎ 01803 856223, ⓦ goldenhind.co.uk

3

Among the trawlers moored up on Brixham's quayside is a full-size reconstruction of the **Golden Hind**, the surprisingly small vessel in which Francis Drake circumnavigated the world in 1577–80, and on board which he was knighted by Elizabeth I on his triumphant return – the ship has no connection with the port, however. Below decks, where up to sixty men were quartered, you can see the extremely cramped surgeon's and carpenter's cabins, and the only slightly grander captain's quarters.

Brixham Heritage Museum

New Rd, TQ5 8LZ • Easter–Oct Tues–Fri 10am–4pm, Sat 10am–1pm • Free • ☎ 01803 856267, ⓦ brixhamheritage.org.uk

From the quayside, steep lanes and stairways thread up to the older town centre around Fore Street, at the top of which an ex-police station now houses the **Brixham Heritage Museum**. Alongside displays of sail-making, tools and navigation aids, and items illustrating the area's social and domestic history, you'll find background on the Reverend Henry Francis Lyte (1793–1847), the first incumbent of the church of All Saints in nearby Church Street and the author of the famous hymn *Abide with Me* (the tune rings out from the church's carillon each day at midday and 8pm).

Berry Head

From Brixham harbour, it's a thirty-minute walk east to the promontory of **Berry Head**. Fortifications built during the Napoleonic Wars are still standing on this southern limit of Tor Bay, which is now a conservation area attracting colonies of nesting seabirds (including the largest guillemot colony on England's south coast) and affording fabulous views. From Berry Head the coast path curves round St Mary's Bay to the south, passes through land managed by the National Trust, and eventually brings you to Kingswear – ten fairly strenuous miles – and the ferry to Dartmouth.

ARRIVAL AND DEPARTURE
BRIXHAM

By bus Most buses arrive in and depart from the upper town, with stops in Town Square and Bank Lane.
Destinations Kingswear (1–2 hourly; 20–30min); Paignton (every 5–20min; 25min); Torquay (every 10–15min; 50min).

By ferry Between April and October you can also get here on motor launches from Torquay's harbour, a 30min crossing (2 hourly; £2–5 one-way, £3–6 return).

INFORMATION AND TOURS

Tourist information Hobb Nobs gift shop, the Quay (daily 10am–5pm; ☎ 01803 211211, ⓦ englishriviera.co.uk).
Boat tours Between April and Oct you can explore the coastline on boat tours from Brixham's harbour, including 2hr mackerel-fishing trips (£15; ☎ 07711 042229, ⓦ funfishtrips.com).

ACCOMMODATION

Sampford House 57–59 King St, TQ5 9TH ☎01803 857761, ⓦsampfordhouse.com. Wake up to stunning views from the front-facing rooms at this B&B, which are smallish but tastefully decorated (book early for rooms with sea views). Breakfasts include home-made yoghurt and jams. Also on site is the Fisherman's Cottage (£97), a self-contained unit with a kitchenette, sleeping two. **£80**

Upton Manor Farm St Mary's Rd, TQ5 9QH ☎01803 882384, ⓦuptonmanorfarm.co.uk. Spacious, well-equipped campsite with a focus on couples and families. It's 1.5 miles south of town and about 10min steep walk from the coast path and the secluded sand and shingle beach at St Mary's Bay. Easter–Oct only. **£18**

EATING AND DRINKING

Blue Anchor 83 Fore St, TQ5 8AH ☎01803 859373. A great spot for a relaxed pint, with low beams, a log fire and black-and-white photos of fisherfolk of old. There are six real ales on tap, and baguettes and a selection of pub classics on the menu (£7–10), plus grills and daily specials. Live music features on Fri and Sat evenings, plus Sun afternoons in summer. Mon–Sat 11am–midnight, Sun 11am–11.30pm.

★ **Rockfish** Fish Market, TQ5 8AJ ☎01803 850872,

ⓦtherockfish.co.uk. For location alone, this place leads the field, set in an airy modern building at one end of the harbour, with lofty views that you can appreciate from its curving deck. It's part of a local chain that specializes in the freshest seafood and fresh-cut chips. Apart from the usual cod, haddock and scampi (£12–17), you can order roast scallops (£10), crab roll (£13) or seafood tacos (£14). There's a take away at street level. Daily noon–9.30pm.

Totnes and around

Five miles inland of Torbay, **TOTNES** has an ancient pedigree, its period of greatest prosperity having occurred in the sixteenth century, when this inland port on the west bank of the River Dart exported cloth to France and imported wine. Some evocative structures from that era remain, but Totnes has since mellowed into a residential market town, its warehouses converted into gentrified flats. The arcaded High Street, secretive flowery lanes, Norman castle and preserved steam railway have attracted some tourist overflow from nearby Torbay, but so far its allure has survived more or less intact – enough, anyway, to attract a host of alternative therapists, craft enthusiasts and crystal-gazers in recent years.

Totnes centres on the long main street that starts off as Fore Street and becomes High Street at the white, castellated **East Gate**, a heavily retouched medieval arch. A number of eye-catching old buildings line both streets; for example, the mustard-yellow, late eighteenth-century **Gothic House** on Fore Street; **16 High St**, a house built by pilchard merchant Nicholas Ball, whose initials are inscribed outside (his wealth, inherited by his widow, was eventually bequeathed by her second husband, Thomas Bodley, to found Oxford's Bodleian Library); and **28 High St**, overhung by curious grotesque masks.

Elizabethan House Museum

70 Fore St, TQ9 5RU • Late March to Sept Mon–Fri 10am–4pm; last entry 3pm • £3 • ☎01803 863821, ⓦtotnesmuseum.org

Many of the buildings in Totnes are Elizabethan in origin, with later facades added, often with a handsome covering of slate tiles. One of the best preserved of these buildings now holds the **Elizabethan House Museum**, packed with an entertaining assortment of domestic objects and furniture that reveal how wealthy clothiers lived at the peak of the town's success.

Rooms in the four-storey building include an Elizabethan "Forehall", a Tudor kitchen and an exhibition devoted to local mathematician **Charles Babbage** (1791–1871), whose "analytical engine", programmed by punched cards, was the forerunner of the computer. His collaborator was Ada, Countess of Lovelace (Lord Byron's daughter), who described the machine as suitable for "developing and tabulating any function whatever", and even mooted its potential for creating computer-generated music. Now, she is widely regarded as the world's first computer programmer.

BLACKPOOL SANDS (P.100) >

3

Church of St Mary

High St, TQ9 5NN • Daily: March–Oct 8.45am–5pm; Nov–Feb 8.45am–4pm • Free • ☎ 01803 865615, ⚓ stmarystotnes.wordpress.com

Beneath East Gate, **Ramparts Walk** trails east along the old town walls, curling round the fifteenth-century **Church of St Mary**, built in vivid red sandstone and enhanced by a tall, pinnacled tower. Inside, the exquisitely carved stone rood screen stretching the full width of the building is the chief highlight.

Guildhall

Ramparts Walk, TQ9 5QH • Early April to Oct Mon–Fri 11am–3pm • Suggested donation £1 • ☎ 01803 862147

Behind the Church of St Mary, the colonnaded **Guildhall** was first constructed in the eleventh century as the refectory and kitchen of a Benedictine priory, was rebuilt in 1553 following the Dissolution, and has been used by the town council ever since. Inside you can view a table used by Oliver Cromwell in 1646, together with the former jail cells and the courtroom, used from 1624 to 1974.

Totnes Castle

Castle St, TQ9 5NU • April–Sept daily 10am–6pm; Oct daily 10am–5pm; Nov–March Sat & Sun 10am–4pm • £4, under-16s £2.40; EH • ☎ 01803 864406, ⚓ www.english-heritage.org.uk/visit/places/totnes-castle

At the top of the town yet almost invisible behind the High Street, **Totnes Castle** is the town's oldest monument, a classic Norman structure of the motte and bailey design, with a simple crenellated keep atop a grassy mound, reached along a winding path from the curtain wall. Though little more than a shell now, the keep ranks as one of the best-preserved in the country, and has superb views of the town and Dart valley from its walls.

ARRIVAL AND INFORMATION
TOTNES AND AROUND

By train Totnes is served by regular trains on the main Exeter–Plymouth line, which stop at the station on Station Road, at the end of Castle Street. Trains from Buckfastleigh on the seasonal South Devon Railway (see box above) stop at Totnes Littlehempston station.
Destinations Exeter (1–3 hourly; 35min); Newton Abbot (2 hourly; 12min); Plymouth (2–3 hourly; 30min).

By bus All buses stop at or near the Plains, at the bottom of Fore St. Frequent services #66, #100 and #GOLD connect with Paignton, #GOLD with Plymouth and Torquay, and

#X64 with Exeter and Dartmouth. National Express coaches also provide a useful link to Exeter, Torquay and Paignton.
Destinations Dartmouth (Mon–Sat 10 daily, Sun 2 daily; 55min); Exeter (7–10 daily; 1hr 15min–1hr 40min); Kingsbridge (Mon–Sat 9 daily, Sun 2 daily; 45min); Paignton (2–4 hourly; 25–40min); Plymouth (1–2 hourly; 1hr 5min); Torquay (1–2 hourly; 50min).

Tourist information See ⚓ visittotnes.co.uk for accommodation, where to eat and local events.

ACTIVITIES

Bike rental Hot Pursuit Cycles, 26 The Stables, Ford Rd on Totnes Industrial Estate, near the train station (☎ 01803 865174, ⚓ hotpursuit-cycles.co.uk). Bikes £15 per day.

Walking Hikers can follow the sixteen-mile, well-waymarked Dart Valley Trail, linking Totnes with Dartmouth. There's a full description at ⚓ southdevonaonb.org.uk.

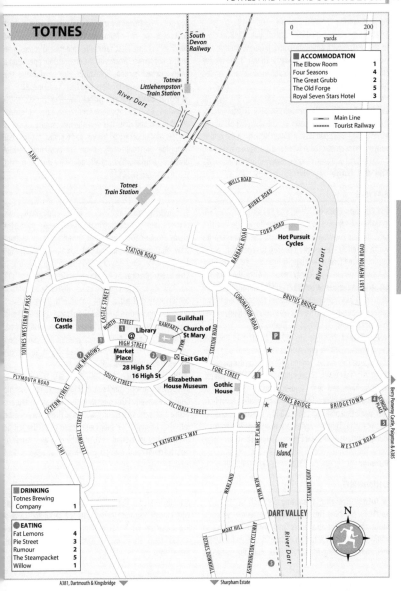

TOTNES

South Devon Railway

Totnes Littlehempston Train Station

River Dart

Totnes Train Station

■ ACCOMMODATION	
The Elbow Room	1
Four Seasons	4
The Great Grubb	2
The Old Forge	5
Royal Seven Stars Hotel	3

| Main Line | |
| Tourist Railway | |

WILLS ROAD
BURKE ROAD
FORD ROAD
BABBAGE ROAD
CORONATION ROAD
A381 NEWTON ROAD
BRUTUS BRIDGE
STATION ROAD
River Dart

Hot Pursuit Cycles

TOTNES WESTERN BY PASS
CASTLE STREET
NORTH STREET
Totnes Castle
Guildhall
RAMPARTS
Church of St Mary
Library @
HIGH STREET
Market Place
THE NARROWS
East Gate
28 High St
16 High St
SOUTH STREET
Elizabethan House Museum
Gothic House
FORE STREET
STATION ROAD
P
Totnes Bridge
BRIDGETOWN
LYMPSTONE PLACE
PLYMOUTH ROAD
CISTERN STREET
A381
LEECHWELL STREET
VICTORIA STREET
ST KATHERINE'S WAY
THE PLAINS
NEW WALK
WARLAND
Vire Island
WESTON ROAD
STEAMER QUAY

Berry Pomeroy Castle, Paignton & A385

■ DRINKING	
Totnes Brewing Company	1

● EATING	
Fat Lemons	4
Pie Street	3
Rumour	2
The Steampacket	5
Willow	1

MOAT HILL
TOTNES DOWNHILL
ASHPRINGTON CYCLEWAY
River Dart
DART VALLEY
N

A381, Dartmouth & Kingsbridge
Sharpham Estate

Markets Market Place, off the High Street, is the venue for a general market every Fri & Sat morning; the Elizabethan Market, a charity market with traders togged up in Elizabethan costumes (May–Sept Tues 9am–3pm), and a Good Food Market on the third Sun of the month from 10am (ⓦtotnesgoodfood.co.uk).

ACCOMMODATION

The Elbow Room North St, TQ9 5NZ ☏ 01803 863480, ⓦtheelbowroomtotnes.co.uk. A good central choice opposite the castle car park, this 400-year-old converted cottage and cider press has two quiet en-suite rooms, and a beamed, high-ceilinged guests' lounge with an array of "character mugs". No credit cards. __£75__

Four Seasons 13 Bridgetown, TQ9 5AB ☎01803 862146, ⓦfourseasonstotnes.co.uk. Friendly B&B close to the centre, with smallish rooms, a guests' lounge and work by local artists on the walls. There's an extensive choice at breakfast, including garden produce, and limited parking. No credit cards. **£90**

★**The Great Grubb** Fallowfields, Plymouth Rd, TQ9 5LX ☎01803 849071, ⓦthegreatgrubb.co.uk. Restful colours, healthy breakfasts and a patio are the main appeal of this friendly, well-equipped B&B, a 15min walk from the centre, with shared or en-suite bathrooms and a family room sleeping three (£109). Local artists' work is displayed in the rooms. **£85**

The Old Forge Seymour Place, TQ9 5AY ☎01803 862174, ⓦoldforgetotnes.com. In a quiet nook a short walk over the river from the Plains, this 600-year-old building has small but tastefully modernized rooms, one with a roof terrace. Rooms on the ground floor open onto a lovely lawned garden. Breakfasts, also overlooking the garden, cater for special diets, and there's parking. **£87**

★**Royal Seven Stars Hotel** The Plains, TQ9 5DD ☎01803 862125, ⓦroyalsevenstars.co.uk. A quirky blend of old and new, this seventeenth-century coaching inn has contemporary bedrooms and a stylish modern bar alongside the traditional *Saloon Bar* and more formal brasserie (both of which are also good for a drink or meal if you're not a guest). **£125**

EATING

Fat Lemons 1 Ticklemore St, TQ9 5EJ ☎01803 866888, ⓦfatlemons-totnes.co.uk. You have to winkle out this café, hidden away on a side street off the Plains, but it's worth the effort – especially if you're into vegetarian, vegan or gluten-free food. Everything is fresh and delicious, from the soups served with crusty bread (£4) to the griddled granary sandwiches (around £7) and the carrot cake. Other than snack lunches, breakfasts, scones and steaming Italian coffees are served, and there's a small, gravelly garden open in summer. Tues–Sat 10am–4.30pm.

★**Pie Street** 26 High St, TQ9 5RY ☎01803 868674, ⓦpiestreet.co.uk. A purveyor of "British soul food", this place specializes in pies (around £10) made on the premises, to eat in or take away. Choices include spicy chicken jalfrezi, chicken, ham and leek, and mushroom *au poivre*, all accompanied by mashed potatoes, chips or salad. Apart from pies, you'll find pork baps, salads and a selection of cheeses on the menu. Timothy Taylors ale is on tap, and there's a lounge upstairs with board games. Mon 11.30am–6pm, Tues–Thurs 11am–8pm, Fri & Sat 11.30am–9pm.

Rumour 30 High St, TQ9 5RY ☎01803 864682, ⓦrumourtotnes.com. With a buzzy atmosphere, this place is ideal for cappuccinos, snacks, make-your-own pizzas (from £7.50) or full meals, including Italian seafood stew. Most mains are around £14. Food served Mon–Sat 10–11.30am, noon–3pm & 6–10pm, Sun 6–10pm.

The Steampacket St Peter's Quay, TQ9 5EW ☎01803 863880, ⓦsteampacketinn.co.uk. Riverside inn with a conservatory and patio, right opposite the river cruisers' dock, serving sandwiches, traditional meals (£10–15) and real ales. Evening meals and Sun lunches are best booked. Mon–Sat 11am–11pm, Sun noon–10.30pm; food served Mon–Fri noon–2.30pm & 6–9.30pm, Sat noon–3pm & 6–9.30pm, Sun noon–8pm.

★**Willow** 87 High St, TQ9 5PB ☎01803 862605. Inexpensive snacks, candle-lit evening meals and organic drinks are served at this mellow vegetarian café-restaurant with a courtyard. Wed is curry night, and there's live acoustic music on Fri night. The soups and mixed salads are terrific (main dishes are around £11), and there's a wide range of teas. No credit cards. Mon, Tues & Thurs 10am–5pm, Wed Fri & Sat 10am–5pm & 6.30–10.30pm.

DRINKING

★**Totnes Brewing Company** 59 High St, TQ9 5PB ☎01803 849290. This pub and microbrewery serves a range of craft ales and ciders from around the world in addition to its own. It has an authentic, spit-and-sawdust feel, and the small garden at the back abuts the castle (it's actually located in the moat). Upstairs, a former ballroom with chandeliers and cinema seats is a venue for DJs and live music on Fri & Sat evenings (ⓦbarrelhousetotnes .co.uk). Mon–Thurs & Sun 5pm–midnight, Fri & Sat noon–midnight.

Dartington Hall

Dartington, TQ9 6EL • Grounds daily dawn–dusk • Free • ☎01803 847514, ⓦdartington.org • By bus from Totnes, take #165 (not Sun), the last one back leaving at around 6pm

A couple of miles north of Totnes, the riverside path passes near the estate of **Dartington Hall**, an arts and education centre set up in 1925 by US millionaire Dorothy Elmhirst and her husband. You can walk through the sculpture-strewn **gardens**, which contain an immaculately kept tiltyard and terraces, at any time and – when it's not in use – visit the fourteenth-century Great Hall, originally built for Richard II's half-brother John Holand and rescued from dereliction by the Elmhirsts.

As well as a constant programme of films, plays, concerts, dance and workshops, the ten-day Ways With Words **literature festival** takes place here in July, featuring big-name writers, and there is a **summer festival** of mainly classical music from late July through to late August.

ACCOMMODATION DARTINGTON

Dartington Hall Dartington, TQ9 6EL ☎01803 847100, ⓦdartington.org. Arranged around the fourteenth-century courtyard of Dartington Hall, two miles north of Totnes, rooms here range from standards with shared bathrooms to en-suite doubles. Breakfast and meals are served in the *White Hart* bar. Accommodation is not available during the Summer School and festivals (including most of July & Aug). **£76**

SHOPPING

The Shops at Dartington Shinners Bridge, Dartington, TQ9 6TQ ☎01803 847500, ⓦdartington .org. Signposted near Dartington Hall on the edge of the estate, this shopping complex retails Devon cider, cakes and biscuits, sportswear and the prized Dartington Crystal glassware, as well as an assortment of upmarket crafts and edible goodies from the farm shop. There's also a branch of the *Venus Café*, and *Cranks*, sole surviving outpost of the 1960s vegetarian restaurant chain. Mon–Sat 9.30am–5.30pm, Sun 10am–5pm.

Berry Pomeroy Castle

Three miles east of Totnes off the A385, TQ9 6LJ • April–Sept daily 10am–6pm; Oct daily 10am–4pm; Nov–March Sat & Sun 10am–4pm • £5.60, under-16s £3.30; EH • ☎ 01803 866618, ⓦ www.english-heritage.org.uk/visit/places/berry-pomeroy-castle • Take bus #66B (Mon–Sat) from Totnes

Surrounded by deep woods, **Berry Pomeroy Castle** is one of Devon's most romantic ruins, a fifteenth-century fortress converted into an Elizabethan mansion by the powerful Seymour family, but never completed and abandoned by 1700. You can enter the gatehouse, walk along the few intact walls – affording great views – and listen on the supplied audioguide to tales of the ghosts said to dwell here.

Sharpham Estate

Three miles downriver of Totnes, near Ashprington, TQ9 7UT • March & April Mon–Sat 10am–5pm; May–Sept daily 10am–6pm; Oct to late Dec Mon–Sat 10am–3pm • Self-guided walks £2.50 • **Guided tours** May–Sept Sat & Sun 3pm; 1hr 30min • £20 • ☎ 01803 732203, ⓦ sharpham.com

Some of England's finest wines are produced at **Sharpham Estate**, which you can explore on rambling trails, self-guided walks or guided tours (no booking required), with tasting and shopping opportunities aplenty. See the website for a full list of options, among them the four-hour "Sharpham Experience", including lunch and tastings (£75; book well ahead).

Dartmouth and around

Seven miles downstream of Totnes and a mile upriver from the sea, **DARTMOUTH** has thrived since the Normans recognized the potential of this deep-water port for trading with their home country. The maritime connection is still strong today: boatyards and marine chandlers abound, and officers are still trained at the imposing red-brick **Royal Naval College**, majestically sited on a hill behind the port.

A number of lopsided but well-preserved old buildings add to Dartmouth's appeal, including the timber-framed **Butterwalk**, overhanging Duke Street on eleven granite columns. The four-storey construction, richly decorated with woodcarvings, was built in the seventeenth century for a local merchant. The Pilgrim Fathers put to shore en route to the New World at **Bayard's Cove**, a short cobbled quay at the bottom of Lower Street, lined with well-restored eighteenth-century houses. Some of Dartmouth's oldest buildings house **pubs** and **restaurants** bristling with character, including a few outstanding ones that have helped to put Dartmouth on the culinary map.

Most of the swimming in these parts takes place south of town at **Start Bay**, particularly the beach of **Blackpool Sands**. Further down, the lagoon and nature reserve at **Slapton Ley** stretches behind Slapton Sands, the scene of World War II operations. A short ride upriver of Dartmouth, Agatha Christie spent her holidays in the tree-encompassed mansion of **Greenway**, while there's a distinctly 1920s feel about **Coleton Fishacre**, a remote country retreat west of Kingswear and close to a fine stretch of coast.

Dartmouth Museum

The Butterwalk, Duke St, TQ6 9PZ • April–Oct Mon & Sun 1–4pm, Tues–Sat 10am–4pm; Nov–March daily noon–3pm • £2 • ☎ 01803 832923, ⓦ dartmouthmuseum.org

Above the shops on the Butterwalk, the compact **Dartmouth Museum** is mainly devoted to maritime curios. The highlight is the King's Room, with its original wood panelling and plaster ceiling, and displays of model sailing ships alongside delicate ivory models of Chinese craft and a man-of-war constructed from bone by French prisoners.

St Saviour's

Anzac St, TQ6 9PZ • Daily 9.30am–dusk • Free • ☎ 01803 835540

Originating in the fourteenth century, **St Saviour's** church was rebuilt in the 1630s when timbers from the captured flagship of the Spanish Armada were incorporated into the gallery occupying the rear of the richly furnished interior. Other highlights include a finely carved and painted stone – not wood, contrary to appearance – pulpit, and a traceried wooden screen, both from the late fifteenth century. Just inside the

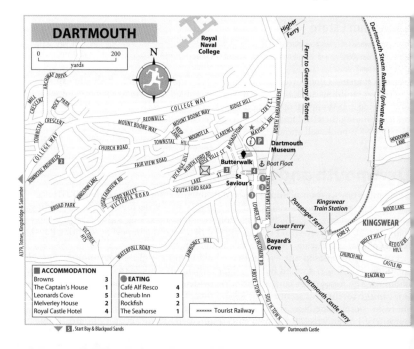

> ## DARTMOUTH'S ROYAL REGATTA
>
> Dartmouth's biggest event, the **Royal Regatta** (ⓦdartmouthregatta.co.uk), takes place over three days around the last weekend of August. The river races, air displays and fireworks attract huge crowds, making accommodation scarce during this period.

entrance, you can admire the superb medieval ironwork on what may have been the church's original outer door (replaced in 1631), showing the elongated leopards of the Plantagenet kings entwined with a tree of life.

Dartmouth Castle

Castle Rd, TQ6 0JN • April–Sept daily 10am–6pm; Oct daily 10am–5pm; Nov–March Sat & Sun 10am–4pm • £6.10, under-16s £3.70; EH • ☎ 01803 833588, ⓦ www.english-heritage.org.uk/visit/places/dartmouth-castle • An easy walk from town, otherwise take the ferry from South Embankment to the creek below the castle (Easter–Oct; £2.50 one-way)

A twenty-minute riverside walk south of Bayard's Cove brings you to **Dartmouth Castle**, one of two fortifications on opposite sides of the estuary (the other is Kingswear Castle, now holiday homes) built in the late fifteenth century. The larger and more complete of the two buildings, Dartmouth Castle was the first in England to be constructed specifically to withstand artillery, but was never tested in action and consequently remains in an excellent state of preservation. Various examples of weaponry are on display, and panels explain the castle's historical function.

3

ARRIVAL AND DEPARTURE   DARTMOUTH

By bus Dartmouth is connected to Totnes by bus #X64, and to Kingsbridge, Torcross and Plymouth by #3; stops are by the car park on Mayor's Avenue. For services to the Torbay towns, take the ferry to Kingswear (see box, p.100). Destinations Brixham via Kingswear (1–2 hourly; 25min);

Kingsbridge (Mon–Sat hourly, Sun 2 daily; 1hr 10min); Paignton via Kingswear (Mon–Sat hourly, Sun 4 daily; 30–50min); Plymouth (Mon–Sat 8 daily; 2hr 20min); Torcross (Mon–Sat hourly, Sun 2 daily; 40min); Totnes (Mon–Sat 8 daily; 50min).

INFORMATION AND ACTIVITIES

Tourist information Mayor's Avenue (Mon, Tues & Thurs–Sat 10am–4pm; ☎ 01803 834224, ⓦ discoverdartmouth.com).

River trips Apart from the river cruises to Totnes (see box, p.94) and to Greenway and Dittisham (see box, p.101), various river, estuary and fishing trips are available from

Dartmouth's quay from around £8.50 for an hour. To add a touch of nostalgia you can join a cruise aboard the UK's last operating coal-fired paddle steamer, the *Kingswear Castle* (Easter & May–Oct 3–4 daily; ☎ 01803 555872, ⓦ paddlesteamerkc.co.uk; from £15).

ACCOMMODATION

★ Browns 27–29 Victoria Rd, TQ6 9RT ☎ 01803 832572, ⓦ brownshoteldartmouth.co.uk. Small, chic hotel, with contemporary decor and helpful and friendly staff. Rooms are compact but perfectly adequate (those at the back are quieter). Tapas are served in the bar and top-notch main meals in the bistro. Two-night minimum stay at weekends. Free parking permits are issued. **£135**

The Captain's House 18 Clarence St, TQ6 9NW ☎ 01803 832133, ⓦ captainshouse.co.uk. If you don't mind the lack of panoramic views and no breakfast, this place offers excellent value for money. Bedrooms are simply but fetchingly decorated in white and pale grey, and you'll find plenty of breakfast venues within an easy walk. Parking available. **£75**

Melverley House Townstal Pathfields, TQ6 9HL ☎ 01803 835756, ⓦ melverleyhouse.co.uk. There are spectacular views over the town and river from the bright, airy rooms of this spacious and elegantly furnished B&B. A choice of continental breakfasts are served in your room at a time of your choosing, and bathrooms are modern and well-equipped. The downside of the lofty views is the steep climb from the centre. **£85**

Royal Castle Hotel 11 The Quay, TQ6 9PS ☎ 01803 833033, ⓦ royalcastle.co.uk. Right in the heart of things, this seventeenth-century inn has a plush and venerable ambience, with antique weaponry on the walls, and low beams. Rooms are contemporary or traditional in style, the more expensive ones with river views, others surrounding a courtyard. Valet parking. **£180**

3

DARTMOUTH FERRIES

Travellers between Torbay and Dartmouth can save time and a long detour through Totnes by using the frequent **ferries** crossing the Dart. Service is continuous from 6.30am (8am on Sun) to around 10.45pm (11.10pm on Passenger Ferry). There is also a ferry to Dartmouth Castle (see p.99), and a service to Totnes (see box, p.94).

Higher Ferry Links with the A379 (foot passengers 60p one-way, cars £5.60 including passengers, bikes free; ⓦ dartmouthhigherferry.com).
Lower Ferry From Kingswear via the minor B3205

(foot passengers £1.50 one-way, cars £4.50 including passengers, bikes free; ⓦ southhams.gov.uk).
Passenger Ferry From Kingswear (£1.50 one-way; ⓦ dartmouthrailriver.co.uk).

EATING

★**Café Alf Resco** Lower St, TQ6 9AN ⓣ 01803 835880, ⓦ cafealfresco.co.uk. Popular and relaxed spot for superb breakfasts – which include their own award-winning marmalade – as well as coffees, freshly baked cakes, lunchtime platters of hams and cheeses, and toasties (£7–10). The outdoor tables fill up fast, and there's usually live music Sun from 11am. Daily 7am–2pm.

Cherub Inn 13 Higher St, TQ6 9RB ⓣ 01803 832571, ⓦ the-cherub.co.uk. An authentically historic inn, low-beamed and full of atmosphere. The local ales include Cherub bitter and Dartmouth Pride, and food choices take in everything from salads and sandwiches to sausages and steaks. There's an evening set menu for £16. Eat in the bar or upstairs for more room. Daily 11am–11pm; kitchen noon–3pm & 6–9pm.

★**Rockfish** 8 South Embankment, TQ6 9BH ⓣ 01803 832800, ⓦ therockfish.co.uk. In a long, shed-like space

with its ceiling festooned with children's crayoned drawings, this posh chippie offers freshly cooked fish and chips. If you want to venture beyond basic cod or haddock (£12–13), sample the red gurnard, plaice or monkfish, or opt for a dish of oysters (£12). An offshoot at 28 Lower Street offers the same meals at lower prices as take aways (noon–9.30pm, reduced hours in winter). Daily noon–9.30pm.

The Seahorse 5 South Embankment, TQ6 9BH ⓣ 01803 628967, ⓦ seahorserestaurant.co.uk. The flagship of chef and restaurateur Mitch Tonks, this is the place to come for the full Dartmouth seafood experience if you've got cash to spare. The ambience is upmarket, but the food is refreshingly simple. Scallops roasted in white port are usually on the menu (£13.50), and mains might include Italian fish stew (£26). Booking advisable. Tues–Sat noon–2.30pm & 6–9.30pm.

Start Bay

The coast path from Dartmouth winds round the rivermouth to **Start Bay**, a long parabola that is home to the best swimming in these parts. It's a great stretch for coast-walkers too, mostly flat until you reach the wild, rocky terrain around the headland of **Start Point**. At the centre of the bay, the A379 is squeezed between the beach on one side and the elongated **Slapton Ley** on the other – Devon's largest natural freshwater lake and a nature reserve since 1896.

Blackpool Sands

Below the pretty hilltop village of Stoke Fleming, **Blackpool Sands** is the most popular of Start Bay's beaches, an unspoilt cove flanked by steep, wooded cliffs. Like all the "Sands" hereabouts, it's actually a shingle beach, and – being sheltered and the winner of a Blue Flag award – popular with families. There's a shop to pick up a bucket and spade or other beach accoutrements, as well as a good café. The beach is around three miles south of Dartmouth; you can walk here in about thirty minutes from Dartmouth Castle, or come by road on the A379.

ACCOMMODATION AND EATING   BLACKPOOL SANDS

Leonards Cove 3 miles south of Dartmouth, in Stoke Fleming, TQ6 0NR ⓣ 01803 770206, ⓦ leonardscove.co.uk. This campsite has fantastic sea views and is within easy walking distance of shops and a pub (and easily

accessible on buses from Dartmouth). As it's so close to Blackpool Sands, it gets pretty packed in summer. Self-catering lodges and bungalows are available all year (from £619/week for 4), but there's no camping Oct–April. **£25**

Venus Café TQ6 0RG ☎01803 770209, ⓦloving thebeach.co.uk. This buzzing, family-friendly café by the beach uses organic and local ingredients in its meals, which span everything from breakfasts to barbies. The burgers and grilled fish are recommended; evening mains are mostly £10–15. Part of a local chain, with another branch at Bigbury-on-Sea (see p.105). Daily: Jan–June & Sept–Dec 8.30am–5pm; July & Aug 8.30am–9.30pm.

Slapton Sands

The three miles of shingle at **Slapton Sands** were used during World War II by US navy and infantry divisions for rehearsing the D-Day landings. Behind the beach, the lagoon of the **Slapton Ley nature reserve** (unrestricted access; free) supports herons, terns, widgeon and great crested grebes.

At the lagoon's southern end, **Torcross** has a memorial to 639 US servicemen killed here when German E-boats succeeded in breaching the coastal defences in 1944, and a Sherman tank that sank in 1944 and was recovered forty years later, its black and oily appearance giving the impression that it has only just been dredged up from the mud.

Greenway

Greenway Rd, Galmpton, TQ5 0ES • Mid-Feb to Oct daily 10.30am–5pm; early Nov to late Dec Sat & Sun 11am–4pm • £10.30; NT • ☎01803 842382, ⓦnationaltrust.org.uk/greenway • Transport options are many and varied (see box below)

Perched above the River Dart, at the top of an 2600ft ascent from the quayside and some three miles north of Dartmouth, **Greenway** is famous as the birthplace of Walter Raleigh's three seafaring half-brothers, the Gilberts, and was later rebuilt for Agatha Christie as a holiday home (see box, p.86). The house is little changed from its 1950s appearance, and displays the diverse collections of archeology, china and silver that Christie and her archeologist husband acquired, as well as a few photos and letters relating to the author. The panoramic wooded grounds hold rich growths of camellias and magnolias, with terrific river views.

Coleton Fishacre

Brownstone Rd, near Kingswear, TQ6 0EQ • Mid-Feb to Oct daily 10.30am–5pm; Nov to late Dec Sat & Sun 11am–4pm • £10.30; NT • ☎01803 842382, ⓦnationaltrust.org.uk/coleton-fishacre

The D'Oyly Carte family, founders of the eponymous opera company associated with Gilbert and Sullivan's late nineteenth-century success, had their holiday retreat in **Coleton Fishacre**, a couple of miles east of Kingswear by footpath (slightly more by road). The house was built in the Arts and Crafts style, but the interior furnishings are predominantly Art Deco from the 1920s. Theatrical guests were encouraged to don gloves and wellies to help tend the thirty acres of terraced garden, where the mild, sheltered sea climate has allowed the growth of some brilliantly colourful plants. Steep trails lead down to the sea at **Pudcombe Cove** (though there's no access to the beach).

GETTING TO GREENWAY

Although it is possible to reach Greenway **by car** along the extremely narrow local lanes, parking places are few and must always be booked in advance by phone (☎01803 842382) or online (ⓦwww.nter.org.uk). It's far more fun anyway to arrive **by boat**; the main ferry service is operated by Greenway Ferry (☎01803 882811, ⓦgreenwayferry.co.uk), with 5–8 departures daily from Dartmouth (£8.50 return). There are also frequent ferry crossings from the very quaint village of Dittisham on the west bank of the Dart, again reachable by Greenway Ferry (£2 each way).

Alternatively you can reach Greenway **on foot** from Dartmouth or Totnes along the Dart Valley Trail (2–3hr), or in around 30min from Greenway Halt, a stop on the Dartmouth Steam Railway (☎01803 555872, ⓦdartmouthrailriver.co.uk). There's also a free **shuttle bus** service laid on for steam railway passengers, leaving from the stations at Churston and Greenway Halt (board at Churston to be sure of a seat).

Kingsbridge

Fine Tudor and Georgian buildings distinguish the "capital" of the South Hams region, **KINGSBRIDGE**, a busy, working market town at the top of the Kingsbridge estuary. You'll find a good selection of shops along steep Fore Street, where every front displays a different style and historical period. Near the top stands the colonnaded **Shambles**, the former market building, largely Elizabethan at street level, with an upper floor added at the end of the eighteenth century supported on granite pillars. At the bottom, the Quay overlooks the Kingsbridge estuary, the scene of markets and the location of the bus station, from where local services to Salcombe, Bantham and other villages of the South Hams depart.

Kingsbridge Cookworthy Museum

108 Fore St, TQ7 1AW • Mon–Sat: April–Sept 10.30am–5pm; Oct 10.30am–4pm • £3 • ☎ 01548 853235, ⓦ kingsbridgemuseum.org.uk

You can immerse yourself in the history and culture of the South Hams at the **Kingsbridge Cookworthy Museum**, housed in a seventeenth-century grammar school and holding more than 14,000 photos from 1870 onwards, a display of costumes and changing exhibitions. The museum is named after the locally born scientist and Quaker William Cookworthy (1705–80), most famous for developing and processing the china clay extracted in Cornwall to make porcelain.

Markets

Next to the Shambles on Fore Street, the town hall hosts various **markets**: a flea market on Mondays (May–Oct), country produce on Wednesdays (year-round) and crafts on Fridays (Easter–Christmas). There are also regular markets on the Quay, including a street market on Tuesdays (also Thurs March–Dec & Mon May–Sept), and a **Farmers' Market** on the first and third Saturday of the month.

ARRIVAL AND DEPARTURE   KINGSBRIDGE

By bus Stagecoach service #3 runs between Plymouth, Kingsbridge, Torcross and Dartmouth, #164 links Kingsbridge with Totnes, and #606 goes to Salcombe (as does #164 on Sun). Stops are on the Quay.
Destinations Dartmouth (Mon–Sat hourly, Sun 2 daily; 1hr 10min); Salcombe (Mon–Sat hourly, Sun 2 daily; 25min); Totnes (Mon–Sat 8 daily, Sun 2 daily; 45min).

By ferry The Rivermaid (☎ 01803 834488 or ☎ 01803 853607, ⓦ kingsbridgesalcombeferry.co.uk) connects Kingsbridge's Quay Steps or Boatyard Quay (depending on the tide) with Salcombe most days June–Sept, departing up to four times daily and taking 35min. Tickets cost around £7 single, £10 return.

INFORMATION

Tourist information The Quay (Easter–Sept Mon–Sat 9am–5pm; Oct–Easter Mon–Fri 9am–5pm, Sat 9am–1pm; ☎ 01548 853195, ⓦ welcomesouthdevon.co.uk). Provides information on the whole South Hams region.

EATING

Crabshell Inn Embankment Road, TQ7 1JZ ☎ 01548 852345, ⓦ thecrabshellinn.com. Right by the water's edge on the southern outskirts of town, this airy, modern pub enjoys fantastic creek views from its upper terrace and outdoor decking. Pizzas are the top choice on the menu (£9–13), otherwise you can order a burger (£9.50), moules frites (£14) or steak (£17). Gets very busy. Daily 10am–midnight; kitchen noon–9.30pm.

Salcombe and around

Devon's southernmost resort, **SALCOMBE** occupies a superb location almost at the mouth of the Kingsbridge estuary, five miles downriver of Kingsbridge and reachable from there on a seasonal ferry. Although there is still some fishing activity, the town is mostly devoted to leisure, its steep and narrow lanes – with designer shops every few yards – mobbed with holidaymakers in summer. Amateur sailors are drawn to the place year-round, which accounts for the myriad small craft strewn across the deep, clear waters of the estuary and the boatyards along its banks. The entrance to the harbour is overlooked by the ruined **Fort Charles**, a Civil War relic that injects a touch of romance amid the villas and hotels.

Salcombe Maritime Museum

Market St, TQ8 8DE • Easter–Oct daily 10.30am–12.30pm & 2.30–4.30pm • £2 • ☎ 01548 843080, ⊚ salcombemuseum.org.uk

Below the tourist office, off the north end of Fore Street, you can bone up on boating and local history at the **Salcombe Maritime Museum**, a tiny space jam-packed with nautical mementos, including paintings, models and gold coins and other items retrieved from the seabed.

ARRIVAL AND DEPARTURE   SALCOMBE AND AROUND

By car Parking is a perennial problem in Salcombe; use the Park-and-Ride at the top of town, connected to the centre by frequent minibuses.
By bus Bus services #606 (Mon–Sat) and #164 (Sun) connect Salcombe with Kingsbridge (Mon–Sat hourly, Sun

2 daily; 25min). The stop is above the church on Shadycombe Rd.
By ferry The summer ferry connection with Kingsbridge makes a great way to experience the estuary (see opposite).

GETTING AROUND

By ferry There is a passenger ferry to East Portlemouth from Jubilee Pier or in winter from Whitestrand Quay, both off Fore St (March–Oct Mon–Fri 8am–7pm, Sat & Sun

8am–7.30pm, continuous service, weather permitting; Nov–Feb Mon–Fri 8am–5.30pm, Sat & Sun 9am–6pm, every 30min; £1.60; ☎ 07769 319375).

INFORMATION AND ACTIVITIES

Tourist information Market St (Easter–Oct daily 10am–5pm; Nov–Easter Mon–Sat 10am–3pm; ☎ 01548 843927, ⊚ salcombeinformation.co.uk).
Boat tours and sailing Ask at the quays below Fore St about fishing excursions and other boat trips exploring the estuary and coast. Whitestrand Boat Hire (☎ 01548

843818, ⊚ whitestrandboathire.co.uk) on Whitestrand Quay arranges two-hour fishing trips (£20) and rents out rowing boats and motorboats (£30–50/hour). You can pick up the basics of sailing at the Island Cruising Club, based on a converted ferry in the estuary and with an office at 28 Island St (☎ 01548 844631, ⊚ islandcruisingclub.co.uk).

ACCOMMODATION

Higher Rew Rew Cross, TQ7 3BW ☎ 01548 842681, ⊚ higherrew.co.uk. A mile southwest of Salcombe and about the same distance from South Sands beach and Soar Mill Cove, this panoramic site is well equipped but not very sheltered. Facilities for tennis, table tennis, skittles and pool are available. Three-night minimum stay in high season. No credit cards. Closed Nov to mid-March. **£21**
Victoria Inn Fore Street, TQ8 8BU ☎ 01548 842604, ⊚ victoriainn-salcombe.co.uk. Two stylish, cosy (but not cramped) rooms in "The Hobbit House", a pub annexe,

provide Salcombe's most central lodging. There's no parking, and no breakfast – though rooms have tea- and coffee-making facilities and there are plenty of breakfast options close by. **£70**
Waverley Devon Rd, TQ8 8HL ☎ 01548 842633, ⊚ waverleybandb.co.uk. Rooms in this airy B&B are clean and en suite, and there's plenty of choice at the ample breakfasts, when guests share one large table. It's less than a 10min (steep) walk to the centre. Self-catering also available. No credit cards. Closed Dec–Feb. **£80**

EATING AND DRINKING

Captain Flint's 82 Fore St, TQ8 8BY ☎ 01548 842357, ⊚ captainflints.co.uk. You'll find a lively, family-friendly atmosphere and a piratical theme at this restaurant specializing in pastas, pizzas and burgers (all £7–11), though steaks are also available (around £16). Bookings aren't taken, so be prepared to queue. Easter–Oct &

school hols daily 6–9.30pm; may close Mon–Wed in quiet periods.
Ferry Inn Fore St, TQ8 8JE ☎ 01548 844000. The broad riverside terrace is the best feature of this pub, a convivial venue for a drink of Palmer's beer and a meal from the extensive menu – perhaps a baguette (£5.50–7.50), a grilled

---

WALKS AROUND SALCOMBE

The **coastline** around Salcombe offers superb **walking** on either side of the Kingsbridge estuary. **Bolt Head**, two miles south of South Sands, marks the western end of the estuary, and the start of a magnificent, moderately challenging six-mile, three-hour hike to the massive cliffs of **Bolt Tail**. Along the way, you'll see shags, cormorants and other marine birds swooping above the ragged coast, and wild thyme and sea thrift underfoot.

Across the estuary, you can follow the coast path from the hamlet of **East Portlemouth** – also accessible by ferry (see p.103) – past the craggily photogenic **Gammon Point** to Devon's southernmost headland, **Prawle Point**, about five miles' walk in all.

---

goat's cheese salad or the pie of the day (£8–12). Look out for monthly live music evenings. Daily 11am–midnight.

★ **No 55** 55 Fore St, TQ8 8JE ☎ 01548 842646, ⓦ no-55.co.uk. This bright, modern bistro on two levels serves beautifully prepared, Italian-influenced dishes that include moreish mushroom linguine, delicious fish pie and some awesome puds. Starters are £6–8, mains around £15. Service is friendly and relaxed. Easter–June Tues–Sat 6.30–11pm; July–Sept Tues–Sun 5.30–11pm; Oct–Easter Thurs–Sun 5.30–11pm.

Overbeck's Museum and Garden

Sharpitor, TQ8 8LW • Mid-March to Oct daily 11am–5pm • £8, children £4; NT • ☎ 01548 842893, ⓦ nationaltrust.org.uk/overbecks • You can reach the house and garden via tiny, steep lanes signposted from Salcombe, or on foot from South Sands (a 10min ascent)

A couple of miles south of Salcombe on the western side of the estuary, an elegant Edwardian house on a height above South Sands beach holds the excellent **Overbeck's Museum and Garden**. The one-time home of Otto Overbeck, a research chemist and eccentric inventor, the museum is mainly dedicated to natural history, with collections of eggs, butterflies, beetles, shells and stuffed birds. But the most intriguing displays illustrate Overbeck's less conventional interests, such as the polyphon – a nineteenth-century gramophone that is regularly played for the benefit of visitors – and his own most celebrated invention, the "rejuvenating machine", with the aid of which, he claimed, people could live to the age of 350. Elsewhere, you can view collections of toys, nineteenth-century dolls and model vessels.

Below the house, a luxuriant **subtropical garden** extends down the slope, holding a number of colourful Mediterranean species as well as Japanese banana and flax, and affording wonderful estuary views.

The beaches

You'll find excellent **beaches** south of Salcombe at **North Sands**, a small sandy strip adjacent to Fort Charles, beyond which is the more extensive **South Sands**, about a mile's pleasant stroll from Salcombe's centre and also accessible via seasonal ferries (see below). Both places, and the adjacent **Splat Cove**, are scenic, sheltered and sandy, making them popular in summer. There are shops, cafés and pubs, and **kayaking**, **windsurfing** and **sailing** sessions are available.

GETTING AROUND   THE BEACHES

By ferry Between Easter and Oct you can reach South Sands on the South Sands ferry (£3.60; ☎ 01548 561035, ⓦ southsandsferry.co.uk), sailing from Salcombe's Whitestrand Quay every 30min between 9.45am and 5.15pm (5.45pm in Aug).

ACCOMMODATION AND EATING

South Sands South Sands Beach, TQ8 8LL ☎ 01548 859000, ⓦ southsands.com. In a prime position right on the beach, this boutique hotel sports an airy "New England" style, enlivened with the odd nautical touch and a grand spiral staircase. You can hear the waves from your window, bathrooms are modern and spacious, and there's a fab restaurant. It's hugely expensive, with beach-facing rooms charging premium rates, though

prices drop in low season. £215
Winking Prawn North Sands, TQ8 8LD ☎01548 842326, ⓦwinkingprawn.co.uk. Right across from the beach, this is a great stop for a breakfast, baguette or ice cream by day, or to sample the steaks or a cassoulet of scallops and chorizo in the evening (mains £17–25). Popular barbecues take place most evenings June–Sept (£19; no booking). Mon–Thurs 8.45am–8.30pm, Fri–Sun 9.30am–8.30pm.

Bigbury-on-Sea and around

The level sands and sheltered waters on the west side of the Avon fronting **BIGBURY-ON-SEA** are great for sunbathing, swimming and poking about the rock pools and caves. The village itself is modern and brash, but visual interest is provided by **Burgh Island**, a few yards out to sea, dominated by the grand Art Deco *Burgh Island Hotel*. There's public access to most of the green and rocky promontory, whose shores are lined with low cliffs. East of the Avon estuary, **Bantham** has a small quay and another wide stretch of sand favoured by families and surfers (ⓦbanthamdevon.co.uk).

3

ARRIVAL AND DEPARTURE BIGBURY-ON-SEA AND AROUND

On foot/by ferry Walkers approaching from the east can cross the Avon estuary to Bigbury-on-Sea easily enough at low tide, and at high tide from late April to mid-Sept can use the ferry between the hamlets of Bantham (half a mile upstream) and Cockleridge (Mon–Sat 10–11am & 3–4pm; £2.50).

By car Westward-bound drivers will have to take the long way round, making a left turn off the A379.

BURGH ISLAND

On foot/by tractor You can walk to this tiny islet from Bigbury-on-Sea at low tide; otherwise jump on the high-rise tractor-like vehicle that operates when the tide is in (£2; check times for the last ride back).

ACTIVITIES

Surfing Discovery Surf School (☎07813 639622, ⓦdiscoverysurf.com) rents surfboards (£12/2hr), bodyboards (£6/2hr), paddleboards (£25/2hr), wetsuits (£6/2hr) and kayaks (£20/hr) from its base at Bigbury; they also have a branch in nearby Challaborough Bay. Call at any time for kit rental and lessons.

ACCOMMODATION

Burgh Island Hotel Burgh Island, Bigbury-on-Sea, TQ7 4BG ☎01548 810514, ⓦburghisland.com. Occupying its own offshore isle, this renowned celebrity haunt is a dazzling display of Art Deco finery, with a glass dome over the cocktail bar and authentic period furnishings. Agatha Christie's *Evil Under the Sun* was filmed here in 2001, so a stay here feels like being on set. Oozing romance, it's a once-in-a-lifetime splurge. Book well ahead to stay in one of the themed suites. £400

Pennymoor Near Modbury, PL21 0SB ☎01548 830542, ⓦpennymoor-camping.co.uk. There are no campsites in the immediate vicinity of Bigbury-on-Sea, so campers should head for one of the sites around Salcombe (see p.103) or this one, five miles north of Bigbury and two miles east of Modbury, on a gently sloping field with modern and clean facilities, caravans to rent (from £300/week) and a shop. Closed mid-Nov to mid-March. £22

EATING

Oyster Shack Stakes Hill, Bigbury, TQ7 4BE ☎01548 810876, ⓦoystershack.co.uk. About three miles inland, off the A379, is this busy, informal seafood restaurant with nets on the ceiling and plastic crabs and lobsters scattered around. Lobster, tiger prawns and crab are regulars on the menu, too, as well as oysters prepared in various ways, all locally caught (main courses £15–19). Booking essential. June–Sept daily noon–9pm; Oct–May Mon–Sat noon–3pm & 6–9pm, Sun noon–3pm.

Venus Café The Warren, Bigbury-on-Sea, TQ7 4AZ ☎01548 810141, ⓦlovingthebeach.co.uk. Right above the beach, this place – part of a chain, with another branch at Blackpool Sands (see p.101) – serves up daytime refreshments including breakfasts, baguettes, burgers and pasties, all under £10. Daily: July & Aug 9am–6pm; Sept–June 10am–5pm.

Dartmoor

LYDFORD GORGE

Dartmoor

Covering the sweep of country between Exeter and Plymouth, Dartmoor is southern England's greatest expanse of wilderness – some 365 square miles of raw granite, barren bogland, grassland, deep-wooded and heather-strewn moor. Things weren't always so desolate though, as testified by the numerous remnants of scattered prehistoric settlements, and the ruined relics of nineteenth-century quarrying and tin-mining industries. Today, desultory flocks of sheep and groups of ponies are virtually the only living creatures you'll see wandering over the central regions of the National Park, with solitary birds wheeling and hovering high above.

For many, the emptiest parts of Dartmoor are the most appealing, uncrossed by roads and miles from the nearest villages. These are mainly in the most northern and southern reaches, appearing as bare tracts on the map, and characterized by tumbling streams and high tors chiselled by the elements. The moor's specific attractions are mostly concentrated on the periphery of the National Park, though the central east–west belt has villages with accommodation and some famous beauty spots, making viable starting points for walks into the core of Dartmoor. In the heart of the moor, **Princetown** provides direct access to the moor and has the main National Park information office. On the edges of the moor, **Okehampton** is the major centre to the north, **Tavistock** to the west and **Moretonhampstead** to the northeast. **Ashburton** and **Buckfastleigh** to the southeast provide useful facilities for sleeping and eating.

The original Dartmoor Forest – a royal hunting zone in Saxon times – has largely disappeared, with only about eleven percent of the moor nowadays defined as woodland. Since the fourteenth century, the area has been owned by the Duchy of Cornwall, but public access is almost unlimited today, provided certain guidelines are followed: parking overnight in unauthorized places is prohibited; vehicles are not allowed further than fifteen yards from any road; and, though "wild camping" is permitted out of sight of houses and roads, fires are strictly forbidden. Parts of the moor are designated as firing ranges by the military (see box, p.113), and should be avoided at specific times.

ARRIVAL AND GETTING AROUND   DARTMOOR

Available from mid-May to mid-September on Sun and bank hols, the **Sunday Rover ticket** (£10) covers all transport using Stagecoach South West buses and GWR trains (including the Dartmoor Line and the Tamar Valley Line) – however, with Sun bus services on and around the moor being so limited, it's mainly useful for train travel. For an overview of routes, tickets and passes, see ⓦ journeydevon.info; for schedules, consult ⓦ www.travelinesw.com.

WALKERS ON DARTMOOR

Highlights

❶ Walking on Dartmoor The best reason for coming here – it's easy to lose sight of civilization in this remote and surprisingly varied granite landscape. **See p.112**

❷ Wistman's Wood This ancient, tangled wood in the heart of the moor is an easy destination for a walk and a picnic. **See p.114**

❸ Hound Tor With the remains of a medieval village on its flank and marvellous views, this makes a great target for a ramble. See p.116

❹ A meal at Gidleigh Park Treat yourself to a memorable dinner – or a considerably less expensive lunch – at this Michelin-starred restaurant, run by super-chef Michael Caines and reckoned to be one of the best in the country. **See p.125**

❺ Castle Drogo This neo-medieval extravagance has an undeniable impact in this lush corner of the moor. **See p.126**

❻ Lydford Gorge This deep ravine makes a secluded beauty spot, the dense woods rising above a churning river. **See p.132**

HIGHLIGHTS ARE MARKED ON THE MAP ON P.110

BY TRAIN

Apart from the private heritage line connecting Buckfastleigh with Totnes (see p.94), there are a couple of train services that may help to provide access from Exeter and Plymouth, both operated by Great Western Railway (☎ 0345 700 0125, �🌐 gwr.com). The Dartmoor Line, along an old goods line, links Okehampton with Exeter via Crediton in about 50min (mid-May to mid-Sept Sun), while the Tamar Valley Line runs daily all year along the Tamar River between Plymouth and Gunnislake, five miles southwest of Tavistock, just over the Cornish side of the river.

BY BUS

There's only a very sketchy bus network within Dartmoor, and almost no Sun services. Bus #173 from Exeter runs to Castle Drogo, Chagford and Moretonhampstead, on the northeast side of the moor. Okehampton is linked by #178 to Bovey Tracey, Chagford and Moretonhampstead and by #46 to Tavistock via Lydford. Bus #98 connects Postbridge, Two Bridges, Princetown and Merrivale with Tavistock, and #1, #X1 and #46 link Tavistock and Plymouth. The #271 Haytor Hoppa circular bus links Newton Abbot, Bovey Tracey, Haytor, Widecombe, Hound Tor and Manaton on Sat (June to mid-Sept; £3–5). Services #6 and #6A, between Exeter and Bude via Okehampton, are the only ones to run on Sun. Apart from these, there's little except once-weekly runs to remote villages.

DARTMOOR

HIGHLIGHTS
1. Walking on Dartmoor
2. Wistman's Wood
3. Hound Tor
4. A meal at Gidleigh Park
5. Castle Drogo
6. Lydford Gorge

- - - - - Tourist Railway

0 — 3 miles

The longer one stays here the more does the spirit of the moor sink into one's soul, its vastness, and also its grim charm. When you are once out upon its bosom you have left all traces of modern England behind you, but on the other hand you are conscious everywhere of the homes and the work of the prehistoric people… If you were to see a skin-clad, hairy man… fitting a flint-tipped arrow on to the string of his bow, you would feel that his presence there was more natural than your own.

Arthur Conan Doyle, *The Hound of the Baskervilles*

BY CAR

Running diagonally across the moor, the B3212 and B3357 provide drivers with easy access to Dartmoor. Other roads can be extremely narrow. The speed limit throughout the moor is 40mph, and drivers should beware of ponies, sheep and other livestock straying onto the roads, particularly in early autumn, when they find it the warmest place to be. If you hit an animal, or come across an injured one on the road, contact the police on ☎ 101 (24hr). Note that Chagford is currently the only place within the National Park that has fuel; fill up at garages in Bovey Tracey, Dunsford, Okehampton, Tavistock and other towns on the periphery.

INFORMATION

Tourist information General and practical information relating to Dartmoor is available at Princetown's helpful High Moorland Visitor Centre (see p.113), or at tourist information offices in the towns and larger villages. Apart from the invaluable National Park website ⊚ dartmoor-npa.gov.uk, the official tourism site ⊚ visitdartmoor.co.uk has events, attractions, accommodation and pubs; ⊚ dartmoor accommodation.co.uk also has links to a wide range of accommodation and some food outlets, and ⊚ dartmoorsociety.com has discussions on the history, culture and other aspects of the moor.

Maps The 1:25,000 Ordnance Survey *Explorer* Map OL28 is of must use to walkers on Dartmoor.

4

ACCOMMODATION

Dartmoor has a fairly good range of accommodation, from classy country hotels to rudimentary campsites, much of it concentrated in and around the towns on the moor's periphery and larger villages such as **Princetown** and **Chagford** (the websites above include a range of options). As availability can be extremely restricted in high season, it's always advisable to book ahead, particularly at weekends. Walkers especially may be interested in Dartmoor's **camping barns** (around £10/night) and **bunkhouses** (around £15/night), offering warm dorms, toilet facilities and sometimes cooking equipment. Again, always book ahead.

Princetown and around

PRINCETOWN, not far from the middle of the moor, owes its growth to the presence of **Dartmoor Prison**, whose grim spirit seeps into the place; some of the drab granite buildings – like the parish church of St Michael – were even built by French and American inmates at the beginning of the nineteenth century. The somewhat oppressive air of the village, not improved by the tall TV mast towering above it on **North Hessary Tor**, does not invite much lingering, though you'll find most of the facilities you'll need around the Square (site of the main National Park information office and the intersection with the B3212) and on Tavistock Road, running alongside. For quick access to the moor, take the path on the left immediately after the fire station on Station Road, which leads onto open moorland.

Dartmoor Prison

Half a mile up Tavistock Road from the Square (heading west), Dartmoor Prison originated as one of the schemes instigated by **Thomas Tyrwhitt**, appointed auditor for the Duchy of Cornwall in 1786. He began work on the prison in 1806, and two years later it was home to 2500 captured French soldiers, and later still, to American prisoners from the 1812 war. The prison brought unprecedented commercial activity to this empty heart of the moor, and the weekly market held within its confines attracted traders from throughout the region.

ACTIVITIES ON DARTMOOR

WALKING

For most visitors, walking is the main reason to be on the moor. Ranging from short and simple jaunts to more challenging treks over long, isolated stretches of rugged uplands, a web of trails crisscrosses what many regard as the country's most inspiring wilderness. Much of it is open access, with the granite tors providing invaluable landmarks; broadly speaking, the gentler contours of the southern moor provide less strenuous rambles, while the harsher northern tracts require more skill and stamina.

The website ⓦdartmoor.gov.uk has downloadable audioguides for walks, as well as routes for the less mobile; for all excursions, a compass and a good map are essential. We've outlined some simple hikes in this chapter, but detailed itineraries are widely available, from specific Dartmoor walking guides (see p.349) to pamphlets. This guide also covers "letterboxing" (see box, p.132) and some of the health hazards to be aware of while walking on the moor (see p.35).

Long-distance trails Seasoned hikers might link up with some of the longer-distance walks intersecting with the trail; for example the Tarka Trail, the Templer Way and the Two Moors Way.

Maps Although some walks are signposted or waymarked with painted stones, map-reading abilities are a prerequisite for all but the shortest of strolls here, and a good deal of experience is essential for longer distances – search parties seeking hikers gone astray are not uncommon. The single-sheet, double-sided 1:25,000 Ordnance Survey *Explorer* map OL28 is impressively detailed, giving copious information, down to the level of field boundaries. Map references (following Ordnance Survey grid references) are provided in this guide for some of the main off-road destinations.

Guided walks You can see an extensive programme of walks conducted year-round by knowledgeable guides and mostly from two to six hours (£5–10) on ⓦmoorlandguides.co.uk. The Devon Wildlife Trust (☏01392 279244, ⓦdevonwildlifetrust.org) and the Royal Society for the Protection of Birds (☏01392 432691, ⓦrspb.org.uk) also organize guided walks.

Walking Festival Dartmoor has its own Walking Festival, taking place over nine days in late Aug/early Sept. As well as a programme of Ranger-led walks for all ages and abilities, the festival includes Nordic walking, climbing, themed talks and presentations. See ⓦdartmoorwalkingfestival.co.uk and *Dartmoor Magazine* (ⓦdartmoormagazine.co.uk) for full details.

CYCLING

Cyclists are well served on Dartmoor, with several dedicated cycle routes, including the Granite Way, an eleven-mile cycle- and walkway from Okehampton to Lydford, and the 21-mile Drake's Trail, from Tavistock to Plymouth (both part of NCN 27). The 95-mile Dartmoor Way (ⓦdartmoorway.co.uk) traces the periphery of the moor – the circular route takes in Tavistock, Okehampton, Chagford, Moretonhampstead, Bovey Tracey, Ashburton and Buckfastleigh – on quiet lanes and dedicated tracks, with a 27-mile High Moorland link crossing through the centre of the moor via Holne and Princetown. You can pick up leaflets outlining these and other routes and regulations from tourist offices. Another really useful tool is Harvey's 1:40,000 map, *Dartmoor for Cyclists* (£13), showing off- and on-road routes, and on sale at tourist offices and local bookshops.

HORSERIDING

Arguably, there's no more invigorating way to experience Dartmoor than on horseback. Several stables are dotted over the moor, and we've mentioned the best in the text, where you can expect to pay around £20 for an hour's ride. The website ⓦridedartmoor.co.uk provides routes, lists riding schools and riding clubs, and suggests where to stay and eat.

CLIMBING

Dartmoor holds some of the UK's finest climbing and bouldering spots. There is no one particular part of the moor that is particularly suitable, but many climbers flock to the crags around Haytor, Sheeps Tor, East Mill Tor and Dewerstone – see ⓦthebmc.co.uk for recommended sites.

In the twentieth century, it held World War I conscientious objectors and Irish nationalists (Eamon de Valera was detained here). It has witnessed several **riots** over the years – one major "mutiny" in 1932 reduced it to ruins, while a more recent riot in 1990 led to extensive refurbishment, though prison conditions continue to be criticized in official reports. Nowadays it houses about 640 inmates, mostly for non-violent and "white-collar" offences.

Dartmoor Prison Museum

Tavistock Rd, PL20 6RR • Mon–Thurs & Sat 9.30am–12.30m & 1.30–4.30pm, Fri & Sun 9.30am–12.30pm & 1.30–4pm; last entry 30min before closing • £3.50 • ☎ 01822 322130, ⓦ dartmoor-prison.co.uk

You can learn much more about life inside at the **Dartmoor Prison Museum**, just past the main prison gate. Displayed within are captured escape tools, an assortment of improvised weapons from knuckle-dusters to blades, and some pretty lethal-looking makeshift tattooing tools, as well as a flogging frame and a cat-o'-nine tails once used to punish prisoners. You can view a mock-up of a cell and of the quarry where prisoners once laboured, and a film showing interviews with contemporary inmates. It's probably not what you came to Dartmoor to see, but it's a sobering and informative diversion when weather conditions preclude outdoor pursuits.

ARRIVAL AND DEPARTURE   PRINCETOWN

By bus Buses leave from outside the Visitor Centre on Tavistock Rd.
Destinations Exeter (late May to mid-Sept Sun 1 daily; 1hr 40min); Merrivale (Mon–Sat 3 daily; 10min);

Moretonhampstead (late May to mid-Sept Sun 1 daily; 45min); Postbridge (Mon–Sat 2 daily, late May to mid-Sept Sun 1 daily; 20min); Tavistock (Mon–Sat 3 daily; 30min).

INFORMATION

Tourist information High Moorland Visitor Centre, The Square (April–Sept daily 10am–5pm; Oct daily 10am–4pm; Nov–March Thurs–Sun 10.30am–3.30pm, daily in school hols; closed 1 week late Feb/early March;

☎ 01822 890414, ⓦ dartmoor-npa.gov.uk). Publications about Dartmoor and walking aids are on sale, and there's an exhibition area and an auditorium showing short films.

ACCOMMODATION AND EATING

Duchy House Tavistock Rd, PL20 6QF ☎ 01822 890552, ⓦ duchyhouse.co.uk. This solid Victorian B&B 250m from Princetown's centre has five traditionally furnished rooms, including a family room (£100), with modern bathrooms. There's a spacious guests' lounge too. **£75**

Fox Tor Café Two Bridges Rd, PL20 6QS ☎ 01822 890238, ⓦ foxtorcafe.co.uk. This warm and welcoming

café is a perfect stop after the rigours of hiking, providing such inexpensive pick-me-ups as all-day breakfasts, soups, pasties and home-made scones – and there's free wi-fi. Above are three bunkrooms with four beds each (which can be booked for just two people; £36.50), and self-catering facilities. Bedding £3.50 per person for first night, then £1. Mon–Fri 9am–5pm, Sat 7.30am–6pm, Sun 7.30am–5pm. Dorms **£11**

FIRING RANGES ON DARTMOOR

The main restrictions to access on Dartmoor are the Ministry of Defence **firing ranges** that, much to the irritation of locals and visitors alike, take up significant portions of the northern moor, an area that contains Dartmoor's highest tors and some of its most famous beauty spots. The ranges are marked by red-and-white posts; when firing is in progress, red flags by day or red lights at night signify that entry is forbidden. As a general rule, assume that if no warning flags are flying by 9am between April and September, or by 10am from October to March, there is to be no firing on that day. August is usually a firing-free month. You'll find an overview of military activity on Dartmoor on the National Park website (ⓦ dartmoor-npa.gov.uk) and **firing schedules** are posted on the website of the Ministry of Defence (ⓦ mod.uk), in local newspapers, on BBC Radio Devon, on village noticeboards, in some pubs and post offices and in tourist offices; alternatively, call ☎ 0800 458 4868.

The Oratory Tavistock Rd, PL20 6RP ☎01822 890273, ⓦtheoratorydartmoor.co.uk. On the outskirts of Princetown, within walking distance of the pubs, shops and the moor, this airy, spacious, self-contained and fully equipped annexe has a separate guests' entrance and access to the garden. There's a kitchenette and lounge area, and a bathroom with a roll-top bath and underfloor heating. Continental breakfasts cost £5 per person extra. **£70**

Plume of Feathers Plymouth Hill, PL20 6QQ ☎01822 890240, ⓦtheplumeoffeathersdartmoor.co.uk. This traditional pub off the Square claims to be the oldest building in town, dating from 1795, with open fires and slate floors. As well as staple pub grub – mains from £7 – and beers including Jail Ale, several accommodation options are offered: B&B in plain, pine-furnished, en-suite rooms; bunkrooms with two, four or ten beds (book well ahead), and a basic campsite. Mon–Thurs & Sun 8am–11pm, Fri & Sat 8am–midnight; kitchen 8am–9pm. Doubles **£85**, dorms **£10.50**, camping/person **£7**

Two Bridges

TWO BRIDGES, at the intersection of the B3212 and the B3357, represents Dartmoor's centre point. Only one of its bridges now remains, a five-span clapper bridge (see below) that crosses the **River Cowsic** (the other originally crossed the West Dart), and there's little else here now other than the *Two Bridges Hotel* (see below), useful for rest and refreshment before or after a wander.

ACCOMMODATION AND EATING   TWO BRIDGES

The Cherrybrook PL20 6SP ☎01822 880260, ⓦthecherrybrook.co.uk. A couple of miles northeast of Two Bridges, set back from the B3212 Postbridge road and surrounded by moorland, this renovated farmhouse offers a friendly ambience, comfy rooms (choose a front-facing one for the moor views) and a pretty garden. Evening meals are available too, at £20 for two courses. **£90**

Spirit of Adventure Powdermills, off the B3212, PL20 6SP ☎01822 880277, ⓦspirit-of-adventure.com. Two and a half miles northeast of Two Bridges, this bunkhouse near the ruins of an old gunpowder factory provides clean and comfortable accommodation (bedding not supplied) with cooking facilities and a warm lounge. Reserve early, as it's often booked up by groups. The owners have a second bunkhouse on the southwestern edge of the moor, near Yelverton. Ask here about activity holidays in the area. Bunkhouse **£15**

Two Bridges Hotel PL20 6SW ☎01822 892300, ⓦtwobridges.co.uk. In sixty acres of private land beside the West Dart River, this makes a luxurious place to stay, with four-poster beds, leather sofas and blazing fires. Local ales, bar snacks and formal dinners (£37.50 for three courses) are also available here to guests and nonresidents. The cream teas are worth trying too. Noon–2.30pm & 7–9pm. **£140**

Postbridge and around

Right at the heart of Dartmoor, three miles northeast of Two Bridges, the largest and best preserved of Dartmoor's **clapper bridges** crosses the East Dart River at **POSTBRIDGE**, an otherwise nondescript hamlet to which it gives its name. First used by tin-miners and farmers in medieval times, these simple structures consist of huge slabs of granite supported by piers of the same material. This one, standing tall over the water close to the main road bridge, makes a good starting point for walks up and down the East Dart.

A WALK TO WISTMAN'S WOOD

The favourite excursion from Two Bridges is to head for the misshapen dwarf oaks of **Wistman's Wood**, little more than a mile north via a footpath running parallel to the West Dart from the small car park opposite *Two Bridges Hotel*. Cluttered with lichen-covered boulders and a dense undergrowth of ferns, it's an evocative relic of the original Dartmoor Forest, and lies on the **Lych Way** – once a route for transporting the dead to **Lydford** (see p.131), where all inhabitants of Dartmoor Forest were buried until 1260. The woods are reputed to have once been the site of druidic gatherings, a story unsupported by any evidence but which feels quite plausible in this solitary spot.

WALKS FROM POSTBRIDGE

North of Postbridge, along a riverside path on the eastern side of the road bridge (turn immediately left into the field), you can hike as far as **Fernworthy Reservoir** (3.5 miles), which is surrounded by woodland and lies in the midst of stone circles and rows. Southwards, you can take an easier option by following the broad track (turn left at the cattle-grid by the Bellever turning) through **Bellever Forest** to the open moor beyond. Waymarked circular routes loop through the forest, starting from a forestry car park by the river (about a mile south of Postbridge, on the Bellever road); one finger-posted path brings you up to the open moorland around **Bellever Tor** (1453ft; map ref SX644764), from where there are outstanding views in all directions.

ARRIVAL AND DEPARTURE
POSTBRIDGE

By bus Service #98 is Postbridge's only bus connection, running to Princetown (15min) and Tavistock (25min) twice daily Mon–Sat.

INFORMATION

Tourist information The visitor centre is in the main car park, near the bridge (April–Sept daily 10am–5pm; Oct daily 10am–4pm; Nov–March Thurs–Sun 10.30am–3.30pm, daily during school hols; ☎ 01822 880272, ⦿ dartmoor.gov.uk).

ACCOMMODATION

Beechwood PL20 6SY ☎ 01822 880332, ⦿ beechwood -dartmoor.co.uk. Near the church, this friendly, cottagey B&B with exposed granite walls and a guests' lounge offers plain rooms with shared or private bathrooms. Breakfast, made using home-produced ingredients, is taken in the conservatory overlooking the garden, and cream teas and evening meals (two courses £20) are available. £76

Runnage Farm PL20 6TN ☎ 01822 880222, ⦿ runnagecampingbarns.co.uk. Close to Bellever Forest on the Widecombe road, this cattle and sheep farm offers two camping barns, a bunkhouse sleeping 12 and a campsite in a meadow next to a stream (at weekends the bunkhouse and camping barns are only for groups).

Electricity and heating cost extra in bunkhouse and barns, and cooking facilities are available but not crockery, cutlery or pots (there's also a pub nearby). Minimum two-night stay at weekends. Bus #98 stops a mile away. Per person: camping £6, camping barns £10, bunkhouse £15

YHA Dartmoor PL20 6TU ☎ 0845 371 9622, ⦿ yha.org .uk. Located a mile south of Postbridge, on the edge of Bellever Forest and on the banks of the East Dart River, this hostel supplies a welcoming log fire, meals and a wealth of information on the moor. Bikes are also available to rent. Take bus #98 from Tavistock or Princetown to Postbridge and walk a mile southeast (signposted). Dorms £23

Dartmeet

Four miles south of Postbridge and the same distance southeast of Two Bridges off the B3357, the East and West Dart rivers merge at **Dartmeet** after tortuous journeys from their remote sources. A place of rocky shallows and with the full range of river-crossings – stepping stones over the **West Dart**, a humpback bridge and the remains of a clapper bridge over the **East Dart** – this beauty spot is a magnet for crowds, but the valley is memorably lush and you don't need to walk far to leave the car park and ice-cream vans behind.

Widecombe-in-the-Moor and around

Around eight miles east of Two Bridges, in a hollow amid high, granite-strewn ridges, **WIDECOMBE-IN-THE-MOOR** is a candidate for most-visited Dartmoor village. Its church of **St Pancras**, dubbed the "cathedral of the moor", provides a famous local landmark. Its lofty pinnacled tower dwarfs the fourteenth-century nave, whose spacious interior boasts a barrel roof with vigorously carved and painted roof bosses depicting a green man, a pelican and, above the communion rail, three hares, or the "Tinners' Rabbits" – the emblem of the local tin-miners who funded the tower.

WIDDICOMBE FAIR

Widecombe's major claim to fame is as the inspiration for the **traditional song** *Widdicombe Fair*, a celebration of the event that has been held in the village since at least the nineteenth century. The popular ballad, published in 1880, relates the journey of Uncle Tom Cobley and companions to the annual fair:

Tom Pearse, Tom Pearse, lend me your grey mare,
All along, down along, out along, lee.
For I want for to go to Widdicombe Fair,
Wi' Bill Brewer, Jan Stewer, Peter Gurney, Peter Davey, Dan'l Whiddon, Harry Hawke,
Old Uncle Tom Cobley and all,
Old Uncle Tom Cobley and all.

Widecombe Fair still takes place annually in a field outside the village on the second Tuesday of September – rather commercialized now, it is still fun, with vintage tractors, tugs-of-war, bale-rolling and sheep-shearing, as well as morris dancing and folk bands in the beer tent. Entry is free but car parking is £15 for the day (see ⓦwidecombefair.com for details).

ARRIVAL AND DEPARTURE
WIDECOMBE-IN-THE-MOOR

By bus Just two weekly bus services connect Widecombe to the outside world: the #271 to Newton Abbot (June to mid-Sept Sat 4 daily; 55min), with stops at Manaton (20min) and Bovey Tracey (30min), and the #672 (year-round Wed; 1 daily) to Buckland-in-the-Moor (13min), Holne (25min), Buckfastleigh (35min) and Ashburton (45min).

INFORMATION AND ACTIVITIES

Tourist information The website ⓦwidecombe-in-the-moor.com is stuffed with local information for residents and visitors.
Horseriding Shilstone Rocks Riding Centre (☏01364 621281, ⓦwww.dartmoorstables.com) offers horseriding for all ability levels. It's just outside the village: take the turning opposite the *Old Inn*, with the church on the left – the stables are at the first junction on the left.

ACCOMMODATION

Higher Venton Farm TQ13 7TF ☏01364 621235, ⓦventonfarm.com. This thatched longhouse dating from the sixteenth century lies fifteen minutes' walk from the village and has an outdated feel – but no less charming for that. The smaller and cheaper rooms have shared bathrooms. Packed lunches, fabulous cream teas and evening meals are available by arrangement. No wi-fi. **£65**

★Manor Cottage TQ13 7TB ☏01364 621218, ⓦmanorcottagedartmoor.co.uk. Centrally located (past the *Old Inn* on the right), this place has a double/twin bedroom in a converted barn with private facilities, and two doubles with a shared bathroom. Breakfast is taken by the inglenook fireplace in the dining room, and there's a large garden. No credit/debit cards. **£50**

EATING AND DRINKING

Old Inn TQ13 7TA ☏01364 621207. Deceptively large, with numerous nooks and dining areas as well as a garden, this modernized fourteenth-century pub can still get packed out with walkers and groups, but the beer's good, and the menu ranges from wraps to pasties, burgers and fish pie (£7–11). Kitchen daily noon–9pm.
★Rugglestone Inn TQ13 7TF ☏01364 621327, ⓦrugglestoneinn.co.uk. One of Dartmoor's finest pubs, the secluded and unspoilt *Rugglestone* (signposted 300m south of the village towards Venton) has local ales straight from the barrel and serves up meals like steak and Stilton pie or spicy meatballs (around £11) as well as bar snacks. There's a sheltered garden across a stream. Kitchen daily noon–2pm & 6.30–9pm.

Hound Tor

According to one version, the original inspiration for Conan Doyle's tale *The Hound of the Baskervilles* was **Hound Tor** (1362ft; map ref SX743790), a crumbly outcrop midway between Widecombe and Manaton, three miles southeast of Grimspound. According to local legend, phantom hounds were sighted racing across the moor here to hurl themselves on the tomb of a hated squire after his death in 1677. Just southeast of the tor, you can see the remains of a **medieval village**, now no more than a collection of low walls – with entrances and fireplaces in evidence – enclosing patches of grass, lapped on all sides by a sea of bracken.

ACCOMMODATION   HOUND TOR

Great Hound Tor Camping Barn Less than half a mile northeast of Hound Tor towards Manaton, TQ13 9UW ☎ 01647 221202, ⓦ yha.org.uk. If you're looking for basic accommodation on this remote moorland tract, look no further than this ancient farmhouse converted into a camping barn. It has simple sleeping platforms, minimal cooking facilities, a hot shower, a stash of wood for the fire and an agreeable medieval vibe. **£7**

Haytor

About two and a half miles east of Widecombe and reached along the B3387 (itself paralleled for part of the way by a footpath), the dramatic and much-frequented **Haytor** (1489ft; map ref SX757770) makes an excellent vantage point over the open moor, the views south sometimes extending as far as the coast. The granite quarries here were worked in the nineteenth century, providing stone for the British Museum and the 1831 version of London Bridge, which now resides in Arizona after being purchased by a US tycoon.

ARRIVAL AND INFORMATION   HAYTOR

By bus The Haytor Hoppa (see p.118) runs here in summer (Sat only).
National Park Visitor Centre Lower car park

(April–Sept daily 10am–5pm; Oct daily 10am–4pm; Nov– March Thurs–Sun 10.30am–3.30pm; ☎ 01364 661520, ⓦ dartmoor.gov.uk).

Grimspound

North of Widecombe-in-the-Moor, a four-mile hike on marked tracks across Hamel Down (or a three-mile drive along the minor road connecting the village with the B3212) takes you to **Hameldown Tor**, on whose flank lies the Bronze Age village of **Grimspound** (map ref SX701809). If you're travelling on the B3212, you'll find the site about 1.5 miles south of the junction at Challacombe Cross; heading north from Widecombe, look out for five granite steps leading off on the right soon after the entrance to Headland Warren Farm – you can park in a small lay-by opposite.

A brisk ten-minute upward walk brings you to a rough granite track on the left ascending to **Hookney Tor**, whose fortress-like rock formations offer stunning views for miles beyond. To the right, you'll soon see the extensive stone periphery of the village. Inhabited some three thousand years ago, when Dartmoor was fully forested and enjoyed a considerably warmer climate than it does today, it is the most complete example of the moor's prehistoric settlements, with its comparative remoteness helping to protect it from plundering. A stone wall up to 9ft thick surrounds the foundations of 24 circular huts scattered within the four-acre enclosure, several of which have raised bed-places, and you can see how the villagers ensured a constant water supply by enclosing part of a stream with a wall. Grimspound is thought to have been the model for the prehistoric settlement in which **Sherlock Holmes** camped out in *The Hound of the Baskervilles* (see box, p.118).

WALKING FROM WIDECOMBE-IN-THE-MOOR TO GRIMSPOUND

Walkers from Widecombe-in-the-Moor to Grimspound should take the Natsworthy road past the *Old Inn*, turning left at the playing fields (signposted Grimspound) and following the track across open moorland at the top. The long uphill climb is rewarded by a superb panorama. Scenes from Steven Spielberg's **War Horse** were filmed in the area.

DARTMOOR'S GREATEST YARN: THE HOUND OF THE BASKERVILLES

As recent revivals on film and TV have shown, there's still an endless appetite for Sherlock Holmes stories, though nothing approaching the public frenzy that accompanied the publication of *The Hound of the Baskervilles* in 1901. In this, fiction's most famous detective was resurrected eight years after **Arthur Conan Doyle** – hoping to concentrate on more serious works – had killed him off by having him fall to his death at the Reichenbach Falls. The detective's demise had sparked off something approaching national mourning, with reports of clerks going to work wearing black armbands, and Conan Doyle himself received sackfuls of letters of complaint. The fact that *The Hound of the Baskervilles* was said to predate Holmes's death did not lessen the public's interest in it. In fact, at its conception, the detective had not even featured in the tale: Holmes was drafted in to fill the leading role and solve the mystery as the story took shape.

The tale has diverse roots. The inspiration for it came from Bertram Fletcher Robinson, a young journalist and author, who related a legend from the Dartmoor countryside where he had been brought up, in which a phantom dog – "**Black Shuck**", a terrifying creature, big as a calf and with eyes that bled fire – was said to haunt the moors; anyone unfortunate enough to meet this apparition was sure to die. At Robinson's invitation, Conan Doyle travelled to Dartmoor, the two men staying in Princetown's Duchy Hotel (now refurbished as the High Moorland Visitor Centre), where much of the book was written. From here they roamed the moor, guided by Harry Baskerville, Robinson's coachman. They took in such locations as the Bronze Age site at **Grimspound** – described by Robinson as "one of the loneliest spots in Great Britain" – and **Fox Tor Mire**, setting of the tale's climax, where it is known as Great Grimpen Mire.

As for the Hound itself, Dartmoor has no shortage of folklore relating to creatures that might fit the bill. Many of these myths centre on the mysterious **Dewer**, a huntsman who terrorizes the local countryside accompanied by a pack of savage, red-eyed hounds said to live in **Wistman's Wood** (see p.114) during daylight hours. It is said that anyone attempting to follow these "Whist Hounds" across the moors will meet his death by plunging over a cliff, known as the **Dewerstone**, on Dartmoor's southern tip, to the supernatural accompaniment of thunder, lightning, sinister laughter and mournful baying.

EATING AND DRINKING
GRIMSPOUND

Warren House Inn B3212, PL20 6TA, 2 miles northeast of Postbridge ☏ 01822 880208, ⊛ warrenhouseinn.co .uk. In a bleak tract of moorland a mile and a half west of Grimspound, this solitary pub offers warm shelter (the fire's been kept burning for over 170 years), West Country ales and a menu that includes rabbit, homity pie and braised lamb shank (£9–15). By road from Grimspound, turn left onto the B3212; you'll come to the inn two miles before Postbridge. Easter–Oct daily 11am–10pm; Nov–Easter Mon & Tues 11am–3pm, Wed–Sat 11am–10pm, Sun noon–10pm.

Bovey Tracey

Despite the surrounding steep wooded valleys, **BOVEY TRACEY** (pronounced "Buvvy"), built at a crossing over the **River Bovey** on the eastern edge of the moor, has an open, spacious feel. Drifting lazily through, the stream contributes to the town's leisurely air, and its craft shops and cafés – most concentrated along Fore Street – make this a favourite stop-off for coach parties. South of town off the A382, family-friendly indoor entertainment is provided at the **House of Marbles** (Mon–Sat 9am–5pm, Sun 10am–5pm; free), a factory, museum and shop where you can watch gigantic glass marbles whizz down convoluted tracks and view the machine that made the world's biggest marble. There are also daily glass-blowing and marble-making demonstrations.

ARRIVAL AND INFORMATION
BOVEY TRACEY

By bus Service #39 runs between Exeter, Bovey Tracey and Newton Abbot. The Haytor Hoppa (#271) runs on Saturdays in summer on a circular route that takes in Haytor and Widecombe-in-the-Moor (see p.115). The town's bus stops are in Union Square.

Destinations Exeter (Mon–Sat hourly, Sun every 2hr; 45min); Haytor (June to mid-Sept Sat 4 daily; 10min); Moretonhampstead (Mon–Sat 2 daily; 20–25min);

Widecombe-in-the-Moor (June to mid-Sept Sat 4 daily; 20min).

Tourist information Car Park, Station Rd (Easter–Oct

Mon–Fri & Sun 10am–4pm, Sat 9.30am–3.30pm; Nov to mid-Dec & Feb–March Sat 10am–2pm; ☎ 01626 832047, ⓦ boveytracey.gov.uk).

EATING AND SHOPPING

Devon Guild of Craftsmen Fore St, TQ13 9AF ☎ 01626 832223, ⓦ crafts.org.uk. Housed in an ex-mill, this complex of shops, workshops and exhibition space invites you to linger, featuring a range of enticing, locally produced craftwork for sale, from quirky ceramics to innovative quilts and alpaca socks. The *Terrace Café* has inexpensive meals cooked with local ingredients – including cider – and offers vegan and gluten-free options. Daily 10am–5.30pm.

House of Marbles Pottery Rd, TQ13 9DS ☎ 01626 835285, ⓦ houseofmarbles.com. Traditional games, puzzles, glassware and, of course, marbles are sold at this place less than a mile south of Bovey off the A382. It's also an entertaining museum (see opposite). The *Old Pottery* restaurant has soups, sandwiches, light meals (a beef and mushroom pie for £12) and teas, with a conservatory and outdoor seating. Mon–Sat 9am–5pm, Sun 10am–5pm.

Ashburton and around

Thankfully bypassed by the A38 on the southeastern edge of the moor, **ASHBURTON** is a pleasing ensemble of slate-hung buildings with projecting first storeys and oriel windows. One of Dartmoor's four **Stannary towns**, where tin was brought to be assayed and taxed, it was also an important centre for the wool trade during the Middle Ages, when nine cloth mills were at work.

It's still the largest town within the National Park, but there's a more leisurely feel to the place these days, inviting a stroll among the antique shops and cafés. The oldest buildings reflect Ashburton's former wealth: most strikingly, the fifteenth-century parish church of **St Andrew** on West Street, marked out by its lofty tower and typical Devon barrel (or cradle) roof with fine bosses. The town's mercantile traditions are also on display during the **bread-weighing and ale-tasting ceremony** that takes place annually on the third Saturday of July.

St Lawrence Chapel

St Lawrence Lane, TQ13 7DD • May–Sept Tues, Thurs & Fri 2–4pm, usually closed late June to early July • Free • ☎ 01364 652768, ⓦ stlawrencechapel.org.uk

On a turning off West Street, the fourteenth-century **St Lawrence Chapel** was originally the private chapel of a former Bishop of Exeter, but it became a school before the Reformation and remained such until 1938. Relics of the school are on show today, but more impressive is the delicate pendant plasterwork around the walls, placed here when the chapel was largely rebuilt around 1740. It is also the meeting place of the **Court Leet**, a judicial court of Saxon origin, where the Portreeve – the local market official and representative of the monarch (now an honorary position) – is still sworn in, along with his entourage of ale tasters, bread weighers, pig drovers and tree inspectors, on the fourth Tuesday in November each year.

ARRIVAL AND INFORMATION

ASHBURTON

By bus Bus service #88 connects Ashburton with Totnes, Buckfastleigh and Newton Abbot. #X38 buses between Exeter and Plymouth stop at Ashburton, Buckfastleigh and Ivybridge.

Destinations Buckfastleigh (Mon–Sat 1–2 hourly, Sun 6 daily; 15–20min); Exeter (Mon–Sat 7 daily, Sun 2 daily; 45min); Ivybridge (Mon–Sat 7 daily, Sun 2 daily; 30min);

Newton Abbot (Mon–Sat 2 hourly, Sun 4 daily; 20min); Plymouth (Mon–Sat 8 daily, Sun 2 daily; 55min); Totnes (Mon–Sat hourly; 40min).

Tourist information Behind the town hall, off North St (Easter to mid-Oct Mon–Sat 9.30am–4.30pm; mid-Oct to Easter Mon–Fri 9.30am–3.30pm, Sat 9.30am–1pm; ☎ 01364 653426, ⓦ ashburton.org).

ACCOMMODATION

Elmcote 34 North St, TQ13 7QD ☎01364 654115, ⓦelmcote.webs.com. Small, homely Victorian B&B in the centre of town, with two rooms: one has its own dressing room and a spacious bathroom, while the other is at the top of the house and has a modern wet room. Breakfasts include home-made bread and lemon curd. No credit cards. **£80**

Old Coffee House 27–29 West St, TQ13 7DT ☎01364 652539, ⓦtheoldcoffeehouse.co.uk. This friendly and inexpensive B&B offers four plain, pine-furnished en-suites

above a tearoom, with soothing views over the adjacent churchyard. **£60**

Summerhill Farm TQ13 7NN ☎01364 652642, ⓦsummerhillfarmcampsite.com. Less than a mile west of town, this basic, good-value campsite offers complete tranquillity despite being on a working farm. Facilities are clean and pitches can be as big as you like. There's also a "shepherd's hut" to rent (£45 for 2 people), with bedding and cooking equipment. There's no shop, restaurant or wi-fi on site. No credit cards. Closed Oct–March. **£12**

EATING

The Brick House 26 East St, TQ13 7AE ☎01364 653939, ⓦthebrickhouseashburton.co.uk. Popular daytime pit stop for breakfasts, toasties, panini, snack lunches (£7–9) and cream teas, and evening venue for stone-baked pizzas (£6–7) or dishes like sausage stew and sweet potato burger with goat's cheese (both £11). You can sit in front of the fire, in the conservatory or in the long garden where ducks, rabbits and guinea pigs roam. Mon–Wed 9am–4.30pm, Thurs & Fri 9am–10.30pm, Sat 10am–10.30pm, Sun 11am–5pm.

Moorish 11 West St, TQ13 7DT ☎01364 654011, ⓦmoorishrestaurant.co.uk. Mellow café/restaurant with

a Spanish–North African flavour, offering tasty tapas at around £5 each, as well as a small selection of full-size dishes (around £13) such as chicken tagine and salmon and prawn skewers. It's a good spot for breakfast, too. Tues–Sat 10am–2.30pm & 6.30–10pm.

Number 14 14 North St, TQ13 7QD ☎01364 653057. For a quiet coffee, a simple meal or just a glass of wine, head for this café/restaurant and wine bar with sofas, a small garden and a cool vibe. The menu has nibbles and full dishes like Mediterranean tartlet and lobster ravioli for around £12. Gets busy at weekends. Mon–Fri 11am–11pm, Sat 10am–11pm; food served until 9pm.

Buckland-in-the-Moor

BUCKLAND-IN-THE-MOOR, three miles northwest of Ashburton, is one of the prettiest of the cluster of moorstone-and-thatch hamlets on this eastern side of Dartmoor. Though surrounded by open country, the scattered village lies enveloped

HUT CIRCLES, STONE ROWS AND CAIRNS ON DARTMOOR

Any glance at a map of Dartmoor will reveal a wealth of remains from the Bronze and Iron Ages, taking a variety of forms. Among the most arresting – and most numerous – items are the five thousand or so **hut circles** that pepper the landscape. Some are freestanding, others in groups, enclosed by circular stone walls or by the walls of fields. One of the biggest concentrations can be found on and around **Buttern Hill**, west of the hamlet of Gidleigh (two miles west of Chagford), but those at **Grimspound** (see p.117) are in far better condition.

Often found in proximity to hut circles, some 75 **stone rows** are known to exist on Dartmoor (over half of the total number in England). No one knows what purpose was served by these uneven lines of rock, often in the remotest areas and ranging from 100ft to 2miles in length. You can find double and triple rows, as well as circular arrangements – **stone circles**. Long treks over rough terrain are required to visit the most striking examples, but those at **Merrivale** (see p.133) are more accessible, close to a main road.

Around 1500 **cairns**, or mounds of rough stones used as landmarks and monuments, have been found on Dartmoor, mostly 3000–5000 years old. Often dramatically placed on tors and ridges, many mark the burial places of Bronze Age men and women, though most have been pillaged over the centuries, leaving behind an untidy heap of grey rocks around a hole, at the bottom of which the slabs of a cist (a stone burial chamber) may sometimes be seen.

Aside from these, **menhirs** (standing stones), **barrows** (burial chambers), **hillforts**, **stone ramparts**, **defensive ditches** and **reaves** (earth-covered field boundaries) can all be encountered on the moor, though you may need a knowledgeable guide to identify them.

CLOCKWISE FROM TOP LEFT DARTMEET (P.115); WIDECOMBE-IN-THE-MOOR (P.115); DARTMOOR PONIES (P.123) >

within thick woods in the winding **Webburn valley**, through which Webburn Water flows south to join the Dart after a mile and a half, accompanied for part of the way by the road.

St Peter's church

TQ13 7HP · Daily dawn–dusk · Free · ☎ 01364 652968

At Buckland's western end, the restored fourteenth-century church of **St Peter** is the main point of interest, with a medieval rood screen painted on both sides and a good Norman font. The clock on its castellated tower has "MY DEAR MOTHER" replacing the numbers on its face – it was a gift in 1939 to the parish from the local lord of the manor William Whitley. Whitley was also responsible for inscribing two slabs of granite with the Ten Commandments on top of **Buckland Beacon**, a mile east of the hamlet on the Ashburton road, in celebration of the rejection of the new Prayer Book in 1928. They're still there today, and the view from this high point is rated as one of Dartmoor's best.

Holne

About three miles southwest of Buckland and the same distance west of Ashburton, the village of **HOLNE** is enclosed on three sides by wooded slopes. The vicarage here was the birthplace of **Charles Kingsley**, author of such Devon-based tales as *Westward Ho!*, who is commemorated by a window in the village church. In the churchyard, you'll also see a whimsical – though badly weathered – epitaph on the grave of **Edward Collins**, landlord of the next-door *Church House Inn* until 1780.

Buckfastleigh

Given its somewhat subdued air, it's hard to believe that **BUCKFASTLEIGH**, three miles southwest of Ashburton on the A38, was once Devon's most important wool-manufacturing town and a major staging post between Plymouth and Exeter. Nowadays it's best known for the imposing abbey just outside, though its quiet Fore Street is worth a stroll for its unusual museum and a handful of shops and cafés.

Valiant Soldier

80 Fore St, TQ11 0BS · Easter–Oct Mon, Tues, Thurs & Fri 12.30–4.30pm, Wed & Sat 10.30am–4.30pm · £4 · ☎ 01364 644522, ⓦ valiantsoldier.org.uk

In contrast to the haughty majesty of its famous abbey, Buckfastleigh also offers a much humbler but surprisingly engaging nostalgia-fest in the form of the **Valiant Soldier**. Having called last orders for good in the 1960s, the pub remained untouched until its sympathetic restoration in the late 1990s, which has retained all the bric-a-brac of a working-man's taproom in the mid-twentieth century, when a pint of mild cost 1s 4d. Knowledgeable volunteers offer plenty of period detail. Your ticket also covers entry to the next-door **heritage centre**, displaying remnants of the town's woollen trade among other items.

Buckfast Abbey

Buckfast Rd, TQ11 0EE · Abbey and grounds daily 9am–6pm · Free · ☎ 01364 645500, ⓦ buckfasttourism.org.uk · Bus #88 from Newton Abbot, Totnes and Buckfastleigh stops here hourly (Sun 4 daily); on selected weekends in summer, an old London double-decker bus operates between the South Devon Railway station (see opposite), Buckfastleigh, Ashburton and the abbey

Most of the tourist traffic hereabouts converges a mile north of Buckfastleigh, where the River Dart weaves through a green wooded valley to enter the grounds of **Buckfast**

DARTMOOR PONIES

There have been ponies on Dartmoor since the **Bronze Age**: small of stature, strong and hardy, they were traditionally used as working and pack animals, and for transporting granite and tin from the moor's quarries and mines. With the decline of mining and the fall in demand for **horsemeat**, numbers have dwindled from thirty thousand in 1950 to fewer than three thousand today, and few of these are of the original hardy stock, as much cross-breeding has taken place over the years. Contrary to popular belief, Dartmoor ponies are not wild, merely unbroken; all have an owner and sport a brand, cut or tag to indicate who they belong to. During the "**drifts**" – roundups that take place each September and October – the ponies are herded into yards, grouped according to ownership and, in some cases, sold on.

As they can bite and kick, you should steer clear of the ponies, and above all don't feed them – it encourages them to approach traffic and is against the law. For more information, see ⓦdpht.co.uk, the website for the Dartmoor Pony Heritage Trust, and ⓦdartmoor.gov.uk, the National Park site.

Abbey. This imposing modern monastic complex occupies the site of an abbey that was founded in the eleventh century by King Cnut, abandoned two hundred years later, refounded, and finally dissolved by Henry VIII. The present buildings were the work of a handful of French Benedictine monks who, in 1932, consecrated the new abbey, built in a traditional Anglo-Norman style that followed the design of the Cistercian building razed in 1535. It's a pretty clinical exercise, which doesn't invite much lingering, though there are good examples of the monks' renowned proficiency in the art of stained-glass windows. The vivid slabs of red, blue and yellow glass in the chapel and the huge corona of lights in front of the high altar are at their best in daylight, though for atmosphere, come to the candlelit compline here at 9pm.

As well as stained glass, the monks are known for their **bee-keeping** skills, and more notoriously as producers of **Buckfast Tonic Wine**, a fortified wine with added caffeine. Honey and tonic wine are both retailed in the abbey's shop.

South Devon Railway

Buckfastleigh station, TQ11 0DZ • Mid-March to Oct plus school hols & weekends in Dec, 3–9 departures daily • £14 return • ⓣ01364 644370, ⓦsouthdevonrailway.org

The restored steam trains of the **South Devon Railway** offer a wonderfully scenic way to view the Dart valley to the southeast. The trains leave from Buckfastleigh station, a mile east of town, and run alongside the River Dart as far as Littlehempston station outside Totnes (30min). On selected weekends in summer, a free double-decker bus service transports ticket-holders between Buckfastleigh station, Buckfast Abbey, Ashburton and the *Valiant Soldier* at Buckfastleigh (see ⓦsouthdevonrailway association.org for dates).

ARRIVAL AND INFORMATION   BUCKFASTLEIGH

By bus Service #X38 links Buckfastleigh with Plymouth, Exeter and Ashburton, and #88 goes to Totnes, Ashburton and Newton Abbot. The town's bus stops are on Plymouth Rd and Dart Bridge Rd.
Destinations Ashburton (Mon–Sat 1–2 hourly, Sun 6 daily; 15–20min); Exeter (Mon–Sat 7 daily, Sun 2 daily; 1hr); Newton Abbot (Mon–Sat hourly, Sun 4 daily; 30min);

Plymouth (Mon–Sat 7 daily, Sun 2 daily; 1hr); Totnes (Mon–Sat hourly; 20min).
Tourist information *Valiant Soldier*, 80 Fore St (April–Oct Mon, Tues, Thurs & Fri 12.30–4.30pm, Wed & Sat 10.30am–4.30pm; Nov–March Wed 10.30am–4.30pm; ⓣ01364 644522).

ACCOMMODATION AND EATING

★**Beara Farm** Colston Rd, TQ11 0LW ⓣ01364 642234. A mile and a half south of town on the banks of

the Dart is this year-round campsite – a rare thing in these parts. It's fairly basic (with no hook-ups) and the pitches are on a slope, but it's sheltered, scenic and relaxed – though the peace and quiet is occasionally interrupted by the steam trains of the South Devon Railway passing nearby. Call ahead in winter. No credit cards. Per person **£5.50**

★**Riverford Field Kitchen** Wash Farm, TQ11 0JU ☎01803 762074, ⊕riverford.co.uk. Buried in a rural spot less than two miles east of town (signposted off the A384), this renowned provider of organic food operates a restaurant where the mainly vegetarian dishes are always fresh, seasonal and inventive. Set-price three-course lunches and dinners are £23.50 and £27.50 respectively. There's a great atmosphere: tables are communal and everyone is served at the same time. Booking required. Arrive early for a walk around the farm. Daily: lunch usually 1pm, dinner usually 7.30pm.

Moretonhampstead

At the intersection of the B3212 and the A382, which cuts across the northeastern wedge of the moor, **MORETONHAMPSTEAD** is an essentially unspoilt market town that makes an attractive entry point from Exeter – and, incidentally, shares with Woolfardisworthy (near Bideford) the honour of having the **longest single-word place name** in England. Apart from its arcaded stone almshouses in Cross Street, dated 1637, the town is not particularly noteworthy architecturally. It does, however, have a range of facilities that make it a useful base for stocking up or staying overnight.

ARRIVAL AND DEPARTURE

MORETONHAMPSTEAD

By bus The #359 is the most useful bus to/from Exeter, while bus #173 takes a more circuitous route between Exeter, Chagford and Moretonhampstead, and the rare #178 links Moretonhampstead with Bovey Tracey, Newton Abbot and (even more rarely) Chagford and Okehampton. The bus stop is on the Square.

Destinations Bovey Tracey (Mon–Sat 2 daily; 25min); Chagford (Mon–Sat 3 daily; 15min); Exeter (Mon–Sat 7 daily; 50min–1hr 20min); Newton Abbot (Mon–Sat 2 daily; 50min); Okehampton (Mon–Sat 1 daily; 1hr 15min).

INFORMATION

Tourist information 11 The Square (March–Oct daily 9.30am–5pm; Nov–Feb Thurs–Sat 10am–4.30pm, Sun 11am–3pm; ☎01647 440043, ⊕visitmoretonhampstead .co.uk). Has a computer with internet access.

ACCOMMODATION

Old Post House 18 Court St, TQ13 8LG ☎01647 440900, ⊕theoldposthouse.com. At the western edge of the town with direct access to the moor, this friendly B&B is particularly welcoming to walkers. The spacious, top-floor family room (£75) enjoys wonderful moorland views, and there's a comfortable guests' lounge. Room-only rates and reductions for longer stays are available. No debit/credit cards. **£55**

Sparrowhawk Backpackers 45 Ford St, TQ13 8LN ☎01647 440318, ⊕sparrowhawkbackpackers.co.uk. Centrally located hostel with a dormitory and large kitchen in a converted stone stable, and a double/family room in the main house. Showers are solar-heated and there's a spacious yard for sitting and eating in summer. No debit/ credit cards. Dorms **£17**, double **£38**

EATING AND DRINKING

The Horse 7 George St, TQ13 8PG ☎01647 440242, ⊕thehorsedartmoor.co.uk. A traditional pub at the front with a restaurant in a converted barn at the back, this is a great venue for a pint and a meal. Apart from panini and sandwiches at lunchtime, the menu mixes traditional English dishes (£12–19) with tapas (around £4) and thin and crispy pizzas (around £11) – only pizzas are available Sun & Mon evenings. There's live folk on the last Mon of the month. Kitchen Mon 6.30–9pm, Tues–Sun 12.30– 2.30pm & 6.30–9pm.

White Hart The Square, TQ13 8NQ ☎01647 440500, ⊕whitehartdartmoor.co.uk. This posting inn dating from the seventeenth century is now a smart hotel, pub and restaurant with plenty of character. Alongside the real ales, you'll find pies and local meat and seafood dishes for around £12, and there's a daily-changing specials menu. Alternatively, settle down on a comfy sofa for a cream tea. Kitchen Mon–Sat noon– 2.15pm & 6–8.30pm, Sun 12.30–2.15pm & 6.30–8.30pm.

Chagford and around

Moretonhampstead has a historic rivalry with neighbouring **CHAGFORD**, a Stannary town (see p.119) that also enjoyed prosperity from the local wool industry. Standing on a hillside above the River Teign, the village has a pointy "pepperpot" **market house** from 1862 at its centre, said to have been modelled on the Abbot's Kitchen at Glastonbury Abbey.

St Michael the Archangel

High St, TQ13 8BN • Daily 9am–dusk • Free • ☎ 01647 432265, ⓦ chagfordchurch.com

The fine, mainly fifteenth-century church of **St Michael the Archangel** stands in the centre of Chagford, surrounded by thatch-roofed houses, pubs and hotels. The church's sanctuary has an inscription dedicated to Mary Whiddon, a member of a powerful local family who was shot and killed outside the church following her marriage on 11 October 1641 – apparently the victim of a jealous suitor (the tale may have been the inspiration for R.D. Blackmore's classic romance *Lorna Doone*). In front of the church at 3 High Street, the sixteenth-century **Endecott House** (not open to the public) is claimed to be the birthplace of John Endecott, a Pilgrim Father who was governor of the Massachusetts Bay Colony 1649–65.

ARRIVAL AND DEPARTURE

CHAGFORD

By bus Chagford is accessible on bus #173 from Exeter and the even less frequent #178 from Okehampton; both connect with Moretonhampstead.

Destinations Exeter (Mon–Sat 5 daily; 1hr 5min); Moretonhampstead (Mon–Sat 3–4 daily; 20min); Okehampton (Mon–Sat 1 daily; 1hr).

ACCOMMODATION

Cyprian's Cot 47 New St, TQ13 8BB ☎ 01647 432256, ⓦ cyprianscot.co.uk. A relaxed, homely atmosphere prevails in this snug sixteenth-century cottage where you can warm your bones at the inglenook fireplace in the guests' sitting room. Just two small rooms are available, and there's a pretty, secluded garden where you can breakfast in fine weather. No credit cards. £70

Globe Inn 9 High St, TQ13 8AJ ☎ 01647 433485, ⓦ theglobeinnchagford.co.uk. Traditional accommodation facing the village church, offering smart, spacious rooms with modern decor – the family room (£130) in the attic is

especially comfortable. Bring earplugs if you're likely to be bothered by the hourly chiming of the church clock. £95

Woodland Springs Venton, Drewsteignton, EX6 6PG ☎ 01647 231695, ⓦ woodlandsprings.co.uk. A quiet, adults-only campsite with modern and clean facilities. It's a couple of miles north of Chagford as the crow flies, but further by road (B3206 to the A382, then two miles northwest) and accessible on the #178 bus route. There's a small shop on site, and the excellent *Post Inn* is a mile north in Whiddon Down. £20.50

EATING AND DRINKING

The Chagford Inn 7 Mill St, TQ13 8AW ☎ 01647 433109, ⓦ thechagfordinn.com. Chic gastropub with slate floors, wooden tables and seating, and local art on the walls. Come by at lunchtime for Welsh rarebit, smoked roast ham or a meat or cheese platter (all about £10), or in the evening to sample local meat and seafood dishes (around £16), or the separate beef menu, which offers different cuts of a locally reared steer over the course of a week. Kitchen daily noon–2.30pm & 6–9pm.

★**The Courtyard Café** 76 The Square, TQ13 8AE ☎ 01647 432571. Pies, mixed salads, veggie burgers, fresh fruit and various wholefoods are sold here for around £5, for the most part local, organic and Fairtrade. Buy to take away or sit down to eat in the small yard. Arts and crafts are

on display inside. Mon–Sat 9am–4.30pm, Sun 9.30am–12.30pm.

★**Gidleigh Park** TQ13 8HH ☎ 01647 432367, ⓦ gidleigh.com. For a one-off splurge, head to the moor's most celebrated restaurant – and one of the best in the country – a couple of miles west of Chagford, set within 45 acres of riverside and woodland gardens. Under the guidance of the Michelin-starred chef Michael Wignall, the restaurant offers unexpected and eclectic combinations in dishes that use the best local ingredients; seven-course tasting menus are £118 in the evening or £75 for lunch, slightly more affordable three-course lunches are £50, and afternoon teas are £37.50 per person. There are rooms here too (from £315). Daily noon–2pm, 3.30–5pm & 7–9pm.

4

THE TWO MOORS WAY AND THE COAST TO COAST WALK

The major walking route linking North and South Devon, the **Two Moors Way** (ⓦtwomoorsway.org) stretches for roughly a hundred miles between Ivybridge on Dartmoor's southern edge and Lynmouth (see p.168) on Exmoor's coast. The southern end of the walk links with the Erme–Plym Trail between Ivybridge and Plymouth (13 miles) and a two-mile stretch between Plymouth and Wembury to form the **Coast to Coast Walk** from Wembury to Lynmouth (116 miles). The walking is good: much of the Dartmoor section follows a disused tramway, before switching to the **Abbot's Way**, the ancient track between Buckfast and Tavistock abbeys, then passes through Holne (usually regarded as the first overnight stop), Widecombe-in-the-Moor, Chagford and Castle Drogo. There are also link paths to other routes, for example the **Tarka Trail**, the **Templer Way** (a granite tramway from Haytor to Teignmouth) and the **Exe Valley Way**.

The best **maps** to use are 1:25,000 Ordnance Survey *Explorer* maps numbers OL28, 113, 114, a very small section of 127, and OL9; map number 20 covers the Erme–Plym Trail. The various walking guides – all titled *The Two Moors Way* – are essential companions, and one or more should be available from local tourist offices, along with leaflets on the Erme–Plym Trail. The **tourist office** at Ivybridge (Mon–Fri 9.15am–5pm, Sat 9.15am–1pm; ☎01752 897035, ⓦivybridge-devon.co.uk), situated at the start of the Two Moors Way in The Watermark centre (next to the River Erme on Leonard's Rd), can also supply plentiful information on the route and accommodation options. Luggage transfer outfits are available to minimize the weight you carry (see p.34).

Castle Drogo

4

Drewsteignton, EX6 6PB • **Castle** Early March to Oct daily 11am–5pm; Nov to mid-Dec Sat & Sun tours 11am–4pm • £9 (including gardens); NT • **Gardens** Early March to Oct daily 10am–5.30pm or dusk; Nov to early March daily 11am–4pm • £5.70; NT • **Grounds** Daily dawn–dusk • Free; NT • Parking free • ☎01647 433306, ⓦnationaltrust.org.uk/castle-drogo • Bus #173 from Exeter, Chagford and Moretonhampstead (Mon–Sat) stops outside the entrance, a 10min walk from the property; discounted tickets for anyone arriving on public transport or by bike

Stupendously sited above the Teign gorge three miles north of Chagford, the granite extravaganza of **Castle Drogo** was the vision of grocery magnate Julius Drewe. Having retired at the age of 33, Drewe unearthed a link that suggested his descent from a Norman baron (Drogo) and set about creating a twentieth-century castle befitting his pedigree. The project was begun in 1910 to a design by Sir Edwin Lutyens, but complications arose, costs escalated and the money ran out in 1930. Though the original plans were never completed, the result is still a striking synthesis of medieval and modern elements, with 6ft-thick walls in the main complex enclosing cold and austere rooms (130 electric fires were installed to heat the place). The living rooms are furnished for the most part with tapestries and other items bought wholesale from a bankrupt Spanish financier. Look out for the forerunner of Subbuteo in the library, and the chic 1930s fashions hung on a rail in the bedroom upstairs.

The castle is currently undergoing a thorough programme of **renovation**, intended to resolve long-running structural issues, with the result that most of the building is likely to remain under scaffolding and some rooms will be closed until around 2019. Alternative displays and exhibitions have been arranged, as well as opportunities to view the renovation work close up, though inevitably the impact of the building is reduced while the scaffolding is in place.

The castle **gardens** have not been affected, however. Immaculately clipped yew hedges surround a huge circular **croquet lawn** (mallets and balls are available in summer if you fancy a game) and recur throughout the sunken garden, shrubbery and herbaceous border. Below the terraced gardens, paths lead down to where the River Teign burrows through the gorge, surrounded both by coppiced oak woods – where you might spot the odd fallow deer – and bare heath, with plentiful rambling opportunities.

Fingle Bridge

From the eastern end of the grounds of Castle Drogo, follow **Fisherman's Path** by the riverside, or **Hunter's Path** higher up (both well signposted), to one of Dartmoor's most noted beauty spots, **Fingle Bridge**, a little over a mile east. This simple granite structure over the Teign, with buttresses recessed for packhorses to pass, lies in the midst of woodland that's carpeted with daffodils and bluebells in spring and is a haven for birdlife all year round. Walking westwards along the riverbank path from the bridge, you might have the luck to spot a kingfisher or any of the three species of woodpecker that frequent these shaded green pools in which trout, salmon and even otters can be spotted.

At the bridge, you'll find the *Fingle Bridge Inn*, where **licences to fish** for salmon, brown trout and sea trout are issued (£12.50–25 for a day). The pub's terrace fronting the river is a nice spot for a drink and a snack, though it can get very busy.

Okehampton and around

Straddling the two branches of the River Okement that merge here, **OKEHAMPTON** was dependent on the wool trade in medieval times, and also benefited from its position on one of the principal routes to Exeter, now the A30. A few good-looking old buildings survive from this period, though today Okehampton shows little evidence of either the grace or the pretensions that typify many of Devon's other wool towns.

For the most part an unexceptional working town, Okehampton preserves few vestiges of its long past, though the prominent fifteenth-century granite tower of the chapel of **St James** survives, at the east end of Fore Street. Along with its continuation, West Street, **Fore Street** forms the town's main thoroughfare, lined with shops and banks. A **farmers' market** takes place outside St James every third Saturday of the month. There are numerous walking possibilities from Okehampton (see box below).

4

Museum of Dartmoor Life

₃ West St, EX20 1HQ • Easter–Sept Mon–Fri 10.15am–4.15pm, Sat 10.15am–1pm; Oct to mid-Dec Mon–Fri 10.15am–3.30pm, Sat 10.15am–1pm • £4 • ☎ 01837 52295, ⓦ museumofdartmoorlife.org.uk

Across from the seventeenth-century town hall, a granite archway leads off West Street to the **Museum of Dartmoor Life**, an excellent overview of habitation on the moor since earliest times. Laid out over three floors, the imaginatively presented collection features motley items of antique agricultural equipment alongside everything from a 1922 Morris Cowley farm pick-up to a pump made to keep newly dug graves dry.

Okehampton Castle

Castle Lodge, EX20 1JA • Daily: Easter–June & Sept 10am–5pm; July & Aug 10am–6pm • £4.50; EH • ☎ 01837 52844, ⓦ www.english-heritage.org.uk/visit/places/okehampton-castle

Loftily perched above the West Okement River, a mile southwest of the town centre, Okehampton Castle is the shattered hulk of a stronghold laid to waste by Henry VIII;

A WALK AROUND DARTMOOR'S NORTHERN TORS

A varied seven-mile, three-hour **circular walk** from **Okehampton** skirts the east of the MoD's Okehampton range, brings you within view of the highest points on the moor and then plunges into the recesses of the **East Okement River**, before rounding **Belstone Common** and returning north to Okehampton via the village of **Belstone**. It's not overly arduous, though there are steep stretches along varied terrain, for which a compass and the 1:25,000 *Explorer* OL28 map are essential.

its dramatic ruins include the gatehouse, Norman keep and the remains of the Great Hall, buttery and kitchens. Free audioguides provide plenty of background on the site, and woodland walks and riverside picnic tables invite a gentle exploration of what was once the deer park of the earls of Devon.

Finch Foundry

Sticklepath, EX20 2NW • Early March to Oct daily 11am–5pm • £5.60; NT • ☎ 01837 840046, ⊕ nationaltrust.org.uk/finch-foundry • Take bus #178, #510 or #599 from Okehampton

Agricultural machinery and hand tools for local farmers and miners were once produced at the water-powered Victorian forge at **Finch Foundry**, four miles east of Okehampton. Said to be the last working water-powered forge in the country, it hosts regular talks and demonstrations, and displays examples of tools made here. The garden holds a curious Gothic-style thatched hut known as **Tom Pearse's Summerhouse**, which once belonged to one of the characters named in *Widdicombe Fair* (see box, p.116), a local serge-maker.

Dartmoor Railway

Okehampton station, EX20 1EJ • Okehampton–Meldon Easter–Sept Sat & Sun 4 times daily • £3 one-way, £5 all-day Rover; under-17s £2/£3; families £8/£14 • ☎ 01837 55164, ⊕ dartmoor-railway-sa.org

One way of getting onto the moor quickly is by means of a brief stretch of the **Dartmoor Railway** from Okehampton station to **Meldon** (10min), a couple of miles southwest of town. Meldon station is close to the **Dartmoor Way**, and is also on the **Granite Way** cycle and walking route between Okehampton and Lydford (see p.131), which parallels the rail route as far as Meldon, then continues over the disused railway viaduct – offering superb views over the moors – and along the old train line. Eleven miles in all, it forms part of the NCN27 (Devon Coast to Coast) cycle route.

On Sundays (mid-May to mid-Sept only), Great Western Railway also operates a service from Okehampton to Crediton and Exeter, with a stop at **Sampford Courtenay**, a village famous for its instigating role in the Prayer Book Rebellion against the imposition of the Book of Common Prayer in 1549.

ARRIVAL AND DEPARTURE

By bus Okehampton enjoys good bus connections with Exeter and Bude in Cornwall on services #6 and #6A, and with Lydford and Tavistock on #46, but has just one link daily with Chagford and Moretonhampstead on bus #178. Stops are on West St and Fore St.

Destinations Exeter (Mon–Sat 1–2 hourly, Sun 7 daily; 1hr); Lydford (Mon–Sat 10 daily; 20min); Moretonhampstead (Mon–Sat 1 daily; 1hr 10min); Tavistock (Mon–Sat 10 daily; 45min).

By train On Sun mid-May to mid-Sept, Great Western Railway (☎ 03457 000125, ⊕ gwr.com) provide Okehampton with a useful rail connection along an old goods line to the Tarka Line and Exeter (Sun 4 daily; 45min), stopping at Crediton (Sun 4 daily; 30min). Dartmoor Railway also runs a heritage service from Okehampton to Meldon in summer (see above). Okehampton's station is a 15min walk up Station Rd from Fore St.

INFORMATION AND ACTIVITIES

Tourist information The Museum of Dartmoor Life can answer most travellers' queries, or see ⊕ everything okehampton.co.uk for limited tourist information and local events.

Bike rental Adventure Okehampton, next to the station (☎ 01837 53916, ⊕ adventureokehampton.com; £12/day); Devon Cycle Hire, Sourton Down, about a mile southwest of Meldon off the A386 (April–Sept, also half-

terms Feb & Oct; ☎ 01837 861141, ⊕ devoncyclehire .co.uk; £16/day). Both have direct access to the Granite Way cycle route (see above).

Horseriding For horseriding on the moor, contact Eastlake (☎ 01837 52513, ⊕ eastlakeridingstables .co.uk), east of town in the Belstone/Sticklepath area. Rides cost £13 for 30min, £20 for 1hr, £35 for 2hr.

ACCOMMODATION

Adventure Okehampton Goods Shed, Klondyke Rd, EX20 1EW; Bracken Tor, Saxon Gate, EX20 1QW ☎01837 53916, ⓦ adventureokehampton.com. This YHA hostel occupies two sites, both south of the centre: the *Goods Shed* at the station (and on the Granite Way), where the reception for both is, and *Bracken Tor*, an arts and crafts-style house that's more convenient for the moor. Bunks are in rooms accommodating 2–8 people, many en suite, and camping pitches are also available. The hostels specialize in outdoor activities, including rock climbing, kayaking and cycling. Dorms £26, doubles £65, camping/person £11

Bundu Sourton Down, EX20 4HT ☎01837 861747, ⓦ bundu.co.uk. Four miles southwest of Okehampton off the A386, this small, relaxed campsite has well-kept facilities, but suffers from some traffic noise. It's on the edge of the moor, right on the Granite Way (see opposite), and there's a pub next door. £14

Meadowlea 65 Station Rd, EX20 1EA ☎01837 53200, ⓦ meadowleaguesthouse.co.uk. Clean and warm, this B&B lies a short walk south of the centre, below the train station, and 400m from the Granite Way. Four of the seven rooms are en suite and there's cycle storage. £58

★**Upcott House** Upcott Hill, EX20 1SQ ☎01837 53743, ⓦ upcotthouse.com. Half a mile north of Okehampton's centre, this sturdy Edwardian B&B was once a boarding school. It has amiable, eco-aware hosts, a large garden with pigs and chickens, and spacious, high-ceilinged rooms – some sharing bathrooms, and two of them with a balcony where the substantial breakfasts can be taken. £80

EATING

2Rivers 16 Fore St, EX20 1AN ☎01837 52981, ⓦ 2riversrestaurant.co.uk. Food and refreshments to suit all tastes are available at this simple place with an exposed granite wall, from coffees and cakes to full-blown meals. You'll find ciabatta melts and quiche on the menu at lunchtime (around £6), and such classics as braised beef brisket, pan-fried sea-bass and ribeye steak in the evening (mostly £10–15). Mon 9am–3pm, Tues–Fri 9am–3pm & 5.30–9pm, Sat 9am–3pm & 5.30–9.30pm, Sun noon–2.30pm.

J Street Diner 14 S James St, EX20 1DH ☎01837 52988. Tucked away behind the museum and at the end of the shopping arcade, this US-style 1950s diner is a cheap retreat for all-day breakfasts, burgers and nachos, all under £7. Mon, Tues & Thurs–Sat 9am–5pm, Sun 10am–3pm.

4

Tavistock

On the western extremity of the moor, but just ten miles north of Plymouth, **TAVISTOCK** has its own very separate identity, partly the result of having been the seat of the most powerful abbey in the West Country during the Middle Ages. After the abbey's dissolution by Henry VIII, the town continued to prosper as a tin and wool centre, but it owes its distinctive Victorian appearance to the building boom that followed the discovery of copper deposits in the vicinity in 1844. The cobbled and crenellated, granite **Bedford Square** at the centre of town is reckoned to be one of the country's finest examples of Victorian ensemble building, with an imposing town hall.

St Eustachius

Bedford Square, PL19 8AU • Daily 8am–5.30pm • Free • ☎ 01822 616673, ⓦ tavistockparishchurch.org.uk

At the heart of Tavistock, on a site immediately north of the old abbey, the parish church of **St Eustachius** dates from the fourteenth century, though it was thoroughly restored in the 1840s. To the left of the altar, the St Mary Magdalene Chapel holds a stained-glass window produced by William Morris's studio from designs by Edward Burne-Jones; oddly, among the figures depicted, Moses is shown with a black halo. Elsewhere in the interior are a couple of grandiose memorials to local worthies from the fifteenth and sixteenth centuries and an elaborate Victorian organ screen carved with 48 figures. Some scant remnants of Tavistock Abbey survive in the churchyard.

Pannier Market

Behind Tavistock's town hall, off Bedford Square, the bustling, covered **Pannier Market** (Tues–Sat; ⊛ tavistockpanniermarket.co.uk) has been a Friday fixture since 1105, though the present-day market buildings are nineteenth century. On other days, just the craftwork, antiques and collectables are traded, making for an interesting wander. Stalls spill out from the main building, and you can usually pick up some bargains from farmers or the local Women's Institute.

Goose Fair

Tavistock is also associated with one of Dartmoor's most famous markets, **Goose Fair**, a sprawl of stalls that take over Bedford Square and Plymouth Road on the second Wednesday of October. You may well see some geese among the motley wares on sale, and a funfair sets up for the occasion.

ARRIVAL AND DEPARTURE   TAVISTOCK

By bus The most useful bus services are #46, travelling between Plymouth, Tavistock, Lydford and Okehampton, and #98 to Merrivale and Princetown; #1 and #X1 also connect Tavistock with Plymouth. Bus stops are outside the *Bedford Hotel* on Plymouth Rd.

Destinations Lydford (Mon–Sat 11 daily; 30min); Merrivale (Mon–Sat 3 daily; 20min); Okehampton (Mon–Sat 9 daily; 50min); Plymouth (Mon–Sat 4–5 hourly, Sun hourly; 1hr); Princetown (Mon–Sat 3 daily; 30min).

INFORMATION AND ACTIVITIES

Bike rental Dartmoor Cycles, 6 Atlas House, West Devon Business Park, next to Morrisons supermarket (☎ 01822 618178, ⊛ dartmoorcycles.co.uk; £18/day); Tavistock Cycles, Paddons Row, Brook St (☎ 01822 617630, ⊛ tavistockcycles.co.uk; £20/day).

ACCOMMODATION

★**Harford Bridge** Peter Tavy, PL19 9LS ☎ 01822 810349, ⊛ harfordbridge.co.uk. The area's best campsite occupies a peaceful spot on the banks of the Tavy, off the A386 two miles north of town and a mile from the *Peter Tavy Inn* (see opposite). Pitches are large and facilities modern and clean, and there's tennis and a play area. Closed mid-Nov to mid-March. **£19.50**

Mount Tavy Cottage Off B3357 Princetown road, PL19 9JL ☎ 01822 614253, ⊛ mounttavy.co.uk. About half a mile east of Tavistock, this 250-year-old building enjoys a beautiful setting with a lush garden roamed by geese and guinea fowl. Rooms have pristine white bed-linen and freestanding baths. Breakfasts are mostly organic and dinner can be prearranged (£25) – taken on a pier on the

---

WALKS FROM TAVISTOCK

Running parallel to and between Plymouth Road and the **River Tavy**, the **Tavistock Canal** was built in the early eighteenth century to carry copper ore to **Morwellham Quay**, five miles away. Richly bordered with pampas grass, the towpath now provides a lovely stroll of up to one and a half miles before it disappears underground. Another fine walk is along the **viaduct** that bestrides the town to the north (walk north from Bedford Square, passing under the viaduct, then turn right at Kilworthy Road to gain access). It once carried a train track and now affords marvellous views over the town and moor.

More ambitious excursions starting from Tavistock will bring you onto moorland. North of town, a four-mile lane wanders up to **Brent Tor** (1129ft; map ref SX471804), dominating Dartmoor's western fringes. Access to its conical summit is easiest along a path that gently ascends through the gorse that covers its southwestern side, and leads to the small church of **St Michael** at the top. A couple of miles eastwards you'll see **Gibbet Hill** (1158ft; map ref SX503811) looming over **Black Down** and the ruined stack of the abandoned Wheal Betsy silver and lead mine; it's said to be where criminals were left to die in cages during the Middle Ages.

South of town, **Drake's Trail** (⊛ drakestrail.co.uk) is a 21-mile cycling and walking route between Tavistock and Plymouth that forms part of Route 27 of the National Cycle Network.

lake. Self-catering accommodation also available. **£85**

★**The Priory** Marshal Close, Whitchurch, PL19 9RB ☎07912 498837, ⓦpriorybnbtavistock-dartmoor .co.uk. Tucked away on the outskirts of town, this B&B has a distinct visual impact – not least for its imposing turret (with great views from the top) and, inside, its tiled entrance illuminated by a large stained-glass window. Bedrooms are spacious and gracefully furnished, but there are no communal areas: if you order breakfast (£6/person

extra), it's brought to your room. It's a 20min walk to the centre. No credit cards. **£88**

Rockmount Drake Rd, PL19 0AX ☎07445 009880, ⓦrockmounthotel.co.uk. Chic, modern hotel a couple of minutes north of Bedford Square. The sleek, boutiquey rooms have iPads and other gadgetry, and one is a studio apartment with a kitchenette and private access to the garden (£113). Breakfast is optional, costing £4–10 per person. Online discounts available. **£89**

EATING AND DRINKING

★**Peter Tavy Inn** Peter Tavy, PL19 9NN ☎01822 810348, ⓦpetertavyinn.com. Classic country pub in a village three miles northeast of Tavistock. Alongside the outstanding ales, there are ploughman's lunches with six different types of Devon cheese, and hot meals such as lamb shank, seafood gumbo and vegetable stew, as well as some amazing pies. You'll pay around £6.50 for a baguette, £11 for a main course at lunchtime or £12–20 in the evening (when booking is advisable). Mon–Sat noon–11pm, Sun noon–10.30pm; kitchen noon–2pm & 6.30–9pm.

Robertson's Organic Café 4–8 Pepper St, PL19 0BD ☎01822 612117, ⓦrobertsonstavistock.co.uk. Relaxed spot in the centre of town for a cup of the best coffee in Tavistock, a snack lunch or a full meal. It's most famous for its pizzas (£8–13.50; also available to take away or be

delivered) with delicious and often unusual toppings, but the menu also has, for example, Moroccan meatballs and risotto (£8–12), and there are gluten-free options. A good selection of beers and wines are available, as well as smoothies and juices. Mon–Fri 11am–9pm, Sat 9am–9pm.

Taylors 22 Market St, PL19 0DD ☎01822 613045, ⓦtaylorstavistock.co.uk. This quirky hybrid of café, restaurant, tearoom and cocktail bar close to St Eustachius church mixes old and new decor in a chatty, laidback environment. Standouts on the menu include eggs Benedict, smoked salmon roulade, onion and tomato tart and lemon meringue pie. Mains are around £12/£14 for lunch/dinner, and tapas are also available (£3). Mon–Sat 9am–10pm, Sun 10am–3pm.

ENTERTAINMENT

The Wharf Canal Rd ☎01822 611166, ⓦtavistock wharf.com. Evening entertainment is provided by this arts centre adjacent to the canal, which puts on year-round

films and performances ranging from risqué stand-up to Chinese opera, and from Abba tributes to local bands.

Lydford

Six miles north of Tavistock, **LYDFORD** has an unassuming appearance that gives little hint of its eventful history as a Saxon outpost against the Celts, and one of Alfred the Great's four principal settlements in Devon, founded for defence against the Danes. Traces of the Saxon fortifications – an earth rampart – can still be seen on either side of the main road at the northeastern end of the village, but the Saxon castle was completely destroyed by the Danes in 997.

Lydford lies at the southern end of the **Granite Way** cycle and walking route, running eleven miles as far as Okehampton (see p.127), largely traffic-free and partly along a disused railway line.

Lydford Castle

EX20 4BH • Unrestricted access • Free

Located right next to the *Castle Inn*, Lydford's best-preserved monument is the sturdy but small-scale **Lydford Castle**, a square Norman keep that, until 1800, was used as a prison for offenders against the Stannary, or Tinners' Law, with the Stannary Court on the first floor. The justice administered from here had a fearsome reputation throughout Dartmoor, as described by a local poet in the seventeenth century: "I oft have heard of Lydford Law/How in the morn they hang and draw/And sit in judgement after".

Lydford Gorge

EX20 4BH • Daily: early March to early Oct 10am–5pm; early Oct to early March 10am–4pm • £7.40, £3.50 in winter; NT • ☎ 01822
820320, ⓦ nationaltrust.org.uk/lydford-gorge • The main entrance is a five-minute walk downhill from the village

The chief attraction here is **Lydford Gorge**. Overgrown with thick woods, the one-and-
a-half-mile gorge – said to be the deepest in the South West – was once the hideout of
a large family of outlaws, the Gubbins, who terrorized the neighbourhood and stole
sheep from Dartmoor farms in the seventeenth century. Its very seclusion makes it an
idyllic place to visit, alive with butterflies, spotted woodpeckers, dippers, herons and
clouds of insects – though you may find yourself sharing it with plenty of other
visitors.

A circular walk starts off high above the River Lyd, dropping down to the hundred-
foot **White Lady Waterfall**, and returning along the opposite bank to the foaming
whirlpools of the **Devil's Cauldron**, near the main entrance. The full course would take
you roughly two hours at a leisurely pace, but there's a separate entrance at the south
end of the gorge if you want to visit only the waterfall. In winter months (between Nov
and March), when the river can flood, only the waterfall and top part of the gorge are
open to the public.

ARRIVAL AND DEPARTURE   LYDFORD

By bus There's a stop at Lydford's war memorial for service   (30min) and Okehampton (20min).
#46 (Mon–Sat 10 daily), which runs between Tavistock

INFORMATION AND ACTIVITIES

Tourist information There's useful info on   ⓦ cholwellridingstables.co.uk), near the village of Mary
accommodation, attractions and local history on ⓦ lydford   Tavy, about two miles south of Lydford off the A386, has
.co.uk.   direct access to the moor. An hour's ride costs £22 (no credit
Horseriding Cholwell Farm (☎ 01822 810526,   cards); tuition and all equipment are provided.

ACCOMMODATION AND EATING

Castle Inn EX20 4BH ☎ 01822 820242, ⓦ castle   menus are usually available and bar snacks are around £10.
innlydford.com. Next door to the castle in the centre of the   There's also accommodation, in the form of three spacious
village, this picturesque sixteenth-century pub offers low-   and elegant rooms. Tues–Sat noon–2.30pm & 5.30–
ceilinged, oak-beamed rooms, each one different (one has   9pm, Sun noon–2.30pm. __£115__
a roof terrace), some quite small. The bar has good beers   ★**Lewtrenchard Manor** EX20 4PN ☎ 01566
and a standard pub menu (mains around £10), and there's   783222, ⓦ lewtrenchard.co.uk. Four miles west of
a garden. Kitchen daily noon–3pm & 6–9pm. __£70__   Lydford, this beautifully preserved seventeenth-century
Dartmoor Inn Moorside, EX20 4AY, on the A386   manor was the home of Victorian hymn-writer Sabine
opposite the Lydford turning ☎ 01822 820221,   Baring Gould. Now it's an atmospheric hotel and
ⓦ www.dartmoorinn.com. Classic gastropub, with tables   restaurant that offers immaculately prepared,
in a series of small rooms. Mains are £12–19, set-price   predominantly traditional dishes such as Creedy Carver

---

DARTMOOR'S LETTERBOXES

The pursuit of **letterboxing** – a sort of treasure hunt with a rubber stamp as the prize
– originated on Dartmoor in 1854 when hardy walkers started a tradition of leaving their
calling cards in a jar at **Cranmere Pool** near the head of the West Okement River, then one of
the most inaccessible points on the northern moor. In 1937, a stone "letterbox" was erected
over the spot, and the practice was adopted at other tors. The "letterboxes" gradually
multiplied, and today there are around 4000 of them. Each contains the rubber stamp and
inkpad that are the key elements of this early form of orienteering. The popularity of
letterboxing has much to do with the fact that it needs no organization or set starting point,
though organized walks with a competitive bent also take place occasionally: **tourist offices**
can provide trail leaflets and schedules for forthcoming events (see also ⓦ dartmoorletter
boxing.org and ⓦ letterboxingondartmoor.co.uk).

WALKS FROM MERRIVALE

Merrivale makes a good starting point for several rewarding **hikes**; for instance along the western slopes of the Walkham valley, where the pinnacle of **Vixen Tor** (1050ft; map ref SX542742), a mile southwest of Merrivale's stone rows, crouches inscrutably above the barren moor – from some angles resembling an old woman's head or a humped animal. Access to the privately owned Tor is not possible, though a public footpath runs close by. The walk 1.5 miles northeast of Merrivale to **Great Mis Tor** (1768ft; map ref SX562770) affords more inspiring views, and reveals the distinctive rock basin, **Mistor Pan**, also known as the "Devil's Frying Pan". Check on accessibility, as this lies on the edge of a firing area.

duck and roast loin of venison on fixed-price menus (£21 for two courses or £25 for three at lunch, £49.50 for three courses at dinner). The rooms are suitably grand, overlooking the courtyard or garden. Daily noon–2pm & 7–9pm. **£180**

Lydford Caravan and Camping Park EX20 4BE

📞01822 820497, 🌐lydfordsite.co.uk. Peaceful site, very convenient for the village a few minutes away and the Granite Way. You'll enjoy great views from the tent field, clean and orderly facilities and free wi-fi. There's normally a two-night minimum stay. Closed Nov to mid-March. **£16.90**

Merrivale

The River Walkham crosses the B3357 five miles east of Tavistock at **MERRIVALE**, a hamlet that amounts to little more than the large *Dartmoor Inn*, where you can get basic meals and refreshments. At 1000ft, Merrivale commands views extending – on a very clear day – as far as the Eddystone Lighthouse in Plymouth Sound. The spot's main claim to fame, however, is its proximity to one of Dartmoor's most spectacular prehistoric sites, the **Merrivale Rows**.

Merrivale Rows

The Merrivale Rows are a half-mile west of Merrivale and just a few yards from the B3357 (map ref SX553746); follow signs from the parking area marked out by trees growing out of the wall, east of the *Dartmoor Inn*. Dating from any time between 2500 BC and 750 BC, the double row of upright stones forms a stately procession for 850ft across the bare landscape. Probably connected with ancient burial rites, the rows are known locally as "Potato Market" or "Plague Market" in memory of the time when provisions for plague-stricken Tavistock were deposited here. Halfway along the southern row, a stone circle surrounds a cairn over a cremation pit; blocking stones, *kistvaens* (rough granite box tombs) and hut circles complete the complex.

ARRIVAL AND DEPARTURE   MERRIVALE

By bus Running 3–4 times daily (Mon–Sat), bus #98 connects Merrivale with Tavistock (20min) and, just three miles southeast, Princetown (8min).

Plymouth
and around

SMEATON'S TOWER

5

Plymouth and around

As the largest city in Devon and Cornwall, Plymouth has a very different feel to anywhere else in the region. There could be no greater contrast to the snug villages nearby in the South Hams, or the miles of wilderness in Dartmoor, than the city's urban sprawl or the immensity of Plymouth Sound, with its docks and naval base. Plymouth is an essential component of Devon's seafaring identity, and the city's maritime traditions are most obvious when you're gazing down onto the Sound from historic Plymouth Hoe. While much of modern Plymouth is off-puttingly ugly, the Barbican and Sutton Harbour are as compact and unspoilt as any of the West Country's medieval quarters, and the city's National Marine Aquarium holds one of the country's finest sea-life collections.

Plymouth also serves as a lively base for day-trips. The nearest of the attractions around the city is the wooded Rame promontory across the Sound, where formal gardens give onto a wild coastline at **Mount Edgcumbe**, within easy distance of the best swimming spot hereabouts, Whitsand Bay. Further out lies a ring of elegant country houses, the most dazzling of which is **Saltram House**, an aristocratic pile to the east of the city containing a wealth of work by Robert Adam and Joshua Reynolds. If you find the overstated decor here indigestible, you may get more out of two Tudor mansions north of Plymouth – **Buckland Abbey**, former home of the mariners Drake and Grenville, and **Cotehele**, a rich repository of tapestries, embroideries and sixteenth-century furnishings.

Plymouth

With its historic core intact, a revitalized waterfront area and a handful of absorbing sights, not to mention its supremely panoramic location, **PLYMOUTH** has gone to great lengths to offset the dampening effects of bland architecture and busy roads slicing through its residential and shopping neighbourhoods. Indeed, with your back to the dreary terraces sprawling across the hills, the vista over **Plymouth Sound** – the basin of calm water at the mouth of the combined Plym, Tavy and Tamar estuaries – is indeed glorious, best appreciated from the high grassy expanse of **Plymouth Hoe**, itself largely unchanged since Drake played his famous game of bowls here prior to taking on the Spanish Armada.

The best-preserved remnants of the medieval city lie in a compact area within a short walk of the Hoe, down by **Sutton Harbour** and around the Elizabethan warehouses and inns of the adjacent **Barbican** area, now the focus of the city's nightlife scene. Across from the Barbican, the **National Marine Aquarium** is Plymouth's premier draw, housing a diverse aquatic population in imaginatively re-created watery habitats. But don't confine yourself to this area – at the western end of town, the former naval victualling area (for food and drink provisions), **Royal William Yard**, has been given a smart new facelift, its nineteenth-century buildings now holding restaurants and bars.

Boat trips from the Barbican p.141   **Sir Francis Drake** p.148
Plymouth Gin p.146

NATIONAL MARINE AQUARIUM

Highlights

❶ Plymouth Hoe This historical grassy esplanade offers glorious, occasionally bracing panoramas over Plymouth Sound and the city. **See p.139**

❷ National Marine Aquarium A variety of aquatic environments are imaginatively re-created in one of Europe's top aquariums, right on Sutton Harbour. **See p.141**

❸ Royal William Yard The navy's old victualling depot, dating from the early nineteenth century, has been cleaned up and now provides a smart harbourside locale for some great cafés and restaurants. **See p.142**

❹ Mount Edgcumbe Just a boat ride from the city, this house and its landscaped gardens lie within an expanse of country park, with woodlands and stunning coastal walks all around. **See p.146**

❺ Saltram House This perfectly proportioned mansion east of Plymouth makes a grand setting for paintings by Joshua Reynolds and interiors by Robert Adam. **See p.147**

❻ Cotehele Fascinating Tudor house filled with tapestries, furniture and weaponry in a delightful setting above the River Tamar, where the Cotehele Quay and a water mill provide added interest. **See p.149**

HIGHLIGHTS ARE MARKED ON THE MAP ON P.138

5

Brief history

Plymouth grew from the "littel fishe towne" of Sutton, a site at the mouth of the **River Plym** owned by the monks of **Plympton Priory**. The growing importance of its sheltered deep-water anchorage during the **Hundred Years' War** against France led to the amalgamation of Sutton – freed from monastic rule in 1439 – with other settlements in the estuary, and the town, under its present name, became the first in England to receive a charter by Act of Parliament. Plymouth also prospered as a result of the silting up of the River Plym upstream and the consequent winding-down of the inland ports, making it an important outlet for wool shipments; its

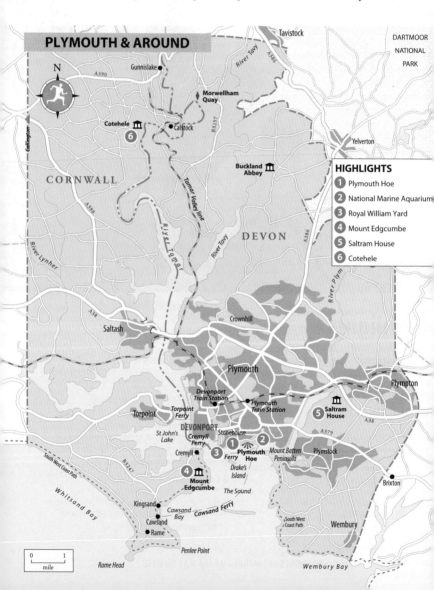

PLYMOUTH & AROUND

N

HIGHLIGHTS
1 Plymouth Hoe
2 National Marine Aquarium
3 Royal William Yard
4 Mount Edgcumbe
5 Saltram House
6 Cotehele

wealth in Tudor times is attested by the grand houses surviving from that era in and around the city.

Alongside its natural attributes, the town owed its leading role as a **naval base** to the fact that it was home to such great mariners as **Hawkins** and **Drake**. The royal fleet was stationed here during the wars against Spain, and it was from here that Drake sailed to defeat the Spanish Armada in 1588. Raleigh and Grenville launched their failed attempts to colonize Virginia from Plymouth, and in 1620 Sutton Harbour was the last embarkation point of the **Pilgrim Fathers** on board the *Mayflower*, whose New Plymouth colony became the nucleus of the English settlement of North America.

After Plymouth sided with the Parliamentarians during the **Civil War**, Charles II prudently commanded the **Royal Citadel** to be built to safeguard against future anti-Royalist eruptions. The construction of the **Royal Naval Dockyard** at the end of the seventeenth century, in what is now the Devonport area, ensured the city's continuing importance. Cook and Darwin both sailed from Plymouth in later eras of discovery, and the town's prestige was further enhanced by the building of the **Royal Albert Bridge** in 1859, spanning the Tamar at Saltash to connect Devon with Cornwall by rail – the last engineering feat of Isambard Kingdom Brunel. Heavy bombing during World War II obliterated Plymouth's Victorian street plan, but the subsequent rebuilding has gone some way to restoring the city centre, while leaving some areas distinctly down-at-heel. Modern-day Plymouth retains its links with the sea: the naval presence is still strong, and the **Devonport dockyards** continue to be a bulwark of the local economy.

Plymouth Hoe

A broad grassy esplanade studded with reminders of the city's great events, **Plymouth Hoe** is a stirring spot to start a tour of the city. Resplendent in fair weather, the Hoe (from the Saxon "high place") can also attract some pretty ferocious winds, making it an unappealing prospect in wintry conditions. The seaward views, however, are stupendous, taking in **Drake's Island** in the centre of the Sound, previously a fortification, then a prison, now in private hands awaiting development. Approaching from the city centre, you'll pass a distinctive tall, white naval cenotaph and smaller monuments to the defeat of the Spanish Armada and to the airmen who defended the city during the wartime blitz, alongside a rather portly statue of Sir Francis Drake gazing grandly out to sea. Appropriately, there's a bowling green back from the brow of the Hoe.

Smeaton's Tower

Plymouth Hoe, PL1 2NZ • Tues–Sun 10am–5pm • £3 • ☎ 01752 304774, ⊛ plymhearts.org/smeatons-tower

In front of the war memorials on the Hoe, the red-and-white-striped **Smeaton's Tower** was originally erected as a lighthouse on the treacherous Eddystone Rocks, fourteen miles out to sea, in 1759. When replaced by a larger beacon in 1882, it was reassembled here, where it now offers the loftiest view over Plymouth Sound from its lantern room, around 72ft high. Living quarters consist of a kitchen, a bedroom with tiny box-beds and a room with the words of Psalm 127 written on the walls: "Except the Lord build the house, they labour in vain that build it."

Tinside Lido

Hoe Rd, PL1 3DE • Late May to late July & early to mid-Sept Mon–Fri noon–6pm (Wed until 7.30pm in good weather), Sat & Sun 10am–6pm; late July to early Sept daily 10am–6pm (Wed until 7.30pm in good weather) • £4.50, under-16s £3.50 • ☎ 01752 261915, ⊛ everyoneactive.com/centre/tinside-lido

Injecting a note of nostalgic glamour to counter Plymouth's more militaristic aspects, **Tinside Lido**, on the seafront below the Hoe, is a rare example of the saltwater lidos that were all the rage in the 1930s. Much work has gone into

5

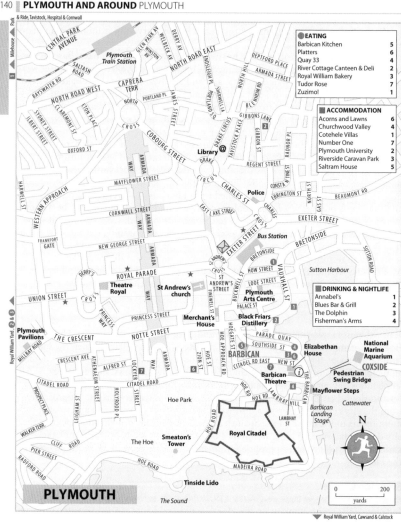

EATING

Barbican Kitchen	5
Platters	6
Quay 33	4
River Cottage Canteen & Deli	2
Royal William Bakery	3
Tudor Rose	7
Zuzimo!	1

■ ACCOMMODATION

Acorns and Lawns	6
Churchwood Valley	4
Cotehele Villas	1
Number One	7
Plymouth University	2
Riverside Caravan Park	3
Saltram House	5

■ DRINKING & NIGHTLIFE

Annabel's	1
Blues Bar & Grill	2
The Dolphin	3
Fisherman's Arms	4

renovating its original Art Deco style, preserving its sleek lines. Even if you don't fancy a dip, it's a great spot for lounging and soaking up the views across Plymouth Sound. Deckchairs are available to rent.

Royal Citadel

East of Plymouth Hoe, PL1 2PD • Tours May–Sept Tues, Thurs & Sun 2.30pm; up to 2hr • £5 • EH • ⓦ english-heritage.org.uk/visit/places /royal-citadel-plymouth; book advance tickets at ⓦ citadel.yapsody.com

On Plymouth's seafront near the Hoe, the **Royal Citadel** is an uncompromising fortress, constructed in 1666 to intimidate the populace of the only town in the South West held by the Parliamentarians during the Civil War; it is still partly in military use. Informative **guided tours** take in the grassy ramparts, seventeenth-century Governor's House and the 1845 Royal Chapel of St Katherine. Cannon buffs will be in their element, and the views over Plymouth and the Sound are superb.

5

BOAT TRIPS FROM THE BARBICAN

The Barbican Landing Stage, by the Mayflower Steps, is the starting point for a range of **boat trips** – mostly in summer, and weather permitting – ranging from one-hour tours around the Sound and Devonport naval dockyard (£8.50) to a four-hour cruise up the Tamar to the Cornish village of **Calstock** (£17.50 return). Get details from Plymouth Boat Trips (☎01752 253153 or ☎07971 208381, ☻plymouthboattrips.co.uk) or at the embarkation point on the Barbican Landing Stage. The same company operates the Cawsand Ferry to **Cawsand beach**, south of Mount Edcumbe on the Rame peninsula (April–Oct; 6 daily; £4), as well as **fishing trips** out to sea: a three-and-a-half-hour mackerel-fishing expedition costs £25, for example.

The **Royal William Yard ferry** to Stonehouse also leaves from here (hourly; single £3; ☻royalwilliamyardharbour.co.uk). If conditions are unsettled, check first at the Barbican Landing Stage or the tourist office (see p.144) for all services.

The Barbican and Sutton Harbour

North of the Citadel, the **Barbican** district is the heart of old Plymouth, with shops and restaurants lining the main Southside Street. The old town's quay at **Sutton Harbour** is still used by Plymouth's sizeable fishing fleet and is the scene of a boisterous early-morning **fish market**. The **Mayflower Steps** here commemorate the sailing of the Pilgrim Fathers in 1620; an inscription lists the names and professions of the 102 Puritans. **Captain Cook**'s voyages to the South Seas, Australia and the Antarctic also set sail from here, as did the nineteenth-century ships that transported thousands of convicts and colonists to Australia.

Elizabethan House

32 New St, PL1 2NA · Closed for renovation · ☎01752 304774, ☻plymhearts.org/elizabethan-house

A former captain's dwelling, the **Elizabethan House** retains most of its original architectural features, including a lovely spiral staircase with what's probably a disused ship's mast for the central newel post and a rope for the rail. The three floors are crammed with fine sixteenth- and seventeenth-century furniture and textiles, including, in the attic bedrooms, a pair of grand beds – an oak-carved canopied tester and a Brittany box-bed with sliding door, decorated with winged cherubs. At the time of writing it was closed for renovation, so call or check online to see when it reopens.

Black Friars Distillery

60 Southside St, PL1 2LQ · Tours hourly: Mon–Sat 10.30am–5.15pm, Sun 11.30am–4.15pm; last tour 45min before closing; 40min · £7; specialist tours £20–40 · ☎01752 665292, ☻plymouthdistillery.com

Plymouth Gin (see box, p.146) has been produced at the **Black Friars Distillery** since 1793. The buildings, which date from 1431, originally housed a monastery and later – following the Dissolution – a prison and a refuge for French Huguenot refugees (the Pilgrim Fathers gathered here before embarking on the *Mayflower* in 1620). The **guided tours** cover the history of gin, the Barbican area and the building itself, ending with a free sampling of the finished product in the wood-beamed *Refectory* cocktail bar. Longer, more in-depth tours that demonstrate the gin-making process are also offered, and gin in its various incarnations is for sale in the on-site shop.

National Marine Aquarium

Rope Walk, Coxside, PL4 0LF · Daily 10am–5pm; last entry 1hr before closing · £14.95, under-16s £10.95 · ☎0844 893 7938, ☻national-aquarium.co.uk

Across the footbridge from the Barbican, the **National Marine Aquarium** is arranged in a series of re-created habitats, with visitors proceeding from the closest to home – the shallows of Plymouth Sound – to the Eddystone Exhibit, before descending to the Atlantic Ocean, the Biozone and lastly the Great Barrier Reef. Among the most popular exhibits are the sharks of various species and sizes that occupy the Atlantic

5

Ocean tank (the country's deepest) along with a variety of rays. Some of the smaller tanks hold equally compelling exhibits – for example, sea horses, anemones, extraordinary frog fish with waving tentacles and stately diamond-like lookdown jacks. The Great Barrier Reef holds Snorkel, a loggerhead turtle washed up on Cornwall's Sennen Cove in 1990. **Talks and presentations** take place throughout the day and **feeding times**, usually accompanied by short talks, are particularly worth catching (the sharks are currently fed Mon, Wed & Thurs at 11am). There are also **daily dives**.

Note that buying a ticket in advance online or from the tourist office will save queuing, and be cheaper; all tickets allow re-entry for one day.

Merchant's House

33 St Andrew's St, PL1 2AX · Closed for renovation · £2.50 · ☎ 01752 304774, ⓦ plymhearts.org/merchants-house

The handsome timber-framed building that now holds the **Merchant's House** dates back to 1608, when it accommodated William Parker, a merchant, privateer and mayor of Plymouth. Preserving the original architecture, the museum displays an engrossing collection of relics from Plymouth's past. Each of the three floors follows a historical theme: the Victorian schoolroom can be quickly passed through, but the photographs documenting the wartime blitz are enlightening, and you can also see the old Barbican ducking stool used to punish alleged miscreants. It was closed for renovation at the time of writing; check online or call to see when the museum is back up and running.

St Andrew's church

Royal Parade, PL1 2AD · Mon–Fri 9am–4pm, Sat 9am–1pm, Sun open for services only · Free · ☎ 01752 661414, ⓦ standrewschurch.org.uk

Plymouth's chief place of worship, **St Andrew's church**, is a reconstruction of the original fifteenth-century building, which was almost completely destroyed by a bomb in 1941. Occupying the role of the Anglican cathedral which Plymouth (strangely) never had, the church has always been at the heart of the city's life: local boy William Bligh, of *Mutiny on the Bounty* fame, was baptized here, and the entrails of the navigator Martin Frobisher are interred within the church, as are those of Admiral Blake, the Parliamentarian who died as his ship entered Plymouth after destroying a Spanish treasure fleet off Tenerife in 1657.

The church's real draw, however, is the set of six **stained-glass windows** installed in 1958 and designed by John Piper (responsible for the more famous stained glass in Coventry Cathedral). Luridly coloured in deep reds and blues, the windows incorporate symbols from the Scriptures and the elements of earth, air, fire and water.

Plymouth Arts Centre

Looe St, PL4 0EB · Tues–Sat 1–8.30pm · Free · ☎ 01752 206114, ⓦ plymouthartscentre.org

You can gain a good insight into the city's contemporary arts scene at **Plymouth Arts Centre**, the venue for a range of exhibitions, films and performances. A compact, relaxed space, it hosts local community projects as well as exhibiting major artists, and the café is conducive to a quiet pause.

Royal William Yard

PL1 3RP · ⓦ royalwilliamyard.com · Bus #34 from Royal Parade every 15min, or hourly waterbus – weather permitting – from The Barbican (see box, p.141)

West of the centre at the mouth of the River Tamar, **Royal William Yard** was originally a victualling – or provisions – depot for the Royal Navy, constructed 1826–35 and named after William IV. It abandoned its original role in 1992 and is now home to wine bars, restaurants, shops, galleries, a yachting marina and fancy apartments. With

5

its waterside views, it's a great place to come at any time, but is especially lively in the evenings. Cantilevered stairs lead to **Devil's Point**, at the southern tip of the promontory, and a **food market** takes place on The Green between 10am and 3pm on the first Sunday of every month.

ARRIVAL AND DEPARTURE   PLYMOUTH

Easily reached by road or rail from Exeter, Plymouth has good public transport connections with all the major centres of the West Country, and the towns and villages of Cornwall's southern coast. Traveline (ⓦ travelinesw.com) has information on all routes.

BY TRAIN
Plymouth's train station is a mile north of the Hoe off Saltash Road. It's the terminus of the Tamar Valley Line (ⓦ greatscenicrailways.com), a hugely attractive route up the river valley as far as Gunnislake.

Destinations Bristol (Mon–Sat 1–2 hourly; 2hr 15min); Calstock (Mon–Sat 8–9 daily, Sun 5 daily; 35min); Exeter (1–3 hourly; 1hr); Gunnislake (Mon–Sat 8–9 daily, Sun 5 daily; 45min); London (Mon–Sat 1–2 hourly; 3–4hr); Penzance (1–2 hourly; 2hr); St Austell (1–2 hourly; 1hr).

BY BUS
Plymouth's bus station on Bretonside, just over St Andrew's Cross from Royal Parade, is more centrally located than the train station.

Destinations Exeter (10–13 daily; 1hr 20min–1hr 50min); Kingsbridge (Mon–Sat hourly; 1hr 15min); Tavistock (Mon–Sat every 15–30min, Sun hourly; 1hr–1hr 15min); Yelverton (Mon–Sat every 20–30min, Sun hourly; 40min).

BY CAR
Parking Drivers may have difficulty in Plymouth as car

parks fill up quickly. You might consider parking at Ivybridge, Liskeard or Gunnislake train stations, from which there are frequent rail and bus services.

Park-and-ride schemes Park-and-ride schemes operate Mon–Sat from Coypool, to the east of the city off the A38 and B3416 near the Marsh Mills roundabout; Milehouse, at the Plymouth Argyle football ground, just north of the train station on the A386 to Tavistock (no Sat service when matches are on); and *The George* hotel, further north on the A386.

Car rental Avis, 20 Commercial Rd, Coxside (ⓣ 0344 544 6090, ⓦ avis.co.uk; closed Sun); Enterprise, 8 The Octagon, off Union St (ⓣ 01752 601000, ⓦ enterprise.co.uk); Thrifty, 15 Sutton Rd, Coxside (ⓣ 01752 207207, ⓦ thrifty.co.uk; closed Sun).

BY TAXI
There are taxi ranks at the train station, as well as at Royal Parade, Raleigh St (off Derry's Cross) and the Barbican. You can also call Taxi First (ⓣ 01752 222222) or Tower Cabs (ⓣ 01752 252525).

GETTING AROUND

By train Plymouth station is connected to Royal Parade by frequent buses, from where it's a brief walk to the Hoe, the Barbican and the bus station.

By bus Useful routes include #21 to Saltram and #34 to Stonehouse, both with stops on Royal Parade. A Dayrider bus pass (from £3.90) allows for a day's unlimited travel on City Buses, available from the bus driver. For schedules, contact Plymouth City Bus (ⓣ 01752 662271, ⓦ plymouthbus.co.uk).

INFORMATION AND ACTIVITIES

Tourist information Plymouth Mayflower, 3–5 The Barbican, off Sutton Harbour (April–Oct Mon–Sat 9am–5pm, Sun 10am–4pm; Nov–March Mon–Fri 9am–5pm, Sat 10am–4pm; ⓣ 01752 306330, ⓦ visitplymouth.co.uk). There's a small interactive exhibition here summarizing the history of the city (£2), and a free accommodation booking service.

Bike rental *Rockets & Rascals*, a café and cycle shop at 7 The Parade, The Barbican (ⓣ 01752 221295, ⓦ rocketsandrascals.com), rents bikes for £15 per day.

ACCOMMODATION

Acorns and Lawns 171 Citadel Rd, PL1 2HU ⓣ 01752 229474, ⓦ acornsandlawnsguesthouse.com. One of a terrace of competitively priced B&Bs close to Plymouth Hoe and the Barbican, offering modern, chintz-free, en-suite rooms, two with views over the Hoe. No one-night bookings May–Sept. **£60**

Churchwood Valley Wembury, PL9 0DZ ⓣ 01752 862382, ⓦ churchwoodvalley.com. On a steep, wooded site just a few minutes from the coast path and the beach at Wembury Bay, this place offers basic cabins and lodges to rent, each equipped with a kitchenette and shower or bath. The price includes bed linen and electricity. There's a shop and laundrette, but limited wi-fi and no mobile signal. Two-night minimum stay. Cabins **£89**, lodges **£118**

5

Cotehele Villas 217 Stuart Rd, Stoke, PL1 5LQ ☎01752 930973, ⓦcotehelevillas.com. This smart and stylish place 10min from the train station is slightly out of the way – a 25min walk to the Hoe and Royal William Yard – but is worth seeking out for its fresh, uncluttered feel. It has three bright, en-suite rooms with wooden flooring, period features and modern bathrooms, to which a light breakfast is brought in the morning. Parking is easy, and there's a two-night minimum stay. **£75**

Number One 1 Windsor Villas, Lockyer St, PL1 2QD ☎01752 212981, ⓦnumberoneplymouth.co.uk. Light, airy and spacious en-suite rooms are offered in this refurbished Regency-style villa on a quiet street close to the Hoe and Barbican, with parking available. French, Spanish and German spoken. No under-8s. **£79**

Plymouth University Gibbon St, PL4 8BT ☎01752 588644. Cheap, clean and functional student accommodation a 10min walk from the Barbican is available during summer holidays (early July to early Sept). All rooms are single and en suite, and guests have access to a gym. Breakfast is provided at an extra cost, but there's a shared kitchen that can be used at any time. Per person **£35**

Riverside Caravan Park Leigham Manor Drive, March Mills, PL6 8LL ☎01752 344122, ⓦriverside caravanpark.com. The nearest campsite to the centre, just north of the Marsh Mills roundabout and close to the Drake's Trail cycle and walking route, this is a convenient spot for reaching the sights by bus or bike. It has quite a rural feel for such an urban site and there are riverside walks and an outdoor pool open in summer. Facilities are very clean. **£15.50**

EATING

Barbican Kitchen 60 Southside St, PL1 2LQ ☎01752 604448, ⓦbarbicankitchen.com. In an attic of the Black Friars Distillery, this relaxed café-bistro offers risottos, burgers and seafood (mostly £8–15) as well as customized steak dishes (£18–28). Lunch and early-evening menus are good value at £9–13 and £10–15 respectively. Have a cocktail in the distillery's atmospheric *Refectory Bar* before or after your meal. Mon–Thurs noon–2.30pm & 6–9.30pm, Fri & Sat noon–2.30pm & 5–10pm.

Platters 12 The Barbican, PL1 2LS ☎01752 227262, ⓦplatters-restaurant.co.uk. Popular, down-to-earth seafood restaurant where diners are surrounded by a plaster relief illustrating the life of a guppy fish. Briskly served, the food, from fish and chips (£7–10) to lemon calamari (£15), is always fresh off the boat, and you can buy it to take away at the next-door counter. Daily 11.30am–9.30pm.

Quay 33 33 Southside St, PL1 2LE ☎01752 229345, ⓦquay33.com. This elegant but informal harbourside spot is ideal for a doorstep sandwich with salad and chips or a plate of pasta for lunch (both around £10), or a more substantial dinner, for which booking is advisable. There's plenty of choice on the menu, usually including Exmouth mussels (£8), mushroom stroganoff (£11), duck leg confit (£14) and a superb fish stew (£17). Sit upstairs for the view. Mon–Sat noon–2.30pm & 5pm–late, Sun noon–3pm & 6–8.30pm.

★**River Cottage Canteen & Deli** Royal William Yard, Stonehouse, PL1 3QQ ☎01752 252702, ⓦriver cottage.net. Celebrity chef Hugh Fearnley-Whittingstall's industrial-looking café and restaurant in the old brewhouse of the ex-naval depot is focused on the organic, local and seasonal. With some tables outside, the place has a pleasant buzz, and the menu ranges from brunches and teas to fried polenta, baked mackerel and venison stew (all £11–15). The deli counter is also worth a linger. Take bus #34 to get here. Mon–Sat 10am–11pm (last orders 9.15pm), Sun 10am–4pm.

Royal William Bakery 3 Bakehouse, Royal William Yard, Stonehouse, PL1 3RP ☎01752 265448. Appetizing aromas of baking bread greet you on arrival at this open-plan bakery and snack-stop in the city's old victualling depot. Serve yourself from a limited but delicious range, from huge croissants to soups, quiches, focaccias and pizzas (all around £7) presented on slabs of wood; sourdough bread, scones and pastries are also on offer. Daily 8.30am–4.30pm.

Tudor Rose 30 New St, PL1 2NA ☎01752 255502, ⓦtudorrosetearoom.co.uk. This traditional English tearoom and restaurant with a secluded garden is tucked up a side-street in the heart of the Barbican. It's renowned for its cream teas with ultra-fresh scones, but you can also come here for breakfast, panini and dishes like seafood platter (£8). Mon–Fri 9am–5pm, Sat & Sun 9am–6pm, closes later July–Sept.

Zuzimo! 153 Vauxhall St, PL4 0DF ☎01752 651300, ⓦzuzimo.co.uk. A good selection of tapas (£4–6) and tagines (£11–15) is served at this convivial place near the bus station. Alternatively, choose from among the eclectic mix of international dishes, such as falafel wrap (£10), crayfish and smoky bacon risotto (£14) and Persian-style hake steak. Various special deals are available during the week. Mon–Sat 5pm–late.

DRINKING AND NIGHTLIFE

Annabel's 86–88 Vauxhall St, PL4 0EY ☎01752 260555, ⓦannabelscabaret.co.uk. Soul, funk, r'n'b, hip-hop, live bands, comedy and sometimes even belly- and burlesque dancers make an appearance at this harbourside club and cabaret bar on three floors, attracting customers of all ages. Usually Fri & Sat 9pm–late.

5

PLYMOUTH GIN

Even without the naval and *Mayflower* connections, the name of Plymouth is familiar worldwide on account of the popularity of **Plymouth Gin**. Soon after **Coates & Co** opened a distillery in the heart of the city's Barbican quarter in 1793, Plymouth Gin began to be exported all over the world. **Royal Navy ships** took the spirit on board before setting sail and, in the 1930s, it became the most widely distributed gin in the world. It owes its flavour to its "magnificent seven botanicals" and soft Dartmoor water, and comes in varying strengths, ranging from 100 percent proof (57 percent ABV) – the version that was supplied to the Navy, who mixed it with Angostura bitters to make pink gin, or "pinkers" (said to be capable of curing everything from indigestion to depression) – to the less daunting 41.2 percent ABV version. The milder version has a richer, more citrusy flavour than London gins, containing less juniper and other bitter botanicals, and makes a pretty perfect **dry martini** or **G&T**. Mixed with cranberry juice, pink grapefruit juice and sloe gin, it also makes a very acceptable Arkansas Breeze. The **Black Friars Distillery** (see p.141) gives the lowdown on the history of gin and the distilling process.

Blues Bar & Grill 8 The Parade, Sutton Harbour, PL1 2JL ☎ 01752 257345, ⊛ bluesbarandgrill.co.uk. Live blues music is played here Tues–Thurs, more mainstream sounds Fri & Sat, and acoustic acts on Sun, all of which you can enjoy while munching on burgers and sipping on drinks. Daily noon–late.

★ **The Dolphin** 14 The Barbican, PL1 2LS ☎ 01752 660876. Unpretentious, old-time fishermen's pub, full of personality, with Tribute and Bass beers straight from the barrel and a mixed clientele. Local artist Beryl Cook set some of her works here (her customary table was on the left, just in from the door). Mon–Sat 10am–11pm, Sun noon–11pm.

Fisherman's Arms 1 Lambhay St, PL1 2NN ☎ 01752 268243, ⊛ fishermansarms.co.uk. Hidden in a side-street next to the Hoe and just up from the harbour, this free house – describing itself as a "country pub" – is worth winkling out for its relaxed vibe, superior pub grub and real ales. The Sunday roasts are especially popular. Mon–Thurs & Sun 11am–midnight, Fri & Sat 11am–1am; kitchen Mon–Sat noon–3pm & 6–9pm, Sun noon–8pm.

ENTERTAINMENT

Barbican Theatre Castle St ☎ 01752 267131, ⊛ barbicantheatre.co.uk. Next to the tourist office off Sutton Harbour, you can see experimental theatre and dance performances here, as well as occasional comedy, jazz and world music.

Plymouth Pavilions Millbay Rd ☎ 0845 146 1460, ⊛ plymouthpavilions.com. The major regional venue for pop, rock, classical and comedy.

Theatre Royal Royal Parade ☎ 01752 267222, ⊛ theatreroyal.com. Mainstream plays, opera, ballet and musicals are staged throughout the year. Also contains the Drum, a more intimate venue showing new and experimental drama.

DIRECTORY

Hospital Derriford Hospital, Derriford Rd, Crownhill, PL6 8DH (☎ 01752 202082), four miles north of the centre, has a 24hr Emergency Department, and there's a Minor Injuries Unit closer to the centre at Cumberland Centre, Damerel Close, Devonport, PL1 4JZ (☎ 01752 434390).

Police Charles Cross, PL4 8HG ☎ 101, ⊛ devon-cornwall .police.uk.

Mount Edgcumbe

Cremyll, Torpoint, PL10 1HZ • **House and Earl's Garden** April–Sept Mon–Thurs & Sun 11am–4.30pm • House £7.20, Earl's Garden £2.50 • Garden tours £1.50; ask at entrance for details • **Country park** Unrestricted access • Free • ☎ 01752 822236, ⊛ mountedgcumbe.gov.uk.

Situated on the Cornish side of Plymouth Sound, **Mount Edgcumbe** is a winning combination of stately home, landscaped gardens and acres of parkland, with access to coastal paths. Though the **house** is a reconstruction of the Tudor original that was gutted by incendiary bombs in 1941, the predominant note inside is eighteenth century, with displays of paintings including works by Joshua Reynolds; there are also sixteenth-century tapestries and items of Plymouth porcelain. Adjacent to the house is

5

the **Earl's Garden**, a formal ensemble of colourful terraces and rare trees, and below it extends the **country park**, which includes immaculate French, Italian and English gardens – the first two a blaze of flowerbeds adorned with classical statuary, the last an acre of sweeping lawn shaded by exotic trees – plus American and New Zealand sections. Also here is the **Amphitheatre** – a series of ponds in a valley garden overlooking Plymouth Sound. Some of the thousand-odd species and varieties of camellias cultivated in the grounds can be seen from January.

The **park** covers the whole eastern side of the **Rame peninsula**, which juts into the estuary to the southwest of Plymouth. A memorable way of taking it all in is by doing the six-mile **circular hike** that follows the coast path from the ferry stop at Cremyll to the village of Kingsand, then heading inland via lanes and paths past Maker church, before reaching the north side of the peninsula where you continue near the water's edge back to the ferry.

ARRIVAL AND DEPARTURE   **MOUNT EDGCUMBE**

By ferry The best way to reach Mount Edgcumbe is on the Cremyll Ferry (£1.50; ⓦcremyll-ferry.co.uk), every 30min until around 9pm (Oct–March 6.45pm), from Admiral's Hard, a small mooring in the Stonehouse district of the city. To reach Admiral's Hard, take the Royal William Yard ferry from the Barbican (see box, p.141), or bus #34 every 30min

from Royal Parade.

By car By car from Plymouth, you'll have to use the Torpoint chain ferry from Devonport (well signposted) to Torpoint (every 10–15min; free from Devonport, £1.50 from Torpoint) then drive around the peninsula, but it's a fairly lengthy route.

Saltram House

Plympton, PL7 1UH • **House** Daily: March–Oct 11am–4.30pm; Nov–Feb 11am–3.30pm • March–Oct £10.70, Nov–Feb £7.50 (includes garden); NT • **Garden** Daily: March–Oct 10am–5pm; Nov–Feb 10am–4pm; last admission 45min before closing • £5.50; NT • **Park** Daily dawn–dusk • Free • Parking £3 • ☎ 01752 333500, ⓦnationaltrust.org.uk/saltram

Three miles east of Plymouth, just south of the A38, the grand, white, eighteenth-century **Saltram House** is Devon's largest country house, and a veritable cornucopia for fans of Neoclassical exuberance. Even non-fans will be seduced by its individual features, not to mention its magnificent grounds.

The original Tudor building received its dramatic Georgian makeover at the hands of the **Parker family**, local bigwigs who numbered **Joshua Reynolds** among their acquaintances. Born nearby in Plympton and a master at the local grammar school, Reynolds was a regular guest at the hunting, shooting and gambling parties held here, and left several works scattered around the house, including fourteen portraits of the family. Saltram's showpiece, however, is the **double-cube Saloon** designed by Robert Adam, supposed to be the perfect embodiment of a classically proportioned room of the era. A fussy but exquisitely furnished room dripping with gilt and plaster, it's an eye-popping sight, set off by a huge Axminster carpet especially woven in 1770. This and other Saltram rooms featured in the 1995 film of *Sense and Sensibility*, in which the house served as Norland Park.

Other high points include works by the eighteenth-century Swiss portraitist **Angelica Kauffman** – one a likeness of her friend and mentor Reynolds – in the staircase hall, where you'll also see George Stubbs' *The Fall of Titan*. The first floor is rich in chinoiserie – wallpaper, mirror paintings and Chinese Chippendale. In the **Great Kitchen**, where the chopping block has been so worn down it resembles a saddle, the scale of entertaining can be judged by the hundreds of items of copperware on display, alongside such curiosities as glass cockroach-catchers, which would be filled with beer to entice the offenders.

Saltram's **landscaped park** provides a breather from this riot of interior design, with garden follies and lovely riverside walks, though it's partially marred by the proximity of the road.

5

ARRIVAL AND DEPARTURE

SALTRAM HOUSE

By bus You can reach Saltram on buses from Plymouth's Royal Parade – most conveniently the #21 (every 10–15min), which stops at Sainsbury's in Marsh Mills, from where it's a pleasant 20min riverside walk.

ACCOMMODATION

St Elizabeth's Hotel Longbrook St, Plympton St Maurice, PL7 1NJ ☎ 01752 344840, ⓦ stelizabeths .co.uk. Six miles east of the centre of Plymouth (off the A38), this luxurious Georgian manor house surrounded by landscaped grounds has elegant rooms with contemporary bathrooms. The main downside is that it is regularly used for wedding receptions at weekends. __£109__

Buckland Abbey

Yelverton, PL20 6EY • Mid-Feb to Oct daily 11am–5pm; Nov Sat & Sun 11.30am–3.30pm; early Dec to late Dec daily 11.30am–3.30pm; last admission 1hr before closing • House & grounds £11; NT • ☎ 01822 853607, ⓦ nationaltrust.org.uk/buckland-abbey

Eight miles north of Plymouth via the A386, **Buckland Abbey** stands right on the edge of Dartmoor, close to the River Tavy. In the thirteenth century, this was the most westerly of England's **Cistercian abbeys**, and was converted after its dissolution into a house by the privateer Richard Grenville (a cousin of Walter Raleigh), from whom **Francis Drake** acquired the estate in 1581. Though it remained Drake's home until his death, the house – a stone Tudor construction with an ungainly central tower – reveals few traces of his residence, as he spent most of his "retirement" years plundering on the Spanish Main. There are, however, numerous maps, portraits and mementos of his buccaneering exploits on show, most famous of which is **Drake's Drum**, said to beat a supernatural warning of impending danger to the country. In the oak-panelled **Great Hall**, dated 1576 but previously the nave of the abbey, you can see a frieze of holly and box interspersed with allegorical scenes, musicians and Sheela-na-gigs (women in less than decorous poses), and there's fine ornamental plasterwork on the ceiling.

The star of Buckland Abbey, however, has nothing to do with Drake or the Elizabethans: a newly restored self-portrait by **Rembrandt** – a painting that was only

---

SIR FRANCIS DRAKE

Born around 1540 near Tavistock (see p.129), **Francis Drake** began his seafaring career at the age of 13, working in the domestic coastal trade before taking part in the first English **slaving expeditions** between Africa and the West Indies, led by his Plymouth kinsman John Hawkins. Later Drake was active in the secret war against Spain, raiding and looting merchant ships in actions unofficially sanctioned by Elizabeth I. In 1572 he became the first Englishman to sight the Pacific, and soon afterwards, on board the *Golden Hind*, was the first one to circumnavigate the world, for which he received a knighthood on his return in 1580.

The following year Drake was made **mayor of Plymouth**, settling in Buckland Abbey, but he was back in action before long – in 1587 he "singed the king of Spain's beard" by entering Cadiz harbour and destroying 33 vessels that were to have formed part of Philip II's Spanish Armada. When the replacement invasion fleet appeared in the English Channel in 1588, Drake – along with Raleigh, Hawkins and Frobisher – played a leading role in wrecking it. The legend that he took his time in finishing a game of bowls on the Hoe before setting sail is probably due to the fact that he was conversant with the tides and could gauge the time. Finally, in 1596 Drake left with Hawkins for a raid on **Panama**, a venture that cost the lives of both captains.

Though Drake has come to personify the Elizabethan Age's swashbuckling expansionism and patriotism, England's naval triumphs were as much the result of **John Hawkins**' humbler work in building a new generation of warships as they were of the skill and bravery of the new ships' captains. Drake was simply the most flamboyant of a generation of reckless and brilliant mariners who broke the Spanish hegemony on the high seas, so laying the foundations for England's later imperialist pursuits.

5

definitively ascribed to the artist and revealed to the public in 2014. Check its whereabouts if you are particularly interested in seeing this, as it spends a lot of time on tour.

ARRIVAL AND DEPARTURE BUCKLAND ABBEY

By bus From Plymouth's Royal Parade, take #1 or #X1 to Yelverton, then change to the #55 minibus (Mon–Sat).
By train You can take a Tamar Valley Line train to Gunnislake or Calstock stations, from where you can get a

bus or walk the last stretch.
By ferry There's a summer ferry service from Plymouth to Calstock (see p.141).

Cotehele

St Dominick, near Calstock, PL12 6TA • **House** Early March to Dec daily 11am–4pm • £10 (includes garden & mill); NT • **Garden** Daily dawn–dusk • £6.50 (includes mill); NT • **Mill** Early March to Sept daily 11am–5pm; Oct daily 11am–4.30pm • £6.50 (includes garden); NT • **Estate** Daily dawn–dusk • Free • Parking £3 • ☎ 01579 351346, ⓦ nationaltrust.org.uk/cotehele

Nestled in the wooded Tamar valley, ten miles northwest of Plymouth, **Cotehele House** is one of the best-preserved and least-altered medieval houses in the country. Built largely between 1485 and 1539, it remained in the **Edgcumbe family** for six hundred years, though their residence at Mount Edgcumbe (see p.146) from the end of the seventeenth century meant that Cotehele remained mostly unmodified, preserving its tranquil Tudor character. Exhibits – chiefly a fascinating collection of needlework, tapestries, weaponry and vigorously carved seventeenth-century furniture – are arranged in an interlinked group of buildings around three courtyards. It's best to visit on a bright day, if you can, as there's no electricity indoors – a contributing factor in the preservation of the textiles.

Each room displays something that grabs the eye. The fine arch-braced **Hall**, with its bare lime-ash floor, has a rare set of folding, mid-eighteenth-century chairs, still with their original leather, while the **Old Dining Room**, hung with Flemish tapestries, leads to the chapel in which you can see the earliest domestic clock in England, dating from 1485 and still in its original position. Upstairs are rooms hung with Jacobean floral crewelwork, stumpwork, gros point and Victorian patchwork. Don't miss the grenade-like Victorian glass fire-extinguishers on the lower landing and, on the upper, the carved Welsh bed-head from 1532, decorated with a hunting and hawking frieze, and a scaly angel expelling Adam and Eve from the Garden of Eden.

The **grounds** are densely wooded and full of surprises. A free shuttle bus or a 500m steep, downhill walk brings you down to **Cotehele Quay** on the Tamar, where there's a restored 1899 sailing barge. The same bus shuttles to **Cotehele Mill** (ⓦnationaltrust.org .uk/cotehele-mill), a working water mill with workshops displaying tools belonging to blacksmiths, carpenters and other craftsmen. It's a flat, fifteen-minute walk through woods between the quay and the mill.

ARRIVAL AND TOURS COTEHELE

By train The Tamar Valley Line runs from Plymouth to Calstock (Mon–Sat 8–9 daily; Sun 5 daily; 35min), from where it's a delightful 1.5-mile riverside stroll.
By bus Service #79A (Mon–Sat) runs to Calstock, 1.5 miles from Cotehele; catch it at Tavistock (#1 or #X1 from Plymouth's train station or Royal Parade), Callington (#12 from Plymouth train station or Royal Parade) or Gunnislake

(on the Tamar Valley Line).
By road To get here by car or bike, you have to negotiate narrow but well-signposted lanes leading off the A390.
Boat tours Plymouth Boat Trips (☎ 01752 253153, ⓦplymouthboattrips.co.uk; £15 return) operates river cruises from Plymouth to Cotehele Quay April–Oct.

Exmoor

TARR STEPS

6

Exmoor

A high, bare plateau sliced by wooded combes and splashing streams, Exmoor boasts tracts of wilderness every bit as forbidding as the South West's other National Park (Dartmoor). It is smaller though, with greater expanses of farmland breaking up the bare moorland. Its long seaboard, from which mists and rainstorms can descend with alarming speed, adds to its distinctive character, affording compelling views over the Bristol Channel. Most of the park is privately owned – including about ten percent held by the National Trust – but there's good access along an extensive network of footpaths and bridleways. Apart from at the moor's famed beauty spots, you'll generally find complete isolation here – with the exception of occasional groups of hikers, photographers, and hunting and shooting folk, who may take up much of the region's accommodation at weekends.

Travellers based at **Dulverton**, on the moor's southern edge and site of the park's main information office, or at **Exford**, at the centre of the moor, will be well placed for **inland Exmoor**'s choicest areas, including such celebrated beauty spots as **Tarr Steps** and the moor's highest point of **Dunkery Beacon**. The hamlets of **Winsford** and **Simonsbath** are smaller, less-frequented starting points for excursions. **Map references** (following Ordnance Survey grid refs) are provided in the Guide for a couple of the main off-road destinations.

The **Exmoor coast**, which includes the tallest sea cliffs in England and Wales, is more easily accessible and can consequently get quite busy, not least around the well-preserved medieval village of **Dunster**, on the northeastern edge of the moor. Nearby **Minehead** marks one end of the **South West Coast Path**, which offers the best way to get acquainted with Exmoor's seaboard. West of here, a string of coastal villages, including **Porlock**, **Oare**, **Lynmouth** and **Lynton**, makes up part of what's known as "**Doone Country**", an indeterminate area that includes some of Exmoor's wildest tracts, and which is now inextricably tied to R.D. Blackmore's tale, *Lorna Doone*. Following its publication in 1869, this romantic melodrama based on local outlaw clans in the seventeenth century quickly established itself in Exmoor's mythology, and is still frequently recalled today.

ARRIVAL AND GETTING AROUND

By train The nearest mainline stations for Exmoor are Taunton and Tiverton. Barnstaple, on a branch line from Exeter, could be a useful access point for western Exmoor. Steam and diesel trains of the private West Somerset Railway (☎ 01643 704996, Ⓦ west-somerset-railway.co.uk) run from late March to October plus some dates in February and December between Bishops Lydeard (with frequent bus connections to nearby Taunton) and Minehead.

DUNSTER CASTLE

Highlights

❶ Riding on the moor Discover the moor on horseback for a memorable and exhilarating experience; stables cater to all ability levels. See p.155

❷ Coastwalking The hogback cliffs at Exmoor's northern edge can be tough going, but the ever-changing views more than compensate. See p.162

❸ Dunster Castle Looming above Dunster's tapering main street, its romantic castle is filled with sixteenth- and seventeenth-century furnishings and works of art. **See p.164**

❹ The cliff railway at Lynton and Lynmouth A steep cliff separates these scenic sister towns, but the water-powered funicular railway makes an effortless and ecofriendly way to move between the two. **See p.169**

❺ Valley of Rocks West of Lynton, this area is encircled by crags and inhabited by feral goats – a great spot for a wander. **See p.170**

❻ Watersmeet Two rivers merge at this renowned beauty spot, from where paths radiate in every direction. There's also a tearoom on hand for refreshments. **See p.172**

HIGHLIGHTS ARE MARKED ON THE MAP ON P.154

EXMOOR

N

West Somerset Railway

Taunton

West Somerset Railway

Dunster

3 Dunster Castle

Minehead

Hurlstone Point

Selworthy

Luccombe

Porlock

Porlock Weir

Wheddon Cross

Brendon Hills

Brompton Regis

Wimbleball Lake

B3224

B3190

B3227

A396

River Exe

Winsford

The Punchbowl

Caratacus Stone

Winsford Hill

Dulverton

Exebridge

B3222

B3222

Dunkery Beacon

Exford

B3224

B3223

EXMOOR NATIONAL PARK

SOMERSET

River Barle

Withypool

Tarr Steps

River Barle

Two Moors Way

Culbone Church

TOLL ROAD

A39

County Gate

Oare

Malmsmead

East Lyn River

B3223

Watersmeet 6

Lynmouth 4

Lynton 5

Barbrook

West Lyn River

Hoar Oak Water

Pinkworthy Pond

EXMOOR FOREST

Simonsbath

Cow Castle

River Exe

B3358

North Molton

DEVON

South Molton

B3227

B3226

A361

A361

Foreland Point

Valley of Rocks 2

Heddon's Mouth

River Heddon

Parracombe

Blackmoor Gate

A39

B3358

Challacombe

A399

Hangman Point

Wild Pear Beach

Great Hangman

Little Hangman

Combe Martin

Ilfracombe

A3123

B3229

South West Coast Path

A3592

Barnstaple

River Taw

A377

A36

A39

B3230

B3232

B3233

HIGHLIGHTS

1 Riding on the moor
2 Coastwalking
3 Dunster Castle
4 The cliff railway at Lynton and Lynmouth
5 Valley of Rocks

0   2
miles

HIKING, BIKING AND OTHER ACTIVITIES ON EXMOOR

Walking is the most popular activity on the moor. You can pick up good, simple route cards of "Golden Walks" (£1) from visitor centres, while the National Park Authority (see p.156) has a full programme of **guided walks** aimed at all abilities. Stables on the moor provide opportunities for **horseriding**, while adventure seekers will find a range of other organized activities available, such as **wildlife safaris**. Despite some serious-looking hills, there are also **cycling** possibilities.

GUIDED WALKS

The National Park Authority and other local organizations have also put together a programme of **guided walks**, graded according to distance, speed and duration and costing £3–5 per person depending on the length of the walk. For more details, and for specific schedules, contact any of the Exmoor visitor centres or see the *Exmoor* free newspaper or the website ⓦexmoor-nationalpark.gov.uk.

CYCLING

Exmoor has some of the UK's best mountain-biking terrain, though you need to stick to bridleways, byways and recognized bike routes. See ⓦexmoor-nationalpark.gov.uk for information on the 60-mile on-road **Exmoor Cycle Route**. Exmoor Adventures at Porlock Weir (ⓣ07976 208279, ⓦexmooradventures.co.uk) rents out bikes and provides a delivery and collection service, plus luggage transfer.

HORSERIDING

The number of stables on Exmoor has declined in recent years (we've listed one of the main ones on p.157), but those still operating are experienced and professional, offering individual and group instruction and escorted field hacks onto the moor. Prices are usually £25–35/hour.

LAND ROVER TOURS

One of the best ways to enjoy the full range of outdoor activities on Exmoor is as part of an organized group. Park visitor centres can supply a full list, but the most appealing options include the partly off-road **Land Rover tours** to view Exmoor ponies, red deer and other wildlife. The main operators are: Barl Valley Safaris (ⓣ07977 571494, ⓦexmoorwildlifesafaris .co.uk), which leave from Dulverton, Exford, Wheddon Cross and Dunster; Exmoor Safari (ⓣ01643 831229, ⓦexmoorsafari.co.uk), which start their tours at the *White Horse Inn* in Exford, where you can also book; Red Stag Safari (ⓣ01643 841831, ⓦredstagsafari.co.uk), leaving daily from various departure points; and Discovery Safaris based in Porlock (ⓣ01643 863444, ⓦdiscoverysafaris.com), leaving from outside Porlock's tourist office (or any other prearranged spot). Excursions generally last 2–3 hours and cost £25–35 per person.

BY BUS

The bus network in the Exmoor area is sparse, with some lines running in summer only, all services reduced in the winter months, and few buses running on Sundays at any time. The most useful year-round routes are #198 between Minehead, Dunster, Wheddon Cross, Exford, Winsford and Dulverton (currently operated by Somerset County Council), and #398 between Tiverton, Exebridge and Dulverton (Dartline Coaches; ⓣ01392 872900, ⓦdartline -coaches.co.uk). Route #28 connects Dunster and Minehead with Taunton (Buses of Somerset; ⓣ01823 211180, ⓦfirstgroup.com/somerset). Along the coast, bus #10 runs between Minehead and Porlock Weir (Buses of Somerset), while the very limited, summer-only #300 "Exmoor Coastlink" is split between the route from Minehead to Selworthy, Porlock and Lynmouth (Quantock Heritage; ⓣ01984 624906, ⓦquantockheritage.com) and one between Lynmouth, Lynton, Combe Martin and Ilfracombe (Filers; ⓣ01271 863819, ⓦfilers.co.uk). See ⓦtravelinesw.com for all schedules. You can flag down a bus anywhere within the National Park, providing it is safe for it to stop. There's also a useful on-demand service, Moor Rover, which allows you to book a ride between 8am and 8pm to and from anywhere on the moor at least one day before travel (lines open Mon–Fri 9am–5pm; ⓣ01643 709701, ⓦatwest.org.uk).

BY CAR

Running parallel to the sea, the A39 links Exmoor's coastal towns and villages; inland, some of the best walking country can be accessed from the B3223, B3224 and B3358 roads, traversing the moor in a roughly east–west direction. Drivers should beware of sheep and ponies straying over the roads; after dark you may even come across sheep lying down on the tarmac.

INFORMATION

Tourist information Information on the whole moor is available at National Park visitor centres at Dulverton (see opposite), Dunster (see p.166) and Lynmouth (see p.170), and on the website ⓦ exmoor-nationalpark.gov.uk.
Maps The 1:25,000 Ordnance Survey *Explorer* map OL9 is of most use to walkers on Exmoor.

Inland Exmoor

6

Watered by 325 miles of river and crossed by some 600 miles of public footpaths and bridleways, the upland plateau of inland Exmoor reveals rich swathes of colour and an amazing diversity of wildlife. There are four obvious bases for excursions: **Dulverton**, in the southeast and connected by bus to Taunton, Tiverton and Minehead, makes a good starting point for visiting the seventeen-span medieval bridge at **Tarr Steps**, about five miles to the northwest; you could also reach the spot from **Winsford** via a circular walk which takes in the prehistoric Wambarrows on the summit of Winsford Hill and the ancient Caratacus Stone; **Exford** is convenient for the heart of the moor; and **Simonsbath**, further west, makes an excellent starting point for exploring the Barle valley and **Exmoor Forest**, though it has few accommodation options.

Bear in mind that over seventy percent of the National Park is privately owned and that access is theoretically restricted to **public rights of way** and designated Access Land; both are shown on Ordnance Survey maps. Special permission should certainly be sought before doing anything like camping or fishing.

Dulverton

On the banks of the River Barle on Exmoor's southern edge, **DULVERTON** is one of the main gateways to the moor, and, as home to the National Park Authority's headquarters, makes a useful port of call before further explorations. The town has a quietly purposeful air and is centred around Fore Street and High Street, which run parallel from the river towards the hilltop parish church. Fore Street has most of the shops and pubs, plus the post office, a bank with a cash machine and the Exmoor Visitor Centre.

Guildhall Heritage Centre

7–9 Fore St, TA22 9EX • Mon–Fri 10.30am–4.30pm, Sat 10.30am–1pm, Sun 2–4.30pm • Free • ☏ 07969 243887, ⓦ dulvertonheritagecentre.org.uk

Behind the visitor centre, and accessible from it, the **Guildhall Heritage Centre** has an absorbing collection of items to do with Dulverton and Exmoor, including a film showing aspects of moor management, a gallery of local art and a reconstructed

USEFUL EXMOOR WEBSITES

ⓦ **enhs.org.uk** Website of the Exmoor Natural History Society, with an overview of wildlife and habitats, and a calendar of events.

ⓦ **everythingexmoor.org.uk** Wide-ranging, community-based directory and encyclopedia, including events and local news.

ⓦ **exmoor-accommodation.co.uk** Efficient directory of all types of accommodation, including campsites and self-catering options.

ⓦ **exmoor-nationalpark.gov.uk** Official National Park site – comprehensive and reliable. The **Active Exmoor** pages are a useful resource for outdoor pursuits on Exmoor, from coasteering and mountain biking to fly-fishing.

ⓦ **visit-exmoor.co.uk** Official tourist website, useful for news about attractions, events, food, drink and accommodation.

ⓦ **whatsonexmoor.com** General information on the moor, with links for attractions, accommodation, eating out, transport, activities and weather forecasts.

Victorian kitchen and bedroom. An archive room holds an extensive photographic collection, tapes of oral history and films, and there are regular Exmoor-themed exhibitions.

ARRIVAL AND DEPARTURE

DULVERTON

By bus Services #198 and #398, with a stop on the High Street. Note that there are no Sunday services.
Destinations Dunster (Mon–Sat 2–3 daily; 35min–1hr);

Exford (Mon–Fri 2 daily, Sat 1 daily; 30min); Minehead (Mon–Sat 2–3 daily; 1hr–1hr 15min); Winsford (Mon–Fri 1–2 daily, Sat 2 daily; 20min).

6

INFORMATION AND ACTIVITIES

Exmoor Visitor Centre 7–9 Fore St (daily: April–Oct 10am–5pm; Nov–March Mon–Wed, Fri & Sat 10am–2.30pm; 01398 323841, exmoor-nationalpark.gov.uk). Itineraries for local waymarked circular walks taking in Tarr Steps are available here.

Horseriding West Anstey Farm, 2 miles west of Dulverton, offers moorland rides for all abilities (01398 341354, westansteyridingstables.co.uk). Prices are £25 per hour, or £45 for 2 hours.

ACCOMMODATION

Lion Hotel Bank Square, TA22 9BU 01398 324437, lionhoteldulverton.com. This central inn should suit anyone hankering for beams and four-posters, though it could do with a refurb; room 9 and the slightly larger number 11 have a nice prospect over the street. Two-night minimum stay at weekends. **£88**

Old Sawmills Pixton Weir, TA22 9NB 01398 323363, theoldsawmills.co.uk. Located 2 miles southeast of town off the A396, this rural B&B offers luxurious, tastefully furnished rooms with large, modern bathrooms and a garden on the banks of the Exe. Breakfasts at a time of your choosing include home-produced eggs and preserves. **£95**

★ Town Mills High St, TA22 9HB 01398 323124, townmillsdulverton.co.uk. A burbling stream runs through the garden of this elegant Georgian mill house. The good-sized, pine-furnished bedrooms include a suite with

garden access, and all are spotlessly clean. No under-12s. **£95**

CAMPING

Exe Valley Caravan Site Bridgetown, TA22 9JR 01643 851432, exevalleycamping.co.uk. This clean and spacious adults-only site sits by the Exe, some 5 miles north of Dulverton on the A396. Pitches are a generous size, and the *Badgers Holt* pub is just a 2min walk away. Closed mid-Oct to mid-March. **£20**

Northcombe Farm Hollam Lane, TA22 9JH 01398 323602, northcombecampingbarns.co.uk. These two YHA-affiliated camping barns 1 mile north of Dulverton (take the road left of the *Rock House Inn*) are available for individuals Sun–Thurs, and for groups at weekends. There are partitioned sleeping areas, cooking facilities and hot showers, but no bed linen and no wi-fi. Per person **£9.50**

EATING

Mortimer's 13 High St, TA22 9HB 01398 323850. Serves hot and cold snacks, including a range of rarebits made with ham, brie and local cider (£5–8), and "moo burgers" (£8). There's a choice of cream teas, and a courtyard garden. Mon, Tues & Thurs–Sun 9.30am–5pm.

Tongdam 26 High St, TA22 9DJ 01398 323397, tongdamthai.co.uk. Take a break from English country cooking at this Thai outpost, where dishes such as coconut red curry go for around £11.50 and marinated duck and stir-fried black tiger prawns are £16.50. European dishes such as chicken stroganoff and lasagne are sold at lunchtime for £7–10, and there's a takeaway service. You

can eat alfresco on the small patio in warm weather. Daily noon–3pm & 6–10pm.

★ Woods 4 Bank Square, TA22 9BU 01398 324007, woodsdulverton.co.uk. With wooden tables, chairs and floor, and a scattering of antlers, boots and riding whips, this gastropub offers a mix of traditional country classics and quality cuisine, with such dishes as grilled sole, slow-roast belly of pork and guineafowl (around £16 in the evening). Baguettes are sold at lunchtime and the bar (open till 11pm) dispenses West Country draught ales. There's also a small garden. Kitchen daily noon–2pm & 6–9.30pm (Sun from 7pm).

Tarr Steps

Nestling in the deeply wooded Barle valley, seven miles northwest of Dulverton, **Tarr Steps** is one of Exmoor's most popular beauty spots. The ancient woodland around the much-photographed **clapper bridge** largely consists of sessile oak – formerly coppiced for tanbark and charcoal production – and a sprinkling of beech, but you'll also see a mix of

6

A WALK FROM TARR STEPS

Tarr Steps makes a great destination on foot from Dulverton or Winsford (see opposite), and you can extend the walk by combining it with this exhilarating five-mile circular walk, which takes in Winsford Hill, near Winsford. It's not particularly challenging, and should take under four hours.

Follow the riverside path upstream from Tarr Steps, turning right about half a mile along Watery Lane, a rocky track that deteriorates into a muddy lane near Knaplock Farm. Stay on the track for three-quarters of a mile until you reach a cattle-grid on open moorland. Turn left here, cross a small stream and climb up **Winsford Hill** for 360-degree moorland views and to explore the **Wambarrows** (see opposite), a group of prehistoric burial mounds. If you want a refreshment stop, you can descend the hill on the other side to Winsford.

A quarter of a mile due east of the barrows, following any of the broad grassy tracks, you'll come to an abrupt, 200ft descent to **the Punchbowl**, a bracken-grown, amphitheatre-like depression. Keep on the east side of the B3223 which runs up Winsford Hill, following it south for a mile to the Spire Cross road junction where you should look out for the nearby **Caratacus Stone** (see opposite), partly hidden among the gorse. Continue south on the east side of the road, cross it after about a mile, and pass over the cattle grid on the Tarr Steps road, from where a footpath takes you west another one and a half miles back to the river crossing.

downy birch, ash, hazel, wych elm and field maple, often with a thick covering of lichen. The hazel coppice forms an important habitat for dormice, and you may spot red deer on the riverbanks. Birds breeding hereabouts include redstarts, wood warblers and pied flycatchers, and you may also catch sight of dippers, grey wagtails and kingfishers.

There's a choice of **walks** to embark upon from Tarr Steps: either to Winsford Hill (see box above); upstream as far as Withypool (4 miles); or downstream to Dulverton. To walk here from Dulverton, simply follow the riverside track upstream; by road it's a left turn from Fore Street and another left five miles along the B3223.

The bridge

Positioned next to a ford, the ancient **clapper bridge** at Tarr Steps is said to be the finest of its type in Britain, constructed of huge gritstone slabs that are fixed onto piers by their own weight – which can be as much as two tonnes. Over 180ft long with seventeen spans, it's normally about 3ft above water level – much lower than when originally built due to the river silting up. **Floodwaters** now frequently cover the bridge, often causing damage – all but one of the slabs were washed away on the night of the 1952 Lynmouth deluge (see p.169). When this happens, however, the stones seldom travel far, and they are now numbered for easy repair; they're also protected by upstream cables that help to arrest flood debris charging down the river.

The bridge's age has been much disputed, with some claiming prehistoric origins – apparently backed up by the Bronze Age tracks found converging on the crossing, and its name, derived from the Celtic *tochar*, meaning causeway. But there's no proof of a construction before this one, the earliest record of which is from Tudor times. Most now agree that, like the clapper bridges on Dartmoor, it is likely to be **medieval**.

According to legend, the bridge was made by the **devil** as a place to sunbathe. The Prince of Darkness vowed to destroy any creature attempting to cross, and when a parson was sent to confront him he was met by a stream of profanities. When the abuse was returned in good measure, the devil was so impressed he allowed free use of the bridge.

ACCOMMODATION AND EATING   TARR STEPS

Tarr Farm TA22 9QA ☎ 01643 851507, ⟲ tarrfarm .co.uk. Above the Steps, this sixteenth-century riverside inn, restaurant and tearoom provides an excellent spot to contemplate the river, and also serves light lunches and teas, as well as evening meals (mains mostly £12–17), for which booking is advised. Upmarket accommodation is available in modern, fully equipped rooms. No under-10s. Kitchen daily noon–3pm & 6.30–9.30pm. **£150**

Winsford

Five miles north of Dulverton, signposted a mile west of the A396, **WINSFORD** lays good claim to being the moor's prettiest village. A scattering of thatched cottages ranged around a sleepy green, Winsford is watered by a confluence of streams and rivers – one of them the Exe – giving it no fewer than seven bridges. Dominated, as it has been for centuries, by the rambling, thatched *Royal Oak* inn, the village was the childhood home of the great trades union leader and Labour politician Ernest Bevin (1881–1951) – his birthplace, bearing a plaque, is across from the post office and shops.

6

Winsford Hill

Once you've admired Winsford's charms the best plan is to abandon them in favour of the surrounding countryside. The obvious walking excursion from the village is the climb up **Winsford Hill**, a heather moor cut through by the B3223 and reached on foot by taking the Tarr Steps road past the *Royal Oak*; turn off onto the moorland where the road turns sharp left after about three-quarters of a mile. About the same distance further west, the hill's round 1400ft summit is invisible until you are almost there, but your efforts are repaid by views as far as Dartmoor, and you can clamber around three Bronze Age burial mounds known as the **Wambarrows**.

The Caractacus Stone

A mile southeast of the summit of Winsford Hill, near the turning for Tarr Steps, the B3223 runs close to the **Caractacus Stone**, an inscribed monolith thought to date from between 450 and 650 and referred to in medieval documents as the Longstone. It is not immediately easy to spot among the vegetation, though you'll probably pick out the roof of the comical "bus shelter" canopy built over it in 1906. The damaged inscription on the greyish-green, 4ft-high monolith reads "Carataci Nepos" – that is, "kinsman of Caracatus", the last great Celtic chieftain who was defeated by the Romans in 46 AD. It's an easy walk from here to Tarr Steps (see box opposite).

ARRIVAL AND DEPARTURE WINSFORD

By bus #198 is Winsford's only service, stopping at Dulverton (Mon–Sat 2 daily; 20min); Dunster (Mon–Sat 1–2 daily; 45min); Exford (Mon–Sat 1–2 daily; 12min); and Minehead (Mon–Sat 1–2 daily; 55min).

ACCOMMODATION AND EATING

Halse Farm TA24 7JL ☏ 01643 851259, ⓦ halsefarm.co.uk. Not very well sheltered and with fairly basic but clean facilities, this smallish campsite a mile southwest of Winsford (reached from Halse Lane) is right on the edge of the moor and convenient for walkers. It's a steep uphill walk from Winsford. Closed Nov to mid-March. **£16**

EXMOOR WILDLIFE

The establishment of the National Park here has done much to protect Exmoor's diverse **wildlife**, from otters and buzzards to fritillary butterflies and dormice. The management of the coastal heath that makes up most of the terrain has allowed certain species of bird to thrive, while the gorse covering large parts has especially favoured the diminutive blue Dartford warbler and the orange-breasted stonechat. Most celebrated of the moor's mammals, though, are **Exmoor ponies**, a unique native species closely related to prehistoric horses. Commonly found in the treeless heartland of the moor around Exmoor Forest, Winsford Hill or Withypool Common, these short and stocky animals are not difficult to spot, though fewer than twelve hundred are registered, and of these only about 170 are free-living on the moor. You probably won't get close to them, but if you do, don't try to feed them (bearing in mind that their teeth are sharp enough to tear up the tough moorland plants). Much more elusive is the **red deer**, England's largest native wild animal, of which Exmoor supports the country's only wild population (about 3000).

6

HUNTING ON EXMOOR

For many, outdoor sports on Exmoor means **hunting** and **shooting**, practices which have been at the heart of local communities for centuries. Shooting mainly takes place between September and January, but hunting can go on all year – though mostly in winter. The hunts play a central social role in the area, too, since most hunts have full calendars of events. The voice of local hunt supporters is loud and clear: the **Countryside Alliance** (ⓦcountryside-alliance.org) pro-hunting lobby has strong support, and "Fight Prejudice" stickers are evident everywhere.

In contrast, the true number of local **opponents** to the hunt will never be known, as few want to risk taking a stand in Exmoor's close-knit communities. Alongside the cruelty argument, the two reasons most often cited for opposing hunting are the damage caused to farmland and gardens by dogs and horses, and the chaos created by the hunt followers – many of them city-folk – whose cross-country manoeuvrings can block up roads and show scant regard for either countryside or property. The National Trust's ban on stag-hunting on its land has added more fuel to the debate, since it has virtually ended the practice in many places.

What cannot be denied is the heavy dependence of Exmoor's economy – more than most other hunting areas in Britain – on the sport, not least in such villages as Exford, home to the kennels and stables of the Devon and Somerset Staghounds. If you're looking for a quiet time in these parts, you're best off keeping your views on the matter to yourself, since feelings run high.

You can find out about hunt meets in the local press or on the website ⓦdevonandsomersetstaghounds.net, alongside news of the local hunt's puppy and horse shows, point-to-point races and other summer events. For the case against hunting, see the website of the **League Against Cruel Sports** (ⓦleague.org.uk).

Royal Oak TA24 7JE ☏01643 851455, ⓦroyaloakexmoor.co.uk. This ancient inn offers Exmoor ales, snacks and full restaurant meals (most mains £10–15) for which booking is advisable in the evening. The accommodation is plush, with spacious – but slightly more expensive – four-poster rooms also available. Front-facing rooms get some bar noise at night. Kitchen daily noon–2pm & 6–8.30pm £100

Exford

At an ancient crossing point on the River Exe, **EXFORD**, four miles northwest of Winsford, preserves an insular air, its sedate cottages and post office ranged around a tidy village green. A part of the Royal Forest of Exmoor from Saxon times until the early thirteenth century, Exford prospered as a junction for packhorse trains carrying wool and cloth. During the nineteenth century, it grew as a **sporting centre** and local life today is still intimately involved with the **hunt**, particularly during the long season (early August to late April).

Dunkery Beacon

Exford is a popular starting point for the hike to **Dunkery Beacon**, Exmoor's highest point at 1704ft (map ref SS891415). A four-mile hike to the northeast, the route is clearly marked along a track that starts from Combe Lane, just past the post office (turn right at the end of the playing fields). The bridleway here eventually becomes a rough track, which winds slowly round to the summit of the hill – a steady uphill trudge. A substantial cairn sits at the top, from where a majestic vista unfolds, with lonely moorland all about and South Wales often visible; there's also easy access by car, with a road passing close to the summit.

ARRIVAL AND DEPARTURE   EXFORD

By bus Service #198 stops by the green and connects Exford with Dulverton (Mon–Sat 2 daily; 35min); Dunster (Mon–Sat 1–2 daily; 30min); Minehead (Mon–Sat 1–2 daily; 40min); and Winsford (Mon–Sat 2 daily; 15min).

ACCOMMODATION

Crown Hotel TA24 7PP ☎01643 831554, ⓦ crown hotelexmoor.co.uk. With friendly staff and a log fire in the lounge, this elegantly old-fashioned, rather upper-crust inn has quiet and spacious rooms, some of which have views over the green. It's worth negotiating for the best rate. **£155**

Exmoor Lodge Chapel St, TA24 7PY ☎01643 831694, ⓦ exmoor-lodge.co.uk. Small, plain and friendly B&B backing onto the village green, with most rooms en suite and lots of local information on hand. There's a garden where you can have a cup of tea, and packed lunches can be arranged. Discount for two nights or more. **£90**

Exmoor White Horse Inn TA24 7PY ☎01643 831229, ⓦ exmoor-whitehorse.co.uk. Impressively timbered and creeper-covered, this coaching inn right by the bridge is traditional in style, and a favourite with the huntin' and shootin' crowd (there's a stables right next door). Rooms are mostly spacious and with views, and some have four-posters. **£180**

YHA Exford Exe Mead, TA24 7PU ☎01643 831229, ⓦ yha.org.uk/hostel/exford. Exmoor's main hostel occupies a gabled Victorian house near the centre of the village on the banks of the Exe. Most rooms have four to six beds, and there's a kitchen and restaurant. Camping is also possible, and bell tents are available to rent between June and October. The hostel is owned and operated by the *White Horse*, just across the bridge, where you should go to check in. Dorms **£20**, doubles **£50**, camping/person **£10**

CAMPING

★ **Westermill Farm** Edgcott, TA24 7NJ ☎01643 831238, ⓦ westermill.co.uk. Two and a half miles northwest of Exford, this tranquil campsite on the banks of the Exe has waymarked walks over the surrounding five-hundred-acre farm, plus a small, seasonal shop selling local meat. Facilities are modern and clean, and self-catering cottages are also available. Per person **£6.50**

EATING

Crown Hotel TA24 7PP ☎01643 831554, ⓦ crown hotelexmoor.co.uk. You can choose between the hotel's bar menu or the restaurant, where modern and classic local favourites are on the menu offered, from an outstanding beef and ale pie (£14) to loin and shoulder of lamb (£18). The garden makes this a nice spot for afternoon tea, too, and the convivial bar serves Exmoor ales. Bar kitchen daily noon–2.30pm & 6.30–9.30pm; restaurant daily 7–9pm.

Exmoor White Horse Inn TA24 7PY ☎01643 831229, ⓦ exmoor-whitehorse.co.uk. Basic bar meals popular with walkers, hunters and hostellers are offered here, including the ever-popular venison pie (£10.50). It also serves afternoon teas, as well as some 150 malt whiskies, and there are tables outside by the river. The more sedate restaurant offers such dishes as "typsy pheasant" and salmon steak, and has a set-price three-course dinner for £45. Bar kitchen daily noon–9pm; restaurant daily 7–9pm.

Exmoor Forest

At the centre of the National Park, **Exmoor Forest** is the barest part of the moor, scarcely populated except for roaming sheep and a few red deer – the word "forest" denotes simply that it was formerly a hunting reserve. It's also one of the moor's wettest and boggiest zones – walkers should carry waterproofs whatever the conditions.

Simonsbath

In the middle of the area, and just over five miles west of Exford on the B3223, **SIMONSBATH** (pronounced "Simmonsbath") consists of little more than a couple of hotels, a pottery and a sawmill at a crossroads between Lynton, Barnstaple and Minehead on the River Barle. The chief appeal is its location, ideal for hiking excursions to some of Exmoor's remotest nooks (see box below).

WALKS FROM SIMONSBATH

Paths radiate out across epic moorland from **Simonsbath** (park visitor centres can supply walking itineraries). One easy waymarked route starts from opposite the *Exmoor Forest Inn* and leads through Birchcleave Wood, running more or less parallel to the Barle for a couple of miles to **Cow Castle**, site of an old hillfort, and four miles further to Withypool.

In the opposite direction, you can follow the River Barle upstream from Simonsbath for about four miles to the dark, still waters of **Pinkworthy Pond** – keep a lookout for red deer drinking here in summer. The B3358 passes within a couple of miles of the lake.

6

Brief history

Simonsbath was home to Midlands ironmaster John Knight, who purchased Exmoor Forest in 1819 and, by introducing tenant farmers, building roads and importing sheep, brought systematic agriculture to an area that had never before produced any income. The Knight family also built a wall round their land – parts of which can still be seen – as well as the intriguing dam at Pinkworthy (pronounced "Pinkery") Pond, part of a scheme to harness the headwaters of the River Barle, though its exact function has never been explained.

ACCOMMODATION AND EATING   **SIMONSBATH**

Boevey's TA24 7SH ☎01643 831622. In a converted barn next to Simonsbath House, this handy tearoom and restaurant can refuel hungry hikers with everything from baguettes to salads and pasta dishes – all around £6–10. The giant toasted teacakes are also worth sampling. Daily 10.30am–5pm, till 4.30pm in winter; closed Dec to mid-Feb.

Exmoor Forest Inn TA24 7SH ☎01643 831341, ⓦexmoorforestinn.co.uk. This friendly village inn has plain but clean, comfortable and good-sized rooms with decent bathrooms and moorland views, and there are also a couple of free camping pitches (but with no dedicated facilities; call ahead). The bar serves a good selection of local ales, while the restaurant offers pasties and burgers made with locally sourced lamb or beef (£10–15) and dishes such as braised lamb shank (£15). There are some tables outside. Kitchen daily noon–2.30pm & 6–9pm. **£75**

★**Simonsbath House** TA24 7SH ☎01643 831259, ⓦsimonsbathhouse.co.uk. Former home of the Knight family and now a cosy, upmarket bolt hole offering plush, spacious rooms with glorious moorland views. Self-catering cottages in a converted 350-year-old barn are also available. In the refined, romantic setting of the restaurant, set-price three-course dinners cost £24.50 (otherwise you'll pay £14–20 for main courses a la carte). The menu is local and seasonal, and might include rack of lamb, guinea fowl and venison, followed by some fabulous puddings. Booking required. Daily 7–8.30pm. **£120**

The Exmoor coast

The thirty-odd miles between Minehead and Combe Martin form the highest section of **coastline** in England and Wales, with cliffs rising to 1043ft. With gentle upper slopes but steep ridges, the hills make for some fairly strenuous hiking if you're following the **South West Coast Path**, and long stretches of woodland add variety to an already diverse landscape. The narrow, stony strips of beach here don't compare with those in other parts of the West Country, but the **sea** is still the central attraction, with an ever-changing shoreline and constant views across the Bristol Channel to the Welsh coast.

Minehead itself has little to warrant an extended stay, but its good transport links make it a useful gateway to northeastern Exmoor and the coast west. It's also conveniently close to **Dunster**, three miles southeast, an unmissable stop for its flamboyant castle. West of Minehead, **Selworthy** scores highly on the charm scale, but **Porlock** has a stronger flavour of the moor and makes a great base for excursions to places such as **Culbone Church**, deeply hidden in woods to the west.

THE SOUTH WEST COAST PATH

Minehead is one end of Britain's longest National Trail, the **South West Coast Path**, which tracks the coastline along Somerset and Devon's northern seaboard, round Cornwall, back into Devon, and on to Dorset, where it finishes close to Poole Harbour – a total of 630 miles, all waymarked with the National Trail acorn symbol. As little of it is level for very long, it ranks among the country's toughest trails, and some degree of **planning** is essential for any long hike: **accommodation** should be booked ahead and you should bone up on local transport schedules, and ask at tourist offices or look online for **luggage-transfer operators** (see p.34). See Contexts (p.349) for publications, including those of the **South West Coast Path Association** (☎01752 896237, ⓦswcp.org.uk).

West of Foreland Point, there are more terrific walks to be enjoyed from **Lynton** and **Lynmouth** – sibling villages which occupy a niche in the cliff wall with woodland and moorland on all sides. Two of the easiest excursions present Exmoor's most contrasting faces: west to the dramatic **Valley of Rocks** and inland to **Watersmeet**, where two of the moor's rivers merge. Nine miles west, **Combe Martin** marks the edge of the moor and the end of one of the toughest sections of the coastal walk.

Minehead

MINEHEAD's role as the most traditional of seaside resorts sits comfortably alongside the vestiges of its genteel Victorian identity. The latter is most evident in the well-to-do area of **Higher Town** on the slopes of North Hill, holding some of the oldest houses and offering splendid views across the Bristol Channel. Steep lanes link the quarter with **Quay Town**, the harbour area and the starting point of the South West Coast Path (see box opposite), the spot marked by huge sculptured hands holding a map. Science fiction fans might like to know that author **Arthur C. Clarke** was born opposite the public gardens at 13 Blenheim Road. The visitor centre housed within the *Beach Hotel* on the seafront incorporates a small **museum** (April–Oct Tues–Sat 10am–4pm, Sun 10am–4pm; free), giving an overview of the town's history and showing regular exhibitions.

ARRIVAL AND DEPARTURE   MINEHEAD

By train Minehead is a terminus for the private and seasonal West Somerset Railway (☎01643 704996, ⓦwest-somerset-railway.co.uk), which runs to Bishops Lydeard (near Taunton; late March to Oct 4–6 daily; 1hr 20min). The station is located across from the seafront off the Esplanade.

By bus Most bus stops are on or around the Parade, at the southern end of the Avenue.

Destinations Dulverton (Mon–Sat 3–4 daily; 55min–1hr 20min); Dunster (Mon–Sat 2–3 hourly, Sun hourly; 10min); Lynmouth (mid-July to early Sept Mon–Fri 2 daily; 1hr 5min); Porlock (Mon–Sat 6–8 daily; 15min); Taunton (Mon–Sat every 30min, Sun hourly; 1hr 15min).

INFORMATION

Tourist information *Beach Hotel*, The Avenue, opposite the West Somerset Railway station (Easter–Oct Tues–Sat, also Mon in summer school hols 10am–4pm, Sun 11am–4pm; Nov–Easter Sat & Sun noon–3pm; ☎01643 702624, ⓦvisitminehead.org).

ACCOMMODATION

★**Baytree** 29 Blenheim Rd, TA24 5PZ ☎01643 703374, ⓦbaytreebandbminehead.co.uk. This Victorian B&B facing public gardens offers spacious rooms with private bathrooms, including a family suite. There's parking available, a discount for staying more than one night, and a two-night minimum stay at weekends in July & Aug. No under-10s. No credit cards. Closed Nov–March. **£70**

Old Ship Aground Quay St, TA24 5UL ☎01643 703516, ⓦtheoldshipaground.com. A useful choice for the coast path, this pub has clean and comfy rooms, some huge with harbour views and balconies, though bathrooms are on the small side. **£79**

YHA Minehead Alcombe Combe, TA24 6EW ☎0845 371 9033, ⓦyha.org.uk/hostel/minehead. Midway between Minehead and Dunster, this hostel is beautifully situated in a secluded combe on the edge of Exmoor. Most rooms have four beds, and the garden has bell tents to rent, each with a double bed and sleeping up to five (£89). There's a kitchen and restaurant. Buses from Minehead, Dunster and Taunton stop a mile away at Alcombe. Dorms **£13**, doubles **£49**

CAMPING

★**Minehead Camping and Caravanning** North Hill, TA24 5LB ☎01643 704138, ⓦcampingandcaravanning club.co.uk. High above town on the edge of Exmoor, this clean, well-equipped and panoramic site is well placed for hiking excursions. A footpath leads to town in 20–30min. Turn up Martlet Road off Blenheim Road to get here. Closed Oct to mid-April. **£19**

EATING

Fausto's 4 Holloway St, TA24 5NP ☎01643 706372, ⓦfaustos.co.uk. With its low prices and friendly service, there's usually a crowd at this Italian restaurant which offers everything from pizzas (from £5) to pastas and risottos (£8–10), as well as seafood and such dishes as *pollo e miele* (chicken with honey and mustard sauce, £13).

Occasional live music. Mon–Sat 6.30–8.45pm, Tues–Sat noon–3pm & 6.30–8.45pm.

★**Toucan Café** 3 The Parade, TA24 5NL ☏ 01643 706101, ⓦ toucanwholefoods.co.uk. In three individually themed rooms above a wholefoods store, you can tuck into falafels, bean burgers and quesadillas (around £6), or just a Fairtrade tea or organic coffee. Also offered are healthy smoothies with names like Flu Fighter and Kale Kick, as well as organic wines and ciders. Mon–Sat: March–Oct 8.30am–5.30pm; Nov–Feb 8.30am–4.30pm.

6

Dunster

Preserving its medieval lines, **DUNSTER** reached its peak of wealth as an important cloth centre in the sixteenth century. Its broad High Street is dominated at one end by the towers and turrets of **Dunster Castle**, while at the other end the octagonal **Yarn Market**, dating from 1609, recalls its wool-making heyday, its conical roof supported by hefty oak beams. Just north of the village, the hilltop folly of **Conygar Tower** (1776) is worth the brief ascent for excellent views.

Dunster Castle

Entrance at the top of High St for those arriving on foot, but the entrance for drivers is off the A39, TA24 6SL • **Castle** Early March to Oct daily 11am–5pm; early to mid-Dec Sat & Sun 11am–3pm • **Grounds** Daily: early March to Oct 10am–5pm; Nov, Dec & Feb to early March 11am–4pm • House, grounds and Dunster Water Mill £10.30; grounds and mill only £7.20; discounts for passengers on some services of West Somerset Railway (see p.152); NT • ☏ 01643 821314, ⓦ nationaltrust.org.uk/dunster-castle

Dunster's chief attraction, **Dunster Castle**, occupies what was once a Saxon frontier post against the Celts. The fortification was rebuilt by the Normans, but almost nothing of these earlier constructions survived the thorough pasting it received during the Civil War. The building owes its present castellated appearance to a radical remodelling in around 1870, though this itself was little more than a veneer on what remains essentially a stately home, and is predominantly Jacobean within. The formidable battlemented **gatehouse** has a greater claim to authenticity, dating back to 1420 and flanked by a pair of squat towers that formed part of the Norman construction.

The interior

The highlights of the castle's **interior** are all sixteenth or seventeenth century – most prominently the grand oak and elm **staircase**, magnificently carved with hunting scenes (a recurrent theme throughout the house). Alongside the stags' heads are numerous portraits of the **Luttrells** – the family that owned the property from 1376 until the National Trust took over in the 1970s – including one that shows the sixteenth-century John Luttrell wading Triton-like across the Firth of Forth. "Thrown" chairs of ash, pearwood and oak are displayed in the Inner Hall, while rare **gilt-leather hangings** in the upstairs Gallery vividly depict the story of Antony and Cleopatra.

The gardens

The castle grounds include sheltered, terraced **gardens** from where paths lead down to the River Avill. Oranges and lemons have been growing here since 1700, including what is claimed to be Britain's oldest lemon tree, and there's a renowned collection of strawberry trees. Mimosas and palms contribute a subtropical ambience.

Dunster Water Mill

Mill Lane, off West St, TA24 6SW • Early March to Oct daily 10am–5pm • Entry fee included with Dunster Castle tickets; NT • ☏ 01643 821759, ⓦ nationaltrust.org.uk/dunster-working-watermill

You can absorb the mysteries of milling and view a small array of agricultural tools at the village's 300-year-old **Dunster Water Mill**. It's still used commercially for milling the grain that goes to make the flour and muesli sold in the shop and riverside café, though milling does not take place every day – it's usually the first Wednesday of the month

CLOCKWISE FROM TOP LYNMOUTH HARBOUR (P.168); VALLEY OF ROCKS (P.170); WATERSMEET (P.172) >

between April and September, plus some additional days (call for dates). A path along the Avill from the mill soon brings you to **Gallox Bridge**, a quaint packhorse bridge from the eighteenth century, surrounded by woods.

St George's

Church St, TR24 6RY • Daily 9am–5pm • Free • ☎ 01643 821812, ⓦ stgeorgesdunster.co.uk

Originally a Norman priory church, **St George's** has a fine, bossed wagon-roof and a magnificent rood screen from about 1500, said to be the widest in the country, with its own miniature fan-vaulting. Among the tombs of various Luttrells, look out for a group at the top of the south aisle that includes an alabaster floor slab inscribed to Elizabeth Luttrell, from 1493. The sloping chest here is thought to be unique, and was probably used by the Benedictine monks of the priory in the fifteenth century.

Behind St George's church, the sixteenth-century **Tithe Barn** has been renovated as a community centre. The **Priory Garden** next to it makes a pleasant spot for a picnic, and opposite you can peek into the circular **dovecote** that may date back to the fourteenth century. It was maintained by the monks – the only people allowed to keep doves, as they damaged farmers' crops.

ARRIVAL AND DEPARTURE
DUNSTER

By train Dunster is a stop on the West Somerset Railway (see p.152), but the station is a mile north of the village, near Dunster Beach.

By bus Dunster is connected to Minehead, Dulverton, Exford and Winsford by bus #198 (from High St); the much more frequent #28 also goes to Minehead, though the stop is on the A39, a 5–10min walk from Dunster.

Destinations Dulverton (Mon–Sat 3–4 daily; 40min–1hr 10min); Exford (Mon–Sat 2 daily; 30min); Minehead (Mon–Sat 2–3 hourly, Sun hourly; 10min); Taunton (Mon–Sat every 30min, Sun hourly; 1hr 10min); Winsford (Mon–Sat 2 daily; 45min).

INFORMATION

Exmoor Visitor Centre Dunster Steep (Easter–Oct daily 10am–5pm; Nov & late Feb to Easter Sat & Sun 10am–2pm; ☎ 01643 821835, ⓦ exmoor-nationalpark .gov.uk). Has general information on Exmoor and details of guided walks on the moor and a self-guided walk around the village. The centre also houses a free exhibition with background on the local wool and timber industries, and an overview of local conservation issues. Information on Dunster is also on hand at ⓦ visitdunster.co.uk and ⓦ discoverdunster.info.

ACCOMMODATION AND EATING

Luttrell Arms 25–31 High St, TA24 6SG ☎ 01643 821555, ⓦ luttrellarms.co.uk. Right by the Yarn Market, this traditional and atmospheric fifteenth-century inn has open fires and beamed rooms, some with four-posters and some with views towards the castle. Standard rooms are more ordinary, mostly smaller and lacking views. Guests and others can eat in the bar, which has a garden, or in the more refined *Psalters* restaurant, where robust English classics are served (mains around £17). Bar kitchen daily 11.30am–9.30pm; Psalters noon–2pm & 6–9.30pm. **£105**

★ **Old Priory** Priory Green, TA24 6RY ☎ 01643 821540, ⓦ theoldpriory-dunster.co.uk. Parts of this B&B behind St George's church date back to the twelfth century – otherwise it's mainly from 1660, when it was converted into a farmhouse. It's all immaculately preserved, with a gigantic fireplace in the guests' sitting room. One of the three bedrooms has an arched roof and a four-poster, and there are no TVs anywhere. Breakfast is largely local and organic, and the pretty garden has its own door to the next-door church garden. No credit cards. **£100**

Reeves 20 High St, TA24 6SG ☎ 01643 821414, ⓦ reevesrestaurantdunster.co.uk. This cosy restaurant with a low beamed ceiling and Moroccan-style touches in the decor serves some of the best food on Exmoor. Expertly prepared and beautifully presented, dishes include sea-bass fillet and roast rump of lamb (around £18), as well as a superb Sunday lunch. The garden is good for an aperitif or lunch in summer when hours are extended. Tues–Sat 7–9pm, Sun noon–2pm; summer school hols also Thurs–Sat noon–2pm.

Selworthy

Five miles west of Dunster, the National Trust-owned village of **SELWORTHY** is a sequestered nook of thatched, custard-coloured cottages and a church with a notable barrel-vaulted ceiling. It's a charming ensemble, if a trifle over-manicured. There are walking routes all around this area, including a signposted path leading through thick woods to **Selworthy Beacon** (1012ft; map ref SS918479).

ARRIVAL AND DEPARTURE	SELWORTHY

By bus Services #10 (not Sun) and #300 (mid-July to early Sept Mon–Fri 2 daily) connect Selworthy, Porlock and | Minehead; #300 also runs to Lynmouth.

ACCOMMODATION

6

Selworthy Farm TA24 8TL ☎01643 862577, ⓦselworthyfarm-exmoor.co.uk. You'll find true tranquillity at this elegant farmhouse from 1870, offering | two traditionally furnished rooms with private or en-suite facilities. It's below the church, on the way into the village. No under-16s; no credit cards. **£80**

Porlock and around

A couple of miles further west of Selworthy, cupped on three sides by Exmoor's hogbacked hills, the thatch-and-cob houses and dripping charm of **PORLOCK** are a magnet for tourists. Some are also drawn by the village's literary links: according to Coleridge's own less than reliable testimony, it was a "person on business from Porlock" who broke the opium trance in which he was composing *Kubla Khan*, while the High Street's ancient *Ship Inn* prides itself on featuring prominently in the Exmoor romance *Lorna Doone*. In real life, the inn sheltered the poet Robert Southey, who staggered in rain-soaked from a ramble on Exmoor and wrote a sonnet here ("Porlock, thy verdant vale so fair to sight...").

Dovery Manor Museum

Doverhay, TA24 8QB • May–Sept Mon–Fri 10am–5pm, Sat 10am–4.30pm • Free • ⓦ doverymanormuseum.org.uk

Housed in a charismatic but cramped fifteenth-century cottage, Porlock's **Dovery Manor Museum** displays traditional domestic and agricultural tools of Exmoor – including a mantrap – together with some material on the local wildlife and a few photos and portraits. The most impressive items, however, are the building's beautiful mullioned window and the huge fireplace on the ground floor. There's a herb garden, and the volunteer staff are knowledgeable.

Porlock Weir

You can escape Porlock's high-season crush by heading two miles west along reclaimed marshland to the tiny harbour of **PORLOCK WEIR**, whose sleepy air gives little inkling of its former role as a hard-working port trafficking with Wales. With its thatched cottages and stony foreshore, it's a peaceful, atmospheric spot, giving onto a bay that enjoys the mildest climate on Exmoor. A room at one end of the toilets in the car park houses the **Natural History Centre** (May–Sept Wed & Thurs 1.30–5pm; free; ⓦenhs.org.uk), focusing on the local fauna and flora.

An easy two-mile stroll west from Porlock Weir along the coast path brings you through woods once inhabited by charcoal burners to **Culbone Church** (always open), claimed to be the country's smallest church.

ARRIVAL AND DEPARTURE	PORLOCK AND AROUND

By bus Service #10 connects Porlock and Porlock Weir with Selworthy and Minehead (not Sun), and the summer-only #300 runs between Porlock, Selworthy, Minehead and Lynmouth on weekdays. | **Destinations** Lynmouth (mid-July to early Sept Mon–Fri 2 daily; 50min); Minehead (Mon–Sat 8–10 daily; 15min); Porlock Weir (Mon–Sat 6 daily; 10min); Selworthy (Mon–Sat 8–10 daily; 6min).

INFORMATION

Tourist office West End, High St (Easter–Oct Mon–Fri 10am–12.30pm & 2–5pm, Sat 10am–5pm; Nov–Easter | Tues–Fri 10am–12.30pm, Sat 10am–1pm; ☎01643 863150, ⓦporlock.co.uk). Free wi-fi available.

6

ACCOMMODATION

The Gables Doverhay, TA24 8LG ☎01643 863432, ⓦthegablesporlock.co.uk. Classically thatched seventeenth-century cottage near Porlock's museum, with four restful rooms (including a family suite) that all have bathrooms. There's a small garden, and abundant breakfasts include yoghurt, fruit and smoked salmon. Two-night stays are preferred at weekends, and self-catering accommodation is also available. **£70**

★**Glen Lodge** Hawkcombe, TA24 8LN ☎01643 863371, ⓦglenlodge.net. You'll find perfect seclusion plus comfort and character at this beautifully furnished

Victorian country B&B a few minutes from the High Street (up Parson's Street). There is a well-stocked library, healthy breakfasts, distant sea views from the rooms, a hot tub in the garden and direct access to the moor. **£100**

Sparkhayes Farm Sparkhayes Lane, TA24 8NE ☎01643 862470, ⓦsparkhayes.co.uk. This small campsite is little more than a couple of fields with basic washing facilities and a laundry room, but it's clean, friendly and extremely handy for the village, signposted off the High St. Closed Jan. Per person **£8**

EATING

The Bottom Ship Porlock Weir, TA24 8PB ☎01643 863288, ⓦshipinnporlockweir.co.uk. Crab sandwiches (£6.50) are a lunchtime favourite at this oak-beamed pub, with its outdoor tables by the harbour. A range of other bar food including cream teas is also available, and a good choice of beers and ciders. Kitchen daily noon–2.45pm & 6–8.45pm.

★**The Café** Porlock Weir, TA24 8PB ☎01643 863300, ⓦthecafeporlockweir.co.uk. Despite its unassuming name, this small and elegant restaurant with sea views offers quality cuisine using local ingredients (main courses

around £16). You can settle down to a lunch of sandwiches or grilled oysters, or a delicious afternoon tea. Rooms are available too (from £99). Noon–8pm (last orders): March–Oct Wed–Sun; Nov–Feb Fri–Sun.

The Ship Inn High St, TA24 8QD ☎01643 862507, ⓦshipinnporlock.co.uk. Exmoor ales, table skittles and occasional folk evenings are the draws at this thirteenth-century tavern, known locally as the "Top Ship". The food's not bad either, with sandwiches and hot dishes (mostly £9–14), and there's a garden. Kitchen daily noon–2.30pm & 6.30–8.30pm.

Doone Country

West of Porlock, the A39 climbs over 1300ft in less than three miles – cyclists and drivers might prefer either of the gentler and more scenic **toll roads** to the direct uphill trawl, one from Porlock (a right turn off the A39, after the *Ship Inn*; cars £2.50, bikes £1), the other narrower and much rougher-going from Porlock Weir (cars £2, bikes free), both passing mainly through woods.

Oare and around

Just before the Devon–Somerset border at **County Gate** – marked by little more than a café and car park – the minuscule church in the hamlet of **OARE** is famous in the annals of Lorna Doonery as being the scene of the heroine's marriage, and where she was shot. R.D. Blackmore's grandfather was rector here, and it's likely that the author derived much of the inspiration for his border tale from the local stories told to him on his visits. The area is now identified as the heart of "**Doone Country**", rich with echoes of Blackmore's fictional Doone Valley, particularly Badgworthy Water and the valleys of Lank Combe and Hoccombe Combe. If you want to explore further, head three-quarters of a mile west to the hamlet of **Malmsmead**, from where you can follow Badgworthy Water upstream; Porlock's tourist office (see p.167) can supply a detailed route.

Lynmouth

Eleven miles along the coast from Porlock, at the junction and estuary of the East and West Lyn rivers, **LYNMOUTH** was described by Gainsborough as "the most delightful place for a landscape painter this country can boast". Shelley honeymooned here (see box opposite) – two different houses claim to have been the Shelleys' love nest – and R.D. Blackmore, author of *Lorna Doone*, stayed in **Mars Hill**, Lynmouth's oldest part, where creeper-covered cottages are framed by the cliffs behind the Esplanade.

Both Lynmouth and its sister-village Lynton (see p.171) attract visitors year-round for the walking trails that radiate out onto Exmoor and along the coast. Lynmouth itself is the start (or end) of the **Two Moors Way**, a 103-mile walking route linking Exmoor with Dartmoor (see p.126), part of it along the Tarka Trail (see p.179). Lynmouth also stands at one end of the **Coleridge Way**, a 51-mile route from Coleridge's former home in Nether Stowey, taking in a good stretch of the Quantock and Brendon Hills as well as Exmoor. Literature describing both walks is available at the visitor centre.

6

Brief history

Beset by cliffs, Lynton and Lynmouth have been relatively isolated for most of their **history**, but the villages struck lucky during the Napoleonic Wars when frustrated Grand Tourists unable to visit their usual continental haunts discovered here a domestic piece of Swiss landscape. **Coleridge**, **Southey** and **Hazlitt** trudged here at different times, and **Shelley** spent his honeymoon in Lynmouth in 1812, but the greatest spur to the area's popularity was the 1869 publication of *Lorna Doone*, which led to swarms of literary tourists in search of the book's famous settings.

Disaster struck in August 1952 when nine inches of rain fell onto Exmoor in 24 hours and Lynmouth was almost washed away by **floodwaters** raging down the valley. Huge landslips carried hundreds of trees into the rivers, all the bridges in the area were swept away, houses were demolished and 34 people lost their lives. Since the disaster, **rumours** have circulated regarding one possible cause of the inundation, relating to secret tests that were then being carried out by the Ministry of Defence in the Exmoor area, which involved sending pilots to "seed" clouds with dry ice to make them rain. The story has been denied by the MoD, but the suspicions remain.

Lynton & Lynmouth Cliff Railway

The Esplanade, EX35 6EQ • Daily: mid-Feb to late March & Oct 10am–5pm; mid-April to early June & mid- to late Sept 10am–6pm; late March to mid-April, early June to late July & early to mid-Sept 10am–7pm; late July to Aug 10am–9pm; early Nov 10am–4pm • £3.70 return, under-14s £2.30 return • ☎ 01598 753486, ⓦ cliffrailwaylynton.co.uk

Opened in 1890, the **cliff railway** makes the most memorable way to move between Lynton and Lynmouth, about 500ft below. The ingenious hydraulic system consists of two carriages on separate rails, counterbalanced by water tanks that fill up at the top with water piped from the West Lyn River. As the bottom carriage empties its load (sometimes the weight of passengers at the top makes this unnecessary), the water-powered brakes are released and the top carriage descends. It's fast, scenic, virtually noise-free and ecologically sound.

SHELLEY IN LYNMOUTH

In the summer of 1812, Percy Bysshe Shelley, aged 20, stopped in Lynmouth in the company of his 16-year-old bride Harriet Westbrook, Harriet's sister Eliza and Dan Healy, their Irish servant. This, Shelley decided, would be the place to establish the commune of free-thinking radicals that he had long contemplated. Although this vision never materialized, Shelley used his nine-week stay – in what is now *Shelley's* hotel – to work on his polemical poem *Queen Mab* and to compose his seditious manifesto, or *Declaration of Rights*, which declared, among other things, that "titles are tinsel, power a corrupter, glory a bubble, and excessive wealth a libel on its possessor". Copies of the *Declaration* were attached to balloons, inserted into bottles launched from Lynmouth's harbour and distributed in nearby Barnstaple (for which Healy was arrested and imprisoned). Now under observation, Shelley and his entourage took flight soon after, hiring a boatman to ferry them to Wales, where the poet continued to work on *Queen Mab*.

6

Glen Lyn Gorge

Watersmeet Rd, EX35 6ER • Easter–Oct daily 10am–4.30pm, summer school hols 10am–5.30pm, reduced opening in winter, usually Sat & Sun 10am–3pm • £5 • ☎ 01598 753207, ⓦ www.theglenlyngorge.co.uk

The most vivid reminders of Lynmouth's 1952 flood are the boulders and other rocky debris still strewn along the **Glen Lyn Gorge**, a steep wooded valley through which the destructive torrent took its course. A deeply tranquil air now pervades the gorge, the walks and waterfalls upstream ideal for picnics. Displays on the uses and dangers of water power include water-cannons and a small hydroelectric plant that provides electricity for the local community.

ARRIVAL AND DEPARTURE   LYNMOUTH

By bus The stop is in the Lyndale car park. For services to Combe Martin and Ilfracombe, change at Barnstaple. Connections to Porlock and Minehead are summer-only. Destinations Barnstaple (Mon–Sat 4 daily; 55min–1hr 10min); Ilfracombe (mid-July to early Sept Mon–Fri 2 daily; 1hr); Lynton (Mon–Sat 4–6 daily; 8min); Minehead (mid-July to early Sept Mon–Fri 2 daily; 1hr 5min); Porlock (mid-July to early Sept Mon–Fri 2 daily; 50min).

INFORMATION AND TOURS

National Park Visitor Centre The Pavilion, The Esplanade (daily 10am–5pm; ☎ 01598 752509, ⓦ exmoor-nationalpark.gov.uk).
Boat trips Exmoor Coast Boat Cruises run 45-minute excursions from Lynmouth's harbour to Lee Bay (£10), usually setting off at 11am or noon (April–Sept; ☎ 01598 753207).

ACCOMMODATION

Rising Sun Harbourside, EX35 6EG ☎ 01598 753223, ⓦ risingsunlynmouth.co.uk. Rooms in this fourteenth-century inn have all the requisite beams and sloping floors. It's touristy and expensive but steeped in atmosphere, and has a superb location by the harbour. It's a popular dining spot too (see below). **£160**

EATING

7theBistro 7 Watersmeet Rd, EX35 6EP ☎ 01598 753302, ⓦ 7thebistro.com. This small place focuses on fresh seafood, including memorable seafood crêpes (£15.50), and locally sourced meat dishes, such as beef stroganoff (£17). Finish off with a lemon posset or the cheese board. April–Oct Tues–Sun 6.30–9pm; Nov–March Fri–Sun 6.30–9pm.
Rising Sun Harbourside, EX35 6EG ☎ 01598 753223,

WALKS FROM LYNTON AND LYNMOUTH

The major year-round attraction in these parts is **walking**, not only along the coast path but also inland. Most trails are waymarked, and you can pick up route maps from the tourist office or Park Visitor Centre. One of the most popular walks is about two miles eastward, either along the banks of the River Lyn or high up above the valley along the Two Moors Way to **Watersmeet** (see p.172), itself the starting place for myriad trails (see box, p.172); from Lynmouth, the path starts from the Lyndale car park opposite *Shelley's Hotel*.

Another easy expedition takes you west out of Lynton along the North Walk, a mile-long path leading to the **Valley of Rocks** (a route shared with the South West Coast Path), a steeply curved heathland dominated by rugged rock formations. The poet Robert Southey summed up its raw splendour when he described it as "the very bones and skeleton of the earth, rock reeling upon rock, stone piled upon stone, a huge terrific mass". At the far end of the valley, herds of wild goats range free as they have done here for centuries; a short climb up Hollerday Hill yields a terrific view over the whole area.

Lynmouth is the best starting point for **coastal walks**. Tiny coves are easily accessible on either side of the estuary, including the sheltered shingle beach at the foot of **Countisbury Hill**, which you could reach en route to the lighthouse at **Foreland Point**, a little over two miles away. Westwards towards Combe Martin (see p.172), the coast path traces some of Devon's most majestic and unspoilt coastline, crossing the River Heddon a short way upstream of **Heddon's Mouth**, site of an old lime kiln and ringed by treacherous rocks. The deep, wooded **Heddon Valley** can be reached by road from the *Hunter's Inn*, signposted off the A39.

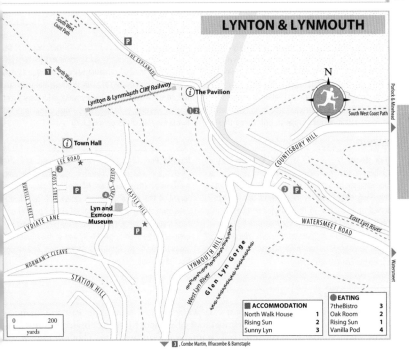

LYNTON & LYNMOUTH

■ ACCOMMODATION		● EATING	
North Walk House	1	7theBistro	3
Rising Sun	2	Oak Room	2
Sunny Lyn	3	Rising Sun	1
		Vanilla Pod	4

3, Combe Martin, Ilfracombe & Barnstaple

ⓦrisingsunlynmouth.co.uk. The traditional bar of this thatched inn (see opposite) serves local ales, and you can lunch on sandwiches or sample the menu of classic English dishes such as roast lamb and duck breast (£14–19). Book early for the restaurant, otherwise take a chance at the bar. Kitchen daily noon–2.30pm & 6–9pm.

Lynton

Perched above a lofty gorge with dramatic views over the sea and its sister resort of Lynmouth, **LYNTON** has a prosperous Victorian–Edwardian air epitomized by the imposing faux-medieval **town hall** from 1900 on Lee Road. It was the gift of publisher George Newnes, who also funded the nearby cliff railway (see p.169).

Lyn and Exmoor Museum

Market St, EX35 6AF • Easter–Oct Mon–Sat 10.30am–1.30pm & 2–5pm • £2

One of Lynton's oldest houses – probably from the early eighteenth century – holds the **Lyn and Exmoor Museum**, a must for fans of small and quirky local collections. The whitewashed cottage is stuffed to the gills with a miscellany of relics from the locality, and has a reconstructed Exmoor kitchen from around 1800 on the ground floor. Upstairs are samples of local rocks, fossils and minerals, and stuffed birds and small animals. Old paintings and prints illustrate domestic and social life, and agricultural tools recall how most locals made a living before the invention of tourism.

ARRIVAL AND INFORMATION   LYNTON

By bus Buses stop in Castle Hill car park and on Lee Road. Destinations Barnstaple (Mon–Sat 11 daily; 55min); Ilfracombe (mid-July to early Sept Mon–Fri 2 daily; 50min; Lynmouth (Mon–Sat 4–6 daily; 8min).

Tourist office Town hall, Lee Rd (Mon–Sat 10am–1pm & 2–4pm, Sun 10am–2pm; ☎01598 752225, ⓦlynton -lynmouth-tourism.co.uk).

6

ACCOMMODATION

★ **North Walk House** North Walk, EX35 6HJ ☎ 01598 753372, ⓦ northwalkhouse.co.uk. Top-quality B&B in a panoramic position overlooking the sea, and convenient for the coast path. The three stylish rooms have pine floors and rugs, abundant breakfasts are taken at a communal table or on the sea-facing terrace, and delicious organic dinners are available for £29/person. There is also self-catering accommodation available all year. B&B closed Dec–Feb. __£134__

★ **Sunny Lyn** Lynbridge, EX35 6NS ☎ 01598 753384, ⓦ caravandevon.co.uk. You can pitch next to the West Lyn River at this tranquil campsite halfway between Lynton and Barbrook off the B3234, with an on-site shop and café (closed in low season), and lodges available for weekly rent all year. It's small, so booking is essential. Camping closed Nov to early March. Per person __£7.75__

EATING

Oak Room Lee Rd, EX35 6HW ☎ 01598 753838, ⓦ theoakroomlynton.co.uk. Convivial tearoom and Spanish tapas bar with small wooden tables and a sofa or two. Tasty dishes such as meatballs or calamari can be served as tapas (£4–7) or in bigger portions as main courses (around £15). Mid-Feb to Nov Mon & Thurs–Sun 10.30am–2.30pm & 6pm–late, Tues & Wed 6pm–late (also lunchtime in summer school hols); kitchen 11.30am–2.30pm & 6–9pm.

Vanilla Pod 10–12 Queen St, EX35 6AA ☎ 01598 753706, ⓦ thevanillapodlynton.co.uk. Good wholesome meals with Mediterranean and Middle Eastern leanings are served at this friendly, modern eatery. You can choose between a platter of meze to share (£23 for 2 people) or a combination of meze, starter and main (£22); otherwise, evening mains such as pork belly and seafood broth are around £16. Daily: April–Oct 10am–4pm & 6–9pm; Nov–March 10am–4pm.

Watersmeet

The East Lyn River is joined by Hoar Oak Water one and a half miles east and inland of Lynton and Lynmouth at **Watersmeet**, one of Exmoor's most celebrated beauty spots. The tranquillity of the place can be utterly transformed after a bout of rain, when the rivers become roaring torrents and the usually crystal-clear water is stained brown with moorland peat. Drivers can leave vehicles at a car park off the A39, and follow the path down through oak woods to the two slender bridges where the rivers merge.

EATING

Watersmeet House Watersmeet Rd, EX35 6NT ☎ 01598 753348. This old fishing lodge now owned by the National Trust dispenses teas and snacks, which you can consume on the veranda. Daily: mid- to late March & Oct 10.30am–4.30pm; April–Sept 10.30am–5pm.

Combe Martin

In a sheltered valley at the western edge of Exmoor's seaboard, **COMBE MARTIN** is memorable for its prodigiously long and straggling main street, which follows the combe for about a mile down to the seafront. The **beach** here is sandy at low tide, with rock pools and secluded coves on either side.

A WALK FROM WATERSMEET

A web of **signposted paths** surrounds Watersmeet, many of them established as donkey tracks when the local charcoal and tanning industries flourished in the nineteenth century. One short route from the bridge takes you south up Hoar Oak Water to **Hillsford Bridge**, the confluence of Hoar Oak and Farley Water, while the **Fisherman's Path** leads east along the East Lyn River above one of the river's most dramatic stretches. Another marked route strikes off from the Fisherman's Path after only a few hundred yards, zigzagging steeply uphill to meet the A39, about a mile north of Watersmeet and 328ft east of the *Sandpiper Inn*. Opposite the pub, a path leads a quarter of a mile north to meet the coast path and gives access to **Butter Hill** which, at over 984ft, affords stunning views of Lynton, Lynmouth and the North Devon coast. You can pick up pamphlets with full details about all the various routes at *Watersmeet House* (see above).

A COASTAL HIKE FROM COMBE MARTIN

A spectacular stretch of coast extends east of **Combe Martin**, notably around Wild Pear Beach to Little Hangman and Hangman Point, part of the **Hangman Hills**. The waymarked path – a section of both the South West Coast Path and the Tarka Trail – is signposted off the north end of the car park behind the *Foc's'le Inn*. It's a gruelling route, involving a two-mile uphill slog (with no refreshment stops) to the great gorse-covered headland of **Great Hangman** – at 1043ft, the highest point on the South West Coast Path. The payback is the incredible panorama, occasionally taking in glimpses of the Gower peninsula in Wales. From here you can retrace your steps or complete a circle by veering inland round Girt Farm and west down Knap Down Lane to Combe Martin; the whole well-marked circuit adds up to about six miles.

6

Pack o' Cards Inn

About halfway along the High Street, look out for the unusual **Pack o' Cards Inn**, supposed to have been built by a gambler in the eighteenth century with his winnings from a card game. Originally possessing 52 windows (some were later boarded up), it has four storeys – decreasing in size as they get higher – each with thirteen doors, and chimneys sprouting from every corner; it's now a pub (see below).

Combe Martin Museum

Cross St, EX34 0DH • Mid-March to Oct Mon–Sat 10.30am–5pm, Sun 11.30am–2pm; Nov–Easter Tues–Thurs 10.30am–3pm • £2.50, under-16s £1.50 (free if accompanied by an adult) • ☏ 01271 889031, ⓦ combe-martin-museum.co.uk

Behind the seafront and next to the tourist office, the **Combe Martin Museum** is more modern and child-friendly than most Exmoor collections. Distributed on three floors, items illustrate the silver mining that has taken place here since Roman times, as well as lime quarrying, agriculture, horticulture and maritime history.

ARRIVAL AND INFORMATION   COMBE MARTIN

By bus Buses run from the stop on the High Street; service #300 goes to Lynton, #301 runs to Barnstaple, and both services go to Ilfracombe.
Destinations Barnstaple (Mon–Sat 8 daily; 55min); Ilfracombe (Mon–Sat 11–13 daily; 20min); Lynmouth (mid-July to early Sept Mon–Fri 2 daily; 40min); Lynton (mid-July to early Sept Mon–Fri 2 daily; 35min).

Tourist office Cross St (mid-March to Oct Mon–Sat 10.30am–5pm, Sun 11.30am–2pm; Nov–Easter Tues–Thurs 10.30am–3pm; ☏ 01271 883319, ⓦ visit combemartin.co.uk).

ACCOMMODATION AND EATING

Pack o' Cards Inn High St, EX34 0ET ☏ 01271 882300, ⓦ packocards.co.uk. This eccentric construction has more conventional rooms than its appearance might suggest – on the small side but clean and comfortable (one, boldly pink, has a four-poster). The bar and restaurant are popular with families, and there's a riverside garden and a skittle alley with a small exhibition of the building's history. It's not very convenient for the seafront though. Kitchen daily noon–3pm & 5.30–9pm, school hols noon–9pm. **£75**

North Devon and Lundy

SURFERS AT WOOLACOMBE SANDS

North Devon and Lundy

Extending southwest from Exmoor to the Cornish border, the North Devon region encompasses a motley range of landscapes, from picture-postcard villages to run-of-the-mill beach resorts, and wind-lashed rockscapes to broad, family-friendly beaches. Apart from a few pockets of more intense activity, it's a tranquil, unhurried region, less touristy than Devon's southern coast, but with plenty of opportunities for activity enthusiasts too, in the form of walking and cycling trails and some of the South West's best surf breaks.

The chief town, **Barnstaple**, at the end of a branch line from Exeter, is a good place to get started, with extensive transport connections and plentiful accommodation and eating options. From here it's an easy run to some of Devon's best beaches, at **Croyde**, **Woolacombe** and **Saunton Sands**, all hugely popular with surfers. **Ilfracombe**, on the other hand, is a traditional tourist resort with strong Victorian trappings; to the east, the hilly seaboard stretching as far as the Exmoor coast provides a strenuous but stimulating hiking route.

Enjoying a fine site on the Torridge River, the working town of **Bideford** is mainly a transit centre, with some decent accommodation and bus connections to all the towns on Bideford Bay; easiest to reach is **Appledore**, sheltered in the mouth of the Torridge estuary. Inland, **Great Torrington** makes a good stop for walkers or bikers following the **Tarka Trail** (see box, p.179), which passes through some of the region's loveliest countryside. West of Appledore, **Westward Ho!** has a magnificent swathe of sand to compensate for the ugly holiday developments.

The coast along the furthest reaches of Bideford Bay is dominated by cliffs, where the quiet hamlet of **Buck's Mills** and the tourist honeypot of **Clovelly** cling to the steep slopes amid thick woods. If you're put off by the crowds and artifice of the latter, follow the bay round to stormy **Hartland Point** at Devon's northwestern corner, an intensely rural area that is well off the beaten track, offering bracing cliff walks southwards as well as the more temperate appeal of Hartland Abbey. For remoteness, though, you can't beat **Lundy Island**, a tract of wilderness in the middle of the Bristol Channel that makes a great bolt hole for a night or two, and affords tremendous views of England, Wales and, westwards, the Atlantic Ocean.

Barnstaple

At the head of the Taw estuary, **BARNSTAPLE** has been North Devon's principal town since at least Norman times. Its role as a port was largely lost in the nineteenth century, however, when the river silted up, preventing large ships from docking. The local Taw and Torridge river mouths are the source of the red clay used in the **pottery** that has been produced in the area since the thirteenth century and was later exported all over northern Europe and the New World; examples of the local **Barum ware** art pottery that was fashionable in the late nineteenth century can be seen in the **Museum of North Devon**.

GREY SEAL, LUNDY ISLAND

Highlights

❶ **The Tarka Trail** This extensive walking and cycling route provides the ideal way to explore North Devon's coast and interior. **See p.179**

❷ **Barnstaple Pannier Market** The biggest of Devon's ancient covered markets offers a few bargains alongside local craftwork and produce. **See p.180**

❸ **Surfing in Barnstaple Bay** Wave enthusiasts flock to the beaches at Croyde, Woolacombe and Saunton for Devon's best surf. **See p.181 & p.184**

❹ **A stroll through Appledore** The narrow lanes of this old port have an almost Mediterranean flavour, terrific estuary views and an engaging maritime museum. **See p.191**

❺ **Westward Ho!** Beyond the dreary bungalows, there's a magnificent, wild beach beloved of watersports fans and backed by the sand dunes, salt marshes and meadows of Northam Burrows. **See p.193**

❻ **Lundy Island** The ultimate escape, this flat splinter of land is broadside on to the Atlantic and dotted with unusual accommodation. **See p.195**

HIGHLIGHTS ARE MARKED ON THE MAP ON P.178

Blackmoor Gate

Combe Martin

Combe Martin Bay

Watermouth

Rillage Point

Hillsborough

Hele Bay

Ilfracombe

Tunnels Beach

Mortehoe

Bull Point

Rockham Bay

Morte Point

Morte Bay

Woolacombe Sands

Baggy Point

Putsborough

Georgeham

Croyde

Saunton

Saunton Sands

Muddiford

Braunton

Braunton Great Field

Braunton Burrows

Barnstaple

Bishop's Tawton

Tarka Line

River Taw

Tarka Trail

Instow

Tapeley Park

Appledore

Northam Burrows

Westward Ho!

Bideford

Weare Gifford

Great Torrington

Rosemoor

River Torridge

Barnstaple or Bideford Bay

South West Coast Path

Buck's Mills

Woolfardisworthy

Clovelly

Higher Clovelly

Clovelly Cross

Hartland

Shipload Bay

Titchberry

Hartland Point

Hartland Abbey

Stoke

Hartland Quay

Speke's Mill Mouth

Elmscott

South West Coast Path

Lundy

HIGHLIGHTS

1 The Tarka Trail
2 Barnstaple Pannier Market
3 Surfing in Barnstaple Bay
4 A stroll through Appledore
5 Westward Ho!
6 Lundy Island

0   2
miles

N

THE TARKA LINE AND TARKA TRAIL

Henry Williamson's classic 1927 tale *Tarka the Otter* (see p.349), partly set in the Taw valley, has lent its name to the **Tarka Line** – the scenic Exeter–Barnstaple rail route that follows the Taw for half its length – and the **Tarka Trail**, a 180-mile route that tracks the otter's wanderings in a giant figure-of-eight centring on the town of Barnstaple. Marked by an otter's-paw symbol, the trail offers an excellent opportunity to get a close-up look at the wildlife of the Taw estuary. It also touches on Exmoor and Dartmoor, follows part of the old Barnstaple–Ilfracombe rail line, and passes through Instow, Bideford and Williamson's home village of Georgeham. The 21 miles that follow former rail lines are ideally suited to **bicycles**, and you'll find rental shops at Barnstaple (see p.180), Bideford (see p.190), Braunton (see p.182) and Great Torrington (see p.192). Space for a maximum of two bikes is available on Tarka Line trains on a first-come-first-served basis, though if there's space more may be allowed. Avoid busy times and you should be alright.

Local tourist offices issue leaflets with a route map covering the whole trail, and you can pick up the more comprehensive *Tarka Trail Guide* (£6.95) from local shops and tourist offices or from the website ⓦ www.tarkatrailguide.co.uk. Route descriptions and information about accommodation are also available at ⓦ devon.gov.uk/tarkatrail (and in paper form at outlets along the Trail), while free **audioguides** can be downloaded from both of these websites as well as from ⓦ northdevonbiosphere.org.uk.

7

Remote from the region's other main centres, Barnstaple has developed a very separate identity from Devon's south coast towns, though, with some notable exceptions, reveals surprisingly little of great age or interest. It's a busy, virtually tourist-free working town, a useful hub for the area, and worth a swift exploration. The **Tarka Trail** runs through the centre, allowing for a pleasant riverside stroll or a cycle further afield.

Museum of North Devon

The Square, EX32 8LN • Mon–Sat: mid-March to Oct 10am–5pm; Oct–March 10am–4pm • Free • ☎ 01271 346747, ⓦ barnstaplemuseum.org.uk

On the riverbank at the end of Boutport Street, the lively miscellany of militaria, nature and pottery at the **Museum of North Devon** makes an absorbing introduction to Barnstaple and North Devon. The ground floor illustrates **local wildlife**, focusing on the ecosystems of North Devon's estuaries and coastline. Upstairs, you'll find a room devoted to **Barum ware**, the colourful pottery created by C.H. Brannam's studio, featuring lurid lizard and fish designs in greens and ochre-reds. You can also see examples of sgraffito, a traditional North Devon technique achieved by scratching through the slip to show the red clay underneath.

Other first-floor rooms display **war memorabilia** – uniforms, flags, guns – connected to the Devonshire regiment and the Royal Devon Yeomanry, formed two centuries ago to protect the coast from Napoleon.

St Anne's Chapel

Paternoster Row, EX31 1BJ • Tues 11am–3pm, Thurs 11am–1pm • Free • Council office ☎ 01271 373311, ⓦ barnstapletowncouncil.co.uk

Between the High Street and Boutport Street, a grassy pedestrian area holds a trio of clerical buildings, most notably the fourteenth-century **St Anne's Chapel**. This oddly shaped, part-battlemented chantry chapel (thought to be the sole survivor of its type nationally) was converted into a grammar school in 1549, later numbering John Gay (1685–1732), author of *The Beggar's Opera*, among its pupils. It's now an arts and community centre, mainly used for events and exhibitions, worth visiting also for its original architectural features as well as some material on John Gay and the **Huguenot refugees** who settled in Barnstaple during the seventeenth century, one of whose number married Samuel Pepys.

The chapel lies across from Barnstaple's **parish church**, conspicuous for its curiously twisted "broach" spire (octagonal and rising from a square tower).

Pannier Market

Butchers Row, EX31 1BW • General goods and local produce Mon (April–Dec), Tues & Thurs–Sat; arts and crafts Mon (April–Dec) & Thurs; antiques and collectables Wed • Free • ⊛ barnstaplepanniermarket.co.uk

Barnstaple's centuries-old role as a marketplace for local foodstuffs is perpetuated in the daily bustle around the huge timber-framed **Pannier Market**, off the pedestrianized High Street – the model for similar structures throughout North Devon. The market offers antiques, arts and crafts, fresh local produce and general bric-a-brac. Friday is the liveliest day, attracting vendors and customers from throughout the region. Alongside the market runs **Butchers Row**, a few of its 33 archways still holding butchers' shops. The creamy white, Neoclassical **Guildhall** on the corner is currently being developed to hold an exhibition of the town's heritage, due to open around 2017.

7

ARRIVAL AND DEPARTURE

BARNSTAPLE

By train Terminus of the Tarka Line, Barnstaple's train station is on the south side of the Taw, a 5min walk from the centre.
Destinations Crediton (Mon–Sat hourly, Sun 7 daily; 50min); Exeter (Mon–Sat hourly, Sun 7 daily; 1hr 10min).
By bus The town's bus station lies between Silver Street and Belle Meadow Road.
Destinations Appledore (hourly; 55min); Bideford (Mon–Sat every 10min, Sun every 30min; 35min); Braunton (Mon–Sat every 10min, Sun 2–3 hourly; 20min); Clovelly (Mon–Sat 4 daily; 1hr 10min); Croyde (Mon–Sat hourly,

Sun late May to mid-Sept 5 daily; 35min); Exeter (Mon–Sat 8 daily; 2hr 5min); Great Torrington (Mon–Sat 1–2 hourly; 35–50min); Hartland (Mon–Sat 6 daily; 1hr 25min); Ilfracombe (Mon–Sat 4 hourly, Sun every 30min; 40min); Instow (Mon–Sat every 10min, Sun every 30min; 25min); Lynton (Mon–Sat hourly; 50min); Saunton (Mon–Sat hourly, Sun late May to mid-Sept 6 daily; 30min); Tiverton (Mon–Sat 12 daily, Sun 4 daily; 50min–1hr 25min); Westward Ho! (Mon–Sat every 20min, Sun hourly; 50min); Woolacombe (Mon–Sat 5 daily; 45min–1hr 5min).

INFORMATION AND ACTIVITIES

Tourist information Museum of North Devon, The Square (Mon–Sat: April to late Oct 10am–5pm; late Oct to March 10am–4pm; ☎ 01271 375000, ⊛ staynorthdevon .co.uk).
Bike rental Local outfits include Tarka Trail Cycle Hire, train station (mid-March to mid-Nov daily; ☎ 01271

324202, ⊛ tarkabikes.co.uk; £12/day), and Biketrail Cycle Hire, 3 miles west at Fremington (☎ 01271 372586 or ☎ 07788 133738, ⊛ biketrail.co.uk; £12.50/day); both provide a delivery and collection service and free route maps. Spares and repairs can be had at Bike Shed, The Square (☎ 01271 328628, ⊛ bikesheduk.com).

ACCOMMODATION

★ **Broomhill Art Hotel** Muddiford, EX31 4EX ☎ 01271 850262, ⊛ broomhillart.co.uk. Set in lush woods 2 miles north of Barnstaple and signposted off the A39, this place is a striking combination of gallery, restaurant and hotel, where the spacious rooms overlook an impressive modern sculpture garden. There are also modern artworks all over the house, and the food's terrific too (see opposite). The frequent #301 Barnstaple–Ilfracombe buses (not Sun) stop outside. **£75**
Lee House Near Marwood, EX31 4DZ ☎ 01271 374345, ✉ michael.darling74@gmail.com. For true rural remoteness, you can't beat this stately manor house, 3.5 miles northwest of town in the deepest wilds of Devon. The house has origins in Elizabethan times, and the guests' sitting room has a Jacobean fireplace and plasterwork ceiling. The rooms – one with a four-poster bed – overlook the lawned garden and ranks of rolling green hills, and the

walls are adorned with the artwork of the owner, a cartoonist for London magazines. No credit cards. **£70**
Old Vicarage Barbican Terrace, EX32 9HQ ☎ 01271 328504, ⊛ oldvicaragebarnstaple.co.uk. Central but quiet Victorian B&B with period features and five spacious rooms, including a family suite. Back-facing rooms overlook the large garden and the adjacent church. There are lots of nice touches, like complimentary home-baked cakes, and parking is available. **£89**
Yeo Dale Hotel Pilton Bridge, on the A39 Ilfracombe road, EX31 1PG ☎ 01271 342954, ⊛ yeodalehotel .co.uk. Prominently sited near the River Yeo and the Tarka Trail, this Georgian building has variously sized, smart, modern rooms with or without bathrooms. The owners are sociable, locally sourced breakfasts (optional, £5/person) are a treat, and evening meals can be requested with notice. Limited parking. **£75**

EATING

The Glasshouse 2 Cross St, EX31 1BA ☎ 01271 323311, ⓦ claytonsbarnstaple.co.uk. The glass-roofed attic space above *Clayton's Lounge Bar* (open all day) provides a classy setting for drinks and tapas or a meal of hake fillet or Exmoor lamb (around £14). The small terrace makes a great suntrap. Mon–Thurs noon–3.30pm & 6–9.30pm, Fri & Sat noon–9.30pm.

Monty's Caribbean Kitchen 19 Tuly St, EX31 1DH ☎ 01271 372985, ⓦ montyscaribbeankitchen.co.uk. Patties, jerk chicken, and ackee and saltfish feature on the menu of this modern Jamaican restaurant with small wooden tables, off Boutport St. *Rasta chana* (with chick peas, £10) is always popular, as is coconut king prawn (£14). Drinks range from *ital* carrot juice to rum punch. Tues–Thurs 11.30am–3pm, Fri & Sat 11.30am–3pm & 6–11pm.

Tea by the Taw The Strand, EX31 1EU ☎ 01271 370032. Right on the Tarka Trail, but in the centre of town, this riverside café serves panini, baguettes and cream teas, as well as quiches, salads and ploughman's lunches (£7–10). There's wi-fi, and outdoor seating to enjoy the river views. Mon–Sat 10am–5pm.

Terra Madre Muddiford, EX31 4EX ☎ 01271 850262, ⓦ broomhillart.co.uk. Part of the *Broomhill Art Hotel*, gallery and sculpture garden (see opposite), this relaxed place north of town specializes in tasty Mediterranean-style cuisine in the form of lunchtime tapas in the bar (£10 for 3) or set-price three-course lunches (£17) and evening meals (£25) in the restaurant. Look out for live jazz evenings accompanied by a Mediterranean buffet, which need advance booking. Wed–Sat 12.30–1.30pm & 7–8.30pm, Sun 12.30–1.30pm.

Croyde and around

Eight miles northwest of Barnstaple, village gentility collides with youth culture at **CROYDE**, a huddle of cottages alongside a leat, or channelled stream, that empties into the sea half a mile away at **Croyde Bay**. Backed by grassy dunes, the firm, sandy **beach** here has retained its secluded, undeveloped appeal, enhancing its role as a favourite **surfing** spot (it's lifeguarded May–Sept 10am–6pm). Drivers can park to the north of the sands at the bottom of Moor Lane – also a good departure point for exploring **Baggy Point**, a headland whose vertical cliffs are swirling with fulmars, shags, wheatears, kestrels, pipits and shearwaters. Out to sea lies the flat silhouette of Lundy Island, and in clear weather you can see across Bideford Bay to Hartland Point.

Georgeham

A mile inland of Croyde, the pretty hamlet of **GEORGEHAM**, a scattering of thatched and beflowered cottages around a typical Devon church, holds a couple of noteworthy pubs as well as **Skirr Cottage**, where Henry Williamson wrote *Tarka the Otter* (see p.349). He's buried in the churchyard of St George's.

Saunton Sands

South of Croyde, surfing is again much in evidence at **Saunton Sands**, a long strand magnificently exposed to ranks of Atlantic breakers. Saunton is said to have one of the

SURFING IN CROYDE

Croyde Bay is rated as one of the UK's best beach **surf breaks**. However, it's not the easiest for beginners, and you should be especially wary at low tide, which has accounted for quite a few broken bones over the years. **Tuition** is provided between April and October by Surf South West, based in the Burrows Beach car park on the northern side of the bay (☎ 01271 890400, ⓦ surfsouthwest.co.uk; around £34/half-day). You can rent **surf equipment** from beach stalls in the summer, otherwise try Ralph's Surf Shop on Hobbs Hill (☎ 01271 890147), open all year (but weekends only Jan & Feb); a board and wetsuit together cost around £12/half-day, or £18/day. For the latest on local **surf conditions**, check out the surf reports and webcams at ⓦ surf-forecast.com, ⓦ eyeballhq.tv and ⓦ magicseaweed.com.

longest right-hand surf breaks on Devon's north coast, ideal for classic longboard surfing, though it's a long paddle out.

Braunton

Three miles inland of Saunton Sands and five miles from Croyde, the small town of **BRAUNTON** is notable mostly for **Braunton Great Field**, a 340-acre area to the west of the Velator level crossing that's one of the few remaining open-field systems surviving in the country. It's still strip-farmed according to medieval methods, the strips divided by grass balks, or ridges. You can view the field from Braunton Beacon, at the top of West Hill.

Braunton Museum

Bakehouse Centre, Caen St, EX33 1AA • Mon–Fri 10am–3pm or 10am–4pm in July & Aug, Sat 10am–1pm; closed part of Jan • Free • ☎ 01271 816688

The small collection of items in **Braunton Museum** is worth a glance for its panoramic sweep of local history. As well as old agricultural implements, model ships, maritime art and military memorabilia, there are regular exhibitions on such themes as local railways and *Tarka* author Henry Williamson. The building also holds Braunton's tourist office.

Museum of British Surfing

The Yard, EX33 1AA • April–Oct Thurs–Sat 10am–3pm; extended hours in summer; call ahead for winter opening • £2 • ☎ 01271 815155, ⓦ museumofbritishsurfing.org.uk

In an old railway building in Braunton's Caen Street car park, Britain's first museum dedicated to surfing showcases what has evolved from a weird Californian cult to an intrinsic element of the West Country's economy. The collection at the **Museum of British Surfing** includes more than thirty boards on display (check out the "coffin lid" board from 1920), as well as posters, T-shirts, board shorts and wetsuits – just part of the UK's most extensive collection of vintage surfboards, literature and memorabilia. There are talks and films, plus exhibitions on related subjects such as "The Art of Surf", highlighting the contributions of artists, film-makers and photographers.

Braunton Burrows

Between Braunton and Saunton Sands extend the substantial sand dunes and mud flats of **Braunton Burrows**, constituting England's largest sand dune system. The bleak but flora-rich area lies at the heart of the UNESCO-designated North Devon Biosphere Reserve, and is interwoven with walking trails: the Tarka Trail and coastal path cut right across, and you can join guided walks in summer – see ⓦ northdevonbiosphere .org.uk for details.

ARRIVAL AND DEPARTURE   CROYDE AND AROUND

By bus Services #21, #21A and #21C link Barnstaple, Braunton, Saunton, Croyde and Georgeham.
Destinations Barnstaple (Mon–Sat hourly, Sun late May to mid-Sept 5 daily; 40min); Braunton (Mon–Sat hourly,

Sun late May to mid-Sept 5 daily; 20min); Saunton (Mon–Sat every 30min, Sun late May to mid-Sept 5 daily; 10min).

INFORMATION AND ACTIVITIES

Tourist information Braunton Museum, Bakehouse Centre, Caen St, Braunton (Mon–Fri 10am–3pm or 10am–4pm June–Oct, Sat 10am–1pm; closed part of Jan; ☎ 01271 816688, ⓦ visitbraunton.co.uk). The websites ⓦ croydedevon.co.uk and ⓦ croyde-bay.com cover events,

accommodation, food and drink, and all things surf in Croyde and around.
Bike rental Otter Cycle Hire, Station Rd, Braunton (March–Nov; ☎ 01271 813339; £13/day).

ACCOMMODATION

HOTELS AND B&BS

Parminter 16 St Mary's Rd, EX33 1PF ☎01271 890030, ⓦparminter.co.uk. Beside the stream, this friendly place has three large, spotless rooms (one can be a family room) in tastefully converted barns and stables, with mini-fridges and modern bathrooms. Superb breakfasts are served in the conservatory. Two-night minimum stay at weekends in high season. No credit cards. **£75**

Saunton Sands Hotel Saunton Sands, EX33 1LQ ☎01271 890212, ⓦsauntonsands.co.uk. Although its marriage of old-fashioned and modern styles doesn't always work, this luxury four-star merits a splurge if only for its superb position overlooking one of the West Country's most spectacular beaches. Indoor and outdoor pools, tennis court, gym and spa facilities are additional draws. Sea-facing rooms cost £40 more. **£190**

Woodstock Stentaway Lane, EX33 1NH ☎01271 890236, ⓦwoodstockcroyde.co.uk. Just 5–10min walk from the beach, shops and pubs, but far enough to enjoy total peace and quiet, this B&B has wonderful views over fields and sea from its rooms – best of which is the suite at the top of the house, with a lounge, kitchenette and balcony. There's a great selection of food for breakfast including home-made bread and granola. No credit cards. **£80**

HOSTEL

Baggy Lodge Moor Lane, EX33 1PA ☎01271 890078, ⓦbaggys.co.uk. Clean and friendly hostel right above Croyde's beach, with three bunkrooms and four stylish doubles, mostly with great views; prices include a simple breakfast. There's a café, and surfboard and wetsuit hire are available. Closed Jan & Feb. Dorms **£33**, doubles **£110**

CAMPING

Bay View Farm EX33 1PN ☎01271 890501, ⓦbay viewfarm.co.uk. Five minutes from the centre of Croyde at the southern end of the village, this family-friendly site is clean and well maintained, and offers wooden pods as well as standard pitches. There's a small shop, and fish and chips and pizzas are available at weekends and in the peak period (when there are minimum-length stays). No groups. Closed early Oct to Easter. Pitches **£26**, pods **£75**

Ocean Pitch Moor Lane, EX33 1NZ ☎07581 024348, ⓦoceanpitch.co.uk. Small, clean and ideally placed for the beach (a 2min walk), this campsite has sea views, friendly staff and good showers. As well as standard pitches, you can rent a comfortable bell tent (two-night minimum stay), with breakfast delivered in a hamper, or stay in a classic VW camper van. Surfing tuition and board hire are available. Closed Sept to early June. Camping/pitch **£26**, bell tents **£85**

EATING

The Blue Groove 2 Hobbs Hill, EX33 1LZ ☎01271 890111, ⓦblue-groove.co.uk. There's a young, funky ambience here in low season and at night, but it gets pretty overwhelmed at peak times. The menu ranges from sandwiches, salads, burgers and seafood to five-bean enchiladas and Caribbean lamb curry, with most evening mains £12–15; alternatively, drop by for a smoothie, beer or cocktail. Sit inside or on the terrace. March–Nov daily 9am–late, Dec Fri–Sun 9am–late; kitchen open until 9pm.

The Manor 39 St Mary's Rd, EX33 1PG ☎01271 890241, ⓦthemanorcroyde.com. A family-friendly alternative to Croyde's more youth-orientated bars, this pub-restaurant at the top of the village has a decent range of beers and meals, including sandwiches and grills, with most mains £12–16. There's a beer garden, a conservatory restaurant, takeaway snacks in summer, games and live music nights (usually every alternate Sat). Kitchen daily noon–10pm.

DRINKING

The Rock Inn Rock Hill, Georgeham, EX33 1JW ☎01271 890322, ⓦtherockinn.biz. Seventeenth-century inn, highly popular with locals and visitors alike, with real ales, excellent bar meals and a conservatory. Booking recommended for dinners, when such dishes as local sausages, pies and seafood are around £13. Daily noon–midnight.

The Thatch 14 Hobbs Hill, EX33 1LZ ☎01271 890349, ⓦthethatchcroyde.com. At the heart of the local scene, this pub with a patio is a buzzing surfers' hangout, with breakfasts, coffees, cream teas and meals (mostly £10–15) throughout the day, and live music (usually Fri). Mon–Thurs & Sun 8am–11pm, Fri & Sat 8am–midnight.

GOLDCOAST OCEANFEST

The biggest annual event hereabouts, the **GoldCoast Oceanfest** (ⓦgoldcoastoceanfest .co.uk), takes place in Croyde Bay over a weekend in mid-June. As well as some twenty bands, the festival features a range of water- and beach-sports competitions – surfing, of course, but also beach soccer, volleyball and skateboarding, plus demonstrations and workshops. Tickets are around £55 for the weekend, with early-bird discounts. Tickets should be booked early – as should accommodation.

Woolacombe Sands

Surfers and family groups alike congregate at **Woolacombe Sands**, a broad, Blue Flag-awarded expanse of beach stretching north from Baggy Point. At its southern end, the pick of the swimming spots is **Putsborough**, sheltered by the promontory and less crowded than the more developed north. At the opposite end of the bay, a break in the rocks makes space for pocket-sized **Barricane Beach**, famous for the tiny tropical shells washed up here from the Caribbean by Atlantic currents, and a favourite swimming spot.

Woolacombe

The northern end of Woolacombe Sands is dominated by the resort of **WOOLACOMBE**. Despite its splendid position at the bottom of a valley, it's an uninspiring spot, devoid of much charm or character, though serving its function as a surfing centre well enough, and you'll find an upbeat, animated vibe here in summer. Shops on West Road and Barton Road rent and sell surf gear (there are also outlets on the beach).

ARRIVAL AND DEPARTURE   WOOLACOMBE

By bus Services to #31 to Ilfracombe and #303 to Braunton and Barnstaple pull in right by Woolacombe's seafront. Destinations Barnstaple (Mon–Sat 5 daily; 40min); Braunton (Mon–Sat 4 daily; 20min); Ilfracombe (Mon–Sat 10 daily; 25min).

INFORMATION

Tourist information The Esplanade (late May to early Sept daily 10am–5pm; early Sept to late May Mon–Fri 10am–noon; ☎01271 870553, ⓦwoolacombetourism .co.uk). Offers an accommodation booking service, tickets to Lundy, and internet.

ACCOMMODATION

The Imperial Bayview Rd, EX34 7DQ ☎01271 870594, ⓦtheimperialwoolacombe.co.uk. Located above and behind the tourist office, this Victorian B&B boasts the best beach views in Woolacombe. Spacious rooms have stripped pine floors and antique furniture, and there's a panoramic patio with a hot tub. Two-bedroom apartments are also available. No credit cards. __£70__

★ **Rocks Hotel** Beach Rd, EX34 7BT ☎01271 870361, ⓦtherockshotel.co.uk. A smart, surfer-friendly place close to the beach, this B&B has smallish, en-suite bedrooms, a self-catering apartment and a breakfast room in the style of a 1950s American diner, complete with Wurlitzer jukebox. Free loan of wetsuits and boards. Two-night minimum stay at weekends in July & Aug. __£79__

EATING

Bar Electric Beach Rd, EX34 7BP ☎01271 870429. This hangout buzzes till late, offering snacks, comfy chairs and beach views from its terrace. Food choices include baguettes, gourmet burgers and pizzas (£8–12), also a curry buffet on Wed (£7), and there's live music Wed eve and Sun lunchtime, and DJs Fri and Sat eves. Wed, Fri & Sat 9am–midnight, Thurs & Sun 9am–11pm (late July to early Sept also Mon & Tues 9am–11pm); kitchen 9am–9pm.

Doyle's South St, EX34 7BN ☎01271 870388. For a change from burgers and chips and a contrast with Woolacombe's prevailing tone, head for this period-style restaurant within the Victorian *Woolacombe Bay Hotel*. Despite the rather posh setting, such dishes as roast rack of lamb (£14) or the Mediterranean vegetable platter for two (£17.50) are quite reasonably priced, and you can enjoy views over the sward of lawn and the sea beyond. The same menu is available in the hotel's *Bay Brasserie*, also open at lunchtime. Daily 7–9pm.

Red Barn Barton Rd, EX34 7DF ☎01271 870264, ⓦredbarnwoolacombe.co.uk. Just up from the beach surf dudes and families mingle at this bar and restaurant with ranks of surfboards in the roof. It provides good beers, all-day breakfasts, salads, steaks, burger and seafood platters (all around £9), and live music on Fri. Kitchen Mon–Thurs until 9pm, Fri–Sun until 9.30pm.

Mortehoe

The beaches of Woolacombe Sands may be the main attraction hereabouts, but the rocky coastline on either side holds equal appeal, not least around **MORTEHOE**, a steep mile north of Woolacombe. This ancient village, whose churchyard holds the graves of shipwrecked mariners, lies just inland of the grassy and gorsy headland of **Morte Point**, which marks the northern end of Woolacombe Bay and from where you can spot **Morte Stone** out to sea, part of a menacing sunken reef that has caused many a shipwreck over the centuries – supposedly inspiring the Normans to dub it "Death Stone".

North of Morte Point, walkers can take in some splendid rock contortions and abundant wildlife at **Rockham Bay**, with its rock pools and secluded beach (also accessible by footpath from Mortehoe), and a mile or so north around **Bull Point**, where a lighthouse warns ships off the fractured reefs tapering away out to sea.

ARRIVAL AND DEPARTURE   MORTEHOE

By bus Service #31 connects Mortehoe with Ilfracombe (Mon–Sat 10 daily; 25min), and #31 and #303 go to Woolacombe (Mon–Sat 11 daily; 10min).

ACCOMMODATION

★**North Morte Farm** EX34 7EG ☎01271 870381, ⓦnorthmortefarm.co.uk. One of North Devon's most peaceful and panoramic sites, with static caravans available for weekly rent. It's fairly unsheltered, but it has a good shower block with free hot showers, and lies 500yd from the coast path and the beach at Rockham Bay and a 5min walk from the pubs of Mortehoe. Closed Nov–Easter. Per person **£8**

★**Victoria House** Chapel Hill, EX34 7DZ ☎01271 871302, ⓦvictoriahousebandb.co.uk. For true tranquillity and the best vistas, seek out this upmarket B&B overlooking Grunta Beach, about a mile north of Woolacombe. Just one room is available, the Beach House, which has its own terrace and terrific sea views. Breakfast, served between 8am and 11.30am, includes fresh fruit, home-baked bread and pancakes or toasted bagels with smoked salmon. No credit cards. **£120**

DRINKING

Chichester Arms EX34 7DU ☎01271 870411. Mortehoe has a few excellent spots for a pint – this traditional place by the church is arguably the best. There's a patio, a good selection of local ales and a menu that includes crab cakes (most dishes around £10). In summer, food orders should be made early as it gets busy. Daily 11am–11pm.

Ilfracombe and around

Squeezed between hills and sea five miles east of Morte Point, **ILFRACOMBE** is North Devon's most popular resort. With large-scale development restricted by the cliffs, the town is essentially little changed since its evolution into a tourist destination in the nineteenth century, since when it has established itself as a full-on family resort. More recently, Ilfracombe has started to attract the surfer crowd and a hipper image, symbolized by the dramatic **Damien Hirst sculpture** *Verity*, installed at the end of the compact harbour: essentially a giant, half-flayed, pregnant woman, trampling on law tomes and with a sword upthrust – said to be an allegory of truth and justice.

Ilfracombe's **harbour** is sheltered by the grassy mound of Lantern Hill, a headland surmounted by the fourteenth-century **St Nicholas Chapel**, once a refuge for pilgrims en route to Hartland Abbey (see p.195) and later used as a lighthouse. There's usually some low-key fishing activity on the quayside, where crab and lobster are hauled up, and in summer it's the departure point for cruises to Lundy (see p.195), coastal tours and fishing trips.

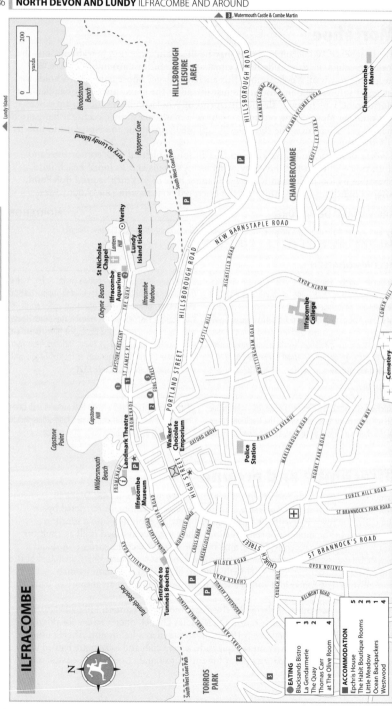

3 Watermouth Castle & Combe Martin

7

ILFRACOMBE

● EATING
Blacksands Bistro   1
La Gendarmerie   3
The Quay   2
Thomas Carr
at The Olive Room   4

■ ACCOMMODATION
Epchris House   5
The Habit Boutique Rooms   3
Little Meadow   2
Ocean Backpackers   1
Westwood   4

Ilfracombe Aquarium

The Pier, EX34 9EQ • Daily: mid-Feb to Easter & Nov 10am–3.30pm; Easter to late May 10am–4pm; late May to late July 10am–5pm; late July to early Sept 10am–5.45pm; early Sept to Oct 10am–4.30pm • £4.50, under-16s £3.50 • ☎ 01271 864533, ⓦ ilfracombeaquarium.co.uk

A former lifeboat house on the harbourside now holds **Ilfracombe Aquarium**, where a variety of watery habitats have been re-created, from stream and rock pool to Lundy Island and the open sea. It's all very small-scale, and it gets congested in high season, but it makes a diverting and instructive rainy-weather attraction.

Ilfracombe Museum

Wilder Road, EX34 8AF • April–Oct daily 10am–5pm; Nov–March Tues–Fri 10am–1pm • £3 • ☎ 01271 863541, ⓦ ilfracombemuseum.co.uk

In a former hotel laundry room, the multifarious **Ilfracombe Museum** is crammed with photos and Victoriana relating to the area, alongside a wealth of material about the local wildlife. You'll see a bat cupboard, giant stuffed gulls, thousands of butterflies, moths and beetles in cases, and a small section devoted to Lundy Island.

7

Tunnels Beaches

Bath Place, EX34 8AN • April–Sept daily 10am–6pm (till 7pm in summer school hols); Oct Tues–Sun 10am–5pm • £2.50, under-16s £1.95 • ☎ 01271 879882, ⓦ tunnelsbeaches.co.uk

West of Ilfracombe's centre, past Wildersmouth Beach, **Tunnels Beaches** take their name from the four tunnels bored through the cliffs by Welsh miners in the nineteenth century – still the main means of access. Privately owned, the clean, sand-and-shingle beaches have a protected rock bathing pool at low tide that's perfect for young children.

Walker's Chocolate Emporium

6 High St, EX34 9DF • Mon 10am–4pm, Tues–Sat 9.30am–5pm • Free • ☎ 01271 867193, ⓦ chocolate-emporium.co.uk

Among the drab shops on Ilfracombe's High Street, **Walker's Chocolate Emporium** stands out, specializing in quality confectionery handmade on the premises. At the back, a small chocolate museum shows old packaging and advertisements and a 6ft chocolate man, and a window lets you view the chocolate-making process live. Sugar-, gluten- and dairy-free products are also sold.

Chambercombe Manor

Chambercombe Lane, EX34 9RJ • Easter–June, Sept & Oct Mon & Fri 11am–3.30pm, Tues–Thurs guided tours only 11am–3pm (last tour), Sun guided tours only noon–3pm (last tour); July & Aug Mon & Fri 10.30am–4pm, Tues–Thurs guided tours only 10.30am–4pm (last tour), Sun guided tours only noon–4pm (last tour) • £5, or £9 for guided tour • ☎ 01271 862624, ⓦ chambercombemanor.org.uk

A mile east of Ilfracombe's centre, off the A399 Combe Martin road,

---

ALONG THE COAST TO COMBE MARTIN

East of Ilfracombe, one of Devon's loveliest **coastal walks** extends five miles to Combe Martin, on the edge of Exmoor, taking in some strenuous uphill stretches that are rewarded by stupendous views. Following the signposted South West Coast Path from the harbour, the stiff ascent to the grassy heights of **Hillsborough**, about a mile from the centre, offers a perfect prospect over the town. Beyond lies **Hele Bay**, its deep waters and pretty shingle beach almost encircled by cliff – the first of a sequence of undeveloped coves and inlets surrounded by jagged, slanting rocks and heather-covered hills. **Rillage Point** offers the occasional seal sighting, while the sandy beach at **Watermouth Bay**, three miles east of Ilfracombe, is sheltered by yet more dramatic cliffs and rocky outcrops. From here it's a couple of miles further to Combe Martin (see p.172). Watermouth Bay and Combe Martin can also be reached on bus #300 from Ilfracombe and Lynmouth, and #301 from Ilfracombe and Barnstaple.

Chambercombe Manor holds Ilfracombe's finest collection of antiques and paintings. Parts of this whitewashed huddle of buildings around a cobbled courtyard originate from the eleventh century, but the furnishings are mostly Elizabethan and Jacobean. Past owners of the manor include a string of smugglers and wreckers as well as the father of Lady Jane Grey, and it's also reputed to be one of Britain's most haunted houses. To get the full story – and some choice spooky tales – join one of the fifty-minute guided tours. The three acres of gardens and some twenty-five acres of woods are an added draw.

Watermouth Castle

Berrynarbor, EX34 9SL • Mon–Fri & Sun: Easter to late July 10.30am–5.30pm, last admission at 3pm; late July & Aug 10am–6pm, last admission at 3.30pm; early Sept to late Oct 10.30am–5pm, last admission at 3pm • £13.50; children under 92cm free • ☎ 01271 867474, ⊛ watermouthcastle.com

Rearing unexpectedly behind Watermouth Bay, the imposing, castellated facade of **Watermouth Castle** dates from 1825, but the amusements within are modern, rip-roaring fun – especially if you're under ten years old. Kids will appreciate the gnomes, dungeons and water rides, while even oldies may be seduced by the Victorian slot machines. Gardens and views offer relief from the mechanical mayhem.

ARRIVAL AND DEPARTURE

ILFRACOMBE AND AROUND

By bus Services #21 for Barnstaple, #31 for Woolacombe, the summer-only #300 (Mon–Fri) for Lynton, and #301 for Barnstaple and Combe Martin all have stops near the harbour on Wilder Road or on the parallel High Street. Destinations Barnstaple (Mon–Sat 3–4 hourly, Sun every 30min; 45min); Braunton (2–3 hourly; 30min); Combe Martin (Mon–Sat 11–13 daily; 15min); Lynton (mid-July to early Sept Mon–Fri 2 daily; 45min); Woolacombe (Mon–Sat hourly; 20–25min).

INFORMATION AND TOURS

Tourist information Landmark Theatre on the seafront (Mon–Fri 9.30am–4.30pm, Sat & Sun 10.30am–4.30pm, Nov–Easter closed Sun; ☎ 01271 863001, ⊛ visitilfracombe .co.uk). Provides local information, bus timetables and tickets for coaches and the boat for Lundy.

Boat tours The Ilfracombe Princess (☎ 01271 879727 or ☎ 07837 569667, ⊛ ilfracombeprincess.co.uk) offers cruises and coastal excursions lasting 1hr 30min (£14).

ACCOMMODATION

Epchris House Torrs Park, EX34 8AZ ☎ 01271 862751, ⊛ epchrisguesthouse.co.uk. In a leafy and well-to-do area of town, a 10min uphill walk from the harbour, this Victorian villa has two acres of gardens, including a paved terrace – where breakfast may be taken in good weather – and a heated pool. There are great views from the rooms, and a two-night minimum stay in summer. No under-10s. **£85**

The Habit Boutique Rooms 46–48 Fore St, EX34 9HR ☎ 01271 863272, ⊛ thehabitboutiquerooms.com. The name says it all – opulent rooms with smart, minimalist decor, contemporary bathrooms and lofty views out to sea. It's centrally located – just up from the harbour – and there's a chic bar and restaurant, garden seating, treatment rooms and a Pilates studio. **£160**

★**Little Meadow** Watermouth, EX34 9SJ ☎ 01271 866862, ⊛ littlemeadow.co.uk. Friendly, low-key campsite 3 miles east of Ilfracombe off the A399, and connected by footpath to Watermouth Castle and the beach. There are exhilarating sea views, a shop selling baguettes and croissants, and a good pub within walking distance. Buses to Ilfracombe and Combe Martin stop right outside. Book well ahead in summer. Closed Oct to mid-March. **£25**

★**Ocean Backpackers** 29 St James Place, EX34 9BJ ☎ 01271 867835, ⊛ oceanbackpackers.co.uk. Excellent independent hostel centrally positioned near the bus station and harbour. A favourite with surfing folk, it has a drying-room for wetsuits, surf DVDs to watch and a well-equipped kitchen. Rooms are mostly six-bed. Limited parking. Dorms **£18**, doubles **£48**

Westwood Torrs Park, EX34 8AZ ☎ 01271 867443, ⊛ west-wood.co.uk. A sojourn in this high-end B&B is like staying in a style magazine, with boldly decorated, good-size rooms, a large lounge and terrific views. The owners are friendly, and provide delicious and generous breakfasts. The converted Victorian house is in a quiet area, a 10min walk from the centre and close to the coast path. **£95**

EATING

Blacksands Bistro 3 St James Place, EX34 9BH ☎01271 523296. Cosy and welcoming restaurant with a small selection of thoughtfully prepared items. Try the baked blue-cheesecake, made with Stilton and leeks, or the roast mackerel with a spiced aubergine ragu, both around £13. There's a warm atmosphere and some tables outside on the heated terrace. Thurs 5–10pm, Fri & Sat 11am–11pm, Sun noon–5pm.

La Gendarmerie 63 Fore St, EX34 9ED ☎01271 865984, ⓦlagendarmerie.co.uk. Ex-Victorian police station converted into a smart brasserie, with dark grey walls, exposed stone walls and a relaxed ambience. Set-price menus (£29 for two courses, £35 for three) might include such dishes as chargrilled beef fillet, Creedy Carver duck breast, sea bream and some divine desserts. June–Aug Tues–Sat 7–9.30pm; Sept–May Thurs–Sat 7–9.30pm.

The Quay 11 The Quay, EX34 9BJ ☎01271 868090, ⓦ11thequay.co.uk. By the harbour, co-owned by artist Damien Hirst (whose works are displayed), this place serves drinks and snacks in the relaxed ground-floor bar, and you can order from the full restaurant menu either here or in the more sedate restaurant upstairs, which overlooks the beach and harbour to either side. Pastas and salads are around £10, and most mains are £15–20. Daily 10am–late; kitchen noon–2.30pm & 6–9pm; reduced hours in winter.

Thomas Carr at The Olive Room 56 Fore St, EX34 9DJ ☎01271 867831, ⓦthomascarrchef.co.uk. Local ingredients livened up with culinary artistry go into the dishes at this sober-looking bistro near the harbour. The six-course taster menu (£50) showcases the creative flair at work in the kitchen, otherwise mains are around £20–25. Feb & March Wed–Sat 6.30–9pm; Easter–Oct Tues–Sat 6.30–9pm; Nov & Dec Thurs–Sat 6.30–9pm.

Bideford

Serenely spread out along the west bank of the River Torridge, the estuary port of **BIDEFORD** formed an important link in the North Devon trade network. The tree-lined quayside retains its role as the town's focal point today, while its **Long Bridge**, first built around 1280 but reconstructed in stone in the following century, still straddles the broad expanse of the Torridge. The bridge was subsequently reinforced and widened – hence the irregularity of its 24 arches, no two of which have the same span.

In Market Place, Bideford's **Pannier Market** is a diminutive version of the one in Barnstaple, open for crafts and produce on Tuesdays, Fridays and Saturdays. Across Long Bridge, **East-the-Water** holds Bideford's disused station– the **Tarka Trail** runs alongside the river on this side.

Brief history

From the Norman era until the eighteenth century, Bideford was the property of the Grenville family, whose most celebrated scion was **Sir Richard Grenville**, commander of the ships that carried the first settlers to Virginia and later a major player in the defeat of the Spanish Armada. Grenville also featured in *Westward Ho!*, the historical romance by Charles Kingsley who wrote part of the book in Bideford and is commemorated by a statue at the quay's northern end. Behind it, extending up the riverbank, **Victoria Park** contains guns captured from the Spanish in 1588.

Burton Art Gallery and Museum

Kingsley Rd, EX39 2QQ • Mon–Sat 10am–4pm (till 5pm Aug), Sun 11am–4pm • Free • ☎01237 471455, ⓦburtonartgallery.co.uk
Backing onto Victoria Park, the **Burton Art Gallery and Museum** exhibits paintings from the eighteenth century to modern times and has regular exhibitions. Craftwork is also represented, including examples of the local slipware – once prized even more highly than that of Barnstaple. The museum section focuses on local personalities including Richard Grenville, and on such trades as lime-burning, saddlery, and glove- and collar-making; items on display include the original town charter sealed by Elizabeth I in 1583, and a scale model of Long Bridge at every stage from its beginnings to the present day.

ARRIVAL AND DEPARTURE

BIDEFORD

By bus All buses stop on Bideford Quay; #16 and #19 go to Appledore (#21A on Sun), #16 and #21 go to Westward Ho!, #319 goes to Clovelly and Hartland, and there are various services to Barnstaple and other local destinations.

Destinations Appledore (1–2 hourly; 15–35min); Barnstaple (Mon–Sat every 5–20min, Sun every 30min, 30min); Clovelly (Mon–Sat 6 daily; 40min); Exeter (Mon–Sat 7 daily; 2hr 10min); Great Torrington (Mon–Sat 1–2 hourly; 15–20min); Hartland (Mon–Sat 5 daily; 55min); Westward Ho! (Mon–Sat 3–4 hourly, Sun hourly; 10min).

INFORMATION AND ACTIVITIES

Tourist information Inside the Burton Art Gallery and Museum (see p.189), with the same hours (☎01237 477676; ⌨burtonartgallery.co.uk). You can buy day-return boat tickets to Lundy Island (see p.195) here as well.

Bike rental Bideford Bicycle Hire, Torrington St, East-the-Water, 150yd south of the bridge (daily 9am–5pm; ☎01237 424123, ⌨bidefordbicyclehire.co.uk); £8.50 per half-day, £11.50 per day. Surfboards and kayaks can also be rented.

ACCOMMODATION AND EATING

★**Bideford Beehives** Higher Fordlands, Heywood Rd, Northam EX39 3QA ☎01237 421139, ⌨bidefordbee hivesbb.co.uk. North of the centre, close to the A39, this first-rate rural B&B offers two twin or double rooms with a shared bathroom – it's ideal for a family or small group, but if just one room is wanted the other is left empty to give exclusive bathroom use. Guests are presented with a cream tea and, at breakfast, home-produced honey. No credit cards. **£75**

Mariners 4 Cooper St, EX39 2DA ☎01237 476447, ⌨marinersbideford.com. This relaxed restaurant just up from the Quay is the place to come for local and seasonal meat and seafood, such as fishcakes, pan-fried scallops with chorizo, and venison steak (mains mostly £12–17), as well as some scrumptious desserts. While you eat you can acquaint yourself with the snippets of local history written on the walls. Wed–Sat 6.30–8.30pm (last orders).

The Mount Northdown Rd, EX39 3LP ☎01237 473748, ⌨www.themountbideford.co.uk. Handsome Georgian guesthouse set in its own walled gardens, with elegantly furnished rooms and a grand piano in a separate guests' lounge. It's in a quiet area a few minutes outside the centre, linked by a footpath. **£90**

★**Velvet & Vanilla** 12 Cooper St, EX39 2DA ☎01237 420444. Small and snug spot in the centre for wonderful soups and toasties, luscious cakes, and evening meze (£3–5) and stone-baked pizzas (£7–10). Good-value set-price deals are sometimes available, and there's wi-fi access. Mon–Sat 10am–4pm, also May–Sept Fri & Sat 7pm–late.

Appledore

A picturesque vestige of North Devon's maritime heritage lies a couple of miles downstream of Bideford at **APPLEDORE**, near the estuary of the combined Taw and Torridge rivers. Until recently home to England's last commercial shipbuilders, the port is now a harmonious ensemble of pastel-coloured Georgian cottages alongside a placid quayside, with a warren of tiny back lanes straggling up the hill. The **Appledore Book Festival** takes place over ten days in late September/early October (⌨appledorebookfestival.co.uk), and there's a ten-day **regatta** in mid-August (⌨www.appledoreinstowregatta.org.uk).

North Devon Maritime Museum

Odun Rd, EX39 1PT · Late March to Oct daily 10.30am–5pm · £3 · ☎01237 422064, ⌨northdevonmaritimemuseum.co.uk

Housed in one of a row of elegant villas a few minutes' walk up from the Quay, Appledore's **North Devon Maritime Museum** lends absorbing insights into the town's seafaring past and into maritime matters generally. Past the ship's figurehead, cannon and anchors arrayed outside, there are roomfuls of salvaged equipment, model ships, shipwrights' tools, faded old photos of Appledore in a reconstructed Victorian kitchen and a pair of mud shoes for walking in the sticky stuff.

ARRIVAL AND DEPARTURE

APPLEDORE

By bus From Richmond Road, by the museum, bus #19 goes to Barnstaple and Bideford (#21A on Sun); for Westward Ho! take #19 to Northam (#21A on Sun) and change onto #21.

Destinations Barnstaple (hourly; 50min); Bideford (hourly; 15–20min); Northam (hourly; 5–10min).

GETTING AROUND AND TOURS

By ferry Between April and October, a passenger ferry shuttles between Appledore and Instow, operating continuously on most days for about 3hr at high tide (check ☞ appledoreinstowferry.com for times; crossings may be cancelled in bad weather). Embark opposite *Johns* delicatessen and café on the quayside; tickets cost £1.50.

Boat tours Between Easter and September, you can join two-hour fishing trips and estuary and river cruises (£12/person each) at Appledore's quayside; ask at Appledore Quay Gift Shop at 15 The Quay or call ☏ 01237 4223071 for information and tickets.

ACCOMMODATION

The Seagate The Quay, EX39 1QS ☏ 01237 472589, ☞ theseagate.co.uk. You can enjoy magnificent estuary views from this quayside inn, which offers ten smart rooms, including family accommodation. It's worth spending extra for more space and the best vistas. Food and drink are available in the popular bar/restaurant downstairs. **£92**

★**Torridge House** 19 Bude St, EX39 1PS ☏ 01237 477127, ☞ torridgehouseappledore.com. Homely Georgian B&B in a quiet lane near the riverfront, offering three en-suite rooms with a mix of antique and modern furnishings. There's a guests' lounge, a garden with chickens and a conservatory where breakfast is taken around a communal table. Evening meals can be arranged too. No credit cards. **£90**

EATING AND DRINKING

Beaver Inn Irsha St, EX39 1RY ☏ 01237 474822, ☞ beaverinn.co.uk. At the northern tip of Appledore, this traditional pub has wonderful estuary views from its outdoor tables, live music (usually Sat, Sun & Mon) and a friendly mix of visitors and locals. You can eat in the bar or the separate restaurant; snacks cost under £10, a seafood main is around £15. Daily 11am–11pm.

The Coffee Cabin 22 The Quay, EX39 1QS ☏ 01237 475843. Here's a handy stop for a coffee or tea with a wedge of cake, an all-day breakfast or a lunch of quiche, smoked haddock chowder or a zingy crab sandwich (£8.50). There are colourful cushions, art on the walls, a seating area upstairs and wi-fi. Daily 9am–5pm.

Instow and around

On the eastern side of the Torridge estuary, **INSTOW** has an even calmer feel than Appledore. The sandy beach, chosen by the US army for D-Day rehearsals during World War II, broadens to a muddy flat at low tide and is backed by a long quay dating from the seventeenth century. A ferry links Instow with Appledore in summer (see above).

Tapeley Park

Near Instow, EX39 4NT • Late March to Oct Mon–Fri & Sun 10am–5pm • £6 • ☏ 01271 860897, ☞ tapeleygardens.com

A mile south of Instow, the ten acres of gardens at **Tapeley Park** feature Italianate lawns overlooked by palm trees and topiary, descending in ornamental terraces to a lake surrounded by huge *Thuja plicata* trees – the oldest of their kind in the country. There's an ilex tunnel; a brick, igloo-shaped Ice House; a Shell House plastered with broken shells and conches; and a walled kitchen garden. The red-brick, much-altered **Queen Anne house** (open only to groups) has been the home for three centuries of the Christie family – John Christie was the moving spirit in setting up Glyndebourne Opera, in Sussex, in 1934. The present owner has given the place a strong eco-efficient direction; consult the website for details of the events and exhibitions taking place throughout the summer.

ACCOMMODATION AND EATING   INSTOW AND AROUND

Instow Arms Marine Parade, EX39 4JJ ☏ 01271 860608, ☞ instowarms.com. Across from the beach, this elegant pub with St Austell and Dartmoor ales has an upstairs dining area (book early for window tables) and outdoor seating. Snack on a wrap or ciabatta, or order a main course for £12–15. Kitchen daily noon–9pm.

Wayfarer Inn Lane End Road, off Marine Parade, EX39 4LB ☏ 01271 860342, ☞ thewayfarerinn.co.uk. The rooms above this pub are light and modern, some with great sea views, and there's a family suite. The owners are friendly and quality bar food is served downstairs. **£80**

Great Torrington and around

Five miles up the River Torridge from Bideford, connected by the Tarka Trail and the A386, **GREAT TORRINGTON** is a sleepy market town surrounded by woods and hills carpeted in gorse and bracken. It's a small, low-key place, though the central **Square** makes a handsome ensemble, with the pink Georgian facade of the long Pannier Market and a porticoed town hall. The beamed *Black Horse* here is one of Torrington's oldest buildings (probably sixteenth-century), briefly serving as the headquarters of General Fairfax during the Civil War.

Brief history

Torrington changed hands several times during England's **Civil War**, and was the scene of the last great battle in 1646, at the end of which the New Model Army under Thomas Fairfax and Oliver Cromwell occupied the town. Two hundred Royalist soldiers were imprisoned in St Michael's church, just north of the Square, where, unknown to their captors, eighty barrels of gunpowder had also been stored; somehow (for reasons never discovered) it was ignited, the ensuing explosion killing them all. In the churchyard of the rebuilt St Michael's, a large cobbled mound near the main entrance is reputed to be the burial place of the victims.

Rosemoor

A3124 Exeter road, EX38 8PH • Daily: April–Sept 10am–6pm; Oct–March 10am–5pm; last entry 1hr before closing • £10, or £7.50 if arriving by bus or bike • ☎ 0845 265 8072, ⓦ rhs.org.uk • Bus #5B (not Sun)

In a steep wooded valley a mile south of Torrington, the gardens at **Rosemoor** encompass a huge range of plants, but are most famed as a centre of rose cultivation, notably in summer when 2000 roses in 200 varieties are on display. However, the garden – one of five managed by the Royal Horticultural Society – makes a good outing at any time for its woodland walks, Winter Garden, Hot Garden, Model Gardens, numerous tropical species and the exuberant herbaceous borders.

ARRIVAL AND DEPARTURE

GREAT TORRINGTON AND AROUND

By bus Great Torrington is connected by services #5B, #71 and #72 to Barnstaple, and by #5B, #75 and #75A to Bideford; #5B also stops at Instow and continues to Exeter. There are no Sunday services.

Destinations Barnstaple (Mon–Sat 1–2 hourly; 45min); Bideford (Mon–Sat 1–2 hourly; 20min); Exeter (Mon–Sat 7 daily; 1hr 50min); Instow (Mon–Sat 6 daily; 25min).

INFORMATION AND ACTIVITIES

Tourist information Castle Hill car park (Mon, Tues, Thurs & Fri 10am–4pm, Wed & Sat 10am–1pm; ☎ 01805 626140, ⓦ great-torrington.com).
Bike rental Torrington Cycle Hire at the old station,

a mile or so north of Great Torrington off the Bideford road (daily 9.30am–5pm, check Nov–Jan; ☎ 01805 622633, ⓦ torringtoncyclehire.co.uk), rents bikes for £12 per day.

ACCOMMODATION AND EATING

Browns 37 South St, EX38 8AB ☎ 01805 622900, ⓦ brownsdelicatessen.co.uk. You can pick up delectable picnic items at this deli, including rolls filled with Devon Blue or Devon Brie cheeses, local pâté and cured salmon rolls. There are some tables at the back for coffees, teas and light snacks such as soup, quiche and spinach and feta pie (£5–8). Tues–Sat 9.30am–5.30pm.
Puffing Billy Old Torrington Station, EX38 8JD ☎ 01805 623050, ⓦ puffingbilly.co.uk. Tarka Trailers will appreciate this refreshment stop serving panini, jacket

potatoes, pasties and pies (around £6). It's in the waiting rooms at the old station just north of Great Torrington. Daily 9am–5pm.
Windsor House New Rd, EX38 8EJ ☎ 01805 623529, ⓦ windsorhousebandb.co.uk. This friendly B&B at the edge of town is in a rather grand ex-farmhouse whose good-size rooms have private bathrooms. Snooker, darts, table football, gym equipment, a lock-up for bikes and evening meals on request are also available. **£70**

ENTERTAINMENT

Plough Arts Centre Fore St, off the Square ☎ 01805 624624, ⓦ theploughartscentre.org.uk. Friendly spot with a gallery showing arts and craftwork exhibitions, and a lively programme of films, comedy, theatre and music. The relaxed café serves snacks and full meals, and has wi-fi. Tues–Sat: bar 10am–late; kitchen noon–3pm & 6.15–8.30pm (call to check evenings).

Westward Ho!

Three miles northwest of Bideford and less than two miles southwest of Appledore, **WESTWARD HO!** is the only English town to be named after a book. **Charles Kingsley**'s bestselling historical romance, which he wrote while staying at Bideford, was set in the surrounding country, and it wasn't long after its publication in 1855 that speculators recognized the tourist potential of what was then an empty expanse of sand and mud pounded by Atlantic rollers. **Rudyard Kipling** spent four years of his youth here, as recounted in his novel *Stalky and Co.*, describing the place as "twelve bleak houses by the shore".

When Kingsley got round to visiting the new resort, he didn't think much of it either, and he probably wouldn't care for it now, with its unsightly muddle of holiday chalets, Victorian villas, modern blocks and the Royal North Devon Golf Club – the country's oldest course, dating from 1864. Once you get past these, however, the broad sandy seafront has an undeniable grandeur. Popular with kite-flyers and kitesurfers, the **Blue Flag beach** offers fabulous swimming, surf and great views across Bideford Bay.

Behind the sands, protected from the sea by the long rocky foreshore and a high ridge of large pebbles, **Northam Burrows** is a flat, marshy expanse of dunes and meadows, rich in flora and fauna and attracting plenty of migratory birds.

Clovelly and around

Off A39, EX39 5TA • Daily: April to late July & early Sept to Oct 9.30am–5pm; late July to early Sept 9am–6.30pm; Nov–March 10am–4pm; closing times may vary • £7 • ☎ 01237 431781, ⓦ clovelly.co.uk

The impossibly picturesque village of **CLOVELLY** was put on the map in the second half of the nineteenth century by two books: Charles Dickens' *A Message From the Sea* and, inevitably, *Westward Ho!* – Charles Kingsley's father was rector here for six years. To an extent, the archaic tone of the village has been preserved by restricting hotel accommodation and shops, and banning holiday homes and traffic. Nonetheless, in the tourist season, when the village is overrun by streams of visitors, it's hard to see beyond the artifice, but come out of season or after hours, and you'll find genuine charm.

Unless you're coast-pathing, you have to pass through the oversized visitor centre to enter Clovelly, where you're charged for access to shops, snack bars, an audiovisual show and use of the car park, as well as for entering the village itself (although it's free after hours). Immediately below the visitor centre, **Hobby Drive** is a three-mile walk along the cliffs, through woods of sycamore, oak, beech, rowan and the occasional holly, with grand views. Also below the visitor centre, the cobbled, traffic-free **High Street**, known locally as Up-along or Down-along (according to which way you are going), plunges down past neat, flower-smothered cottages where battered sledges are tethered for transporting goods – the only way to carry supplies since the use of donkeys ceased. One building holds an exhibition devoted to **Charles Kingsley**, another has been restored as a nineteenth-century fisherman's home.

At the bottom of the village, Clovelly's stony beach and tiny **harbour** lie snuggled in a cleft in the cliffs. A handful of fishing boats and piles of lobster baskets are the only remnants of a fleet that provided the village's main business before the herring and mackerel stocks dried up in the first half of the twentieth century.

7

ARRIVAL AND GETTING AROUND

CLOVELLY

By bus Service #319 (not Sun) stops at the visitor centre on its route between Barnstaple, Bideford and Hartland.
Destinations Barnstaple (Mon–Sat 4 daily; 1hr 10min); Bideford (Mon–Sat 5 daily, 45min); Hartland (Mon–Sat 5 daily; 15min).

Land Rover service A shuttle service operates continuously between the harbour and the visitor centre (March–October; £2.50).

INFORMATION AND TOURS

Tourist information Visitor centre (daily: April to late July & early Sept to Oct 9.30am–5pm; late July to early Sept 9am–6.30pm; Nov–March 10am–4pm; ☎01237 431781, ⓦ clovelly.co.uk).
Boat tours In summer, boat trips advertised at the harbourside provide an excellent way to experience the bay and coastline. Independent Charters (☎01237 431374,

ⓦ independentcharters.co.uk) offers two-hour cruises to Hartland Lighthouse (£25) and trips to Lundy Island (see p.195), which include at least six hours on shore plus an hour's sailing each way (£40). Tickets cost £40 plus a £6 per person landing fee that is waived for National Trust cardholders. Fishing trips are also available (4hr inshore for £35, full-day offshore for £60). All prices are per person.

ACCOMMODATION AND EATING

★ East Dyke Farmhouse Higher Clovelly, EX39 5RU ☎01237 431216, ⓦ bedbreakfastclovelly.co.uk. A 200-year-old building with a beamed and flagstoned dining room and three spacious guest rooms with fridges and private bathrooms. Breakfasts are outstanding. No credit cards. **£65**

Red Lion The Quay, EX39 5TF ☎01237 431237, ⓦ stayatclovelly.co.uk. Superbly positioned, this harbourside hotel has a traditional, slightly clubby atmosphere, but friendly staff and great views from the bedrooms. Pies and sandwiches are available in the *Harbour Bar*, while the semiformal restaurant upstairs provides two- or three-course dinners for £26 or £30. Restaurant daily 7–8pm (last orders); bar kitchen noon–2.30pm & 6–8.30pm. **£156**

Buck's Mills

Five miles east along the coast from Clovelly, **BUCK'S MILLS** lies at the bottom of thick woods that are tended by the Woodland Trust and crossed by waymarked paths. A fast-flowing stream gushes through the valley, alongside the village's sloping street, and thundering down to a stony beach that's overlooked by the ivy-covered, castle-like ruin of a **lime kiln**, thought to date from 1760. Limestone and coal were brought here by boat from south Wales and burned in the local kilns to produce slaked or quicklime, used in limewash, limewater and as fertilizer for the local acidic soil.

From the beach, you may be able to pick out the **Gore**, a submerged pebble bank that stretches out to sea for a quarter of a mile. This may have been man-made, though local lore attributes it to the devil, who started building it as a causeway to Lundy, eighteen miles distant, but gave up when the handle of his Devon shovel broke.

Hartland and around

Four miles west of Clovelly and about three from the coast, **HARTLAND** has a quiet, insulated air, remote from the main routes of the West Country. The village has three pubs and a couple of stores to supply nourishment, but it's the coast to the north and west that provides the main incentive for being here, reached – unless you're on the coastal path – along narrow, high-hedged lanes.

Hartland Point

Three miles northwest of Hartland, the Atlantic meets Bideford Bay at **Hartland Point**, one of Devon's most dramatic headlands. A solitary lighthouse, 350ft high, overlooks jagged black rocks battered by the sea, and when conditions are clear, the bare horizon is interrupted only by the long, low profile of Lundy Island. Seals can sometimes be seen here. A mile east, **Shipload Bay** is the only sandy beach between Westward Ho! and Cornwall.

Hartland Quay

A couple of miles south of Hartland Point, **Hartland Quay** is a scatter of houses around the remains of a once-busy port, financed in part by the mariners Raleigh, Drake and Hawkins, but mostly destroyed by storms in the nineteenth century. The slate in the cliffs to either side reveals cross-sections of spectacularly contorted rock strata, though its instability makes it inadvisable to approach the edge, climb or sit under the cliffs.

Hartland Abbey

Near Hartland, EX39 6DT • House Easter–Sept Mon–Thurs & Sun 2–5pm; gardens Easter–Sept Mon–Thurs & Sun 11.30am–5pm • £12, grounds only £8 • ☎ 01237 441496, ⓦ hartlandabbey.com

A mile or so west of Hartland, gardens and lush woodland surround **Hartland Abbey**, an eighteenth-century country house incorporating the ruins of an abbey dissolved in 1539. It's an endearing old place, displaying fine furniture, old photographs and recently uncovered Victorian murals on Arthurian themes, copied from the House of Lords. The Regency library has portraits by Gainsborough and Reynolds, and George Gilbert Scott designed the vaulted Alhambra Corridor and outer hall. From the house, a path leads a mile through woodland strewn in spring with bluebells and primroses to cliffs and a small bay that's sandy at low tide.

7

ARRIVAL AND INFORMATION

HARTLAND AND AROUND

By bus Hartland is served by bus #319, running east to Clovelly, Bideford and Barnstaple and south to Bude, and buses #217 and #219 to Bude.

Destinations Barnstaple (Mon–Sat 4 daily; 1hr 25min);

Bideford (Mon–Sat 5 daily; 1hr); Bude (Mon–Sat 3–6 daily; 30min); Clovelly (Mon–Sat 6 daily; 15min).

Tourist information The website ⓦ hartlandpeninsula .co.uk has pages of useful information on the area.

ACCOMMODATION

★ **Two Harton Manor** The Square, off Fore St, EX39 6BL ☎ 01237 441670, ⓦ twohartonmanor.co.uk. Congenial choice with three rooms (one a single, one en suite with a four-poster) above an artist's studio and close to a good pub. Organic, locally sourced and Aga-cooked breakfasts are eaten in the flagstoned kitchen. Woodcut printmaking courses are also offered. No credit cards. **£72**

YHA Elmscott Bunkhouse Elmscott, EX39 6ES ☎ 01629 592700, ⓦ yha.org.uk/hostel/elmscott -bunkhouse. Located 3.5 miles southwest of Hartland and about 0.5 mile inland, this remote bunkhouse with a self-catering kitchen and small shop occupies a converted Victorian schoolhouse. Dorms **£22**, twin rooms **£42**

Lundy Island

Disembarking on windswept **LUNDY ISLAND**, twelve miles northwest of Hartland Point, induces something close to culture shock. A granite sliver roughly three miles long and half a mile wide, the island today has no roads, one pub, one shop and some twenty full-time residents. Most of Lundy consists of grass, heather and bog that's crossed by dry-stone walls and grazed by ponies, goats, deer and rare Soay sheep. The shores – mainly cliffy on the south and west, softer and undulating on the east – shelter a rich variety of **birdlife**, including kittiwakes, fulmars, shags and Manx shearwaters, which often nest in rabbit burrows. The most famous birds, though, are the **puffins**, which can be sighted in April and May when they come ashore to mate. Offshore, **basking sharks**, which can grow to 25ft, can be seen from early July to mid-August, and grey seals can be observed all the year round. You'll find a few pockets of beach to swim off, but the cold waters are not exactly inviting, and swift currents are a risk, particularly at the northern end of the island.

Brief history

Named from the Norse *Lunde* (puffin) and *ey* (island), Lundy was home to an early Christian community in the fifth and sixth centuries. The piratical **Marisco family** established itself here in the twelfth century, making use of the coves and shingle beaches to terrorize shipping up and down the Bristol Channel. The family's reign ended in 1242 when one of their number, William de Marisco, was found to be plotting against the king, whereupon he was hanged, drawn and quartered at Tower Hill in London.

After the Mariscos, Lundy's most famous inhabitants were **Thomas Benson**, MP for Barnstaple in the eighteenth century – mainly remembered for using slave labour to work the island's granite quarries and for his part in a massive insurance fraud – and **William Hudson Heaven**, a clergyman from Bristol who bought the island in 1834 and established what became known as the "Kingdom of Heaven". He reopened the quarries, which are said to have provided the tough granite for the Thames Embankment in London, though they closed soon afterwards.

In 1969, Lundy was acquired by the National Trust and it's now managed by the **Landmark Trust** with the aim of restoring the many relics of former habitation that are scattered around – several of them converted into holiday accommodation – and preserving the primitive character of the place.

The village

The island's "**village**" is a uniform cluster of buildings including the pub and shop. Just east of the pub stands **Millcombe House**, an incongruous piece of Georgian architecture in these bleak surroundings that was the home of William Hudson Heaven. South of the pub, the square-towered church of **St Helena** was built in 1896 by his son, Hudson Grosett Heaven, to the design of the eminent Victorian architect John Norton.

The Devil's Limekiln

Southwest of the church, around the island's southern tip, the **Devil's Limekiln** should be approached with care: it's a pit more than 300ft deep, into which the sea enters from the bottom.

Marisco Castle

A short walk up from the landing jetty on the island's southeastern corner, **Marisco Castle** was erected by Henry III in 1244, following the downfall of the Mariscos, and was paid for from the sale of rabbits – Lundy was a Royal Warren. The small keep has walls 3ft thick, constructed of local granite and all inclining inwards, and was probably the main building on the island until the late eighteenth century. Rebuilt in the Civil War, it's now restored as holiday accommodation.

The northern end of the island

Lundy's main track heads along the north–south axis of the island, across the springy turf and heather of **Ackland's Moor** to the first of the island's three dividing walls. After the first or "quarter wall", climb down a steep path to the right to see the **quarries** – last used in 1911 – and adjacent beach. At the western end of the wall, granite steps lead down to the remains of the cottages, magazine and gun-station which make up the **Battery** (dating from 1863), from which a cannon was fired every ten minutes in foggy conditions: the cannons are still there. Half a mile to the north, **Jenny's Cove** is named after a vessel reputed to be carrying ivory and gold that was wrecked here in the seventeenth century, and is the haunt of razorbills, guillemots and puffins.

ARRIVAL AND INFORMATION

LUNDY ISLAND

By boat The MS *Oldenburg* crosses to Lundy up to three times weekly from Bideford and Ilfracombe between April and October, with a journey time of around two hours from either town. Day-return tickets cost £36, open returns £64 (discounts apply to families and, on day-return tickets, senior citizens, students and National Trust members).

By helicopter Between November and March, a helicopter service from Hartland Point (see p.194) takes over, taking just seven minutes (currently Mon & Fri at 11am, £112 return).

Travel and tourist information For sailing and flight reservations, and to check departures (sailings are dependent on the state of the seas, though cancellations are rare) call ☎ 01271 863636; day-returns can also be booked from Ilfracombe and Bideford tourist offices. Consult ⊛ lundyisland.co.uk for information on transport, accommodation and activities.

ACCOMMODATION

B&B accommodation must be booked within two weeks of your stay, but **self-catering** accommodation can be booked at any time. Bookings made within two weeks of your stay can be arranged at the Landmark Trust's shore offices on Bideford's Quay or, between April and October, Ilfracombe Harbour (☎ 01271 863636 for both); otherwise, contact the Trust's main office (☎ 01628 825925, ⊛ landmarktrust.org.uk).

7

SELF-CATERING

Prices Accommodation on Lundy can be booked up months in advance, but it's always worth enquiring about last-minute vacancies. Self-catering is the main option, with accommodation prices for two at around £685–985/week in midsummer, £366–469/week in winter (three- or four-night stays are also possible).

Accommodation options Choices include the two-storey granite *Barn*, a hostel sleeping fourteen; the *Old House*, where Charles Kingsley stayed in 1849; and the *Old Light*, a lighthouse built in 1820 by the architect of Dartmoor Prison (one of the three lighthouses on the island – the other two are in use). The remotest place is the *Tibbetts*, about 1.8 miles from the village along the main track to the north, and lit by calor gas rather than

electricity; it sleeps four in bunks. A single person will find the *Radio Room* cosy; it once housed the transmitter that was the island's only link with the outside world.

B&B

B&B – with breakfast in the *Marisco Tavern* – is available only in the rare gaps between rentals, and can only be booked within two weeks of the proposed visit (around £75 per night for a double room).

CAMPING

There's a campsite near the *Marisco* (Easter–Oct; £6–10/person). It's surrounded by a protective wall but can still get pretty wet and windswept in stormy weather.

EATING

The **village shop** (open daily) has a good range of provisions and, if you're staying on the island, you can arrange to have groceries delivered.

Marisco Tavern High St, EX39 2LY ☎ 01237 431831. The convivial atmosphere in this pub/community centre is only slightly dampened by the display of life-preservers from some of the ships that have foundered off the island's coasts. The burgers, pasties (around £6) and St Austell ales are good enough to discourage some trippers off the ferry from venturing any further on the island. Kitchen daily 8.30am–10am, noon–2pm & 6–8.30pm.

Southeast Cornwall

FOWEY

Southeast Cornwall

Nearly all of Cornwall's rivers empty into the sea along the county's southern coast, providing a succession of estuaries that shelter the numerous small fishing ports strung along the seaboard. This combination of natural beauty and quaint old villages has ensured that the area is popular with visitors, and most places are touched by commercialization to a degree. Nonetheless, the thrilling cliff-hung coastline – the best sections of which are accessible only on the South West Coast Path – always provides a refreshing escape.

Tourism has certainly stamped its imprint on medieval ports such as **Looe** and **Polperro**, but their charm is well-nigh irresistible in low season, when they revert to the sleepy state that suits them best. The estuary town of **Fowey**, however, is big enough to transcend the summer influx, and as a working port has an agreeably self-sufficient air, while the quiet appeal of inland **Lostwithiel** is mostly lost on travellers hurrying through on the A390. West of here, **St Austell**, the capital of Cornwall's china-clay industry, lacks much intrinsic interest, but it's just a stone's throw from the unspoilt Georgian harbour village of Charlestown – the most appealing of the resorts on St Austell Bay – and the extraordinary **Eden Project**, the region's most-talked-about attraction.

8

On a smaller scale, the Lost Gardens of Heligan, further west, are also spectacular: this salvaged Victorian garden contains immaculate shrubs alongside swampy, jungle-like tracts. Close by, **Mevagissey** preserves a genuine allure, with the added bonus of some fine restaurants. To the south, **Veryan Bay** is a sequestered nook that is mostly off the tourist track, though its gorgeous beaches are popular in summer.

Continuing west along the coast, Carrick Roads, the complex estuary basin that forms one of the finest deep-water anchorages in Britain, has pockets of frantic tourist activity counterbalanced by the rural calm of its creeks and muddy inlets. At its top, the county capital of **Truro** has Cornwall's best museum and one of Britain's most striking – and newest – neo-Gothic cathedrals, but the major resort in these parts is **Falmouth**, at the bottom of the estuary, where the mighty Pendennis Castle occupies a commanding site at the end of the promontory. Its sister-fort lies across the estuary mouth at **St Mawes**, the biggest village on the **Roseland Peninsula**, a sequestered and undeveloped area of secretive lanes, waterside churches and rocky coast.

Looe

LOOE was drawing crowds as early as 1800, when the first bathing machines were wheeled out, but the arrival of the railway in 1879 was what really packed its beaches. The town stands where the mouths of the East and West Looe rivers meet, the combined waterway dividing East Looe, where most of the action is, from quieter West

Highlights

❶ The Eden Project This disused clay pit is now home to exotic plants and crops, many reared in vast domes, and offers an extraordinary display of biodiversity. **See p.209**

❷ Fowey With its beautiful location, this classic riverside town and its environs invite an extended exploration. **See p.205**

❸ Lost Gardens of Heligan Exuberant and intriguing, this historic garden ranks among the country's finest. **See p.215**

❹ Caerhays Castle This remote stately home and its extensive grounds, leading down to a beach on one of Cornwall's loveliest coasts, repay a leisurely wander. **See p.215**

❺ The Roseland Peninsula Seclusion and serenity reign in this remote haven, which also offers fabulous coastal walking. **See p.219**

❻ Oyster Festival, Falmouth A convivial celebration of local seafood and gastronomy – a must for foodies. **See p.226**

HIGHLIGHTS ARE MARKED ON THE MAP ON P.202

Looe. On the East Looe side, the main **Fore Street** runs south from the bridge, a long gaudy parade of shops and cafés that ends at the web of narrow lanes around the beach. It's East Looe's long **harbour** that holds most of the interest, however, its quays stacked with crates and lobster baskets, serving the sixty-odd fishing vessels that continue to work from here. When the tide's right, crossing by **ferry** (40p) from here saves you the trek round by bridge to West Looe.

Old Guildhall Museum

Higher Market St, PL13 1BW • Easter–Oct daily 11am–4pm • £2 • ☎ 01503 263709

On two floors, the **Old Guildhall Museum** sums up Looe's history by means of a motley collection of maritime models, household knick-knacks, World War II mementos, and Punch and Judy puppets. It's the building itself that impresses most, however – a timber-framed fifteenth-century construction that once housed a magistrates' court and jail cells. You can see the magistrates' bench at one end, and below, alongside a set of stocks, a couple of the cells.

The beaches

Projecting south from the harbour, Banjo Pier – named for its shape – separates the river mouth from **East Looe Beach**. This is the handiest stretch of sand but it gets pretty congested. At the far end of the beach, try instead the quieter (and rockier) **Second** or **Sanders Beach**, reached through a break in the rocks. More secluded and sandier beaches are accessible from here at low tide and also via the coastal path from Looe or by road. One of the best is **Millendreath**, a crescent of sand and shingle less than a mile east of Looe, backed by concrete terraces and holiday chalets but still scenic, with scattered rocks and green hills on either side. West Looe's long **Hannafore Beach** at the end of Marine Drive has good views over to Looe Island; shingly at high tide, it reveals rock pools when the tide's out.

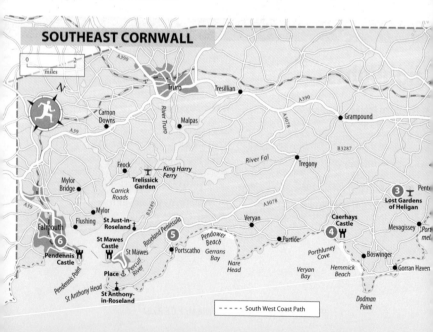

LOOE ISLAND

One of the most popular excursions from Buller Quay is out to **Looe Island** (also called St George's Island), a mile or so offshore. Once the site of a Benedictine monastery, the low, green hump, just a few hundred yards across, was bombed in World War II by Germans who mistook it for a warship. In 1965 it was bought by two doughty sisters who lived there for nearly forty years, as recounted in *We Bought an Island* by Evelyn Atkins (see p.348). Now a bird sanctuary owned by Cornwall Wildlife Trust, the island is great for a gentle ramble on a trail that takes in its highest point (500ft), and allows you to observe Cornwall's second-largest breeding colony of great black-backed gulls. The rat population is a constant threat to the nesting birds; according to the nineteenth-century novelist Wilkie Collins, rats were caught on the island, "smothered in onion" and "eaten with vindictive relish by the people of Looe".

Boat trips take place between Easter and September (£7 return, plus a £4 landing fee), allowing you a two-hour stay; the excursions are highly dependent on the tides, but departures should be posted up on the quayside (near the lifeboat station) or you can call the operator (☎07814 264514). Guided walks, once or twice monthly, can be booked at ⓦ cornwallwildlife trust.org.uk (£25). Take food and drink, as there's nothing available on the island.

ARRIVAL AND INFORMATION
LOOE

By train The Looe Valley Line makes a scenic run along the course of the East Looe River from Liskeard (April–Oct Mon–Sat hourly & Sun 8 daily, Nov–March Mon–Sat hourly; 30min).

By bus All bus services stop just north of the bridge, including the #71 to Plymouth, #71A and #72 to Plymouth and Polperro, #73 to Polperro and Liskeard, and #481 to Polperro and Polruan.

Destinations Liskeard (Mon–Sat hourly, Sun every 2hr; 30min); Plymouth (Mon–Sat 2 hourly, Sun every 2hr; 1hr 10min–1hr 35min); Polperro (Mon–Sat 2–3 hourly, Sun 1–2 hourly; 15–25min); Polruan (Mon–Fri 4 daily; 40min).

By car Drivers should head for the Millpool car park at the approach to Looe, as the car park near the bridge fills up quickly.

Tourist information New Guildhall, Fore St, East Looe (Easter–Oct daily 10am–5pm; ☎01503 262072, ⓦ looeguide.co.uk). Offers an accommodation booking service (£3 plus ten percent of per-night room price).

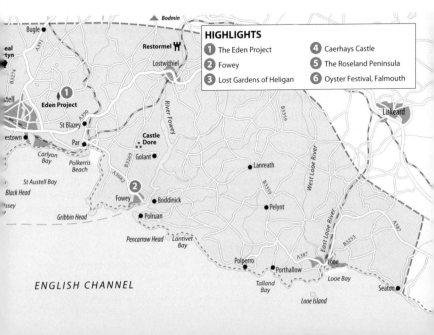

HIGHLIGHTS

① The Eden Project ④ Caerhays Castle

② Fowey ⑤ The Roseland Peninsula

③ Lost Gardens of Heligan ⑥ Oyster Festival, Falmouth

ENGLISH CHANNEL

TOURS AND ACTIVITIES

Boat tours Buller Quay is the embarkation point for various boat tours in summer. Looe Island (see box, p.203) is one of the most popular destinations; other tours include a cruise to Polperro (£18 return), and river and estuary trips (around £8). The various departure times are listed on the quay, where you can sign up to reserve a place.

Fishing trips Looe offers opportunities to go on sea-fishing jaunts (around £35/6hr), though the more modest two-hour mackerel-fishing expeditions (£12) are enough for most. Consult the boards at the quayside for days and times.

ACCOMMODATION

Bay View Farm St Martin's, PL13 1NZ ☎ 01503 265922, ⓦ looebaycaravans.co.uk. As the name suggests, the biggest draw at this friendly clifftop campsite is the fabulous view over the coast, though it's not very sheltered when the wind's up, and much of it slopes. It's right on the coast path, two miles east of Looe, and also offers "snugs" – wooden shacks with futons provided. Camping £22, snugs £50

Meneglaze House Shutta, East Looe, PL13 1LU ☎ 01503 269227, ⓦ looebedandbreakfast.com. Guests at this B&B near the station are greeted with fresh flowers and home-made biscuits. Rooms have fridges and Egyptian cotton bed-linen, and breakfasts include hog's pudding. Parking available. £95

Schooner Point 1 Trelawney Terrace, West Looe, PL13 2AG ☎ 01503 262670, ⓦ schoonerpoint.co.uk. Just 100yd from Looe Bridge, this family-run guesthouse has great river views from most of its rooms, which include a single. Banana pancakes are a speciality at breakfast. Access is via steep steps. £75

EATING

Old Sail Loft The Quay, PL13 1AP ☎ 01503 262131, ⓦ theoldsailloftrestaurant.com. This oak-beamed former warehouse on two floors offers fresh seafood, local meat and lots of antique atmosphere. Choose between the brasserie menu (£20 for three courses) or a la carte, allowing you to sample a lamb shank or the catch of the day (£18). Mon, Wed, Thurs & Sun 5.30–9pm, Fri & Sat 11.30am–2pm & 5.30–9pm.

Squid Ink Lower Chapel St, PL13 1AT ☎ 01503 262674, ⓦ squidinklooe.co.uk. You'll find a calm, stylish ambience at this smart little café/restaurant that serves tasty dishes of lamb and pork belly as well as a range of seafood dishes (around £20). Set-price menus are £20 or £26.50 for two or three courses. Feb–Dec Mon & Wed–Sat noon–11pm; food served Feb–Dec Mon & Wed–Sat noon–2pm & 6–9pm.

Trawlers on the Quay The Quay, PL13 1AH ☎ 01503 263593, ⓦ trawlersonthequay.co.uk. Behind a large window overlooking the harbour, this friendly bistro focuses on seafood, with blackboards showing the daily specials. Regular items include tempura soft-shell crab, grilled sardines and lemon sole goujons, served in large (£12–17) or small (£6–9) portions. Meat and vegetarian options are available too, and there's some outdoor seating. March–Oct daily 11am–late; food served March–Oct daily 11am–3pm & 6pm–late.

Polperro and around

Smaller and quainter than Looe, with tightly packed houses rising on each side of a stream that empties into a minuscule harbour, **POLPERRO**, four miles east, is little changed since its heyday of smuggling and pilchard fishing. However, its straggling main street, the Coombes, is now an almost unbroken row of gift shops and cafés that can get overwhelmed by the summer crowds. Come in the evening or at any time out of season and you'll fall under the spell of this undeniably pretty spot. The coast-walking, too, is outstanding: the five miles west of Polperro to **Polruan**, on the Fowey estuary, are among the most scenic stretches of South Cornwall's coastal path, giving access to some beautiful, secluded sand beaches.

POLPERRO'S FISHERMEN'S CHOIR

If you're in the area in the summer, it's worth catching a **quayside concert** by the Polperro Fishermen's Choir. They usually take place during July and August on Wednesdays at 7.30pm in Polperro, and at other local villages on different evenings. Look out for posters for details, or there may be a notice outside Polperro's chapel on Fore Street (where they perform in bad weather).

Heritage Museum of Smuggling and Fishing

The Warren, PL13 2RB • Easter–Oct daily 10.30am–4.30pm; summer school hols daily 10am–5pm • £3 • ☏ 01503 273005,
Ⓦ polperro.org/museum.html

You can get some good background on the village at the **Heritage Museum of Smuggling and Fishing**, housed in an old pilchard factory on the eastern side of the harbour. Focusing on the fishing and smuggling communities that once inhabited Polperro's packed cottages, it's a pretty low-key display, but you'll find some intriguing photos from the 1860s, including some showing the local fishermen wearing their traditional "knitfrocks" (knitted sweaters), examples of which are also on display here.

ARRIVAL AND DEPARTURE

POLPERRO AND AROUND

By bus Bus service #73 goes to Looe and Liskeard, and the #71A, #72, #73, and #481 go to Looe and Polruan from the stop at the top of the village. From the car park here, electric "trams" (Easter–Oct; £1.20) provide an alternative

to the 10min walk alongside the River Pol to the harbour.
Destinations Liskeard (Mon–Sat hourly, Sun 7 daily; 1hr 10min); Looe (1–3 hourly; 15–25min); Polruan (Mon–Fri 4 daily; 25min).

INFORMATION AND TOURS

Tourist information Visit the community website Ⓦ polperro.org, or consult the knowledgeable and helpful staff at the post office on Fore St for information on the whole area.

Boat trips Half-hour coastal jaunts cost £6, or you can board a boat bound for Looe (£18 return) or Fowey (£20 return). Most excursions are between Easter and October; call ☏ 07966 528045 to book.

ACCOMMODATION

8

The Cottles Loongcoombe Lane, PL13 2PL ☏ 01503 272578, Ⓦ cottles-polperro.co.uk. Above the car park at the top of the village this B&B has three rooms, with a conservatory (where breakfast is taken) and a deck with leafy views. **£75**
The House on the Props Talland St, PL13 2RE ☏ 01503 272310, Ⓦ houseontheprops.co.uk. Staying at this quirky B&B right on the harbour is a bit like being on a boat, with

wonky floors and unrivalled views from its snug rooms – some of which jut out over the Pol, supported by ancient struts. There's a tearoom and restaurant on board. **£80**
Penryn House The Coombes, PL13 2RQ ☏ 01503 272157, Ⓦ penrynhouse.co.uk. One of Polperro's most congenial options, this is dead central yet has a calm feel, with cosy modern rooms, a comfy guests' lounge and friendly management. **£75**

EATING AND DRINKING

★**Blue Peter** The Quay, PL13 2QZ ☏ 01503 272743, Ⓦ thebluepeterinn.yolasite.com. Snug pub above the harbour where you can pick up a doorstep crab sandwich (£9.50) or a seafood platter (£18). The beers are excellent, and there's live jazz or acoustic music at weekends. Mon–Sat 10.30am–11pm, Sun noon–11pm; kitchen daily noon–3pm & 6–9pm, winter noon–2.30pm & 6.30–8.30pm.
Couch's Saxon Bridge, PL13 2QT ☏ 01503 272554, Ⓦ couchspolperro.com. With its beamed ceiling and flickering stoves, this place has a warm, romantic

ambience, the perfect setting for its inventive dishes highlighting local produce, like scallops, duck breast and roast sea-bass fillet. You'll pay £28 or £35 for three or five courses – book ahead. May–Sept Mon–Fri 6.30–9pm; Oct–April Wed–Sat 6.30–9pm.
Old Millhouse Inn Mill Hill, PL13 2RP ☏ 01503 272362, Ⓦ theoldmillhouseinn.co.uk. Family-friendly pub with ancient stone walls, sofas, a separate restaurant area and a garden. Cornish and guest ales are served, as well as breakfasts, snacks and speciality grills (most mains around £10). Daily 9am–11pm; kitchen daily 9am–8.30pm.

Fowey and around

First views of the inland port of **FOWEY** (pronounced "Foy") reveal a cascade of neat, pale terraces at the mouth of one of the peninsula's grandest riverscapes. Having become Cornwall's major south-coast port in the fourteenth century, the town became ambitious enough for Edward IV to strip it of its military capability, though it continued to thrive commercially and became the leading port for china-clay exports in the nineteenth

---

COASTAL WALKS AROUND FOWEY

At its southern end, the Esplanade shrinks to a footpath that gives access to some exhilarating **coastal walks**. On the right, look out for the remains of a **blockhouse** that once supported a defensive chain hung across the river's mouth; a few minutes' walk past this will bring you to the small beach of **Readymoney Cove**. As the only town beach, it doesn't take long to get jam-packed, but you can escape along the wooded path that climbs steeply above the southern end of the cove to enjoy fine estuary views from the scant ruins of **St Catherine's Castle**, built by Thomas Treffry on the orders of Henry VIII – little more than a wall or two remain today.

The coast path weaves west to **Gribbin Head**, which marks the eastern bracket of St Austell Bay. Near the headland stands Menabilly House, the home of **Daphne du Maurier** for 24 years and the model for "Manderley" in *Rebecca*. The house is not open to the public and not visible from the path, but you can see where Rebecca met her watery end at **Polridmouth Cove**.

Facing Fowey across the rivermouth, **Polruan** is worth a visit for the magnificent views towards Fowey harbour and far beyond, stretching south as far as the Lizard peninsula. From the small port, a two-mile signposted coastal walk curls east to **Lantic Bay**, sheltering a beautiful and relatively quiet beach; beware that currents can be very strong here, though.

---

century. Fowey retains its strong maritime flavour today, its harbour crowded with yachts and motor launches – bulky freighters dock at the wharves north of town.

The town has close connections with **Daphne du Maurier** (1907–89), who wrote many of her novels in "Ferryside", on the water's edge at Bodinnick, and later lived at Menabilly, north of Gribbin Head (see box above). Fans can explore the links with her and other literary figures at the **Fowey Festival of Arts and Literature** (☎01726 879500, ⓦfoweyfestival.com), which takes place over eight days in mid-May and encompasses talks, walks and music.

St Fimbarrus and around

Dominating the steep centre, the fifteenth-century church of **St Fimbarrus** marks the traditional end of the ancient **Saints' Way** from Padstow (see p.298), linking the north and south Cornish coasts. Below the church, the *Ship Inn*, sporting some fine Elizabethan panelling and plaster ceilings, was originally home to the Rashleighs – a recurring name in the local annals – and was the Roundheads' HQ during the Civil War. Behind the church, **Place House**, an extravagance belonging to the local Treffry family, has a Victorian Gothic tower grafted onto the fifteenth- and sixteenth-century fortified building.

ARRIVAL AND INFORMATION

FOWEY AND AROUND

By bus Buses #24 and #25 connect Fowey with St Austell and Par train stations. The stop is outside the *Safe Harbour* pub on Lostwithiel St. Cross the river to Polruan for services to Polperro and Looe.

Destinations Par (Mon–Sat every 30min, Sun hourly; 15min); St Austell (Mon–Sat every 30min, Sun hourly; 45min).

By ferry Coming from the east, Fowey can be reached by ferry from Polruan or Bodinnick (see box, p.208). The Fowey–Mevagissey ferry (late April to Sept 3–5 daily;

35min; ☎07977 203394, ⓦmevagissey-ferries.co.uk), from Whitehouse Slip, makes an excellent way to travel between the villages and a great opportunity to view St Austell Bay, with the possibility of spotting the odd basking shark. Tickets cost £8 one-way, or £14 return.

By car The Caffa Mill car park by the Bodinnick ferry crossing fills up quickly (though there's an overflow car park nearby); there's more space at the central car park off Hanson Drive and at the third, more distant, one above Readymoney Cove; both are well signposted. A minibus

---

FOWEY REGATTA WEEK

Fowey's prosperous air is most conspicuous at its premier annual event, the **Royal Regatta and Carnival**, taking place over a week in mid-August. The sailing extravaganza, with river races and a gleaming display of fancy yachts, is topped off with aerial displays, bands, fireworks and a lively carnival night. See ⓦfoweyroyalregatta.co.uk for details.

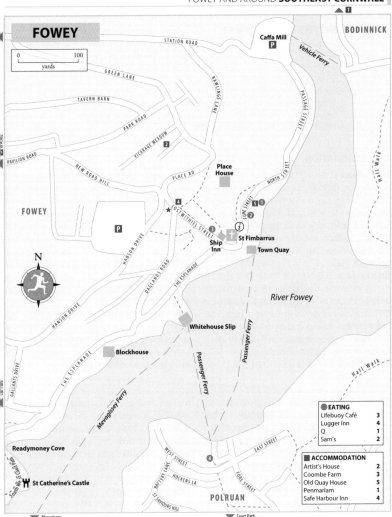

EATING

Lifebuoy Café	3
Lugger Inn	4
Q	1
Sam's	2

ACCOMMODATION

Artist's House	2
Coombe Farm	3
Old Quay House	5
Penmarlam	1
Safe Harbour Inn	4

shuttles between the main car parks and St Fimbarrus (March–Oct Mon–Sat 10am–6pm, Sun noon–5pm; Nov–Easter Tues–Sat 10am–4pm; £1–£1.50; ☎ 07703 292531).

Tourist information 5 South St (Mon–Sat 9.30am–5pm, Sun 10am–4pm, reduced hours in winter; ☎ 01726 833616, ⓦ fowey.co.uk).

TOURS AND ACTIVITIES

Boat trips The Town Quay is the departure point for river and sea tours between Easter and October. They make a great way to explore the harbour, the river as far as Lostwithiel and the coast, where you can sometimes glimpse dolphins and basking sharks; prices start at £7 for a 45-minute harbour and estuary cruise (☎ 07776 685941, ⓦ foweycruise.com).

Boat rental Self-drive motorboat rental is available between April and October from Town Quay Boat Hire (☎ 07989 991115, ⓦ fowey-boat-hire.co.uk; £30/1hr, £60/4hr, including petrol).

Canoe trips For accompanied canoe trips between April and September, contact Fowey River Expeditions (☎ 07515 353936, ⓦ foweyexpeditions.co.uk), or Encounter Cornwall (☎ 07976 466123, ⓦ encountercornwall.com). Three-hour trips cost £25 per adult, and both outfits also offer kayak hire.

CROSSING THE RIVER FOWEY

A car and passenger ferry runs between the village of **Bodinnick** and Caffa Mill, at the north end of Fowey (May–Sept Mon–Sat 7am–8.45pm or dusk, Sun 8am–8.45pm or dusk; Oct–April Mon–Fri 7am–7pm, Sat 8am–7pm, Sun 9am–7pm; £4.60 one-way for a car, driver and passenger, £1.80/foot passenger).

A passenger ferry connects **Polruan** with Fowey's Whitehouse Slip or Town Quay (May–Sept Mon–Fri 7.15am–11pm, Sat 7.30am–11pm, Sun 9am–11pm; Oct–April Mon–Fri 7.15am–7pm, Sat 7.30am–7pm, Sun 10am–5pm; £1.80 one-way, bikes £1).

For information on both ferry services, call ☎01726 870232 or see ⓦctomsandson.co.uk.

ACCOMMODATION

Artist's House 40 Vicarage Meadow, PL23 1EA ☎01726 833680, ⓦartists-house.co.uk. This B&B a short walk up from the centre displays work by the owner, a textile artist, among other eclectic bits and bobs. The two en-suite rooms have garden or river views, there's fresh produce for breakfast, and dinners and picnic lunches can be arranged. Two-night minimum stay. No debit/credit cards. Closed Nov–March. **£88**

Coombe Farm Lankelly Lane, PL23 1HW ☎01726 833123, ⓦcoombefarmbb.co.uk. Perfect rural isolation is available here, just twenty minutes' walk west of town, at the end of a lane off the B3269. The two en-suite rooms have sea views, and there's a bathing area at Coombe Haven 300m away. Cream teas are available in the walled garden in summer. No under-12s. No debit/credit cards. **£70**

Old Quay House 28 Fore St, PL23 1AQ ☎01726 833302, ⓦtheoldquayhouse.com. Right on the river, this elite boutique hotel offers abundant style, blending traditional with contemporary decor, and a fantastic restaurant (see below). Most of its eleven opulent rooms have patios and stunning estuary views, though some are quite small. **£190**

Penmarlam Bodinnick, PL23 1LZ ☎01726 870088, ⓦpenmarlampark.co.uk. Three-quarters of a mile up from the Bodinnick ferry crossing on the east bank of the river, this is a peaceful spot with a well-stocked shop and clean facilities. Bodinnick's *Old Ferry Inn* is a steep descent away. Closed Nov–Easter. **£23**

Safe Harbour Inn 58 Lostwithiel St, PL23 1BQ ☎01726 833379, ⓦsafeharbourinn.co.uk. A brisk walk up from Fore St, but right in front of the bus stop, this pub has decent-sized accommodation including family, triple and single rooms – and there's parking. **£100**

EATING

Lifebuoy Café 8 Lostwithiel St, PL23 1BD ☎07715 075869, ⓦthelifebuoycafe.co.uk. Delightfully decorated with quirky retro knick-knacks, books and games, this tiny place serves strong mugs of tea or coffee to go with the big breakfasts (served till noon) or cream teas. Lunch options include crusty sandwiches and crabcakes with a butterbean salad (£8). Easter–Oct daily 9am–5pm; late Feb to Easter & Oct–Dec reduced opening.

Lugger Inn The Quay, Polruan, PL23 1PA ☎01726 870007, ⓦluggerinnpolruan.co.uk. Traditional no-frills waterside pub, with well-kept Cornish ales, delicious scallops and mussels, and a great fish stew (mains around £12). Children welcome. Kitchen daily noon–2.30pm & 6–9pm.

★Q 28 Fore St, PL23 1AQ ☎01726 833302, ⓦtheoldquayhouse.com. With a waterside terrace, this contemporary, elegant restaurant at the *Old Quay House*

hotel (see above) ranks among the fancier places in town, specializing in inventive takes on traditional meat and seafood dishes. At lunchtime you can just have a sandwich (around £10) or tackle the set-price menu (£22 for two courses, £26 for three); in the evening the menu is £32.50 for two or £40 for three courses. Easter–Sept Mon & Tues 6.30–9pm, Wed–Sun 12.30–3pm & 6.30–9pm; Oct–Easter daily 6.30–9pm.

Sam's 20 Fore St, PL23 1AQ ☎01726 832273, ⓦsamscornwall.co.uk. Popular burger bar and bistro adorned with rock'n'roll memorabilia. The meat and fish burgers (£9–15) are first class, and there's usually bouillabaisse available (£29 for two). It doesn't take bookings, so arrive early if you don't want to queue, or wait in the lounge bar upstairs (which stays open late). Daily noon–late.

Lostwithiel and around

Five miles north of Fowey, **LOSTWITHIEL** is an old market town and tin-exporting port on the lowest bridging point of the River Fowey, with an appealing mix of comely Georgian houses, antiques shops and cobbled passageways. The main A390 passes through the centre of town along Queen Street, east of which lies Fore Street, where you'll find **St Bartholomew's church**, with its thirteenth-century (but much rebuilt) Breton-inspired octagonal spire. The church is dedicated to the patron saint of tanners (tanning was a major industry here until the late 1800s). The parallel North Street leads to a fifteenth-century granite **bridge** over the river.

Restormel Castle

Restormel Rd, PL22 0EE • April–June & Sept daily 10am–5pm; July & Aug daily 10am–6pm; Oct daily 10am–4pm • £4; EH • ☎ 01208 872687, ⓦ www.english-heritage.org.uk/visit/places/restormel-castle

South Cornwall's military heritage is vividly captured in the imposing ruins of **Restormel Castle**, crowning a hill a mile or so north of Lostwithiel. Thought to have been built by a Norman baron around 1100 to protect the port, and enlarged at the end of the thirteenth century, Restormel preserves the shale-built shell of its huge circular keep, surrounded by a deep moat. By the time of the Civil War, the castle was already in a sorry state, and Royalist forces under Sir Richard Grenville found it easy to prise it out of the hands of the Earl of Essex's Parliamentarian army in 1644, the last time Restormel saw any service – and the last time that it was inhabited, since the Royalists abandoned it almost immediately. It's a peaceful, panoramic spot, an easy walk from Lostwithiel and good for a picnic.

ARRIVAL AND INFORMATION   LOSTWITHIEL AND AROUND

By train Lostwithiel's station is a short walk from the centre of town and across the river.
Destinations Bodmin (Mon–Sat 13 daily, Sun 7 daily; 5min); Par (Mon–Sat 14 daily, Sun 6 daily; 10min); St Austell (Mon–Sat 12 daily, Sun 6 daily; 15min).
By bus Bus services #423 and #928, and National Express

coaches to and from St Austell (Mon–Sat 7 daily, Sun 4 daily; 25–40min) stop at Liddocoat Rd, near Fore St. Change at St Blazey for connections to Bodmin and Fowey.
Tourist information See ⓦ lostwithiel.org.uk for local events and where to eat and sleep.

ACCOMMODATION AND EATING

Calogero's 35 Fore St, PL22 0BN ☎ 01208 873070, ⓦ calogeros.co.uk. Modern Italian café-bistro serving breakfasts, coffees, snacks and meals, including ciabatta melts (£7), pork meatballs (£11) and seafood risotto (£14.50). There are pizzas, too, and a good children's menu. Mon–Sat 10am–late, Sun 10am–3pm; food served Mon–Sat 10am–2pm & 6.30–9pm, Sun 10am–3pm.
Penrose 1 The Terrace, PL22 0DT ☎ 01208 871417, ⓦ penrosebb.co.uk. Well-preserved Victorian B&B with a

garden on three sides and well-sized rooms, some of them enjoying amazing views. It's off the A390 southwest of the centre, from which it's less than a 5min uphill walk. **£80**
★ **Trewithen** 3 Fore St, PL22 0BP ☎ 01208 872373, ⓦ trewithenrestaurant.com. Dishes at this elegant and intimate restaurant with a courtyard garden are globally inspired and locally sourced – for example artichoke and bean tart (£14.50) and lemon and tarragon chicken (£16.50). Two-course lunches are £14.50. Tues–Fri 11.30am–2pm & 6.30–9pm, Sat 6.30–9pm.

8

The Eden Project

Bodelva, PL24 2SG • April–Oct daily 9.30am–6pm, may close later during school hols; Nov–March Mon–Fri 10am–4pm, Sat & Sun 9.30am–6pm; last entry 1hr 30min before closing; check website for precise times • £25, under-16s £14 (book online for discount); £21 if arriving by bike, by bus or on foot • ☎ 01726 811911, ⓦ edenproject.com

Showcasing the diversity of the planet's plant life in an innovative, sometimes wacky style, the **Eden Project** was the brainchild of Tim Smit, the leading light in the rescue of the Lost Gardens of Heligan (see p.215), who first envisaged the potential of this disused clay pit, 160ft deep and covering 34 acres. The awesome scale of the project becomes apparent only once you have passed the entrance at its lip, from where the whole site is revealed, stunningly landscaped with an array of crops and flowerbeds on scimitar-shaped terraces.

There's plenty to see and do here and it's worth setting aside a full day for a thorough exploration – ideally with frequent breaks, as the whole experience can prove quite exhausting. Weekends are always the most congested time to visit (especially during school holidays), while things are generally quietest either earlier or later in the day. Ideally, visit in different seasons to see the different sides of Eden's constantly evolving "living theatre". Fresh **sculptures** and new hands-on activities are regularly added, many of them aimed at children, who will also appreciate the grand exhibition space and workshops (among other amenities) in **The Core** educational centre. Abundant good food is readily available, and there's a free **Land Train** shuttling between the entrance and the bottom of the pit in case your feet give up.

The biomes

Taking centre stage at Eden are the geodesic "biomes" – vast conservatories made up of ecofriendly, Teflon-coated, hexagonal panels. The **Mediterranean Biome** holds groves of olive and citrus trees, cacti and other plants more usually found in the Mediterranean, southern Africa and southwestern US. Connected to it by a common entrance, the larger **Rainforest Biome** – claimed to be the biggest greenhouse in the world – contains plants from the tropics, including teak and mahogany trees, and there's even a waterfall and river gushing through. Things can get pretty steamy here, but you can take cool refuge in an air-conditioned bunker halfway along the course.

The grounds

Described by Smit as "Picasso meets the Aztecs", the **external grounds** of the Eden Project hold impressive plantations of bamboo, tea, hops, hemp and tobacco, interspersed with brilliant swathes of flowers and eye-catching artworks, from intricate wire animals to cork and deadwood sculptures of woodland species. Informative panels outline some of the more pressing ecological issues around the world, and helpful guides are on hand to provide information. Timed **talks** and "story-telling" sessions are advertised on noticeboards.

In the midst of the complex, a lawned, open-air **arena** is the venue for free events by day and full-on concerts on summer evenings (see box below). In winter (Oct–Feb), this becomes a skating rink. On winter weekends, you can also try out the **Skywire**, England's longest zipwire (660m), for a breathtaking bird's-eye view of the site.

ARRIVAL AND DEPARTURE   **THE EDEN PROJECT**

By bus The #101 runs between the Eden Project and St Austell (hourly; 20min).

On foot/by bike Eden is accessible on the Clay Trails cycle paths (see box, p.213) and on a network of footpaths and road routes from St Austell and Par (local tourist offices can

provide maps).

By car Four miles northeast of St Austell off A390 and A391, Eden is well signposted, and there are plenty of parking spaces on site.

THE EDEN SESSIONS

The amphitheatre-shaped arena in the centre of the Eden Project has become one of Cornwall's premier concert venues for its **Eden Sessions** (ⓦedensessions.com). Held every June and July, the events attract big-name artists (Manic Street Preachers and Elton John are among recent acts) and can book up months ahead. Check the website or call ☎01726 811972 for news of events. Ticket prices are £35–40, with priority given to "Inside Track" members (£15 annual subscription); ticket-holders get free admission to the Eden Project on the day of the concert and the following day. Concerts start at 8pm or later; check the website for details of **bus services** to St Austell after the show.

ACCOMMODATION

YHA Eden Project Bodelva, PL24 2SG ☎ 01629 592675, ⓦ yha.org.uk/hostel/eden-project. The Eden Project's only on-site accommodation is provided at this hostel, where you can sleep either in "snoozeboxes" – ex-shipping containers holding 1 to 5 people (from £30 for a single) – or in the campsite, where you can pitch your own tent or rent a bell tent (sleep up to 5). Breakfasts and snacks are available. Camping/person **£11.50**, bell tents **£85**

St Austell and around

Six miles west of Fowey and the nearest town to the Eden Project, **ST AUSTELL** is an unprepossessing place that often gets gridlocked during the summer months. The town developed on the strength of the china-clay industry after deposits were found locally in the eighteenth century (see box below), and the conical spoil heaps left by the mines are still a dominant feature of the local landscape, especially on Hensbarrow Downs to the north, where the great green-and-white mounds make an eerie sight. The main reason to come to St Austell, however, is for the access it provides to choicer destinations nearby on the coast or inland.

St Austell Brewery

63 Trevarthian Rd, PL25 4BY • **Brewing Experience** Mon–Sat 9am–5.30pm, last tour 4.30pm; 1hr • £12 • **Access All Areas** Fri 2pm; 2hr 30min • £25 • ☎ 01726 66022, ⓦ staustellbreweryvisitorcentre.co.uk

Ever wondered where the West Country's most ubiquitous beer comes from? The **St Austell Brewery**, at the top of the town (5min walk north from the station), is still owned by the same Hicks family who established the brewery in 1893, and is open to beer aficionados and others interested in seeing the brewing process at first hand. The **Brewing Experience** tour provides a fascinating insight into ale brewing, including stops at the exhibition and museum and a tutored beer sampling. For the full lowdown on the brewer's art, though, you should join the **Access All-Areas** tour, which takes you through the process step by step with numerous tastings – numbers are limited, so book ahead.

Wheal Martyn

Carthew, PL26 8XG • Mid-Jan to late March Mon–Fri & Sun 10am–4pm; late March to Oct daily 10am–5pm; Nov to late Dec daily 10am–4pm; last entry 1hr 30min before closing • £9.75, under-16s £5 • ☎ 01726 850362, ⓦ wheal-martyn.com • From St Austell train station, you can follow the "Green Corridor", a two-mile walk or bike ride that forms part of the Clay Trails (see opposite)

Two and a half miles north of St Austell on the B3274, the museum at **Wheal Martyn** reveals everything you ever wanted to know about Cornwall's china-clay industry. It's an extensive and absorbing exhibition, allowing a close-up view of how the pits were operated; you can explore the old clay workings, along with the original locomotives and wagons

---

CHINA CLAY

The extraction of **china clay**, or kaolin, is a Cornish success story. An essential ingredient in the production of porcelain, until the mid-eighteenth century kaolin had only been produced in northern China, where a high ridge, or *kao-lin*, was the sole known source of the raw material. In 1756, **William Cookworthy** discovered deposits of kaolinite near Helston and subsequently in the hills west of St Austell, kicking off the industry in Cornwall. The china clay was originally extracted to supply ceramics producers such as Wedgwood and Spode, but further uses were soon found. Among its many applications today, china clay goes into paper, paint, rubber and plastics, fertilizers, insecticides, toothpaste and medicines (notably for quelling upset stomachs). Its most important use, though, is in **paper production**, and it remains the most widely used material after wood pulp. Cornwall continues to export some 80 percent of its china clay through the ports of Fowey and Par to western Europe and Scandinavia.

used in the pits. The site encompasses 26 acres of wooded country park, including nature trails, picnic areas and children's amusements, so allow plenty of time to see everything.

ARRIVAL AND INFORMATION   ST AUSTELL

By train Trains on the main Penzance line stop at St Austell station on Station Approach, in the centre of town off High Cross Street.

Destinations Bodmin (hourly; 20min); Plymouth (hourly; 1hr); Truro (hourly; 15min).

By bus Most buses stop on South St or at the train station, including #24 and #25 for Charlestown, Par and Fowey (#24 also goes to Mevagissey) and National Express coaches.

Destinations Charlestown (Mon–Sat 2 hourly, Sun hourly; 10–15min); Eden Project (9 daily; 20min); Fowey (Mon–Sat

every 30min, Sun hourly; 45min); Lostwithiel (4 daily; 15min); Mevagissey (Mon–Sat 2–3 hourly, Sun hourly; 20min); Newquay (Mon–Sat 2 hourly, Sun every 2hr; 55min); Par (Mon–Sat every 30min, Sun hourly; 30min); Truro (Mon–Sat 2 hourly, Sun every 2hr; 35min–1hr 10min).

Tourist information St Austell's main tourist office lies half a mile southeast of the centre behind the Texaco garage on Southbourne Road, the A390; there's also a kiosk at the train station (both daily 9am–5pm; ☎ 01726 879500, ⓦ www .staustellbay.co.uk).

Charlestown

St Austell's nearest link to the sea is at **CHARLESTOWN**, an unspoilt port that's an easy one-mile walk downhill from the centre. It's named after the entrepreneur Charles Rashleigh who in 1791 began work on the harbour of what was then a small fishing community, widening its streets to accommodate the china-clay wagons that passed through daily. Still used until the 1990s for shipping clay, the wharves appear oversized beside the tiny jetties, and are often dressed up by elaborate old-fashioned film sets – it's a favourite location for TV and film productions (scenes from the swashbuckling BBC drama *Poldark* were shot here). The company Square Sail now owns the dock, and you'll often see the company's square-rigger, *Phoenix*, in situ.

To either side of Charlestown, the coarse-sand and stone **beaches** are sprinkled with small rock pools, above which cliff walks lead to the beaches around St Austell Bay.

Shipwreck and Heritage Centre

Quay Rd, PL25 3NJ • March–Oct daily 10am–5.30pm • £5.95 • ☎ 01726 69897, ⓦ shipwreckcharlestown.com

Housed in an old "dry" house for china clay behind Charlestown harbour, the **Shipwreck and Heritage Centre** is entered through tunnels once used to convey clay to the docks. It's an eclectic and rather random collection of photos and relics, with an informative section on diving and tableaux of historical scenes, as well as material on Charlestown and the china clay shipments.

ARRIVAL AND DEPARTURE   CHARLESTOWN

By bus The #24 (hourly) and #25 (Mon–Sat hourly) run to St Austell, Par and Fowey; #24 also goes to Mevagissey.

ACCOMMODATION AND EATING

★ **Broad Meadow House** Quay Rd, PL25 3NX ☎ 01726 76636, ⓦ broadmeadowhouse.com. This small and friendly campsite offers pitches in a meadow with glorious sea views, as well as "tent and breakfast" (May–Sept; three-night minimum stay; £95 for two) in a pre-pitched "posh tent", to which breakfast is brought in the morning,

and with its own washing facilities. Regular campers, for whom there is a two-night minimum stay at weekends, can also order breakfast hampers for £8.50 each, and a "posh shed" is available for weekly stays by up to four people (£845). Closed Nov–Easter. Per person **£15**

Pier House Hotel Harbourfront, PL25 3NJ ☎ 01726

THE CLAY TRAILS

The **Clay Trails** (ⓦ www.claytrails.co.uk) are a network of mainly off-road cycle routes linking up St Austell and the area to the north, including the Eden Project and the China Clay Country Park. Mostly gravel-surfaced, the trails are equally good for walkers and bike riders – St Austell's tourist office (see p.213) has route maps.

67955, ⓦpierhousehotel.com. This smart, traditional hotel has a range of rooms, the best with outstanding sea views. The bar-bistro serves snacks – including sandwiches (around £7.50) – and meals, while the restaurant has dishes such as pork medallions and "Seafood Frenzy" for around £20. Bar-bistro daily 11am–11pm, food served noon–9.30pm; restaurant daily 6–9pm. **£125**

Rashleigh Arms Charlestown Rd, PL25 3NJ ☎01726 73635, ⓦrashleigharms.co.uk. Friendly inn with St Austell and guest ales, plus reasonably priced food (mains £10–16) including sandwiches, vegetarian dishes and a Sunday carvery. It's family-friendly and has outdoor seating. Rooms are available upstairs or in a Georgian annexe in front. Daily 11am–11pm; kitchen noon–9pm. **£120**

Mevagissey and around

Until the nineteenth century, **MEVAGISSEY**, five miles southwest of Charlestown, was famed for the fast ships constructed here and used for transporting contraband as well as pilchards. Today, the tiny port might display a few stacks of lobster pots, but the real business is tourism, with day-trippers converging on the harbour and overflowing into its surrounding labyrinth of alleys, a tight cluster of picturesquely flower-draped fishermen's cottages. Despite the crowds, the minute inner harbour – separated from the larger outer harbour by a pair of breakwaters – has an irresistible charm, with its clamour of swirling gulls amid the apparatus of the small fishing fleet.

Many visitors to Mevagissey end up on the broad, sandy **Pentewan Beach**, 1.5 miles to the north, much of which is dominated by a camping and caravan site. It also makes a good base for heading to the fascinating and historic **Lost Gardens of Heligan** nearby.

8

Mevagissey Museum

East Wharf, PL26 6QR · Daily: Easter–June, Sept & Oct 11am–4pm; July & Aug 10am–5pm · Free · ☎01726 843568, ⓦmevagisseymuseum.co.uk

At the end of the harbour, **Mevagissey Museum** is housed in a building that has as much history as the exhibits inside; it was built in 1795 for the construction and repair of smugglers' boats, with most of its roof beams recycled from the same. The contents are a fascinating miscellany, from net-making machinery to a cider-press, a five-barrelled mousetrap and a plethora of evocative photographs. One display is devoted to Andrew Pears, a local barber-turned-chemist who created the world's first transparent soap in 1789.

ARRIVAL AND DEPARTURE   MEVAGISSEY AND AROUND

By bus Service #24 to and from St Austell and Charlestown (1–2 hourly; 20min) stops off Market Square. For Fowey, change at St Austell.

By ferry Between late April and September, a ferry operates daily between Mevagissey and Fowey (see p.206).

INFORMATION AND ACTIVITIES

Tourist information The Candy Shop, on East Quay, has local info (daily 11am–8.30pm; ☎07883 096116, ⓦmevagissey-info.com).

Bike rental Pentewan Valley Cycle Hire, Pentewan, two miles north of Mevagissey on the B3272 (☎01726 844242, ⓦpentewanvalleycyclehire.co.uk); £14 per day.

ACCOMMODATION

Old Parsonage 58 Church St, PL26 6SR ☎01726 843709, ⓦoldparsonage.net. Back from the harbour, this brightly renovated Victorian B&B has friendly owners and five smallish but pleasantly furnished rooms. Multiple breakfast choices include fresh fruit salads and compotes. **£90**

Pentewan Sands Pentewan, PL26 6BT ☎01726 843485, ⓦpentewan.co.uk. There are cheaper campsites around, but this is one of the closest to Mevagissey (1.5

miles south) and right on Pentewan Beach. Facilities are good, and prices plummet in low season. Closed Nov to mid-March. **£36**

Wild Air Polkirt Hill, PL26 6UX ☎01726 843302, ⓦwildair.co.uk. Away from the crowds and just up from the harbour, this B&B has three tastefully furnished rooms, all with en-suite or private bathrooms and amazing views over the coast. No kids, and no one-night stays in winter. **£85**

EATING AND DRINKING

Alvorada 5 East Quay, PL26 6QQ ☎01726 842055. You'll find a strong Portuguese flavour in the food and decor of this casual, family-run restaurant on the harbour. Dip into delicious tapas (around £7.50) at lunchtime, or sample such specialities such as *feijoada a mar* (seafood bean casserole) and oven-cooked turbot for around £15. Feb–Oct Tues–Sat noon–2pm & 6.30pm–late; may close Tues in winter.

Fountain Inn Cliff St, PL26 6QH ☎01726 842320. Economical lunches and evening meals are served in this fifteenth-century tavern, with all dishes £8–15; takeaway fish and chips are also available. Beers include Tribute, HSD and Mena Dhu stout, and on Monday evenings the local male choir sings shanties. Daily noon–midnight; kitchen Mon–Sat noon–2pm & 6–9pm, Sun noon–2pm.

★**Number Five** Market Square, PL26 6UD ☎01726 844422, ⓦnumberfiveinmevagissey.co.uk. Bright and buzzy place with sofas, and local art on the walls – an ideal stop for breakfast, coffee or lunch, when choices include the best crab sandwiches in Mevagissey (£6.50). Evening mains such as pork escalope and surf'n'turf are around £17. Daily 9am–8.30pm (last orders); reduced hours in winter.

Lost Gardens of Heligan

Pentewan, PL26 6EN • April to mid-July & Sept daily 10am–6pm; mid-July to Aug Mon 9.30am–6pm, Tues–Sun 10am–7.30pm; Oct–March daily 10am–5pm; last entry 1hr 30min before closing • £13.50 • ☎01726 845100, ⓦheligan.com • Take bus #24 or #471 from Mevagissey or St Austell, alternatively walkers and cyclists can use a virtually traffic-free trail from either place – local tourist offices can supply a route map

The awesome display of greenery at the **Lost Gardens of Heligan** lies two miles northwest of Mevagissey via the B3273. At their prime in the late 1800s, the gardens later fell into neglect and were only rediscovered beneath a 10ft covering of brambles in 1990. Tim Smit, of Eden Project fame (see p.209), was largely responsible for their restoration, and the marvellously abundant palm trees, giant Himalayan rhododendrons and immaculate vinery appear today as if they've been transplanted from warmer climes. Near the entrance, the northern gardens contain huge flower and vegetable plots, including pineapple pits dating from 1720, where the first pineapples in 150 years were coaxed into life a few years ago by the original manure heating system. A boardwalk takes you past interconnecting ponds, through a jungle and under a canopy of bamboo, ferns and palms down to the Lost Valley, where there are lakes, a wildflower meadow and leafy oak, beech and chestnut "rides". **Guided tours** are available daily, and you can sample produce from the gardens at the *Stewardry* and *Heligan* tearooms.

Veryan Bay

Curving west between Dodman Point and Nare Head, the five-mile parabola of **Veryan Bay** has been barely touched by commercialism. Bounding the bay on the east, **Dodman Point** ranks as one of South Cornwall's most dramatic headlands, its gorse-covered heights topped by a stark granite cross built by a local parson as a seamark in 1896, close to the substantial remains of an Iron Age **fort**. Splendid views take in a chaos of reefs and rocks that have been the cause of many a wreck. Less than a mile west, sandy **Hemmick Beach** makes an excellent swimming spot, with rocky outcrops affording a measure of privacy.

Caerhays Castle

Gorran, PL26 6LY • House tours Mid-March to mid-June Mon–Fri 11.30am, 1pm & 2.30pm; 45min • £9 (£14 including gardens) • Gardens Mid-Feb to mid-June daily 10am–5pm; last entry 4pm • £9 (£14 including house) • ☎01872 501310, ⓦwww.caerhays.co.uk

In a beautiful setting of woodland and pasture, a mile or so west of Hemmick Beach, the sandy beach at **Porthluney Cove** is backed by the battlemented **Caerhays Castle**, built in 1808 by John Nash. The house **tours** (call to reserve a place) are chiefly of interest to fans of Hitchcock's 1940 film, *Rebecca*, which was shot here. The beautiful wooded garden is more compelling, displaying world-famous collections of camellias, magnolias and rhododendrons.

Portloe

Three miles west of Caerhays Castle, the minuscule and whitewashed village of **PORTLOE** is fronted by jagged black rocks that throw up fountains of sea spray, giving it a bracing, end-of-the-road kind of atmosphere. The deep cove once sheltered a thriving fleet, but little more than crab- and lobster-fishing now remains. The zigzagging, three-mile coastal hike to **Nare Head** takes you down to some lovely coves.

Veryan and around

A mile or so inland of Portloe, **VERYAN** has a pretty village green and pond, but is best known for its five circular, white **houses**, built some two hundred years ago by one Reverend Jeremiah Trist – apparently to guard the village from devils, which would be unable to hide in corners. For additional protection, the thatched roofs are topped by crosses.

Pendower Beach

A lane from Veryan leads less than a mile down to **Pendower Beach**, one of southern Cornwall's cleanest swimming spots. Backed by dunes, Pendower joins with neighbouring **Carne Beach** at low tide to create a long sand-and-shingle continuum nearly a mile long.

About halfway between the village and beach, a footpath provides access to the conspicuous mound of **Carne Beacon** – one of the country's largest Bronze Age barrows. According to local legend, it contains the tomb of the Cornish king of the Dumnonii, Geraint, killed in 710 fighting against the West Saxons.

Truro

On a wedge of land separating the Allen and Kenwyn rivers, **TRURO** is something of a historical hotchpotch. On the city's higher slopes, stately Georgian dwellings look down on a cobbled centre that retains traces of the medieval town's lanes, where

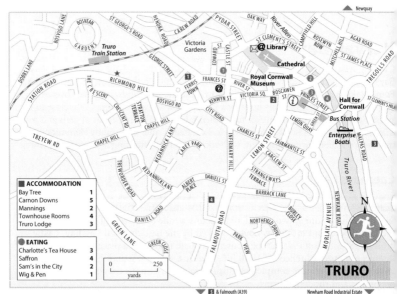

"kennels" or water channels still burble in the streets. Centre-stage is Truro's chronologically confused **Cathedral** – a twentieth-century version of a medieval edifice – which is one of the town's two big draws, alongside the **Royal Cornwall Museum**. Otherwise, the city is more of a tourist crossroads than a holiday centre, lacking enough diversion to keep you away from the coast for long. In its favour, Truro has reasonably priced accommodation and a good range of pubs and restaurants.

A flea **market** takes place inside the Hall for Cornwall, Boscawen St (Tues, Wed & Sat), while nearby Lemon Quay is the venue for a farmers' market (Wed & Sat), both 9am to 4pm.

Brief history
Connected to the Carrick Roads estuary by the Truro River, Truro developed as a protected inland port shipping tin to Europe and copper to Wales. One of Cornwall's original Stannary towns, it was a long-standing rival to Falmouth, but declined in the seventeenth century with the silting of the river. Truro's prosperity returned with the tin-mining boom of the 1800s, and the arrival of the railway in 1859 – followed by the granting of city status in 1877 – confirmed its role as Cornwall's commercial and administrative centre, and it remains today the county's only city.

The Cathedral

St Mary's St, TR1 2AF • Mon–Sat 7.30am–5pm, Sun noon–4pm • Guided tours April–Oct Mon–Thurs 11am • Free, but donations welcomed • ☎ 01872 276782, ⊚ trurocathedral.org.uk

8

A neo-Gothic confection of local granite and Bath stone, the tall exterior of Truro's **Cathedral** sprouts dramatically up from the city's modern shopping centre. Completed in 1910, the building aroused controversy from the off – the result of architect John Loughborough Pearson's decision to revert to the Early English style, rather than something more in keeping with Truro's predominantly Georgian lines. It makes a powerful impact though, and lacking the "close" usually surrounding English cathedrals, it also appears slightly hemmed in – in fact, the building had to be shoe-horned into the available space, accounting for the skewwhiff alignment noticeable in the nave. Apart from this slight aberration, the overall effect is of orderly, clean-cut lines – a rather academic exercise in Gothic church-building which, a century later, has not noticeably mellowed or blended with the city to any degree.

The interior
With its emphatically pointed arches and elaborate roof vaulting, the airy **interior** is notable for its Victorian **stained-glass** windows, considered the finest collection in the country. The most impressive include the rose window of the west front, depicting the Creation, and those in the north and south transepts. The south (right) aisle has a fine **baptistry**, with arcading, and a font with pillars fashioned from Cornish serpentine. Further up on the same side, to the right of the choir, **St Mary's Aisle** is a relic of the Perpendicular church that formerly occupied the site, mostly demolished to make way for the new construction. You can see etchings of its original appearance at the back of the aisle, where there's also a copy of a letter of thanks from Charles I to the Cornish for their loyalty during the Civil War. The medieval-looking triptych behind the altar here is the work of Frank Pearson, the son of the cathedral's architect, who completed the project after his father's death.

More fragments of the original church are scattered about, and there are some colourful Jacobean tombs worth viewing. In a different vein, look out for the **matchstick model** of the cathedral in the south aisle: it took 1600 hours and some 42,000 matches to assemble.

Royal Cornwall Museum

River St, TR1 2SJ • Aug Mon–Sun 10am–4.45pm; Sept–July Mon–Sat 10am–4.45pm • £4.50 • ☎ 01872 272205, ⓦ www. royalcornwallmuseum.org.uk

As the county's premier museum, the **Royal Cornwall Museum** provides essential context to your travels through the region. The **main gallery** on the ground floor illustrates aspects of Cornwall's past and includes a Celtic inscription found at Tintagel that may refer to King Arthur. To either side, the **Nature Gallery** and the **Mineral Gallery** illuminate the county's natural history and geological make-up. The latter's collection of specimens is internationally important and includes examples of cassiterite (the only tin mineral of economic importance), mirror-surfaced iron pyrites and copper, asbestos and, in its various mottled forms, serpentine from the Lizard peninsula. You can also learn about Delabole slate and china clay via a diorama of a china-clay pit.

The Egyptian and Philbrick galleries

Upstairs, past the unwrapped mummy and two detached feet from Roman-period mummies in the **Egyptian Gallery**, the **Philbrick Gallery** features some outstanding paintings by the Newlyn School, including Harold Harvey's famous *St Just Tinminers*, work by Stanhope Forbes and some sentimental but occasionally striking paintings by Henry Scott Tuke. Three further rooms show Old Master drawings and items from the museum's collections of textiles and costumes.

ARRIVAL AND DEPARTURE   TRURO

8

By train Truro's station lies a few minutes' walk west of the centre on Station Rd, at the top of Richmond Hill.
Destinations Bodmin (hourly; 35min); Exeter (hourly; 2hr 10min–2hr 30min); Falmouth (Mon–Sat every 30min, Sun 11 daily; 20min); Liskeard (hourly; 50min); Penzance (hourly; 45min); Plymouth (hourly; 1hr 15min).

By bus National Express coaches for Penzance, Plymouth and London, and bus services for Falmouth, Newquay and St Mawes stop at the bus station on Green St; some services also stop near the train station on Richmond Hill.
Destinations Falmouth (Mon–Sat every 30min, Sun hourly; 35–50min); Newquay (Mon–Sat 5 hourly, Sun 2 hourly; 35min–1hr 20min); Penzance (Mon–Sat every

30min, Sun hourly; 1hr 45min); Plymouth (5 daily; 1hr 40min–2hr 20min); St Austell (2 hourly, Sun 8 daily; 40min–1hr 10min); St Ives (Mon–Sat every 30min, Sun hourly; 1hr 40min); St Mawes (4–7 daily; 55min).

Boat excursions Enterprise Boats (☎ 01326 741194, ⓦ falriver.co.uk) operate river trips from Truro's Town Quay to Falmouth 3–5 times daily (late March to October; £10 one-way, £15 return; 1hr 20min–1hr 45min) and St Mawes 3 times daily (late May to September; same fares; 1hr 15min), or you can just go as far as Trelissick Garden (£6 one-way, £10 return). At low tide, departures are from Malpas, a village a couple of miles downstream, connected by a free shuttle bus.

INFORMATION AND GETTING AROUND

By car Avis, Tregolls Rd ☎ 0344 544 6109, ⓦ avis.co.uk; Hertz, train station ☎ 0843 309 3077, ⓦ hertz.co.uk; Enterprise, Newham Road Industrial Estate ☎ 01872 262211, ⓦ enterprise.co.uk.

By taxi A2B ☎ 01872 272989; Spikes ☎ 01872 271017. Ranks at Boscawen Street and Quay Street.
Tourist information Boscawen St (Mon–Fri 9.30am–5pm, Sat 9am–4pm; ☎ 01872 274555, ⓦ visittruro.org.uk).

ACCOMMODATION

Bay Tree 28 Ferris Town, TR1 3JH ☎ 01872 240274, ⓦ baytree-guesthouse.co.uk. Old-fashioned but homely B&B near the centre, with three rooms sharing a bathroom and a chatty landlady full of local knowledge. Rough Guide readers get a discount. No debit/credit cards. **£60**

Carnon Downs Carnon Downs, TR3 6JJ ☎ 01872 862283, ⓦ carnon-downs-caravanpark.co.uk. Three miles southwest of Truro on the A39 Falmouth road, this large, flat campsite has sheltered pitches and first-class washing facilities. It's one of the few sites in the area that remain open all year. **£26**

Mannings Lemon St, TR1 2QB ☎ 01872 270345, ⓦ manningshotels.co.uk. Very central, this hotel in a handsome Georgian building has been given a stylish, modern makeover. Rooms are well-equipped (choose one at the back for a quieter night), and there are spacious apartments (£135), parking and an excellent brasserie. **£105**

★Townhouse Rooms 20 Falmouth Rd, TR1 2HX ☎ 01872 277374, ⓦ trurotownhouse.com. A short walk uphill from the centre, this quiet, three-storey B&B with a lovely garden mixes modern decor with traditional furnishings. Buffet breakfasts can be had at a time of your

choosing, and the breakfast/dining room has kitchen equipment and is free to use during your stay. Complimentary cakes and scones are a further draw. **£79**
★**Truro Lodge** 10 The Parade, TR1 1QE ☎07813 755210, ⓦtrurolodge.co.uk. Relaxed B&B in a large

Georgian terraced house in a quiet lane close to the centre, with period features and a pleasant veranda. The rooms are with shared or en-suite bathrooms, breakfasts are DIY, and you can use the kitchen with its Aga stove for self-catering. **£45**

EATING

Charlotte's Tea House Coinage Hall, Boscawen St, TR1 2QU ☎01872 263706. The ideal spot for toasted teacakes, muffins and cream teas, in a gloriously Victorian setting, and there's a superb secondhand bookshop in the corridor. Mon–Sat 10am–5pm.

Saffron 5 Quay St, TR1 2HB ☎01872 263771, ⓦwww .saffronrestauranttruro.co.uk. An eclectic mix of meat and seafood dishes is offered at this congenial spot – for example, fish stew or slow-cooked lamb shank (around £15). There are good-value lunch and early-evening menus (£12.50 and £15 respectively for two courses), and hearty Saturday brunches. Mon–Sat 10am–10pm; food served 11am–3pm & 5–9pm.

Sam's in the City 1–2 New Bridge St, TR1 2AA ☎01872 859819, ⓦsamscornwall.co.uk. An offshoot of the Fowey

burger bar (see p.208), this place offers a similar line in music and film memorabilia, cool cocktails and ace burgers. "Samsburger" (£8–12) and steaks (£15–20) are perennial favourites on the menu, but the seafood dishes are excellent too. Vegans and vegetarians should look elsewhere. Daily 11.30am–late.

Wig & Pen 1 Frances St, TR1 3DP ☎01872 273028, ⓦwigandpentruro.co.uk. Useful, centrally located pub, serving St Austell ales, brunches, cream teas and excellent meals (build-your-own-burgers and ploughman's lunches are £7–10). It's child-friendly and has some outdoor seating. Mon–Thurs 11.30am–11pm, Fri & Sat 11.30am–midnight, Sun 11.30am–8pm; kitchen Mon–Sat noon–3pm & 6–9pm, Sun noon–3pm.

ENTERTAINMENT

Hall for Cornwall Back Quay ☎01872 262466, ⓦhallforcornwall.co.uk. The main regional venue, the

Hall for Cornwall stages a programme of concerts and plays throughout the year.

DIRECTORY

Hospital 24hr accident and emergency department at the Royal Cornwall Hospital, Treliske, TR1 3LJ (☎01872 250000), about a mile west of the centre on the A390

Redruth road.
Police 74–75 Lemon St ☎101, ⓦwww.devon-cornwall .police.uk.

The Roseland Peninsula

A deeply serene area of unspoilt fishing hamlets and idyllic waterside retreats, the backwaters of the **Roseland Peninsula** make an irresistible excursion for anyone not averse to narrow winding lanes. Biking and walking are the best means of exploring the area – whose name probably derives from the Celtic *Rhosinis* meaning "moorland isle" – with the coast path providing access to some extremely select and secluded patches of beach.

St Mawes

In a secluded spot at the mouth of the Percuil estuary and facing Falmouth across the neck of the Carrick Roads, **ST MAWES** is a select enclave of cottages, villas and abundant gardens, sloping above a simple harbour. A stroll around the village could take in **St Mawes Castle**, a good spot to soak up the stirring estuary views.

St Mawes Castle

Castle Drive, TR2 5DE • April–Sept daily 10am–6pm; Oct daily 10am–5pm; Nov–March Sat & Sun 10am–4pm • £5; EH • ☎01326 270526, ⓦwww.english-heritage.org.uk/visit/places/st-mawes-castle

At the western end of St Mawes, the small and pristine **St Mawes Castle** was, like Falmouth's Pendennis (see p.225), built during Henry VIII's reign from 1539 to 1543, based on designs by the king's German military architect Stefan von Haschenberg.

Both castles adhere to the same clover-leaf design, with a central round keep surrounded by robust gun emplacements. St Mawes, however, has more architectural interest, with three semicircular bastions surrounding the four-storey central tower, and some of the best examples of decorative stonework of all Henry's fortified works (look out for a Latin inscription to Henry, with a back-to-front "S", at the entrance). Although its design was considered revolutionary at the time, the castle retained such medieval features as the *oubliette*, a deep, square shaft just inside the entrance on the right where prisoners were detained, now covered by a glass roof.

The castle lacks much drama, partly on account of its immaculate condition which it owes to its early surrender when placed under siege by General Fairfax's Parliamentary forces in 1646. The bloodless takeover eased the way for Fairfax's harder-fought conquest of Pendennis Castle a few weeks later. The free audioguide fills you in on this, as well as much else about the castle's background and local history.

ARRIVAL AND DEPARTURE ST MAWES

By bus Bus #50 links St Mawes with Truro every 2hr (1hr).
By ferry Tickets are available from the harbour at the ferry departure point. See ⓦ falriver.co.uk for routes and schedules. Destinations Falmouth (1–2 hourly; 20min); Place (late March to Sept daily every 30min or on demand; 10min); Trelissick Garden (late May to Sept Mon–Sat 4 daily, late

June to early Sept Sun 4 daily; 40min–1hr 20min); Truro (late May to Sept Mon–Sat 4 daily, late June to early Sept Sun 4 daily; 1hr 25min–2hr).
Tourist information The websites ⓦ stmawesandthe roseland.co.uk and ⓦ stmawes.info are useful for places to stay and eat, and for general information.

ACCOMMODATION

Hotel Tresanton Lower Castle Rd, TR2 5DR ☎ 01326 270055, ⓦ tresanton.com. Cornwall doesn't get much ritzier than this – a slice of Mediterranean-style luxury with bright, sunny rooms, all with sea views, and a yacht and speedboat available in summer to guests. There's a fabulous restaurant, too (see below). **£270**
Little Newton Newton Rd, TR2 5BS ☎ 01326 270664, ⓦ little-newton.co.uk. Two small but smart and modern en-suite rooms are available at this B&B, just off Castle Rd (easily accessed by drivers without having to enter the

village), or a steep 10min walk up from the seafront behind the *Victory Inn*. Rooms have peaceful views over the Percuil River or the garden. No credit cards. Closed Nov–Feb. **£60**
Trethem Mill St Just-in-Roseland, TR2 5JF ☎ 01872 580504, ⓦ trethem.com. You'll find large pitches and immaculately clean, modern facilities at this quiet campsite three miles north of St Mawes, signposted off the A3078 and B3289. Closed early Oct to late March. **£23**

EATING

Café Chandlers Marine Parade, TR2 5AA ☎ 01326 270998, ⓦ cafechandlers.co.uk. Located right on the seafront with tables outside, this is a perfect place for a breakfast, light lunch or coffee – or just for contemplating the view. Pizzas are available (£9–11), and the "cheese tea" makes a nice change from the cream variety. Daily 8.30am–5pm.
★ **Tresanton** Lower Castle Rd, TR2 5DR ☎ 01326 270055, ⓦ tresanton.com. This restaurant offers chic cuisine with a Mediterranean slant, strong on seafood and local meat. At lunchtime you can have a sandwich for around £15 or order

the set menu (£23 for two courses), while evening mains range from beef burger (£12) to half a lobster and chips (£42). There are spectacular views and terraces for dining alfresco, and you can stay here (see above). Daily 7.30am–9.30pm.
Victory Inn Victory Steps, TR2 5DQ ☎ 01326 270324, ⓦ victory-inn.co.uk. Atmospheric, oak-beamed pub a few steps up from the harbour, serving good Tribute and Betty Stoggs ales. Fresh seafood meals are served at the bar or in the more formal restaurant upstairs (mains £10–15). Daily 11am–11pm; kitchen daily noon–2pm & 6–9pm.

THE KING HARRY FERRY

On the B3289, 4 miles north of St Mawes, the chain-driven King Harry ferry across the River Fal significantly shortens the route to Truro or Falmouth. It runs roughly every twenty minutes (April–Sept Mon–Sat 7.30am–9.30pm, Sun 9am–9.30pm; Oct–March Mon–Sat 7.20am–7.30pm, Sun 9am–7.30pm; cars £6 one-way, £8 day return; bikes £1 one-way; foot passengers free; ☎ 01872 862312, ⓦ falriver.co.uk).

St Anthony-in-Roseland and around

Ferry services from St Mawes daily every 30min: late March–May & Oct 9am–4.30pm; June–Sept 9am–5.30pm • £5 one-way, bikes £2 one-way, £6.50 return

In summer a ferry crosses the Percuil River from St Mawes harbour to Place, a ten-minute crossing. A short walk up from the ferry landing brings you to the village of **ST ANTHONY-IN-ROSELAND**; from here the coast path follows the Roseland Peninsula's rocky littoral round **St Anthony Head**, where a lighthouse marks the entry to the Carrick Roads estuary and there are throngs of nesting seabirds.

The village is also home to one of Cornwall's most picturesque churches, **St Anthony-in-Roseland** (TR2 5EZ; daily 9am–dusk; free; ☎0117 929 1766). This twelfth- to thirteenth-century construction is joined at its northern transept to turreted Place House – site of the former priory – and has a fine late-Norman south entrance.

St Just-in-Roseland

St Anthony-in-Roseland's charm is if anything eclipsed by that of a second church, **St Just-in-Roseland** (TR2 5JD; daily 9am–dusk; free; ☎01326 270248, ⊚stjust .roselandchurches.co.uk). On the shore of a creek surrounded by palms and subtropical shrubbery, with granite gravestones tumbling right down to the water's edge, the small grey church dates from 1261 but has a fifteenth-century tower. The village of **ST JUST-IN-ROSELAND** (not to be confused with St Just-in-Penwith) lies ten minutes' walk to the east of the church.

Trelissick Garden

Feock, TR3 6QL • Daily: mid-Feb to Oct 10.30am–5.30pm or dusk; Nov to mid-Feb 10.30am–4.30pm or dusk • £9.05; NT • ☎01872 862090, ⊚nationaltrust.org.uk/trelissick • Accessible via bus #493 (Mon–Sat) from Truro, or, in summer, boats from Truro (see p.218), Falmouth (see p.226) and St Mawes (see p.220)

Midway between St Mawes and Truro, close to the King Harry ferry crossing (see box, p.220), **Trelissick Garden** is celebrated for its hydrangeas, rhododendrons and camellias, and species more usually found in the Mediterranean or more exotic climates. Spacious lawns, four summerhouses and splendid woodland and riverside walks make this a perfect venue for a picnic and stroll, while occasional exhibitions are held in **Trelissick House** (March–Oct Tues–Sun).

Falmouth and around

The construction of Pendennis Castle on the western side of the Carrick Roads estuary mouth in the sixteenth century prepared the ground for the growth of **FALMOUTH**, then no more than a fishing village. The building of its deep-water harbour was proposed a century later by Sir John Killigrew, one of a mercantile dynasty that long dominated local life, and Falmouth's prosperity was assured in 1689 when it became chief base of the fast Falmouth packet ships, which sped mail and bullion to the Mediterranean and the Americas.

In the twentieth century, Falmouth evolved into a full-time tourist resort, and the town has latterly assumed a more cosmopolitan identity as a centre of the **local arts scene**, fuelled by its prestigious art college and providing a vital antidote to the predominant eating-and-shopping tone of the busy **High Street** and its continuations Market and Church streets, running parallel to the harbour. Some enticing beaches and excellent eating and sleeping options add to Falmouth's appeal, not to mention the choice of river and sea cruises available for exploring the ins and outs of the Carrick Roads.

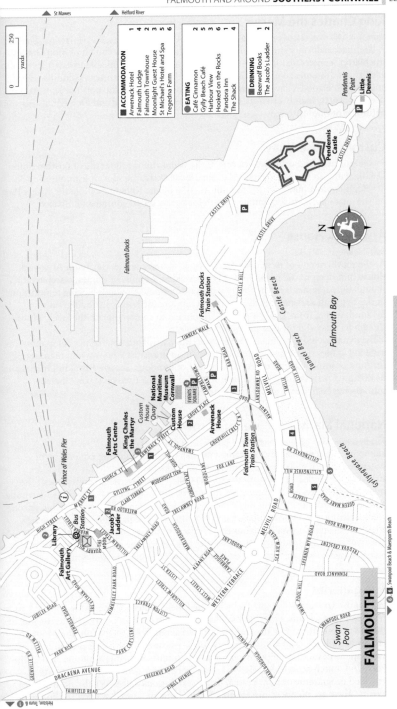

St Mawes   Helford River

0   250
    yards

ACCOMMODATION
Arwenack Hotel	1
Falmouth Lodge	4
Falmouth Townhouse	2
Moonlight Guest House	3
St Michael's Hotel and Spa	5
Tregedna Farm	6

EATING
Café Cinnamon	2
Gylly Beach Café	5
Harbour View	3
Hooked on the Rocks	6
Pandora Inn	1
The Shack	4

DRINKING
Beerwolf Books	1
The Jacob's Ladder	2

Pendennis Point

Little Dennis

Pendennis Castle

CASTLE DRIVE

Falmouth Docks

Castle Beach

Falmouth Docks Train Station

CASTLE HILL

CASTLE DRIVE

N

Falmouth Bay

8

TINNERS WALK

BAR ROAD

Prince of Wales Pier

Falmouth Arts Centre

King Charles the Martyr

Custom House Quay

National Maritime Museum Cornwall

Custom House

Arwenack House

EVENTS SQUARE

CAMPFIELD TOWN WALK

GROVE PLACE

BERKELEY VALE

TINNERS WALK

Tunnel Beach

CHURCH ST

ARWENACK ST

QUAY ST

SWANPOOL ST

MARKET ST

THE MOOR

GYLLING STREET

CLARE TERRACE

WODEHOUSE TERR

TRELAWNEY ROAD

FOX LANE

GROVEHILL CRESCENT

LANSDOWNE RD

MELVILL ROAD

TUNNEL

CASTLE

CLIFF ROAD

Falmouth Town Train Station

GYLLYNGVASE RD

Gyllyngvase Beach

GYLLYNGVASE HILL

GYLLYNGVASE RD

STRACEY ROAD

QUEEN MARY ROAD

BOSCAWEN ROAD

HIGH STREET

Library

Falmouth Art Gallery

Bus Station

WELLINGTON TERRACE

THE QUARRY

Jacob's Ladder

WATERLOO RD

KILLIGREW RD

TRELAWNEY ROAD

MARLBOROUGH ROAD

WOODLANE

ALBANY ROAD

LISTER ST

CAMBRIDGE PLACE

RIVER ROAD

WOODLANE

MELVILL ROAD

SEA VIEW ROAD

SPERNEN WYN ROAD

TREDOVA CRESCENT

PENNANCE ROAD

Swanpool Beach & Maenporth Beach

FRETHAM ROAD

KIMBERLEY PARK ROAD

PENROSE ROAD

TELLAM RD

GREENBANK ROAD

JUBILEE ROAD

PARK RISE

PARK CRESCENT

CLIFTON TERRACE

KILLIGREW STREET

WESTERN TERRACE

WEST STREET

ALBANY ROAD

KINGS AVENUE

TREGENVE ROAD

FAIRFIELD ROAD

DRACAENA AVENUE

SWANPOOL ROAD

SWAN POOL HILL

MARLBOROUGH AVENUE

Swan Pool

FALMOUTH

Helston, Truro 8

Swanpool Beach & Maenporth Beach

King Charles the Martyr

Church St, TR11 3DX • No fixed opening • Free • ☎ 01326 319141

A landmark halfway along the main drag is Falmouth's parish church of **King Charles the Martyr**, consecrated in 1665 when the town was once again able to assert its royalist allegiances. It's unusual for its round arches and huge granite Tuscan columns within, and has some good Victorian stained and enamelled glass in the north aisle, worth a peek. **Concerts**, mainly classical, take place here between April and October, usually on Saturdays at noon (free).

Custom House Quay

At the southern end of Arwenack Street, the white-columned facade of **Custom House** (1820) stands in front of the busy **Custom House Quay**, the spur of Falmouth's development as a port after it was built in 1670 by the Killigrews. Note the King's Pipe on the quayside, a brick chimney used to incinerate seized contraband tobacco.

Arwenack House

Grove Pl, Arwenack St, TR11 4AU

At the southern end of Arwenack Street, the Killigrews' home, the Tudor **Arwenack House** (not open to the public) is Falmouth's oldest example of domestic architecture, though only fragments of the fourteenth-century house remain following remodelling in the sixteenth and eighteenth centuries. Opposite the house, the odd granite pyramid, dating from 1737, is probably intended to commemorate the local family, though its exact significance has never been clear.

The dynasty's most eminent member was Thomas Killigrew, a former companion-in-exile to Charles II and an indifferent Restoration dramatist who was also manager of the king's company of actors. As the founder of London's Theatre Royal in Drury Lane, he obtained permission to use female actors for the first time on stage – thereby introducing Nell Gwyn to the king's notice.

National Maritime Museum Cornwall

Discovery Quay, TR11 3QY • Daily 10am–5pm • £12.50 • ☎ 01326 313388, ⓦ nmmc.co.uk

Falmouth's **National Maritime Museum Cornwall** offers a fascinating exploration of water-borne craft, with diverse examples from all over the world. Many of these are strikingly suspended in midair in the **Flotilla Gallery**, the cavernous centrepiece of the museum, where vessels can be viewed from three different levels. The exhibits are rehung annually to illustrate different maritime themes. In addition, there are numerous smaller galleries that focus on boat-building and repairing skills, seafaring history, Falmouth's packet ships and Cornwall's various other links with the sea, including fishing. There's plenty of interactive gadgetry, a below-water area, and at one end of the museum a lighthouse-like lookout tower offers lofty views over the harbour and estuary.

The galleries

Falmouth's arts scene – largely fuelled by the presence here of one of the country's most prestigious art schools, University College Falmouth – presents a very different side to the town. You can sample the end product at **Falmouth Art Gallery** on The Moor (☎ 01326 313863, ⓦ falmouthartgallery.com), whose collection ranges from the Pre-Raphaelites to contemporary art, and which hosts regular exhibitions, and at **The Poly**, 24 Church St (☎ 01326 319461, ⓦ thepoly.org), a general arts centre with a crowded programme of film, drama, dance, exhibitions, talks, recitals and live-music events. There are plenty of private art galleries in town, as well as open studio events publicized on flyers, posters and at the tourist office, often showing a more dynamic slant than much of the artwork on display at the region's other arts centre, St Ives.

Pendennis Castle

Pendennis Head, TR11 4LP • April–Sept daily 10am–6pm; Oct daily 10am–5pm, Nov–March Sat & Sun 10am–4pm; last entry 1hr before closing • £7.90; EH • ☎ 01326 316594, ⓦ www.english-heritage.org.uk/visit/places/pendennis-castle • Buses #367 and #400 stop nearby

Falmouth's most monumental attraction, **Pendennis Castle**, occupies the tongue of land at the eastern end of town whose Cornish name, Pen Dinas, or "fort on the hill", testifies to the presence of a fortification here up to two thousand years ago. Standing sentinel at the entrance to Carrick Roads, the current structure is a less refined contemporary of the castle at St Mawes (see p.219), but the site wins hands down, the stout ramparts offering superb all-round views. Although now much more extensive and imposing than St Mawes Castle, Pendennis was originally the same size, consisting of the circular keep and curtain wall erected by Henry VIII. Spurred to action by the Spanish Armada and Spain's attack on Penzance in 1595, Elizabeth I added the bastioned outer defences, which were to prove crucial during the Civil War a half-century later, when it endured a five-month siege by the Parliamentarians that ended only when nearly half its defenders had died and the rest had been starved into submission.

Displays of jousting and open-air evening **concerts** and theatre productions are sporadically staged in Pendennis Castle grounds in summer, and there are ghost tours in winter; see the website or call for dates and details.

The interior

The central **Keep** now holds a collection of cannonry, and its upper gun room is the scene of a battle re-enactment, with a gun crew, sound effects and the whiff of cordite. The structure formerly housed the garrison as well as the guns, and is joined to a domestic block that accommodated the governor, and also army officers during both world wars (accounting for the somewhat incongruous panelling in some rooms).

Near the keep, the fifteenth-century **Gunshed** has an exhibition where you can hone your Morse code and aiming abilities. In front, next to the One-Gun Battery, the Sally Port is the entrance to tunnels leading to the camouflaged **Half-Moon Battery**, first built in 1793 as a cannon platform, after which it remained the castle's most important gun emplacement for some 150 years. Together with the battery on St Anthony Head, on the opposite side of the estuary, Pendennis provided Falmouth's main defence during both world wars, though the guns visible now are 1946 models. There's a good view out to sea from the **Battery Observation Post**, where sightings were taken and relayed to the battery itself; it's now restored to how it might have looked during World War II, with instruments and charts, radio equipment and taped conversations adding to the ambience.

Little Dennis

Out on the headland, beyond the walls, **Little Dennis** is the original blockhouse (rudimentary defensive structure) built by Henry VIII before Pendennis was constructed. Reachable from Castle Drive outside the castle, it's a breezy, exposed point to visit at any time, with terrific views of Falmouth Bay and the estuary.

The beaches

West of Pendennis Point stretches a series of long sandy bays. The most central and popular of the **beaches** is **Gyllyngvase Beach** (locally known as Gylly), which was awarded a Blue Flag in 2016, though neighbouring **Swanpool Beach** – accessible by coast path from Gyllyngvase – is pleasanter, with an inland lake and a great café/restaurant (see p.227). You'll find another enticing stretch of sand a couple of miles further on at **Maenporth Beach**, from where there are some fine clifftop walks.

ARRIVAL AND DEPARTURE

BY TRAIN

A branch line from Truro (Mon–Sat every 30min, Sun 11 daily; 25min) runs to Falmouth, stopping at both Falmouth Town, nearest the beaches, and Falmouth Docks, nearest the castle. Both stations are around a 10-minute walk from the centre.

BY BUS

Buses #U1 from Truro, #2 from Helston and Penzance, #35 and #35A from Helston, and National Express coaches stop on the Moor.

Destinations Helston (Mon–Sat 12 daily; Sun 2 daily; 40min–1hr 20min); Penzance (Mon–Sat 6 daily, Sun 1 daily; 1hr 45min); Plymouth (2 daily; 2hr 35min); St Austell (2 daily; 1hr 5min); Truro (Mon–Sat every 30min, Sun hourly; 55min).

BY FERRY

From the Prince of Wales Pier, below the Moor, or (late March to Oct only) from Custom House Quay, ferries leave for St Mawes once or twice an hour (20min; £6.50 one-way,

FALMOUTH AND AROUND

£9.50 return, bikes free) between 8.30am and about 5.15pm (check last departures). Between late March and October, ferries from Prince of Wales Pier also connect with Truro three–five times daily (1hr 15min–1hr 45min each way; £10 one-way, £15 return), with a stop at Trelissick Garden (around 35min; £6 one-way, £10 return). In addition, there are once- or twice-hourly crossings to the placid hamlet of Flushing, across the Penryn River (daily 8.30am–5.45pm, Nov–March Mon–Sat until 5.15pm; 10min; £2.50 one-way), and various cruises, including to the Helford River (Easter–Oct; 2hr 10min; £16 round trip), bookable from kiosks on the pier. Consult ⓦ falriverlinks .co.uk for full schedules.

Boat rental Self-drive motorboats carrying up to six people are available from Falmouth Boat Hire at Custom House Quay (☎ 07951 610247, ⓦ falmouthboathire.co.uk; £95/4hr), for which no experience is necessary.

Car rental Enterprise, Kernick Rd, Penryn ☎ 01326 373355, ⓦ enterprise.co.uk; Cornwall Car Hire (☎ 01637 850971, ⓦ cornwallcarhire.co.uk) will deliver anywhere.

INFORMATION AND GETTING AROUND

By bus Local buses are useful for linking the various parts of town: chiefly #367 (Mon–Fri) between the Moor, the National Maritime Museum, Pendennis Castle, Gyllyngvase Beach and Swanpool Beach, and (#400) (daily) between the Moor, Pendennis Castle and Gyllyngvase Beach – both hourly.

Tourist information Prince of Wales Pier (April–Sept Mon–Sat 9.30am–4pm, Sun 9.30am–1pm; Oct–March Mon–Fri 10am–3pm; ☎ 01326 741194, ⓦ falmouth .co.uk).

ACCOMMODATION

Arwenack Hotel 27 Arwenack St, TR11 3JE ☎ 01326 311185. It's basic and desperately dated, but this place offers clean, central and good-value en-suite accommodation, including two rooms at the top with great views. Parking available. No credit cards. **£64**

Falmouth Townhouse 3 Grove Place, TR11 4AL ☎ 01326 312009, ⓦ falmouthtownhouse.co.uk. Central, clubby hotel in a Georgian building, decked out in a cool retro style – more thrift shop than boutique – with spacious guestrooms and a friendly vibe. There's a buzzing bar downstairs, which, together with street noise, can make for occasional noisy evenings for residents. **£115**

Moonlight Guest House 6 Anwyn Cottages, Avenue Rd, TR11 4BA ☎ 01326 315262, ⓦ moonlight guesthouse.co.uk. Convenient for the centre, station, beaches and castle, this budget guesthouse has six en-suite rooms with woody decor, the best of them (slightly more

expensive) the spacious attic. Breakfast is not provided, but rooms have basic self-catering facilities. Profits from the business are donated to charities. No credit cards. **£40**

THE BEACHES

★ **Falmouth Lodge** 9 Gyllyngvase Terrace, TR11 4DL ☎ 01326 319996, ⓦ falmouthbackpackers.co.uk. Clean and friendly hostel near the beach, decorated with memento of Africa and the Caribbean, and with a sociable lounge and kitchen and free wi-fi. The attic room (sleeps 2–6; from £56) is worth booking ahead. Dorms **£19**, doubles **£48**

St Michael's Hotel and Spa Gyllyngvase Beach, TR11 4NB ☎ 01326 312707, ⓦ stmichaelshotel.co.uk. Sleekly luxurious seaside hotel, very close to the beach and with an excellent range of spa facilities, including an indoor pool. Rooms are bright and contemporary, the cheapest being compact "cabin rooms". The *Flying Fish* bistro provides

FALMOUTH'S OYSTER FESTIVAL

Marking the start of the oyster-dredging season, Falmouth's **Oyster Festival** (ⓦ falmouthoysterfestival.co.uk), stretching over four days in October, features celebrity chefs, seafood-cooking demonstrations and an abundance of oysters, as well as races in the harbour, live music and other entertainments. The main venue is Events Square.

quality modern cuisine with sea views. **£180**

Tregedna Farm Maenporth, TR11 5HL 01326 250529, tregednafarmholidays.co.uk. More tent-friendly than the other overdeveloped caravan parks around Falmouth, this campsite, 2.5 miles from town and half a mile from Maenporth Beach and the coast path, is fairly basic, but it also has bunkrooms. There is a better-equipped inland site between Falmouth and Truro, *Carnon Downs* (see p.218). No credit cards. Camping closed Nov–March. Camping/person **£8.50**, dorms **£20**, doubles **£60**

EATING

Café Cinnamon Old Brewery Yard, TR11 2BY 01326 211457. Wholefood vegetarian and vegan café with courtyard seating that offers a delicious soup of the day and a selection of inexpensive bites, including toasted panini, Greek salad, lentil burger and aubergine curry (£5–8). Local beers and ciders are also available. Tues–Sat 10am–4pm.

Harbour View 24 Arwenack St, TR11 3JB 01326 315315, harbourdining.com. With a shady terrace overlooking the sea, this place has a relaxed Mediterranean feel. Come for breakfasts, snacks and drinks during the day, or an evening meal of well-prepared meat or seafood dishes, mostly £10–15. Summer daily 9am–9pm or later; winter Mon & Tues 9am–3pm, Wed–Sun 9am–9pm.

Pandora Inn Restronguet Creek, Mylor Bridge, TR11 5ST 01326 372678, pandorainn.com. Four miles north of Falmouth, a narrow lane off the A39 leads to this riverside pub, where Rattlers cider, bar snacks, cream teas, and meat and seafood dishes (mostly £10–15) are served in the bar, in the upstairs restaurant and at waterside tables. Daily 10.30am–11pm; kitchen daily 10.30am–9.30pm.

The Shack Events Square, TR11 3XP 01841 212800, theshackfalmouth.co.uk. With a casual style and warm ambience that matches its name, this shellfish bar next to the Maritime Museum offers locally sourced scallops (3 for £8), oysters (£2 each) and mussels (£9–15), plus dressed crab and lobster. The menu also finds space for a few non-seafood items, such as risotto and moussaka. Mon–Thurs & Sun noon–3pm & 6–9pm, Fri & Sat noon–3pm & 6–10pm.

THE BEACHES

Gylly Beach Café Gyllyngvase Beach, TR11 4PA, 01326 312884, gyllybeach.com. Right on the beach with a decked area outdoors, this cool hangout serves everything from iced drinks to sandwiches, burgers and grills, with lunch dishes around £9 and evening mains £13–20. A good spot for breakfast or a summer barbecue (from 5pm), and there's live music on Sun evenings. Daily 9am–late.

Hooked on the Rocks Swanpool Beach, TR11 5BG 01326 311886, hookedcornwall.com. This mellow café and restaurant with a panoramic terrace has a stunning location above Swanpool Beach, and a menu that focuses on fish, including its signature seafood platter (£20). Tapas (£3–4), fish and chips (£12) and Goan seafood curry (£15) are also delicious, and there are meat and veggie dishes too. Book early for the best tables. Mid-Feb to May & Oct–Dec Thurs–Sat 10am–3pm & 5pm–late, Sun 10am–3pm; June–Sept Mon–Fri 10am–3pm & 5pm–late, Sat & Sun 10am–late; kitchen mid-Feb to May & Oct–Dec Mon–Sat noon–2.30pm & 6–9pm, Sun 10am–3pm; June–Sept daily noon–2.30pm & 6–9pm.

DRINKING

Beerwolf Books Bells Court, off Market St, TR11 3AZ 01326 618474, beerwolfbooks.com. Here's a novel concept – a free house and bookshop combined. Set in a beautifully restored old building, with tables in a secluded courtyard, it makes a relaxing ambience for a drink, with a great selection of local beers. Mon–Sat 10am–midnight, Sun noon–11pm.

The Jacob's Ladder 1–2 Chapel Terrace, TR11 3BQ 01326 311010, thejacobsladderinn.co.uk. Popular with the local students, this pub sits at the top of the daunting 111-step Jacob's Ladder from the Moor. With its sofas and armchairs, it's got a great atmosphere, with live music Thurs–Sat, guest ales, pizzas and burgers in the evening (around £6) and wi-fi. Mon–Thurs 4pm–midnight, Fri–Sun noon–midnight; kitchen Mon–Fri 6–9pm, Sat noon–3pm & 6–9pm, Sun noon–9pm.

8

The Lizard and Penwith peninsulas

VIEW OF ST MICHAEL'S MOUNT

9

The Lizard and Penwith peninsulas

Jutting like pincers into the Atlantic, the twin prongs of the Lizard and Penwith peninsulas (respectively the mainland's most southerly and westerly points) comprise one of the country's most scenically spectacular coastal areas, a succession of wave-pounded cliffs interspersed by a variety of exquisite beaches, and backed by wild expanses of undeveloped moorland. The stunning scenery is enhanced by the range of exotic and multicoloured vegetation that the mild climate makes possible, with fiery monbretia and rich, purple foxgloves crowding every roadside, and bright geraniums and lobelia spilling from the window boxes of the grey, rough-hewn cottages. As well as the ubiquitous granite, evident everywhere from farmsteads to dry-stone walls, churches and castellated cliffs, greenish-brown serpentine can also be discerned – a soft hydrated magnesium silicate that's sometimes mottled or spotted like a serpent's skin (hence the name) and is the staple material of craft-shop trinkets on the Lizard peninsula.

The **Lizard peninsula** is the less developed of the two, its mostly flat and bare interior encompassed by precipitous bluffs and cliff-girdled coves. Most of the holiday traffic is concentrated around these rugged bays with their superb beaches – like **Kynance Cove**, theatrically framed by rocky pinnacles and serpentine cliff walls – though of course there's always a stream of pilgrims to **Lizard Point**, at the southern tip of the peninsula. Apart from the region's chief town of **Helston** and its nearby port of **Porthleven**, where a small fishing fleet lends a slightly brisker feel, most of the spartan villages hereabouts are tiny, remote havens buried away at the end of narrow lanes, such as **Mullion Cove** and **Coverack**. The South West Coast Path provides access to all of these, and is usually the only way to view the awe-inspiring scenery that separates them along the coast.

The raw granite landscape predominates once more on the **Penwith peninsula**, where there are also some cracking sandy beaches that attract throngs of tourists in summer. The principal town, **Penzance**, is large enough to preserve an independent identity, however, and has a first-rate museum that gives a fascinating insight into the cultural life that existed here at the turn of the twentieth century. Many artists congregated in the neighbouring port of **Newlyn**, now the South West's biggest fishing centre, where there still exists a good collection of contemporary art, while later waves of artists were attracted across the neck of the peninsula to the busy holiday town of **St Ives**, where a branch of the Tate Gallery showcases their work within earshot of the sea.

The peninsula's main draw, however, is its dramatic coastline – an inhospitable ring of cliffs, unbroken on the northern coast, but punctuated by some of Cornwall's best sandy beaches to the south – for instance at **Porthcurno**. Most visitors bypass the most

---

THE MINACK THEATRE

Highlights

① Lizard Point England's southernmost cape preserves a bracing, windswept appeal, with exhilarating walks and a diverse range of flora. **See p.238**

② Kynance Cove One of Cornwall's grandest beaches, framed by dramatic cliffs and rocky isles. **See p.239**

③ St Michael's Mount This partly fortified isle enjoys a commanding position in Mount's Bay, with rooms packed with interest and panoramic views. **See p.247**

④ An evening at the Minack Theatre A unique open-air venue for drama and other performances, perched right on a cliff edge. **See p.252**

⑤ Tate St Ives Newly expanded gallery on Porthmeor Beach, a perfect place to view some of the vivid and colour-drenched art that was created in this quirky resort. **See p.261**

⑥ Barbara Hepworth Museum Absorbing St Ives gallery and subtropical garden packed with the sculptor's abstract works, often inspired by the Penwith landscape itself. **See p.262**

HIGHLIGHTS ARE MARKED ON THE MAP ON P.232

THE LIZARD & PENWITH PENINSULAS

Falmouth
Penryn
Redruth
Camborne
Rosemullion Head
Mawnan
Porthallow
Porthoustock
Coverack
B3294
Glendurgan Garden
Helford Passage
Helford
Manaccan
St Keverne
B3293
Porth Navas
River Helford
Trelowarren House
Kennack Sands
Cadgwith
Landewednack
Constantine
Cornish Seal Sanctuary
Gweek
Mawgan
Lizard Peninsula
GOONHILLY DOWNS
Stithians Reservoir
A394
Helston
A3083
Mullion
2
Lizard
Poldhu Cove
Polurrian Cove
Mullion Cove
Loe Pool & Bar
Leedstown
B3302
Breage
A394
Porthleven
Cove
Godrevy Point
St Ives Bay
Hayle
St Erth
River Hayle
B3280
Cudden Point
Kenneggy Praa Sands
Rinsey Head
Trewavas Head
Mount's Bay
Porthmeor Beach
St Ives
5
6
B3306
Zennor Quoit
Zennor
Zennor Head
Chysauster
Nine Maidens
Men-an-Tol
Lanyon Quoit
Badger's Cross
Madron
B3311
Marazion
St Michael's Mount
3
Penzance
Newlyn
Mousehole
Paul
Lamorna Cove
Lamorna
St Loy's Cove
Men Scryfa
Morvah
Pendeen
Pendeen Watch
Chun Castle
Chun Quoit
Penwith Peninsula
Carn Euny
Pipers
Merry Maidens
B3315
B3071
Geevor Tin Mine
Levant Mine and Beam Engine
Botallack Head
Botallack Mine
Botallack
St Just-in-Penwith
Cape Cornwall
Carn Brea
A30
B3306
St Buryan
Sennen
Whitesand Bay
Sennen Cove
Land's End
Porthcurno
Minack Theatre
4
Porthgwarra

HIGHLIGHTS

1. Lizard Point
2. Kynance Cove
3. St Michael's Mount
4. An evening at the Minack Theatre
5. Tate St Ives

N

Isles of Scilly

interesting bits on their way to **Land's End**, whose position at Britain's westernmost point has endowed it with a mythic significance, and also with a brash entertainment complex. However, the jagged coast on either side has been spared, and offers some of the most rewarding coastal walking in the county. North of Land's End, **Cape Cornwall** retains its desolate air, the abandoned chimney stacks of Penwith's once-flourishing mining industry only adding to the majesty. You can soak up the flavour of the interior at villages such as **Zennor**, whose granite integrity attracted D.H. Lawrence during World War I, or by exploring the remnants of the peninsula's prehistoric societies amid bleak, hilly moorland.

The Lizard peninsula

The bare plateau of the **LIZARD PENINSULA** – from the Celtic *lys ardh*, or "high point" – has plenty of primitive appeal, but you'll need to make a little effort to unearth some of the more out-of-the-way places. If the peninsula can be said to have a centre, it is **Helston**, a useful transport hub and best known for its folk museum and the centuries-old tradition of the Furry (or Flora) Dance. From here, the solitary A3083 cuts across the broad, largely treeless landscape as far as the southern headlands and the village known simply as **the Lizard**. On either side of the A3083, roads branch off westwards towards obvious attractions such as **Loe Pool**, Cornwall's largest natural lake and a haven for wildlife, and to remote hamlets such as **Mullion Cove**, little more than a scattering of cottages set around a thick-walled harbour. Though the neighbouring beaches of **Polurrian** and **Poldhu** are more popular with surfers, **Kynance Cove**, west of Lizard village, is the peninsula's most appealing place to swim. The eastern coast is also sparsely settled, though such villages as **Coverack** attract a good deal of summer traffic for their lovely secluded settings. In contrast, the **Helford River**'s insular communities and secretive creeks have a very different tone; its muddy banks harbour Cornwall's most famed oyster beds.

INFORMATION   THE LIZARD PENINSULA

Tourist information Brief descriptions of the main villages, local walks and accommodation options can be found at ⓦ www.lizard-peninsula.co.uk.

Helston

Three miles from the sea at the northern end of the Lizard peninsula, quiet, hilly **HELSTON** preserves few traces of the intense activity that formerly characterized it when (as Hellaz) it was a busy port on the River Cober. This function ended in around 1300, when Helston's sea outlet was silted up by deposits from upstream tin-workings, resulting in both the formation of Loe Pool (see p.235) and the frequent flooding that afflicted the town until the 1980s. These days the water level is controlled by a sluice and culvert at Loe Bar (see p.235) and by giant tanks in the town. Despite losing its role as a port, Helston remained an important centre as a Stannary town (where tin was brought to be assayed and taxed), as recalled in the name of its broad main thoroughfare, **Coinagehall Street**, which meets Helston's second axis, Meneage Street, at the Neoclassical **Guildhall**, itself the starting point for the town's celebrated **Furry Dance** (see box, p.234).

Helston lay at the centre of one of Cornwall's most intensely mined regions, near to the biggest tin mine in the country, owned by the mighty Godolphin family, who had their townhouse in what is now the *Angel Hotel* (see p.234). At the bottom of Coinagehall Street, the arched and turreted **Grylls Monument**, erected in 1834 in honour of a local banker and benefactor, occupies the former site of Helston's castle, which once guarded the Cober valley but was already a ruin by the sixteenth century.

9

HELSTON'S FURRY DANCE

Helston is most famous for its annual **Furry Dance** (also called Flora Dance), a complex ritual held on Flora Day (May 8, unless this date falls on a Sun or Mon, in which case the procession takes place on the previous Sat). It's the high point on the town's calendar, for which preparations are made months in advance. It is said to commemorate an apparition by St Michael, the town's patron saint, but the revelry probably predates Christianity as a spring fertility ritual; it formerly involved a ceremony in the woods close to town followed by a dance back to the centre, now commemorated by the Hal-an-Tow ceremony, the second dance of the day. Of the five separate dances, the first begins at 7am, and is the least crowded; others take place at 8.30am, 9.30am, noon and 5pm. The midday dance is the most important: a stately procession of top-hatted men and summer-frocked women solemnly twirling through the town's streets, gardens and even houses, led by the Helston Brass Band. Give yourself plenty of time to guarantee a good viewing spot.

Helston Museum

Market Place, TR13 8TH • Mon–Sat 10am–4pm • Free • ☎ 01326 564027, ⊛ helstonmuseum.co.uk

Housed in former market buildings behind the Guildhall, the eclectic and engrossing **Helston Museum** explains and illustrates aspects of the town's history and social make-up. The long exhibition space, leading up through the old butter market to the fish and meat markets, is filled with a happy assortment of bric-a-brac relating to local trades, and includes sections on Helston's Furry Dance and on the telegraphy pioneer Marconi, whose early experiments in transatlantic radio telegraphy were conducted in the vicinity. There's also some fascinating material on Helston's native son, **Bob Fitzsimmons** (1863–1917), the first boxer to be world middleweight, light heavyweight and heavyweight champion, and the only Briton to achieve this triple. The reconstructed Victorian classroom, with examples of canes and a leather tawse for beating children, and an upstairs section on mining and quarrying, are also worth a look.

ARRIVAL AND DEPARTURE
HELSTON

By bus Most buses stop on Coinagehall Street, including the #2 to Falmouth and Penzance, #35 and #35A to Falmouth, #36 to Coverack and Truro, and #37 to Mullion and The Lizard.

Destinations Coverack (Mon–Sat 5 daily; 25–40min);

Falmouth (Mon–Sat 11 daily, Sun 2 daily; 25min–1hr 15min); The Lizard (Mon–Sat 12 daily, Sun 5 daily; 50min); Mullion (Mon–Sat 12 daily, Sun 5 daily; 30min); Penzance (Mon–Sat hourly, Sun 7 daily; 50min); Truro (5–6 daily; 1hr).

ACCOMMODATION

Angel Hotel 16 Coinagehall St, TR13 8EB ☎ 01326 569393, ⊛ angelhotelhelston.co.uk. Slightly tired-looking coaching inn, with spacious bedrooms. Retains some features from its five-hundred-year history, including a minstrels' gallery and a deep well in the bar. **£88**

No. 52 52 Coinagehall St, TR13 8EL ☎ 01326 562821, ⊛ spingoales.com/B&B.html. Smart B&B with solid old furnishings in four good-sized, en-suite rooms to the front and rear, and abundant breakfasts. Ask at the adjacent *Blue Anchor* if there's no reply. **£70**

EATING AND DRINKING

★ **Blue Anchor** 50 Coinagehall St, TR13 8EL ☎ 01326 562821, ⊛ spingoales.com. An essential stop for pub connoisseurs, this ancient alehouse was a fifteenth-century monks' rest house, and now has a series of snug flagstoned rooms, a skittle alley and a small garden. The excellent Spingo beer is brewed on the premises, available in three strengths (plus an extra-strength version at Christmas). Live music Thurs–Sat. Mon–Thurs & Sun 10am–midnight, Fri & Sat 10am–1am.

Henlys 2 Church St, off Coinagehall St, TR13 8TG ☎ 01326 561141, ⊛ henlysbarandrestaurant.co.uk. At this relaxed restaurant and cocktail bar, opposite the museum, you can sit in booths on the ground floor for drinks and snacks or sit upstairs for a more substantial menu of fish pie or steaks (around £15). Mixologists are on hand to deliver some classic cocktails. Daily 11am–late; food served noon–3pm & 6–9pm.

Porthleven and around

9

Three miles southwest of Helston on the B3304, **PORTHLEVEN** is a sizeable port that once served to ship tin ore from the inland mines. The harbour is of most interest, healthily packed with fishing boats and protected by two sets of stout sea walls. A brace of cannons sits on the outer walls, salvaged from the HMS *Anson*, a frigate wrecked on Loe Bar in 1807 with the loss of 120 sailors; the guns are said to have fired on Napoleon's navy at the Battle of Brest.

ARRIVAL AND DEPARTURE

PORTHLEVEN

By bus Service #2 (Mon–Sat hourly, Sun every 2hr) connects Porthleven with Helston (10min) and Penzance (45min).

ACCOMMODATION

An Mordros Peverell Terrace, TR13 9DZ ☎01326 562236, ⓦanmordroshotel.com. On a hill above Porthleven and close to Porthleven beach, this traditional hotel has great views across the harbour and sea; it's definitely worth paying a little extra for the sea-facing rooms. **£78**

Kota Harbour Head, TR13 9JA ☎01326 562407, ⓦkotarestaurant.co.uk. There are two rooms above this restaurant (see below), one smaller with no view, and a larger one benefiting from a glorious vista for which you will pay £20 more. Closed Jan to mid-Feb. **£75**

Wellmore End Cottage Methleigh Bottoms, TR13 9JP ☎01326 569310, ⓦwellmoreend.com. Two neat, en-suite rooms are offered in this fisherman's cottage, close to the harbour and convenient for the coast path. Generous breakfasts include vegetarian and vegan options, and there's a garden. No credit cards. **£80**

EATING

Kota Harbour Head, TR13 9JA ☎01326 562407, ⓦkotarestaurant.co.uk. This semiformal restaurant offers an intimate, unhurried setting for its exquisite meat and seafood dishes. Mains cost around £20, and there are good-value set menus for £20 and £25. Mid-Feb to Dec Tues–Sat 6–9pm.

Kota Kai Harbour Head, TR13 9JY ☎01326 574411, ⓦkotakai.co.uk. Modern and buzzy offshoot of *Kota*, a few steps away, with a lounge-bar which has great harbour views. Expect Asian-inspired dishes such as massaman chicken curry, as well as burgers for £12–15. Mon, Tues & Thurs–Sat (plus Wed in school hols) 11am–11pm, Sun 11am–3pm; food served Mon–Sat noon–2pm & 5.30–9pm, Sun noon–2.30pm.

SeaDrift Kitchen Café Fore St, TR13 9HJ ☎01326 558733, ⓦseadriftporthleven.co.uk. Unpretentious but top-quality café-restaurant, serving breakfasts, filled baps, and some excellent seafood dishes, such as grilled tiger prawns in garlic butter (£8) and pan-roasted hake (£17). Set-price lunches and dinners are £12 and £18 respectively. Wed 5.30pm–late, Thurs–Sat 10am–10pm; food served Wed 5.30–9pm, Thurs–Sat 10am–2pm & 5.30–9pm.

Loe Bar

One and a quarter miles southwest of Porthleven, **Loe Bar** is a lovely bank of sand and shingle accessible via the coast path from the village's harbour – though swimming here is not recommended, due to the steeply shelving bottom and strong currents.

Loe Pool

The Bar separates the sea from the freshwater **Loe Pool**, a lake stretching one and a quarter miles inland, and formerly extending much further up the valley of the River Cober towards Helston. Loe Pool is one of two places where it is claimed King Arthur's sword Excalibur was restored to its watery source – the other is on Bodmin Moor (see p.325). Another local superstition warns that the pool claims a victim every seven years. A five-mile waymarked path round its perimeter allows you to explore the surrounding creeks and woods, accessible also from Helston (from the park on the Porthleven road).

Praa Sands and around

There are plenty of good **beaches** within easy reach of Porthleven, including **Praa Sands**, three miles northwest, the best surfing beach hereabouts. Reached via the coast path beyond it, **Kenneggy Sands** is a wide sandy bay with rock pools, though access – via a chain ladder – might be tricky for families. There are also some good coast walks around **Rinsey Head**.

9

EATING

Sandbar Praa Sands, TR20 9TQ ☎01736 763516, ⓦsandbarpraasands.co.uk. Floor-to-ceiling windows overlooking the beach, tables on the terrace and local ales and ciders set the tone at this lively bar/restaurant. There is plenty of local seafood on offer, going into Mediterranean-style dishes such as crab and prawn linguini (£14.25), and live music Fri evenings (May–Sept) and Sun lunchtime. Daily 10am–11pm, closes midnight during summer school hols, and reduced opening in winter; food served until 9pm.

Mullion and around

The inland village of **MULLION**, five miles south of Helston, consists of little more than a church, a pub and a couple of shops, but it makes a useful base for visiting the beaches and coves hereabouts. If you're rambling in the area, look out for peregrine falcons and choughs – the latter have recently begun to breed locally.

St Mellanus

Churchtown, TR12 7HQ • Daily 9am–5pm • Free • ☎01326 240325

At the centre of Mullion, a triangle of quiet roads encloses the fifteenth- to sixteenth-century church of **St Mellanus**, dedicated to the Breton St Mellane (or Malo). The short tower is partly constructed of serpentine, and the interior boasts a good set of knobbly oak bench-ends illustrating Jonah and the whale, and other biblical scenes, as well as some more idiosyncratic carvings – a jester, a monk and cherubs with a chalice and barrel. Look out, too, for the dog-flap in the south door, originally for the ejection of unruly shepherds' dogs.

TOURS AND ACTIVITIES

Boat tours Fishing trips and pleasure cruises to local sea caves operate from Mullion Cove between Easter and October (☎01326 240345 or ☎07974 803924; £25/person).

Horseriding Newton Farm, on Polhorman Lane (a right turn off the Poldhu road from Mullion), offers lessons and hacks in the area (☎01326 240388, ⓦnewton-equestrian .co.uk): £10 per lesson, £20 per 1hr ride or £30 per 1hr 30min ride on the beach.

ACCOMMODATION AND EATING

Mullion Cove Hotel Mullion Cove, TR12 7EP ☎01326 240328, ⓦmullion-cove.co.uk. This Victorian hotel is spectacularly situated high above the harbour, with its own diminutive outdoor pool. It's a bit old-fashioned, but the views are fantastic; sea-facing rooms cost more, and an extra £28 per person gets you an excellent evening meal. **£155**

Old Inn Churchtown, TR12 7HN ☎01326 240240, ⓦoldinnmullion.co.uk. You'll find an agreeably antique atmosphere at this thatched sixteenth-century pub, which has ranks of tables outside. St Austell's Trelawny beer and Rattler cider are served alongside menu items ranging from ploughman's lunch to cajun spiced chicken and avocado, and a trio of sausages (all £11–13). Mon–Thurs & Sun noon–11pm, Fri & Sat noon–midnight; kitchen daily noon–2.30pm & 6–9pm.

Old Vicarage Nansmellyon Rd, TR12 7DQ ☎01326 240898, ⓔbandbmullion@hotmail.com. A large, elegant building fronted by a lawn and enclosed within a tall hedge garden at the centre of the village, this B&B offers four bright and spacious rooms, either en suite or with private bathroom. **£90**

SHOPPING

The Old Cider Barn Just south of Mullion on the A3083, TR12 7AU ☎01326 241309, ⓦtheoldciderbarn .co.uk. Local ciders, wines, meads and liqueurs are sold here, with free tastings. There's a tearoom and craft shop too. Easter–Sept daily 11am–5pm.

Mullion Cove

Signposted a mile and a quarter southwest of the village, a scattering of picturesque cottages amid gorse- and bracken-smothered slopes look down on the tiny but gorgeous harbour of **Mullion Cove** (also known as Porthmellin). A handful of fishing boats shelter behind thick, brick jetties and rocky outcrops.

EATING **MULLION COVE**

Porthmellin Tea Rooms Mullion Cove, TR12 7ES ☎ 01326 240941. You can sample fresh crab sandwiches, pasties, pizzas, cream teas and delicious cakes right by the harbour at this relaxed spot. Most items £5–10. Easter to late Oct daily 9.30am–4.45pm.

Polurrian and Poldhu coves

There's good swimming at cliff-flanked **Polurrian Cove**, a popular surfing beach less than a mile north of Mullion Cove along the coast path, while a further mile or so north, **Poldhu Cove** is a generous expanse of sand wedged between acres of wild moorland. Both beaches are accessible on the minor Mullion–Helston coast road (from Mullion, take The Commons, which turns into Poldhu Road).

Marconi Monument

If you're following the coast path north from Polurrian, you'll pass, on Poldhu's southern cliff edge, the **Marconi Monument**, a solitary obelisk erected in 1937 to mark the spot from where the first transatlantic radio transmission was said to have been made by Guglielmo Marconi in 1901 (some sceptics deny that this early attempt was in fact successful). Poldhu continued as a commercial radio station until 1922, and during World War II was a vital link between Britain and the Atlantic convoys bringing men, munitions and food.

EATING **POLDHU COVE**

Poldhu Beach Café Poldhu Cove, TR12 7JB ☎ 01326 240530, ⊚ poldhu.com. Energizing breakfasts, good-quality coffee, restorative hot chocolates and locally produced ice creams are served at this shack. Ciabatta melts and burgers are around £5. Daily: March, April & Oct 9.30am–5pm; May, June & Sept 9.30am–5.30pm; July & Aug 9.30am–6pm; Nov–Feb 9.30am–4pm.

The Lizard and around

Around four miles south of Mullion, at the end of the A3083, the nondescript village of **THE LIZARD** was likened by John Betjeman to "an army housing scheme given over to visitors". Its shops and handful of places to sleep and eat give it a strictly functional appeal, and unless you're looking for serpentine souvenirs, refreshment or a bed for the night, you're unlikely to linger long. It's the coast that holds all the appeal – but beware of fierce currents and creeping tides if you're spending any time on the beaches.

ARRIVAL AND DEPARTURE **THE LIZARD**

By bus The #37 bus (Mon–Sat hourly, Sun 5 daily) links The Lizard to Mullion (10min) and Helston (45min–1hr).

ACCOMMODATION

Caerthillian TR12 7NQ ☎ 01326 290019, ⊚ the caerthillian.co.uk. This grand, Wedgwood-blue Victorian B&B in the centre of the village has clean, bright rooms with en-suite bathrooms – room 3 has gorgeous views to Kynance Cove – and great breakfasts. No credit cards. **£80**

★ **Henry's** Caerthillian Farm, TR12 7NX ☎ 01326 290596, ⊚ henryscampsite.co.uk. Not your usual kind of campsite – with quirky art scattered about, free-ranging chickens and pitches bordered by subtropical plants – this spot just a few minutes' walk from the village centre has a friendly, laidback ambience. There's a small shop and basic, but adequate, unisex washing facilities. No credit cards. Per person **£11**

Penmenner House Penmenner Rd, TR12 7NR ☎ 01326 290370, ⊚ penmenner-house.co.uk. The poet Rupert Brooke once stayed in this lovely house on the edge of the village, which has four en-suite guest rooms, a spacious guests' lounge and sea views. Closed Jan & Feb. **£80**

★ **YHA Lizard** Lizard Point, TR12 7NT ☎ 0845 371 9550, ⊚ yha.org.uk/hostel/lizard. This hostel occupies a former Victorian hotel right on the coast, with majestic views. There's a shop and self-catering kitchen but no restaurant. Books up quickly. Dorms **£19**, doubles **£69**

EATING

Coast Coffee Bar & Bistro TR12 7NJ ☎ 01326 290400, ⊚ coastthelizard.co.uk. Friendly, modern café with outside seating, selling salads, pastas and burgers (around £10), as well as smoothies and cream teas. April,

May & early Sept to Oct Mon & Sun 9.30am–5pm, Tues–Sat 9.30am–8pm; June to early Sept daily 9.30am–8.30pm; Nov–March Wed–Sun 9.30am–5pm. **Top House** TR12 7NQ ☎01326 290974, ⍟thetop houselizard.co.uk. At the centre of the village, the mainland's southernmost pub serves snacks and full meals (evening mains around £12). It has a few outside tables and live folk music on Monday nights. Daily 11.30am–11pm; kitchen Mon–Thurs 11.30am–8.30pm, Fri & Sat 11.30am–9pm, Sun noon–8.30pm.

Witchball Lighthouse Rd, TR12 7NJ ☎01326 290662, ⍟www.witchball.co.uk. Traditional locals' pub and restaurant, where you can tuck into fish and chips (£12), huge Texas-style "Voodoo Burgers", pastas and pizzas (all around £12). Beers and ciders come from Cornish Chough and other local breweries. Easter–Oct daily noon–11pm; Nov–Easter Mon–Wed 4.30–11pm, Thurs–Sun noon–11pm; kitchen daily noon–3pm & 7–9pm.

Lizard Point

A web of footpaths radiates out from the village towards the sea; the most popular route is the mile-long track running parallel to the road that leads to mainland Britain's southernmost tip, **Lizard Point**. Here, a couple of low-key cafés and gift shops look down on a churning sea and a tiny sheltered cove holding a disused lifeboat station. It's all quite unspoilt – a far cry from the paraphernalia surrounding Land's End (see p.253) – and the coast on either side is no less impressive: a succession of rugged chasms and caves hollowed out by the sea, where you can occasionally glimpse grey seals, basking sharks and dolphins.

Lizard Lighthouse

Lizard Point, TR12 7NT • **Heritage Centre** Late March to Oct Mon–Thurs & Sun 11am–5pm • £3 • **Lighthouse tours** Mon–Thurs & Sun hourly; 45min • £7.50 (includes Heritage Centre) • ☎01326 290202, ⍟trinityhouse.co.uk

The distinctive twin towers of the **Lizard Lighthouse**, dating from 1752, dominate the headland. In the old engine room, the Heritage Centre displays restored lighthouse equipment, and has interactive gizmos that will appeal to children. You can view the adjoining lighthouse on a guided **tour**, and enjoy amazing vistas from the lantern room, where the five-tonne lens structure floats on a tank of mercury.

Housel Cove

From Lizard Point, the coast path leads east past the **Lion's Den**, a huge cavity in the cliffs caused by the collapse of a sea cave, to **Housel Cove**, where Marconi conducted his early radio experiments from a bungalow that's still visible above the small sandy beach (accessed via a steep cliff path). Beyond Marconi's bungalow, the prominent white, castellated building on **Bass Point** was constructed by Lloyd's insurers in 1872 to enable its company agents to semaphore passing ships and relay news of cargoes to merchants in London; it's now a private house.

Church Cove

Half a mile further east and north of Bass Point, **Church Cove** is the site of the lifeboat station that replaced the one at Lizard Point. The cove lies at the end of a lane linking it

---

THE LIZARD'S COASTAL FLOWERS

Much of the Lizard peninsula is designated a Site of Special Scientific Interest (SSSI) and is a protected nature reserve, with a total of eighteen nationally rare plant species growing locally, making this one of the top ten botanical sites in Britain. Ever since John Ray ("the father of British botany") discovered the fringed rupture-wort and the very rare wild asparagus at Lizard Point in 1667, visitors have flocked to the area in search of **cliff flowers**, many of them Mediterranean in origin. The hottentot fig, a showy South African succulent with pink and white flowers, which was introduced in the nineteenth century, now dominates large areas of the cliffs despite efforts by the National Trust and Natural England to control its spread, while bluebells and thrift create extravagant swathes of colour in spring. Look out, too, for dropwort, harebells, bloody cranesbill and the rare and colourful Cornish heath that grows only on the magnesium-rich serpentine and gabbro rocks hereabouts.

with the hamlet of **LANDEWEDNACK**, whose fifteenth-century church, St Wynwallow, is said to be the last place where a sermon was preached in the Cornish tongue, in 1674.

Cadgwith

From Church Cove, continue northeast along the coast path for about a mile to reach **CADGWITH**, an idyllically snuggled fishing village, whose thatched roofs nestle between headlands. Just before the village you can look down from the top of the cliff into the **Devil's Frying Pan**, where waves swirl around a collapsed sea cave.

Kynance Cove

A mile northwest of the Lizard, the peninsula's best-known beach, **Kynance Cove**, lies at the end of a toll road, signposted west off the A3083. In all, it's about a forty-minute walk from Lizard Point, including a final fifteen-minute clamber down steep steps to the shore. The white-sand beach is encircled by sheer 200ft cliffs in which the olive-green serpentine is flushed with reds and purples, and faces the stacks and arches of offshore islets that are joined to shore at low tide; the biggest of these, **Asparagus Island**, takes its name from the wild asparagus that grows there. Masses of other wild flowers adorn the rocks on every side, giving the scene a wild grandeur. The water quality is excellent, too, though bathers should take care not to be stranded on the islands by the sea, which submerges the entire beach at **high tide**. Kynance Cove has an excellent seasonal café (ⓦwww.kynancecovecafe.co.uk) and there are toilets.

Coverack

East of the A3083 Helston–Lizard road, the lonely B3293 crosses the broad windswept plateau of **Goonhilly Downs**, where the futuristic saucers of an extensive satellite station and the nearby ranks of wind turbines make somewhat spooky intrusions. A right fork onto the B3294 brings you to the sequestered fishing port of **COVERACK**, once a notorious centre for contraband. The village presents a placid picture, its thatched and lime-washed granite cottages overlooking a bay where you might spot dolphins frolicking, and a curve of beach that disappears to almost nothing at high tide. Small boats are moored in the tiny walled harbour, where there's a small selection of cafés and restaurants.

INFORMATION AND ACTIVITIES

COVERACK

Tourist information Check out the community website ⓦcoverack.org.uk for information on accommodation and local activities.

Windsurfing The Coverack Windsurfing Centre, at Cliff Cottage in the village centre, offers RYA-recognized windsurfing courses at all levels, with equipment provided (April–Oct; ☎01326 280939, ⓦwww.coverack.co.uk). You can also rent kayaks and paddleboards (£10/hr).

ACCOMMODATION

Boak House School Hill, TR12 6SA ☎01326 280329. G&Ts await guests arriving at this B&B, which has four white-walled rooms with sea views and shared or private bathrooms. The Juliet room has a small terrace, and guests have use of the dining room and conservatory. No debit/credit cards. **£90**

Fernleigh Chymbloth Way, TR12 6TB ☎01326 280626, ⓦfernleighcoverack.co.uk. Just up from Harbour Road, this homely B&B has three spacious rooms (with private or en-suite bathroom), a small garden with bay views and an amiable host who can provide an excellent supper (£18) as well as packed lunches, luggage transfers and a clothes-washing service. No debit/credit cards. **£75**

Little Trevothan TR12 6SD ☎01326 280260, ⓦlittletrevothan.com. Under a mile inland (signposted on the right of the B3293 as you approach Coverack, near the St Keverne fork), this quiet campsite has level pitches and caravans for weekly rental from £290. Closed Jan & Feb. **£17**

YHA Coverack School Hill, TR12 6SA ☎0845 371 9014, ⓦyha.org.uk/hotel/coverack. A short walk uphill from the harbour, this hostel has panoramic views, and accommodation in dormitories, en-suite private rooms or in a campsite where you can rent bell tents sleeping up to five (£99). Meals are available, or you can self-cater. Nov–Feb groups only. Dorms **£19**, doubles **£75**

9

EATING

Lifeboat House The Cove, TR12 6SX ☎ 01326 281400, 🌐 thelifeboathouse.co.uk. This modern restaurant by the harbour serves superb fresh seafood as well as tagines (mains £11–15); booking is recommended. You can get a decent breakfast here too, and there's an attached take away for fish and chips (daily noon–9pm). Easter–Oct daily 9.30am–9pm; reduced opening in winter; take away same days noon–9pm.

Paris Hotel The Cove, TR12 6SX ☎ 01326 280258, 🌐 pariscoverack.com. Right above the harbour, Coverack's social hub enjoys wonderful views and has good beers, lunchtime snacks, bar meals (mains around £15) and a garden. Small but comfortable rooms are also available (£90). Daily 11am–11pm; kitchen Mon–Sat noon–2.30pm & 6–9pm, Sun 12.30–3pm & 6–9pm.

St Keverne and around

Five miles north of Coverack, the inland village of **ST KEVERNE** is set around a pretty square holding a couple of pubs and the church of **St Akeveranus**. The church's ribbed, octagonal spire has served as a marker for sailors over the centuries, and the adjoining churchyard holds the tombs of those who drowned off this treacherous stretch of coast. The carved fifteenth-century bench-ends inside the church are also worth a look.

The beaches

Several mainly stony **beaches** lie within a short distance of the village, and are perfect for a swim if you don't mind the rocks. The nearest of these is **Porthoustock** (pronounced "P'rowstock"), a mile east of St Keverne, via the road to the right of the *White Hart* (turn off along the signposted lane to the right). It's a stone-and-shingle strip flanked by quarry workings, which faces the dreaded Manacles rocks three miles offshore – the cause of numerous shipwrecks. Alternatively, stay on the road from the *White Hart* for a couple of miles to reach **PORTHALLOW**, where there's a small grey-sand beach and a cluster of cottages around the harbour.

Roskilly's

Tregellast Barton, TR12 6NX • Mon–Wed & Sun 10am–6pm, Thurs–Sat 10am–8pm • Free • ☎ 01326 280479, 🌐 roskillys.co.uk

Less than a mile south of St Keverne (signposted off the Coverack road), **Roskilly's** produces some of Cornwall's most lip-smackingly delicious ice cream, available in more than thirty flavours and mainly organic. You can sample these, as well as frozen yoghurt, fudge and other goodies, in the shop and the *Croust House* café/restaurant (see below). The surrounding ponds, glades and wetlands, created to shelter wildlife, make for a pleasant wander.

ARRIVAL AND DEPARTURE   ST KEVERNE AND AROUND

By bus St Keverne is connected by bus #36 to Helston (Mon–Sat 6 daily; 35min) and Coverack (Mon–Sat 2 daily; 10min).

ACCOMMODATION AND EATING

The Croust House Tregellast Barton, TR12 6NX ☎ 01326 280479, 🌐 roskillys.co.uk. At Roskilly's (see above), this farmhouse restaurant has excellent pasties, burgers and baguettes (mostly around £10), not to mention the creamiest ice creams and the fruitiest sorbets. You can eat inside or under the pergola, and children's portions are available. On summer evenings, stone-baked pizzas are served from the wood-burning oven (around £7) and there's weekly live music. Daily 9am–6pm; summer school hols 9am–9pm.

Five Pilchards Inn Porthallow, TR12 6PP ☎ 01326 280256, 🌐 thefivepilchards.co.uk. Just off the beach, this no-frills free house serves succulent, fresh-off-the-boat fish (around £10) and sizzling steaks (£17), and has spacious rooms with grand views. Easter–Oct daily noon–3pm & 6–11pm; Nov–Easter Mon 6–11pm, Wed–Sat noon–2.30pm & 6–11pm, Sun noon–11pm; kitchen Feb–Dec Mon 6–9pm, Wed–Sun noon–2pm & 6–9pm. **£75**

★**The Greenhouse** 6 High St, TR12 6NN ☎ 01326 280800, 🌐 tgor.co.uk. Local, organic and seasonal food is served at this cottage restaurant off the main square; for example slow-roasted jerk pork belly (£15) – a signature dish – and monkfish and clams (£18). Two- and three-course set-price menus ring in at £15 and £18.50, and local

9

beers and ciders are offered alongside reasonably priced wine. Wed–Sat 6.30–9.30pm.

Old Temperance House The Square, TR12 6NA ☎ 01326 280986, ⓦ oldtemperancehouse.co.uk. In the centre of the village, this neat B&B has four smallish but spotless rooms (choose "Bailey's" for more space) and great breakfasts. There's also a self-catering cottage sleeping three (£385–525 per week). No under-12s. **£90**

Helford River and around

Marking the northern edge of the Lizard peninsula, the **Helford River** – actually a ria or drowned river valley – reveals a range of different faces along its length, from sheltered muddy creeks upstream, to its rocky, open mouth, all of which repay exploration on foot or by boat. Oak woods, meadows and small beaches line the riverbanks, from where herons, egrets, cormorants and curlews are a common sight.

Helford

Surrounded by woods and lying at the bottom of a steep and narrow lane, the agreeable old smugglers' haunt of **HELFORD** has a neat, gentrified appearance nowadays, immersed in a comfortable lethargy. You can cross to the Helford River's north bank – the route of the South West Coast Path – by seasonal passenger ferry to the hamlet of **HELFORD PASSAGE**. Both Helford and Helford Passage make good starting points for riverside rambles, and you can **rent boats** or **kayaks** from Helford River Boats (see below).

GETTING AROUND AND TOURS HELFORD

By ferry A passenger ferry runs from Helford (south bank) to Helford Passage: April–June, Sept & Oct 9.30am–5pm; July & Aug 9.30am–9pm (£4 one-way, £6 return; ☎ 01326 250770, ⓦ helford-river-boats.co.uk).

Boat tours Helford River Boats, Helford Passage (☎ 01326 250770, ⓦ helford-river-boats.co.uk), operates a kiosk in front of the *Ferryboat Inn*. Motorboats cost £60 for 2 hours (fuel included), kayaks £12 per hour; paddleboards and rowing boats are also available.

EATING

Ferryboat Inn Helford Passage, TR11 5LB ☎ 01326 250625, ⓦ thewrightbrothers.co.uk. Idyllically situated on the river, this pub run by the operators of the nearby Duchy of Cornwall Oyster Farm (the source of many of the dishes here) makes a fine spot to soak up the atmosphere. Mains are £9–13, and good sandwiches are also available (£7–10). Gets busy, so orders may be slow coming. Daily 11am–11pm; food served noon–9pm.

New Yard Trelowarren, southwest of Helford, TR12 6AF ☎ 01326 221595, ⓦ newyardrestaurant.co.uk. For brief refreshments or sophisticated dining, drop in at this classy café/restaurant in a converted coach house on the Trelowarren estate, near Mawgan off the B3293. Local ingredients go into the breakfasts, snacks and supper dishes; for example wild garlic soup with yoghurt, pearl barley risotto with goat's curd, and various tapas (mains £11–17). Pizzas are served in the evenings on Sunday and, in summer, Wednesday (call first to check). You can sit outside in warm weather. Feb–Easter & Oct–Dec Wed & Thurs 10am–2.30pm, Fri & Sat 8.30am–9pm, Sun 8.30am–2.30pm; Easter–Sept Mon–Thurs 10am–9pm, Fri & Sat 8.30am–9pm, Sun 8.30am–2.30pm.

Frenchman's Creek

On the river's south side and one of a splay of inlets, **Frenchman's Creek** was the inspiration for Daphne du Maurier's novel of the same name, and her evocation of it still holds true: "still and soundless, surrounded by the trees, hidden from the eyes of men". Less than a mile west of Helford, the creek is on a footpath signposted from the *Shipwright's Arms*.

Cornish Seal Sanctuary

Gweek, TR12 6UG • Daily: summer 10am–5pm, winter closes 3.30/4pm • £15.50, under-16s £12.95 • ☎ 01326 221361, ⓦ sealsanctuary.co.uk

Nestled outside the village of **GWEEK** in a tranquil riverside setting, the **Cornish Seal Sanctuary** is a rehabilitation and release centre for the increasing number of injured seals being rescued from around Cornwall and beyond. Without the need for glitz or technology, the centre provides an informative insight into the lives of seals and the measures taken to care for them. There's plenty of entertainment in watching the seals at play – especially the pups – which can usually be seen between September and February. The ultimate aim is to get the seals back in the wild, but as this is sometimes impossible on account of their condition, the centre also offers a "retirement home". Other creatures, such as sea lions, otters, penguins, ponies and goats, are also cared for.

Glendurgan Garden

Mawnan Smith, TR11 5JZ • Mid-Feb to July & early Sept to Oct Tues–Sun 10.30am–5.30pm or dusk; Aug to early Sept daily 10.30am–5.30pm • £8.10; NT • ☎ 01326 252020, ⓦ nationaltrust.org.uk/glendurgan-garden

On the northern shore of the Helford River, **Glendurgan Garden** is one of Cornwall's most glorious gardens. Indeed, there is little in the way of labelling or information about the giant gunnera, tulip trees, Chilean flamebushes and Mexican pines that thrive in this sheltered spot, but this adds to the appeal. Steep paths trail down the glen, past a maze, to the tiny hamlet of Durgan on the riverbank, where there's a beach and a small café selling tea, coffee and (in summer) ice cream.

Mawnan

In contrast to these inland locations, the village of **MAWNAN** stands close to the mouth of the Helford River, a couple of miles east of Helford Passage. Set apart on a height, the granite church of St Maunanus has a Cornish inscription above the lychgate: *Da thymi nesse the Dhu* ("It is good to draw nigh to the Lord"). From here the coast path heads northeast for about a mile to **Rosemullion Head**, jutting out into Falmouth Bay and strewn with wild flowers in spring and summer. The path continues for just over a mile to the beach at Maenporth and beyond to Falmouth (see p.222).

The Penwith peninsula

Though more densely populated than the Lizard, and absorbing a heavier tourist influx, the **Penwith peninsula** (also known as West Penwith, or the Land's End peninsula) retains the elements that have always marked it out – craggy, wave-pounded granite cliffs and a string of superlative sand beaches encompassing wild, untrammelled moorland. The main town, **Penzance**, preserves a lively, unpretentious feel as well as some handsome Regency architecture, and makes a useful starting point for forays to nearby sights: the offshore bastion of **St Michael's Mount**, the Iron Age settlement of **Chysauster**, the neighbouring fishing centre of **Newlyn**, and, just beyond, bijou **Mousehole**. Further round the coast, **Porthcurno** has a five-star beach and one of the country's most famous performance venues, the cliff-hewn **Minack Theatre**.

The raw appeal of Penwith's rugged landscape is still encapsulated by **Land's End**, though the headland's commercialization leads many to prefer the unadulterated beauty of **Cape Cornwall**, four miles north. Inland **St Just-in-Penwith** is the largest village hereabouts, from where you could explore the remnants of the local mining industry around **Pendeen**, a scattering of **prehistoric remains** and the compact granite village of **Zennor**. Penwith's northern seaboard has few beaches to write home about, with the notable exception of the generous sands surrounding **St Ives**, whose tight knot of flower-filled lanes and Mediterranean ambience have long made it a magnet for artists and holiday visitors alike.

Penzance

Occupying a sheltered position in Mount's Bay, **PENZANCE** has combined a busy working atmosphere with the trappings of the holiday industry since the rail link to London was established in the 1860s. Most traces of the medieval town were obliterated at the end of the sixteenth century by a Spanish raiding party, and the predominant style now is Regency and Victorian – most conspicuously on the broad promenade west of the harbour and in the centre.

9

Market House and around

Climbing up from the bus and train stations, Market Jew Street (from *Marghas Jew*, meaning "Thursday Market") rises to the pillared **Market House**, dating from 1836 and now a bank, its silver dome conspicuous for miles around. In front there stands a statue of pioneering scientist Sir Humphry Davy (see box, p.245).

Chapel Street

Swinging back downhill from the top of Market Jew Street, elegant **Chapel Street** has some of the town's finest buildings, including the flamboyant **Egyptian House**, built in the 1830s as a museum but subsequently abandoned until its restoration by the Landmark Trust (ⓦlandmarktrust.org.uk) forty-odd years ago; they now rent the house out as three excellent holiday apartments (sleeping 2–4 people each). It's colourfully daubed with lotus-bud capitals – an "Egyptian" style harking back to the vogue spawned by Napoleon's campaign in Egypt in 1798.

Across the street from the Egyptian House, the seventeenth-century **Union Hotel** originally held the town's assembly rooms, where news of Admiral Nelson's victory at Trafalgar and the death of Nelson himself was first announced in 1805.

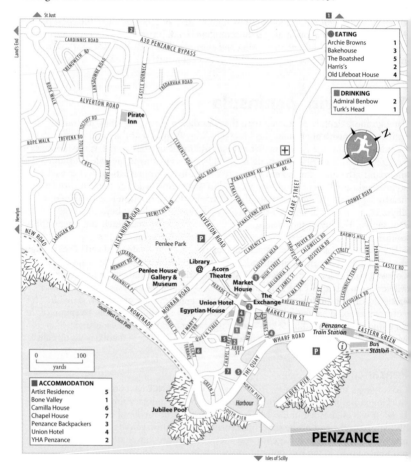

EATING

Archie Browns	1
Bakehouse	3
The Boatshed	5
Harris's	2
Old Lifeboat House	4

DRINKING

Admiral Benbow	2
Turk's Head	1

ACCOMMODATION

Artist Residence	5
Bone Valley	1
Camilla House	6
Chapel House	7
Penzance Backpackers	3
Union Hotel	4
YHA Penzance	2

PENZANCE

The Exchange

Princes St, TR18 2NL • 10am–5pm: late March to late Oct Mon–Sat; late Oct to late March Tues–Sat • £3.50, including Newlyn Art Gallery (see p.248); valid 7 days • ☎ 01736 363715, ⓦ newlynartgallery.co.uk

A turning at the top of Chapel and Market Jew streets brings you to **The Exchange**, a strikingly refurbished telephone exchange that now holds Devon and Cornwall's largest contemporary art gallery, with regular exhibitions of local, national and international artists.

Jubilee Pool

The Promenade, TR18 4UU • Late May to mid-Sept daily 10.30am–6pm, Tues closes 8pm • £4.75, or £3.10 after 3.30pm • ☎ 01736 369224, ⓦ jubileepool.co.uk

Sited on a small promontory bulging out into Mount's Bay, the Art Deco **Jubilee Pool** is a tidal, saltwater (though chlorinated) open-air swimming pool, built to mark the Silver Jubilee of George V in 1935. It's a classic example of the style, and non-swimmers can stroll around as a visitor (£2) to get a closer view of the pool and bay. Deckchairs can be rented for 50p.

Penlee House Gallery and Museum

Morrab Rd, TR18 4HE • Mon–Sat: April–Oct 10am–5pm; Nov–March 10.30am–4.30pm • £4.50 • ☎ 01736 363625, ⓦ penleehouse.org.uk

A must for anyone interested in the art scene that flourished in and around Penzance in the late nineteenth century, **Penlee House Gallery and Museum** holds the country's largest collection of Newlyn School artworks (see p.345), though only a limited number are on display at any time. Frequently sentimentalized but bathed in an evocatively luminous light, impressionistic maritime scenes rub shoulders with portraits of Newlyn's fishing community by the likes of Stanhope Forbes and Norman Garstin – whose atmospheric masterpiece *The Rain It Raineth Every Day* is here – while temporary exhibitions highlight particular artists or themes. The museum has displays on local history.

Penlee House itself is a creamy Italianate Victorian villa from 1865, inherited in 1918 by Alfred Branwell, a keen horticulturalist who introduced rare trees and shrubs from China, South America and Australia into its surrounding gardens – perfect for a picnic.

ARRIVAL AND DEPARTURE   PENZANCE

By train Penzance train station is at the eastern end of town next to the tourist office and bus station.
Destinations Bodmin (hourly; 1hr 20min); Exeter (hourly; 3hr); London (11 daily; 5–6hr); Plymouth (hourly; 2hr); St Ives, most via St Erth (1–2 hourly; 20–40min); Truro (hourly; 40min).

By bus All services arrive at and leave from the bus station, right by the train station.
Destinations Helston (Mon–Sat hourly, Sun every 2hr; 50min); Land's End (hourly; 55min); Mousehole (Mon–Sat 4 hourly, Sun every 30min; 15min); Newquay (5 daily;

1–2hr); Plymouth (6 daily; 2hr 45min–4hr 10min); St Ives (Mon–Sat 3–4 hourly, Sun 1–2 hourly; 30–50min); St Just (Mon–Sat 1–2 hourly, Sun every 2hr; 25min); Truro (Mon–Sat every 30min, Sun hourly; 1hr 35min).

By car There are car parks by the seafront and a cheaper one off Alverton Rd (convenient for Penlee House). Travellers to the Isles of Scilly can deposit their vehicles at Isles of Scilly Parking (☎ 01736 332727, ⓦ islesofscillyparking.co.uk), either very near the harbour (from £7.50/day) or at a more distant site connected to the harbour by a shuttle service (from £6/day). Booking essential.

LOCAL BOY MADE GOOD: HUMPHRY DAVY

Penzance's statue of **Humphry Davy** (1778–1829) remembers the local woodcarver's son who became one of the leading scientists of the nineteenth century. A pioneer in the field of electrochemistry, he identified six new elements including potassium and sodium, discovered the use of nitrous oxide ("laughing gas") for anaesthetic use in 1798, and invented the life-saving miners' safety-lamp, which bears his name and which his statue holds.

9

GETTING AROUND

By car You can rent cars from Europcar (train station; ☎0371 384 5975, ⌨europcar.co.uk) or Enterprise (The Forecourt, Long Rock; ☎01736 332000, ⌨enterprise .co.uk).

By bike Penzance Bike Hire, Torwood House, Alexandra Rd (☎07764 225535, ⌨penzancebikehire.co.uk); £15 per day.

By taxi There are taxi ranks at bus and train stations, or you can call the Penzance Taxi Company (☎01736 366366).

INFORMATION AND TOURS

Tourist information Station Approach (Easter–Sept Tues–Fri 10am–5pm, Sat 10am–4pm, Sun 10am–2pm; Oct–Easter Mon–Sat 10am–4pm; ☎01736 335530, ⌨lovepenzance.co.uk).

Hospital West Cornwall Hospital, St Clare St, TR18 2PF ☎01736 874000. 24hr accident and emergency department.

Boat tours Mermaid Pleasure Trips (☎07901 731201, ⌨cornwallboattrips.co.uk) and Marine Discovery (☎07749 277110, ⌨marinediscovery.co.uk) offer coastal cruises, fishing trips and wildlife-watching in search of seals, seabirds, dolphins, porpoises, sharks etc. Trips last from 1hr 30min (£15–18/person) to 4hr (£35–45/person), leaving from the harbour.

Minibus tours Western Discoveries (☎01736 362763, ⌨westerndiscoveries.co.uk) run 4hr minibus tours of the Penwith peninsula, taking in prehistoric remains and local wildlife, leaving from the tourist office (£35/person).

ACCOMMODATION

★**Artist Residence** 20 Chapel St, TR18 4AW ☎01736 365664, ⌨arthotelcornwall.co.uk. Artistic licence has been given free rein at this central hotel, where each room is designed and decorated by a different artist and has its own aesthetic. Themes range from Indian- and Aboriginal-inspired through to cool minimalist and street art. The staff are friendly and helpful, and the breakfasts are fabulous. **£125**

Bone Valley Heamoor, TR20 8UJ ☎01736 360313, ⌨bonevalleyholidaypark.co.uk. The nearest campsite to Penzance lies two miles north of town, and can be reached on buses #10 and #10A. It's sheltered, clean, friendly and well equipped, but small, so call ahead at any time of year. **£14**

Camilla House 12 Regent Terrace, TR18 4DW ☎01736 363771, ⌨camillahouse.co.uk. Just off the seafront Promenade, this elegant Regency B&B is convenient for the harbour and has sea views from most rooms (the top rooms are cosiest). There's usually a three-night minimum stay. Closed Nov–March. **£92**

★**Chapel House** Chapel St, TR18 4AQ ☎01736 362024, ⌨chapelhousepz.co.uk. This refurbished Georgian townhouse has the wow-factor in spades, from its white-walled, antiques-furnished drawing room to the six airy and elegant, individually styled guest rooms with state-of-the-art bathrooms and terrific views over Mount's Bay. There's a peaceful, multilevel garden, brilliant breakfasts, and kitchen suppers can be arranged. **£170**

Penzance Backpackers Alexandra Rd, TR18 4LZ ☎01736 363836, ⌨pzbackpack.com. One of the region's tidiest hostels, with en-suite dorms, doubles and family rooms (£72 for 4 people), a clean, well-equipped kitchen and a large lounge. Dorms **£16**, doubles **£36**

Union Hotel Chapel St, TR18 4AE ☎01736 362319, ⌨unionhotel.co.uk. This Georgian coaching inn is a fine place to soak up some local history, with breakfast served in the *Victorian Theatre Bar* and drinks in the *Nelson Bar* (dinners are available in the modern *Hamiltons Restaurant*). It's all a bit weathered, but friendly and good value. **£85**

YHA Penzance Castle Horneck, Alverton TR20 8TF ☎0845 371 9653, ⌨yha.org.uk/hostel/penzance. Clean and friendly hostel housed in a Georgian mansion with an airy bar/restaurant, a well-equipped kitchen, camping pitches and bell tents to rent. It's a 25min hike from the stations, or a short bus ride (#5 or #6 as far as the *Pirate Inn*, from where it's signposted). Dorms **£19**, doubles **£59**, camping/person **£12**, bell tents **£59**

EATING

★**Archie Browns** Bread St, TR18 2EQ ☎01736 362828, ⌨archiebrowns.co.uk. Vegans, vegetarians and wholefood fans will be happy in this café above a health-food shop, with a relaxed, friendly vibe and local art on the walls. Choices include quiches, falafel, mixed salads and homity pie (£5–8). Mon–Sat 9am–5pm.

THE ART PASS

Not to be confused with the National Art Pass, Cornwall's **Art Pass** (£15) allows unlimited access over seven days to six galleries in West Penwith: Penlee House, The Exchange and Newlyn Art Gallery in Penzance and Newlyn, and Tate St Ives, the Barbara Hepworth Museum and the Leach Pottery in St Ives. Pass-holders also get a discount on shop purchases at The Exchange and Newlyn Art Gallery. Pick one up at any of the galleries.

GOLOWAN FESTIVAL

A dynamic mix of traditional and contemporary arts, Penzance's **Golowan Festival** (☎01736 369686, ⓦgolowanfestival.org) features torchlit processions, folk music, workshops, ceilidhs and other entertainments over nine days in mid- to late June. Events take place in pubs and churches, Greenmarket car park, Morrab Gardens, Penlee Park and down at the harbour, and the festival culminates on **Mazey Day**, with parades and performances all over town.

Bakehouse Chapel St, TR18 4AE ☎01736 331331, ⓦbakehouserestaurant.co.uk. In a former bakery in a secluded courtyard, this place has a modern Mediterranean feel, offering dishes including Helford mussels (£14), hake fillet with Tuscan stew, and some of the best steaks you'll ever have (£12–20). The early-bird menu (available Tues–Fri before 7pm) is especially good value, at £13 for two courses. Mon–Sat 6–9pm.

The Boatshed Wharf Rd, TR18 4AS ☎01736 368845, ⓦboatshed.org.uk. With granite walls and ships' timbers decorating the interior, this relaxed café-bar and restaurant by the harbour serves daytime snacks as well as pastas, burgers and pizzas (around £8), steaks and seafood (£9–16). Choose between booth seating or tables outside. Jan & Feb Fri & Sat 6.30–9.30pm; March–June & Oct–Dec daily 6.30–9.30pm; July–Sept daily 11am–3pm & 6.30–9.30pm.

Harris's 46 New St, TR18 2LZ ☎01736 364408, ⓦharrissrestaurant.co.uk. Quality cuisine in formal surroundings. Seafood is the speciality, for instance grilled scallops, crab florentine and roast John Dory, though meat dishes such as grilled fillet steak with Béarnaise sauce are also available. Main courses cost around £22. Tues–Sat noon–2pm & 7–9.30pm.

Old Lifeboat House Wharf Rd, TR18 4AA ☎01736 369409, ⓦoldlifeboathouse.co.uk. On the seafront, this charmingly converted café-bistro delivers seafood dishes at reasonable prices (around £15 on the evening menu). Apart from the daily specials, you'll find fish pie and a fish medley, as well as a couple of meat and vegetarian options. You can also drop by for breakfast, a well-filled sandwich or coffee and cake. Tues–Sat 9.30am–9pm, Sun 9.30am–4pm.

DRINKING

Admiral Benbow 46 Chapel St, TA18 4AF ☎01736 363448. Crammed with gaudy ships' figureheads and other nautical items, this historic pub has a restaurant made to resemble a ship's galley. The meals are family-friendly but fairly mediocre – lunchtime dishes cost around £10, while in the evening Newlyn cod or steak and ale pie are £10–15. Look out for the armed smuggler on the roof. Mon–Sat 11am–11pm, Sun noon–10.30pm; kitchen daily noon–2.30pm & 6–9.30pm.

★**Turk's Head** 49 Chapel St, TA18 4AF ☎01736 363093, ⓦturksheadpenzance.co.uk. The town's oldest pub, reputed to date back to the thirteenth century, makes a great place for a drink or meal, with a maze of low-ceilinged rooms and a small walled garden. The beer selection is good (including Turk's Head Ale, naturally) and menu items range from sandwiches to seafood pie and coq au vin (£11–14). Daily 11.30am–11.30pm; kitchen daily noon–2.30pm & 6–10pm.

St Michael's Mount

Marazion, TR17 0HS • **Castle** Mid-March to June, Sept & Oct Mon–Fri & Sun 10.30am–5pm; July & Aug Mon–Fri & Sun 10.30am–5.30pm • £9 (£12.50 with gardens); NT • **Gardens** Mid-April to June Mon–Fri 10.30am–5pm; July & Aug Thurs & Fri 10.30am–5.30pm; Sept Thurs & Fri 10.30am–5pm; call for winter opening • £6 (£12.50 with castle); NT • ☎01736 710507, ⓦstmichaelsmount.co.uk • Bus #2 or #17B Penzance–Marazion. Walk along the causeway at low tide; at high tide frequent ferries make the crossing (£2 one-way)

Five miles east of Penzance, some 400yd from the mainland village of **MARAZION** atop a promontory, **St Michaels' Mount** presents a fine spectacle – an irresistible lure to anyone travelling along the long curve of Mount's Bay. As well as the castle, the lush gardens are well worth exploring. The site can be accessed on foot along a cobbled causeway, or by ferry at high tide. A couple of cafés provide refreshments, and local bands play at the harbour on most Sundays in July and August.

Brief history

Bronze Age finds recently unearthed testify to settlement of this site stretching back at least three millennia, but it was supposedly a vision of the archangel Michael to some local fishermen that led to the construction of a church on this granite pile in the fifth century, and within three centuries a Celtic monastery had been founded here. The

9

present building derives from a chapel raised in the eleventh century by Edward the Confessor, who handed over the island to the Benedictine monks of Brittany's Mont St Michel, an island-abbey also inspired by a vision of St Michael. Based on Mont St Michel, the new Benedictine abbey complex was later appropriated by Henry V during the Hundred Years' War, and it became a fortress following its dissolution a century later. During the Civil War it was used to store arms for the Royalist forces, and it subsequently became the residence of the St Aubyn family, who still inhabit parts of the castle today.

The castle

Above the island's harbour – historically used by the fishermen of Marazion, as their village never possessed its own – it's a steep climb to the **castle** itself, up the cobbled **Pilgrims' Steps**. The series of surprisingly small rooms within displays a wealth of weaponry and military trophies, period furniture and a feast of miniatures and larger paintings. The highlight of the tour is undoubtedly the **Chevy Chase Room**, the former monks' refectory given a seventeenth-century makeover. Its name has no connection to the actor, referring instead to a medieval hunting ballad, illustrated by a simple plaster frieze on the walls of the room ("Chevy" is either from the Cheviot Hills or the French *chevaux*, horses). Apart from this, the room is dominated by the royal coat of arms given by Charles II in recognition of the St Aubyns' support during the Civil War.

The family is well represented in portraits covering the walls elsewhere in the castle, and in the inscriptions in the battlemented **chapel** that crowns the island's summit. The Georgian finery and "Gothick" style of the **Blue Drawing Room**, embellished with Rococo twirls and fancy plasterwork, makes a refreshing contrast to all the militaria, while the model of the house made of champagne corks in the **Map Room** also suggests less-than-martial pursuits.

The castle's primary function, however, is remembered in the **Garrison Room**, where the Armada was first sighted on July 30, 1588; the beacon fire that was lit was the first to warn the nation that the Spanish invasion had come.

Newlyn

Immediately south of Penzance, and well protected behind two long piers, **NEWLYN** is Cornwall's biggest fishing port and an important market for the catches of smaller West Cornwall ports. **William Lovett** (1800–77), leader of the radical Chartist movement, was born here in Church Lane, the son of a master mariner, and the town later became the focus of Cornwall's first "artists' colony" (see p.345), when a group of artists gathered here in the wake of the painter Stanhope Forbes in the late nineteenth century.

Newlyn's artistic profile, however, is dwarfed today by its **fishing** business, whose vitality – despite huge problems concerning falling stocks, quotas and foreign (particularly Spanish) competition – is a refreshing contrast to the dwindling activity evident in most of Cornwall's other ports. You can sample the local catch at the various shellfish and seafood outlets scattered around the harbour.

Newlyn Art Gallery

24 New Rd, TR18 5PZ · 10am–5pm: late March to late Oct Mon–Sat; late Oct to late March Tues–Sat · £3.50, including The Exchange (see p.245); valid 7 days · ☎ 01736 363715, ⓦ newlynartgallery.co.uk

> **THE NEWLYN FISH FESTIVAL**
>
> Newlyn's seafood catch is celebrated at the **Newlyn Fish Festival** (ⓦ newlynfishfestival.org.uk; £6), taking place on the late August Bank Holiday Monday in and around the fish market, with food stalls, cooking demonstrations and local seafood to sample. But there's plenty more besides, in the form of crafts, Cornish dancing, busking, gig-racing and other entertainment.

CHRISTMAS AT MOUSEHOLE

It's particularly worth stopping over in Mousehole during the Christmas and New Year period, when the **Christmas illuminations** are a regular crowd-puller. Reckoned to rival those of Manchester and Oxford Street, the lights are erected all over the village, including on the harbour walls and out to sea, and can be seen in all their glory every evening between the middle Saturday of December and the Friday at the end of the January's first week. The dazzling displays range from spouting dolphins to dancing reindeer, a multicoloured serpent and a Christmas pudding. You can even take a helicopter flight from Penzance to view the illuminations from above – contact Penzance tourist office (see p.246) for details.

The climax of the events is on **Tom Bawcock's Eve**, on December 23, to commemorate the stormy night long ago when a local fisherman – Tom Bawcock – managed to haul in enough fish to feed the hungry village. A local seafood dish known as Stargazy (or Starry Gazy) pie is prepared at the *Ship Inn* and brought out at midnight amid much carousing, and an image of the pie is always to be seen in lights. Nearby **Newlyn** (see opposite) has its own version of the Christmas illuminations.

The work of the Newlyn School is displayed at Penlee House in Penzance (see p.245), but Newlyn's pioneering artistic spirit is perpetuated at the **Newlyn Art Gallery**, occupying a detached Victorian building on the seafront. Elegantly modernized within, the gallery concentrates on contemporary works, but its regular exhibitions often focus on local artists, giving an insight into how local tradition has evolved.

Mousehole and around

Accounts vary as to the derivation of the name **MOUSEHOLE** (pronounced "Mowzle"), located three miles south of Penzance. Previously known as Porth Enys ("port of the island") – a reference to St Clement's Isle, a low, bare reef a few hundred yards offshore – the village may have taken its present name from a nearby sea-cave or from a small brook running through the settlement. In any case, the name perfectly encapsulates the village's minuscule round harbour, cradled in the arms of a granite breakwater and encircled by a compact huddle of cottages. As the village attracts more visitors than it can handle, you'd do well to avoid the peak holiday periods when exploring its tangle of lanes, where many of the neat whitewashed or granite-grey cottages are draped with jasmine, fuschia and even cacti; most are rented out as holiday homes, giving the place a rather artificial air in season, and an almost ghostly feel in the winter months.

Outside the tight knot of cottages, further diversion can be had poking around the rocky foreshore north of the harbour, where there are good views across the bay to St Michael's Mount.

Keigwin House

A stroll through the village will soon bring you to Keigwin Place, just up from the harbour, and site of Mousehole's oldest house, the porched **Keigwin House** (closed to visitors). Dating from the fourteenth century, it survived the famous raid on July 23, 1595, when four hundred Spanish arquebusiers and pikemen landed in the village and set upon the local inhabitants, slaying Squire Jenkyn Keigwin but sparing his house. The rest of the village and the church in nearby Paul were torched.

ARRIVAL AND DEPARTURE   **MOUSEHOLE**

By bus Mousehole is linked to Penzance by frequent buses (mostly #5 and #6) stopping at the harbour and the Parade north of the centre.

By car If you're driving into Mousehole from the north, it's best to park on the roadside or in the car park before entering the village, from where steps lead down to a waterside path that takes you directly into the village.

9

2 Fore St TR19 6QU ☎01736 731164, ⓦ2forestreet.co.uk. Relaxed modern bistro just back from the harbour, where you can dine on fresh seafood (around £15 for mains) in the sheltered, gravelly garden. Coffees and teas available during the day. Late Feb to Dec daily 10am–late; food served daily noon–3.30pm & 5–9.30pm.

Old Coastguard The Parade, TR19 6PR ☎01736 731222, ⓦoldcoastguardhotel.co.uk. Mousehole's swishest hotel lies just north of the centre, backed by a sloping subtropical garden that gives access to the coast path. Most rooms have stunning sea views, and some have balconies (open to all), or you can drop by for a full meal of seafood freshly landed at Newlyn or local meat dishes (mains around £17). Daily 8am–late; food served daily 8am–9.30pm. **£135**

Rock Pool The Parade, TR18 6SB ☎01736 732645, ⓦfacebook.com/rockpoolmousehole. Cute, vintage style café overlooking Mousehole's rockpool, with tables outside for the best views across Mount's Bay. It's not much more than a shack, but the staff are lovely and the crab sandwiches (£10.50) and cream teas are tasty; drinks range from hot chocolate to cocktails. It's at the bottom of the car park next to the *Old Coastguard*, also reachable by the footpath from the harbour. Daily 10.30am–6pm; reduced hours in winter.

Ship Inn Harbourside, TR19 6QX ☎01736 731234, ⓦshipinnmousehole.co.uk. Overlooking the village's boats, this traditional pub is the perfect spot for a pint of Tribute and a ploughman's lunch (£9.50) or fish pie (£12.50). Accommodation is available in modern en-suite rooms, some in an annexe (those with a view cost extra). Mon–Sat 11am–11pm, Sun 11am–10.30pm; kitchen daily noon–2.30pm & 6–8.30pm (longer hours in summer). **£110**

Paul

Half a mile inland of Mousehole, at the top of steep Mousehole Hill, the churchyard wall in the village of **PAUL** holds a memorial to **Dolly Pentreath**, a Mousehole resident who died in 1777 – reputedly aged 102 – and is claimed to have been the last person to speak in Cornish as a first language. Whether or not this is true, the tablet has become a symbol of the near extinction of the language, and the inscription includes a Cornish translation of a verse from the Bible.

Lamorna Cove and around

Four miles southwest of Mousehole, **Lamorna Cove** is squeezed between granite headlands and accessible along a deeply wooded lane from the old *Lamorna Wink* pub – as the sign shows, it was the wink that signified that contraband spirits were available. Placid and unspoilt, the cove has a small crescent of sand that's covered at high tide, and is sheltered by a sturdy pier and backed by a disused granite quarry gouged out of the rock. The spot makes a nice starting point for exploring the coast path: following it westwards for a couple of miles takes you round Boscawen Point to **St Loy's Cove**.

Standing stones: The Merry Maidens and the Pipers

If you're following the B3315 running parallel to the coast, it's easy to drop in on the signposted **Merry Maidens**, a ring of nineteen stones in an open field about a mile west of the road junction for Lamorna (there's a small lay-by for parking). The rough-hewn circle is said to be all that remains of a group of local women turned to stone as a punishment for dancing on a Sunday.

Half a mile to the north, in a field on the other side of the road, the **Pipers** are two tall upright stones supposedly representing the musicians petrified by the same spell. Other than the likelihood that the ring and uprights date from some time between 2400 and 800 BC, nothing is known about their origin or significance, though they were probably the focus of some ceremonial function.

Porthcurno and around

Five miles west of Lamorna, the scattered settlement of **PORTHCURNO** stands above a succession of picturesque coves and generous sand beaches set against a jagged granite

BOTALLACK MINE (P.256) >

9

backdrop. The village is famous in the annals of telecommunications, both as a terminus for transatlantic cables and for the experiments in wireless telegraphy that took place here

Protected by high cliff walls and composed of coarse shell sand, **Porthcurno Beach** is one of the most scenic – and most popular – of Penwith's beaches, though bathers should beware of strong currents.

Telegraph Museum Porthcurno

TR19 6JX • Late March to Oct daily 10am–5pm; Nov to late March Mon, Sat & Sun 10am–4pm, daily during school hols; last admission 1hr before closing • £8.50 • ☎ 01736 810966, ⓦ porthcurno.org.uk

The history of Porthcurno's cable telegraphy station, including the serious competition it faced from Marconi's innovations in wireless transmissions, is related in the **Telegraph Museum Porthcurno**, just up from Porthcurno Beach. Brass and mahogany instruments and etchings give a vivid sense of the pioneering work undertaken by the marine engineers and the problems they faced with cables getting broken or snagged – one photo from 1947 shows a fisherman staring in dismay at a tangle of trawl gear entwined with cable. Most cables today are buried under the seabed; a model of one of the submersible vehicles used for putting them in place is also on show. Most of the displays are underground, in a system of bomb-proof, gas-proof **bunkers** from where a secret communications system was operated during World War II.

Minack Theatre

TR19 6JU • Exhibition centre daily: Mid-March to Sept 9.30am–5.30pm, closes noon when there are matinée performances (usually late May to Sept Tues & Thurs); Oct 10am–4.30pm; Nov to mid-March 10am–3.30pm • £4.50 • ☎ 01736 810181, ⓦ www.minack.com

At the top of steep steps on the western side of Porthcurno Beach 60yd above the sea, Porthcurno's famous **Minack Theatre** was founded by local benefactor Rowena Cade as a venue for amateur plays put on by her friends and family. The theatre staged its first production (*The Tempest*) in 1932, and subsequently expanded as its fame spread – it now holds 750 seats, though the basic Greek-inspired design remains intact. The spectacular backdrop of Porthcurno Bay makes this one of the country's most inspiring theatres and the eclectic programme of plays, operas and musicals frequently sells out during the season (Easter–Sept; see box opposite). The weather can be cold and blowy

---

COASTAL WALKS FROM PORTHCURNO

Plenty of splendid swimming spots can be reached along the South West Coast Path from Porthcurno. Westwards, with your steps accompanied by the whistling buoy at the Runnel Stone a mile offshore, it's around half a mile to **Porthchapel**, a wedge of smooth, clean sand, beyond which the path runs to the much narrower cleft in the cliffs at **Porthgwarra**, where a tunnel has been bored through a huge boulder to the rocky shore. Continuing west from here brings you to a sandy beach at **Nanjizal**, and eventually to **Land's End** – all in all, one of the best stretches of coastal walking anywhere.

Heading east from Porthcurno, a **white pyramid** adjacent to the coast path marks the spot where a transatlantic undersea telegraph cable was landed in 1870, recalling Porthcurno's role as a terminus for a network of cables that reached across the world. Further along, the headland forming the eastern prong of Porthcurno Bay was once occupied by the Iron Age fort of **Treryn Dinas**, leaving earthworks comprising a ditch and bank visible today. Above it and a few steps back on a cluster of granite slabs stands **Logan's Rock**, a seventy-tonne monster that for centuries rocked – reputedly at the merest touch – until it was knocked off its perch by a nephew of playwright Oliver Goldsmith and a gang of sailors in 1824. In the outcry that followed, the culprits were made to replace the boulder, but it rocked no more.

From Treryn Dinas, the coast path skirts the beach of **Pednevounder**, a steep climb down and traditionally popular with naturists. Half a mile beyond, the path sweeps down to more sandy beaches near the cluster of cottages and handful of fishing vessels at **Penberth Cove**, which is blissfully unspoilt. The heavy wooden capstan once used to haul boats up the slipway has been restored by the National Trust.

9

PERFORMANCES AT THE MINACK

Performances at the **Minack Theatre** generally take place between Easter and September; programmes are available from local tourist offices and on the website. **Tickets** for afternoon (1.30 or 2pm) or evening (7.30 or 8pm) shows cost £11.50 for the main auditorium or £9 for upper-terrace seating. Book by phone or in person at the box office (Easter–Sept Mon–Fri 10am–8pm, Sat & Sun 10am–5pm; Oct–Easter Mon–Fri 10am–4pm; ☎ 01736 810181, ✆ minack .com), or on the website. You can hire or bring your own cushion, and a blanket might also be advisable; you can also bring your own food and drink (but don't bring a bulky hamper).

but cancellations are rare. If you can't make it to a performance, you can at least nose around the site and follow the story of the theatre's creation at the **Exhibition Centre**.

ARRIVAL AND DEPARTURE   PORTHCURNO

By bus Service #1A stops at Porthcurno on its daily run between Penzance and Land's End.

ACCOMMODATION AND EATING

Cable Station Inn The Valley, TR19 6JX ☎ 01736 810479, ✆ cablestationinn.co.uk. Useful refreshment stop, serving baguettes (£6), standard bar meals (£9–14), cream teas, and Tribute and Betty Stoggs beers. There's a terrace, a playroom for kids, a pool table and darts (you can also apply here to use the nearby tennis courts). March–Oct: daily noon–1am; kitchen daily noon–9pm.

Sea View House The Valley, TR19 6JX ☎ 01736 810638, ✆ seaviewhouseporthcurno.com. Four hundred yards from the beach, this B&B has small but clean rooms with views, and provides picnics and cream teas. They also provide laundry facilities, packed lunches and a luggage transfer service for walkers. No credit cards. **£78**

Land's End and around

It would be hard to compromise the potency of the majestic headland of **Land's End** – England's extreme western tip, around four miles west of Porthcurno – though the hotel and amusements complex that dominates the land approach comes pretty close. Once past it, however, you can relax: 60ft-high turf-covered cliffs provide a platform to view the Irish Lady, the Armed Knight, Dr Syntax Head and the other wind-eroded outcrops scattered out to sea, beyond which you can spot the Longships lighthouse, a mile and a half out, and sometimes the Wolf Rock lighthouse, nine miles southwest (flashing every fifteen seconds), or even the dim outline of the Isles of Scilly, 28 miles away.

You'll almost always have to share the point with crowds of other visitors queuing for the traditional Land's End souvenir – a photo taken next to a signpost showing distances to New York (3147 miles), John o' Groats (874 miles) and whichever other place they select – but you can avoid much of the hoo-ha by opting to visit via the coast path. Tracking the **coast** will also enable you to take in the area's richly diverse **wildlife**, from busy fulmars and herring gulls, to Atlantic grey seals "cottling" out to sea (drifting, as though asleep, with just their heads above the water). In early September, colonies of seals haul themselves out of the water to breed on the rocks below Longships lighthouse. Other regular passengers on the fast currents include dolphins, porpoises and basking sharks, for which a pair of binoculars would be useful.

Land's End Experience

Sennen, TR19 7AA • Mid-Feb to Oct daily 10am–4pm, closes 6pm in summer school hols, 8pm on fireworks nights; last admission 1hr before closing • All attractions £12, or £10.80 online; individual attractions £4 • ☎ 01736 871501, ✆ landsend-landmark.co.uk

Although no substitute for the real "Land's End experience" – the view from the headland – the **Land's End Experience** amusement park will be a hit with younger children, not least for the panoply of lasers and sound effects in the various themed shows such as Arthur's Quest (an interactive retelling of the King Arthur story), the *Lost World* (a 4-D film about dinosaurs) and the Shaun the Sheep Experience. One exhibition is dedicated to the

9

"end-to-enders" – those who have walked, ridden or driven from Land's End to John o' Groats (or vice versa) – showing some of the various means of transport used; for example a motorized bar stool and a powered supermarket trolley. In July and August, live music and **fireworks displays** take place on Tuesday and Thursday evenings.

ARRIVAL AND DEPARTURE
LAND'S END

By bus Land's End can be reached via buses #1 and #1A from Penzance (hourly; 50min), or the summer-only open-top #300 (late May to mid-Sept 4–5 daily), which follows a circular route taking in Sennen Cove (10min), St Just (25min), Zennor (1hr) and St Ives (1hr 20min).

By plane Land's End Airport (ⓦ landsendairport.co.uk), on the B3306 midway between Land's End and St Just, is served by Skybus (ⓣ 01736 334220, ⓦ ios-travel.co.uk) for year-round flights to and from the Isles of Scilly (see p.268).

INFORMATION AND ACTIVITIES

Tourist information The websites ⓦ landsendcornwall .co.uk and ⓦ cornwallfarwest.co.uk are useful resources for all types of accommodation.
Scenic flights You can enjoy bird's-eye views of the

area on scenic flights from Land's End Airport; a 20min flight costs from £50 per person (minimum £180 for a flight; ⓦ islesofscilly-travel.co.uk). Call ⓣ 01736 785231 to book.

EATING

Apple Tree Café Trevescan, TR19 7AQ ⓣ 01736 872753, ⓦ appletreecafe.co.uk. Half a mile inland of Land's End, this fresh-looking café with garden seating offers filling and healthy breakfasts, huge sandwiches and cream teas, as well as lunches of crab and saffron soup, beef

burgers, mussels and vegetarian risotto (all £6–9). It opens for occasional bistro evenings with live music in summer (£25 for three courses). Wed–Sun 10am–5pm, daily in summer school hols; reduced opening in winter.

Whitesand Bay

The rounded granite cliffs hereabouts fall away a mile and a quarter northeast of Land's End at **Whitesand Bay** to reveal a glistening mile-long shelf of sand – the only substantial beach at this end of the peninsula, and one of the largest in West Cornwall. The rollers here make for good surfing, and boards can be rented and lessons arranged at the more popular, southern end of the beach, **Sennen Cove**.

ACTIVITIES
WHITESAND BAY

Surfing Sennen Surfing Centre (ⓣ 01736 871227, ⓦ sennensurfingcentre.com), operating from the beach, provides lessons and courses between April and October,

with all equipment provided. Alternatively, hire a wetsuit and board (£7–16 each) or a paddleboard (£30).

ACCOMMODATION AND EATING

Ben Tunnidiffe on the Beach Sennen Cove, TR19 7BT ⓣ 01736 871191, ⓦ benatsennen.com. Occupying a prime position on the beach, this busy café/restaurant serves brunches, lunches and dinners – beef burgers, mussels and rump steak are all on the menu (£11–17). There's live music on Wed in summer. Mon–Sat 10am–8.30pm (last orders); Sun 10am–6pm; summer school hols daily 9.30am–9pm; reduced hours in winter.

Old Success Inn Sennen Cove, TR19 7DG ⓣ 01736 871232, ⓦ oldsuccess.co.uk. Excellent seaside pub offering St Austell ales, baguettes (£6–7) and above-average bar meals such as smoked haddock chowder, *moules frites* and fish pie (all around £14). Eat in the bar, in the separate restaurant or outside. Rooms are also available. Daily 11am–11pm; kitchen daily noon–9pm. **£110**

Sunny Bank House Sea View Hill, Sennen, TR19 7AR ⓣ 01736 871278, ⓦ sunnybankhousebandb.com. A steep 15min hike from Sennen Cove, this friendly B&B with distant sea views has clean rooms, including for families (£128 for 3 people) and singles (£35); some rooms and en-suite bathrooms are small. Packed lunches and home-cooked suppers (£15) can be arranged. **£79**

Trevedra Farm Sennen, TR19 7BE ⓣ 01736 871818, ⓦ trevedrafarm.co.uk. Scenically located, this clifftop campsite has level pitches, simple, clean facilities, a café and a shop. It's a 15min walk down to Sennen Cove. Closed Nov–March. **£17.50**

Whitesands Sennen, TR19 7AR ⓣ 01736 871776, ⓦ whitesandshotel.co.uk. This place offers accommodation either in themed en-suite guestrooms (minimum two-night stay) or in a surf-lodge with bunkrooms and a self-catering kitchen. Breakfasts cost extra, taken in the café/restaurant, which is open to all and also offers tacos, tapas, grilled meat and seafood (most mains £10–15); it has outdoor seating

and regular barbecues in summer. Restaurant daily 8.30am–11pm. Dorms £25, doubles £70

St Just-in-Penwith and around

Three miles north of Whitesand Bay and half a mile inland from the sea, **ST JUST-IN-PENWITH** is the main centre at the peninsula's western end. Once a close-knit mining community serving the local tin and copper industry, St Just (not to be confused with St Just-in-Roseland) retains its rows of trim grey cottages, radiating out from the central Market and Bank squares. Just off the squares, behind the clocktower, **Plen-an-Gwary**, or "play place", is a grassy open-air theatre that was once a venue for old Cornish miracle plays and was later used by Methodist preachers as well as local wrestlers; these days, the occasional concert or play is staged here.

Cape Cornwall

There could be no greater contrast to the prosaic tenor of St Just than the dramatic coastline two miles west at **Cape Cornwall** (reachable from Cape Cornwall St, off Bank Square). For years this desolate rocky headland – topped by the stack of the Cape Cornwall Mine (closed in 1870) – was thought to be England's westernmost point, until more accurate means of measurement decided the contest in favour of Land's End. In many ways, though, Cape Cornwall is the more evocative of the two promontories: there are no towering outcrops or lighthouses to look out onto, but neither are there cafés, entertainments or car parks to distract from the vista. Sheltered by the cape, the cove has a few boats hauled up and a foreshore with plenty of rock pools to explore, though there's no beach to speak of.

ARRIVAL AND DEPARTURE
ST JUST-IN-PENWITH AND AROUND

By bus St Just is reachable from most places in Penwith on buses #10, #10A, #300 (summer only) and #509. The bus stand is on Market St.

Destinations Penzance (Mon–Sat 1–2 hourly, Sun 6 daily; 30min); St Ives (late May to mid-Sept 5 daily; 55min); Zennor (Mon–Sat 5–10 daily, late May to mid-Sept Sun 5 daily; 35min).

ACCOMMODATION

The Commercial Market Square, TR19 7HE ☎ 01736 788455, ⊛ commercial-hotel.co.uk. The best of the two inns on St Just's central square has plain but modern en-suite rooms, and friendly staff. Rooms at the top, including one budget double (£79), are accessed via steep stairs. £95

Kelynack Caravan and Camping Park Kelynack, TR19 7RE ☎ 01736 787633, ⊛ kelynackholidays.co.uk. This secluded campsite is one of the few sheltered ones on Penwith, about a mile south of St Just. It's clean, with good amenities and a small but well-stocked shop. There are also caravans (£390/week) and self-catering rooms available. Camping/person £8, doubles £70

★ **Old Fire Station** Nancherrow Terrace, TR19 7LA ☎ 01736 786463, ⊛ oldfirestationstjust.co.uk. Boldly

renovated B&B near Market Square, with an open-plan lounge and breakfast room, and three smallish but airy en-suite bedrooms, the top two of which have distant sea views. Mainly vegetarian breakfasts include croissants, fresh fruit and cheeses. No credit cards. Closed mid-Oct to Easter. £75

YHA Land's End Letcha Vean, TR19 7NT ☎ 0845 371 9643, ⊛ yha.org.uk/hostel/lands-end. Less than a mile south of St Just and a convenient half-mile from the coast path, this hostel has camping facilities with a bell tent to rent (July–Sept; £100), a kitchen and cooked meals. On foot, take the left fork past the post office to get here; by road, take the B3306 Land's End route, turning right at Kelynack. Oct–March groups only. Dorms £20, doubles £40, camping/person £12

EATING

The Cook Book 4 Cape Cornwall St, TR19 7JZ ☎ 01736 787266, ⊛ thecookbookstjust.co.uk. For coffee and home-made cake, plus breakfasts, brunches and lunches of soups, salads and fry-ups (around £7), this easy-going café

should satisfy. There are secondhand books for browsing, local pictures and prints on the walls, and tables outside. Daily: Feb–June & mid-Sept to Dec 10am–4pm; July to mid-Sept 9am–5pm.

9

Kegen Teg 12 Market Square, TR19 7HD ☎01736 788562. Fresh, local food and great coffees are served here – the menu includes falafel, Welsh rarebit, stews and burgers (all around £8), with plentiful veggie options. Tasty breakfasts, cakes, smoothies and cream teas are also available. Mon–Sat 10am–5pm.

Star Inn 1 Fore St, TR19 7LL ☎01736 788767,

ⓦ thestarinn-stjust.co.uk. Old-school gem of a pub, full of traditional character, where you can savour Tribute, HSB and Proper Job ales. No food is served, but you can bring in a pasty or other non-odorous snack. There's a rear yard, and live music on Mondays, Thursdays and some Saturdays. Daily 11am–midnight.

The Tin Coast

North of Cape Cornwall, the coast path takes in some spectacular cliff scenery towards **Pendeen**, passing close to one of Cornwall's most dramatic engine houses near **Botallack Head**. The mine here is just one of a cluster along this coast that have been restored and opened to the public, constituting what the marketeers have branded Cornwall's **Tin Coast** – a fascinating insight into Penwith's industrial history.

Botallack Count House

Botallack, TR19 7QQ • Daily 10am–4pm • Free • ☎01736 786004, ⓦ cornish-mining.org.uk

The evocative, cliff-clinging remains of **Botallack Mine**, dating from the 1860s, are the only visible part of a complex of tunnels and workings that extended under the sea. The restored **Count House** (the old accounting office) now contains displays on the area's mining history, geology and wildlife, and you can enter the "labyrinth chambers" – the decontaminated arsenic works.

Levant Mine and Beam Engine

Trewellard, TR19 7SX • Late March to Oct daily 10.30am–5pm; Nov to early Dec & early Jan to late March Fri 10.30am–4pm • £7.20; NT • ☎01736 786156, ⓦ nationaltrust.org.uk/levant-mine-and-beam-engine

From Botallack Head, a three-quarter-mile walk north along the coast path brings you to Levant, where, perched on the cliff edge, the brick buildings of a former mine head hold Cornwall's oldest beam engine, the **Levant Beam Engine**, now restored and functioning. Already famous for the number of its "cappens" (captains, or foremen) and for its use of pit ponies – rare in Cornwall – Levant was the scene of a major disaster in 1919, when the beam holding the "man-engine", or mechanical lift, broke away from its upper coupling, resulting in the deaths of 31 men and serious injuries to many others. The mine closed eleven years later. The engine is in operation, or "steaming", from 11am daily (winter Fri only), and there's a free **tour** (1hr 15min; last one at around 3pm in summer, 2pm in winter) and an explanatory film. Watch out for nesting choughs on the cliffs hereabouts.

Geevor Tin Mine

Pendeen, TR19 7EW • April–Oct Mon–Fri & Sun 9am–5pm; Nov–March Mon–Fri & Sun 10am–4pm; last entry 1hr before closing • Tours usually 11am, 1pm & 3pm outside peak season only; 30min • £12.95 • ☎01736 788662, ⓦ geevor.com

Two miles north of St Just on the B3306, **Geevor Tin Mine** was Penwith's last working mine, ceasing operations in 1990. Since then, the building has been restored and opened up to visitors to allow a fascinating close-up view of the Cornish mining industry. You can wander at will among the surface machinery (or join a **tour** in winter) and through the vast mill where the 98 percent of valueless rock was separated from the tin ore, but the most thrilling part is the adit, or horizontal passage running into the rock (the main underground area is now flooded to sea level). Here, the hellish working conditions of a tin miner are graphically described by the knowledgeable guides, and you can peer down into the murky depths of vertical shafts, or up them to the sky. A small **museum** shows a model of the mine and explains the complex process of tin production. Consult the website for weekly **events** – mostly during the summer school holidays – such as pasty-making, Poldark Days, stone-carving and miners' talks.

Inland Penwith: prehistoric sites

9

The hilly, granite moorland of **inland Penwith** is an apt setting for a cluster of remote and enigmatic relics of Cornwall's **prehistory**, worth winkling out if only for their resonant, lonely settings. With a good map and a compass to hand, the sites can be visited on foot across country, or by road from one of the very minor routes linking the B3306 with Penzance or the A30. Apart from Chysauster, the sites are always open and free. Ordnance Survey grid references are given for the locations. Alternatively, join a guided tour of the sites in Penzance (see p.246) or St Ives (see p.264).

Chun Quoit

From the B3318 less than a mile southeast of Pendeen, a lay-by marks the start of a track that winds onto the moor and to **Chun Quoit** (map ref SW402339), one of the most dramatic of Penwith's "quoits" – dolmens, or granite rocks arranged into what may have been burial chambers, whose outer covering of earth has washed away over the centuries. Chun resembles a giant mushroom from afar, the capstone poised precariously on four upright slabs, together enclosing a chamber within which bones of ancestors may have been laid.

Chun Castle

Less visually arresting remains of Penwith's past inhabitants can be reached along a path that threads about a quarter of a mile eastwards from Chun Quoit to the top of a hill, where a rubble of rocks and two upright stones marking a gateway are all that's left of the Iron Age **Chun Castle** (map ref SW405339). At this ancient hillfort, archeologists have found traces of slag in smelting pits, suggesting that tin mining existed here at least two thousand years ago.

Men-an-Tol

From the minor Morvah–Madron road, a signposted track wanders northeast for just under a mile to where a marked path to the right goes through fields to **Men-an-Tol** (map ref SW426349), or "stone of the hole". Also called the "Devil's Eye", this rock hoop in open moorland – probably the remains of a Neolithic tomb – suggests nothing so much as a giant doughnut. Similar "hole stones" have been found elsewhere as entrances to burial chambers, and in the Middle Ages this one was thought to have great healing powers: people crawled through the hole to rid themselves of rheumatism, spine troubles or ague, while children with scrofula or rickets were passed through it three times before being dragged round it through the grass.

The Nine Maidens and Men Scryfa

Five minutes' walk east from Men-an-Tol brings you to the **Nine Maidens**, also known as Boskednan stone circle (map ref SW434351). Once probably consisting of twenty-two upright stones, only six remain. The same distance northwest of Men-an-Tol lies **Men Scryfa** (map ref SW427353), a standing stone with a Latin inscription commemorating "Rialobran, the son of Cunoval" – probably a reference to a sixth-century Celtic chieftain.

Lanyon Quoit

Less than two miles northwest of Madron along the Morvah–Madron road, **Lanyon Quoit** (map ref SW430337) has a convenient roadside location – partly accounting for its status as the best known of Cornwall's quoits. Its local name, "Giant's Table", is a plain reference to its form – a broad top slab balanced on three upright stones. The quoit has not survived intact, however: in 1815 a storm caused the structure to collapse, and it was re-erected nine years later with only three of its original four supports. Consequently it is not as high as it once was, thought it still presents an arresting sight in the midst of the moor.

9

Chysauster

Newmill, TR20 8XA • Daily: April–June & Sept 10am–5pm; July & Aug 10am–6pm; Oct 10am–4pm • £4.20; EH

The best known and most visited of Penwith's ancient remains – and arguably the best-preserved ancient settlement in the South West – **Chysauster** occupies a windy hillside with views over Penzance. It lies one and three-quarter miles from the turn-off from the B3311 Penzance–St Ives road at Badger's Cross.

The village (map ref SW472350), from around the first century BC, consists of the shells of eight stone buildings, each holding an open courtyard from which small chambers lead off. The largest structures are likely to have been **farm dwellings**, probably thatch-roofed with walls coated with wattle and daub, while other rooms were probably barns, stalls or stables, or even protected vegetable gardens. Huts three, four and six are the best preserved and give the most vivid impression of the grandeur of the dwellings, where open hearths, covered drains, and stone basins for grinding corn have been identified.

The site was used as an open-air pulpit by **Methodist preachers** at the beginning of the nineteenth century and was first excavated in the 1860s. The surrounding heather and gorse give the place a bracing, wild feel, though it's a mystery why the original inhabitants would have chosen such a high, exposed position for their village.

Carn Euny and Carn Brea

Two more ancient sites lie further west towards Land's End, between the A30 and A3071 roads. Like Chysauster, **Carn Euny** (map ref SW402288) is a wonderfully well-preserved and atmospheric Iron Age settlement, but it is even older, first built around 200 BC. The site includes a **fogou**, or underground passageway, which you can enter. A mile to the southwest, a path links Carn Euny with the hilltop chambered tomb of **Carn Brea** (map ref SW386280), from where there are sweeping views over the whole of Penwith.

Zennor and around

The coastal B3306 snakes five or so miles eastward from Morvah to **ZENNOR**, an ancient village known for its associations with **D.H. Lawrence** (see box below). The

D.H. LAWRENCE IN ZENNOR

Seeking an escape from the London literary scene, as well as inspiration from the "fine thin air which nobody and nothing pollutes", D.H. Lawrence came to live in Cornwall in December 1915, settling in Zennor the following March. Installed with his wife **Frieda** at Higher Tregerthen, one of a group of cottages about a mile east of the village, he was evidently smitten by the place, describing it in a letter to **John Middleton Murry** and **Katherine Mansfield** in March 1916 as "a tiny granite village nestling under high shaggy moor hills, and a big sweep of lovely sea, lovelier even than the Mediterranean… It is all gorse now, flickering with flowers, and then it will be the heather; and then, hundreds of foxgloves. It is the best place I have been in, I think." The following month Murry and Mansfield came to join the Lawrences in what Lawrence envisaged as a writers' community to be called **Rananim**. The experiment was unsuccessful, however; alienated by Lawrence and Frieda's violent quarrels and by Lawrence's evident disapproval of the newcomers' own relationship, Murry and Mansfield left after two months for a more sheltered spot near Falmouth. Lawrence stayed on to write **Women in Love**, spending a year and a half in Zennor in all, though his enthusiasm for the place was gradually eroded by the hostility of the local constabulary and the residents, who took a dim view of the couple's unorthodox lifestyle, not to mention Frieda's German associations (her cousin was air ace Baron von Richtofen, the "Red Baron"). In October 1917, after police had ransacked their cottage, the Lawrences were brusquely given notice to quit. His Cornish experiences were later described in **Kangaroo**, while Mansfield and Murry were peeved to find themselves characterized as Gudrun and Gerald in **Women in Love**, with the Lawrences themselves re-created as Birkin and Ursula.

WALKS FROM ZENNOR

Behind the *Tinners Arms*, a fairly level path leads less than a mile northwest to the sea at **Zennor Head**, where there is some awe-inspiring cliff scenery above sandy **Pendour Cove** (the fabled home of Zennor's mermaid). The six-and-a-half-mile coastal hike to St Ives from here is testing but highly rewarding, taking three or four hours. If you're doing a round trip, you might consider the inland route for one leg, taking the path between Zennor's churchyard and the village hall across fields and through a sequence of tiny hamlets. The path passes close to **Higher Tregerthen**, where D.H. Lawrence lived after his stay at the *Tinners Arms*, and is reachable in about fifteen minutes from Zennor. Above the house, another path leads south off the St Ives road behind the Eagle's Nest – for many years the home of St Ives painter **Patrick Heron** – for around a mile to **Zennor Quoit** (map ref SW469380). This chambered tomb, which has one of the widest roof slabs of all Cornwall's quoits – at an angle, as it has slipped over time – is a rare example of a quoit with two central chambers, thought to be some 4500 years old.

village retains no trace of Lawrence's presence today, though you might invoke his memory in the *Tinners Arms* (see below) – the pub that lent him the title of a short story which historian A.L. Rowse grudgingly conceded to be "more true to Cornish life than most other things written about us by foreigners".

St Senara

TR26 3BY • Daily 9am–dusk • Free • ⓣ 01736 786425

The simple granite church of **St Senara** has a barrel-vaulted roof typical of many of Penwith's churches, but its most famous feature is the **Mermaid Chair**, made from two sixteenth-century bench-ends carved with an image of a mermaid holding a mirror and a comb. The carving relates to a local legend, according to which a mermaid was so entranced by the singing of a chorister in the church choir that she lured him down to the sea, from which he never returned – though his singing can still occasionally be heard. On the left of the church doorway, a plaque commemorates the memory of John Davey of Boswednack, supposed to be the last person to possess a working knowledge of the Cornish language when he died in 1891 – one of several claiming this honour.

ARRIVAL AND DEPARTURE — ZENNOR AND AROUND

By bus From Penzance and St Ives, buses #508 and the summer-only #300 run to Zennor. The bus stop is on the main B3306.

Destinations Land's End (April–Sept 3–5 daily; 1hr 15min); Penzance (Mon–Sat 6–9 daily, Sun April–Sept 5 daily; 30min–1hr 15min); St Ives (Mon–Sat 5–10 daily, Sun April–Sept 3–5 daily; 25min).

ACCOMMODATION AND EATING

Cove Cottage Gurnard's Head, Treen, TR26 3DE ⓣ 01736 798317, ⓦ www.cornwall-online.co.uk/cove-cottage. A mile and a half west of Zennor, this classy B&B has two elegant rooms with outstanding views over an isolated cove where you can enjoy peaceful swimming and sunbathing. Breakfast can be taken on the terrace. Two-night minimum stay. No under-10s. No credit cards. **£125**

Gurnard's Head Treen, TR26 3DE ⓣ 01736 796928, ⓦ gurnardshead.co.uk. This classic gastropub west of Zennor offers rooms, good beers and ciders (the local Skreach cider is recommended) and simple but expertly prepared and locally sourced dishes (set-price lunches cost £16/£19 for two/three courses, otherwise mains cost £14–20). Worth booking ahead for food and accommodation. Daily 11am–11pm; kitchen spring, autumn & winter daily 12.30–2.30pm (Sun from noon) & 6.30–9pm, summer daily noon–2.30pm & 6–9pm. **£115**

Tinners Arms TR26 3BY ⓣ 01736 796927, ⓦ tinnersarms.com. Historic and homely spot for a drink and a meal, with a separate dining area and some outdoor tables. Among the beers are Tinners Ale and Zennor Mermaid, and the food includes ploughman's lunch (£10.25) and leek and Stilton crumble (£11.50). There's live folk music on Thursdays. There's accommodation in an adjacent building: two en-suite doubles and two singles with a shared bathroom. Mon–Sat 11.30am–11pm, Sun noon–10.30pm; kitchen noon–3pm & 6–9pm (Sun until 8.30pm). **£100**

9

Tregeraint House TR26 3DB ☎01736 797061, ⓦwww.cornwall-online.co.uk/tregeraint-house. A quarter of a mile west of Zennor, by the turn-off to the village from the B3306, this remote place is run by a potter and boasts clifftop vistas from two of its three rooms, all of which have washbasins and share a bathroom. Breakfast is served in a conservatory with panoramic views. No credit cards. £80

Zennor Chapel Guesthouse TR26 3BY ☎0173⟨ 798307, ⓦzennorchapelguesthouse.com. This forme⟨ Wesleyan chapel provides comfortable accommodation i⟨ small, simply furnished rooms (3 of them sleeping 4 peopl⟨ each). There are various choices of breakfast for guests⟨ costing an extra £5, while the café (open to nonguests) ha⟨ baguettes, cream teas and dishes like homity pie (£5⟨ April–Oct daily 9am–5pm. £80

St Ives and around

Penwith's chief resort, **ST IVES**, has little in common with the rest of the peninsula, its higgledy-piggledy flower-decked lanes, ubiquitous galleries and the contemporary lines of the Tate putting it into an altogether different category from the austere granite villages and jagged cliffs that characterize most of West Cornwall. Squeezed between steep slopes, headlands and no fewer than four beaches – if you count the sands of the harbour – St Ives

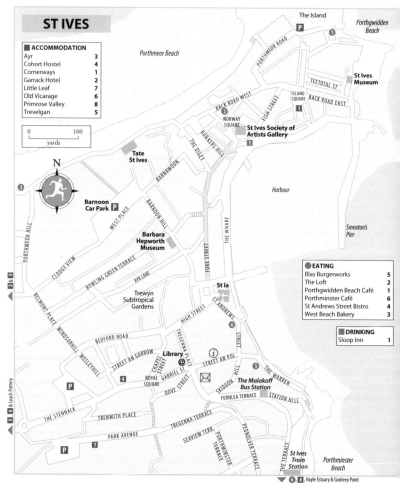

ST IVES

◼ ACCOMMODATION	
Ayr	3
Cohort Hostel	4
Cornerways	1
Garrack Hotel	2
Little Leaf	7
Old Vicarage	6
Primrose Valley	8
Trevelgan	5

0   100
yards

● EATING	
Blas Burgerworks	5
The Loft	2
Porthgwidden Beach Café	1
Porthminster Café	6
St Andrews Street Bistro	4
West Beach Bakery	3

◼ DRINKING	
Sloop Inn	1

is a town of picturesque nooks and eye-catching vistas. Pedestrianized **Fore Street** threads through its centre and is usually a mass of shuffling tourists who spill out onto the wide harbour, where the piercing shrieks of gulls add to the hubbub. Above and at either end of the main drag is a disorientating maze of lanes bearing such melodious names as Teetotal Street and Salubrious Place, and sprinkled with restaurants, bars and galleries.

Brief history

At heart, St Ives has always been a traditional **fishing community** thanks to its protected harbour. So productive were the offshore waters that a record sixteen and a half million fish were caught in one net on a single day in 1868, and the diarist Francis Kilvert was told by the local vicar that the smell was sometimes so great as to stop the church clock. Virginia Woolf, who spent every summer here to the age of twelve, described St Ives as "a windy, noisy, fishy, vociferous, narrow-streeted town; the colour of a mussel or a limpet; like a bunch of rough shell fish clustered on a grey wall together".

By the time the pilchard reserves dried up in the early 1900s, St Ives was beginning to attract a vibrant **artists' colony** (see p.347), precursors of the wave later headed by Ben Nicholson, Barbara Hepworth, Naum Gabo and the potter Bernard Leach, who in the 1960s were followed by a third wave including Terry Frost, Peter Lanyon and Patrick Heron. The town's pivotal role in the local arts scene was recognized and formalized by the opening of a branch of the Tate in 1993, by which time the town was firmly established as one of Britain's favourite holiday haunts, perennially popular with families and the cool surfer set alike.

Tate St Ives

Porthmeor Beach, TR26 1TG • March–Oct daily 10am–5.20pm; Nov–Feb Tues–Sun 10am–4.20pm; closes for one week three times a year • £7.50; combined ticket with Barbara Hepworth Museum £10 • ☎ 01736 796226, ⊛ tate.org.uk/stives

Providing a bold architectural backdrop to the broad sands of Porthmeor Beach, the town's greatest cultural asset, **Tate St Ives**, consummately fulfils its role as the region's primary showcase for challenging, locally based art. The airy white building, refurbished and expanded in 2017, takes its form from the gasworks that previously occupied the site, and provides the perfect context for viewing the collection's paintings, sculptures and ceramics; most of these date from 1925–75, and they were often inspired by St Ives itself.

The works

The gallery's tone is set by a massive stained-glass window by **Patrick Heron** near the entrance, said to be the largest unleaded stained-glass piece in the world, whose great slabs of colour recall the brilliance of the sun, sand and sea outside. The work of local naive painter **Alfred Wallis**, whose *St Ives* was one of the first paintings he sold (bought by Ben Nicholson on his visit to the town in August 1928), is well represented. You'll detect the influence of Wallis's diagrammatic designs in some of the other work here, for example *Island Sheds* by **Wilhelmina Barns-Graham** and *St Ives from the Cemetery* by **Bryan Pearce**. Search out, too, Lanyon's tall, chaotic, partly abstract harbour view, *Porthleven*, and **John Wells**' *Seabird Forms*, which strikingly depicts the movement and flight patterns of seabirds, in a similar blend of figurative and abstract ideas.

As well as the paintings, the gallery holds important displays of sculpture; for example **Barbara Hepworth**'s *Sea Form (Porthmeor)* – her response to the beach – while her *Menhirs*, carved from a single piece of slate, and *Landscape Sculpture*, a bronze from the late 1950s, take their inspiration from what she called "the pagan landscape" of the Penwith peninsula. The interplay between different generations of artists can be seen in the painted aluminium and wood *Construction* by **Peter Lanyon**, which shows a debt to the constructivist **Naum Gabo**, who lived in St Ives during World War II (and is also represented here). Lastly, don't miss pottery and stoneware by **Bernard Leach** and his school (including **Michael Cardew** and **Shoji Hamada**) – mostly very simple designs of jugs, cups, plates and bowls.

9

ST IVES SEPTEMBER FESTIVAL

Over a fortnight in September, you can catch a range of jazz, blues, classical and roots music at the **St Ives September Festival** (Ⓦ stivesseptemberfestival.co.uk), one of Cornwall's liveliest cultural gatherings. Although the focus is on music, there's plenty more on hand – comedy, cabaret, exhibitions, talks, films and open studio events. The main venues are the Guildhall on Street-an-Poll and the *Western Hotel* on Royal Square. Tickets can be booked online or from local tourist offices, or can be bought at the venue on the night if available.

Ask at the entrance or consult the website about free half-hour **tours** of the gallery (usually twice daily).

Barbara Hepworth Museum and Sculpture Garden

Barnoon Hill, TR26 1AD • March–Oct daily 10am–5.20pm; Nov–Feb Tues–Sun 10am–4.20pm; closes at dusk if sooner; closes for one week three times a year • £6; combined ticket with Tate £10 • Tours daily 1pm; 45min • ☎ 01736 796226, Ⓦ tate.org.uk/stives

If your appetite has been whetted by Hepworth's elemental sculptures on view in Tate St Ives, the **Barbara Hepworth Museum and Sculpture Garden** is the essential next stop. One of the foremost nonfigurative sculptors of her time, Hepworth lived in the building (Trewyn Studio) from 1949 until her death in a fire here in 1975. Apart from the sculptures, the museum has background on her art, from letters to catalogues and reviews; her photos of Cornish quoits and landscapes provide clues to the inspiration behind her sleek monoliths.

The clean all-white space is a superb setting for such works as *Infant*, a shiny, alien-looking child carved from Burmese wood. In the adjoining garden, a lush area planted with subtropical trees and shrubs, Hepworth herself arranged her stylistically diverse works in striking settings, with, at their centre, the most massive work, *Four Square (Walkthrough)*. Hepworth's famous "wired" pieces, in which different planes are linked by threaded cord, are also well represented.

There are a few other Hepworth works dotted around St Ives, including the rather uncharacteristic *Madonna and Child*, a tender work in memory of her son killed during RAF service in 1953, and donated to the harbourside church of **St Ia** (Ⓦ stiveschurch .org.uk) – the steel candlesticks standing in front of the work are also by the sculptor).

St Ives Society of Artists Gallery

Norway Square, TR26 1NA • Early Jan, March, Nov & Dec Mon–Sat 10.30am–5.30pm; April–Oct Mon–Sat 10.30am–5.30pm, Sun 2.30–5.30pm • Free • ☎ 01736 795582, Ⓦ stisa.co.uk

The **St Ives Society of Artists Gallery** has occupied the old Mariners' Church since 1945, when the Society's members included Lamorna Birch, Barbara Hepworth and Ben Nicholson. Following a split within the Society in 1948, when the more abstract artists disassociated themselves from the group, the gallery has shown chiefly figurative work, much of it of a high quality. In the main gallery upstairs, the members' paintings and sculptures – virtually all on local themes – are constantly replaced by new works, giving a good overview of the group's varying styles, while the **Crypt Gallery** below is mainly used for private exhibitions.

St Ives Museum

Wheal Dream, TR26 1PR • Easter–Oct Mon–Fri 10.30am–4.30pm, Sat 10.30am–3.30pm • £3 • ☎ 01736 796005

Housed in an old Sailors' Mission between the harbour and Porthgwidden Beach, **St Ives Museum** will appeal to anyone with a magpie curiosity and lots of energy. A wide-ranging trawl through Cornish history, and more particularly that of Penwith and St Ives, the densely crowded rooms on two floors throw up such nonessential bric-a-brac as a collection of kettles, a bardic robe, a turtle that had wandered over to Cornwall from Mexico and was subsequently stuffed, and a collection of photos, including some of the St Ives artists. Grittier aspects of local life are illustrated by sections devoted to the railway in Cornwall, the pilchard industry and of course mining, with a model of the Levant mine "man-engine" which crashed in 1919 (see p.256). One of the most curious exhibits is a stuffed dog called Tiny, just a few inches tall.

From outside the museum, views stretch out over tiny **Porthgwidden Beach**, a sheltered spot for a quiet paddle on a hot day, and across the bay to Hayle Sands.

Leach Pottery

Higher Stennack, TR26 2HE • March–Oct Mon–Sat 10am–5pm, Sun 11am–4pm; Nov–Feb Mon–Sat 10am–5pm • £4.50 • Tours Easter– Oct Wed & Fri 11am • ☎ 01736 799703, ⓦ leachpottery.com

Devotees of Bernard Leach's Japanese-inspired ceramics can visit his studio, the **Leach Pottery**, three-quarters of a mile outside St Ives' centre on the Zennor road. You can see the original workshops used by Leach and Shoji Hamada in 1920, and later by Michael Cardew, Janet Leach and others, as well as an exhibition room, contemporary gallery and shop.

Trewyn Subtropical Gardens

Off Bedford Rd, TR26 1AD • Daily 8am–sunset • Free

When you need relief from the claustrophobic lanes of St Ives, take a picnic or just a breather in **Trewyn Subtropical Gardens**, a miniature haven cocooned from the crowds above the High Street. It's furnished with wooden sculptures of musicians round the lawns and banana trees.

The Island

For an invigorating leg-stretch, you can't do better than a brisk climb up to **The Island**, the undeveloped, heathy headland (also known as St Ives Head) at the northern tip of the town. **St Nicholas Chapel** sits in solitude on the promontory, and there are inspiring views across St Ives Bay.

The beaches

The wide expanse of **Porthmeor Beach** dominates the northern side of St Ives, exposed to Atlantic rollers that make it popular with surfers (boards can be rented below the Tate). **Porthminster Beach**, south of the train station, is an even longer stretch of smooth yellow sand, but more sheltered and suitable for sunbathing and swimming. Unusually for town beaches, the water quality at both is excellent, and both were awarded Blue Flag status in 2016. A third town beach, the bijou, family-friendly **Porthgwidden**, lies in the lee of The Island. All three beaches have excellent cafés. Further east, some of the region's most enticing beaches lie to either side of the **Hayle estuary**, with three miles of pearly sands extending northeast from the estuary – another favourite venue for surfers.

At the eastern end of St Ives Bay, **Godrevy Point** is a great spot for wildlife-watchers, with dolphins, porpoises and seabirds to be seen, and a large grey seal colony in nearby Mutton Cove. Perched on an isle three miles offshore, **Godrevy Lighthouse** was the inspiration for Virginia Woolf in her novel *To The Lighthouse* (though she located it in the Hebrides).

ARRIVAL AND DEPARTURE	ST IVES AND AROUND

By train A branch line connects St Ives with Penzance (25min–1hr) hourly, usually with a change at St Erth (15min); the St Ives–St Erth section is highly scenic. The train station in St Ives lies at the eastern end of town, behind Porthminster Beach and below Station Hill.

By bus Long-distance buses and National Express coaches pull in near the train station on The Malakoff, Station Hill. Many local services stop at Royal Square, at the bottom of The Stennack.

Destinations Land's End (late May to mid-Sept 4 daily; 1hr 20min); Newquay (5 daily; 1hr 15min–2hr); Penzance (Mon–Sat 4 hourly, Sun 2 hourly; 30–45min); Plymouth (3 daily; 3hr 30min); St Just (late May to mid-Sept 4 daily; 55min); Truro (Mon–Sat every 30min, Sun hourly; 1hr 35min); Zennor (Mon–Sat 3–7 daily, late May to mid-Sept Sun 4 daily; 20–35min).

By car Drivers should park as soon as possible on entering the town, or, better still, use the car park at Lelant Saltings

9

(or one of the other stations on the branch line from St Erth) and take the train in. Alternatively, park at Carbis Bay and walk a mile along the coast from there, an easy and pleasant stroll. From the B3306 there is a good park-and-ride on Alexandra Road at St Ives Rugby Football Club (Easter–Oct; £5/day, buses into town £1 one-way).

GETTING AROUND

By bus Most local services, run by St Ives Bus Company (☎01736 798837, ⊛sttivesbuses.co.uk) and Royal Buses (☎01736 797982, ⊛www.royalbuses.co.uk), stop at Royal Square, at the bottom of The Stennack.

By taxi Taxis in St Ives are generally cheap. You'll find ranks at the bus and train stations, and outside the cinema on Dove St (☎07530 710707); firms include Ace Cars (☎01736 797799), DJ Cars (☎01736 796633) and St Ives Taxi Co (☎01736 799200).

INFORMATION

Tourist information The Guildhall, Street-an-Pol (May & June daily 10am–4pm, but Sun 10am–3pm in May; July–Sept Mon–Sat 10am–5pm, Sun 10am–4pm; Oct–April Mon–Sat 10am–3pm; ☎0905 252 2250, ⊛visitstives.org .uk). They offer an accommodation booking service (£5) and luggage storage (each item £2/day).

Hospital The Minor Injury Unit at Stennack Surgery, at the bottom of Bullans Lane on The Stennack (☎01736 793333), can deal with most problems; otherwise head for Penzance (see p.246).

Market A farmers' market takes place at the Guildhall, Street-an-Pol (Thurs 9.30am–2pm).

TOURS AND ACTIVITIES

Boat tours A range of excursions is touted at the harbour in summer; an hour-long ride to Seal Island or Godrevy Point costs £12–14, a 1hr 30min fishing trip £18 (☎07770 040303).

Prehistoric monument tours Ancient Stones of Kernow (☎01736 797312, ⊛ancientstonesofkernow .co.uk) explores the prehistoric monuments of the Penwith peninsula: a five-mile walking tour costs £20 per person (minimum four people), and full-day car or minibus tours are £45 per person; book 24hr ahead. See Penzance listings for an alternative local outfit (see p.246).

Walking tours Walking tours focusing on the history and culture of St Ives and its environs take place all year round on Wednesdays, also on Mondays and Thursdays March–October, meeting outside the tourist office at 11am (1hr 15min–1hr 30min; £5; ☎07816 180639, ⊛guidedtoursofstives.co.uk).

Ghost walks Ghost walks of St Ives start from the car park behind the *Sloop Inn*, on The Wharf (Easter & June–Oct Wed 8.30pm; Aug & Halloween Wed & Thurs 8.30pm; 1hr 15min–1hr 30min; ⊛ghosthuntingcornwall.com; £6).

Horseriding Penhalwyn Trekking Centre, Halsetown (☎01736 796461), offers hourly, half-day and day treks over Penwith's moors.

Surfing St Ives Surf School (☎01736 793938, ⊛stives surfschool.co.uk), based ion Porthmeor Beach, offers 2hr lessons for all levels for £35; outside town Shore Surf (☎01736 755556 or ☎07855 755556, ⊛shoresurf.com) offers half-day (£30) or full-day (£50) surfing courses from *St Ives Bay Holiday Park* or Godrevy car park, both between Hayle and Gwithian. Both outfits also rent out equipment (wetsuits and bodyboards each £5/2–3hr, longer boards £7–12) and offer paddleboarding, while St Ives Surf School leads sea-kayaking tours from Porthminster beach.

ACCOMMODATION

★**Cohort Hostel** The Stennack, TR26 1FF ☎01736 791664, ⊛stayatcohort.co.uk. Restored Wesleyan chapel school from 1845, usefully located in the centre of St Ives, with a clean, modern feel, a sociable environment and surf and watersports packages available. There are mixed or single-sex dorms, double and twin rooms, a bar and a kitchen. Nov–Feb groups only. Dorms £25, doubles £50

Cornerways 1 Bethesda Place, TR26 1PA ☎01736 796706, ⊛cornerwaysstives.com. Daphne du Maurier once stayed in this tasteful cottage conversion, which has friendly management and contemporary but mostly small en-suite rooms named after characters and places in du Maurier books – ask for the top room, "Sandra", for the best views. No credit cards. £100

Garrack Hotel Burthallan Lane, TR26 3AA ☎01736 796199, ⊛garrack.com. Suitably secluded for a pampered stay, but within easy walking distance of Porthmeor Beach, this sedate, family-run hotel has a variety of rooms plus an indoor pool, a sauna, an excellent restaurant and lovely sea views. Buses #5 and #6 stop nearby. £120

★**Little Leaf** 16 Park Avenue, TR26 2DN ☎01736 795427, ⊛littleleafguesthouse.co.uk. With friendly young hosts and local art on the walls, this ecofriendly guesthouse is worth the steep climb from the centre. There are six en-suite rooms, including a family suite (£110), two with fantastic views and one with its own patio. Breakfasts are fresh and local. Two- to three-night minimum stay March–Oct. £75

Old Vicarage Parc-an-Creet, Lelant, TR26 2ES ☎01736 796124, ⊛oldvicarage.com. Away from the bustle in its own abundant wooded garden, this nineteenth-century, period-furnished former rectory is a 15–20min uphill walk from the centre of St Ives (or a cheap bus- or taxi-ride).

Healthy, Aga-cooked breakfasts are served, and there's a bar-lounge and ample parking. Closed Dec. **£90**

Primrose Valley Porthminster Beach, TR26 2ED ☎01736 794939, ⓦprimroseonline.co.uk. Stylish and relaxed boutique hotel, a level walk from the centre, and close to the train station and Porthminster Beach (from which it's separated by the railway). The chic, contemporary rooms, some with balconies, are fresh and light; four have (sideways) sea views, though some are small and viewless. No under-12s. Closed Dec & Jan. **£160**

CAMPING

Ayr Higher Ayr, TR26 1EJ ☎01736 795855, ⓦayr holidaypark.co.uk. St Ives has no campsites right on the seafront, but this large complex half a mile west of the centre above Porthmeor Beach has a great sea prospect and good facilities; downsides are that it's expensive, gets crowded, and doesn't have much in the way of shelter. It's near to the coast path, and buses #5 from Royal Square and #10 from Porthmeor Beach stop outside. **£24.50**

★ **Trevalgan** Off B3306, TR26 3BJ ☎01736 792048, ⓦtrevalgantouringpark.co.uk. A couple of miles west of St Ives and 10min from the coast, this spacious site has level, partly sheltered pitches and clean, modern facilities. It's family-friendly, with a play area and games room, and the six-times-daily #44 bus (late June to late Sept) connects the site with Porthmeor Beach. Closed Oct–April. **£30**

EATING

★ **Blas Burgerworks** The Warren, TR26 2EA ☎01736 797272, ⓦblasburgerworks.co.uk. This "alternative burger bar" with a boisterous atmosphere doles out what might just be the finest burgers you'll ever have, using the best local ingredients and costing £10–12. Try the truffle with blue cheese, or the beet, with beetroot. There's just one small room with five communal tables made from reclaimed materials and barrels and crates to sit on; you can also buy to take away. No reservations. Mid-Feb to June & mid-Sept to early Nov daily 5.30–9.30pm; July to mid-Sept daily noon–9.30pm.

The Loft Norway Lane, TR26 1LZ ☎01736 794204, ⓦtheloftrestaurantandterrace.co.uk. Stylish, modern restaurant set in a long, conservatory-like space with an outdoor terrace. It's known for its ethically sourced seafood dishes and rare-breed steaks, and the menu might include line-caught pollack, pan-fried turbot (£17.50 and £24.50 respectively), beef fillet with asparagus (£24.50), and some dazzling desserts. Wed–Sun: mid-March to April & Oct–Dec 11am–3pm & 6–9pm; May–Sept 10am–10pm.

★ **Porthgwidden Beach Café** Porthgwidden Beach, TR26 1PL ☎01736 796791, ⓦporthgwiddencafe.co.uk. Overlooking St Ives' smallest beach, in the Downalong area of town, this bustling place with a stone terrace offers baguettes and salads, as well as burgers, fish pie and paella (£11–14). Breakfasts include scrambled egg and smoked salmon (£6); or just order a coffee or tea. Easter–Oct & school hols daily 9am–late; Nov–Easter term-time Tues, Wed & Sun 9am–3pm, Thurs–Sat 9am–3pm & 6pm–late; kitchen Easter–Oct & school hols daily 9–11am, noon–3pm & 6–9pm; Nov–Easter term-time Tues, Wed & Sun 9–11am & noon–3pm, Thurs–Sat 9–11am, noon–3pm & 6–9pm.

Porthminster Café Porthminster Beach, TR26 2EB ☎01736 795352, ⓦporthminstercafe.co.uk. With its fantastic beach location, this makes a superb spot for breakfasts, coffees, lunches, teas and evening meals. Seafood is king on the lunchtime and evening menus, featuring dishes such as smoked haddock chowder (£8), crab linguine (£15), monkfish curry (£19) and baked halibut fillet (£22). Jan–Easter Tues, Wed & Sun 9am–4pm, Thurs–Sat 9am–late; Easter–Oct daily 9am–late; Nov & Dec Tues & Wed 9am–3pm, Thurs–Sat 9am–late, Sun 9am–4pm; kitchen Mon–Fri 9–11am, noon–3pm & 6–9.30pm, Sat & Sun noon–4pm & 6–9.30pm (winter closed Mon–Wed & Sun).

St Andrews Street Bistro 16 St Andrews St, TR26 1AH ☎01736 797074, ⓦbistrostives.com. Rugs and quirky *objets* on the tall white walls set the tone here. Among the dishes on the varied, French-inspired menu you'll find shellfish bisque, roast fillet of hake, linguine with mushrooms and blue cheese, slow-roasted belly pork and coq au vin. Most mains cost £14–17, and fixed-price deals are often available. June–Sept Mon–Fri 6–10pm, Sat & Sun noon–2.30pm & 6–10pm; Oct & Dec–May daily 6–10pm, with extended opening during school hols.

West Beach Bakery Porthmeor Beach, TR26 1JZ ☎01736 795843, ⓦwestbeachbakery.com. Brilliantly sited on the emptier, western end of Porthmeor Beach, this wonderful shack does a great line in breakfasts, from bacon rolls to burritos, as well as baguettes for lunch (around £4), delicious pizzas (noon–9pm; £8–10) and, in the evening, tasty curries (£10.50–12.50). It's outdoor seating, on decking directly over the sand. Mid-May to early Sept daily 9am–10pm.

DRINKING

Sloop Inn The Wharf, TR26 1LP ☎01736 796584, ⓦsloop-inn.co.uk. This centuries-old harbourfront pub has slate floors, beams and work by local artists on display. It's best out of season when it's less busy and you can soak up the scene from outdoor tables while sampling from the extensive bar menu (most dishes around £10). There's live music from 9pm at weekends, and free wi-fi. Daily 9am–midnight; kitchen daily 9–11am, noon–3pm & 5–10pm.

The Isles of Scilly

CROMWELL'S CASTLE, TRESCO

The Isles of Scilly

Lying 28 miles southwest of Land's End, the Isles of Scilly (locals dislike the term "Scilly Isles") are a compact archipelago of between 100 and 150 islands – counts vary according to the definition of an island and the height of the tide. None is bigger than three miles across, and only five of them are inhabited. Though they share a largely treeless and low-lying appearance – rarely rising above 100ft – each island nonetheless has a distinctive character, revealing new perspectives over the extraordinary rocky seascape at every turn.

10

Free of traffic, theme parks and amusement arcades, the Scillies provide a welcome respite from the mainland tourist trail. The energizing briny air is constantly filled with the cries of seabirds, while the beaches are well-nigh irresistible, ranging from minute coves to vast untrammelled strands – though swimmers must steel themselves for the chilly water. Other attractions include Cornwall's greatest concentration of prehistoric remains, some fabulous rock formations, and masses of flowers, nurtured by the long hours of sunshine. Along with tourism, the main source of income here is flower-farming, and the heaths and pathways of the islands are also dense with a profusion of wild flowers, from marigolds and gorse to seathrift, trefoil and poppies, not to mention many more exotic species introduced by visiting foreign vessels.

The majority of the resident population of just over two thousand is concentrated on the biggest island, **St Mary's**, which has the lion's share of facilities in its capital, Hugh Town. Among the "off islands", as the other inhabited members of the group are known, **Tresco** is the largest, whose subtropical botanical gardens are the archipelago's most popular attraction. West of Tresco, **Bryher** has the smallest population and a bracing, back-to-nature feel that is nowhere more evident than on the exposed western shore, where Hell Bay sees some formidable Atlantic storms. East of Tresco, **St Martin's** has impressively wild beaches and stunning views from its cliffy northeastern end. On the southwest rim of the main group, the tidy lanes and picturesque cottages of **St Agnes** are complemented by the weathered boulders and craggy headlands of its indented shoreline.

A visit to the islands would be incomplete without a sortie to the **uninhabited isles**, sanctuaries for seals, puffins and a host of other marine birdlife. On the largest of them, Samson, you can poke around prehistoric – and more recent – remains of former settlement. Some of the smaller islets also repay a visit for their delightfully deserted beaches, though the majority amount to no more than bare rocks. This chaotic profusion of rocky fragments – each bearing a name – is densest at the archipelago's extremities: the Western Rocks, lashed by ferocious seas and the cause of innumerable wrecks over the years, and the milder Eastern Isles.

Brief history

In the annals of folklore, the Scillies are the peaks of the submerged land of **Lyonnesse**, a fertile plain that extended west from Penwith before the ocean broke in, drowning the land and leaving only one survivor to tell the tale. The story may not be complete fantasy, insofar as the isles form part of the same granite mass as Land's End, Bodmin Moor and Dartmoor, and may well have been joined to the mainland in the distant past.

Flower-farming in the Scillies p.271
Gig racing p.272

Sir Cloudesley Shovell p.273

ABBEY GARDENS, TRESCO

Highlights

❶ Gig racing All of the islands participate in these exciting boat races – Scilly's primary sport – best viewed from accompanying boats out at sea. **See p.272**

❷ Tresco Abbey Gardens An oasis of exotic greenery built around the ruins of an old priory. **See p.276**

❸ Great Bay, St Martin's Among the dozens of stunning beaches in the Scillies, this crescent of creamy white sand takes some beating. **See p.280**

❹ Diving The clarity of the waters and the numerous wrecks make the archipelago one of Britain's best dive sites. **See p.280**

❺ Samson A ramble over this now uninhabited isle reveals abandoned dwellings from the nineteenth century just a short distance from prehistoric burial chambers. **See p.282**

❻ Boat excursions to the Western Rocks This remote and scattered rockscape has been the scene of countless shipwrecks, and today is a teeming sanctuary for birds and seals. **See p.283**

HIGHLIGHTS ARE MARKED ON THE MAP ON P.270

10

Early history

The early human history of the Isles of Scilly is equally obscure. The archipelago may have been the group of islands referred to in classical sources as the Cassiterides, or "Isles of Tin", where the Phoenicians and Romans obtained their supply of the precious metal – though no trace of tin mining remains today. Some have also identified the Scillies as the legendary "Isles of the Blest" to which the dead heroes and chieftains of mainland Britain were conveyed in order to find peace and immortality. This theory is apparently supported by the unusual quantity of **Bronze Age** burial chambers found here, though it is more likely that these were rather the tombs of the first Scillonians between 1900 and 800 BC. Patchy evidence exists of **Roman occupation** from the third and fourth centuries AD, when the isles are thought to have been used as a place of exile for undesirables.

From the Middle Ages to the Civil War

In the twelfth century Henry I granted the islands to the Benedictine abbey of Tavistock, in Devon, whose monks established a priory on Tresco. Although the **Benedictines** had nominal control for the next four hundred years, the resident monks

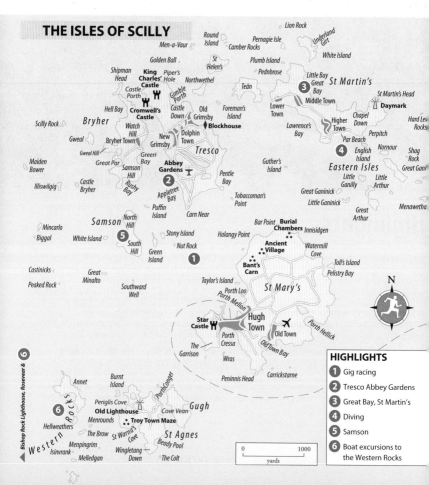

THE ISLES OF SCILLY

HIGHLIGHTS

1 Gig racing
2 Tresco Abbey Gardens
3 Great Bay, St Martin's
4 Diving
5 Samson
6 Boat excursions to the Western Rocks

FLOWER-FARMING IN THE SCILLIES

After tourism, **flower-farming** is the most important commercial activity on the isles. The flower farms shape much of the landscape with their narrow fields, or "pieces", intricately divided by tall windbreaks of hardy veronica, pittosporum, euonymus and escallonia, lending a maze-like appearance to some of the inland tracts. Most of the crop consists of various species of **narcissus**, first appearing well before Christmas and creating a spectacular effect in March and April when they are in full flower. Harvesting takes place throughout the winter, just before they flower, when the crop is flown or shipped directly to markets in London and other mainland centres.

10

lived a hazardous existence, menaced by pirates and oppressed by the extremely tough conditions, so that they probably welcomed the opportunity to return to the mainland following the Dissolution in 1539. The construction of Star Castle on St Mary's in 1593 was at the behest of Elizabeth I, motivated by the fear of Spanish invasion. The presence of the fort ensured that Hugh Town, rather than Tresco, should be the islands' capital. It also meant that the islanders were left alone by the pirates, and stability reigned until the eruption of the **Civil War**, when the Scillies upheld the Royalist cause long after the mainland had capitulated to the Parliamentarians. After a brief sojourn by the Prince of Wales (later Charles II) in 1646, the archipelago was occupied by a Roundhead army, whose legacy was Cromwell's Castle on Tresco.

Modern times

Maladministration and corruption of their local stewards combined with regular crop failure reduced the local population to a fruitless struggle for subsistence over the next couple of centuries. Conditions improved only with the arrival in 1834 of a new leaseholder, **Augustus Smith**, who, despite his despotic methods, implemented far-reaching reforms that included the construction of roads, the overhaul of the land-tenure system and the introduction of compulsory education thirty years before it became law on the mainland.

Smith's work was continued after his death in 1872 by his nephew Lieutenant Dorrien-Smith, who was mainly responsible for introducing **flower-farming** to the archipelago (his descendant, Robert Dorrien-Smith, is the current leaseholder of Tresco and owner of Bryher's *Hell Bay Hotel*); this quickly became the economic lifeblood of the community and continues to be of prime importance today. The growth of the holiday industry dates chiefly from the 1960s, when the islands were the favourite resort of the Labour prime minister Harold Wilson. Since then, tourism has transformed the economy, most conspicuously on St Mary's, though development of the "off islands" has been much less conspicuous.

ARRIVAL AND DEPARTURE

BY FERRY

Travelling by sea is the cheapest way of getting to the islands, though the crossing is often nauseatingly rough. Ferries to St Mary's are operated between mid-March and early November by Isles of Scilly Travel (☎ 01736 334220, ⓦ islesofscilly-travel.co.uk) from Penzance's Lighthouse Pier, where there's a ticket office. On embarkation, luggage will be clearly marked by the baggage-handlers with the name of the island to which you want it delivered.

Days of operation Mid-March & mid-Oct to early Nov Mon, Wed, Fri and Sat; April–June and mid-Sept to mid-Oct Mon–Sat; July to mid-Sept daily. There is no service between early Nov and mid-March. Departures are mainly at 9.15am, depending on the tide, with most returns from St Mary's at 4.30pm; the journey time is about 2hr 45min.
Fares One-way ticket from £45; day return £40.

BY PLANE

Arriving by air is expensive, but quick and memorable, affording a terrific overview of the archipelago and its surrounding litter of rocks. Skybus flights are operated by Isles of Scilly Travel (see above). Schedules listed below apply to the April–October season; a significantly reduced service operates in winter. Fares shown are one-way; day-return tickets are also available, costing £105 from Land's End and £120 from Newquay. Alternatively, you can choose

10

GIG RACING

If you're coming to the Isles of Scilly between May and September, try to time your visit to be here on a Wednesday or Friday evening to witness the **gig races**, the most popular sport on the Scillies. Some of the gigs – six-oared vessels some 30ft in length – are over a hundred years old, built originally to carry pilots to passing ships. Women race on Wednesdays, men on Fridays; routes vary but many start off from Nut Rock, to the east of Samson, finishing at St Mary's Quay, and all can be followed on launches that leave about twenty minutes before the start of each race (£6, pay on board).

the "Fly+Sail Combo", allowing you to fly from Land's End and return to Penzance on the ferry for £78 (including the Penzance–Land's End transfer). Land's End Airport offers parking on site (£7.50/day, £6.50 if booked in advance; call

☎ 01736 334220).

Destinations Exeter (Mon–Sat 3–5 daily; 1hr; from £135); Land's End Airport (Mon–Sat 7–23 daily; 20min; from £70); Newquay (Mon–Sat 4–6 daily; 30min; from £95).

GETTING AROUND

Inter-island launches Most passenger boats between the islands are operated by St Mary's Boatmen's Association (☎ 01720 423999, ⓦ scillyboating.co.uk). Leaving from St Mary's quayside, launches for the "off islands" start from 10.15am and continue throughout the day, services increasing as the season progresses. All departures are tide-dependent, and there is a much-reduced service November–March, and none at all in bad weather. Tickets cost £9 return, £13 for a two-island trip.

INFORMATION

Tourist information The comprehensive website ⓦ visitislesofscilly.com should be your first port of call. Less up-to-date ⓦ scillyonline.co.uk can also be useful. The information office on St Mary's (see p.275) covers the whole archipelago.

ACCOMMODATION AND EATING

Hotels and B&Bs Advance booking is always essential. Many B&Bs on the "off islands" require a three-night minimum stay (or a week in high season), and often insist on a dinner, bed and breakfast package. Most hotels and B&Bs close in winter.

Self-catering The majority of the accommodation on Scilly is self-catering; stays are usually available by the week and you'll need to book some time in advance.

Camping You'll find campsites on St Mary's, St Martin's, St Agnes and Bryher, mostly unsheltered but with good facilities. They're often fully booked six months ahead for the peak period, and all of them close during winter. Camping elsewhere is not allowed.

Food All five inhabited islands have pubs, cafés and restaurants, and you'll find basic groceries on each (though at higher prices than on the mainland). In winter most places close, and pubs have reduced opening hours.

St Mary's

Measuring about three miles across at its widest point, **ST MARY'S** is the largest of the Isles of Scilly and holds the vast bulk of the archipelago's population and facilities. The island's port, Hugh Town, is pleasant enough, but the best attractions – notably a handful of prehistoric remains and some enticing beaches – are dispersed around the island, reachable by easy hikes, and some accessible by bus or bike.

Hugh Town

Straddling the low-lying isthmus that connects the island's western limb, **HUGH TOWN** can get inundated by ambling tourists in summer yet never feels overwhelmed in the way that many mainland towns do – partly on account of the absence of much motor traffic. The twin centres of activity are **Hugh Street**, lined with shops and pubs, and the **harbour**, where the coming and going of ferries, launches and yachts creates a mood of quiet purposefulness. Of the local **beaches**, the best for bathing is **Porthcressa Beach** (located in Porth Cressa Bay), a sandy hollow in the sheltered bay on the south of the isthmus.

The Garrison

From the western end of Hugh Street, Garrison Hill climbs up to the **Garrison**, named for the ring of fortifications erected around this headland in the eighteenth century. The promontory was already the site of the archipelago's major defensive structure, **Star Castle**, built in the shape of an eight-pointed star in 1593 after the scare of the Spanish Armada. Now an atmospheric hotel and restaurant (see p.275), the castle once sheltered the future Charles II when he was on the run from Parliamentary forces in 1646, and later became the headquarters of the Royalist privateer, Sir John Grenville, under whom it was the last Cavalier stronghold until stormed by Admiral Blake in 1651. Beyond the castle, a circular **rampart walk** around the headland – which can be completed in less than an hour – affords spectacular views over all the islands and the myriad rocky fragments around them.

10

Isles of Scilly Museum

Church St, TR21 0JT • Easter–Sept Mon–Fri 10am–4.30pm, Sat 10am–noon; Oct–Easter Mon–Sat 10am–noon • £3.50 • ☎ 01720 422337, Ⓦ iosmuseum.org

The engaging **Isles of Scilly Museum** is well worth an hour or two's wander for historical background on the archipelago and a close-up view of some of its oddities. Many of the exhibits are relics salvaged from the numerous ships that have foundered on or around the islands, such as the ragbag of finds recovered from the *Cita*, which sank off St Mary's Porth Hellick in March 1997 – much of the cargo, ranging from tobacco and trainers to Toyota car spares, found its way into the islanders' homes. Roman brooches, pottery and stuffed birds are also on show, and downstairs is a gig from 1877 and the Gannex raincoat and pipe belonging to the Labour prime minister Harold Wilson, whose holiday home was here.

Around the island

East of Hugh Town, St Mary's is a chequerboard of meadows and hedged-in flower plantations. The most attractive parts are all on the coast, which is best

---

SIR CLOUDESLEY SHOVELL

Of all the wrecks that litter the seabed around the Isles of Scilly, the most famous are those belonging to the fleet led by Rear-Admiral **Sir Cloudesley Shovell** (1650–1707), a hero of many naval battles, including an attack on Tripoli and the capture of Gibraltar and Barcelona. On September 19, 1707, a month after sailing for England from Gibraltar, 21 ships of the Mediterranean squadron under Shovell's command were beset by gales and fog, which made accurate navigation impossible. The concerned commander convoked a meeting on board his flagship, the HMS *Association*, to establish their position, at which the consensus was that they were off the island of Ushant, 26 miles northwest of Brittany, with the English Channel open and clear before them. In fact they lay some hundred miles north of that position, so when Shovell issued the command to steer in a northeasterly direction, the fleet converged directly onto the Isles of Scilly. In all, **five ships** and nearly **2000 men** were lost; four ships foundered on the Western Rocks, two – including the *Association* – with all hands lost.

Despite his evident responsibility for the tragedy, Shovell's reputation was, if anything, enhanced by it, and he was glorified as a much-decorated war hero who went down with his ship: Queen Anne ordered that his body be exhumed and conveyed to London for an elaborate funeral in Westminster Abbey, where his tomb lies to this day. In 1967, local divers recovered many of the **treasures** carried in his fleet, which included a hoard of Spanish **"pieces of eight"** – one of the greatest troves ever found around the British Isles.

explored on foot. From Hugh Town's Porthcressa Beach, a path wanders south, skirting the jagged teeth of **Peninnis Head**, and passing some impressive sea-sculpted granite rocks on the way. Look out in particular for the formation known as the **Kettle and Pans**, 100yd north of Peninnis lighthouse, where immense basins have been hollowed out by the elements.

Old Town

10

Past Peninnis Head, placid **Old Town Bay** has a scatter of modern houses that make up **OLD TOWN**, giving little hint that this was the island's chief port before Hugh Town took over that role in the seventeenth century. These days, Old Town has a couple of cafés, and behind its sheltered south-facing **beach** the church cemetery holds the grave of Labour politician **Harold Wilson**, Prime Minister 1964–70 and 1974–76.

The south coast

Three-quarters of a mile east of Old Town, beyond the airport, **Porth Hellick** holds a rugged quartz monument to the fantastically named Admiral Sir Cloudesley Shovell (see box, p.273), just back from the beach, and the rock formation known as the **Loaded Camel**. At the eastern end of the bay, a gate leads to a path over the hill, from where a signpost points right to a 4000-year-old **barrow** probably used by the Scillies' first colonists. The grave is covered by a circular mound some 40ft in diameter, with a curving passage leading to a central chamber composed of large upright stones and four large slabs for a roof.

The east coast

On the **eastern side** of St Mary's, less than two miles from Hugh Town and a mile north along the coast from Porth Hellick, **Pelistry Bay** is one of the most secluded spots on the island, its sandy beach and crystal-clear waters sheltered by the outlying **Toll's Island**. The latter, joined to St Mary's at low tide by a slender sandbar, holds the remains of an old battery known as **Pellow's Redoubt** as well as several pits in which kelp was burned to produce a substance used for the manufacture of soap and glass. Grey seals are also a common sight here.

The north coast

The most evocative remnants of early human settlement on the Scillies are in the north of St Mary's, a mile or so north of Hugh Town. Overlooking the sea near the island's tall TV mast and dating from around 2000 BC, **Halangy Down** holds an extensive complex of stone huts, the largest of which gives onto a courtyard with interconnecting buildings. Above the village at the top of the slope, you'll find **Bant's Carn**, a long rectangular chamber topped by four large capstones. Part of a much earlier site, the Carn is probably contemporaneous with the barrow at Porth Hellick and was used for cremations. Further east, past the lovely sand beach at **Bar Point**, lie two more well-preserved "entrance graves" (as these burial chambers are known) just up from **Innisidgen**, a rubble of rocks that becomes an island at high tide.

GETTING AROUND   **ST MARY'S**

By bus The Community Bus service operates a circular route around the island, leaving from outside the town hall on the Parade in Hugh Town (Easter to mid-Oct Mon–Sat 7 daily, Sun 5 daily; £2; ☎07810 435417). There are no stops – flag it down at a safe spot. The tourist office has timetables.

By taxi DJ Cabs (☎01720 423775); Island Taxis (☎01720 422126); Toots Taxis (☎01720 422142).

By bike St Mary's Bike Hire, Porthmellon Business Park, behind Hugh Town's fire station. Operates between Easter and November (☎07796 638506, ⓦ stmarysbikehire.co.uk; £6/4hr, £12/24hr; no debit/credit cards). Book a Bike will deliver to and collect from your accommodation (☎01720 422661, ⓦ bookabikeonscilly.co.uk; £12.50/day).

INFORMATION AND ACTIVITIES

Tourist information Porthcressa Bank, above Porthcressa Beach (March–Oct Mon–Sat 9am–5.30pm, plus Sun May–Oct 9am–2pm; Nov–Feb Mon–Fri 10am–2pm; ☎ 01720 424031, ⌨ visitislesofscilly.com). Provides info on all the islands, including accommodation, activities and transport. Further news and information (including boat times) can be found by tuning in to Radio Scilly (107.9 FM).

Watersports The Sailing Centre based at Porthmellon Beach, east of Hugh Town's centre (☎ 01720 422060, ⌨ sailingscilly.com), offers sailing dinghies, kayaks, paddleboards and windsurf equipment to rent, as well as sailing tuition. Wetsuits and snorkelling gear are also available.

TOURS

Bus tours Island Rover offers bus tours with commentary, running from Holgate's Green on the Strand, Hugh Town, and lasting around 1hr 10min (Mon–Sat 10.30am & 1.30pm; £8; ☎ 01720 422131, ⌨ islandrover.co.uk).

Boat tours You'll get a good taster of the islands and the wildlife around them on tours lasting about 2hr 30min aboard the glass-bottomed *Sea Quest* (☎ 07484 718182; £16/person return), usually departing at 10.30am from Hugh Town's harbour. Island Sea Safaris at Old Town (☎ 01720 422732 or ☎ 07747 615732, ⌨ islandseasafaris .co.uk) offers one- or two-hour excursions to reefs (£24)

and wrecks (£33) around the uninhabited islands; it also rents out wetsuits and snorkelling equipment.

Wildlife walking tours Nature specialist Will Wagstaff (☎ 01720 422212, ⌨ islandwildlifetours.co.uk) leads wildlife tours around St Mary's and other islands (April to mid-Oct Mon–Fri; £12/day, plus ferry fares to the "off islands"). Tours of St Mary's normally meet behind the town hall above Porthcressa Beach at around 10am, those for the other islands at the Quay at 9.45am. Dates and times are advertised at the tourist office and St Mary's Quay.

ACCOMMODATION

★**Mincarlo** Carn Thomas, Hugh Town, TR21 0PT ☎ 01720 422513, ⌨ mincarlo.info. With modern decor in a traditional building, this B&B at the top of the Strand and at the eastern end of Town Beach has fantastic views. All rooms are en suite and most have big windows, though the cheapest (on the ground floor) don't overlook the sea. The terrace is a great suntrap, and top-quality meals are available some evenings. Closed Dec–Feb. **£85**

Old Chapel Old Town Lane, Old Town, TR21 0NA ☎ 01720 422100, ⌨ schiller-scilly.co.uk. A fifteen-minute walk east of Hugh Town and just five minutes from the airport, this former Wesleyan meeting hall has two rooms, both spacious, each with a wrought-iron bed and one (costing more) with a separate sun lounge. You can sit outside in the lush garden or in the conservatory. Minimum two-night stay, no under-10s. No debit/credit cards. **£100**

★**Star Castle** The Garrison, TR21 0JA ☎ 01720 422317, ⌨ star-castle.co.uk. The island's most luxurious and atmospheric hotel, offering a range of rooms: those in the castle have more character; modern, more spacious ones in the annexe have garden or sea views, and some have a private garden area or veranda. There's a fabulous indoor pool, two great restaurants (see p.276) and a *Dungeon Bar*. Closed Jan to mid-Feb. **£278**

Tolman House Old Town, TR21 0NH ☎ 01720 422967,

⌨ tolmanhouse-scilly.co.uk. A 15min walk from Hugh Town, this friendly B&B has great views over the bay (binoculars are provided) and breakfast includes kippers, croissants and home-made preserves. No under-12s. No debit/credit cards. **£92**

CAMPING

Garrison Campsite The Garrison, TR21 0LS ☎ 01720 422670, ⌨ garrisonholidays.com. The island's main campsite is just outside Hugh Town and has large, flat pitches, panoramic views and a small shop. Pre-erected tents and self-catering units – including in a refurbished lookout tower – are also available, and there's a baggage-transfer service from the port. Closed Nov–Easter. Per person **£11.50**

Peninnis Farm Luxury Camping Church Rd, Hugh Town, TR21 0NA ☎ 01720 421008, ⌨ peninnisfarm luxurycamping.co.uk. Glamping on this farm half a mile west of the town centre is more like staying in canvas holiday homes than in tents. Sleeping up to six, each unit consists of three rooms, kitchen and bathroom, plus a lounge with a log-burner. An honesty shop on the site provides locally produced eggs and meat. A week's minimum stay applies in Aug, three nights at other times, and there are discounts for couples outside school holidays. Closed Oct–Easter. From **£185**

EATING

Carn Vean Pelistry, TR21 0NX ☎ 01720 423458. A couple of minutes up from Pelistry Bay (signposted), this café with a large garden makes the perfect mid-point stop on a round-island walk. Crab sandwiches, delicious pasties,

huge salads (£6–8) and sticky cakes are on the menu. April–Sept daily 10.30am–4.30pm.

Dibble and Grub Porthcressa Beach, TR21 0JQ ☎ 01720 423719, ⌨ dibbleandgrub.co.uk. This place

10

housed in an ex-fire station has a casual Mediterranean feel, a mellow musical soundtrack and superb views, with tables outside. It's open during the day for fresh fruit juices, wraps and smoothies, in the evening for tapas (£4–6), succulent steaks, seafood and vegetarian dishes (mostly £12–18). Easter–Oct daily 10am–10pm, last orders 8.30pm.

Juliet's Garden Restaurant Porthloo, TR21 0NF ☎01720 422228, ⊛julietsgardenrestaurant.co.uk. With stunning views out to sea, this restaurant with garden-terraces just outside Hugh Town is one of the archipelago's most congenial eateries. By day it serves salads, home-made pâtés, scrumptious cakes and teas, with dishes such as braised organic beef, pan-roasted bream fillets, and mushroom and chestnut crumble (mostly £13–18) in the evenings. Monday is steak night. Late March to Oct Mon & Wed–Sun 10am–9pm, Tues 10am–5pm.

★**Spero's** Porthmellon Beach, Hugh Town, TR21 0JY ☎01720 422521, ⊛speros.co.uk. With a prime location in a converted boathouse, this café-bistro has sandwiches and crabcakes among other snacks during the day, and a more expensive evening menu (most dishes £12–18), which might include chargrilled rump steaks. Glass doors give onto a decked area right on the beach. March–Oct Tues–Sat 10am–9pm.

★**Star Castle** The Garrison, TR21 0JA ☎01720 422317, ⊛star-castle.co.uk. Superb food is available in three different venues here. The traditional *Castle Dining Room* specializes in high-quality meat dishes, while the airier, less formal *Conservatory*, adorned with a thick vine trailing in from the garden, concentrates on seafood. Set-price menus at both places are £33 for two courses, £39 for three courses and £45 for four; booking is essential. The *Dungeon Bar* is good for snack lunches and pre- or post-prandial drinks, and has tables on the ramparts. Mid-Feb to Oct daily: restaurants 6.30–8.30pm (last seating); bar noon–late, food served noon–2pm.

Tresco

Measuring two miles by one mile, **TRESCO** is the second-largest island of the archipelago, and also the most visited of the "off islands". Once the private estate of Devon's Tavistock Abbey, and later the home of the "benevolent despot" Augustus Smith and his family, Tresco retains a privileged air, with accommodation mainly confined to self-catering and timeshare apartments. Most of the activity here revolves around the famous Abbey Gardens and **NEW GRIMSBY**, midway along the island's western coast, where there's a store, a gallery and a pub. To the north, tidy fields give way to the heathland of **Castle Down**, an elemental expanse of granite, gorse and heather crossed by narrow paths. According to the tide, **boats** pull in at New Grimsby, Old Grimsby on the east coast, or Carn Near at Tresco's southernmost point.

Abbey Gardens

TR24 0QQ • Daily 10am–4pm • £15 • ☎01720 424108, ⊛tresco.co.uk/enjoying/abbey-garden

The sparse ruins of the Benedictine priory of St Nicholas lie amid a rich array of subtropical plants at **Abbey Gardens**, first laid out by Augustus Smith in 1834. Immediately on taking up office as Lord Proprietor of the islands, Smith established his residence in the present abbey, a tall Victorian mansion to the west of the gardens, and set about clearing the wilderness of undergrowth that then covered most of the island's southern half. Planting belts of cypress and Monterey pines from California as windbreaks, and erecting a tall wall, he introduced plants and seeds from London's Kew Gardens, which formed the core of the botanical garden. His work was continued by his successors and augmented by seedlings brought from Africa, South America and the Antipodes, often by local mariners. Today's dense abundance of palms, aloes, cacti and other tropical shrubs lends an almost jungle-like air, with some strategically sited statuary adding to the exotic ambience. The entry ticket also admits you to **Valhalla**, a colourful collection of figureheads and nameplates taken from vessels that have come to grief around the islands.

Beaches

Tresco's most alluring **beaches** are all on the southern end of the island. One of the best, **Appletree Bay**, a dazzling strip of white sand and shells, is only a few steps from the boat landing at Carn Near, and there's another gorgeous sandy bay at **New Grimsby**, further up the island's western shore. From this cluster of cottages, a lane heads across the narrow waist of the island through **DOLPHIN TOWN** – named after an early Lord Proprietor of Scilly, Sir Francis Godolphin – to Tresco's eastern side, where **OLD GRIMSBY**'s pier is flanked by more sandy beaches. South of here, a string of wide strands ends at the glorious curve of **Pentle Bay**.

Fortifications

Tresco preserves a motley collection of military **fortifications**, though all are now in a very rudimentary condition. On the high ground at the southern end of Old Grimsby's harbour, it's easy to visit the **Blockhouse**, a gun platform built to protect the harbour in the sixteenth century.

Skirting Castle Down from New Grimsby, a path traces the west coast to the scanty ruins of **King Charles' Castle**, built in the 1550s to cover the lagoon-like channel separating Tresco and Bryher. However, poor design meant that its guns were unable to lower far enough to be effective, and it was superseded in 1651 by the much better preserved **Cromwell's Castle** nearby, a round, granite gun-tower built at sea level next to the pretty sandy cove of **Castle Porth**.

Piper's Hole

From Castle Porth the shore path continues round the serrated northern edge of Tresco to **Piper's Hole**, a long cave accessible from the cliff edge, and variously identified as the abode of mermaids, ghosts or smugglers. The entrance can be a little difficult to negotiate but it's worth pressing ahead to the freshwater pool some 60ft within, for which a torch is essential. South of here, the deep indentation of **Gimble Porth** is one of the few sheltered inlets of this northern promontory, with a sand-and-stone beach that's ideal for a quick dip.

INFORMATION AND ACTIVITIES   TRESCO

Tourist information The island's website ⓦ tresco.co.uk has information on activities and accommodation.

Bike rental Estate office at New Grimsby (☎ 01720 422849); £12 per day.

ACCOMMODATION AND EATING

New Inn New Grimsby, TR24 0QQ ☎ 01720 422849, ⓦ tresco.co.uk. Airy, spacious rooms with sea views, attentive staff, prodigious breakfasts and an outdoor pool add up to a great stay – but it doesn't come cheap. Fresh seafood and Tresco beef take pride of place in the bar and restaurant, where most mains are £14–16 and a crab and prawn sandwich will set you back £10. Guest ales are always available in the bar, and there's patio seating. Kitchen noon–5pm & 6.30–9pm: Feb–Oct daily; Nov & Dec Thurs–Sun. **£220**

Bryher

Covered with a thick carpet of bracken, heather and bramble, **BRYHER** is the smallest of the populated islands, and also the wildest. The prevailing feeling here is of a struggle between man and the environment, with the cultivable parts of the island regularly threatened by the encroaching sea.

Bryher's eighty-odd inhabitants are mostly concentrated in the scattering of houses just up from the main quay that makes up the grandly named **BRYHER TOWN**, facing Tresco on Bryher's eastern side.

The north of the island

To the north of Bryher Town, flower plantations creep up **Watch Hill**, one of the island's five Scillonian-scale "hills", whose comparatively steep slopes make it seem taller than its 138ft. A brief ascent allows you to take in a grand panorama of the whole group of islands.

Barren heathland soon asserts itself to the north, extending as far as the impressive granite promontory of **Shipman Head**, another terrific vantage point offering dizzying views over the foaming Atlantic. Bryher's exposed western seaboard takes the full brunt of the ocean, nowhere more spectacularly than at the aptly named **Hell Bay**, cupped by a limb of land below Shipman Head, and frequently blasted by ferocious winds and savage waves.

10

Rushy Bay

In contrast to the sound and fury of Bryher's western shores, peace usually reigns in south-facing **Rushy Bay**, a small, sheltered, sandy crescent, surrounded by a mass of flowers. Its name is derived from the rushes, marram grass and other plants grown here by Augustus Smith in the 1830s in order to stabilize the shore against erosion. Above the bay, **Samson Hill** has a few megalithic barrows submerged beneath a coating of gorse, foxgloves, campion and other wild flowers, and boasts views as good as those from Watch Hill.

ACTIVITIES

BRYHER

Boat rental Bennett Boatyard (☎07979 393206, ⊛bennettboatyard.com) at Green Bay, south of the main quay on Bryher's eastern side, offers boats to rent – mainly kayaks (£10–20/hr or £20–30/4hr) and sailing dinghies (£20–35/hr or £35–65/4hr). Paddleboards and wetsuits can also be hired (respectively £10 and £3/hr).

ACCOMMODATION

Bank Cottage Western side, near Great Par Beach, TR23 0PR ☎01720 422612, ⊛bank-cottage.com. This guesthouse has a patio and luxuriant garden with wonderful sea views. Guests have use of a kitchen to prepare light meals, a barbecue, fishing rods and a rowing boat. Three-day minimum stay, or one week (from Sat) May–Aug. No under-10s. No debit/credit cards. Closed Oct–April. £124

★**Bryher Campsite** Watch Hill, TR23 0PR ☎01720 422068, ⊛bryhercampsite.co.uk. This relatively sheltered site on the eastern side of the island (a couple of minutes from the pub) has hot showers, laundry facilities and fabulous views towards Tresco. Closed Nov–March. Per person £10.25

EATING

Fraggle Rock Bar North of the main quay, near Bryher Town, TR23 0PR ☎01720 422222, ⊛bryher.co/fraggle-rock. Famous for its crab sandwiches (£8), this is one of Bryher's social hubs. Other dishes average around £6 at lunchtime and £10 in the evening, when booking ahead is advised – especially for fish and chips on Fridays (also Mon during main season). There's a bright, wood-floored upstairs area, tables on a panoramic terrace and wi-fi. Daily 10.30am–4.30pm & 7–11pm, reduced opening in winter; food served noon–2pm & 7–8.30pm.

Hell Bay Hotel Western side, near Great Par Beach, TR23 0PR ☎01720 422947, ⊛hellbay.co.uk. This extremely swish hotel has a bar and high-end restaurant, both open to nonresidents. You can order a salad or sandwich (around £10) or a bacon cheeseburger (£14) for lunch; in the evening, choose between the bar menu and the set-price restaurant menu (£45 for three courses), for which early booking is essential. There's also the stripped-down *Crab Shack* (from 6.15pm: Tues–Thurs in summer, also Mon in July & Aug) for freshly caught crab, mussels and scallops, with just five tables – and aprons provided. Again, book well ahead. Mid-March to late Oct noon–2pm & 6.45–9pm.

Vine Café Below Watch Hill, TR23 0PR ☎01720 423168. This traditional spot sells hot snacks, sandwiches and cakes during the day and has set evening meals (£20; served at 7pm sharp) for which booking is essential – bring your own beer or wine. Special diets catered for. No debit/credit cards. March–Oct: during school hols Mon, Wed, Thurs & Sun 10.30am–4pm & 7pm–late, Fri & Sat 10.30am–4pm; term time Mon & Thurs–Sat 10.30am–4pm, Wed & Sun 10.30am–4pm & 7pm–late.

St Martin's

A mile east of Tresco, **ST MARTIN'S** is a narrow ridge some two miles in length, its northern side wild and rugged, the southern side sloping gently to the sea and chiefly given over to flower-growing. Free of plankton or silt, the waters around St Martin's are said to be among the clearest in Britain, and are much favoured by scuba enthusiasts. The main quay is on the promontory jutting out from the more sheltered side, at the head of the majestic sweep of **Par Beach**, a bare wedge of pure-white sand. A second landing stage is located at the western end of the island.

From the main quay, a road leads uphill to **HIGHER TOWN**, the island's main concentration of houses and the location of the only shop. Beyond the church, a road runs westwards along the island's long spine to **MIDDLE TOWN** – actually little more than a cluster of cottages and a few flower-packing sheds – and from there to the western extremity of the isle. Here, **LOWER TOWN** has a slightly larger collection of houses and a pub nestled below Tinkler's Hill, all overlooking the uninhabited isles of Teän and St Helen's (see p.282). From Lower Town, there's easy access to the long, sandy continuum of **Lawrence's Bay** on St Martin's southern coast, backed by large areas of flowerbeds.

The northern coast

The best beaches – among the grandest ones in the Scillies – lie on the desolate northern side of the island, reachable via paths branching north off the main east–west track: the beautiful half-mile recess of sand at **Great Bay** and adjacent **Little Bay**, utterly secluded, backed by grassy dunes, and ideal for swimming. From Little Bay, you can climb across boulders at low tide to the hilly and wild **WHITE ISLAND** (pronounced "Wit Island"), on the northeastern side of which you'll find a vast cave, **Underland Girt**; it's accessible at low tide only, so take care not to be stranded by the returning high waters.

East of Great Bay, paths weave round rocky coves and the heathland of **Chapel Down** to the island's northeastern tip, where a conspicuous red-and-white Daymark, erected in 1683 (not 1637 as inscribed) as a warning to shipping during the day, stands above the sheer cliffs of **St Martin's Head**. On a clear day you can make out the foam breaking against the Seven Stones Reef seven miles distant, where the tanker *Torrey Canyon* was wrecked in 1967, causing one of the world's worst oil spills.

INFORMATION AND ACTIVITIES   ST MARTIN'S

Tourist information The website ⓦ stmartinsscilly.co.uk has details of accommodation and services on the island, plus a useful map.

Diving Scilly Diving, Higher Town (ⓣ 01720 422848, ⓦ scillydiving.com), offers scuba and snorkelling excursions with equipment to rent, as well as tuition.

ACCOMMODATION

Fuchsia Cottage Middle Town, TR25 0QN ⓣ 01720 422023, ⓦ scillyman.co.uk. This simple, whitewashed cottage has two rooms with en-suite or shared facilities, and home-made bread for breakfast. No debit/credit cards. Closed mid-Oct to March. **£70**

Polreath Higher Town, TR25 0QL ⓣ 01720 422046, ⓦ polreath.com. Three smartly furnished rooms with sea views are available at this B&B, with a conservatory and a separate garden for guests. Daytime meals are served in the

popular tearoom, as well as evening meals three times a week. The minimum stay is five days in April, one week (from Fri) at other times. Cash or debit cards only. Closed Oct–March. **£120**

St Martin's Campsite Middle Town, TR25 0QN ⓣ 01720 422888, ⓦ www.stmartinscampsite.co.uk. Right by Lawrence's Bay, protected by tall hedges, this is the best equipped of the Scillies campsites, and there's a self-catering chalet as well. Book well ahead. Closed early Oct to mid-March. Per person **£11.50**

EATING

★ **Adam's Fish and Chips** Higher Town, TR25 0QN ⓣ 01720 423082, ⓦ adamsfishandchips.co.uk. The freshest and tastiest fish and chips on the archipelago can

be ordered here, to eat in (£9.50; booking required) or take away (£8.50). Lobster tails and scampi are also available, and local spuds are used, while puddings, beers and wine are from a neighbouring vineyard. You can sit at outdoor tables. Easter to end of April Tues & Thurs 6–8.30pm; May, June & Sept Tues, Thurs & Sat 6–8.30pm; July & Aug Tues–Thurs & Sat 6–8.30pm, Sun noon–2pm.

★ **Little Arthur Farm** West of Higher Town, TR25 0QL ☎ 01720 422457. Rustic-looking wholefood café offering a range of delicious cakes and organic, farm-grown snacks by day, and bistro food one evening a week (mains £9–14). It's somewhat remote – about 30min from Lower Town on the side of a steep hill – but with sweeping views. No debit/credit cards. April–Sept Mon–Thurs 10.45am–4pm,

Fri 10.45am–4pm & 6–9pm.

Seven Stones Inn Lower Town, TR25 0QW ☎ 01720 423777. Situated on a ridge overlooking St Mary's, this place boasts the best views of any Scillies pub, and offers a good selection of ales and traditional meals. Soups, salads, crab sandwiches and fish chowder are served at lunchtime, while the evening menu features burgers, and dishes like couscous with halloumi (all £7.50–12). There's a flower-filled garden, and occasional live music and film screenings (the pub hosts a film festival in early Oct). April–Oct Mon–Sat 11am–11pm, Sun noon–10.30pm; Nov–March Wed & Fri 6–11pm, Sun noon–6pm.

10

St Agnes

The southern- and westernmost of the inhabited isles, **ST AGNES** is also the craggiest, its rocks weathered into fantastic shapes. Visitors disembark at **Porth Conger** in the north of the island, from where a road leads inland past the most significant landmark on St Agnes, the disused **Old Lighthouse** – dating from 1680, it's one of the oldest in England.

Periglis Cove and St Warna's Cove

From the lighthouse, paths radiate to picturesque **Periglis Cove** on the northwestern side of the island, and south to **St Warna's Cove**, where the patron saint of shipwrecks is reputed to have landed from Ireland (the exact spot is marked by a holy well). Between the two coves the coastal path passes the **Troy Town Maze**, a miniature maze of stones thought to have been created a couple of centuries ago, but possibly much older. Kept in good order over the years, the circular formation appears rather paltry relative to the mighty granite boulders nearby.

Cove Vean and Gugh

The **eastern** side of St Agnes shelters one of the island's finest beaches, the small, sheltered **Cove Vean**. Between the cove and Porth Conger, a broad sandbar appears at low tide to connect the islet of **GUGH** (pronounced to rhyme with Hugh), creating another lovely beach. Gugh merits a wander for its scattering of untended Bronze Age remains – including the **Old Man of Gugh**, a tilting standing stone on the eastern side – and the memorable panorama from its northern end. Take care not to be marooned by the incoming tide, which creates an extremely fierce current over the bar. Swimming is not advised at high tide.

Wingletang Down and around

South of St Warna's Cove, spectacular views take in the Western Rocks (see p.283). The island's southern segment is mostly taken up by the wild heathland of **Wingletang Down**. At its tip, the headland of **Horse Point** has more tortuously wind-eroded rocks.

On the eastern side of Wingletang Down the inlet of **Beady Pool** gained its name from a trove of beads washed ashore from the wreck of a seventeenth-century Dutch trader – some of the reddish-brown beads still occasionally turn up. Above the cove, the **Giant's Punchbowl** is one of the island's most remarkable rock sculptures: two immense boulders, one poised above the other, with a wide basin – 3ft deep – in its top.

TOURS

ST AGNES

Boat tours Weather permitting, there are boat trips to all the islands from Porth Conger, as well as tours to the Bishop Rock lighthouse (£16.50). Schedules are posted at all St Agnes accommodation and at the *Turk's Head* pub, or you can call ☎07990 742982. See at ⍉stagnesboating.co.uk for this and other trips.

ACCOMMODATION AND EATING

Covean Cottage Above Porth Conger, TR22 0PL ☎01720 422620, ⍉coveancottage.com. Friendly B&B with three small but comfortable rooms, with en-suite or shared bathrooms. Breakfasts are real feasts and pizza nights (pizzas £9) are organized once or twice a week (at time of writing Mon, plus Sat in school hols; check in advance). There's a conservatory and tea garden for home-made cakes, lemonade and traditional cream teas. Two-night minimum stay. Tearoom early April to late Oct Tues & Thurs–Sat 2–5pm. **£88**

Troytown Farm Periglis Cove, TR22 0PL ☎01720 422360, ⍉troytown.co.uk. This campsite is fairly exposed, but right at the water's edge, and also enjoying first-rate views over to the Western Rocks. Home-produced beef, pork, vegetables and milk – which also goes into lip-smacking ice cream – are sold at the farm shop. Pre-erected bell tents are also available to rent (May–Sept, £500/week), and you can have your baggage transferred from the quay (£3.50). Additional tent charge (£2–8) mid-July to Aug. Closed Nov–March. Per person **£9.50**

★**Turk's Head** Porth Conger, TR22 0PL ☎01720 422434. This perfectly sited pub just above the jetty is reckoned to be the best on the islands, with plenty of outdoor seating to soak up the views. Local beers are served to accompany superb St Agnes pasties (£4.75) as well as a range of meat, seafood and veggie dishes (around £11). April–Oct: Mon–Sat 10.30am–11.30pm, Sun 10.30am–10.30pm; kitchen daily noon–2.30pm & 6–8pm.

The uninhabited isles

Many of Scilly's **uninhabited isles** were previously settled and reveal fascinating traces of former habitations and commercial activities. The prevailing impression, though, is of nature holding sway, from the teeming birdlife perched on every ledge to the ocean in full spate beating against the exposed shores.

Samson

From Bryher's quay it's just a quick hop to **SAMSON**, the largest of the uninhabited isles and marked out by its mammary-like twin hills. The island has been abandoned since 1855 when the last impoverished inhabitants were transferred to other islands. Wildlife reigns supreme, the slopes thickly grown with gorse and sea holly and populated chiefly by dive-bombing gulls and colonies of black rabbits.

Boats usually pull up on a beach on the island's eastern side, from where a path leads up over **North Hill**, the site of several primitive burial chambers dating from the second millennium BC. One of these – without its cover and exposed to the elements – is thought to be the sepulchre of a tribal chief. Most of the abandoned cottages of the nineteenth-century inhabitants are on **South Hill**, many still with limpet shells piled outside their doors, left over from when these were collected and traded.

TOURS

SAMSON

Boat tours There are usually daily departures from St Mary's for Samson at 10.15am and 2pm, weather and numbers permitting, costing £9 per person (return). Contact the St Mary's Boatmen's Association (☎01720 423999) to check.

Teän and St Helen's

There are regular excursions from Lower Town in St Martin's to the uninhabited isles of Teän and St Helen's, just a quarter of a mile away. **TEÄN**, flattish and with several crescents of sandy beach, was formerly used by St Martin's families for burning kelp and grazing their cattle; their ruined cottages can still be seen.

Behind Teän, **ST HELEN'S** holds the remains of the oldest church on the archipelago, a tenth-century oratory, together with monks' dwellings and a chapel. At the base of the island's hill, which reaches almost 150ft, you can see the melancholy ruins of a "pest house" built in 1756 to house plague-carriers entering British waters.

TOURS	TEÄN AND ST HELEN'S
Boat tours There are no scheduled services to these islands, but – when there is sufficient demand and weather permitting – trips are run by independent operators like	Calypso (☎ 01720 422187 or ☎ 07778 198454; £27/person day-trip).

The Western Rocks

Out beyond St Agnes, the **Western Rocks** are a horseshoe of islets and jagged rocks that have been the cause of innumerable wrecks, from Cloudesley Shovell's *Association* (see box, p.273) to the American schooner *Thomas W. Lawson*, the largest pure sailing vessel ever built and the only one with seven masts; it came to grief here in 1907, creating what may have been the world's first spillage disaster when its cargo of crude oil washed up on St Agnes.

The biggest of the outcrops is **ANNET**, probably never inhabited and notable as a nesting place for a rich variety of **birds**, such as the stormy petrel and Manx shearwater, as well as colonies of puffins and shags. The island cannot be visited during the breeding season (mid-April to mid-August), which is probably just as well, as the screeching clamour and stench of avian effluvia are said to be unbearable.

The islands forming the western arm of the group are the best place in the archipelago to see **grey seals**, which prefer these remote outposts for breeding.

Bishop Rock Lighthouse

A lonely column five miles out, **Bishop Rock** is the tallest lighthouse in the British Isles at 175ft and the westernmost one on this side of the Atlantic. The men who built it between 1847 and 1850 lived on the nearby rocky islet of **ROSEVEAR** – hard to believe, given the extremely harsh conditions. Even more incredibly, they grew their own vegetables here, established a blacksmith's shop and even organized a ball to which guests from the other islands were invited. Remains of their constructions can still be seen.

The Eastern Isles

Scattered between St Martin's and St Mary's, the **Eastern Isles** are mere slivers of rock to which boat-trippers make forays to view puffins and grey seals. Protected from the Atlantic currents, these outcrops generally have more soil than the Western Rocks, and several have excellent beaches – notably **GREAT ARTHUR** and **GREAT GANILLY**. Both of these also have prehistoric remains; on **Nornour**, reached at low tide along a rocky bar from Great Ganilly, dwellings have been unearthed which date back to the first century AD – the finds are now on show in the museum on St Mary's (see p.273).

TOURS	THE WESTERN ROCKS AND EASTERN ISLES
Boat tours Weather permitting, there are regular boat excursions from Hugh Town (on St Mary's) to the Western Rocks and Eastern Isles, run by the St Mary's Boatmen's	Association (☎ 01720 423999), and also services from the nearest inhabited islands. The fare for a "circular" ticket from St Mary's is £15.

Cornwall's Atlantic coast

PORT ISAAC

Cornwall's Atlantic coast

Bleaker and cliffier than the county's southern seaboard, North Cornwall's Atlantic coast is punctuated by a sequence of small resorts that have sprung up around some of the finest beaches in England. These sandy strands are especially popular with surfers, but they attract beach connoisseurs of all ages, drawn as much to their dramatic settings as to the swimming possibilities. Standing aloof from the holiday traffic are the derelict stacks and castle-like ruins of the engine houses that once powered the region's mining industry, complemented by grey Methodist chapels that testify to the impact of the great evangelist John Wesley on the local communities.

11

Much of the local copper and tin production was concentrated around **Redruth** and **Camborne**, though you'll find a more rewarding setting for the relics of both mining and Methodism in the area around **St Agnes**, a steep and dispersed village to the north that preserves its old miners' dwellings. On the nearby coast, the accent is on recreation, especially surfing. Surrounded by splendid beaches, **Newquay** is acknowledged as the country's surfing capital, and has become the centre of Cornwall's party culture. The surf scene extends north to the beaches around the fishing port of **Padstow**, on the Camel estuary, though the town itself has forged a separate identity as a gastronomic hotspot, thanks largely to the efforts of chef Rick Stein, who has carved out a veritable empire here with the emphasis firmly on fresh seafood. Another reason to come to Padstow is for the Camel Trail, a cycle and walking route that weaves inland along the Camel River to Wadebridge, and eventually to Bodmin Moor.

North of the Camel, from the beach resort of **Polzeath** to the secluded village of **Morwenstow**, the coast is an almost unbroken line of cliffs. The gaunt, exposed terrain shelters peaceful nooks such as **Port Isaac**, and makes a theatrical setting for **Tintagel**, whose atmospheric ruined castle and mythical links with King Arthur have made it the most popular sightseeing destination on this coast. Squeezed into a craggy valley, the neighbouring village of **Boscastle** has strong associations with Thomas Hardy that can be traced on an inland riverside walk. Sand and surf re-establish themselves at **Bude**, though there are also some memorable cliff paths to be enjoyed hereabouts, particularly those running due north to the Devon border, seven miles away.

Camborne, Redruth and around

Ten miles west of Truro, the unprepossessing towns of **REDRUTH** and neighbouring **CAMBORNE** are largely bypassed by tourists speeding down the A30, but there are a few spots in the neighbourhood that merit a stop for anyone interested in Cornwall's industrial history. Nowadays an amalgamated conurbation spreading for six miles

Highlights

The beaches The cliffy, west-facing beaches
ning Cornwall's Atlantic coast are not only
pectacular but ideal for swimming and surfing.
See p.291, 292, 294, 302, 304 & 312

Seafood in Padstow This busy harbour
own boasts an extraordinary concentration of
gastronomic excellence, well worth a splurge.
See p.301

Camel Trail One of Cornwall's most satisfying
walking and cycling routes, extending from
Padstow along the River Camel to Bodmin Moor.
See p.301

❹ St Enodoc Burial place of John Betjeman, this
ancient church nestles in a peaceful spot within
sight of the sea. **See p.304**

❺ Tintagel Castle A romantically ruined
fortress on the cliff edge, rich in Arthurian
associations. **See p.306**

**❻ Museum of Witchcraft and Magic,
Boscastle** Delve into the world of sorcery at
this fascinating collection right next to
Boscastle's pretty harbour. **See p.310**

HIGHLIGHTS ARE MARKED ON THE MAP ON P.288

along the A3047, the towns once accounted for two-thirds of the world's copper production, the 350 pits in the area employing some fifty thousand workers in the 1850s. Many of the miners were forced to emigrate when cheaper deposits of tin and copper were discovered overseas at the end of the nineteenth century; the area has never fully recovered, as the numerous ruins of engine houses dotting the area bear eloquent testimony.

East Pool Mine

Trevithick Rd, Pool, TR15 3NP • Late March to late Oct Tues–Sat 10.30am–5pm • £7.20; NT • ☎ 01209 315027, ⓦ nationaltrust.org.uk/east-pool-mine

You can get an intriguing insight into Cornish mining at the **East Pool Mine**, about a mile west of Redruth's centre on the A3047 (reached through the *Morrisons* car park, where you can leave your vehicle). At the entrance, the Discovery Centre provides an audiovisual overview of the history of mining and miners in Cornwall that's worth taking in, though the main points of interest are the two dramatic beam engines. **Taylor's Shaft**, adjacent to the visitor centre, is one of the largest Cornish engines ever to be constructed (and the last), originally built in 1892 to pump water from the nearby Carn Brea mines. Now immaculately restored with gleaming brass and wood trimmings, the gigantic cylindrical apparatus is viewable on three levels within the engine house.

Michell's Engine House

Across the road from East Pool Mine you can see **Michell's Engine House** with the winding engine or "whim" in clanking action. It was originally used to haul men and ore up from the mine shaft and was then worked by steam – it's now powered by electricity.

Gwennap Pit

Busveal, outside St Day, TR16 5HH • Daily 24hr • Free • ⓦ gwennappit.co.uk

A couple of miles southeast of Redruth, the grassy, terraced hollow of **Gwennap Pit** was the scene of huge gatherings of miners and their families who came to hear John Wesley preach between 1762 and 1786. The first visits to Cornwall by the co-founder of Methodism were met with derision and violence, but he later won over the tough mining communities who could find little comfort in the gentrified established Church. At one time Wesley estimated that the congregation at Gwennap Pit exceeded

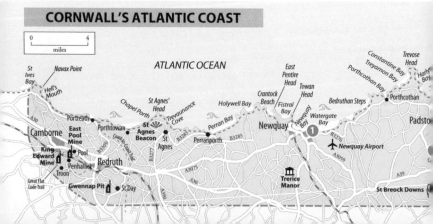

CORNWALL'S MINING TRAILS

Built in the heyday of the mining era between 1750 and 1860 for the transportation of tin and copper ore, Cornwall's Mineral Tramways, or **Mining Trails**, have been restored as mainly off-road **walking**, **cycling** and **horseriding routes**. Some of the tracks follow old railway lines – the Redruth and Chacewater Railway, built to carry ore from the mine at Gwennap to the coast (becoming Cornwall's first proper railway when it converted to steam in 1853), and the rival Portreath Tram Road, to Portreath harbour on the northern coast – and most are partly on-road. One, the circular **Great Flat Lode Trail** (7.5 miles) around Carn Brea hill, can be accessed from King Edward Mine (see below), while the **Coast to Coast Trail** links Portreath with Devoran at the top of the Carrick Roads estuary on the south coast (11.5 miles).

Books and route maps can be bought at local tourist offices or from local **bike rental** shops such as Bike Chain at Bissoe, signposted off the A393 near Gwennap (☏ 01872 870341, ⓦ bikechainricci.co.uk), and The Bike Barn, at Elm Farm, outside Portreath (☏ 01209 891498, ⓦ elmfarm.biz); both are on the Coast to Coast Trail and rent out bikes from £15 per day.

11

thirty thousand, noting in his diary, "I shall scarce see a larger congregation till we meet in the air." The present tiered amphitheatre was created in 1807, with seating for twenty thousand, and is today the venue of Methodist meetings for the annual Whit Monday service, drawing adherents from all over Cornwall.

King Edward Mine

Outside Troon, TR14 9DP • 10am–5pm: May Wed, Thurs, Sat & Sun; June Wed–Sun; July–Sept Mon & Wed–Sun; last admission 4pm • £7 • ☏ 01209 614681, ⓦ kingedwardmine.co.uk

King Edward Mine is Cornwall's oldest complete mine site, and now a museum where you can view the machinery and devices used to break down and sort the tin ore, and tour the various parts of the site. You can also learn about the network of **Mining Trails** that provide a useful way of accessing King Edward Mine and exploring the area (see box above).

Portreath

Redruth's former harbour lies two and a half miles northwest at **PORTREATH**. Shipments from here ceased in the 1960s, and nowadays the village has a rather rundown feel, its sand-and-shingle beach a draw for surfers despite the occasional presence of large amounts of seaweed.

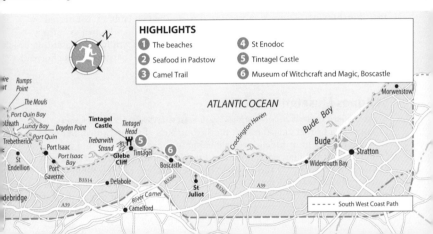

HIGHLIGHTS

1. The beaches
2. Seafood in Padstow
3. Camel Trail
4. St Enodoc
5. Tintagel Castle
6. Museum of Witchcraft and Magic, Boscastle

Porthtowan

Three miles north of Redruth, **PORTHTOWAN** is one of the choicest surfing beaches on this stretch of coast – and that's saying something. The steep terrain has helped to preserve the village without too much development, lending the place an appealingly remote feel, and unlike many of the cliff-bordered beaches around here it still catches the late afternoon sun. The good water quality merited a Blue Flag award in 2016.

ARRIVAL AND DEPARTURE   PORTHTOWAN

By bus Porthtowan is connected with Redruth train station and St Agnes by bus #315, and with St Ives, St Agnes and Newquay by the seasonal #57.
Destinations Newquay (June–Aug 2 daily; 1hr); Redruth (Mon–Sat 5 daily; 20min); St Agnes (Mon–Sat 4–8 daily, June–Aug Sun 2 daily; 10–15min); St Ives (June–Aug 2 daily; 1hr).

ACTIVITIES

11

Surfing Surf gear can be rented from Tris Surf Shop on the beach (Easter–Oct; ☎ 01209 890990, ⓦ trissurfshop.com; £4/hr, £16/day for board and wetsuit). They also offer surfing lessons (£15/hr including equipment).

ACCOMMODATION AND EATING

★**Blue Bar** Eastcliff, TR4 8AW ☎ 01209 890329, ⓦ blue-bar.co.uk. The perfect beachside stop, this congenial place much favoured by the surf crowd has drinks, breakfasts and a good choice of snacks such as fajitas, curries and burgers (all £9–11). Live bands play Sat evenings in summer. Daily: Feb, March, Nov & Dec 10am–6pm; April–Oct 10am–late; kitchen daily: Feb, March, Nov & Dec 10am–3pm; April–Oct 10am–9pm.

Cambrose Touring Park Portreath Rd, TR16 4HT ☎ 01209 890747, ⓦ cambrosetouringpark.co.uk. Between Porthtowan and Portreath, this small, clean campsite has well-sheltered pitches, free hot showers, a heated outdoor pool, a games room and a small store. Closed Nov–Easter. **£18.50**

Unicorn Beach Rd, TR4 8AD ☎ 01209 890244, ⓦ theunicornporthtowan.co.uk. It's not particularly inspiring but this pub close to the beach has clean and adequate accommodation in double and family rooms (£110), as well as in bunkrooms with a kitchen and common room available. You can eat here too; pizzas and burgers are £8–11. Daily noon–11pm; kitchen daily noon–9pm. Dorms **£22.50**, doubles **£85**

St Agnes and around

Five miles north of Redruth and a mile from the coast, the old mining town of **ST AGNES** gives little hint today of the grim, impoverished conditions in which its population once lived. Immaculate flower-filled gardens front the straggling streets of grey-slate and granite cottages in **Peterville**, the lower part of the village, and **Churchtown**, the upper, more central part. The two ends are connected by the steep Town Hill, with its picturesque terrace of cottages known as "Stippy-Stappy", a Cornish colloquialism for going uphill. The town has a pleasant, laidback appeal, and it's just a hop away from some superb cliffy coastline and a choice of beaches.

St Agnes Museum

Penwinnick Rd, TR5 0PA • Easter to late Oct daily 10.30am–5pm • Free • ☎ 01872 553228, ⓦ stagnesmuseum.org.uk

Occupying a former chapel of rest on the outskirts of Churchtown, **St Agnes Museum** holds a multitude of items relating to the area's history and culture. Apart from the expected material on mining, exhibits include a model of the harbour before its destruction by the sea in 1916, a self-portrait of John Opie – the first Cornish Royal Academician who was born in the vicinity (see p.345) – and a giant, stuffed leatherback turtle that was washed up on Porthtowan Beach, dead from ingesting a plastic bag.

St Agnes Beacon

The best place from which to take it all in is **St Agnes Beacon** (630ft), a ten-minute walk up from the car park on Beacon Drive, a mile west of the village. One of Cornwall's most famous vantage points, it affords views extending down the coast to St Ives and inland to Bodmin Moor and even across the peninsula to St Michael's Mount. The base of the mound holding the trig point contains the remains of a Bronze Age **barrow**, and cairns nearby indicate others.

St Agnes Head and the beaches

Footpaths from Beacon Drive lead a mile or so northwest of the Beacon to **St Agnes Head**, a knuckle of land surrounded by cliffs that support the area's largest colony of breeding kittiwakes, fulmars and guillemots. There are good beaches to either side: to the east, a mile north of St Agnes, **Trevaunance Cove** is popular with surfers and boasts excellent water quality; while south of the headland, beneath the clifftop relics of **Wheal Coates** tin mine, **Chapel Porth** is a wide expanse of white sand at low tide – swimmers and surfers should be wary of the strong currents and undertows.

11

ARRIVAL AND DEPARTURE   ST AGNES

By bus St Agnes is connected to Redruth train station and Porthtowan by service #315, and the seasonal #57 (to Perranporth, Porthtowan & Newquay) and #87 (to Perranporth & Truro) run from Peterville and Vicarage Rd, Churchtown.

Destinations Newquay (hourly; 50min); Perranporth (hourly; 15min); Porthtowan (Mon–Sat 4–8 daily, June–Aug Sun 2 daily; 10–15min); Redruth (Mon–Sat 5–6 daily; 35min); Truro (hourly; 30min).

INFORMATION AND ACTIVITIES

Tourist information For where to stay and eat, activities and events, see ⓦ st-agnes.com.

Surfing Boards and wetsuits can be rented from Aggie

Surf Shop, 4 Peterville Square (☎ 01872 552574), for £10 and £8 respectively.

ACCOMMODATION AND EATING

★ **Driftwood Spars** Trevaunance Cove, TR5 0RT ☎ 01872 552428, ⓦ driftwoodspars.com. This white-washed hotel, pub and restaurant just up from the beach started out in the seventeenth century as a tin miners' warehouse. Hot and cold dishes are served at the three bars and in an upstairs bistro in summer from around £7 (evening mains £10–17). There's an on-site microbrewery and, at weekends, live music. The restaurant also runs a takeaway chippie across the road. Rooms are comfortable, some – which cost more – facing the sea. Mon–Thurs 8am–11pm, Fri 8am–midnight, Sat 8am–1am, Sun 11am–11pm; kitchen daily noon–2.30pm & 6–9pm, bistro Easter–Sept Thurs & Fri 6–9pm. £92

★ **Penkerris** Penwinnick Rd, TR5 0PA ☎ 01872 552262, ⓦ penkerris.co.uk. At the southern edge of the village, this creeper-clad, spacious and delightfully old-fashioned Edwardian B&B has log fires in winter and a garden for badminton and barbecues. £70

Presingoll Farm Penwinnick Rd, TR5 0PB ☎ 01872 552333, ⓦ presingollfarm.co.uk. A mile south of St Agnes, this is a useful, immaculately clean campsite

attached to an organic farm, with level pitches, laundry facilities, free hot showers and a small shop. No debit/credit cards. Closed Nov–Easter. Per person £7.50

Tap House Peterville Square, TR5 0QU ☎ 01872 553095, ⓦ www.the-taphouse.com. This pub with a veranda attracts a young, lively crowd thanks largely to its burgers and stonebaked pizzas (mostly £8.50–12.50). More substantial dishes such as Malaysian beef rendang curry and seafood chowder (both £13) are also available, and there's a fixed-price lunch for £7.50. Live music takes place on Thursdays in summer. Daily noon–3pm & 5.30–late; kitchen Mon–Sat noon–2pm & 5.30–9pm.

Taste 40 Vicarage Rd, TR5 0TF ☎ 01872 552194, ⓦ bit.ly/taste-st-agnes. Small, welcoming restaurant with starters including fishcakes and steamed mussels (both £6.50), and grilled lobster thermidor (£16.50) among the mains. You can just have a panino or a "Taste Plate" selection for lunch, and there are set-price menus (£14.50 for two courses, £17.50 for three). Tues–Sat 10.30am–2pm & 6–9pm, Sun 10.30am–2pm.

Blue Hills Tin Streams

Wheal Kitty, TR5 0YW • Mid-April to mid-Oct Tues–Sat 10am–2pm • £6.50 • ☎ 01872 553341, ⓦ cornishtin.com

You can pick up the basics of tin extraction at **Blue Hills Tin Streams**, a wild spot a mile or so northeast of St Agnes off the B3285. A member of the resident family will guide you through the processes of vanning, panning and jigging and point out examples of tin in its various smeltings in the workshop. You're free to wander around the site, and tin products are for sale in the shop.

Perranporth

Past the old World War II airfield three miles northeast of St Agnes, the resort of **PERRANPORTH** lies at the southern end of Perran Beach, a three-mile expanse of sand enhanced by caves and natural rock arches, and backed by grass-covered dunes. Once devoted to tin and copper mining, it's now a compact holiday resort that hasn't changed much since the 1930s, when John Betjeman poured scorn on its "bungalows, palm-shaded public conveniences and amenities, and shopping arcades in the cheapest style so that Newquay looks almost smart by comparison". However, the resort's aesthetics have little impact on the thousands of surfers who flock here year-round, drawn by the long ranks of rollers coming in straight off the ocean – boards can be rented at the beach.

11

ARRIVAL AND DEPARTURE   PERRANPORTH

By bus Perranporth is connected to St Agnes by the seasonal #57 and #87, to Newquay by the same services plus #86, and to Truro by #86 and #87. There's a stop near the beach on Tywarnhayle Square.

Destinations Newquay (1–2 hourly; 35min); St Agnes (hourly; 15min); Truro (1–2 hourly; 35–45min).

ACCOMMODATION AND EATING

Perranporth Camping and Touring Park Budnick Rd, TR6 0DB ☎ 01872 572174, ⓦ perranporth-camping .co.uk. Given its location close to the centre of town at the base of Budnick Hill and just a few minutes' walk from the beach, this campsite is surprisingly quiet and relaxed. It's got a laundrette, bar and shop, and there's an outdoor pool. Closed Oct–Easter. **£24**

Watering Hole Perranporth Beach, TR6 0BH ☎ 01872 572888, ⓦ the-wateringhole.co.uk. This slightly tacky, tropical-themed place right on the sand is a useful stop for breakfasts, giant ciabattas (£7–11) and burgers (£9), or just for a drink. It's busy year-round, with live music – everything from folk to funk – on Saturdays (more

often in summer months) and barbecues in summer. Easter–Oct daily 9am–midnight, Nov–Easter Mon–Thurs 9am–6pm & Fri–Sun 9am–midnight; food served summer daily 9am–9pm, winter Mon–Thurs 9am–3pm & Fri–Sun 9am–9pm.

YHA Perranporth Droskyn Point, TR6 0GS ☎ 0845 371 9755, ⓦ yha.org.uk/hostel/perranporth. Housed in a former coastguard station on a clifftop west of the centre and on the coast path, this small, friendly hostel enjoys superb views. It has two four- and two eight-bed rooms, family rooms (£99), a kitchen and very limited camping facilities. Nov–Feb groups only. Dorms **£19**

Newquay and around

Straddling a series of rocky bluffs seven miles north of Perranporth, **NEWQUAY** has an exuberantly youthful air, its string of beaches and steady inflow of Atlantic rollers making it North Cornwall's premier resort for **surfers**. Its natural advantages are undeniable, enhanced by ornamental gardens and sloping lawns on the clifftops. However, its partly

GIG RACES IN NEWQUAY

Thrilling harbour races by **pilot gigs** (simple six-oared rowing boats) take place from May to September. The boats are relics of the days when trading schooners and ketches needed to be guided into harbour, hiring the first gig to reach them. For details of **fixtures**, contact Newquay Rowing Club (☎ 01637 876810, ⓦ newquayrowingclub.com).

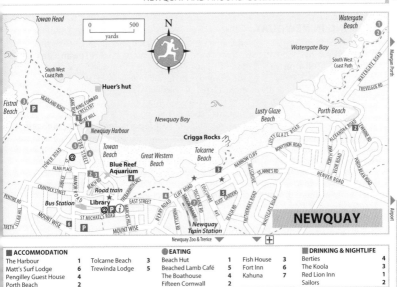

■ ACCOMMODATION			
The Harbour	1	Tolcarne Beach	3
Matt's Surf Lodge	6	Trewinda Lodge	5
Pengilley Guest House	4		
Porth Beach	2		

● EATING			
Beach Hut	1	Fish House	3
Beached Lamb Café	5	Fort Inn	6
The Boathouse	4	Kahuna	7
Fifteen Cornwall	2		

■ DRINKING & NIGHTLIFE	
Berties	4
The Koola	3
Red Lion Inn	1
Sailors	2

NEWQUAY

11

pedestrianized centre is a somewhat tacky parade of shops and fast-food outlets, and despite the infiltration of a few interesting bars and restaurants, Newquay has so far resisted all attempts to inject a cool, modern vibe. A popular destination for stag and hen parties, schoolkids celebrating the end of exams, and busloads of partygoers from throughout the region, it can get pretty boisterous – not least at weekends.

For most, however, Newquay's remarkable coastline is the number one attraction, which you can sample on an easy walk around the cliffs of **Towan Head** (from Fore Street's western end, continue on to Beacon Road and turn right at King Edward's Crescent). En route you'll pass the whitewashed **huer's hut**, a reminder of the town's former fishing role, where a "huer" would be stationed as a lookout for pilchard shoals; on sighting a shoal he would send the fleet docked in the port into action by his cry of "heva!" ("found!"), bellowed through a 3ft-long horn.

Brief history

It's hard to imagine the town enjoying any history extending more than a few decades back, but in fact the "new quay" was built as long ago as the **fifteenth century**. By then there was already a long-established fishing port here, previously known more colourfully as **Towan Blystra** (Cornish for "boat cove in the sand hills"), and concentrated in the sheltered west end of the bay. Newquay's thriving pilchard industry reached its peak in the late eighteenth century, when large quantities of the fish were exported to the Mediterranean (principally Italy).

A century later, the **harbour** was expanded for coal imports and a **railway** was constructed across the peninsula to carry shipments of china clay from the pits around St Austell to Newquay for export. With the trains came a swelling stream of seasonal visitors, drawn to the town's superb position and fine golden sands, since when the town has not looked back, its beaches and **club culture** continuing to pull the crowds today.

Blue Reef Aquarium

Towan Beach, TR7 1DU • Daily: March–Oct 10am–6pm; Nov–Feb 10am–4pm; last entry 1hr before closing • £10.50, under-12s £8.25; online discounts available • ☎ 01637 878134, ⓦ bluereefaquarium.co.uk

---

SURFING IN NEWQUAY

Newquay's surfing buzz is infectious enough to tempt scores of non-surfheads to try their hand every summer. Close to the centre of town, the sheltered beaches of **Towan**, **Great Western** and **Tolcarne** are suitable for beginners with bodyboards, while further to the north **Watergate Bay** is slightly more exposed, and good for intermediates. Experts should head for **Fistral Bay** to the west of the town, which gets fast hollow waves (especially when the wind comes from the southwest), and is the focus for national and international championships. The beach is under the surveillance of up to ten lifeguards – conditions are most dangerous at low tide, especially mid-afternoon on the spring tide. For **surf reports**, **forecasts** and **webcam** images, see Ⓦa1surf.com, Ⓦeyeballhq.tv and Ⓦmagicseaweed.com. If you can, try to arrange your visit to Newquay to coincide with one of the **surfing competitions** and events that run right through the summer – contact the tourist office for dates.

A range of **surfing equipment** is available to rent or buy from beach stalls and shops along Fore St, Tower Rd and Cliff Rd; you'll pay £5–15 a day to rent boards and wetsuits. Dozens of local outfits arrange **surfing coaching and courses** year-round. Some of the best include: Kingsurf, based at Mawgan Porth Beach, north of Watergate Bay (Ⓣ01637 860091, Ⓦkingsurf .co.uk); Fistral Beach Surf School at Fistral Beach (Ⓣ01637 850737, Ⓦfistralbeach.co.uk); O'Neill Surf Academy at Watergate Bay (Ⓣ01841 520052, Ⓦoneillsurfacademy.co.uk); and Hibiscus (Ⓣ01637 879374, Ⓦhibiscussurfschool.co.uk), for women-only surf courses. Equipment is provided, and most schools can arrange weekend or week-long packages including accommodation. **Prices** range from around £30 for a two-and-a-half-hour group session to £145–200 for a week-long course.

A guaranteed wet-weather attraction, the **Blue Reef Aquarium** at the bottom of Beach Road re-creates Cornish coastline, Mediterranean and Caribbean seas and a coral reef, in large, open-top tanks. Underwater tunnels allow you close-ups of tropical fish, and talks and feeding sessions take place hourly throughout the day.

Newquay Zoo

Trenance Gardens, off Edgcumbe Ave, TR7 2NN • Daily: 10am–5pm, last admission 4pm • £12.35, under-15s £9.25 • Ⓣ0844 474 2244, Ⓦnewquayzoo.org.uk

Small and somewhat overpriced, **Newquay Zoo** has subtropical lakeside gardens, a maze and play areas for children. Times of talks and feeding times are supplied with your ticket, and provide a useful opportunity to learn about the zoo's conservation and breeding programmes. You can upgrade your ticket for free return visits within seven days.

Newquay Bay beaches

Sheltered by the massive headland and adjacent to the town's small harbour, Newquay's most central swimming spot, **Towan Beach**, is a smooth sandy expanse reached from the bottom of Beach Road off Fore Street. It's bound on its eastern side by a tall crag connected to the promenade above by a quaint replica of Bristol's Clifton Suspension Bridge. A favourite with families, and with the full range of equipment-rental facilities, the beach can get unbearably crowded in high season, and you'll get more elbow room on any of the succession of firm sandy beaches that extend for seven miles to the northeast. Nearest are **Tolcarne**, reached by steep steps from Narrowcliff, and, past Crigga Rocks, the evocatively named **Lusty Glaze**, accessible from Lusty Glaze Road – both well protected from the wind by the bordering cliffs. You can reach these spots along the sandy shore at low tide, but for some of the more distant beaches, such as **Porth Beach**, with its grassy headland, or the extensive **Watergate Bay**, a glorious expanse of fine sand two and a half miles north of the centre, you could use local bus #56.

All the main beaches are **lifeguarded** in season, and you should heed any warning flags. All except Porth merited a Marine Conservation Society recommendation in 2016, but none received a Blue Flag award.

Fistral Bay and the beaches south

All of the town's beaches are popular with **surfers**, particularly Watergate, but the most challenging break is **Fistral Bay**, to the west, which you can reach on foot past Towan Head or across the golf links. Fully exposed to the Atlantic, the fierce breakers make it an ideal venue for surfing championships, but the violent rip currents are hazardous. On the far side of East Pentire Head from Fistral, **Crantock Beach** – reachable over the Gannel River by regular passenger ferry in season, by upstream footbridge or on bus #85 or #415 – is usually less packed, and has a lovely backdrop of dunes and undulating grassland. Further west, past Kelsey Head, **Holywell Bay** (bus #85) was the setting for the opening sequence of the James Bond film *Die Another Day*.

ARRIVAL AND DEPARTURE
NEWQUAY

11

By plane Newquay Cornwall Airport (☎01637 860600, ⓦcornwallairportnewquay.com) is at St Mawgan, five miles northeast of town, linked by bus #56. Flybe (☎0371 700 2000, ⓦflybe.com) operates 2–3 flights daily to and from London Gatwick and up to 8 weekly to Manchester, as well as seasonal flights (usually summer only) to Aberdeen, Belfast, Birmingham, Edinburgh, Glasgow, Liverpool and Newcastle. Skybus (☎01736 334220, ⓦislesofscilly-travel.co.uk) has frequent, year-round connections with St Mary's, in the Isles of Scilly (Mon–Sat).

By train Newquay's train station lies close to the seafront off Cliff Rd; services run to Par (Mon–Sat 6–7 daily, Sun

3–6 daily; 50min).

By bus The bus station is on Manor Rd, close to Fore St and 5min from the tourist office, though most buses also stop on Cliff Rd and its extension Narrowcliff.

Destinations Padstow (hourly; 55min–1hr 30min); Perranporth (1–2 hourly; 35min); St Agnes (hourly; 50min); St Austell (Mon–Sat 2 hourly, Sun 5 daily; 55min–1hr 10min); Truro (2–4 hourly; 50min–1hr 25min).

By car Parking near the central beaches and Fore St can be tricky; it's easiest to leave your vehicle in one of the car parks off Mount Wise and St Michael's Rd, or behind Fistral Beach.

GETTING AROUND

By road train The kiddie-sized hop-on, hop-off Surf Rider road train circulates around Newquay's main attractions – including the aquarium and zoo – hourly in summer (Easter–Oct; £6 day-ticket).

By car You can rent cars from the Europcar offices at the airport (☎03713 843415) and 8a Quintrell Rd (☎0371 384

5973, ⓦeuropcar.co.uk); alternatively, Newquay Car Hire are based at the train station and airport (☎01637 850971, ⓦnewquaycarhire.co.uk).

By taxi A2B Taxis (☎01637 877777) and Trenance Taxis (☎01637 262626) operate a 24hr service.

INFORMATION

Tourist information Marcus Hill (April–Sept Mon–Fri 9.15am–5.30pm, Sat & Sun 10am–4pm; Oct–March Mon–Fri 10am–4pm, Sat & Sun 10am–3pm; ☎01637 854020, ⓦvisitnewquay.org). There's a left-luggage service here (£3/item for first hr, then £1/hr). The website

ⓦnewquay.co.uk also has copious local info.

Hospital Newquay Community Hospital, St Thomas Rd, TR7 1RQ ☎01637 834800, has a minor injuries unit (daily 8am–10pm; ☎01637 834820).

TOURS AND ACTIVITIES

Fishing trips From May to September, half- (£25) or full-day (£45) fishing trips can be arranged from the harbour. Contact Newquay Boatmen's Association (☎07771 966485, ⓦnewquay-harbour.com) or Paddlefish Adventure (☎07803 955923, ⓦpaddlefishadventure.co.uk) for details.

Watersports For high-octane thrills such as kitesurfing, land-yachting, wave-skiing, surf canoeing, paragliding,

coasteering and zip-wiring, as well as bodyboarding and surfing, try Lusty Glaze Adventure Centre (☎07497 005899, ⓦlustyglazeadventurecentre.co.uk), on Lusty Glaze beach and especially good for children and groups; Newquay Activity Centre, 22 Headland Rd, Fistral Beach (☎01637 877722, ⓦnewquayactivitycentre.co.uk), or the Extreme Academy, Watergate Bay (☎01637 860840, ⓦextremeacademy.co.uk).

11

NEWQUAY'S FESTIVALS

Touted as Europe's biggest surf, skate and music festival, Newquay's **Boardmasters festival** spreads over five days in August. There are two main venues, connected by shuttle buses: Watergate Bay, where big-name acts perform everything from grime to hip-hop and acoustic music (and where the campsite is located), and Fistral Beach for surfing, skateboarding and BMX competitions and the musical Beach Sessions. Advance tickets for the whole event cost around £150 (including camping), while tickets for single days and the weekend cost less, but are more expensive at the gate (if still available). Book early at ⓦboardmasters.co.uk.

A smaller shindig takes place on Fistral Beach over a couple of days in early July: the **Electric Beach festival** (ⓦelectricbeachfestival.co.uk), which has previously attracted such big names as De La Soul and the Levellers. Tickets cost £50, or £25–35 when bought in advance.

Lastly, Newquay hosts the **Lowender Peran festival** over five days in early November, a celebration of all things Cornish and Celtic. Featuring workshops, craft displays, ceilidhs and concerts, the festival has its main hub at the *Atlantic Hotel* above Fistral Beach; you can buy a ticket which covers all events for £53, a weekend ticket for £42, an evening ticket for £8–12 or one just for Friday daytime (£3). For information, call ☎01872 553413 or see ⓦlowenderperan.co.uk.

ACCOMMODATION

There is plenty of accommodation in all categories, though rooms are at a premium in July and August, when it's strongly advisable to book ahead. Newquay has the West Country's biggest choice of **independent hostels**, some fairly scruffy and jam-packed in peak season, but all with TVs, kitchens and places to store your surfboard. In some, regular stag and hen parties can make for disturbed nights, however. **Campsites** in the area are mainly mega-complexes, many of them geared to families and unwilling to take same-sex groups, or even couples, in order to minimize rowdy behaviour. The majority are located east of the centre, and are closed in winter.

The Harbour North Quay Hill, TR7 1HF ☎01637 873040, ⓦharbourhotel.co.uk. Select and compact hotel with stunning views over the harbour from its five stylish rooms, all of which have balconies. A couple of the rooms are small, so check first. There's a classy restaurant, too. **£135**

Matt's Surf Lodge 110 Mount Wise Rd, TR7 1QP ☎01637 874651, ⓦmatts-surf-lodge.co.uk. In a quiet spot fairly close to the centre, this hostel is clean and orderly, with friendly staff and a licensed bar. Free tea and coffee are available, and prices include a simple Continental breakfast. No debit/credit cards. Dorms **£20**, doubles **£45**

Pengilley Guest House 12 Trebarwith Crescent, TR7 1DX ☎01637 872039, ⓦpengilley-guesthouse.co.uk. Very close to the main town beach and with friendly management, this has tastefully decorated, en-suite rooms – one has an antique brass bed and the single at the top has a small balcony – and a guests' lounge. Breakfast includes home-laid eggs. No debit/credit cards. **£85**

Porth Beach Porth, TR7 3NH ☎01637 876531, ⓦporthbeach.co.uk. A stone's throw from Porth Beach, this site has a villagey feel, with a stream running through and ducks waddling around. It's on the B3276, half a mile from the A3058 turn-off, with a bus stop right outside for frequent connections to Newquay's centre and Padstow. Glamping pods with bunks are available, and the beachside

Mermaid pub is just opposite. No singles or same-sex groups. Closed Nov–Feb. Camping **£30**, pods **£65**

Tolcarne Beach Narrowcliff Rd, TR7 2QN ☎01637 872489, ⓦtolcarnebeach.com. You can drift off to the sound of the surf at these clean and compact en-suite cabins right on the beach. Each one can accommodate two people, and four- to eight-person apartments are also available (from £175). There's a minimum week-long stay in late July and Aug. Closed Oct–March. **£100**

Trewinda Lodge 17 Eliot Gardens, TR7 2QE ☎01637 877533, ⓦwww.trewinda-lodge.co.uk. In a quiet street close to the train station, town centre and Tolcarne Beach, this B&B with en-suite rooms has friendly owners who can give informed advice to surfers (they also run Dolphin Surf School). Rooms are on the small side but clean, and breakfast includes fruit salad and warm croissants. **£60**

OUT OF TOWN

★**The Scarlet** Tredragon Rd, Mawgan Porth, TR8 4DQ ☎01637 861800, ⓦscarlethotel.co.uk. This is the ultimate coastal idyll for those for whom money is no object – a clifftop spa retreat with stunning views from its spacious rooms and restaurant, located near the airport six miles north of town. Rooms over five levels have balconies and private courtyards, service is discreetly relaxed and the spa facilities are luxurious. No under-16s. **£320**

EATING

Beach Hut Watergate Bay, TR8 4AA ☎01637 860877, Ⓦwatergatebay.co.uk/food-and-drink/the-beach-hut. A great location for a sundowner looking over the bay, this scenic spot also has delicious burgers (around £12) as well as grilled fish masala, crab spaghetti (both £17) and steaks (£22). To warm up post-swim, the Extreme Hot Chocolate is just the ticket. Gets very busy. Mid-March to Nov daily 9am–late; food served until 9pm.

★**Beached Lamb Café** 72–74 Fore St, TR7 1EY ☎01637 872297. Cool and quirky café-restaurant that specializes in wonderful smoothies and milkshakes. More solid sustenance comes in the form of surfer breakfasts, mega-sandwiches, nachos and burgers (£6–12), with vegan and vegetarian diets well catered for. In the evening, drop by for a blended mango mojito in the Thai-inspired chill-out lounge. Daily: March–July & Oct–Dec 9am–5pm; Aug & Sept 9am–9pm.

The Boathouse Newquay Harbour, TR7 1HT ☎01637 874062, Ⓦthe-boathouse-newquay.co.uk. The most atmospheric restaurant in town sits right by the old harbour, with crabs and lobsters scurrying around in the adjacent tanks and the local catch landed just yards away. Crawfish, hake and fish stew appear regularly on the menu (mains mostly £11–18), and sandwiches are available at lunchtime (£7–10). March, Oct & Nov Wed–Sun 10am–3pm & 6–10pm; April–Sept daily 10am–11pm; kitchen March, Oct & Nov Wed–Sun noon–2.30pm & 6–9pm; April–Sept daily noon–9pm.

Fifteen Cornwall Watergate Bay, TR8 4AA ☎01637 861000, Ⓦfifteencornwall.co.uk. Opened by Cockney super-chef Jamie Oliver on an inspired site overlooking the beach, this contemporary-looking place showcases the culinary talents of local trainee chefs in the form of inventive, Italian-influenced dishes made with seasonal Cornish ingredients. An evening tasting menu of five courses will set you back £65, or £115 including select wines. During the day you can have breakfast or lunch (£26 for a two-course set menu). Well worth the splurge. Daily 8.30am–late; food served daily 8.30–10am, noon–2.30pm & 6.15–9.15pm.

★**Fish House** Fistral Beach, TR7 1EW ☎01637 872085. With white-painted walls made from salvaged wood, this small place overlooking acres of beach has the feeling of a shack, and an appealingly casual atmosphere to match. The seafood on offer is authentically fresh and tasty, from *moules frites* (£8.50 or £16.50) and crispy squid (£8) to fish curry and roast hake fillet (£16–17). There are a few tables outside, and memorable sunset views. March–Dec daily noon–3.30pm & 6–9pm.

Fort Inn 63 Fore St, TR7 1HA ☎01637 875700, Ⓦfortinnnewquay.co.uk. Good for families and with grand sea views from its ranks of outdoor tables, this pub has St Austell ales, a range of food (£10–12) and Sunday carveries in winter. Daily 11am–11pm; food served daily noon–9pm.

Kahuna Station Parade, TR7 2NG ☎01637 850440, Ⓦkahunarestaurant.co.uk. After a day in the surf, this spacious Pan-Asian restaurant with contemporary decor is the perfect spot for a meal of pad Thai, Malaysian beef rendang curry or seafood laksa (£11–17). The cocktails are worth sampling, and take aways are also available. Daily 5.30pm–late, reduced opening in winter; food served until 9.30pm.

DRINKING AND NIGHTLIFE

Berties East St, TR7 1DB ☎01637 872255, Ⓦfacebook .com/bertiesnightclub. Newquay's largest nightclub – two clubs in one – attracts stag and hen parties and plays chart sounds, R&B, party anthems and drum'n'bass. Mainly Fri & Sat until late.

The Koola 12 Beach Rd, TR7 1ES ☎01637 873415, Ⓦchybarandkitchen-newquay.co.uk. This two-level club is stylishly done up with industrial-chic decor. Celeb DJs spin hip-hop, funk, urban and house music, and there are occasional live bands. Nightly in summer 10pm–late; reduced opening in winter.

Red Lion Inn North Quay Hill, TR7 1HE ☎01637 872195, Ⓦredlionnewquay.co.uk. This large pub close to the harbour is popular with surfers and locals alike, getting lively in the evenings without being rowdy. There's a choice of sandwiches (£5–6), grills and bar meals (£8–12), and live bands Friday & Saturday. Daily noon–midnight.

Sailors 15 Fore St, TR7 1HB ☎01637 872838, Ⓦsailorsarms.com. This popular club caters to a mainly young crowd with chart and house sounds – expect long queues in summer. The next-door *Sailors Arms* is a lively pub with a lofty panoramic terrace, DJs and live bands to listen to, and tapas, pizzas and grills to eat. Club Fri & Sat 10.30pm–4am; pub daily 8am–late.

Trerice

Kestle Mill, TR8 4PG • March–Oct daily 11am–5pm; Nov to mid-Dec (Great Hall only) Sat & Sun 11am–4pm • £7.65, Nov to mid-Dec £3.85; NT • ☎01637 875404, Ⓦnationaltrust.org.uk/trerice • From Newquay take bus #25 (Mon–Sat) or #90 to Kestle Mill, nearly a mile distant

If you feel like escaping the seaside crowds, you'll appreciate the tranquillity of **Trerice**, three miles southeast of Newquay, and reachable by road on the A392 and

A3058. Little changed since it was built by Sir John Arundell in 1571, the manor house has a Dutch gabled facade and a sequence of period-furnished rooms, the most impressive of which are the **Great Hall** on the ground floor, and the magnificent **Great Chamber** upstairs, both with ornate plaster barrel ceilings with pendants. The Great Hall also boasts a latticed window that preserves much of the original glass in its 576 panes, and displays a rare set of fat sixteenth-century wooden skittles, or "kayles", with necks on top and bottom, similar to those used by Francis Drake when playing "bowls" on Plymouth Hoe (see p.139); visitors can try their hand at "kayling" or "slapcock" – a version of badminton – on the bowling green.

Padstow

Twelve miles northeast of Newquay, **PADSTOW** almost rivals its larger neighbour in popularity, but its compact dimensions and harbour ambience lend it a very different feel. Enclosed within the estuary of the **Camel** – the only river of any size that comes out on Cornwall's northern seaboard – the town was for a long time the main fishing port on this coast, and it still shelters a small working fleet.

In recent years, the town has acquired a reputation for its **gourmet restaurants**, most famously those run by superstar chef Rick Stein, whose various outlets are scattered throughout town. There are some first-class **beaches** within a short distance on the predominantly cliffy coast (see p.302), and in addition the town hosts one of Cornwall's most famous **festivals**, the Obby Oss, a costumed May Day parade with medieval origins (see box, p.300).

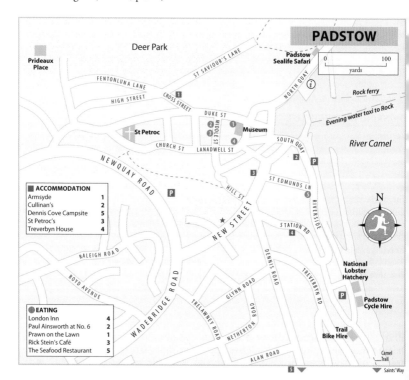

The harbour

With its medieval warren of largely traffic-free lanes, which are draped for much of the year with window-boxfuls of hydrangeas, fuchsias and geraniums, Padstow makes a pleasant place to wander. The focal point is, of course, the **harbour**, which is usually jammed with small craft, and the surrounding quaysides, which tend to be equally crowded with people. Between June and mid-September, weather permitting, **brass-band concerts** take place here on Wednesdays 6.30 to 8.30pm and on Sundays at 2.30 to 4pm and 6.30 to 8pm (sometimes a silver band or choir will appear instead).

National Lobster Hatchery

South Quay, PL28 8BL · Daily: Easter to late Oct 10am–5pm, school hols 10am–7pm; late Oct to Easter 10am–4pm · £3.75 · ☎ 01841 533877, ⓦ nationallobsterhatchery.co.uk

The **National Lobster Hatchery** offers insights into the life of these lugubrious crustaceans, from tiny juveniles to hoary old giants. The centre plays an active role in promoting lobster conservation; fishermen hand in females with eggs, which hatch and are released into the sea after three months, measuring around half an inch long.

11

St Petroc

Church Lane, PL28 8BG · Daily 9.30am–5pm, until 4pm in winter; tours May–Sept Wed 11.30am; 1hr · Free · ☎ 01841 533776, ⓦ padstowparishchurch.org.uk

Above and behind the harbour, the parish church of **St Petroc** stands amid the slate tombstones of mariners within a wooded churchyard. A large, mostly slate construction, the church is dedicated to St Petroc, a Welsh or Irish monk who landed here in the sixth century, founded a monastery on this site and eventually became Cornwall's most important saint, bequeathing his name – "Petrock's Stow" – to the town. Inside there's a fine fifteenth- or sixteenth-century font with the twelve apostles, three on each side, carved from Catacleuse stone, and a Tudor-period wineglass pulpit. Look out, too, for a lively medieval bench-end to the right of the altar depicting a fox preaching to a congregation of geese. The walls are lined with monuments to the local Prideaux family, who still occupy nearby Prideaux Place.

Prideaux Place

Tregirls Lane, PL28 8RP · **Grounds** Easter & early May to early Oct Mon–Thurs & Sun 12.30–5pm · £4 · **House tours** Easter & early May to early Oct Mon–Thurs & Sun 1.30pm–4pm; 1hr · £9 (includes grounds) · ☎ 01841 532411, ⓦ prideauxplace.co.uk

A superbly preserved example of an Elizabethan manor house, **Prideaux Place** boasts grand staircases and richly furnished rooms plastered with portraits and with fantastically ornate ceilings, all viewable on the house tours. Outside, you can wander through the formal gardens, and an ancient deer park that affords sweeping views over the Camel estuary. You might recognize some parts of the estate, which is used extensively for location filming, appearing in a plethora of films including *Twelfth Night* and *Oscar and Lucinda*.

ARRIVAL AND DEPARTURE

PADSTOW

By bus Padstow is linked to Newquay by bus #56 (hourly; 50min–1hr 15min), and to Bodmin (45min) and Wadebridge (25min) by #11A (Mon–Sat hourly, Sun 6 daily). There's a stop by South Quay.

By car Drivers will find the most convenient parking right by the harbour on South Quay.

On foot Padstow is the start of two of the West Country's best-known long-distance trails: the seventeen-mile Camel Trail (see box, p.301) and the Saints' Way, an old pilgrims' route that extends for nearly thirty miles across the peninsula to Fowey (see p.205) – the tourist office has itineraries for both.

INFORMATION AND ACTIVITIES

Tourist information North Quay (April–Sept Mon–Fri 10am–5pm, Sat & Sun 10am–4pm, but summer school hols Mon–Fri 9.30am–5.30pm, Sat & Sun 10am–5pm; Oct–March Mon–Sat 10am–4pm; ☎ 01841 533449,

11

THE OBBY OSS FESTIVAL

Padstow's chief annual festival, the **Obby Oss**, is a May Day romp whose origin is obscure, but has been variously interpreted as a welcome to summer, a rainmaker, a fertility ritual and even a strategy to ward off the French. The event takes place on May 1 – or May 2 if May 1 is a Sunday – but celebrations kick off at midnight of the preceding day with a **procession** around town to the accompaniment of a special "Night Song", lasting until the early hours. Later in the morning, the "Obby Osses" – circular contraptions draped in shiny black material and hoisted onto fearsomely masked locals – make their appearance in streets bedecked with greenery. Two teams – all dressed in white with red or blue ribbons and bunches of spring flowers pinned to lapels – follow their own obby oss as it prances through the town on set routes, preceded by a club-wielding "teazer" and accompanied by a retinue of **musicians**, **singers** and twirling **dancers**. The strains of the May Song resound all day:

Unite and unite and let us all unite,
For Summer is a-come in today.
And whither we are going we all will unite,
In the merry morning of May.

You'll need to **book accommodation** well ahead if you wish to attend, and it's worth being there the day before to savour the excitement of the preparations. Even if you can't make the festival, you can see an authentic oss in the town **museum**, near the harbour (Easter to mid-Oct Mon–Fri 10.30am–4.30pm, Sat 10.30am–1.30pm; free; ⓦ padstowmuseum.co.uk).

ⓦ padstowlive.com).

Boat tours Padstow's harbour is jammed with boats advertising cruises and fishing trips in Padstow Bay, including excursions to view seals, cormorants and occasionally (between May and July) puffins, razorbills and guillemots. Padstow Sealife Safaris (ⓣ 07754 822404, ⓦ padstowsealifesafaris.co.uk) offers one-hour powerboat tours (£25) and two-hour wildlife-watching excursions

(£39), among other trips.

Bike rental Try Trail Bike Hire (ⓣ 01841 532594, ⓦ trail bikehire.co.uk; £14/day) or Padstow Cycle Hire (ⓣ 01841 533533, ⓦ padstowcyclehire.com; £15/day) on Padstow's South Quay. In Wadebridge, the first stop after Padstow on the Camel Trail and on the A39, Bridge Bike Hire has a large selection (ⓣ 01208 813050, ⓦ bridgebikehire .co.uk; £12–14/day). All shops are open daily.

ACCOMMODATION

Armsyde 10 Cross St, PL28 8AT ⓣ 07872 029992, ⓦ armsydebandbpadstow.co.uk. A mix of traditional furnishings and chic, modern colours, this B&B has oak-floored rooms with contemporary bathrooms, and there's a family suite on the top floor. Get advice for parking. **£99**

Cullinan's South Quay, PL28 8BY ⓣ 01841 532383, ⓦ southquaybedandbreakfastpadstow.co.uk. You'll find this three-storey B&B right on the harbour next to the Old Custom House. The top bedroom has a prodigiously wide double bed, private bathroom and a French window leading onto a balcony; a cheaper and quieter room faces the back. No parking. No debit/credit cards. **£75**

Dennis Cove Campsite Dennis Lane, PL28 8DR ⓣ 01841 532349, ⓦ denniscovecampsite.co.uk. In a quiet field above the estuary, about a 10min walk south of town along the Camel Trail, this sheltered, well-maintained and picturesque site caters mainly for tents. There are

discounts for carless campers, but the site fills up quickly so book ahead. No shop. Closed Oct–April. **£24.50**

St Petroc's 4 New St, TR28 8EA ⓣ 01841 532700, ⓦ rickstein.com/stay/st-petrocs/hotel. As well as classy dining, restaurateur Rick Stein offers stylish accommodation, including this chic little hotel away from the harbour. The Georgian house has crisply contemporary decor, a small courtyard and outstanding breakfasts. **£135**

★**Treverbyn House** Station Rd, PL28 8DA ⓣ 01841 532855, ⓦ treverbynhouse.com. This beautifully furnished Edwardian house preserves its original character with working fireplaces in the spacious bedrooms. Ask for the Turret Room or Yellow Room, which both have balconies. When weather permits, breakfast is served on the terrace, which has river views. There's usually a two-night minimum stay. No debit/credit cards. **£125**

EATING

Foodies know Padstow best for its gourmet **restaurants** – particularly those associated with chef **Rick Stein**, who has reigned for more than forty years in Padstow, giving rise to the town's local nickname: Padstein. As Stein's TV fame has grown, his *Seafood Restaurant* has been joined by various offshoots, including a fish-and-chip shop and a deli on South Quay and a patisserie on Lanadwell Street, and has also spawned some healthy competition from other cafés and restaurants. Be prepared to blow your budget to sample the culinary excellence, and always book ahead, especially in summer and at weekends.

London Inn Lanadwell St, PL28 8AN ☏01841 532554, ⓦpadstowlondoninn.co.uk. Without airs or graces, this locals' pub dating from 1803 has wood panelling, nautical memorabilia and a friendly atmosphere. Order sandwiches, a steak and ale pie (£10) or a fish medley (£15) to accompany your St Austell ales. Mon–Sat 11am–11pm, Sun noon–10pm; kitchen daily noon–3pm & 6–9pm.

★**Paul Ainsworth at No. 6** 6 Middle St, PL28 8AP ☏01841 532093, ⓦnumber6inpadstow.co.uk. Top-notch cuisine is served at this rated restaurant in a tastefully converted Georgian townhouse. The modern European dishes are magnificently presented; starters include Porthilly oysters (£14), main courses such as Creedy Carver duck are around £32, and there's a set-price lunch menu (£19 for two courses). Tues–Sun noon–2.30pm & 6–10pm.

Prawn on the Lawn 11 Duke St, PL28 8AB ☏01841 532223, ⓦprawnonthelawn.com. Part fishmonger, part rough-and-ready bistro, this place is usually abuzz with cheerful diners, offering menus that change daily but are based on what's on display. "Small plates" such as spiced mackerel, marinated scallops and Szechuan prawns cost £7–10, larger "platters" are £16–30, and

there's a good dessert menu and wine list. Tues–Sat noon–late.

Rick Stein's Café 10 Middle St, PL28 8AP ☏01841 532700, ⓦrickstein.com/eat-with-us/rick-steins/cafe. The most relaxed of the Stein eateries has bright and breezy Mediterranean-type decor and stays open all day for full breakfasts, coffees and snack lunches (arrive early). In the evening, when booking is necessary, main courses – such as lamb and spinach karahi curry and grilled hake – cost around £14, and there's a set-price three-course menu for £23.50. Daily 8am–9.30pm.

★**The Seafood Restaurant** Riverside, PL28 8BY ☏01841 532700, ⓦrickstein.com/eat-with-us/the-seafood-restaurant. One of the country's top fish restaurants, Rick Stein's flagship is classy without being snooty, with contemporary art on the walls and a bright, modern feel. The extensive menu ranges from grilled scallops to stone bass vindaloo and lobster thermidor. Main mains cost £25–40, or you can opt for cod and chips for a modest £19.50, and there's a three-course lunch menu for £40. Book early – alternatively, you can perch at the central seafood bar for which no reservations are required. Daily noon–2.45pm & 6.30–10pm.

Around Padstow

Padstow is conveniently placed for some of Cornwall's most spectacular **beaches**. Those on the west can be reached on bus #56, though walking is best for appreciating the wonderful coastline. For beaches across the Camel estuary (see p.304), you can use the Rock ferry (see box, p.302).

THE CAMEL TRAIL

The Camel Trail is one of the West Country's most popular **cycle routes**, running a total of seventeen miles from Padstow up the River Camel as far as Poley's Bridge, a mile west of Blisland (see p.324) on the edge of Bodmin Moor. The five-and-a-quarter-mile Padstow–Wadebridge section of the trail follows an old railway line and offers glimpses of a variety of **birdlife** – especially around Pinkson Creek, habitat of terns, herons, curlews and egrets. However, this stretch can get very crowded in summer, and you may choose to join at Wadebridge – from the town centre, follow Eddystone Road (from the south side of the bridge) until you reach the trail. From **Wadebridge**, the route heads five and a half miles southeast towards Bodmin (see p.318), before turning northwards for a further six and a quarter miles to Poley's Bridge, within spitting distance of Wenfordbridge. This, the quieter end of the route, traces the winding river through tranquil woods, always within sight of the moor. The trail is also open to **walkers**, and to **horses** between Padstow and Dunmere, a mile west of Bodmin. You can pick up guides, maps and leaflets from the **tourist offices** at Padstow and Bodmin (see p.299 & p.321).

Doom Bar

Following the coast path northwards out of Padstow for about a mile, look out at low tide for the **Doom Bar**, a sand bar that was allegedly created as a punishment by a mermaid who had been mortally wounded by a fisherman mistaking her for a seal. Apart from thwarting the growth of Padstow as a busy commercial port, the bar has scuppered some three hundred vessels, with great loss of life.

Beaches west of Padstow

Some three miles west of **Stepper Point** (at the top of the Camel estuary) you'll reach the sandy and secluded **Harlyn Bay**, popular with families and surfers. The area's best surfing beach, though, with first-class water quality, is **Constantine Bay**, a mile south of **Trevose Head**, the promontory located two miles west of Harlyn Bay. The surrounding dunes and rock pools make this one of the most appealing bays on the coast, but both here and at adjacent **Treyarnon Bay**, the tides can be treacherous and bathing hazardous at low tide and near the rocks. A mile or so south of Treyarnon, **Porthcothan**, a long narrow beach, with dramatic cliffs and an expanse of sand at low tide, is partly maintained by the National Trust and has a useful pub and village store.

11

ACTIVITIES · BEACHES WEST OF PADSTOW

Surfing Harlyn Surf School (☎ 01841 533076, ⊛ harlynsurfschool.co.uk) offers tuition and rents out boards and wetsuits.

ACCOMMODATION

★**YHA Treyarnon** Tregonnan, Treyarnon, PL28 8JR ☎ 0845 371 9664, ⊛ yha.org.uk/hostel/treyarnon. Nearly five miles west of Padstow, this hostel is housed in a 1930s summer villa in a lofty position overlooking Treyarnon Bay. Dorms have up to six beds, and there are doubles and camping pitches available, with bell tents sleeping up to five for rent (Easter–Sept; £59). There's a kitchen and café-bar. It's half a mile from Constantine Bay, which is on the #56 bus route. Dorms <u>£25</u>, doubles <u>£45</u>, camping/person <u>£15</u>

Bedruthan Steps

One of the West Country's most dramatic beaches lies three or four miles south of Porthcothan: **Bedruthan Steps**. The jagged slate outcrops here were said to be the stepping stones of a giant called Bedruthan, though this legendary figure was actually conjured into existence in the nineteenth century. You can view the grand panorama from the clifftop path, at a point that drivers and travellers on bus #56 can reach on the B3276. From here steep steps lead down the sheer face to the sandy beach, though there is no access between November and February. The beach makes a great place to ramble about, but swimming is dangerous on account of the rocks and often-violent waves, and you should be ultra-careful not to get trapped by the incoming tide.

> ### THE PADSTOW–ROCK FERRY
>
> The easiest way to visit the alluring beaches around Daymer Bay and Polzeath from Padstow is via the regular **ferry** across the estuary between Padstow and Rock (high summer daily 8am–7.30pm from Rock/8am–7.50pm from Padstow; winter 8am–4.30pm from Rock/8am–4.50pm from Padstow; other periods have varying last crossing times; £4 return, bicycles £4 return subject to space; ⊛ padstow-harbour.co.uk). Departures are from Padstow harbour's North Pier, except at low water when ferries leave from near the war memorial further downstream. In summer, an evening water-taxi takes over (continuous service: Easter to mid-July, Sept & Oct 7pm–midnight; mid-July to Aug 7.30pm–midnight; £4 one-way, £7 return; ☎ 07778 105297, ⊛ rock-watertaxi.co.uk), departing from South Slip in the harbour at high tide, or Lower Beach, a few minutes' walk north, at low tide.

Polzeath and around

Situated three miles northeast of Padstow on the east side of the Camel estuary, **POLZEATH** is renowned for its fine, flat beach, which was awarded a Blue Flag in 2016. The slow wave is ideal for wannabe surfers – even the babies turn out in wetsuits – and the sandy beach also attracts sand-yachters, not to mention its fair share of rich kids whose high-spirited shenanigans regularly hit the headlines in the silly season. Surrounded by dunes, and with fine views across the estuary, **Daymer Bay**, a mile or two to the south, is a great place for sunbathing, with shallow waters that are popular with families. Daymer is also a big hit with the **windsurfing** crowd, and equipment is available to rent from stalls in summer.

ARRIVAL AND DEPARTURE   POLZEATH

By bus Polzeath is accessible on the #96 bus from Wadebridge, Camelford and Port Isaac.
Destinations Camelford (4 daily; 45min); Port Isaac (4–5 daily; 20min); Wadebridge (4–5 daily; 25min).
By ferry From Padstow, Polzeath can be reached via the Rock passenger ferry (see p.302).

INFORMATION AND ACTIVITIES

Tourist information Limited information about Polzeath can be found at ⓦ polzeathincornwall.co.uk.
Surfing Surf gear can be rented on the beach, or from Ann's Cottage (ⓣ01208 863317) and TJ's Surf Shop (ⓣ01208 863625), both nearby, or from Surf's Up, at 21 Trenant Close and on the beach (ⓣ01208 862003 or ⓣ07760 126225, ⓦsurfsupsurfschool.com). Surf's Up also runs a range of courses and individual lessons for around £28 for two hours including wetsuits and boards. For local surf reports, see ⓦmagicseaweed.com.

ACCOMMODATION AND EATING

Cracking Crab PL27 6TD ⓣ01208 862333, ⓦ winkingprawngroup.co.uk/cracking-crab. This spacious and airy beach café directly below *Tristram* campsite has fabulous views over Polzeath's beach, the perfect accompaniment for salads, baguettes and wraps during the day. It stays open in the evening for a good choice of dishes, including baked cod (£18.50), monkfish wrapped in bacon (£19.50) and steaks (£19–25). Daily 8.45am–late; reduced opening in winter.
Oyster Catcher Dunders Hill, PL27 6TG ⓣ01208 862371, ⓦoystercatcherpolzeath.co.uk. A short climb up from Polzeath's beach, this pub has a panoramic terrace that fills up with families during the day, and serves sandwiches (£6–7), curries and burgers (around £10). It gets fairly merry at night, with live bands on Saturday nights. Daily 11am–midnight.
Tristram PL27 6TP ⓣ01208 862215, ⓦpolzeath camping.co.uk. On a low cliff above Polzeath beach, this campsite has glorious views, though it can get very crowded and it's pricey; showers cost 50p. Booking essential in July and Aug. No groups. Closed Nov to mid-March. £30
Valley Caravan Park PL27 6SS ⓣ01208 862391, ⓦvalleycaravanpark.co.uk. Signposted from behind Polzeath's beach, just 150yd away, this large, sheltered site has a stream running through it attracting ducks and geese. Like other local sites, it gets teeming in summer. Closed Nov–March. £25

St Enodoc

Trebetherick, PL27 6LD • Daily 7.30am–dusk • Free • ⓣ01208 863778

Long associated with this part of Cornwall, the poet **John Betjeman** is buried in the

---

A WALK FROM POLZEATH

Heading north from Polzeath, the **coastal path** brings you through clifftop growths of feathery tamarisk, which flower spectacularly in July and August. From the headland of **Pentire Point**, views unfold for miles over the offshore islets of **The Mouls** and **Newland**, with their populations of grey seals and puffins. Half a mile east, the scanty remains of an Iron Age fort stand on the humpy back of **Rump's Point**, from where the path descends a mile or so to **Lundy Bay**, a pleasant sandy cove surrounded by green fields. Climbing again, you pass the shafts of an old antimony mine on the way to **Doyden Point**, which is picturesquely ornamented with a nineteenth-century castle folly once used for gambling parties.

thirteenth-century church of **St Enodoc**, the building now incongruously stranded in the middle of a golf course above Daymer Bay. Few people are tempted away from the sand and sea to visit the church, but it's an appealing spot, the walls half buried in the grassy sand dunes and surrounded by a protective hedge of tamarisk. So invasive were the surrounding sands that at one time the vicar and his congregation had to enter through a hole in the roof. It's most easily approached from the Daymer Bay car park, where the footpath is signposted. Alternatively, cross the golf course from Rock, following the white stones and keeping a weather eye out for golf balls.

Port Quin

A mile east of Lundy Bay, the tiny inlet of **Port Quin** has a few placid cottages but no shops, the place having been abandoned in the nineteenth century when the antimony mine at nearby Doyden failed. The land is now managed by the National Trust, who have maintained a tidy appearance. At low tide, you can poke around the patches of sand and the rock pools.

11

Port Isaac and around

Five miles east of Polzeath, the quintessential Cornish fishing village of **PORT ISAAC** is wedged in a gap in the precipitous cliff walls. Already celebrated for its crab and lobster catch, Port Isaac has also achieved fame for its appearances in films and TV productions – including the 1970s **Poldark** series and **Doc Martin** programmes from 2004 to present – as well as for having spawned the **Fisherman's Friends** male choir, whose rollicking sea shanties have become a staple at music festivals.

Consequently, there is a regular trickle – or sometimes a torrent – of day-trippers here, but Port Isaac still preserves its air of seclusion, with granite, slate and whitewashed cottages tumbling steeply down to a largely unspoilt seafront. A pebble beach and rock pools are exposed by the low tide, and **fishing** and coastal **boat trips** are available in summer.

Half a mile to the east, the coast path brings you to **Port Gaverne** (pronounced Gayverne), a small cove with a pebble and sand beach, and sheltered bathing, where you can also grab a bite to eat in the *Port Gaverne Hotel* (see p.306). Head a couple of miles west of Port Isaac and you'll reach Port Quin (see above), and more dramatic coastline.

ARRIVAL AND DEPARTURE
PORT ISAAC AND AROUND

By bus Bus service #96 links Port Isaac with Polzeath, Wadebridge and Camelford; the stop is at the top of the village on New Rd. Change at Camelford for buses to Tintagel.
Destinations Camelford (4 daily; 25min); Polzeath (4–5

daily; 20min); Wadebridge (4–5 daily; 50min).
By car Port Isaac's lanes are impossibly narrow, so drivers should leave their vehicles in one of the car parks at the top of the village.

ACCOMMODATION

★**Old School Hotel** Fore St, PL29 3RD ☎01208 880721, ⦿theoldschoolhotel.co.uk. On the edge of the harbour, this place has exposed oak beams, slate walls and schoolroom memorabilia everywhere. Most bedrooms are quite small (the Mathematics Room is a family suite; £165), but the views are amazing and breakfasts are huge. There's

a good restaurant too. **£115**
Slipway Hotel Harbourfront, PL29 3RH ☎01208 880264, ⦿portisaachotel.com. At the centre of things down by the seafront, this place has small but comfortable rooms, two with harbour views and balconies, though these can suffer from noise from the bar at night. **£110**

EATING AND DRINKING

Golden Lion Fore St, PL29 3RB ☎01208 880336, ⦿thegoldenlionportisaac.co.uk. Traditional harbourside

pub with bare floorboards and nautical bits and pieces in numerous rooms and snugs, and there's a separate upstairs restaurant and a small outdoor terrace. Bar meals are available in generous portions (mostly £11–15), as well as Tribute and HSD ales. Mon–Thurs & Sat noon–11pm, Fri noon–midnight, Sun noon–10.30pm; kitchen daily noon–3pm & 5–9pm.

★**Outlaw's Fish Kitchen** 1 Middle St, PL29 3RH ☏01208 881183, Ⓦ outlaws.co.uk. Celebrity chef Nathan Outlaw has staked his pitch in Port Isaac with this informal, rather cramped fish tapas bar right opposite the harbour. The pricey but delicious taster-size dishes are £9–12 each. The same chef operates a more upmarket place at the top of the village, *Restaurant Nathan Outlaw*

(6 New Rd ☏01208 880896), where the innovative set-price seafood menus roll in at £59 and £119 per person. Noon–3pm & 6–9pm: June–Sept Mon–Sat; Oct–May Tues–Sat.

Port Gaverne Hotel Port Gaverne, PL29 3SQ ☏01208 880244, Ⓦ portgavernehotel.co.uk. This secluded inn just steps up from the beach has St Austell ales on tap, bar snacks (including ciabatta rolls for £6–8), and meat and seafood mains (£14–17), which you can eat in the bar or separate restaurant. There's a garden, too. Daily 11am–11pm; kitchen daily noon–2.30pm & 6–9pm.

Tintagel

Seven miles northeast of Port Isaac, the village of **TINTAGEL** is a magnet for visitors on account of its fabled **castle**, whose scanty ruins stand on an outcrop of the nearby coast. Apart from this and a medieval manor house restored by the National Trust, the village amounts to little more than a dreary collection of bungalows, guesthouses and souvenir shops milking the area's associations with King Arthur for all they're worth. The most evocative approach to the site is from **Glebe Cliff** to the west (accessed off the B3263), where the Norman parish church of **St Materiana** sits in windswept isolation.

Tintagel Castle

Castle Rd, PL34 0HE • April–Sept daily 10am–6pm, Oct daily 10am–5pm, Nov–March Sat & Sun 10am–4pm • £7.90, under-16s £4.70; EH • ☏01840 770328, Ⓦ www.english-heritage.org.uk/visit/places/tintagel-castle • 10min walk from the village; there's a Land Rover service for visually- or mobility-impaired people from the bottom of Fore St (April–Oct; £2 one-way)

Thankfully, none of the local tourist palaver lessens the impact of the forsaken ruins of **Tintagel Castle**, magnificently sited on the black, rocky coast west of Tintagel. Although the castle makes a plausibly resonant candidate for the abode of the "Once and Future King", the remains in fact belong to a Norman stronghold constructed in the thirteenth century and occupied by the earls of Cornwall, most of which had washed into the sea by the sixteenth century. There are some much older fragments, however – notably the ruin of a **Celtic monastery** that occupied this promontory in the sixth century, which has become an important source of information on the set-up of the country's earliest monastic houses. Digs begun in 1998 on the eastern side of the island also revealed glass fragments dating from the sixth or seventh century and believed to originate in Malaga, as well as a 1500-year-old section of slate bearing two Latin inscriptions, one of them attributing authorship to "Artognou, father of Coll's descendant", which some people have taken as a trace of Arthur's existence, though Artognou was quite a common name at that time; the slate is currently on display in

Truro's museum (see p.218). In 2016, further excavations unearthed walls up to 3ft thick – suggesting that this was indeed a royal residence belonging to rulers of the fourth- to eighth-century kingdom of Dumnonia – together with large amounts of pottery from the eastern Mediterranean.

At low tide, you can visit **Merlin's Cave** at the base of the promontory, where the wizard is supposed to have taken the infant Arthur to keep him safe. Look out for the unobtrusive rock carving of Merlin's head at the mouth of the cave, one of several artistic installations dotted around the site which have led to accusations of the "Disneyfication" of Tintagel.

The Old Post Office

Fore St, PL34 0DB • Daily: mid-Feb, mid-March & late Sept to Oct 11am–4pm; mid- March to late Sept 10.30am–5.30pm • £4; NT • ☎ 01840 770024, ⓦ nationaltrust.org.uk/tintagel-old-post-office

Tintagel's **Old Post Office** is a rickety-roofed, slate-built manor house from the fourteenth century, now restored. The original gallery can still be seen, and one room, used in the Victorian era as a post office, preserves its fourteenth-century appearance. Note the huge buttresses propping up the building, visible from the garden.

11

KING ARTHUR IN CORNWALL

The first question always asked about **King Arthur** is: "Did he really exist?" If he did, it is likely that he was an amalgam of two people: a sixth-century Celtic warlord who united local tribes against the invading Anglo-Saxons, and a Cornish saint. Whatever his origins, his role was recounted and inflated by poets and troubadours, particularly in Welsh poems (the earliest of which, *Gododdin*, is thought to date from the sixth century). The basic narrative of Arthur, Queen Guinevere and the knights of Camelot was later elaborated by the twelfth-century chroniclers **Geoffrey of Monmouth**, who first popularized the notion that Tintagel was Arthur's birthplace, and **William of Malmesbury**, who further embroidered the legend that, after being mortally wounded in battle, Arthur sailed to Avalon. Avalon itself was identified with Glastonbury, in Somerset, where the tombs of Arthur and Guinevere were "discovered" by Benedictine monks in the twelfth century. The Arthurian legends were later unfolded in **Thomas Malory**'s epic, *Morte d'Arthur* (1485), heavily romanticized in **Tennyson**'s *Idylls of the King* (1859–1885) and vividly resurrected in **T.H. White**'s saga, *The Once and Future King* (1937–1958).

Numerous places throughout Britain and Europe claim some association with Arthur, not least in Brittany and Wales, but it is England's West Country – and **Cornwall** in particular – that has the greatest concentration of supposed links, and where the spirit of Arthur is said to be embodied in the Cornish chough (a rare bird, once thought to be extinct). The most famous Arthurian site is **Tintagel**, where today every kind of swords-and-sorcery hogwash is peddled, while nearby **Bodmin Moor** is full of places with names like "King Arthur's Bed" and "King Arthur's Downs". Camlann, the battlefield where Arthur was mortally wounded fighting against his nephew Mordred, is thought to lie on the northern reaches of the moor at **Slaughterbridge**, near Camelford, which itself is sometimes identified as Camelot. Nearby, at **Dozmary Pool** (see p.325), the knight Bedivere was dispatched by the dying king to return the sword Excalibur to the mysterious hand emerging from the water – though **Loe Pool** in Mount's Bay also claims this honour (see p.235). According to some, Arthur's body was transported after the battle to **Boscastle** (see p.309), from where a funeral barge carried it to Avalon.

Cornwall is also the presumed home of **King Mark**, at the centre of a separate but later interwoven cycle of myths. It was Mark who sent the knight **Tristan** (or Tristram) to Ireland to fetch his betrothed, **Isolde** (or Iseult). Mark's palace is traditionally held to have been at **Castle Dore** near Fowey. Out beyond Land's End, the fabled, vanished country of **Lyonnesse** is also said to be the original home of Arthur, as well as being (according to **Spenser**'s *Faerie Queene*) the birthplace of Tristan.

King Arthur's Great Halls

Fore St, PL34 0DA • March–Oct Tues–Sun 10am–5pm • £5 • ☏ 01840 770526

You can dip into the world of make-believe at **King Arthur's Great Halls**, created in the 1930s by Frederick Thomas Glasscock, a wealthy London custard manufacturer, and now owned by the Masons (who still meet here). The centrepiece of this slightly cheesy re-creation of King Arthur's court is a medieval-like chamber, the Hall of Chivalry, containing a grandiose throne, a round table and 72 windows by Veronica Whall – a pupil of William Morris – depicting the deeds of the knights.

Trebarwith Strand

South of Tintagel the coast is wild and unspoilt, making for steep and strenuous **walking**, well compensated by some stupendous sandy beaches en route, such as **Trebarwith Strand**, two miles down, with its beautiful rock formations. Reached by a passage through the rocks, the beach here is only accessible at low tide, and is lifeguarded during the summer months. Between half tide and low tide, Trebarwith becomes a magnet for **surfers**, rated as one of the finest beach breaks in the country.

ARRIVAL AND INFORMATION   TINTAGEL

By bus Tintagel is linked to Boscastle and Camelford by buses #95 and #96. Change at Camelford for connections to Port Isaac. Buses stop outside the tourist office on Bossiney Rd, at the top of Fore St.
Destinations Boscastle (4–6 daily; 10min); Camelford (4–5 daily; 15min).

Tourist information Bossiney Rd (daily: Easter–Oct 10am–4pm; Nov–Easter 10am–1pm; ☏ 01840 779084, ⊕ visitboscastleandtintagel.com). As well as selling leaflets on local walks, the office has an informative permanent exhibition explaining and illustrating the area's history and the Arthur saga; there's also wi-fi here.

ACCOMMODATION

The Avalon Atlantic Rd, PL34 0DD ☏ 01840 770116, ⊕ tintagelbedbreakfast.co.uk. Classy guesthouse in the centre of the village, with Gothic-style beds and Victorian fireplaces, but a fresh, contemporary feel. Some rooms are small, but all are spotless and most have amazing views. There's a good choice at breakfast, including awesome porridge. Closed Oct–Feb. **£89**

Bosayne Atlantic Rd, PL34 0DE ☏ 01840 770514, ⊕ bosayne.co.uk. At the eastern end of the village, this solid Edwardian B&B has amiable, eco-aware owners and smallish rooms with sea views and mini-fridges. Breakfasts are mainly organic with home-made bread and cakes. Packed lunches, a luggage transfer service and a self-catering cottage are all available. **£70**

Headland Atlantic Rd, PL34 0DE ☏ 01840 770239, ⊕ headlandcaravanpark.co.uk. Convenient and spacious campsite a few minutes' walk from Tintagel's centre, with

scenic but exposed pitches. There are no frills, but facilities are clean and staff are friendly. Closed late Oct to Easter. **£18**

Michael House Trelake Lane, Treknow, PL34 0EW ☏ 01840 770592, ⊕ michael-house.co.uk. This vegetarian and vegan B&B with good-size rooms stands a mile south of Tintagel and a 15min walk from Trebarwith Strand. Breakfasts are a highlight, and excellent evening meals are available (£16.50/£21 for two/three courses). **£80**

YHA Tintagel Dunderhole Point, PL34 0DW ☏ 0845 371 9145, ⊕ yha.org.uk/hostel/tintagel. Spectacularly sited on Glebe Cliff, three-quarters of a mile south of Tintagel, the offices of a former slate quarry now house this youth hostel with great coastal views. There's a kitchen but no restaurant. Closed Nov to mid-March. Dorms **£19**

EATING

Charlie's Fore St, PL34 0DA ☏ 01840 779500, ⊕ charlies.cafe. This deli and café with outdoor seating has a bright, family-friendly feel, and sources its ingredients locally. Choose from among the pies and Scotch eggs for a superlative picnic, or settle down for brunch, a doorstep sandwich (£4–7) or a delicious pizza (£9–12). Mon–Sat 10am–5pm, plus occasional winter evenings (check website).

Mill House Inn Trebarwith, PL34 0HD ☏ 01840 770200, ⊕ themillhouseinn.co.uk. This secluded stream-side pub ten minutes' walk up from Trebarwith Strand serves Tintagel brewery beers and Rattler cider in the flagstoned bar. You can eat from the lunchtime bar menu or have a fuller evening meal (mains £13–18); Wednesday in winter is "Pauper's Night", with a fixed-price £17.50 menu. Kitchen daily noon–3pm & 6.30–9pm.

The Olive Garden Atlantic Rd, PL34 0DD ☎01840 779270. Small, unfussy restaurant with plain wooden tables, a friendly atmosphere and a Mediterranean menu that includes calamari (£6), pastas (£10–12) and gigantic pizzas (from £8.50). Italian wines and Peroni are also served. Mid-March to mid-Oct daily 6pm–late.

Boscastle

Compressed within a narrow ravine drilled through by the Jordan and Valency rivers, the tiny port of **BOSCASTLE**, three miles east of Tintagel, presents a tidy appearance, its riverbanks lined by thatched and lime-washed cottages. Few traces now remain of the destruction wreaked in 2004, when freak weather conditions created a powerful torrent that surged through the valley, sweeping away much of the orderly riverfront. Although the destruction was immense, the houses have been meticulously repaired or rebuilt.

The village is split between its higher and lower ends, linked by a long, steep road that starts as High Street at the top of the hill, changing its name to Fore Street, Dunn Street and Old Road on the way down. A short walk from the bridge at the bottom will bring you to the rivermouth, especially worth viewing in rough weather an hour either side of low tide, when you'll see the **Devil's Bellows** in action – a blowhole that shoots water across the harbour entrance.

11

Brief history

Boscastle grew up around twin settlements – at the harbour and around **Bottreaux Castle**, built in the twelfth century on a spur above the Jordan valley but now vanished (the site is below the Methodist chapel on Fore Street) – there's a model of its presumed appearance in the tourist office. The port's heyday was during the nineteenth century, when sailing vessels had to be "hobbled" (towed) through the twisty harbour entrance by boats manned by eight oarsmen, and centred in the

---

THOMAS HARDY IN BOSCASTLE

Why go to Saint-Juliot? What's Juliot to me?
Some strange necromancy
But charmed me to fancy
That much of my life claims the spot as its key.   *A Dream or No (1913)*

After eight years working as an architect in London, **Thomas Hardy** came to Boscastle in 1870 to restore the church of St Juliot. It was in the course of this work that he first met **Emma Gifford**, the sister-in-law of the rector, and after return visits he married his "West of Wessex girl" in 1874. A year earlier he had published his third novel *A Pair of Blue Eyes*, which opens with an account of an architect arriving in a Cornish village to restore its church, and which is full of descriptions of the country around Boscastle. Although the marriage to Emma was highly strained, her death in 1912 inspired Hardy to return to the village and write bittersweet love lyrics recalling happier moments in their married life, published in *Poems 1912–1913*, which have been called among the most moving love poems in the English language. In 1916, he erected a plaque to Emma's memory in St Juliot, still visible on the wall of the north aisle.

To take in Boscastle's various Thomas Hardy connections, you can follow a **circular walk** that traces the Valency valley for three miles or so from Boscastle to St Juliot (drivers will find it signposted off the B3263). It's small and nondescript, but pretty much as the young architect left it (Hardy later regretted his draconian restoration). The rectory where he stayed lies a quarter of a mile beyond the church, and is now a comfortable B&B (see p.310). You can pick up a leaflet describing the walk from the tourist office.

channel by gangs of men pulling on ropes. Horses then hauled the goods, which came from as far afield as Canada, up Boscastle's steep inclines, bringing back slate, manganese and china clay in return for export.

Museum of Witchcraft and Magic

The Harbour, PL35 0HD • Easter to early Nov Mon–Sat 10.30am–6pm, Sun 11.30am–6pm • £5 • ☎ 01840 250111, ⓦ museumofwitchcraftandmagic.co.uk

For a break from Hardy, check out the **Museum of Witchcraft and Magic**, an intelligent, comprehensive and non-gimmicky account of witchcraft and sorcery through the ages, displayed in themed galleries. Look out for the "dark mirrors" – which are supposed to see into the future – and "healing poppets" (dolls) used in cursing, with pubic hair and nail clippings sewn onto them. You can even listen to a rare recording of occultist Aleister Crowley intoning his poetry and excerpts from "The Gnostic Mass".

11

ARRIVAL AND INFORMATION

BOSCASTLE

By bus Services #95 and #96 connect Boscastle to Bude, Camelford and Tintagel. Buses stop by the bridge at the bottom of town and on Bossiney St, at the top of Fore St. Destinations Bude (4–6 daily; 40min); Camelford (4–6 daily; 30min); Tintagel (4–6 daily; 10min).

Tourist information The Harbour (daily: March–July, Sept & Oct 10am–5pm; Aug 10am–5.30pm; Nov–Feb 10.30am–4pm; ☎ 01840 250010, ⓦ visit boscastleandtintagel.com).

ACCOMMODATION

Boscastle House Tintagel road, PL35 0HA ☎ 01840 250654, ⓦ boscastlehouse.co.uk. On the edge of the village, a ten-minute uphill walk from the harbour (but with a bus stop outside), this B&B has spacious and chic rooms, most with sea views. Breakfasts are gourmet-standard, and there's a large garden. **£88**

★ **Lower Pennycrocker** St Juliot, PL35 0BY ☎ 07967 605392, ⓦ pennycrocker.com. Signposted two miles out of Boscastle on the B3263 towards Bude, this campsite is quite basic and exposed to the wind, but spacious, friendly and with amazing sea views. Pods (sleeping 2) are available for the tentless. It's a quarter-mile from the #95 and #96 bus stops, and 10min from the coast path. No debit/credit cards. Closed Nov–Easter. Camping/person **£8**, pods **£33**

Old Rectory St Juliot, PL35 0BT ☎ 01840 250225, ⓦ stjuliot.com. For Thomas Hardy fans, this is the only place worth considering, where you can sleep in Hardy's or Emma's bedroom, in the Rector's Room, or in a converted stables with a separate entrance. There's home-grown fruit and fresh eggs for breakfast, meals in the Victorian greenhouse and extensive grounds for roaming. It's outside Boscastle on the St Juliot road, signposted from the B3263. No under-12s. Closed mid-Dec to mid-Feb. **£95**

Wellington Hotel The Harbour, PL35 0AQ ☎ 01840 250202, ⓦ wellingtonhotelboscastle.com. This turreted Victorian hotel has a solid, traditional feel, with plushly elegant rooms (the two spacious turret rooms are most impressive). There's fine dining in its Georgian-style *Waterloo* restaurant, or you can eat and drink more cheaply in the congenial surroundings of the *Long Bar*. **£135**

★ **YHA Boscastle** The Harbour, PL35 0HD ☎ 0845 371 9006, ⓦ yha.org.uk/hostel/boscastle. Characterful old hostel in a former stables, beautifully sited by the river. Family rooms are available (£69), and there's a self-catering kitchen and a comfy lounge. No wi-fi. Dec–Feb groups only. Dorms **£24**

EATING

Cobweb The Bridge, PL35 0HE ☎ 01840 250278, ⓦ cobwebinn.com. Busy but welcoming pub down by the harbour, with two bars, open fires in winter and live music on Saturdays. Cornish Rattler cider and Tintagel beers are dispensed, and you can eat pasties and baguettes (£5–9), pizzas (£6–9) or fresh seafood, veggie and meat dishes (mostly £10–15). As well as the bar, there's a first-floor restaurant and tables outside. Mon–Thurs & Sun 11am–11pm, Fri & Sat 11am–midnight; kitchen Mon–Sat 11.30am–2.30pm & 5.15–9.30pm, Sun noon–

2.30pm & 5.15–9.30pm.

Napoleon Inn High St, PL35 0BD ☎ 01840 250204, ⓦ napoleoninn.co.uk. At the top of the village, this beamed old pub has a huge log fire, a beer garden and such evening diversions as the Boscastle Buoys singing Cornish songs on Tuesdays and live bands Fridays. St Austell ales are served straight from the barrel, and the menu includes burgers (around £10), salads (£13) and pastas (£10–12). Daily 11am–11pm; food served noon–2pm & 6–9pm.

Riverside The Bridge, PL35 0HE ☎ 01840 250216,

ⓦ hotelriverside.co.uk. Pleasant spot where you can watch the Valency flow from the adjacent garden and enjoy a cream tea, a sandwich or a full meal. The evening menu is strong on seafood, from chowder (£8) to baked hake (£15),

and there's a great Sunday carvery (£9) that needs booking. April–Oct daily 8.30am–9pm; Nov–Feb Mon–Thurs & Sun 8.30am–4pm, Fri & Sat 8.30am–9pm.

Bude and around

Just four miles from the Devon border, **BUDE** ranks among Cornwall's premier holiday resorts thanks to the broad, family-friendly sands on either side that are also much beloved of surfers. The town, which is built around the mouth of the River Neet and the parallel Bude Canal, is smaller and quieter than Cornwall's other major seaside resorts. The surrounding cliffy coast preserves a wild beauty, and the canal's towpath provides excellent opportunities for walking and biking.

The biggest event of the year, the **Bude Jazz Festival**, attracts a range of stomping sounds over four days in August/September (ⓦ budejazzfestival.co.uk).

11

Bude Castle

The Wharf, EX23 8LG • Heritage Centre daily 10am–4pm; last entry 3pm • Free • ☎ 01288 357300, ⓦ thecastlebude.org.uk

Prominently sited behind Summerleaze Beach at the confluence of the River Neet and Bude Canal, battlemented **Bude Castle** dates from 1850, apparently constructed here in order to prove that it *was* possible to build a house on sand – albeit on concrete rafts. The grandly named "castle" was in fact the home of the local inventor and philanthropist **Sir Goldsworthy Gurney** (see box below), and now holds a **Heritage Centre**, whose overview of Bude's history includes exhibits relating to the Bude Canal and a section on Gurney himself, whose major invention is commemorated in front of the castle by the **Bude Light**, a tall, stripy cone that comes into its own at night, when a system of fibre optics lights it and the surrounding zodiac circle on the ground in a pattern of constellations. The **gallery** here holds exhibitions of local art, and the *Café Limelight* (daily 10am–5pm) makes a pleasant refreshment stop, with tables on a terrace.

Bude Canal

Extending for nearly 35 miles when it was completed in 1825, the **Bude Canal** originally served to transport lime-rich sand and seaweed inland for improving North Cornwall's acid soil, and carry back slate and granite for export. It was more of a network than a single waterway, with a branch stretching almost as far as Launceston and a feeder arm from Tamar Lake, and it had direct access to the Atlantic via the sea lock at Bude (still operational). With the arrival of the railway in 1898, the canal was gradually abandoned, and only the first couple of miles of the

---

A LOCAL GENIUS: SIR GOLDSWORTHY GURNEY

One of a noble Cornish line of eccentric scientific geniuses, **Sir Goldsworthy Gurney** (1793–1875) is credited with inventing a steam jet, a steam carriage, an oxyhydrogen blowpipe and a bizarre musical instrument consisting of glasses played as a piano. However, he's probably most celebrated for improving the lighting in the House of Commons by replacing the 280 candles with three "Bude Lights" of his own invention, used for sixty years until the arrival of electricity. He adapted his light – which shone extra brightly by means of oxygen injected into the flame – for use in **lighthouses** by placing it in a revolving frame. Each lighthouse had its own sequence of flashes – a principle still in use today. Born near Padstow, Gurney moved to London and later to Bude, where his home, "the castle built on sand", still stands.

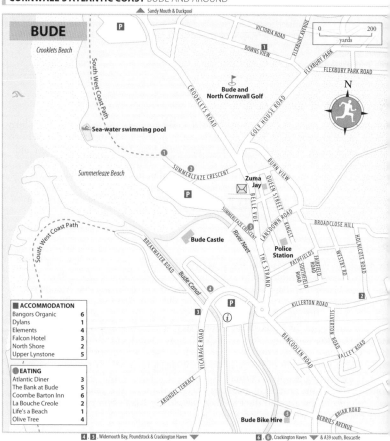

ACCOMMODATION
Bangors Organic	6
Dylans	1
Elements	4
Falcon Hotel	3
North Shore	2
Upper Lynstone	5

EATING
Atlantic Diner	3
The Bank at Bude	5
Coombe Barton Inn	6
La Bouche Creole	2
Life's a Beach	1
Olive Tree	4

waterway now survive, which provide a delightful **towpath trail** – pick up a leaflet at the tourist office (see opposite).

The beaches

Bude has an excellent selection of **beaches** within easy reach. Most central is **Summerleaze**, sheltered, sandy and wide; in fact it grows to such immense proportions when the tide is out that a sea-water swimming pool was installed near the cliffs in the 1930s – and is still much used.

Two and a half miles south of Bude, mile-long **Widemouth Bay** (pronounced "Widmouth") is the main crowd-puller, backed by a straggle of white bungalows, though bathing can be dangerous near the rocks at low tide. Surfers and families also congregate five miles south down the coast at **Crackington Haven**, which has a gently shelving beach and is beautifully set between 425ft crags at the mouth of a lush valley. The cliffs on this stretch include Cornwall's highest (aptly named High Cliff, 700ft) and are characterized by remarkable zigzagging strata of shale, limestone and sandstone.

North of Bude, just beyond Summerleaze Beach, the classic breaks at acres-wide **Crooklets** have made it the scene of surfing and lifesaving demonstrations and competitions in summer. A couple of miles further on, beyond the signposted *Atlantic*

Hills Caravan Park, **Sandy Mouth** is a pristine expanse of sand that's best at low tide, with rock pools and finger-like rock formations beneath encircling cliffs. Less developed and quieter in high season than other local beaches, the tiny sandy cove of **Duckpool**, less than a mile north, is flanked by jagged reefs at low tide and dominated by the 300ft promontory of **Steeple Point**. The beach lies at the mouth of a stream that flows through the **Coombe valley**, once the estate of the Elizabethan master mariner Sir Richard Grenville and now providing excellent walks.

ARRIVAL AND INFORMATION — BUDE

By bus From outside the tourist office, bus #95 goes to Boscastle, #6 and #6A go to Exeter, #216 and #217 go to Morwenstow, and #217 and #219 go to Hartland, Devon.

Destinations Boscastle (4–5 daily; 40min); Exeter (Mon–Sat 11 daily, Sun 3 daily; 2hr–2hr 25min); Hartland (Mon–Sat 1–5 daily; 30–55min); Morwenstow (Mon–Sat 1 daily; 20min).

Tourist information Crescent car park (Mon–Sat 10am–5pm, Sun 10am–4pm; summer school hols daily 10am–7pm; ⓣ01288 354240, ⓦvisitbude.info). You can book beach huts (May–Sept £22–30/day) and accommodation here, and access the internet.

11

ACTIVITIES

Surfing Raven Surf School (ⓣ07860 465499, ⓦravensurf.co.uk) offers some of the best surf courses locally for £35 for the first lesson, £30 for subsequent lessons. Atlantic Pursuits (ⓣ01288 321765 or 07974 718145, ⓦwww.atlanticpursuits.com) runs surfing and body-boarding sessions at Widemouth Bay. DIY-ers can rent surfing gear from Zuma Jay, 20 Belle Vue Lane in Bude's centre (ⓣ01288 354956, ⓦzumajay.co.uk), *Life's a Beach* on Summerleaze Beach, the car park of the *Bay View Inn* in Widemouth Bay, or the beach at Crackington Haven.

Canoeing Atlantic Pursuits (see above) has Canadian canoes on the Bude Canal available for half- or full-day sessions (respectively £30 and £50), with full instruction.

Bike rental You can rent bikes from Bude Bike Hire, Pethericks Mill, by the towpath on National Cycle Route 3 (ⓣ01288 353748, ⓦbudebikehire.co.uk) for £10 per half-day, £14 per day. Download local routes from their website, or see ⓦatlantictrail.co.uk.

ACCOMMODATION

★ **Bangors Organic** Poundstock, EX23 0DP ⓣ01288 361297, ⓦbangorsorganic.co.uk. Four miles south of Bude and a mile inland of Widemouth Bay (bus #95 and #96), this stylish B&B offers two spacious, beautifully designed rooms, a lounge and an excellent licensed restaurant. All food is local and organic, much of it home-grown. No under-10s. **£100**

Dylans 12 Downs View, EX23 8RF ⓣ01288 354705, ⓦdylansguesthouseinbude.co.uk. The best of a tidy row of terraced B&Bs near the centre and overlooking the golf course. This one has stripped wooden floors, spotless, modern rooms, arty decoration and free parking. No debit/credit cards. **£80**

Elements Marine Drive, Upton, EX23 0LZ ⓣ01288 352386, ⓦelements-life.co.uk. Well placed for walkers and surfers, less than two miles south of Bude towards Widemouth Bay, this hip hotel has storage and drying rooms for surfers as well as a sauna and gym, and offers surf packages. Bikes and boards are available to guests, and there's a good Italian café/restaurant, too. **£79**

Falcon Hotel Breakwater Rd, EX23 8SD ⓣ01288 352005, ⓦfalconhotel.com. This turreted, white pile facing the canal claims to be the oldest coaching house in North Cornwall. Rooms are smart, though old-fashioned, and have great views, and there's a garden, bar and restaurant. Tennyson broke his leg while staying here in 1848. **£140**

North Shore 57 Killerton Rd, EX23 8EW ⓣ01288 354256 or ⓣ07970 149486, ⓦnorthshorebude.com. Friendly hostel 5min from the centre of town, which has a kitchen with free tea and coffee, and a large garden including a barbecue area. The clean and spacious bunkrooms have four or six beds and there are doubles with shared or en-suite facilities. Photo-ID required. Dorms **£20**, doubles **£50**

Upper Lynstone Caravan and Camping Park Lynstone Rd, EX23 0LP ⓣ01288 352017, ⓦupperlynstone.co.uk. Three-quarters of a mile south of the centre on the Widemouth Bay road, this family-run site is friendly and well managed, with a children's play area. It's a lovely coastal walk into town. No groups. Closed mid-Oct to March. **£22**

EATING

Atlantic Diner 5–7 Belle Vue, EX23 8JL ⓣ01288 354167. A useful town-centre café, popular with surfers and families, with bright colours, cool music and views from a small veranda. The menu includes breakfasts, salads, burgers, lasagne and beef chilli (all £5–10), with veggie and vegan options. Feb–Easter Mon–Fri

9am–4pm; Easter–Oct daily 10.30am–9pm.

The Bank at Bude Pethericks Mill, EX23 8TF ☎01288 352070, ⊛thebankatbude.co.uk. A bit out of the way – unless you're a cyclist, as it's right on the cycle path – this relaxed place offers tapas and cocktails in a friendly atmosphere. As well as the rich selection of tapas (most around £6), there are paellas and other meat and seafood dishes (£13–24), and you can sip a range of cocktails which watching the river flow. It's just a five-minute walk along the riverbank from the tourist office. Easter–Oct Tues–Sun noon–11pm; Nov–Easter Wed–Sat 5pm–late.

Coombe Barton Inn Crackington Haven, EX23 0JG ☎01840 230345, ⊛coombebarton.co.uk. Just steps from the beach and with unrivalled views, this pub with tables outside serves fresh seafood, chargrilled steaks and a range of Cornish ales, and there are regular music nights. Most mains cost £9–14. Kitchen 12.15–3pm & 5.30–9pm; bar menu available all afternoon in summer.

La Bouche Creole Summerleaze Crescent, EX23 8HJ ☎01288 352451, ⊛labouchecreole.co.uk. This smart restaurant housed within the pink-fronted *Atlantic House* hotel brings a touch of New Orleans to Cornwall, offering dishes such as seafood gumbo, crabcakes and chicken jambalaya (£25 for two courses). Tues–Sun 6–9pm.

Life's a Beach Summerleaze Beach, EX23 8HN ☎01288 355222, ⊛lifesabeach.info. Right on the beach, this place beats all the competition for style, location and cuisine. It's a café by day, offering great baguettes and burgers (£5–9), and in the evening a somewhat pricey but good-quality seafood bistro (mains £18–22). Book ahead for the evening. Easter to late Oct Mon–Sat 10.30am–3.30pm & 6.30–9pm, Sun 10.30am–3.30pm; late Oct to Easter Thurs 7–9pm, Fri & Sat 10.30am–3.30pm & 7–9pm, Sun 10.30am–3.30pm.

Olive Tree Lower Wharf, EX23 8LG ☎01288 359577, ⊛olivetreebude.co.uk. The ideal spot for a daytime snack or informal dinner on the quayside, with sofas and a warm, chatty atmosphere. During the day you can order dishes such as avocado and poached egg on toast in small (£5.50) or large (£7.50) sizes, while evening mains include prawn and mussel risotto (£15) and loin of lamb (£18). There are some outdoor tables too. Mon, Tues & Sun 10am–5pm, Wed–Sat 10am–9pm.

Morwenstow

Tucked into Cornwall's northwest tip, seven miles due north of Bude and just two miles south of the Devon border, **MORWENSTOW** has an appealingly remote feel to it, surrounded by windswept cliffs and fields. The isolated hamlet is best known for its colourful opium-smoking poet-vicar **Robert Hawker**, credited with introducing the custom of the **Harvest Festival** to England in 1843. Hawker's tiny **driftwood hut**, complete with stable door, lies embedded in the cliffs and is accessed via steep steps, 400yd along a footpath from the end of the road (always accessible; free).

The rugged coast on either side of the village makes for strenuous but exhilarating **walking**. Immediately to the north of Morwenstow, **Henna Cliff** has, at 450ft, the highest sheer drop of any sea-cliff in England after Beachy Head.

Church of St Morwenna and St John the Baptist

EX23 9SR • Daily 24hr • Free

Hawker's church of **St Morwenna and St John the Baptist** lies nestled in a wooded combe to the right of where the road through the village peters out. In the graveyard, look out for the white figurehead of the *Caledonia* which serves as a gravestone for its wrecked captain. Numbering a good proportion of smugglers, wreckers and dissenters among his parishioners, Hawker insisted on giving shipwrecked sailors a churchyard rather than a traditional beachside burial, with the result that forty mariners now repose here. If the state of decomposition of the corpse was far advanced, he would encourage his gravediggers with liberal doses of gin. Inside the church are some impressive Norman arches carved with bearded men, menacing bird-like creatures and what is reckoned to be a hippopotamus, plus a wonky tub **font** that's the oldest of its type in the country. Below the church, Hawker's **vicarage** sports a diversity of chimneys in imitation of various church towers known and loved by him.

ARRIVAL AND ACTIVITIES

MORWENSTOW

By bus Services #216 and #217 link Morwenstow and Bude (Mon–Sat 1–2 daily; 20min).

Horseriding Gooseham Barton Stables, two miles east of Morwenstow and signposted from the A39, offers hacks in the area (☎01288 331204, ⊛riding-holidays -cornwall.co.uk; £16/30min, £28/1hr). Self-catering cottages are also available.

EATING

Rectory Tea Rooms Crosstown, EX23 9SR ☎01288 331251, ⊛rectory-tearooms.co.uk. Just by the churchyard, this medieval farmhouse with stone flags and high-backed settles offers top-notch cream teas, either inside or in the garden. Soups, quiches and other wholesome snacks are also available for under £12, with many of the ingredients sourced from the organic garden. Easter–Oct daily 11am–5pm; call for winter opening.

11

Bodmin and Bodmin Moor

STOWE'S HILL

Bodmin and Bodmin Moor

A miniature wilderness just ten miles in diameter and watered by a quartet of rivers – the Fowey, Lynher, Camel and De Lank – Bodmin Moor is the smallest, mildest and most accessible of the West Country's great moors, its highest tor rising to just 1375ft from a platform of 1000ft. Though bisected by the main A30, the moor's bare, desolate appearance conveys a sense of loneliness quite out of proportion to its size, its emptiness only accentuated by the scattered relics left behind by its Bronze Age population. Its remote air has also engendered a slew of literary and legendary associations, notably in the annals of King Arthur and the fiction of Daphne du Maurier. Like Exmoor and Dartmoor, Bodmin Moor has a small population of wild ponies, though its most celebrated animal occupant – if it exists at all – is the Beast of Bodmin, whose phantom presence might add some frisson to your ramblings.

The moor's highest tors lie in its northern reaches, west of the A30 and roughly midway between the archetypal moorland villages of **Blisland** and **Altarnun**. The southeastern moor holds some of Cornwall's most important prehistoric sites, including The Hurlers and Trethevy Quoit, while some of the region's finest examples of fifteenth-century church art can be seen nearby in the attractive village of **St Neot**.

For the best choice of food and lodgings, you might want to base yourself in one of the towns on the moor's perimeter: **Liskeard**, to the south; **Launceston**, near the Devon border; or **Bodmin** itself, southwest of the moor. As well as having the area's widest range of accommodation, Bodmin has several local sights well worth a whirl, including the notorious Bodmin Jail and, outside town, two impressive country piles: Lanhydrock, one of the West Country's grandest mansions, and the more intimate Pencarrow.

INFORMATION AND GETTING AROUND

Tourist information Bodmin's tourist office (see p.321) can supply information on the town and all parts of the moor, including walks, rides, transport and accommodation. The website ⓦ bodminmoor.co.uk has a useful overview of the moor's history and landscape.

Maps For a walk of any length, arm yourself with a good map: Ordnance Survey *Explorer* OL109 takes in the whole moor at a scale of 1:25,000 (grid refs for some of the main hiking destinations are given in this chapter).

By road Bus services are woefully limited, but there's a reasonable road network and there are plenty of places to park.

By bike National Cycle Routes 3, 32 and 327 skirt the west and north of the moor, linking Bodmin with Camelford and Launceston.

Bodmin

The workaday town of **BODMIN** lies two or three miles west of Bodmin Moor proper, equidistant from the north and south Cornish coasts and close to both the Fowey and Camel rivers. This central position encouraged Bodmin's growth as a trading hub; it also became an important ecclesiastical centre with the establishment of a priory by

LANHYDROCK

Highlights

❶ **Bodmin Jail** Eerie and gloomy though this former prison is, it provides a sobering insight into the lives of the poorest sections of Cornish society without gadgetry or gimmicks. See p.321

❷ **Lanhydrock** One of the country's most fascinating and complete nineteenth-century stately homes, stuffed with art and antiques, and surrounded by glorious grounds bordering the River Fowey. **See p.323**

❸ **The hike to Rough Tor and Brown Willy** An easy but rewarding walk that brings you to the highest points of the moor and remnants of Bronze Age settlements. See p.328

❹ **St Neot church** This fifteenth-century church in one of the moor's prettiest villages has a stunning collection of stained glass. See p.329

❺ **Trethevy Quoit** Looming over the moor, this is Cornwall's most striking example of this type of prehistoric tomb. See p.331

HIGHLIGHTS ARE MARKED ON THE MAP ON P.320

Saint Petroc after he moved here from Padstow in the sixth century. Bodmin became Cornwall's county town in 1835, but sacrificed much of its administrative role by refusing land for the Great Western Railway in the 1870s, resulting in most administrative functions and local commerce transferring down the road to Truro. Since then, the town has drifted into a provincial slumber, off the tourist track and looking a little frayed in places – though in many ways it is more authentically "Cornish" than some of the more prettified coastal settlements.

Bodmin's central square, **Mount Folly**, sits at the junction of the main Fore and St Nicholas streets (B3268), and is dominated by the Georgian **Shire House** – formerly the assize court and now part-occupied by the tourist office and council offices.

Bodmin Museum

Mount Folly, PL31 2HQ • Easter–Sept Mon–Fri 10.30am–4.30pm, Sat 10.30am–2.30pm; Oct Mon–Sat 10.30am–2.30pm • Free •
☎ 01208 77067

For a good, all-round introduction to the town, **Bodmin Museum** is well worth a whizz round. Wildlife, geology and Bronze Age culture are all illustrated, alongside features on various local worthies and a miscellaneous collection that includes a sixteenth-century granite font later used as a corn measure, the town's first ramshackle fire engine from the late eighteenth century and a stuffed chough. There's also a reconstructed Cornish kitchen that includes a clome (or cloam) oven, used to make bread and fuelled by gorse and bracken – a fixture in most rural Devon and Cornwall kitchens until the twentieth century

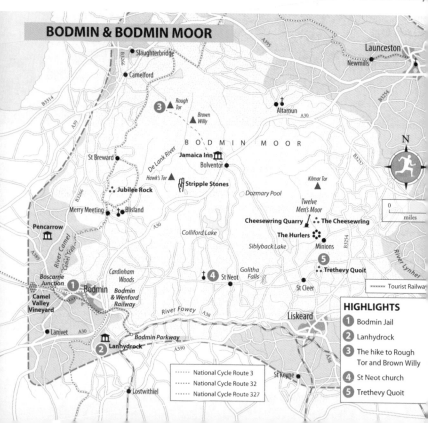

BODMIN & BODMIN MOOR

HIGHLIGHTS

1. Bodmin Jail
2. Lanhydrock
3. The hike to Rough Tor and Brown Willy
4. St Neot church
5. Trethevy Quoit

Courtroom Experience

Mount Folly, PL31 2DQ • Tours 11am–5pm: Easter–Oct Mon–Sat; Nov–Easter Mon–Fri; last tour at 4pm • £3.95 • ☎ 01208 76616

For a fairly prosaic town, Bodmin has quite a few dark secrets lurking. You can unearth one of them at the theatrical **Courtroom Experience**, located within the Shire House. Aided by film and moving waxworks, hour-long tours include a re-enactment of the trial of Matthew Weeks, indicted for the murder of Charlotte Dymond on Bodmin Moor in 1844, a verdict which was widely questioned at the time. Visitors are invited to cast their own vote at the end of the tour, and can visit the holding cells below the courtroom, their ambience enhanced by such refinements as the rancid smell of urine.

St Petroc

Priory Rd, PL31 2DT • April–Sept Mon–Fri 11am–3pm • Free • ⓦ st-petroc-bodmin.co.uk

At the bottom of Turf Road, Priory Road (A389) is dominated by the granite hulk of **St Petroc**, Cornwall's largest parish church. Mainly fifteenth-century but with its Perpendicular windows restored in the nineteenth century, its interior reveals a typical Cornish wagon roof embellished with fine bosses and, in a glass case embedded in the south wall, an ivory casket that once held the bones of Petroc (now lost). Between the chancel and the north chapel is the **Vyvian tomb**, a powerful recumbent effigy of one of the last priors of the abbey carved from black Catacleuse stone. The most striking item here, though, is the formidable **Norman font** near the entrance, its base resting on one column, and its bowl – encrusted with fearsome beasts and deeply carved with interlacing trees of life – supported by four others topped by impassive angels.

12

Bodmin Jail

Berrycombe Rd, PL31 2NR • Daily 10am–dusk • £6.50 • ☎ 01208 76292, ⓦ bodminjail.org

On the northern outskirts of town, **Bodmin Jail** is menacingly redolent of the executions that were once guaranteed to pull the crowds here – to such an extent that special trains were hired. After 1862 the hangings continued behind closed doors until the jail's closure in 1909. You can explore extensive sections of the original eighteenth-century structure, including the treadmills, the flogging posts and the condemned cell – a sombre and somewhat eerie experience in the austere, echoing surroundings. It's low-tech, with mannequins displayed in various poses within the cells, but the pinned-up stories of the inmates – many of them children incarcerated for such crimes as stealing milk from a cow – are chilling. There's also an atmospheric bar/restaurant here.

ARRIVAL AND DEPARTURE

BODMIN

By train Bodmin Parkway train station lies three and a half miles southeast of town, connected to the centre by bus #11A (Mon–Sat hourly, Sun 6 daily).

Destinations Liskeard (1–2 hourly; 12min); Penzance (1–2 hourly; 1hr 20min); Plymouth (1–2 hourly; 40min).

By bus The town's main bus stop is located on Mount Folly, close to the tourist office and the shopping area. Bus #11A provides access to the town from Padstow,

Liskeard and Wadebridge, and #27 from St Austell. National Express coaches stop at Priory Rd, near the church, if coming from the east, or at nearby Dennison Rd, if coming from the west.

Destinations Liskeard (Mon–Sat hourly, Sun every 2hr; 40min); Padstow (Mon–Sat hourly, Sun every 2hr; 45min); St Austell (Mon–Sat hourly, Sun 5 daily; 1hr); Wadebridge (Mon–Sat hourly, Sun 8 daily; 20min).

INFORMATION AND ACTIVITIES

Tourist office Shire Hall, Mount Folly (March–May & Oct Mon–Fri 8.45am–4pm, Sat 10am–5pm; June–Sept Mon–Fri 8.45am–5pm, Sat 10am–5pm; Nov–Feb Mon–Fri 8.45am–2pm; ☎ 01208 76616, ⓦ bodminlive.com). Has

an accommodation booking service (£3) and wi-fi, and sells National Express tickets.

Bike rental Bodmin Bikes, 3 Hamley Court, off Dennison Rd (☎ 01208 73192, ⓦ bodminbikes.co.uk; £14/day).

THE BEAST OF BODMIN MOOR

Of all the many myths and strange stories spawned on the moor, one of the most enduring has been that of the **Beast of Bodmin Moor**. Local farmers were the first to raise the issue of this phantom mauler of their livestock in the 1980s, and there have been around sixty big-cat sightings recorded in the area since then, as well as six-inch paw prints and cat droppings. Although an official investigation in 1995 could not confirm the existence of the so-called beast, some persuasive evidence emerged afterwards: a photograph taken in the St Austell area in 1997 apparently showing two creatures, one an adult female **puma**, possibly pregnant – or anyway looking "very fat, fit and contented" in the words of the curator of Newquay Zoo – and measuring about 2.5ft tall, the other possibly a cub; and a twenty-second video taken the following year that seemed to show a sleek, black animal about 3.5ft long. These two findings prompted a systematic trawl of the moor by **RAF reserve volunteers** in 1999, using state-of-the-art night vision and seismic equipment, but again they failed to unearth any positive proof. All the same, farmers have continued to lose sheep to what they maintain to be a large, savage creature, and there has been ongoing pressure to persuade the government to reopen the inquiry.

The farmers do not entirely lack support within the scientific community, however. Some scientists believe the moor could well be home to a species of wild cat thought to have become extinct, though others maintain that the mysterious beasts sighted in various parts of the country are probably escaped or abandoned **exotic pets**. The puma is the most popular candidate, while the lynx, which would be well suited to cold British weather, also has a strong claim, and it is even possible that jaguars could live in the wild in the British Isles (black-coloured varieties exist). Most likely of all, however, is that any big cat on the moor would be a hybrid – the result of different species **crossbreeding**. Such an animal could easily survive on a diet of rabbits and other mammals and would only attack sheep or other stock in extreme desperation. To date nobody has ever been attacked by a large cat on Bodmin Moor. If you chance to encounter one, your best bet is to walk nonchalantly by – but not before taking a precious photograph of the fabulous beast.

12

ACCOMMODATION

★**Bedknobs** Polgwyn, Castle St, PL31 2DX ☎01208 77553, ⊛ bedknobs.co.uk. A secluded Victorian villa in an acre of wooded garden, *Bedknobs* has three spacious and luxurious rooms; the priciest has its own en-suite "airbath", and all have fridges. Breakfasts are around a communal table. The hosts are friendly and eco-aware, and also offer a self-contained apartment (£630/week). **£95**

Bokiddick Farm Near Lanivet, PL30 5HP ☎01208 831481, ⊛ bokiddickfarm.co.uk. Five miles south of town, two miles outside the village of Lanivet and close to the Lanhydrock estate, this large working farm on the Saints Way boasts fantastic views from the conservatory/breakfast room. Three rooms, including a family room, adjoin the farmhouse or are in a converted barn, and there's also a self-catering option (£675/week). No under-5s. **£90**

Roscrea 18 St Nicholas St, PL31 1AD ☎01208 74400, ⊛ roscrea.co.uk. Central and friendly B&B with tasteful decor in three Victorian rooms full of personal touches. Breakfasts include eggs laid by hens in the garden, and you can request a great two-course dinner for £20 – a good option in Bodmin. No debit/credit cards. **£90**

★**Ruthern Valley** Ruthernbridge, PL30 5LU ☎01208 831395, ⊛ ruthernvalley.com. Three miles west of Bodmin, this secluded, wooded site has a range of accommodation available as well as tent pitches: pods (sleep 4), wooden "wigwams" (sleep 5), caravans (sleep 6, 2-night minimum stay £190), bungalows (sleep 6; 3-night minimum stay £345) and cabins (sleep 6; 3-night minimum stay £375). There's a shop, but no pub within easy walking distance. Bikes can be rented, and the Camel Trail's close by. Camping **£20**, pods **£43**, wigwams **£55**

EATING AND DRINKING

Bosvena Mount Folly, PL31 2DG ☎01208 264561, ⊛ bosvena.com. Bang opposite the tourist office, *Bosvena* is a handy spot for anything from breakfasts to light snacks and full meals. Evening mains include a good selection of seafood, such as roast hake, monkfish wrapped in pancetta, and seared scallops and prawns with risotto (£17–20). As well as the more casual downstairs area, there's an elegant dining room and a small courtyard. Mon–Sat 9am–11pm, last orders 9pm.

Chapel an Gansblydhen Fore St, PL31 2HR ☎01208 261730, ⊛ www.jdwetherspoon.co.uk. At the top of the main drag in a former Methodist chapel dating from 1840, this Wetherspoons pub has retained its atmospheric setting, and has outdoor tables and cheap food and beer all

day. Daily 8am–11pm; kitchen 8am–9.30pm.
Green Frog Café 14 Honey St, PL31 2DN ☎01208 72206. A relaxed spot in the shopping precinct across from St Petroc for breakfasts, panini, wraps and hot snacks (most items £4–7). Wine and beer are served and there's a small outdoor area and wi-fi. Mon–Sat: May–Sept 9.30am–4pm; Oct–April 9am–2pm.
Hole in the Wall 16 Crockwell St, off Fore St, PL31 2DS

☎01208 72397. This pub occupies a former debtors' prison, its exposed fourteenth-century walls now enclosing a collection of antiquities and bric-a-brac. You can enjoy bar food (dishes £7–14) and Doom Bar and Betty Stoggs bitters at the bar, in the upstairs restaurant or on the patio where a stuffed white lion stands sentinel. Kitchen Mon–Sat noon–2.30pm.

Around Bodmin

There are several easy excursions you can make from Bodmin without a car. Further up from Bodmin Jail, Berrycombe Road holds a section of the **Camel Trail** (see box, p.301), linking the town by a one-and-a-half-mile cycleway and footpath to the main route along the River Camel, a mile northwest. You can explore a section of the local area on the heritage **Bodmin & Wenford Railway**, which also offers access to **Cardinham Woods**. The magnificent home and grounds of **Lanhydrock** are easily reachable by bike or on foot, but a car would be useful for visiting two destinations northwest of town: the Georgian stately home of **Pencarrow** and the **Camel Valley Vineyard**, an essential stop for anyone with an interest in British wine in particular or wine-making in general.

Bodmin & Wenford Railway

Bodmin General Station, Harleigh Rd, PL31 1AG · June–Sept & school hols 4–7 daily; sporadic services at other times · £13, under-16s £6, valid all day · ☎01208 73555, ⓦ bodminrailway.co.uk
From Bodmin General station, a few minutes' walk south of the centre off the Lostwithiel road, the steam locomotives of the **Bodmin & Wenford Railway** run northwest to Boscarne Junction (right next to the Camel Trail; 15min) and southeast to Bodmin Parkway station (on the main rail line; 20min). Bodmin General station itself formerly served trains of the Great Western Railway and now has historic mementos dotted about, and offers steam enthusiasts the chance to watch the locomotives being restored in the Engine Shed.

Cardinham Woods

A couple of miles east of Bodmin, **Cardinham Woods** makes a lovely spot for a ramble and a picnic. Waymarked nature trails and cycle tracks wind through this mixed-forest plantation where Douglas fir is grown for the timber industry, and ravines and small streams run down to the main river, Cardinham Water, where there's a small clapper bridge. Deer roam the woods, buzzards wheel overhead, and if you're very lucky you may even catch sight of an otter.
One rewarding way to access the woods is from **Colesloggett Halt**, a stop on the Bodmin & Wenford Railway between Bodmin General and Bodmin Parkway, from where there's a half-mile path.

Lanhydrock

PL30 5AD · **House** March & Oct daily 11am–5pm; April–Sept daily 11am–5.30pm; Nov Sat & Sun 11am–4pm; Dec daily 11am–4pm · £12.65, £7 in winter (includes grounds); NT · **Grounds** Daily dawn–dusk · £7.70, £4 in winter; NT · ☎01208 265950, ⓦ nationaltrust .org.uk/lanhydrock · A walk signposted from Bodmin Parkway station leads less than two miles west to Lanhydrock, and National Cycle Route 3 passes right outside
Perhaps the greatest of Cornwall's country houses, **Lanhydrock** was originally constructed in the seventeenth century, but was totally rebuilt after a disastrous fire in

12

1881. Consequently, much of the house is High Victorian in tone, though the imposing pinnacled gatehouse, most of the granite exterior and the north wing remain true to their original form.

You're free to wander at will around the fifty rooms, where the grand style in which the local Robartes family lived is best illustrated by the quantities of equipment in the nurseries, luggage room, linen lobby and livery room. Most illuminating of all is the **kitchen**, built in the style of a college hall with clerestory windows, and supplemented by an unending series of dairies, sculleries, larders and pantries – and there's even a spit large enough to roast an entire cow. The showpiece of the house, however, is in the north wing, mostly unscathed from the nineteenth-century fire, where a long **picture gallery** on the first floor has a remarkable barrel-vaulted plaster ceiling depicting 24 Old Testament scenes. Note that some rooms are closed in winter. In the north wing, a small **museum** shows sundry photographs and letters relating to the family.

Outside, the thousand acres of gardens and wooded **parkland** bordering the River Fowey are worth a prolonged wander, especially in spring for the spectacular beds of magnolias, azaleas and rhododendrons. A leaflet available at the entrance details the choice of walks you can take.

Pencarrow

Washaway, PL30 3AG · **House tours** Late March to Sept Mon–Thurs & Sun 11am–5pm; last tour 3pm · £10.75 (includes gardens) · **Gardens** March–Oct daily 10am–5.30pm · £5.75 · ☎ 01208 841369, ⓦ pencarrow.co.uk

The mile-long drive at **Pencarrow**, three miles north of Bodmin, might suggest something on the same scale as Lanhydrock, but this country house has a very different, more intimate feel. The Georgian building was begun by Sir John Molesworth, co-founder in 1771 of the banking house that was the forerunner of Lloyds Bank (a portrait of him by Joshua Reynolds is one of many paintings on display here). The present scions of the family have stamped their personality on the house by jauntily placing hats on the busts of the various worthies, though the exquisite carpets and furnishings are what make the deepest impression. **Guided tours** give you the lowdown on the family's history and point out items such as the piano on which Sir Arthur Sullivan, a guest here in 1882, composed much of the music for *Iolanthe*. Leave time to explore the beautiful wooded grounds.

Camel Valley Vineyard

Nanstallon, PL30 5LG · **Vineyard** 10am–5pm: Easter–Sept Mon–Sat; Oct–Easter Mon–Fri · Free · **Tours** 2.30pm: April–Sept Mon–Fri; Oct Mon, Tues, Thurs & Fri; 1hr · £8.50 · **Grand tours** 5pm: April–July, Sept & Oct Wed; Aug Wed & Thurs; 1hr 30min · £15 · ☎ 01208 77959, ⓦ camelvalley.com

Signposted off the A389 Wadebridge road three miles northwest of Bodmin, and easily accessible from the Camel Trail, the **Camel Valley Vineyard** produces some of the region's finest dry white, rosé and sparkling wines. The Lindo family started here in 1989 and now cultivate some 24,000 vines on their south-facing estate – their Cornish Brut and Bacchus wines rival French Champagne and Sancerre. Instructive **tours** of the vineyard and winery end with a tasting (the more expensive Grand Tour has a more in-depth, tutored sampling). If you don't want the tour, you can just stop by to have a glass with olives and grissini on the terrace, or to purchase a bottle or crate.

Blisland and around

Four and a half miles northeast of Bodmin, **BLISLAND**, tucked into the Camel valley on the western slopes of Bodmin Moor, is mostly interesting for its Norman **church**, which sits among the Georgian and Victorian houses scattered around the village green. It has the distinction of being the only one in England dedicated to St Protus and St

> ## DOZMARY POOL: LEGEND AND LITERATURE
>
> According to Arthurian mythology, **Dozmary Pool**, lying at the centre of the moor 1.5 miles south of **Bolventor**, was where Sir Bedivere hurled the sword **Excalibur** at the bidding of King Arthur, to be seized by an arm raised from the depths – Loe Pool, on the Lizard peninsula, also claims the honour (see p.235). The diamond-shaped lake usually preserves an ethereal air, though it's been known to run dry in summer, dealing a bit of a blow to the legend that the pool is bottomless.
>
> The lake is also the source of another, more obviously Cornish, myth, concerning **John Tregeagle**, a steward at Lanhydrock in the seventeenth century, whose unjust dealings with the local tenant farmers are supposed to have resulted in a curse condemning his spirit to endlessly baling out the pool with a perforated limpet shell. As if this were not enough, his ghost is said to be further tormented by a swarm of devils that pursue him as he flies across the moor in search of sanctuary; their infernal howling is claimed to be audible on windy nights.
>
> One possible access point for hikers to the lake is from *Jamaica Inn*, outside Bolventor off the A30. In a previous incarnation the inn was described in **Daphne du Maurier**'s novel of the same name as being "alone in glory, four square to the winds", but it's now a popular coach stop, stripped of any vestigial romance.

Hyacinth, brothers who were martyred in the third century. Sensitively restored at the end of the nineteenth century, the church has a seventeenth-century carved pulpit and a startlingly colourful Victorian Gothic rood screen, while overhead, the beams of the wagon roof are as wildly wonky as the columns in the nave.

Jubilee Rock

You can make an easy and rewarding ramble less than half a mile north of the village to the gigantic **Jubilee Rock** on Pendrift Common, reached along a signposted and well-trodden path across the moor. The rock is inscribed with various patriotic insignia commemorating the 1809 jubilee of George III's coronation, but the view from this 700ft vantage point is the main attraction, looking eastward over the De Lank gorge and the boulder-crowned knoll of **Hawk's Tor**, three miles away. On the shoulder of the tor stand the Neolithic **Stripple Stones**, a circular platform once holding 28 standing stones, of which just four are still upright.

Blisland also lies less than a mile east of the **Merry Meeting** crossroads, a point near the end of the Camel Trail (see box, p.301).

ACCOMMODATION AND EATING | BLISLAND AND AROUND

Blisland Inn The Green, PL30 4JF ☎01208 850739. Traditional village pub on the green, serving eight real ales on tap, including Blisland Bulldog, as well as Cornish fruit wine, bar snacks (£6–8) and full meals (£8–15), with daily changing specials. The interior is festooned with mugs, jugs and pump clips, it has outdoor tables, and there's live music most Saturdays. Kitchen Mon–Sat noon–2pm & 6.30–9pm, Sun noon–2pm.

★**South Penquite** PL30 4LH ☎01208 850491, ⓦsouthpenquite.co.uk. The best campsite locally lies two and a half miles north of Blisland on the St Breward road. A working organic farm with a strong environmental slant, it offers camping pitches plus yurts (sleep 5; available mid-May to Sept) with futons, a woodburner and a stove, plus bunkhouses and a pod sleeping two (available all year). The owners know everything there is to know about Bodmin Moor. Camping closed Nov–Easter. Camping/person £9, yurts £70, pod £40, bunks £15

Altarnun

Three miles northeast of Bolventor off the A30, **ALTARNUN** is a pretty, granite-grey village snugly sheltered beneath the eastern heights of the moor. Its ancient **church** is the main attraction here, situated by a picturesque packhorse bridge over Penpont Water, but its secluded lanes are also worth a wander, the front doors of the cottages approached by slate slabs across a trickling stream. The village is fictionally famous as the home of the albino vicar Francis Davey, head of the "wreckers" who lured ships to their doom in Daphne du Maurier's novel *Jamaica Inn*.

St Nonna

PL15 7SJ • Daily 10am–5pm • Free • ☎ 01579 320472

The fifteenth-century church of **St Nonna** has been dubbed the "cathedral of the moors" on account of its lofty west tower and spacious interior. The church is dedicated to the mother of David, the patron saint of Wales, after whom the village is named ("altar of Non"). Its fine, solid Norman **font** was the prototype of the dozen or so "Altarnun fonts" in the area, characterized by their square shape, with geometric flowers surrounded by snakes on the four sides and rugged faces at the corners.

The highlight of the church, however, is the superb set of 79 **bench-ends** carved at the beginning of the sixteenth century, boldly depicting secular and sacred subjects – saints, musicians, clowns, moorland sheep and even a bagpipe player. Some of the slate **memorials** in the churchyard were carved by local sculptor Nevil Northey Burnard, also responsible for the effigy of John Wesley, the co-founder of Methodism, over the door of the Methodist chapel on the village's main street.

ARRIVAL AND DEPARTURE   ALTARNUN

By bus Service #425 connects Altarnun with Launceston (Mon–Sat 3 daily; 35min).

12

Launceston

Cornwall's capital until 1835, **LAUNCESTON** still retains much of its original architecture, overlaid with a sedate, well-to-do charm. Situated less than a mile from the Devon border, it was, until the construction of its bypass forty years ago, literally the "Gateway to Cornwall", since all traffic entering the county here passed through the narrow twelfth-century **Southgate Arch** – the last remaining of the three original gateways to the county's only walled town.

Launceston Castle

Castle Lodge, PL15 7DR • Daily: Late March to Sept 10am–6pm; Oct 10am–5pm • £4; EH • ☎ 01566 772365, ⓦ www.english-heritage
.org.uk/visit/places/launceston-castle

Launceston developed around its **castle**, which still dominates the skyline from the top of a grassy mound just west of the centre, though all that now remains is the rough-hewn cylindrical keep and round curtain walls. In the thirteenth century this was the chief fortress of Richard, earl of Cornwall and brother of Henry III, but it later fell into decay until repaired by the Black Prince. The sweeping views from the top stretch from Bodmin Moor to Dartmoor. In a sturdy cell near the castle's north gate, **George Fox**, founder of the Society of Friends, or Quakers, was imprisoned in 1656 for "disturbing the peace" in St Ives. Launceston had earlier taken a stand against religious dissenters when St Cuthbert Mayne was hung, drawn and quartered in its main square in 1577 – the first Roman Catholic seminary priest to be executed in England.

Lawrence House Museum

9 Castle St, PL15 8BA • April–Oct Mon–Fri 10.30am–4.30pm • Free • ☎ 01566 773277, ⓦ lawrencehousemuseum.org.uk

North of the castle, Castle Street was described by John Betjeman as the finest Georgian street in Cornwall. Its graceful red-brick buildings include Lawrence House,

GOLITHA FALLS (P.330) >

built in 1753 and now holding the **Lawrence House Museum**, whose three floors are packed with interest: portraits, period furnishings, a polyphon (an early version of a record player) from the 1880s, a reconstructed Victorian kitchen and a collection of Victorian costumes including wedding gowns and mourning clothes. There are also items relating to **John Couch Adams** (1819–92), co-discoverer of the planet Neptune and born in nearby Lidcot, and **Charles Causley** (1917–2003), one of Cornwall's most celebrated poets, who was born, lived and died in Launceston.

HIKING TO ROUGH TOR AND BROWN WILLY

One of the best hikes on Bodmin Moor, and one which can be accomplished without too much difficulty, is to its two highest peaks: **Rough Tor** (locally pronounced Row – to rhyme with "cow" – Tor; 1311ft) and **Brown Willy** (1378ft), accessible either from Camelford or the hotel and pub outside Bolventor, *Jamaica Inn*. The forbidding landscape was the setting for the final climactic scenes of Daphne du Maurier's novel, *Jamaica Inn*. Though the ascents don't present particular hazards, you'll need suitable clothing and footwear, and a good map, such as OS *Explorer* OL109. Do not attempt the walks in poor visibility.

FROM CAMELFORD

Rough Tor (map ref SX146808) lies about a mile south of the car park at Rough Tor Ford, which is three miles southeast of Camelford and reachable on foot or by car from Rough Tor Road, a right turn off Victoria Road at Camelford's northern end. From the bridge over the stream below the car park, walk about a mile over springy turf and a well-worn trail, past a stone monument to Charlotte Dymond (see p.321) and the three boulders of **Showery Tor** (map ref SX149813), before bearing left along the ridge to the slight elevation of **Little Rough Tor** (map ref SX138817). From here, continue in a southeasterly direction to the summit, a gentle but steady uphill trudge over the heath, as often as not accompanied by a biting wind. The sides of Rough Tor are very rocky and the path on the last stretch is not well defined, so care is needed. The piles of flat, precariously balanced rocks crowning the summit present a different aspect from every angle – an ungainly mass from the south, and a nobly proportioned mountain from the west – and were described by Daphne du Maurier as "shaped like giant furniture with monstrous chairs and twisted tables". Nearby are the ruins of a medieval chapel, and the whole area is scattered with Bronze Age remains.

Originally named Bronewhella, or "highest hill", Bodmin's loftiest peak, **Brown Willy** (map ref SX159800), is easily visible less than a mile and a half to the southeast of Rough Tor. Brown Willy, too, shows various faces, its sugarloaf appearance from the north sharpening into a long, multi-peaked crest as you approach. To reach it, continue from the summit of Rough Tor in a southeasterly direction towards a ruined building near which a bridge crosses the upper reaches of the De Lank River. From here the ascent is clearly marked, with the final stretch along a steep but well-defined track. From the summit, the highest point in Cornwall, you get a grand panorama of the rock-strewn, green-and-brown patchwork of high moorland on all sides. Both Rough Tor and Brown Willy can be climbed in a couple of hours (round trip) from the car park.

FROM JAMAICA INN

Brown Willy can also be accessed from *Jamaica Inn*, outside Bolventor – a three-and-a-quarter-mile walk. Turning left out of the car park, follow the old road down the hill, and take the second turning on the left under the A30. From here, take the first turning on the right, then first left, walking along this road for 150yd until you see a signed footpath on the right. Follow this path for the length of three fields until it becomes a broader track, and continue up this, bearing to the right of the buildings in front of you, from where a lane leads to a gate after 750yd. Pass through the gate and onto the moorland, bearing right for 250yd to **Tolborough Tor** (map ref SX175778), the highest point on the surrounding downs and a mile from *Jamaica Inn* as the crow flies (but more like 1.5 miles walking). From here, Brown Willy is clearly visible under two miles to the northwest across bare moor. Walk towards it for another 250yd to a gate, beyond which you should continue for another mile and a half with a wire fence on your left, crossing this over a stile and then climbing the steep slopes of the tor. Allow three to four hours for the whole walk.

12

St Mary Magdalene

Church St, PL15 8AR • Mon–Fri 10am–4pm, Sat 10am–noon, Sun open for services • Free • ⓣ 01566 772771

Launceston's church of **St Mary Magdalene** is unique in England for its prolifically carved exterior walls – no mean feat, considering the unyielding qualities of granite. Completed in 1524, the church was commissioned by one Henry Trecarrel, whose coat of arms and that of his wife can be seen on the upper storey of the south porch, among a profusion of leaves, quatrefoils, pomegranates and heraldic shields. The recumbent figure of Mary Magdalene is carved into the east wall, the subject of a poem by Charles Causley; according to local lore, if you throw a stone over your shoulder and it lands on the effigy's back, you will receive good luck. Highlights inside the church include the fine Perpendicular pulpit that was vandalized by Cromwell's troops – and later restored – and the contrasting Art Nouveau, carved bench-ends.

Launceston Steam Railway

St Thomas Rd, PL15 8DA • 11am–4pm: Easter, late May, July–Sept & late Oct Mon–Fri & Sun; June Mon, Tues & Sun • £10.50, valid all day • ⓣ 01566 775665, ⓦ launcestonsr.co.uk

From the station just west of the castle, **Launceston Steam Railway** runs frequent five-mile round trips to Newmills through the Kensey valley on the original Waterloo to Padstow line. The narrow-gauge steam locomotives, built in the 1880s and 1890s, formerly worked in the slate quarries of North Wales. There are also veteran cars and motorcycles on show in the small transport museum here (same hours; free).

12

ARRIVAL AND INFORMATION — LAUNCESTON

By bus Stops for the #12 to Plymouth (Mon–Sat 1–2 hourly, Sun every 2hr; 1hr 25min), #425 to Altarnun (Mon–Fri 4 daily; 35min), #236 to Liskeard (Mon–Fri 4 daily; 40min–1hr) and #410 to Camelford (Mon–Sat 3 daily; 30min) are on Westgate St.

Tourist information Market House Arcade, Market St (Easter–Oct Mon–Fri 9am–5pm, Sat 10am–4pm; Nov–Easter Mon–Fri 9am–5pm, Sat 10am–1pm; ⓣ 01566 772321, ⓦ visitlaunceston.co.uk).

ACCOMMODATION AND EATING

Jericho's Kitchen 4 Northgate St, PL15 8BD ⓣ 01566 770080, ⓦ jerichoskitchen.co.uk. Upstairs in the old Liberal Club behind St Mary Magdalene, this roomy place with sofas and big windows makes a great daytime stop for sandwiches, a frittata or just a cup of tea, or for a dinner of lamb rump, duck breast, salmon or chicken (£14–17). Mon–Wed 11.45am–3.30pm, Thurs–Sat 11.45am–3.30pm & 6.30–9pm.

Rose Cottage 5 Lower Cleaverfield, PL15 8ED ⓣ 01566 779292, ⓦ rosecottagecornwall.co.uk. North of the centre off the A388 Dutson Rd, this pretty B&B has three rooms – one a single (£38) – with great views of Launceston and the Kensey valley and a good vegetarian breakfast option. The centre is accessed via a steep hill. No under-10s. Packed lunches and a luggage transfer service are available. **£78**

St Neot and around

Seven miles east of Bodmin and reachable from the A38 two miles south, **ST NEOT** makes a good entry point for the southern tracts of Bodmin Moor. As one of the moor's prettiest villages, it also strongly merits a visit in its own right, not least for its fifteenth-century **church**.

St Neot church

PL14 6NG • Daily: Easter–Sept 9am–5pm; Oct–Easter 10am–4pm • Free • ⓣ 01579 320216, ⓦ saintneot.church

You'll find some of the most impressive medieval stained-glass windows of any parish church in the country at **St Neot church**. The set begins with the oldest glass, at the east end of the south aisle, where the fifteenth-century **Creation Window** shows God with mathematical instruments and Seth planting in Adam's mouth the seeds from which the wood of the Cross will grow. The first window in the south aisle, **Noah's Window**, continues the sequence with lively scenes of the ark as a sixteenth-century sailing ship. However, the narration soon dissolves into windows portraying saints and – due to the need of sponsorship when the money ran out – patrons and local bigwigs, as well as the ordinary men and women of the village.

ACCOMMODATION AND EATING   **ST NEOT**

Lampen Farm PL14 6PB ☎ 01579 320284, ⊛ lampen -farm.co.uk. Local accommodation options in the village are limited, but this one, signposted 350yd down a track below the village car park, is a perfect choice – a sixteenth-century farmhouse with Victorian furnishings, three spacious rooms with en-suite or private bathrooms, a lounge and a huge garden. No credit cards. **£85**

London Inn School Hill, PL14 6NG ☎ 01579 326728, ⊛ thelondoninnstneot.com. Next door to the church, this pub provides a cosy setting for Cornish ales, sandwiches and bar meals for around £10. Good-sized rooms are also available. Kitchen Mon–Sat noon–3pm & 6–8.30pm, Sun noon–3pm. **£85**

Golitha Falls

The southern edge of Bodmin Moor is far greener and more thickly wooded than the north due to the confluence of a web of **rivers** into the Fowey, which tumble through the **Golitha Falls**. One of the moor's best-known beauty spots, located below Draynes Bridge a couple of miles east of St Neot, this is actually more a series of rapids than a waterfall, enlivened by the dippers and wagtails that flit through the surrounding beech trees.

Siblyback Lake and around

Just over a mile to the northeast of Golitha Falls, **Siblyback Lake** – actually a dammed reservoir – is an attractive expanse of water surrounded by rolling hills and used for boating and fishing. There's a rewarding woodland walk here from the falls: follow the river up to Draynes Bridge, then walk north up a minor road until a path branches off on the right after a half-mile, leading down to the water's edge.

North of Siblyback Lake, and reachable from the B3254 Launceston road, **Twelve Men's Moor** holds some of Bodmin Moor's grandest landscapes. Though they appear enormous from the north, **Hawk's Tor** (1079ft) and lower **Trewartha Tor** actually have quite modest elevations, and are topped in height by **Kilmar Tor** (1280ft), the highest of the hills on the moor's eastern flank.

Liskeard and around

Off the southern limits of the moor, **LISKEARD** is a small, hilly town worth a brief wander, with a couple of decent pubs and snack stops. It's a useful bus and rail junction at the head of the East Looe valley, connected by a branch line with Looe, on the coast (see p.200).

Magnificent Music Machines

Mill House, St Keyne, PL14 4SH • Easter–Oct daily 11am–4pm • Free, but donations suggested • ☎ 01579 343108, ⊛ pianolarepairs.co.uk

Entertainment and instruction are on hand at **Magnificent Music Machines**, an unusual exhibition of pianolas and a Wurlitzer cinema organ from 1929, three miles south of Liskeard in St Keyne (a request stop on the train line to Looe, and signposted off the B3254). A half-hour's enthusiastic tour includes a demonstration on the Wurlitzer.

12

PREHISTORIC BODMIN MOOR

Four miles north of Liskeard, Cornwall's highest village, Minions, makes a good departure point for exploring a cluster of the moor's important **prehistoric remains**. To get to the closest of these, follow the signposted path a few steps west of the centre of Minions, which brings you after a quarter-mile to **The Hurlers**, a wide complex of three stone circles dating from about 1500 BC. The purpose of these stark upright stones is not known, though local lore declares them to be men turned to stone for playing the Celtic game of hurling on the Sabbath. Following the path a further half-mile or so north, **Stowe's Hill** has a top-of-the-world wilderness feel and is the site of Bodmin Moor's most famous stone pile, **The Cheesewring** (map ref SX258724), a precarious pillar of flat, balancing granite slabs that have been weirdly eroded by the wind to resemble a hamburger in a peaked cap. Gouged out of the hillside nearby, the disused **Cheesewring Quarry** is a centre for rock climbing.

    Trethevy Quoit (map ref SX259688) is another Bronze Age survivor, a chamber tomb 15ft high and surmounted by a massive capstone. Originally enclosed in earth, the slabs have been stripped by centuries of weathering to create Cornwall's most impressive megalithic monument. The quoit lies three miles south of Minions and less than half a mile south of the village of Darite, off the Tremar road.

    There's no direct bus to Minions, but the #74 from Liskeard calls at St Cleer (Mon–Sat 9 daily; 10min) and Darite (Mon–Sat 9 daily; 15min), both of which are close to Trethevy Quoit; alternatively, it's a three-mile walk from Liskeard.

ARRIVAL AND DEPARTURE
LISKEARD

By train On the main Plymouth–Penzance line and the starting-point for the branch line to Looe, Liskeard's station lies a few minutes south of town, over the A38 bridge.
Destinations Bodmin (hourly; 40min); Looe (hourly; April–Oct daily, Nov–March Mon–Sat; 30min); Plymouth (hourly; 25min).

By bus Liskeard's main bus and coach stops are on Barras St. Bus #11A connects the town with Bodmin, and the infrequent #283 with St Neot.
Destinations Bodmin (Mon–Sat hourly, Sun 7 daily; 40min); St Neot (Mon–Sat 2 daily; 20–30min).

12

ACCOMMODATION AND EATING

Fat Frog 6a Market St, PL14 3JJ ☎01579 348818. This colourful, child-friendly café with comfy sofas offers all-day breakfasts, panini, burgers and seafood and vegetarian dishes (mostly £5–9), plus wi-fi. Mon–Sat 8.30am–6pm, Sun 10am–3pm.

Pencubitt House Lamellion Cross, PL14 4EB ☎01579 342694, ⓦpencubitt.com. A grand Victorian guesthouse on the southern outskirts of town (but just a few minutes' walk from the train station), this has a central castellated tower and wonderful views over the Looe valley. Quality meals can be requested (£22.50 for two courses). No under-15s. **£79**

LANYON QUOIT

Contexts

History

Remote from England's main centres of political and industrial activity, the counties of Devon and Cornwall have played a largely peripheral role in the country's history. The region has been most pre-eminent in matters related to the sea, namely fishing, smuggling and buccaneering, while inland, Devon's cloth industry and Cornwall's mines provided a solid economic base for centuries.

Prehistory

The first evidence of human settlement in the region is from around 40,000 BC – a teenager's jawbone found in **Kents Cavern**, Torquay – but the subsequent prehistory of the region is a succession of long blanks of which next to nothing is known. In general, however, it seems likely that England's westernmost counties shared the same experiences as other parts of the land, the scattered tribes relying on hunting and gathering, with a rudimentary social organization. In common with the rest of England, the region was settled by Neolithic tribes from mainland Europe during the fourth millennium BC, who introduced relatively advanced domestic and industrial skills. Strangely, despite the unearthing of large quantities of flints and arrowheads from Neolithic sites, relics of habitation are paltry, though Cornwall has numerous examples of quoits (chambered tombs set in open country with a giant slab, or capstone, for a roof). The beginnings of cereal cultivation and livestock farming are also traced to this period.

Bronze Age settlement

More prolific are finds associated with the **Bronze Age** peoples who began to arrive on the scene during the second millennium BC. These tribes left a rich legacy of granite menhirs, kistvaens, stone rows, stone circles and hut circles throughout the region – more than 1200 barrows (burial mounds) have been discovered in Devon alone, of which a significant number lie on Dartmoor. In Cornwall, remains are concentrated particularly on the Isles of Scilly, the Penwith peninsula and Bodmin Moor, where the Hurlers, a complex of three circles from about 1500 BC, represent a fine example. Most of these sites were rifled centuries ago, and the surviving artefacts have yielded frustratingly little information about the lives and social structures of the people who occupied them.

The Celts

In around 500 BC, another wave of immigrants, the **Celts**, established themselves in the region, bringing with them weapons and tools made of iron. Much given to tribal wars, the Celts constructed sturdy hillforts throughout the peninsula; the best-preserved relic from these times is the village of Chysauster in Penwith, dating from

39,000 BC	50–55 AD	501–600	926
The earliest traces of *Homo sapiens* in northwestern Europe – a fossilized jawbone – found at Kents Cavern, Torquay.	Romans occupy Exeter.	Celts resist the incoming Saxons – the conflict was probably the source of the King Arthur legends.	The Saxons complete their conquest of Cornwall, though without much settlement in the area.

around the first century BC and occupied until long after. Good examples of the form and layout of the fields farmed in these times still exist hereabouts: notably the small, stone-hedged field systems around Zennor.

Roman settlement and the Dark Ages

Recorded history begins with the coming of the **Romans**, who occupied Exeter (or, as they called it, Isca Dumnoniorum) in the first century AD but did not venture much further west. Little interested in this extremity of their empire, the Romans left few traces in Devon and Cornwall, content to establish a strong military presence in Exeter to keep an eye on the Celtic tribes who were left to their own devices further west. Although the region as a whole benefited from the *Pax Romana*, Roman ways were never greatly assimilated, as far as historians can tell, and the Roman interlude left less of an impression here than on most other areas of the country.

The accelerating disintegration of the Roman Empire towards the end of the fourth century led to the withdrawal of the legions and a rapid reversion to pre-Roman practices in the West Country. Almost immediately, incursions were made by the **Saxons**, a Germanic people who settled in much of the region during the sixth and seventh centuries. The invaders were at first unable – or unwilling – to subdue the Britons in the far west, however, making an unconquered enclave of Cornwall. Consequently, while the rest of the country was experiencing the "**Dark Ages**", Cornwall, as the last stronghold of Celtic resistance in England and the torch-bearer of Christianity, enjoyed something of a golden age, during which much of the county's rich folklore originated. In this scantily recorded era, saints and mystics were said to wander the pilgrimage routes between Wales, Ireland and Brittany, and the various strands of the **Arthurian saga** were first woven together – probably based on the exploits of a Celtic chieftain resisting the Saxons. The county's isolation aided the survival of the Celtic tongue, and while **Cornish** has not been spoken as a living language since the eighteenth century, Celtic place names are still much in evidence today.

The Saxons, Danes and Normans

Cornwall was not fully conquered by the Saxons until the time of Athelstan in around 926. In Devon, the local Dumnonii more readily absorbed the Saxon newcomers who, by the **eighth century**, were at least nominally Christians. Much of the work of converting the Saxons was undertaken by such individuals as St Boniface (c.680–754), born Wynfrith in Crediton, who went on to spread the faith in Devon and later among the Frisians in Germany and the Lowlands. The integration of Saxons and Celts was further strengthened by the need to confront the threat of **Danish raids** that afflicted the region, in common with the rest of the country, during the **ninth and tenth centuries**. Unlike in other regions, however, there was little Viking settlement in the West, but a constant skirmishing between invading armies and the forces of the West Saxons under Alfred the Great and his descendants. The Danes occupied Exeter for the last time in 1003, but the Anglo-Saxon state was not to last much longer, for the entire region was shortly to be absorbed into the new Norman kingdom following William the Conqueror's capture of Exeter in 1068.

1068	**1133**	**1497**
A Norman garrison is stationed at Exeter.	Exeter Cathedral is consecrated, having been built by the Normans on the site of an earlier Anglo-Saxon minster.	Uprisings against taxation and the centralizing tendencies of the new Tudor state – the Cornish Rebellion and Warbeck's Rebellion – are both suppressed.

THE ORIGINS OF MINING IN CORNWALL

Although Cornwall played a comparatively minor part in the cloth trade during the Middle Ages, it had a much larger role in the region's **mining** industry. Tin had been extracted here since prehistoric times, when it was alloyed with copper – also found in the region – to make bronze. Though the Romans do not appear to have utilized the resource, the greater level of protection and organization that existed under the Normans made Cornwall Europe's biggest supplier of tin in the twelfth century. Over the next hundred years Helston, Lostwithiel, Truro and Liskeard in Cornwall, plus Ashburton and Tavistock in Devon were made **Stannary towns**, according to which they were granted special privileges and placed by the Crown under the separate legal jurisdiction of the Stannary (tin mine) courts. Stannary towns were visited twice a year by officials from London who came to test the smelted tin, chipping a corner if it was approved – "coigning" it, from the French for "corner", hence the English word *coin*.

The Middle Ages

The **Normans** built castles at Exeter, Totnes, Okehampton, Restormel and Launceston, which acted as nuclei for the growth of towns. This urban development was also spurred on by the **cloth trade**; this was Devon's principal industry at the time, and continued to be so throughout the medieval and early modern periods. Wool from the county's fertile inland pastures was processed locally or in the towns, and exported to mainland Europe from the great estuary ports of the south coast. This established both a robust rural economy and a strong mercantile class in towns such as Topsham, Totnes and Dartmouth. Exeter's primacy in Devon was assured when the bishopric was transferred here from Crediton in 1050, and the great cathedral constructed in the twelfth century.

In Cornwall, the existing Saxon manors were taken over by the Normans to form the basis of an earldom, which was granted to Edward III's son, the Black Prince, in 1337; since then, the earldom has belonged traditionally to the eldest son of the English sovereign, who acts as duke of Cornwall. On the whole, the Norman yoke was accepted here, the greater links with France and centralized economy promoting commerce and the growth of inland ports such as Truro and Fowey.

After farming and mining, the third most important activity in Devon and Cornwall was **fishing**, and many of the ports of the southern coast in particular – such as Beer, Brixham, Polperro and Mevagissey – have retained their medieval layout. In 1272, however, the imposition of custom duties for the first time gave birth to another lucrative spin-off that existed side-by-side with fishing – **smuggling**, for which the inlets and estuaries proved ideal terrain. The activity was to carry on until well into the nineteenth century, and there are even echoes of it in the present era, with shipments of illegal drugs regularly apprehended off the peninsula's coasts.

Popular rebellions

While the region had consolidated its wealth in comparative peace during the later part of the Middle Ages, the **fifteenth and sixteenth centuries** saw Devon and Cornwall increasingly drawn into the turmoil of national events. Stirrings of **revolt** against the new, centralizing Tudor state surfaced in 1497 when Thomas Flamank, a Bodmin

1549	1577–1580	1588
The suppression of the Prayer Book Rebellion, which originated in Sampford Courtenay, near Dartmoor, in reaction to the imposition of a new church liturgy.	Sir Francis Drake sets out from Plymouth to circumnavigate the world.	The Spanish Armada is defeated, with much of the credit due to the actions of Drake and his Plymouth-based fleet.

lawyer, and Michael Joseph, a blacksmith from the Lizard area, led 15,000 Cornishmen to London to protest against high taxation. By the time the force arrived at Blackheath, they were much depleted and easily crushed by Henry VII's army. However, the rejection of the rebels' demands and the execution of their leaders ensured that resentment continued to simmer in Cornwall. This created widespread support for **Perkin Warbeck**, who landed at Whitesand Bay near Land's End just three months later, claiming to be Richard, Duke of York – one of the disappeared "Princes in the Tower" who had in fact probably been dispatched by Richard III in 1483. Warbeck received a rapturous welcome in Bodmin and attracted some support from local gentry who proclaimed the pretender Richard IV. Crossing the Tamar in September 1497, however, the rebels failed to take Exeter and Warbeck's army melted away when confronted by the king's forces at Taunton.

A further revolt took place in 1549 against the Act of Uniformity and its insistence on the Book of Common Prayer, and the simplified service in English rather than the old Latin Mass – a particular aggravation to the non-English-speaking Cornish. The **Prayer Book Rebellion** began in the village of Sampford Courtenay, near Okehampton, and drew support in both Devon and Cornwall. In the end the rebels were defeated in battle at Clyst St Mary, outside Topsham, by Lord Russell – who happened to be the principal beneficiary of dissolved monastery lands in the West Country.

The Tudor navy

As England's defence came to rely more heavily on its maritime prowess, and trade began to focus increasingly on the Atlantic, Devon assumed an important naval role. It was not just the county's geographical position that accounted for its growing significance: some of the greatest mariners of the age – Drake, Grenville and Raleigh, among others – were born and bred in Devon, and all were to take a leading part in the defence of the realm and the expansion of trade to the Americas. Less to their credit, all were also involved in piracy and slavery.

Francis Drake (c.1540–96), born near Tavistock, was plundering the coast of Guinea and the Spanish Main when he was only in his twenties, becoming a popular hero on his return to Plymouth, of which he later became mayor. **Walter Raleigh** (1552–1618), born in Hayes Barton, East Devon, also indulged in piratical activities in addition to his attempts to colonize America, and represented the county in parliament. His cousin **Richard Grenville** (1542–91) commanded the fleet that carried English colonists to Roanoke Island in present-day North Carolina in 1585, and died heroically against overwhelming odds in a celebrated tussle with a Spanish treasure fleet in the Azores – his ship, the *Revenge*, was crewed by "men of Bideford in Devon". Grenville's preparations for a voyage of discovery to the South Pacific were adopted by Drake when the latter circumnavigated the world in 1577–80, the first Englishman to do so.

As the home port of these and other maritime adventurers, **Plymouth** became the western centre of Britain's maritime power and remains a prominent base for the Royal Navy today. Devonport Dockyard here is still one of the area's biggest employers, while **Appledore** on the northern coast also continues its centuries-old shipbuilding activities – though on a much reduced and increasingly precarious scale.

1595	1642–1647	1710	1743–1786
Mousehole, Newlyn and Penzance are torched by the Spanish.	First English Civil War engulfs Devon and Cornwall.	Thomas Newcomen from Dartmouth devises the first steam engine for pumping water out of mines.	The great Methodist evangelist John Wesley spreads the word in Devon and Cornwall.

THREATS FROM ABROAD

Throughout the late fifteenth and sixteenth centuries, defences on the south coast of Devon and Cornwall were strengthened against French and Spanish raids, with fortifications erected or expanded in Dartmouth, Fowey, St Mawes, Falmouth and St Mary's, on the Isles of Scilly. The ever-present fear of Spanish invasion during the second half of the **sixteenth century** was realized in 1588 with the sailing of the **Spanish Armada**, whose approach was first announced from the Cornish coast at the Lizard, and which was eventually scuppered by Elizabeth I's fleet docked in Plymouth – the occasion of Drake's famous sang-froid when he insisted on finishing his game of bowls on Plymouth Hoe before putting to sea to fight the enemy. Far more dangerous for Cornwall than the Armada was the Spanish invasion of **Brittany** in 1590, which provided a convenient base for raids on Cornwall, including a devastating attack in 1595, when two separate Spanish assault parties joined forces to sack and burn the three ports of Mousehole, Newlyn and Penzance.

Civil War

England's **Civil War** engulfed and divided the West Country as it did other regions. Although most places preferred to observe the course of events before rallying to either side, sentiment here was pretty squarely behind the Royalist cause – with the notable exceptions of Exeter and Plymouth, which declared both ways at different times. Where it was necessary to come out in favour of one side over another, most people followed their religious and political beliefs. Thus, in Cornwall Bevil Grenville (celebrated warrior and hero of Robert Hawker's ballad, *Song of the Western Men*), along with many others, sided with the king in defence of the Anglican Church, while Presbyterian merchant Lord Robartes, and others who rejected absolutism, sided with parliament.

The **Royalist mint** was established in Truro in 1642–43 and Cornwall became a major theatre of war. Battles were fought and won by the Royalists at Braddock Down and Stratton in Cornwall and at Lansdown near Bristol, where Bevil Grenville fell. There were two campaigns in 1643, and the following year Charles I defeated the Earl of Essex's army at Lostwithiel. However, Royalist fortunes were reversed when the New Model Army under the command of Thomas Fairfax appeared in the West in 1645. This final brutal campaign culminated in the Royalist surrender at Tressillian, near Truro, on March 12, 1645, although St Michael's Mount, Pendennis Castle and Exeter held out until the following year.

The main legacies of this sequence of sieges and small battles – there was none on the scale of Naseby or Marston Moor – were **harvest failure**, starvation and the destruction of many great houses and forts, though some of the latter were simply decommissioned and converted to domestic use. The **wool trade** in Devon, however, was largely unscathed, and entered a hugely prosperous phase in the second half of the seventeenth century.

Industry and Methodism

Tin and copper **mining** brought a degree of prosperity to Cornwall in the **eighteenth century**, with the introduction of beam engines in 1716 allowing ever-deeper shafts to be excavated, pumped and mined. The more extensive underground networks were largely made possible by the innovations of engineers like **Thomas Newcomen** of Dartmouth

1756	1803–1815	1812	1840
William Cookworthy discovers deposits of kaolinite near Helston, kicking off Cornwall's china clay industry.	The Napoleonic Wars prevent European travel, instigating a fashion for West Country tours.	Richard Trevithick develops the first high-pressure steam engine for use in Cornish mines.	The railway reaches Exeter, opening up Devon and Cornwall to tourism.

(1663–1729), who constructed a steam engine for pumping water out of pits, and the Cornish scientists **Humphry Davy** (1778–1829), famous for his "Davy lamp", and **Richard Trevithick** (1771–1833), who invented a steam carriage for use in the mines. The beam engines were fuelled by coal from South Wales, helping to keep the peninsula's northern ports busy. For the miners themselves, the working conditions were both squalid and dangerous, and the circumstances of their families were equally appalling. These impoverished communities provided a fertile ground for the preaching of **John Wesley**, the co-founder of Methodism, who travelled extensively in Devon and Cornwall between 1743 and 1786. His first visits met with a hostile response, but he later found a receptive audience for his pared-down version of the Christian message, and it is from this period that many of the Methodist chapels dotted around the region date.

The copper and china clay industries

The **copper** industry peaked during the 1840s, focused on the area around Redruth and Camborne, but shortly afterwards the mining industry collapsed when cheaper deposits of both copper and tin were found elsewhere in the world market. Pit closures during the nineteenth and twentieth centuries were followed by large-scale emigration from Cornwall, chiefly to Australia and South America.

On a much smaller scale, the region's extensive deposits of slate and granite continued to be quarried as they had been for centuries, while the eighteenth century also saw the beginning of the **china clay** industry in Cornwall. The deposits were first discovered by **William Cookworthy** (1705–80) of Kingsbridge in the area around Helston, and, more significantly, north of St Austell, where the conical white mountains of debris are still a feature of the landscape (often now coated with greenery), and where extraction remains an important industry. First used in the making of ceramics, the kaolin is now used in a wide range of everyday products.

World Wars I and II

Along with the steady stream of artists who were drawn to Devon and Cornwall, various **writers** became associated with the region in the **twentieth century**, though again these were mainly outsiders who settled in or had links with the West – D.H. Lawrence, Virginia Woolf, Henry Williamson (of *Tarka the Otter* fame), Daphne du Maurier and Agatha Christie, among others.

However, here, as elsewhere in the country, all else was overshadowed during this period by the two world wars. While **World War I** had little direct effect on the region beyond cutting a swathe through its adult male population, the south coast of Devon and Cornwall in particular suffered from both military requisition and enemy bombing during **World War II**. Although most of the West Country was designated safe from German aerial attack – and accordingly received many evacuees – Plymouth suffered the highest bombardment of any British seaport, and Exeter too was targeted in the "Baedeker raids", so-called because they were directed at centres of cultural and historic interest that would have appeared in the Baedeker guidebooks of the time. The subsequent reconstruction in these two cities followed very different paths: more conservative in Exeter, bolder in Plymouth, but arguably less successful. Neither city has escaped the imposition of unsympathetic shopping centres and unsightly car parks.

1884	1914–1918	1916	1928	1939–1945
Stanhope Forbes founds the Newlyn school of art.	World War I.	D.H. Lawrence relocates to Zennor, Penwith.	Ben Nicholson visits St Ives – the first of a group of artists who became known as the St Ives school.	World War II – Exeter and Plymouth are subjected to heavy bombardment.

THE BIRTH OF TOURISM

Devon's seaside towns found a new and valuable source of income in the tourist industry, which expanded throughout the **nineteenth century**. The Napoleonic Wars in 1803–15 prevented society folk from taking the fashionable Grand Tour of continental Europe, so there was an increasing trend to sojourn in the comparatively mild climate of such towns as Torquay, Exmouth and Sidmouth on the south coast, and, on the north, the villages of Lynton and Lynmouth, which were said to recall an Alpine landscape.

The extension of Brunel's railway to Exeter in 1840 had the immediate result of accelerating this phenomenon, and the railway's extension over the Tamar into Cornwall in 1859 and to North Devon in 1872 brought these regions for the first time into the ambit of mass **tourism**. Ilfracombe became an archetypal Victorian seaside resort, while Falmouth, Newquay and St Ives in Cornwall found their full flowering in the twentieth century. Along with the tourists, the railways also brought other groups from metropolitan England: **artists** congregated first in Newlyn, at the end of the nineteenth century, and later in neighbouring St Ives (see pp.345–347).

Modern times

In the 1950s, the designation of Dartmoor and Exmoor as **national parks** was a significant indication of both the new importance of tourism to the area and the urgency of conservation for the future wellbeing of the region. However, the decade was also marred by tragedy when heavy rain on Exmoor in 1952 caused the River Lyn to burst its banks, resulting in the catastrophic flooding of Lynmouth and the loss of 34 lives. The event was echoed more recently by the **flash flood** that engulfed Boscastle, in North Cornwall, in 2004, though unlike the earlier tragedy in Lynmouth, there was no loss of life.

The closure of most local rail lines in the 1960s had no significant impact on the region's economy as it was well compensated for by the huge expansion of motor traffic, encouraged by the extension of the M5 motorway to Exeter and the building of the link road to North Devon. However, the volume of traffic, which intensifies during the peak summer months, has brought its own massive environmental problems, engulfing towns, villages and country lanes that were never built for 4WDs.

Coastal communities in particular have been transformed in the last forty years, with declining fish stocks and the imposition of EU quotas having a powerful impact on the fishing economy. Many in both the farming and fishing sectors have turned to tourism as a source of income, though only a small fraction can benefit from the holiday industry – high-profile tourist developments such as **Tate St Ives** and the **Eden Project** in Cornwall, for example, have not prevented the county from having some of the UK's lowest wages, while the choice of Devon and Cornwall as places of retirement and for **second homes** has also impacted on property values, effectively pricing locals out of the area.

With farming increasingly at the mercy of the giant food retailers and the fishing industry struggling, the region has further been hit by the global **recession** that swept through the UK – and the world – from 2008 onwards, leading many local businesses to go bust and unemployment rates to soar. **Tourism**, at least, has remained strong, with "stay-cationing" Brits pouring into the South West peninsula as a cheaper alternative to foreign holidays, though even this sector cannot be immune to the economic vagaries of an uncertain future.

1952	2004	2008–2009	2016
Lynmouth flood disaster; 34 people lose their lives.	Boscastle's harbour is devastated by flooding.	Recession: the economy goes belly-up, cutting swathes through small businesses in Devon and Cornwall.	Devon (55.3%) and Cornwall (56.5%) vote to leave EU in national referendum.

Landscape and wildlife

Devon and Cornwall are rightly famous for the beauty of their landscapes and the richness of their coastline. Driving a wedge deep into the Atlantic, the South West peninsula lies at the junction of the warm southern, and cool northern, water bodies that ensure a strong maritime influence, with the benevolent effects of the Gulf Stream giving the region's flora and fauna an almost subtropical diversity that's unmatched in the British Isles.

Most people's experience of this rich marine environment is confined to the occasional glimpse of a dolphin or seal, but there is far more to be explored along the region's long **coastline**, where walls of **sea cliffs** are interspersed with bays and estuaries sheltering colourful birdlife, and often fringed by extensive areas of sand dunes. Elsewhere, on or just behind the shoreline, **reedbeds** survive in isolated patches and are an important habitat for a range of rare insects, plants and birds.

Inland, the geological peculiarities of the peninsula have also contributed to its range of habitats. The upland **granite outcrops** that characterize the high moorland were created long ago by violent volcanic intrusion, which also strongly contorted the overlying strata of mudstone and limestone. These bare expanses of **moorland** – primarily Exmoor, Dartmoor and Bodmin Moor – are composed of lowland and upland heaths, and blanket bog fringed by upland oakwoods.

Human activity has played a prominent role, of course – not least in Devon and Cornwall's **agricultural heartland**, where changes in farming practices have squandered vast quantities of species-rich hedges, meadows and banks. Nowadays some of the richest habitats are entirely limited to **nature reserves**, which are precious but increasingly beleaguered resources.

The marine environment

The **marine environment** of Devon and Cornwall constitutes one of the finest to be found around British shores. In spring and early summer especially, the coasts are bright with an abundance of **sea campion, kidney vetch, sea lavender**, orange **lichen** and green **algae**. Rarer flora to look out for include **golden samphire**, a nationally scarce plant quite common along the Cornish coastline where it grows on bare rock just above the high-water mark.

USEFUL INFORMATION SOURCES

Cornwall Wildlife Trust ☎01872 273939, ⊛cornwallwildlifetrust.org.uk
Dartmoor National Park Authority ☎01822 890414, ⊛dartmoor-npa.gov.uk
Devon Wildlife Trust ☎01392 279244, ⊛devonwildlifetrust.org
Exmoor National Park Authority ☎01398 323665, ⊛exmoor-nationalpark.gov.uk
Marine Conservation Society ☎01989 566017, ⊛mcsuk.org
National Trust Devon Regional Office ☎01392 881691; Cornwall Regional Office ☎01208 265200; ⊛nationaltrust.org.uk
Natural England (responsible for most National Nature Reserves) ☎0300 060 3900, ⊛naturalengland.org.uk
Royal Society for the Protection of Birds ☎01392 432691, ⊛rspb.org.uk
WDC (Whale and Dolphin Conservation) ☎01249 449500, ⊛uk.wales.org

Seabirds

Most ubiquitous of the fauna around the coast, from rugged cliff to fishing village, are the various populations of **seabirds** – according to the season they may be nesting or wintering here, or passing through on migration. Among the many species, **fulmars** and **kittiwakes** are numerous around St Agnes Head in Cornwall, while **razorbills** and **guillemots** are plentiful on almost all Cornish coasts. One of the most rewarding birds to look out for is the **gannet**, with long, black-tipped white wings, known for its vertical plunges into the sea as it fishes. The richest variety of marine birds is found on the **Isles of Scilly**, including large flocks of **puffins**, which also breed in April and May on **Lundy Island**.

Of the many species of gull, most common is the **herring gull**, distinguished by its grey mantle, flesh-coloured feet and black-and-white-spotted wing tips. Chiefly a scavenger, its numbers in the region have greatly increased in recent years as a result of expanding food supplies, which include refuse and sewage, though the birds are also known for their trick of dropping shellfish onto rocks to crack them open.

Seals

As for waterborne marine life, **grey seals** may occasionally be seen by observant coastal walkers, though they're most commonly spotted from a boat at sites such as Godrevy Island, Mousehole Rock and Falmouth Bay or, in greater numbers, the Isles of Scilly. Here, you'll encounter them hauled out onto rocks to bask in the sun or on remote beaches where females ("cows") – lighter and smaller than the males ("bulls") – often return each year to give birth. West Country seal pups are smaller than those of other UK populations, and they learn to swim earlier due to the milder conditions.

Dolphins, porpoises and whales

Dolphins and **porpoises** live in family groups with territories covering hundreds of miles, so there are no specific places where sightings can be guaranteed – your best bet for land-based viewing would be at the far west of the peninsula, at Land's End, Sennen Cove, Cape Cornwall or Mount's Bay. The last century has seen a dramatic decline in porpoise and dolphin populations in the English Channel and southern Celtic Sea, partly due to their being a by-catch of fishing boats, but also due to the fact that fish stocks – their prey – have drastically fallen. It's now recognized that almost all the dolphins stranded on our beaches have been caught accidentally in fishing nets. Sightings of **whales**, which have also fallen prey to fishing methods, are quite rare: the best chances of seeing minke, pilot, humpbacked or even orca (killer) whales is from **Sennen Cove**, or else from the ferry en route to the Isles of Scilly.

In summer **basking sharks** follow the warm Gulf Stream currents up Britain's west coast, allowing more than five hundred sightings in a typical year in the South West. A large cartilaginous fish – the world's second largest, at 35ft – they are harmless to humans, as their huge jaws are designed to scoop up plankton (tiny plants and animals that form the basis of the ocean food chain). Less common are **leatherback turtles**, which grow to over 6ft in length and also follow a migration route from their tropical breeding grounds in late summer and early autumn. They're occasionally washed up on Cornish beaches, but you're more likely to see them stuffed in local museums.

Sea cliffs

Robust granite makes up most of the **cliffs** that dominate Devon and Cornwall's coastline – much of it under the protection of the National Trust (see box opposite). The distinctive striated and undulating red cliffs of East Devon, however, are softer sandstone, where landslips have led to the creation of thickly vegetated undercliffs, a dense scrub of **privet**, **dogwood**, **maple** and **spindle** that has encouraged the **nightingale** and the rare **dormouse**. The close-cropped grassland at the clifftops may be home to a rare community of flowers such as **wild thyme** and several species of **orchid**.

One of the best wildlife sites on the south coast is **Berry Head National Nature Reserve** near Brixham, which is home to a substantial **guillemot** colony nesting on cliff ledges, while more unusual **skuas** and **shearwaters** can be seen offshore. The area is also rich in rare plants, with over five hundred species recorded on the cliffs and surrounding scrub and limestone grassland. Many, such as **autumn squill** and the delightfully named **autumn lady's tresses** orchid, are national rarities.

On the peninsula's northern coast, small ledges on the sheer faces of the sea cliffs provide protected habitats for many species of rare plants and nesting sites for birds such as **ravens** and the **peregrine falcon**. On the cliffs of North and West Cornwall, successful attempts have been made to reintroduce the **chough**, a rare, red-billed member of the crow family and the emblem of Cornwall; though virtually extinct here since 1973, the bird is now breeding on the Penwith and Lizard peninsulas.

In West Cornwall, the **Land's End Wildlife Discovery Centre** has nesting **razorbills**, while the **National Nature Reserve** at the Lizard headland holds a fantastic variety of wild flowers. The magnesium-rich **serpentine** which makes up much of the peninsula allows rare species of plants to flourish, such as the colourful **Cornish heath** heather, unique to the Lizard. The magnesium also contributes to the floristically rich grasslands running up to the cliffs, harbouring plants normally found around the Mediterranean.

Estuaries, rivers and reedbeds

Devon and Cornwall's **estuaries** hold some nationally rare species of waders and wildfowl, including beautiful, pure-white **little egrets**. Among the most important areas for wintering wildlife are the **Tamar** complex around Plymouth, the **Hayle estuary** in Cornwall, and, most significantly, the **Exe estuary**, whose broad and shallow waters shelter around 20,000 **waders** as well as **brent geese** and **wigeons** in winter. These last two feed on **zostera**, an unusual flowering marine grass that thrives in the soft, muddy sediments adjacent to the salt marsh and also helps to stabilize the mud. The best site to watch these wintering flocks is **Dawlish Warren** at the mouth of the estuary, where you can usually see around twenty species just before high tide.

Other winter species that frequent the Exe include **shelduck**, **dunlin**, **curlew**, **redshank**, the **black-** and **bar-tailed godwit**, and large flocks of **oystercatcher**, while one of the country's largest winter flocks of the rare and elegant **avocet** is commonly seen higher up the estuary at **Topsham**.

Many of the estuaries of Devon and Cornwall's southern seaboard are **rias**, river valleys drowned long ago by a rise in sea level, which have high levels of salinity. In the **Helford river valley** in West Cornwall, for example, the winding creeks and wooded shorelines are a haven for **eelgrass**, while the salty water is ideal for **cuttlefish** and **oysters**.

Rivers

Fast-flowing and varied in character, the **rivers** of Devon and Cornwall, including the Teign, Dart and Fowey, tend to run south from the high ground of the region's three

---

TOP SPOTS FOR WILDLIFE VIEWING

Exe estuary The best place to see huge flocks of wintering wildfowl. See p.49 & p.81

Dartmoor Southern England's greatest wilderness is home to a rich variety of fauna and flora. See p.108

Braunton Burrows Part of the North Devon Biosphere Reserve, with England's most extensive system of sand dunes. See p.182

Lizard Point Butterflies, birdlife and rare plant species are among the things to look out for on this rugged coast. See p.238

Isles of Scilly Swarming colonies of seabirds, from petrels to puffins, have made this archipelago their own. See p.268

moors. Along their banks, it's not difficult to spot **kingfisher**, **heron**, **dipper**, **sand martin** and **grey wagtail**, among other birds, while in the evening you may glimpse a **Daubenton's bat** skimming low over the water. On Bodmin Moor, the steep-sided **Golitha** gorge, formed by the River Fowey tumbling down a waterfall and rapids, creates the humid conditions that allow **lichens** and **mosses** to thrive.

The most important of the rivers that empty from the region's northern coast are the **De Lank** and **Camel** in Cornwall, and the **Taw** and **Torridge** in Devon, all habitats of the secretive **otter**. Your best chance of spotting these elusive mammals is on a guided excursion organized by the Devon or Cornwall Wildlife Trusts (see box, p.340).

Reedbeds

Reedbeds constitute a highly scarce habitat nationally, much depleted after the drainage and reclamation of wetlands that occurred in previous centuries. However, the National Nature Reserve at **Slapton Ley**, between Dartmouth and Kingsbridge in South Devon, is one of the nation's finest freshwater reedbeds and aquatic areas. Its main feature is the Ley itself, the largest natural lake in southwest England and separated from the sea by only a narrow shingle bar. The extensive areas of reedbed surrounding the lake shelter abundant aquatic flora, including the rare **convergent stonewort** and the only British occurrence of the **strapwort**, while the monotonous call of **sedge** and **reed warblers** can be heard through much of the summer.

You'll also find reedbeds on the **River Exe** just upstream from Topsham on RSPB and Devon Wildlife Trust reserves, and at **Marazion** in Cornwall, which harbours a discreet RSPB reserve where the reedbeds are becoming famous for rare migrant **dragonflies** and **butterflies** such as the migrant **clouded yellow** and **painted lady**.

Sand dunes

Extending northwards from the tip of the Taw/Torridge estuary in North Devon, **Braunton Burrows** is one of the largest **sand dune** systems in Britain, nearly four miles in length and over a mile wide. Forming part of a designated International Biosphere Reserve, the dunes, which reach up to 100ft high, are composed of wind-blown marine sand and crushed shells held loosely together by **marram** grass. These dynamic natural systems are continually – if imperceptibly – on the move, and the site's rich community of highly specialized plant and animal species has excited botanical interest since the seventeenth century. Among the 400-plus species of plant recorded here, the myriad wild flowers include **evening-scented sea-stock**, vivid patches of **biting stone crop**, deep-blue **viper's bugloss**, and the tall, lemon-coloured **evening primrose**, while throughout the summer months the ground is carpeted with an abundance of **bird's-foot trefoil** and **wild thyme**. Other notable dune sites are at **Dawlish Warren**, in South Devon, and on the edges of the **Hayle estuary** in Cornwall, where **kestrels** may sometimes be seen hovering overhead.

Meadows and hedges

Unimproved neutral grassland – or **meadow** – constitutes one of the most picturesque British habitats, sheltering a wealth of colourful flowers and insects (particularly rush pasture, which occurs on poor soils). Flower-rich meadows are plentiful in North Devon where they are known as **Culm grassland**, with a range of attractive and increasingly rare plants such as **devil's-bit scabious**, **meadow thistle** and various **orchids** and **sedges**. Meadows are also very important for the rapidly declining **marsh fritillary butterfly**, whose remaining stronghold is in Devon, notably Exmoor and Dartmoor national parks.

Small fields, woodland and thick, banked species-rich **hedgerows** are characteristic elements of the South West's meadows, harbouring a rich variety of wildlife such as **blackbird**, **bullfinch** and **song thrush**, which nest here. The **buzzard** is a common sight wheeling above these fields and copses, and is one of the region's most common birds of prey.

Upland oakwood

Devon and Cornwall hold some remarkable relics of **upland oakwood**, the majority of which are to be found on Dartmoor, Exmoor and Bodmin Moor. The woods were traditionally managed for charcoal and tanbark through **coppicing** – stimulating woodland plant growth through regular cropping – but recent times have seen a dramatic decline in this form of management and some change of character as the coppice stools grow out and gradually revert to forest. On Dartmoor, **Yarner Wood** has probably existed as woodland since prehistoric times, a mixture of sessile oak, holly, rowan, beech, ash and wych elm with an under-carpet of bilberry. It's rich in woodland **butterflies**, **moths** and **wood ants**. Breeding birds include **sparrowhawks** and all three British **woodpeckers**, while **red**, **roe** and **fallow deer** may occasionally be seen.

Heathland and blanket bog

The South West peninsula's wide swathes of **lowland heath** typically comprise open ground, which is poor in nutrients and dominated by **heathers** and **gorse**, with a scattering of scrub and trees (often Scots pine). There are excellent examples of this habitat near Exmouth in East Devon, where the pebblebed heaths of **Aylesbeare** and **Harpford Common** (RSPB-managed reserves) are a refuge for the nocturnal moth-eating **nightjar**, the **Dartford warbler** and the agile **hobby falcon**.

Maritime heath

The warm and wet climate on Cornwall's Lizard peninsula supports some outstanding examples of **maritime heath** of a type not found elsewhere in Britain. The unusual mix of maritime species creates a glorious spectacle in summer, when the ground is a blue carpet of **autumn** and **spring quill**, **rock sea lavender** and **golden samphire**, and later in the year, when the flowering purple **heathers** and golden **gorse** add a regal blaze. Maritime heathlands also range along the coasts of Penwith and North Cornwall, and on the Isles of Scilly. On the Cornish mainland, **adders** may be found basking on rocks in hot sunny weather, identifiable by their brownish colour and the lozenge pattern down their backs.

Upland heath

In global terms, Britain holds a high proportion of **upland heath**, characterized by poor-quality soil and vegetation consisting of **heather**, **bilberry**, **crossleaved heath** and **western gorse**. The largest area of this type of terrain is on **Exmoor**, where unusual plants like **lesser twayblade** grow, while **crowberry** and **cranberry** occur at the very southern edge of their geographical range. Exmoor is the most important stronghold of the endangered **heath fritillary butterfly** in the UK, but its most famous long-term residents are its **red deer** and ponies. **Exmoor ponies**, descended from wild ponies, have a total population lower than many more recognized rare species, but they are hardy and well adapted to the tough conditions of winter on the exposed hills. The equally robust **Dartmoor ponies**, used for centuries for mining and quarrying, are also greatly reduced in number from previous levels, and most ponies grazing the moor today are not pure-bred.

Blanket bog

Blanket bog is restricted to plateau areas where the wet conditions have allowed a mantle of **peat** to develop, with a high proportion of **heathers**, **cottongrasses** and **bogmosses** and very small populations of breeding **golden plover** and **dunlin**. Other typical birdlife on these moors includes the summer visitors **wheatear** and **ring ouzel**, while **peregrine falcons** occasionally nest on the sheer rock faces.

The arts

Stuck on the margins of British cultural life, Devon and Cornwall have produced few artists of great renown, though the late nineteenth and twentieth centuries saw the establishment of two of Britain's rare "art schools" linked to a particular place – namely, the Newlyn and St Ives schools, both in West Cornwall. The same factors that drew these artists' colonies – a combination of picturesque charm, rugged grandeur and clear light – have continued to work on successive generations of artists, so that the region now has one of the largest arts and crafts communities in the country.

The eighteenth and early nineteenth centuries

Before the advent of the Newlyn and St Ives schools, Devon and Cornwall saw a relatively low level of artistic activity, though in the **eighteenth century**, each of the counties produced one nationally acclaimed figure. Of these, **Joshua Reynolds** (1723–92), born in Plympton, near Plymouth, achieved more lasting fame. After a sojourn in Italy, he found rich patrons who adored his Grand Manner and heroic style. Closely identified with formal "Academy art", Reynolds advocated above all history painting, though he excelled at what he considered the inferior (but better-paid) field of portraiture.

John Opie (1761–1807), the first Cornish artist of any significance, was also highly esteemed for his portraits, though these were of a very different ilk. Something of a child prodigy, the untutored Opie was discovered by the Devon-born political satirist John Wolcot, then practising as a doctor in Truro, who in 1780 accompanied Opie to London to launch his artistic career (and simultaneously Wolcot's own as "Peter Pindar", author of a series of caustic poetical pamphlets). An instant success, the "Cornish wonder" was most comfortable with his portraits of simple country folk – old people and children in particular – for which he used plenty of chiaroscuro in a style reminiscent of Caravaggio and Rembrandt. Although his later work is now deemed undistinguished and repetitive, he was made a professor of painting at the Royal Academy in 1805, and his death two years later was met with universal grief.

Reynolds' and Opie's West Country successors included figures such as the marine artist **Thomas Luny** (1757–1837), associated with Teignmouth, and the Romantic painter **Francis Danby** (1793–1861), who settled in Exmouth in 1847 and was famous for his apocalyptic biblical scenes, but better liked for his sunsets and landscapes.

The Newlyn school

The arrival of the **railway** in Devon and Cornwall in the nineteenth century generated a huge growth of interest in the region. Artists were particularly drawn to the far west of the peninsula, encouraged by the mild climate and exceptional light, which, together with the strong fishing culture, recalled a corner of continental Europe. For many painters, the aim was to immerse themselves in the life of the **fishing community** in order to represent it more faithfully, and their work shows great sympathy with the people of the locality, even if it is occasionally prone to sentimentality.

Two Birmingham artists, **Walter Langley** (1852–1922) and **Edwin Harris** (1855–1906), settled in Newlyn in 1882, but it was the arrival of **Stanhope Forbes** (1857–1947) two years later that really set the ball rolling for the "**Newlyn school**". Inspired by the fishing port's resemblance to villages in Brittany where he had studied, Forbes showed his

---

ART GALLERIES AND MUSEUMS IN DEVON AND CORNWALL

The prolific output of Joshua Reynolds is well represented in stately homes throughout the country, a good number of them in Devon, such as **Hartland Abbey** and **Saltram House**. Most of the region's major public collections also hold examples of his oils, notably Exeter's **Royal Albert Memorial Museum** which, along with Truro's **Royal Cornwall Museum**, is also the place to see works by John Opie. You'll find a few paintings by Thomas Luny, among other local nineteenth-century artists, exhibited in Torquay's **Torre Abbey**.

Most of the important works of the Newlyn school are in major collections, but a good selection is on view in Penzance's **Penlee House**. **The Exchange**, housed in an old telephone exchange in Penzance, is a significant addition to the local arts scene, with a focus on modern art. Just up the road, the **Newlyn Art Gallery** also features contemporary art by local and other artists, while recent years have seen a thriving arts scene emerging in Falmouth, which you can experience at the **Falmouth Art Gallery** and **The Poly**.

The central role of St Ives in the region's art world was confirmed by the siting there of **Tate St Ives**. The Tate also manages the town's **Barbara Hepworth Museum**, which showcases Barbara Hepworth's sculptures, while the **Leach Pottery** is the place to see work by Bernard Leach, Shoji Hamada and their various pupils and disciples. Contemporary work by local artists is on view at the **St Ives Society of Arts Gallery**.

---

fascination with the effects of the luminous light and with the life of the local fishing community in works such as the lively *Fish Sale on Newlyn Beach* (1884). When displayed at the Royal Academy, this established Forbes and the Newlyn school as the most prominent exponents of the new French-influenced styles, which contrasted with the insular and backward-looking tone of most British painting of the time.

Norman Garstin and Henry Scott Tuke

Other prominent members of the Newlyn school included **Norman Garstin** (1847–1926), an Irishman who came to Newlyn in 1886 – supposedly the most "intellectual" member of the group. His most famous work, *The Rain It Raineth Every Day* (1889), was accepted by the Royal Academy but never shown there – it's currently viewable in Penlee House, Penzance. **Henry Scott Tuke** (1858–1929), born in York but brought up in Falmouth and London, had already spent some time painting in Newlyn before he settled in Falmouth in 1885, with the stated intention to "paint the nude in open air". Unable to find suitable models locally, he imported one from London – Walter Shilling – and, though his numerous depictions of nude boys aroused controversy, his work did gain some respectability and was actively encouraged by Stanhope Forbes. Truro's museum has some of his works.

Interior and domestic scenes

Although most Newlyn artists shared Forbes' devotion to open-air painting, another member of the school, **Frank Bramley** (1857–1915), made his reputation with *A Hopeless Dawn* (1888), an interior scene suffused with light from different sources. Elizabeth Armstrong, later to become Stanhope Forbes' wife and better known as **Elizabeth Forbes** (1859–1912), also painted domestic scenes and portraits characterized by a directness and warmth sometimes missing in her husband's works. Her output was at one time valued more highly by the critics than that of her husband, but her career was cut short by her early death.

Dod Proctor and Laura Knight

There was another wave of artists to Newlyn some twenty years after Forbes first arrived in the town – including **Dod Proctor** (c.1890–1972), then known as Doris Shaw, and **Laura Knight** (1877–1970), who, as part of the offshoot Lamorna Group, was one of the protagonists of the 2013 film *Summer in February*. However, Newlyn's golden period had ended by the beginning of the twentieth century and interest subsequently focused on St Ives.

The St Ives School

Across the neck of the Penwith peninsula, **St Ives** attracted the attention of the art world in 1811 with a visit from Turner. With the new age of rail travel, other artists followed in his footsteps, including Whistler and Sickert in 1883–84, who left a few tiny oil studies as evidence. A trickle of English and foreign artists set up studios during the ensuing years, so that by the 1920s there were scores of artists working locally, including many amateurs alongside more well-known names.

Among the established artists in St Ives were **Ben Nicholson** (1894–1982) and **Christopher Wood** (1901–30), who, on a day-trip to St Ives in 1928, were jointly responsible for discovering the work of **Alfred Wallis** (1855–1942), a retired sailor born in Devonport. Having previously worked on fishing boats both inshore and out to sea for over twenty years, Wallis later took up a variety of jobs such as dealing in marine scrap and selling ice cream, and following the death of his wife in 1925, he turned increasingly to painting. His work, often produced on scraps of driftwood, depicted primitive scenes of ships and seascapes around St Ives and the adjacent coasts. Despite the efforts of Nicholson, Wood and others to promote his art, and his subsequent rapid rise to fame as Britain's best-known naive artist, Wallis ended his days in a St Ives workhouse. Wood himself produced some of his best work during his short residence in Cornwall (1929–30), while Nicholson went on to be the guiding spirit of the **St Ives school**, which flourished between the late 1940s and early 1960s.

Abstracts and semiabstracts

Nicholson shared with the other artists of the group a preference for nonfigurative work, and his delicate reliefs and semiabstract still lifes are acknowledged to have had a greater influence on abstract art than any other British artist. Nicholson had settled in the town in 1939, together with his second wife **Barbara Hepworth** (1903–75), a sculptor who had abandoned figure-based art in favour of abstract geometric forms, and whose work was increasingly inspired by the rock and sea landscape of the Penwith peninsula. Nicholson left St Ives in 1958, but Hepworth spent the rest of her life in the town, eventually dying in a fire in her studio there, after which her house and garden became a museum dedicated to her work.

Probably the most influential of the group during the war years was the Russian constructivist **Naum Gabo** (1890–1977), whose spatial geometric sculptures had a profound effect on Nicholson and Hepworth as well as other members of the community. Though Gabo left for the US in 1946, many of his ideas are reflected in the work of younger St Ives artists such as **Wilhelmina Barnes-Graham** (1912–2004), whose work is alternately abstract and figurative, and **Peter Lanyon** (1918–64), who was born in the town and lived there most of his life; such works of his as *Porthleven* (1951) mix abstract themes with allusions to the local landscape.

The St Ives Pottery

On the periphery of the group, **Bernard Leach** (1887–1979) arrived in St Ives from Japan in 1920, accompanied by **Shoji Hamada** (1894–1978). Together they set up the St Ives Pottery which, over the next six decades, remained at the centre of the studio pottery movement in Britain. Among the foremost potters who studied under Leach in St Ives were Michael Cardew and Katherine Pleydell-Bouverie.

Later artists

In the late 1950s and 1960s, a third wave of St Ives artists rose to prominence, including **Brian Wynter** (1915–75), **Roger Hilton** (1911–75), **Terry Frost** (1915–2003) and **Patrick Heron** (1920–99). More recently, locally born **Bryan Pearce** (1929–2007) achieved some prominence, the vibrant colours and simple lines in his still lifes, church interiors and scenes of St Ives recalling those of Alfred Wallis.

Books

We've highlighted a selection of books below that will give you a flavour of Devon and Cornwall, past and present; books marked ★ are particularly recommended. Some of the titles may be out of print, but these are often available from online stores, local libraries or the region's numerous secondhand bookshops – note, however, that local-interest books are usually cheaper (if harder to find) in shops outside the West Country. Many of the memoirs and novels listed here are available as CDs or downloadable audiobooks.

HISTORY, MEMOIR AND BACKGROUND

Simon Armitage *Walking Away*. The next best thing to walking the coast path is reading this vivid account of the Yorkshire poet's hike along part of it – holey boots, weary laments and all.

Evelyn Atkins *We Bought an Island*. Humorous account of the purchase of Looe Island off the coast of Cornwall and the various characters encountered. *Tales from Our Cornish Island* is the sequel.

★**John Betjeman** *Betjeman's Cornwall*. Collection of prose and poetry relating to Cornwall, with illustrations by John Piper and photos. Fans will also be interested in a DVD, *Betjeman's West Country*, a compilation of films about the region made by the poet, intercut by interviews.

Michael Bird *The St Ives Artists: A Biography of Time and Place*. Entertaining and meticulously researched narrative about the waves of artists who settled in St Ives from 1946. It's a fascinating tale, best read in conjunction with a pictorial guide to the works, such as the Tate's *St Ives Artists* series, as it's scantily illustrated.

★**Anthony Burton** *Richard Trevithick: The Man and his Machine*. The extraordinary story of Cornwall's greatest engineer and inventor (1771–1833), who built his first locomotive in 1801 – the first of many innovations for which the world was not ready. He spent ten years wandering South America but died penniless in England.

Marion Dell and Marion Whybrow *Virginia Woolf and Vanessa Bell: Remembering St Ives*. The two sisters of the title spent large parts of their childhood in St Ives, an experience that infused their later work, as this book absorbingly describes by means of extracts from letters, journals and Virginia's own fiction. It's beautifully illustrated, too.

★**Daphne du Maurier** *Vanishing Cornwall*. The book chronicles all aspects of the place where du Maurier lived for most of her life, fusing history, anecdote and travelogue in a plea for the preservation of Cornish culture.

Patrick Hutton *I Would Not Be Forgotten: The Life and Work of Robert Stephen Hawker*. The eccentric vicar of Morwenstow, Hawker (1803–75) was the author of Cornwall's anthem, *The Song of the Western Men*; this biography includes his verse alongside details of his colourful life.

★**Gavin Knight** *The Swordfish and the Star*. A revealing, sometimes shocking, insight into West Cornwall's fishing community, written as a series of far-fetched anecdotes.

★**Philip Payton** *Cornwall: A History*. Learned and comprehensive history of the county, bringing the story up to the present day in a revised and updated edition.

Nikolaus Pevsner and Bridget Cherry *The Buildings of England: Devon*. First published as two volumes in 1952, this single fat volume has been updated and enlarged, and tells you everything you wanted to know about every building of note in the county – and plenty that you probably have no wish to know. It's comprehensive, but cumbersome and expensive.

Nikolaus Pevsner and Enid Radcliffe *The Buildings of England: Cornwall*. The first of the series of Pevsner's monumental guides researched on long car journeys with his wife, this is also one of the slimmest, with few mentions of vernacular architecture or Cornwall's rich heritage of nonconformist chapels.

Tim Smit *Eden*. Often inspiring chronicle of the trials and triumphs that went into the Eden Project; humorously narrated, if sometimes over-burdened with the nitty-gritty. In *The Lost Gardens of Heligan*, Smit has also written about his involvement with his other great project.

C.J. Stevens *The Cornish Nightmare (D.H. Lawrence in Cornwall)* and *Lawrence at Tregerthen*. The story of Lawrence and Frieda's Cornish sojourn during World War I, as told to the author by Stanley Hocking – "the boy" in *Kangaroo* (see opposite) – and others. This is everyday Lawrence seen fondly, sometimes critically and with some amusement, by the Cornish locals.

Carol Trewin *Gourmet Cornwall* and *Cornish Fishing and Seafood*. The first of these is an expert gastro-guide, sumptuously photographed, with well-informed background, while the second takes a well-balanced look at the local fishing industry and speculates about its future; both are laced with recipes.

Mark Wallington *Travels With Boogie: 500 Mile Walkies*. Hilarious account of a low-budget hike on the South West Coast Path in the 1980s, in the company of the dog of the title. A must for anyone familiar with or attempting the coast path.

FICTION

R.D. Blackmore *Lorna Doone*. Swashbuckling Exmoor yarn of romance and inter-clan warfare during the time of the Monmouth Rebellion. Don't let the archaic language and antiquated style put you off this page-turner, which was televised by the BBC in 2000.

★**Daphne du Maurier** Perhaps the author most associated with Cornwall, her best-known works are an irresistible blend of deception, romance and smuggling, notably *Frenchman's Creek*, set during the Restoration; *Jamaica Inn*, set on Bodmin Moor; and *Rebecca*, which gallops along at an unputdownable pace from the famous first line: "Last night I dreamt went to Manderley again…"

Helen Dunmore *Zennor in Darkness*. Dunmore's first novel is an imaginative re-creation of D.H. Lawrence's experience while living in West Cornwall in 1915–17, seen from the perspective of a local girl who falls under his spell. With World War I as a constant background, the haunting atmosphere and erratic protagonists are skilfully depicted.

★**Patrick Gale** *Notes From an Exhibition*. Set amid the local artistic community in the author's hometown of Penzance, this subtle exploration of gay and inter-generational relationships delves into a family's convoluted backstory, with frequent time jumps. Similar themes are pursued in Gale's *Rough Music*, set in a beach house in Cornwall, and also highly readable.

Winston Graham *Poldark* series. *Ross Poldark*, *Demelza* and *The Angry Tide* are among the ten novels set around Perranporth and St Agnes through the late 1700s and early 1800s, and a rampant success when adapted for TV in 2015 and 2016.

Thomas Hardy *A Pair of Blue Eyes*. Partly based on Hardy's own experiences as an architect in Cornwall, this tragic story of Elfride Swancourt, caught between the love of handsome, gentle Stephen Smith and the intellectually superior Henry Knight, sheds light on the struggle between the classes and sexes in the England of that time.

D.H. Lawrence *Kangaroo*. This semiautobiographical tale follows Richard and Harriet Somers arriving in Australia from the decay of postwar Europe and incorporates a nightmare sequence recounting the Lawrences' trauma of being chased out of Cornwall.

Derek Tangye *The Minack Chronicles*. A local hero in West Cornwall, Tangye was a former deb's delight who came to Cornwall to find the "good life", revealing all in his "shocking" tales. Minack is the Cornish flower farm where he and his wife Jeannie lived. Titles in the series include *A Drake at the Door*, *A Gull on the Roof* and *A Cat in the Window*.

Henry Williamson *Tarka the Otter*. The natural history of North Devon is a minutely detailed backcloth to this animal tale, which has spawned an industry.

Virginia Woolf *To the Lighthouse*. Although the novel is set on a Hebridean island, the lighthouse of the title is Godrevy, near Hayle, where Woolf spent her summers, and the story recalls strands of her Cornish sojourns.

GUIDEBOOKS

John Betjeman *Cornwall* and *Devon*. First published in 1933 and 1936 respectively (revised 1953 & 1964) these Shell Guides are now collectors' items, imbued with Betjeman's forthright views on churches and architecture, and still pertinent – a welcome antidote to glossy brochures.

Nick Cotton *Ordnance Survey Cycle Tours: Cornwall and Devon*. Fourteen on-road and ten off-road routes, including rides across Dartmoor and Exmoor and using 1:50,000 Landranger mapping. See also Cotton's *South West Mountain Biking* and *More Cycling Without Traffic: Southwest*, which has around 30 leisurely, off-road rides with families in mind, avoiding hills and difficult terrain.

★**Max Darkins** *Mountain Bike Rides in & around Exmoor & Dartmoor*. Beautifully produced guide to off-road biking in the region – not just on the two moors but as far afield as Saunton and Truro – in a ring binder that can accommodate "expansion packs" (available from ⓦ roughrideguide.co.uk). The OS maps and directions are first-class.

John Earle *Dartmoor: Walks into History*. Mainly short and undemanding hikes on Dartmoor, each based around a place of historical significance – prehistoric sites, castles, old mining remnants, quarries and ancient trackways – with other items of interest pointed out en route.

John Gilman *Exmoor Rangers' Favourite Walks*. Thirty circular walks to get the most out of Exmoor, originally written by a former head ranger and subsequently updated by National Park staff and volunteers. The routes vary from two to eight miles.

John Macadam *The Two Moors Way*. Expert guide to this 90-mile trail using 1:25,000 OS maps and with colour photos.

David Norman and Vic Tucker *Where to Watch Birds in Devon and Cornwall*. An excellent introduction to birdlife and other aspects of the region, including birdwatching sites, information on access for the car-bound or disabled, and an update of recent occurrences at each site.

Various authors *South West Coast Path*. The official National Trail Guide to the coast path in four pocket-friendly volumes, with excellent 1:25,000 Ordnance Survey maps, copious information on background and things to see, and details of circular walks en route.

Small print and index

A ROUGH GUIDE TO ROUGH GUIDES

Published in 1982, the first Rough Guide – to Greece – was a student scheme that became a publishing phenomenon. Mark Ellingham, a recent graduate in English from Bristol University, had been travelling in Greece the previous summer and couldn't find the right guidebook. With a small group of friends he wrote his own guide, combining a contemporary, journalistic style with a thoroughly practical approach to travellers' needs.

The immediate success of the book spawned a series that rapidly covered dozens of destinations. And, in addition to impecunious backpackers, Rough Guides soon acquired a much broader readership that relished the guides' wit and inquisitiveness as much as their enthusiastic, critical approach and value-for-money ethos. These days, Rough Guides include recommendations from budget to luxury and cover more than 120 destinations around the globe, from Amsterdam to Zanzibar, all regularly updated by our team of roaming writers.

Browse all our latest guides, read inspirational features and book your trip at **roughguides.com**.

SMALL PRINT | 351

Rough Guide credits

Editors: Rebecca Hallett, Tim Locke
Layout: Pradeep Thapliyal, Nikhil Agarwal
Cartography: Deshpal Dabas
Picture editor: Michelle Bhatia
Proofreader: Diane Margolis
Managing editor: Natasha Foges
Assistant editor: Payal Sharotri

Production: Jimmy Lao
Cover photo research: Roger Mapp
Photographer: Tim Draper
Editorial assistant: Aimee White
Senior DTP coordinator: Dan May
Programme manager: Gareth Lowe
Publishing director: Georgina Dee

Publishing information

This sixth edition published March 2017 by
Rough Guides Ltd,
80 Strand, London WC2R 0RL
11, Community Centre, Panchsheel Park,
New Delhi 110017, India
Distributed by Penguin Random House
Penguin Books Ltd, 80 Strand, London WC2R 0RL
Penguin Group (USA), 345 Hudson Street, NY 10014, USA
Penguin Group (Australia), 250 Camberwell Road,
Camberwell, Victoria 3124, Australia
Penguin Group (NZ), 67 Apollo Drive, Mairangi Bay,
Auckland 1310, New Zealand
Penguin Group (South Africa), Block D, Rosebank Office
Park, 181 Jan Smuts Avenue, Parktown North, Gauteng,
South Africa 2193
Rough Guides is represented in Canada by DK Canada, 320
Front Street West, Suite 1400, Toronto, Ontario M5V 3B6
Printed in Singapore
© Robert Andrews, 2017
Maps © Rough Guides
Contains Ordnance Survey data © Crown copyright and
database rights 2016

360pp includes index
A catalogue record for this book is available from the
British Library
ISBN: 978-0-24127-032-5
The publishers and authors have done their best to
ensure the accuracy and currency of all the information
in **The Rough Guide to Devon & Cornwall**, however,
they can accept no responsibility for any loss, injury, or
inconvenience sustained by any traveller as a result of
information or advice contained in the guide.
1 3 5 7 9 8 6 4 2

MIX
Paper from
responsible sources
FSC   FSC™ C018179
www.fsc.org

Help us update

We've gone to a lot of effort to ensure that the
sixth edition of **The Rough Guide to Devon &
Cornwall** is accurate and up-to-date. However, things
change – places get "discovered", opening hours are
notoriously fickle, restaurants and rooms raise prices
or lower standards. If you feel we've got it wrong or
left something out, we'd like to know, and if you can

remember the address, the price, the hours, the phone
number, so much the better.

Please send your comments with the subject line
"**Rough Guide Devon & Cornwall Update**" to mail@
uk.roughguides.com. We'll credit all contributions and
send a copy of the next edition (or any other Rough Guide
if you prefer) for the very best emails.

ABOUT THE AUTHOR

From his lair in Bristol, **Robert Andrews** makes frequent forays westward to sniff the air, wallow in the waves and scoff pasties. He has also written for and researched the Rough Guides to England, Italy, Sicily, Sardinia and Bath, Bristol and Somerset.

Acknowledgements

Robert Andrews would like to heartily thank Becca Hallett, for her expert and sensitive editing of this edition, and for her (and her family's) invaluable local tips. Tim Locke's ever-insightful contribution to North Devon and Exmoor is also greatly appreciated. Thanks, too, to the Rough Guide cartography and picture departments for their hard work. Evelina at Visit England provided useful input, while in Devon and Cornwall, the superb but sadly diminishing staff at the region's tourist offices gave huge assistance (and mighty thanks are due to Judy at *Falmouth Lodge*). Lastly, the Emerald Empress performed her usual magic.

Readers' updates

Thanks to all the readers who have taken the time to write in with comments and suggestions (and apologies if we've inadvertently omitted or misspelt anyone's name):

Ben Boyd-Taylor, Ranmal Burkmar, Martin Disney, Colm Magee, Marilyn Meaker, Helen Wilson.

Photo credits

Index

Maps are marked in grey

Map symbols

The symbols below are used on maps throughout the book

State/province boundary
Chapter division boundary
Road
Pedestrianized road
Steps
Path
South West Coast Path
Railway
Tourist railway
Ferry route
Wall

Bus/taxi
Parking
Internet café/access
Post office
Information office
Museum
Hospital
Place of interest
Ferry/boat stop
Bridge
Boat

Waterfall
Surfing beach
Stately home
Castle
Ruin
Lighthouse
Fortress
Abbey
Vineyard
Viewpoint
Gardens

Stone circle
Cliffs
Standing stone
Tin mine
Mine
Church (regional maps)
Church (town maps)
Building
Park
Beach
Cemetery

Listings key

Accommodation
Eating
Drinking/nightlife

ROUGH
GUIDES

ESCAPE
THE EVERYDAY